Law and Society

Foundations of Criminal Law and Procedure

2023 Edition

Lore Rutz-Burri, J.D.

Law and Society
Foundations of Criminal Law and Procedure
2023

Table of Contents

Chapter One: Fundamental Principles of Criminal Law

OVERVIEW AND LEARNING OBJECTIVES

This chapter introduces the fundamental principles of law and the role of criminal law in the administration of justice. After reading this chapter, you should be able to answer the following questions:

> What are the functions of criminal law? What are the things that criminal law can do for individuals or for society?
> What are the limitations of criminal law? What are the things that criminal law cannot do?
> What are the various classification schemes used to organize or think about the criminal law?
> What are the main legal traditions existing today?
> How does criminal law differ from civil law?
> How does criminal law differ from moral codes?
> What is the difference between a felony, a misdemeanor, a violation and an infraction?
> What is the difference between a *mala in se* crimes and a *mala prohibita* crimes?
> What are the differences between substantive law and procedural law?

FUNCTIONS AND LIMITATIONS OF LAW

Law is a formal means of social control. Society uses "laws" or rules designed to control citizen's behaviors so that these behaviors will conform to societal norms, cultures, mores, traditions, and expectations. Because courts must interpret and enforce these rules, law differs from many other forms of social control. Both formal and informal social control have the capacity to change behavior. Informal social controls, including that of social media (including Facebook, Instagram, Twitter, and TikTok) have a tremendous impact on what people wear, how they think, how they speak, what people value, and perhaps how they vote. Social media's impact on human behavior cannot be overstated, but because these "controls" are largely unenforceable through the courts, they are not considered "laws."

Law and legal rules promote social control by resolving basic value conflicts, settling individual disputes, and making rules that even our rulers must follow.[1] Kerper (1979) recognized the advantages of law in fostering social control but identified four major limitations of the law. First, she noted, the law often cannot gain community support without support of other social institutions.[2] Second, even with community support, law cannot compel certain types of conduct contrary to human nature. Third, to resolve disputes the law is dependent upon a complicated and expensive fact-finding process. Finally, the law changes slowly.[3]

Professor Lippman (2015) noted that the law does not always achieve its purposes of social control, dispute resolution, and social change, but rather can harm society. He refers to this as the "dysfunctions of law."

> Law does not always protect individuals and result in beneficial social progress. Law can be used to repress individuals and limit their rights. The respect that is accorded to the legal system can mask the dysfunctional role of the law. Dysfunctional means that the law is promoting inequality or serving the interests of a small number of individuals rather than promoting the welfare of society or is impeding the enjoyment of human rights.[4]

Lawrence Friedman has identified several dysfunctions of law:[5]

- *Harassment.* Legal actions may be brought to harass individuals or to gain revenge rather than redress a legal wrong.
- *Bias.* The law may reflect biases and prejudices or reflect the interest of powerful economic interests.
- *Repression.* The law may be used by totalitarian regimes as an instrument of repression.
- *Rigidity.* The law is based on a clear set of rules. Self-defense requires an imminent and immediate threat of violence. Battered women who have been subjected to a lengthy period of abuse and who, as a result, kill their abuser while they sleep typically are denied the justification of self-defense. The denial of self-defense to "battered women" according to some legal commentators is unfair because the women reasonably can anticipate that the abuser will continue the patter n of violence in the near future.
- *Precedent.* The law, because of the reliance on precedent, may be slow to change. Judges are also concerned about maintaining respect for the law and hesitate to introduce change that society is not ready to accept.
- *Unequal access to justice.* An individual who is able to afford a powerful law firm and talented private attorneys and who can afford to retain experts and investigators has a better chance of being acquitted of a criminal charge or winning a civil suit than an individual who lacks resources. In the criminal arena, a defendant who can afford bail has a better chance of being acquitted than a defendant who is forced to remain in jail while awaiting trial.
- *Conservatism.* Courts are reluctant to second-guess the decisions of political decision-makers, particularly in times of war and crisis. For instance, the U.S. Supreme Court

---

[1] See, Hazel B. Kerper, Introduction to the Criminal Justice System (2d ed., 1979).
[2] Consider *Brown v. Board of Education of Topeka, Kansas,* 347 U.S. 483 (1954), declaring racially segregated schools unconstitutional. The decision was largely unpopular in the southern states, and many had decided to not follow the Court's holding. Ultimately, the Court had to call in the National Guard to enforce its decision requiring schools be integrated.
[3] Kerper, *supra* at 11.
[4] Lippman, M. *Law and Society,* 11 (2015).
[5] *Id.* at 25.

during World War II upheld the internment of 112,000 Japanese immigrants and Japanese Americans (*Korematsu v. United States,* 323 U.S. 214 (1944)).

- *Political activism.* A reliance on law and courts can discourage democratic political activism. Individuals and groups, when they look to courts to decide issues, divert energy from lobbying the legislature and from building political coalitions for elections. The reliance on unelected judges to make public policy decisions is criticized as undemocratic.
- *Impede social change.* The law may limit the ability of individuals to use the law to vindicate their rights and liberties.

CLASSIFICATIONS OF LAW

In this next section you will read about the various classification schemes used to help us organize the criminal law into frameworks for easier comprehension and comparison.

LEGAL TRADITIONS OR FAMILIES OF LAW

Legal traditions are also known as "families of law." Many families of law have existed over the course of history,[6] but most legal scholars today recognize four existing families of law: common law, civil law, socialist law, and Islamic law.[7] The two primary legal traditions are the civil law tradition -- followed in most European, African, and South American countries -- and the common law tradition -- followed in England, Australia, New Zealand, Ireland, Canada, and the United States. The Socialist legal tradition is seen in China, North Korea, and Cuba.[8] Many countries have legal systems that are based purely on religious law (primarily Islamic law) or are based on mixed religious and secular legal practices.[9]

According to Scheb (2013), codes of law developed in Western civilization as leaders formalized and enforced customs that had evolved among their peoples.[10] Examples of such codes are the Code of Hammurabi (circa, 2000 B.C.), the Justinian Code (6th Century), the Draco Code (7th Century), and the Justinian/Napoleonic Code (put into effect by Napoleon in 1804). The legal codes used in Western Europe are frequently referred to as Roman Law. These codes, used in those countries that are part of the civil law tradition, are based on the primacy of statutes enacted by the legislature. The statutes are written generally and are integrated into a comprehensive code that does not require judges to do too much interpretation.

On the other hand, the common law legal tradition is much younger – dating back to the Norman Conquest of England in 1066.

Before the Norman Conquest of 1066 English law was a "patchwork of laws and customs applied by local courts." The Norman kings appointed royal judges to settle disputes based on the customs of the people. By 1300, the decisions of the royal judges were being recorded to serve as precedents to guide judges in future similar cases. Eventually a common body of law emerged throughout the entire

---

[6] Legal scholar John Henry Wigmore identified sixteen legal systems: Egyptian, Mesopotamian, Chinese, Indian, Hebrew, Greek, Maritime, Roman, Celtic, Germanic, Church, Japanese, Mohammedan, Slavic, Romanesque and Anglican.

[7] See, e.g., Philip Reichel, Comparative Criminal Justice Systems: Topical Approach (2002) and Lippman, Law and Society, supra at 11.

[8] Since the re-establishment of diplomatic relations with the United States in 2015, Cuba may be a nation in transition. It is likely, that as its legal system moves away from the Socialist legal tradition (assuming that it does so), it will emerge as a blend of the common law and the civil law systems.

[9] *See,* https://www.law.cornell.edu/wex/legal_systems.

[10] John Scheb, *Criminal Law and Procedure,* 10 (10th ed., 2013).

kingdom, hence the term 'common law.' As the centuries passed, coherent principles of law and definitions of crimes emerged from the judges' decisions. Thus, in contrast with Roman law systems, which are based on legal codes, the common law developed primarily through judicial decisions. . ..

[America's] criminal laws are rooted in the common law as it existed when America proclaimed its independence from England in 1776. After independence, the new American states adopted the English common law to the extent that it did not conflict with new state and federal constitutions. However, the federal government did not adopt the common law crimes. From the outset, statutes passed by Congress defined federal crimes. Of the fifty states, Louisiana is the only one whose legal system is not based on the common law; rather, it is based primarily on the Napoleonic Code.[11]

INQUISITORIAL AND ADVERSARIAL APPROACHES

Within these current legal traditions, two distinct approaches to resolving criminal cases have developed — the inquisitorial approach (sometimes referred to as the accusatorial approach) and the adversarial approach. The differences found in the inquisitorial and adversarial approaches generally involve the roles of judges, attorneys, defendants and witnesses in developing and presenting evidence in the case. No country has a pure form of either inquisitorial model or adversarial model, and the trend has been a significant blending of practices in both models. The inquisitorial approach is used in nations that are part of the civil law tradition and to some extent in nations that follow a religious legal tradition. It places greater emphasis on the pre-trial screening of evidence. Judges, often called "examining magistrates" or "investigating magistrates," direct the investigation of the crime. The truth about the defendant's role in committing the crime is said to emerge through this extensive pre-trial investigation. Trials in the inquisitorial model are more perfunctory and tend to revolve around the appropriate resolution or sanction to be employed.

The adversarial approach is used in nations that are part of the common law tradition. It places greater emphasis on the use of confrontation and cross examination of the witnesses and evidence. The truth about the defendant's role in committing the crime is said to emerge once the defendant has challenged the government's evidence through cross-examination of prosecution witnesses. Trials in the adversarial model place more emphasis on the active role of the attorneys. Because roughly 95% of the cases in the United States are resolved through plea-bargaining and thus never go to trial, the primary truth-revealing stage is rarely reached.

CIVIL LAW, CRIMINAL LAW, AND MORAL LAW

Law is also classified as either private (civil law) or public (criminal law). Even though all legal actions[12] fall into one or the other of these two categories, one act or harm may violate both civil law and criminal law. For example, if Joe punches Sam in the face, Sam may sue Joe civilly, and the state may also criminally prosecute Joe for punching Sam.

CIVIL WRONGS

A civil wrong is a private wrong, and the injured party's remedy is to sue the party who caused the wrong/injury for money called "damages." The injured party (Sam) bringing the suit is called the "plaintiff." The party that caused the harm and is being sued (Joe) is called the

---

[11] *Id.*

[12] Legal actions are called by a variety of names including: "law suits," "cases," "actions," "claims," or "prosecutions."

"defendant" or "respondent." Plaintiffs can be individuals, businesses, classes of individuals (you may have heard of a "class action suit"[13]), or government entities, etc. Defendants in civil actions can also be individuals, businesses, multinational corporations, governments, or state agencies. Civil law covers many types of civil actions or suits including:

> torts (personal injury claims);
> contracts;
> property or real estate disputes;
> family law (divorces, adoptions, and child custody matters);
> intellectual property claims (copyright, trademark, and patent claims);
> and, trusts and estate laws (wills and probate).

The primary purpose of a civil suit is to compensate the injured party. The plaintiff brings the suit in his or her own name -- for example, Sam Smith versus Joe Jones. The amount of "damages," a monetary award, is theoretically related to the amount of harm done by the defendant to the plaintiff. Sometimes, when the jury finds there is a particularly egregious harm, it will decide to punish the defendant by awarding a monetary award called "punitive damages" in addition to general damages. Plaintiffs may also bring civil suits called "injunctive relief" to stop or "enjoin" the defendant from continuing to act in a certain manner. Codes of civil procedure set forth the rules to follow when suing the party who allegedly caused some type of private harm. These codes govern the myriad types of civil actions.

In a civil trial the plaintiff has the burden of producing evidence that the defendant injured or caused the plaintiff harm. To meet this burden, the plaintiff will call witnesses to testify and introduce physical evidence. In a civil case the plaintiff must convince or persuade the jury that it is more likely than not that the defendant caused the harm -- this level of certainty or persuasion is known as "preponderance of the evidence." Another feature in a civil suit is that the defendant can cross-sue the plaintiff (basically claiming that the plaintiff is actually responsible for the harm).

---

[13] On July 14, 2020 the New York Times reported:
"Expressing deep skepticism, a federal judge on Tuesday upended a $25 million proposed civil settlement between Harvey Weinstein, his former film company, and dozens of women who have accused him of sexual harassment and abuse.

In a scathing 18-minute phone hearing on Tuesday morning, Judge Alvin K. Hellerstein of the Southern District of New York picked apart the class-action lawsuit at the heart of the deal, suggesting it was misconceived. He asked why the women were not pursuing individual cases, given how much their allegations varied in severity, and whether the group met the definition of a legal class.

"What is there to make me believe that a person who just met Harvey Weinstein has the same claim as the person who is raped by Harvey Weinstein?" the judge asked.

He went on to question how the women's allegations would be evaluated and the money allocated among them, and called an additional $12 million that would have gone toward legal fees for Mr. Weinstein and his former company directors "obnoxious." He criticized Beth Fegan, the lead counsel for the plaintiffs in the class-action case, saying she wasted time "with settlements and attempts to create a class that doesn't exist.""

CRIMINAL WRONGS

Now that you have a basic idea of the civil or private law, we will turn to the focus of this text: criminal or public law. A crime is an act (or failure to act, generally referred to as an omission to act) that violates society's rules. The government (referred to as "the State" or "the Commonwealth" or "the United States") on behalf of society at large, is the plaintiff and brings the suit. A criminal wrong can be committed in many ways by individuals, groups, or businesses against individuals, businesses, governments or with no particular victim.

Criminal Defendant	Victim	Examples
Individual	self or with no particular victim	Gambling or drug use,
Individual	other individual(s)	assault, battery, theft
Individual	business or government	trespass, welfare fraud, treason
Group of individuals	individual or individuals	conspiracy to commit murder
Group of individuals	government or no particular victim	riot, rout, disorderly conduct
Business entity	Individuals	fraud
Business entity	government or no particular victim	fraud, pollution, tax evasion

Criminal laws reflect society's moral and ethical beliefs. They govern how society through its government agents, holds criminal wrongdoers accountable for their actions. Sanctions or remedies such as incarceration, fines, restitution, community service, and restorative justice program are used to express societal condemnation of the criminal's behavior. Government prosecutors file charges against criminal defendants on behalf of society--not necessarily to remedy the harm suffered by any particular victim. The title of a criminal prosecution reflects this: "State of California v. Jones," "the Commonwealth v. Jones," or "People v. Jones."

In a criminal jury trial or a "bench trial" (a trial in which the judge decides whether the defendant is guilty or not) the prosecutor carries the burden of producing evidence that will convince the jury or judge beyond any reasonable doubt that the criminal defendant committed a violation of law that harmed society. To meet this burden, the prosecutor will call upon witnesses to testify and may also present physical evidence which suggests the defendant committed the crime. Just as a private individual may decide that it is not worth the time or effort to file a legal action, the state may decide not to use its resources to file criminal charges against a wrongdoer. The injured party (the "victim") cannot force the state to prosecute the wrongdoing. Rather, if there is an appropriate civil claim (called a cause of action), the injured party will need to file a civil suit as a plaintiff and seek damages against the defendant. (Often, when the state proceeds with a criminal case, gets a conviction, and the court awards restitution (discussed later), the injured party will decide it is not worth the time and money to file a private suit.)

OVERLAP OF CRIMINAL LAW AND CIVIL LAW

Sometimes the criminal law and civil law overlap, and an individual's action constitutes both a violation of criminal law and civil law. The types of civil claims or civil suits that most resemble criminal law are referred to as "torts." Torts involve injuries inflicted upon a person for which the civil law awards money damages as compensation. In the example of Joe and Sam above, when Joe punches Sam and breaks Sam's nose, Joe's act is both a criminal wrong (criminal assault/battery) and a civil wrong (civil assault/battery). More familiar may be the case involving O.J. Simpson. Simpson was prosecuted for murder for killing his ex-wife, Nicole Brown Simpson, and her friend, Ron Goldman. After the criminal trial, the Brown and Goldman families filed a "wrongful death action" (a civil claim with wrongful death being the cause of action) against Simpson for killing the two.

Sometimes criminal behavior has no civil law counterpart. For example, the crime of possessing burglary tools does not have a civil law equivalent. Conversely, many civil actions do not violate the criminal law. For example, civil suits for divorce, wills, or contracts do not have corresponding criminal wrong. So, even though there is certainly an overlap between the criminal law and the civil law, it is not a perfect overlap.

MORAL WRONGS

Moral wrongs differ from criminal wrongs. "Moral law attempts to perfect personal character, whereas criminal law, in general, is aimed at misbehavior that falls substantially below the norms of the community. Criminal conduct is ordinarily unjustifiable and inexcusable."[14] There are no codes or statutes governing violations of moral laws in the United States. One of the most frequently cited examples of a moral wrong involves the story of thirty-seven neighbors who purportedly did nothing when "Kitty" Genovese was stabbed to death outside their apartment building in New York City in 1964. There are many discrepancies about this story and what the neighbors knew, or didn't know, and what they did, or didn't do, but the general belief is that they had at least a moral obligation to do something (for example, call the police), and by failing to do anything, they committed a *moral* wrong. Ultimately, none of the neighbors had any *legal* obligation to report the crime or intervene to help Ms. Genovese. In 2015 Netflix released a documentary, "The Witness," in which Bill Genovese, Kitty's brother, re-examined what was said, heard, reported about his sister's death and which sheds a new light on whether these neighbors committed even a moral wrong. It appears that 50 years of textbook debate and "neighbor shaming" has been based on very inaccurate information.

CLASSIFICATIONS BASED ON THE SERIOUSNESS OF THE OFFENSE

Legislatures typically distinguish crimes based on the severity or seriousness of the harm inflicted on the victim. The criminal's intent also impacts the crime's classification. Crimes are generally classified as felonies or misdemeanors. Certain, less serious, behavior may be classified as criminal violations or infractions. The term "offense" is a generic term that is sometimes used to mean any type of violation of the law, or it is sometimes used to mean just misdemeanors or felonies. Although these classification schemes may seem pretty straight forward, sometimes states allow felonies to be treated as misdemeanors and misdemeanors to be treated as either felonies or violations. For example, California has certain crimes, known as "wobblers," that can be charged as either felonies or misdemeanors based on the offender's criminal history or the specific facts of the case. In Oregon, state law allows prosecutors to give crimes classified as misdemeanors "violation treatment" (meaning to treat the defendant as if he or she were only charged with a violation rather than a misdemeanor—the difference primarily being that no incarceration occurs with violations.)

The distinction between felonies and misdemeanors developed at common law and has been incorporated in state criminal codes. At one time, all felonies were punishable by death and forfeiture of goods, while misdemeanors were punishable by fines alone. Laws change over time, and as capital punishment became limited to only certain felonies (like murder and rape),

---

[14] Thomas Gardner, *Criminal Law Principles and Cases*, 7 (3d ed., 1985).

new forms of punishment developed.[15] Now, felonies and misdemeanors alike are punished with fines and/or incarceration. Generally, felonies are treated as serious crimes for which at least a year in prison is a possible punishment. In states allowing capital punishment, some types of murder are punishable by death. Any crime subject to capital punishment is considered a felony. Misdemeanors are regarded as less serious offenses and are generally punishable by less than a year of incarceration in the local jail. Infractions and violations--when those classifications exist--include minor acts for which the offender can be cited, but not arrested, and fined, but not incarcerated.

The difference between being charged with a felony or misdemeanor may impact more than just the length of the offender's sentence and whether he or she is sent to prison or jail. For example, in some jurisdictions, the authority of a police officer to arrest may be linked to whether the crime is considered a felony or a misdemeanor. In 2019, for example, the Idaho Supreme Court held that, under the Idaho Constitution, police may only arrest without a warrant an individual for a felony or a misdemeanor committed in their presence.[16] In many states the classification impacts which court will have authority to hear the case. For example, many states allow misdemeanors to be heard in magistrates' courts (a court of "limited jurisdiction") while felonies must be tried by a trial court with felony or "general jurisdiction."[17] In some states, the felony-misdemeanor classification determines the size of the jury.

A number of states have adopted a classification for minor offenses suggested by the Model Penal Code (MPC)[18]. The MPC, which is discussed in greater detail below, treats behavior punishable only by a fine as a violation. Some states have followed this MPC distinction closely. Other states punish violations with both fines and incarceration. In New York, for example, violations include offenses punishable by a fine only or by a sentence of imprisonment that does not exceed fifteen days. As mentioned above, California has "wobblers." In Oregon, because violations or infractions are not considered crimes and are not punishable by incarceration, defendants have no right to appointed counsel when charged with violations or infractions.[19] Some states allow the lowest classification of misdemeanors to be either charged as violations or reduced to violations after sentencing.

MALA IN SE AND *MALA PROHIBITA* CRIMES

Crimes have also been classified as either *mala in se* (inherently evil) or *mala prohibita* (wrong simply because some law forbids them.) *Mala in se* crimes, like murder or theft, are "wrong in themselves." These behaviors are generally recognized by every culture as evil and morally wrong. Most offenses that involve injury to persons or property are *mala in se*. All of the

---

[15] *See*, Matthew Lippman, *Contemporary Criminal Law,* (3rd ed., 2013).

[16] *See*, https://idahonews.com/news/local/idaho-court-officer-didnt-see-misdemeanor-arrest-not-ok

[17] *See* Chapter Three for more on the structure and jurisdiction of courts.

[18] American Law Institute, *Model Penal Code,* 1962.

[19] In *State v. Fuller* (http://www.publications.ojd.state.or.us/docs/S060808.pdf, Oct. 3, 2013) and *State v. Benoit* (http://www.publications.ojd.state.or.us/docs/S060858.pdf, Oct. 3, 2013) the Oregon Supreme Court decided cases involving individuals arrested in 2010 as part of an Occupy Portland movement protest. At arraignment, the prosecutor notified the court that it would be giving these charges "violation treatment." Defense counsel objected and later successfully argued on appeal that it was unfair for the state to treat defendants' Class C misdemeanor charges as violations when they had already been arrested. Although seemingly counterintuitive (why wouldn't a defendant want to have a crime downgraded to a lesser offense—a non-criminal violation?), counsel noted that defendants initially suffered the stigma and pains of arrest and some periods of incarceration and suffered a "double whammy" when they were later denied the right to counsel and a jury trial because their charges were considered mere violations.

common law felonies were considered *mala in se* crimes.[20] *Mala prohibita* crimes, like traffic violations or drug possession, are acts that are not necessarily wrong. The act is not a crime because it is evil, but rather because some law prohibits it. Most of the newer crimes that are prohibited as part of a regulatory scheme are *mala prohibita* crimes.

The distinction between *mala in se* and *mala prohibita* may not be as important as it once was, but some jurisdictions retain different procedures or punishment structures tied to the crime's classification—for example, in some jurisdictions, causing an unintentional death during the course of a misdemeanor may be a homicide if the underlying misdemeanor is a *mala in se* offense but not if it is a *mala prohibitum* offense.

CLASSIFICATIONS BASED ON THE TYPE OF HARM INFLICTED

Almost all state codes classify crimes according to the type of harm inflicted. The MPC uses the following classifications:

- Offenses against persons (homicide, assault, kidnapping and rape, for example),
- Offenses against property (arson, burglary, and theft, for example),
- Offenses against family (bigamy and adultery, for example),
- Offenses against public administration (e.g., bribery, perjury, escape),
- Offenses against public order and decency (e.g., fighting, breach of peace, disorderly conduct, public intoxication, riots, loitering, prostitution).

Classifications based on the type of harm inflicted may be helpful for the purpose of organization, but some crimes such as robbery, may involve both harm to a person and property. Although generally, whether a crime is a person or property crime may not have any legal implications when a person is convicted, it may matter if and when the person commits a new crime. Most sentencing guidelines treat individuals with prior person-crime convictions more harshly than those individuals with only prior property-crime convictions. (That said, it is likely that the defense will argue that it is the facts of the prior case that matter not how the crime was officially classified.)

SUBSTANTIVE AND PROCEDURAL LAW

Another classification scheme views the law as either substantive law or procedural law. Substantive criminal law is generally created by statute (or through the initiative process) and defines what conduct is criminal. Substantive criminal law establishes the possible criminal penalties and identifies any defenses to criminal liability. For example, substantive criminal law tells us that Sam commits theft when he takes Joe's backpack if he did so without Joe's permission and intending to keep it. Substantive criminal law also specifies the punishment Sam could receive for stealing the backpack (for example, a fine up to $500.00 and incarceration of up to 30 days). The substantive law may also provide Sam a defense and a way to avoid conviction--for example, Sam may claim he reasonably mistook Joe's backpack as his own and therefore can assert a mistake of fact defense.

Criminal procedural law establishes the mechanisms to enforce the substantive law. Procedural law governs the process for determining the rights of the parties. It sets forth the rules governing searches and seizures, investigations, interrogations, pretrial procedures, and trial procedures. It may establish rules limiting certain types of evidence at trial, establishing

---

[20] A mnemonic can be used to learn the common law felonies: MR and MRS LAMB (Murder, Rape, Manslaughter, Robbery, Sodomy, Larceny, Arson, Mayhem and Burglary).

time lines, as well require the sharing of certain types of evidence and giving certain type of notice.

WRAP UP

Societies use both informal control and formal control to regulate their members' behavior. The law is a formal means of control. Law is functional when it helps society change, regulates disputes, and maintains order; it is dysfunctional when it represses individuals and limits their rights. Many legal traditions or families of law have existed over time. These legal traditions embrace certain values and approaches to how violations of law or disputes will be handled. Today, most countries follow either the common law traditions or civil law traditions. Criminal wrongs differ from civil or moral wrongs. Criminal wrongs are behaviors that harm society as a whole rather than one individual or entity specifically. When people violate the criminal law there are generally sanctions that include incarceration and fines. Classification schemes allow us to discuss aspects or characteristics of the criminal law: criminal law may be characterized as substantive or procedural; crimes may be felonies or misdemeanors (or wobblers) and either *mala in se* or *mala prohibita*; crimes are classified by their seriousness, by the actor's intent, or by the type of harm that results to persons, property, or the administration of justice.

SOME THINGS TO THINK ABOUT OR EXPLORE

> ➤ What recent events have you seen that reveal a dysfunction of law mentioned by professors Lippman and Freidman?
> ➤ Have you ever seen behavior which you believe is morally wrong, but to your knowledge is not a crime or a civil cause of action?
> ➤ Knowing the little you have read about inquisitorial systems of trial and adversarial systems of trial, which approach do you think is more likely to reveal the truth concerning the facts of the case?

TERMINOLOGY

- action (cause of action)
- adversarial approach/system
- bench trial
- burden of persuasion
- burden of production
- burden of proof
- civil law
- Civil law (legal tradition)
- classifications with legal significance
- Common law (legal tradition)
- criminal law
- damages/general damages
- defendant
- enjoin (injunction)
- felony
- fines
- infraction
- inquisitorial approach/system
- law
- legal tradition (or family of law)
- mala in se crimes
- mala prohibita crimes
- misdemeanor
- moral wrong
- offense
- plaintiff
- procedural law
- punitive damages
- state (government)
- substantive law
- tort
- violation

Chapter Two: The Structure of Government and Its Relationship to the Criminal Law

OVERVIEW AND LEARNING OBJECTIVES

This chapter examines the organization of our government and the role that courts and constitutions play in the administration of justice. After reading this chapter, you should be able to answer the following questions:

➤ How does the governmental structure in the United States influences the workings of the American criminal justice system?
➤ What is the relationship between state and national governments and their criminal justice systems?
➤ What is the rule of law, why is it important, and how do we adhere to the rule of law in the United States?
➤ How do courts ensure that legislative enactments do not violate the Constitution?
➤ How do courts ensure that executive actions do not violate the Constitution?
➤ Where does Congress get its authority to pass federal criminal laws?
➤ Where do state legislatures get their authority to pass state criminal laws?
➤ What happens when state laws and federal laws conflict?
➤ What is constitutional supremacy?
➤ What are the sources of criminal law in the United States?
➤ What is stare decisis?
➤ What tools do judges have to help them when interpreting vague laws or cases of first impression (and what is a case of first impression?)

THE STRUCTURE OF AMERICAN GOVERNMENT

Legal scholar Professor Matthew Lippman stated,

> The genius of the American Constitution is the creation of a governmental structure characterized by separation of powers, checks and balances, and federalism. In this system of divided government, no single branch of government is able to monopolize power or to enforce its will. The branches of the federal government must cooperate with another and with the state governments to govern effectively.[21]

In recent times you may question the accuracy of Lippman's proclamation, but in general it has held true over more than 200 years.

SEPARATION OF POWERS

Federal and state constitutions generally adopt the same governmental structure. These constitutions divide authority among three branches of government. These branches of government--the executive branch, the legislative branch, and the judicial branch--are said to be "separate but equal." By dividing authority among the branches, there is a check and balance on each, and this is referred to as the separation of powers. The legislative branch is responsible for making the laws that specify crimes and their punishments. The executive branch is responsible

---

[21] Lippman, *Law and Society*, supra at 98.

for enforcing the laws and for carrying out the punishments. The judicial branch interprets the laws and ensures that persons charged with crimes receive fair treatment by the criminal justice system and also imposes punishment (carried out by the executive branch).

Whittington and Iuliano note,

> The United States Constitution does not include an explicit provision recognizing the principle of separation of powers, but the commitment to some form of separation of powers across three branches of government is evident throughout the constitutional scheme and various provisions of the constitutional text. Article I of the Constitution specifies that "[a]ll legislative Powers herein granted shall be vested in a Congress of the United States." Article II and Article III include their own vesting clauses, placing "[t]he executive Power" in the hands of the President of the United States and "[t]he judicial Power of the United States . . . in one supreme Court, and in such inferior Courts as the Congress may from time to time ordain and establish." The Constitution thus recognizes the existence of distinct functional powers that can be characterized as either legislative, executive, or judicial and places those powers in hands of different government entities or officials.

> To the extent that the Constitution departs from a pure separation-of-powers model and allows some sharing of powers across the branches of government, those exceptions are spelled out in the text. Whether to introduce some checks and balances into the constitutional system or to take advantage of some potential governmental efficiencies, the President is, for example, given a share of the legislative power through the prerogative of the presidential veto. Similarly, the Senate is given a share of the executive power through the right to advise and consent to the appointment of government officers.

> The sharing of political power across government branches means that the Constitution creates a certain "invitation to struggle" over the control of government policy. However, the Constitution also provides each branch of government a certain core of inalienable power and authority. There is no explicit textual prohibition on the delegation of legislative power to other actors, but such a rule has long been thought implicit in the U.S. Constitution.

> There are a variety of arguments explaining why a principle of nondelegation might be found in these textual provisions and the broader structure of the separation of powers. The very idea of a separation of powers might suggest that executive officials should refrain from, or be barred from, exercising legislative powers. Consolidating the legislative and executive functions in the same hands has long been seen as a serious threat to liberty, and a core principle of liberal constitutional theory was to separate those distinct governmental functions in distinct governmental organs.[22]

As just noted, one issue arising from the separations of powers structure concerns the limits of sharing political power. Generally, lawmakers cannot allow others to make laws. According to what is referred to as the "nondelegation doctrine" the legislative branch cannot

---

[22] Keith Whittington and Jason Iuliano. The Myth of the Delegation Doctrine, *The University of Pennsylvania Law Review*, Vol. 165, No 379 (2017), pp. 379-431 at pp. 388-389.

delegate its lawmaking authority to executive and administrative agencies. When such delegations are challenged in Court, the legal test used by the Court is the "intelligible principle test" which in essence holds that Congress cannot delegate its lawmaking authority to the executive branch unless it provides guidance and directives on how to do so. When authorizing a government official or agency to regulate or otherwise implement the law, Congress must "lay down by legislative act an intelligible principle to which the person or body authorized to [act] is directed to conform.

In June, 2022, the Court decided *West Virginia v. EPA* ___ US ___ (2022)[23] and held that the Environmental Protection Agency exceeded its authority in passing some regulations. The Court found that the EPA and other governmental agencies do not have authority in policy matters of economic and political significance ("major questions") and that these decisions must be made by Congress. Thus, we have a recent case where the new 6-3 conservative Court has, as anticipated, made a significant blow to the "administrative state."

> The US Supreme Court's recent climate change ruling was a setback for climate action and, in the words of one conservative legal scholar, it ignored the legal principles the Court's conservative majority claims to uphold. . . . The Supreme Court elevated a recent judge-made legal framework known as the "major questions doctrine" to find that the EPA's climate pollution standards for existing power plants exceeded its authority. The Court concluded that the particular program design employed by the EPA was a "highly consequential power beyond what Congress could reasonably be understood to have granted." The Court also explained the "major questions" doctrine should be applied only in "extraordinary cases" and such cases necessitated "clear congressional authorization."

> . . .

> The Court did not specify the "best system of emission reduction" EPA should consider in establishing future climate pollution standards for existing power plants. The Court also found that the "EPA itself still retains the primary regulatory role in Section 111(d)," the provisions of the Clean Air Act establishing standards of performance for existing power plants, oil and gas methane, and other similar industrial sources, and therefore the EPA "decides the amount of pollution reduction that must ultimately be achieved" under state implementation plans.[24,25]

---

[23] See, https://www.oyez.org/cases/2021/20-1530

[24] https://www.edf.org/article/supreme-courts-ruling-climate-change-explained?ub_tg=372&ub_o=26&ub_cta=4&utm_source=google&utm_campaign=edf_none_upd_pmt&utm_medium=ad&utm_id=1666800886&gclid=EAIaIQobChMIyrLnm8GN-wIVIiatBh2nUQ7XEAAYASAAEgKIpPD_BwE&gclsrc=aw.ds

[25] See also, https://www.goodstewardsnetwork.org/post/supreme-court-deals-blow-to-energy-policy-in-west-virginia-v-epa?gclid=EAIaIQobChMIyrLnm8GN-wIVIiatBh2nUQ7XEAAYAiAAEgL92PD_BwE; https://pacificlegal.org/apocalypse-west-virginia-v-epa-really-means/?gclid=EAIaIQobChMIyrLnm8GN-wIVIiatBh2nUQ7XEAAYAyAAEgIGrfD_BwE

EXECUTIVE BRANCH

The executive branch at the national level includes the President of the United States and executive agencies. The President is the chief law enforcement officer of the United States and is responsible for ensuring that all laws passed by Congress are enforced and that persons who violate the laws are held accountable. The President relies on the Department of Justice (an executive branch agency), the Attorney General, and the U.S. Attorneys to prosecute violations of federal law. Federal law enforcement officers (for example FBI, DEA, ATF, ICE, EPA, and Homeland Security agents) conduct investigations of federal crimes.

At the state level, the executive branch includes the governor, state attorneys general, local prosecutors, state law enforcement officers, and various executive branch agencies. At the local level, the executive branch comprises city mayors, local solicitors, local prosecutors, local police or sheriffs. At the state and local level, administrative agencies assist in the investigation and prosecution of crimes.

Presidents' Use of Executive Agencies and Executive Orders

United States presidents, through administrative agencies, have the authority to enact regulations that, in effect, create criminal laws (subject to the constraints of the non-delegation doctrine discussed above). Under the Constitution of the United States[26], Congress has delegated substantial authority to presidents to execute laws through the adoption of regulations by administrative agencies. For example, the Department of Fish and Wildlife may enact regulations, whose violations carry criminal penalties.

Additionally, although the Constitution does not specifically permit executive orders, Article II of the Constitution[27] grants executive power to the President. Article II, Section 3 Clause 5 states that the President shall "take Care that the Laws be faithfully executed."[28] Most presidents justify their executive orders as an exercise of their sworn duty and authority to help direct officers of the United States. Executive orders are regarded as having the full force of law either because they are seen as being authorized by some act of Congress that specifically delegates to the President some degree of discretionary power (delegated legislation) or because they are seen as flowing from direct powers to the Executive branch by the Constitution. Executive orders, like other laws, are subject to judicial review, and to the extent that the executive order violates the Constitution, the Court may declare it invalid. For example, in *Hamdan v. Rumsfeld*, 548 U.S. 557 (2006), the Court ruled that military tribunals were neither authorized by federal law nor required by military necessity. The Court found that President George W. Bush's executive order establishing special tribunals to try foreign national accused of

---

[26] This text refers to the federal constitution as "the Constitution" (with a capital C) and sometimes the U.S. Constitution, or federal constitution for clarity. State constitutions will be identified as state constitutions. The Supreme Court of the United States is similarly referred to as the Court (with a capital C), and sometimes as the U.S. Supreme Court. Amendments to the United States Constitution will be referred to by their number; for example, the First Amendment to the United States Constitution will be referred to as simply, "the First Amendment."

[27] U.S. Const. art. II, § 1, cl. 1.

[28] U.S. Const. art. II, § 3, cl. 5.

terrorism against the United States ran afoul of the Geneva Convention's[29] provisions governing the treatment of prisoners of war.

LEGISLATIVE BRANCH

The legislative branch at the national level consists of members of the United States House of Representatives and the United States Senate — collectively referred to as "Congress." Article I of the Constitution governs the structure, authority, and powers of the legislative branch. The role of Congress is to enact laws — called "acts." To become law these acts must generally be passed by a majority vote within each chamber[30] and approved by the President. If the President vetoes the proposed legislation, Congress can override the veto with the vote of two thirds of the members of each house.

At the state level, the legislative branch is comprised of the fifty states' legislative bodies (of various names) that pass state statutes. Except for Nebraska, all states have two chambers that must jointly approve proposed legislation. The state governor must then approve these bills. Once signed and enacted as "statutes," these laws apply throughout the state.

Most states empower local government bodies to enact local laws. At the local level, county commissioners, village and city councilors, and township trustees pass local codes and ordinances. These local ordinances must comply with both state and federal law. (See below, legislative law, ballots, initiatives and referendums).

JUDICIAL BRANCH

The judicial branch is made up of various courts. In Chapter Three you will read more about the organization, structure, and function of "Article I Courts" and "Article III Courts." But succinctly, Article III of the Constitution establishes a Supreme Court and allows that Court to establish lower tribunals (a tribunal is another name for a court). Article I of the Constitution gives Congress authority to establish courts as well. Both Article III and Article I courts are responsible for interpreting congressional acts and ensuring that the laws are applied fairly and consistently. These courts' primary responsibility is to determine what legal rules should be applied to the cases before them. At the trial level, the basic duties of the judicial branch are to determine the relevant rules of law, ascertain the facts involved in the particular case, relate those facts to the relevant law, and enter conclusions consistent with those laws and facts. At the appellate level, the primary duty of the judicial branch is to determine whether there has been a serious legal error at the trial. Since a significant source of error is the trial judge's possible reliance upon the wrong rules of law, the appellate court must also decide and interpret what the applicable rules of law are.

FEDERALISM

In addition to the division of government into three separate branches, the American government is divided into one national government, 50 state governments, one capital district (Washington, D.C.), and several territories. Each governmental division has its own criminal justice system. The national government operates to enforce federal criminal laws,[31] and each sovereign state or territory has its own system of justice to define and enforce its own criminal

---

[29] The Geneva Convention is comprised of four international treaties and three additional protocols that establish standards for the humanitarian treatment of wartime prisoners. The United States is a signatory to the four treaties and to one of the protocols.

[30] When the Senate splits votes and is tied 50-50, the Vice President of the United States casts the controlling vote.

[31] In this text, military and tribal tribunals are being treated as part of the national government.

laws. The division of authority between these state systems and the national system is called federalism. One challenge in dealing with criminal law is being able identify those behaviors which can be governed exclusively by state law, those behaviors which can be governed exclusively by the federal law, and those behaviors which can be regulated by either or both. As will be discussed below, states have broad authority to pass criminal law, but the federal government's authority is much more limited.

> The Constitution gives the national government jurisdiction over activities such as interstate and international commerce, foreign relations, warfare, immigration, and certain crimes committed on high seas and against the 'law of nations.' Individual states are prohibited from entering into treaties with foreign governments, from printing their own money, from granting titles of nobility. States, however, retain the power to make laws regulating or criminalizing activity within their boundaries. The general authority of the states to regulate for health, safety, and welfare of their citizens is the police power.[32]

Although the Constitution carves out significant authority for the federal government to regulate all types of interactions, it does not authorize the federal government to regulate areas that belong exclusively to the states. The Tenth Amendment to the U.S. Constitution protects state sovereignty stating, "the powers not delegated to the United States by the Constitution, nor prohibited by it to the states, are reserved to the states respectively, or to the people."[33]

STATES' AUTHORITY TO PASS CRIMINAL LAWS

States are sovereign and autonomous, and unless the Constitution takes away state power, the states have broad authority to regulate activity within the state. Most state criminal law is derived from the states' general "police powers" to make and enforce criminal law within their geographic boundaries. Police power is the power to control any harmful act that may affect the general wellbeing of citizens within the geographical jurisdiction of the state. A state code may regulate any harmful activity done in the state or whose harm occurs within the state. The states have substantial police power over all individuals within their jurisdictions.

CONGRESS'S AUTHORITY TO PASS LAWS

Federal lawmakers do not possess police power. Instead, Congress must draw its authority to enact criminal statutes from particular legislative powers and responsibilities assigned to it in the Constitution. Congress's legislative authority may be either enumerated in the Constitution or implied from its provisions, but if Congress cannot tie its exercise of authority to one of those powers, the legislation may be declared invalid.

Enumerated powers, for example the power to regulate interstate commerce, are those that are specifically mentioned in Article I Section 8 of the Constitution. Over the years, courts have broadly interpreted the term "interstate commerce" to mean more than just goods and services traveling between and among the states. Instead, interstate commerce includes any activity — including purely local or intrastate activity — that affects interstate commerce. The affectation doctrine[34] maintains that congressional authority includes the right to regulate all

---

32 John Feldmeier and Frank Schmalleger, *Criminal Law and Procedure for Legal Professionals*, 29 (2012).
33 U.S. Const. amend. X.
34 Generally, the "affectation doctrine" means that Congress may regulate any activity when it has a rational basis for concluding that the economic activity being regulated substantially affects interstate commerce. *See*, legallynoted.com/2011/11/05/affectation-doctrine/. *See also*, "affectation doctrine," Bryan Garner, *A Dictionary of Modern Legal Usage.* (2 ed., 1995).

matters having a close and substantial relation to interstate commerce.[35] Although the Court has found limits on what affects interstate commerce, Congress has used its broad power to regulate interstate commerce to criminalize a wide range of offenses including carjacking, kidnapping, wire fraud, and a variety of environmental crimes.

The implied powers of Congress are those that are deemed to be "necessary and proper" for carrying out all the enumerated powers.[36] Article I Section 8 of the Constitution states, "Congress shall have Power . . . to make laws which shall be necessary and proper for carrying into Execution the foregoing Powers, and all other Powers vested by this Constitution." In *McCulloch v. Maryland*, 17 U.S. 316 (1819), United States Supreme Court Chief Justice John Marshall established the implied powers doctrine by stating, "let the end be legitimate, let it be within the scope of the Constitution, and all means which are plainly adapted to that end, which are not prohibited, but consist with the letter and spirit of the Constitution, are constitutional." This implied powers doctrine expands legislative power of Congress. And, for that reason, the Necessary and Proper Clause has often been called the "expansion clause."

Because of the implied powers found in the Necessary and Proper Clause, Congress has authority to pass legislation and regulate a wide variety of activity to the extent that it is able to show that the law furthers one of the enumerated powers. Nevertheless, the Court will overturn acts of Congress when it believes Congress has overstepped its constitutional authority. For example, in *United States v. Lopez*, 514 U.S. 549 (1995), the Court held that Congress exceeded its authority when it passed the 1990 Gun Free School Zones Act that made it a crime to possess a firearm in a school zone. Chief Justice Rehnquist noted, "The challenged statute has nothing to do with 'commerce' or any sort of economic enterprise, however broadly one might define those terms." Similarly, in *Jones v. United States 529 U.S. 848* (2000), the Supreme Court overturned Jones' federal arson conviction for firebombing his cousin's home under a federal statute which makes maliciously damaging or destroying any building in interstate commerce a federal crime. The Court found that the Indiana home was not used in interstate commerce even though, as the federal government argued, the home loan was guaranteed by an out-of-state lender and the home received gas from outside of Indiana. In *United States v. Morrison*, 529 U.S. 598 (2000), the Court invalidated the federal Violence Against Women Act of 1994 that provided victims of gender crimes a civil cause of action (a means to file a civil law suit) against their attackers. The Court found that, because rape is "not, in any sense of the phrase an economic activity," Congress lacked authority to regulate it under the Commerce Clause. So, despite the broad expanse of implied powers, Congress's authority is still limited and by no means as vast as the states' police powers.

> The federal government's authority . . . is limited by the federal constitution's restriction of federal legislation to specified subjects. Congress may deal only with activities that relate to areas specifically entrusted to the federal government by the Constitution. The most significant areas within this federal authority are: the regulation of interstate and foreign commerce; the maintenance and direction of federal service agencies such as the armed forces and the postal services; the coining and distribution of money; the imposition and collection of taxes; the enforcement of civil rights; and the regulation of federal territories. Federal criminal statutes can reach activities anywhere in the United States, but those activities must be related to these special areas of federal concern. . . .

---

[35] Feldmeier and Schmalleger, *supra* at 32.
[36] See, U.S. Const. art. I, § 8.

Viewed in terms of their relationship to particular areas of federal authority, federal crimes tend to fall into three basic categories. First, there are those crimes that relate to the federal government's power to carry out basic federal governmental functions . . . A second, closely related category of federal offenses seeks to protect certain private facilities in which the federal government has a special interest as a result of its close regulation or financial involvement. The prime illustration of such a facility is the federally insured bank . . . .. The third category of federal crimes also tends to overlap with state law. This category is composed of federal offenses based upon Congress's regulatory powers. Thus, Congress, utilizing its authority to enforce civil rights, has made it a crime for state official to intentionally infringe upon civil liberties protected by the federal constitution. Similarly, in the exercise of its authority over commerce between the states, Congress has adopted a wide variety of criminal provisions relating to activities that extend across state lines.

. . .

It should be emphasized that, while the federal criminal code plays a significant role in the overall enforcement of our substantive law, it is far from dominant. For those criminal activities relating to unique federal government functions . . . federal statutes clearly are the primary (and sometimes exclusive) source of prosecution. For most types of criminal activity, however, even where both federal and state laws apply (as in gambling and narcotics), the vast majority of all prosecutions are based on the state codes.[37]

CONSTITUTIONAL SUPREMACY

To the extent that state laws conflict with the federal Constitution, the federal Constitution generally controls. The term "constitutional supremacy" is derived from Article VI, Section 2 of the Constitution which states, "This Constitution . . . shall be the supreme Law of the Land; and the Judges in every State shall be bound thereby, any Thing in the Constitution or Laws of any State to the Contrary notwithstanding."

The Supremacy Clause ensures that federal standards serve as the minimum legal threshold for acceptable criminal practices. State law must give way whenever state law provides fewer individual rights than the federal Constitution. States are, however, free to provide more individual rights and civil liberties than the federal Constitution does. An example may illustrate. In Michigan, law enforcement officials were concerned with the harm caused by drunken drivers, so they developed a roadblock system designed to detect drunken drivers. Rick Sitz was a Michigan citizen with a valid driver's license who, with others, filed a civil suit requesting the court stop the state from erecting the roadblocks; Sitz claimed that the roadblocks were unlawful seizures and thus violated the Fourth Amendment to the U.S. Constitution. Ultimately, the Court found that the Michigan roadblock program did not violate the U.S. Constitution. However, the Court returned the case to Michigan for further proceedings, and upon further review, the Michigan Supreme Court determined that the roadblock program violated Michigan's own constitution, so it disallowed the roadblocks.[38] (Thus Michigan's laws provided more rights than the U.S. Constitution.)

---

[37] Kerper, *supra* at 73-74.
[38] For an examination of Oregon's policy on "DUII" checkpoints *see*,
  http://www.koin.com/news/investigative/oregons-battle-on-sobriety-checkpoints.

Sometimes substantive federal law conflicts with state laws or policies, and sometimes the federal government's interest in prosecuting cases in federal court conflicts with competing interests of the states. One debate surrounds the conflicting federal and state laws governing marijuana use.[39] The case of *Gonzalez v. Raich*, 545 U.S. 1 (2005), started a string of legal battles in the Courts and throughout the states. In *Raich*, the Supreme Court found that the California law protecting the cultivation and use of marijuana for medicinal purposes conflicted with a federal law properly passed under Congress's authority to regulate interstate commerce. The Court stated:

> Given the enforcement difficulties that attend distinguishing between marijuana cultivated locally and marijuana grown elsewhere, and concerns about diversion into illicit channels, we have no difficulty concluding that Congress had a rational basis for believing that failure to regulate the interstate manufacture and possession of marijuana would leave a gaping hole in the . . . [federal government's law].[40]

Between 1996 and November 2022, thirty-six states and the District of Columbia passed laws legalizing the possession of small quantities of marijuana for medicinal purposes for state residents.[41] As of November 2022, 20 states[42] and the District of Columbia allow have legalized marijuana for recreational use by adults in small amounts through the use of legislation and state-wide initiatives and referendums. These laws conflict directly with the federal Controlled Substance Act, 21 U.S.C. 13, § 841, (CSA) which holds that any use or possession of marijuana is a federal crime.[43] Despite the conflict between the state and federal laws on marijuana, the federal government, starting with the Obama administration have embraced a policy of federal self-restraint in prosecution of marijuana law violations in run-of-the-mill cases. Congress followed, and in June 2019, the House of Representatives widely passed a measure which blocks the Department of Justice from enforcing national marijuana laws in states which have legalized marijuana.[44]

In the November 2020 election, Oregon became the first state to decriminalize cocaine, heroin, methamphetamine when voters passed Ballot Measure 110. The ballot measure made possession of personal non-commercial amount of a Schedule I – IV controlled substance (heroin, cocaine and methamphetamine) no more than a Class E violation carrying a maximum fine of $100.00 dollars. It also established a drug addiction treatment and recovery program which was

---

[39] Another recent conflict between federal interests and state interests involves Oregon's physician-assisted suicide law, the "Death with Dignity Act." The Court in *Gonzalez v. Oregon*, 546 U.S. 243 (2006), decided that U.S. Attorney General Ashcroft's threat to revoke the medical licenses of physicians who took part in state-approved physician assisted suicide was an illegal directive. The Court reasoned that the federal Controlled Substance Act of 1970 did not authorize the U.S. Attorney General to regulate medical matters within the states nor did it authorize the Attorney General to declare illegitimate a medical practice authorized under state law.

[40] 545 U.S. at 33 (2005).

[41] See, https://time.com/6231201/marijuana-legal-elections-2022/

[42] See, https://time.com/6231201/marijuana-legal-elections-2022/

[43] When federal law conflicts with state law, the executive branch always has the option to back down. Sometimes it does--as was the case in 2013 when Attorney General Holder issued a statement indicating that the U.S. Department of Justice would let the recreational marijuana laws go into effect. Sometimes it does not--as was the case in 2002 when "the Guru of Ganja" Ed Rosenthal, a California horticulturist well-known as a proponent of legalized medicinal and recreational marijuana, was arrested for cultivating marijuana even though he was validly licensed to do so under state and local laws.

[44] https://www.forbes.com/sites/tomangell/2019/06/20/congress-votes-to-block-feds-from-enforcing-marijuana-laws-in-legal-states/#7a4c1f524b62

to be funded by tax revenue arising from legalized marijuana. Individuals who are found guilty of the violation would either receive a fine or have the option of participating in a health assessment which are to be conducted through addiction recovery centers and include a substance use disorder screening by a certified alcohol and drug counselor to be completed within 45 days of the violation; individuals who were found guilty of manufacture or distribution of the drugs were still subject to criminal penalties.[45]

RULE OF LAW, RECHTSTAAT AND JUDICIAL REVIEW

One of the key features of the American legal system has been its commitment to the rule of law. Rule of law has been defined as a "belief that an orderly society must be governed by established principles and known standards that are uniformly and fairly applied."[46] Philip Reichel, in his text on comparative criminal justice systems,[47] identified a three-step process by which countries can achieve rule of law. The first step is that a country must identify core, fundamental values. The second step is for the values to be reduced to writing—they must be written somewhere that people can point to them. The final step is to establish a process or mechanism whereby laws or governmental actions are tested to see if they are consistent with the fundamental values. When laws and actions embrace the fundamental values, they are considered valid; when the laws and actions conflict with the fundamental values, they are invalid. Does the United States adhere to the rule of law under Reichel's three-step analysis? In theory, yes. First, we have recognized fundamental values--for example, the right to religious freedom, the right to privacy, the right to be free from unreasonable searches and seizures, and the right to assemble. Second, we have reduced our fundamental values to writing and, for the most part, have included them in our Constitution. Third, we have a mechanism--that of judicial review--by which we judge whether our laws and our government actions comply with or violate the Constitution.

Judicial review is the authority of the courts to determine whether a law or action conflicts with the Constitution, and it can be traced to the case of *Marbury v. Madison*, 5 U.S. 137 (1803), in which Chief Justice John Marshall wrote, "It is emphatically the province and duty of the judicial department to say what the law is. Those who apply the rule to particular cases, must of necessity expound and interpret that rule. If two laws conflict with each other, the courts must decide on the operation of each. "

Executive Actions and The Rule of Law

When law enforcement officers arrest an individual, they are engaging in an executive action. A court can review these actions to see if the police behavior complies with the values set out in the Constitution. Similarly, when a prosecutor takes a long, long time to bring a case to trial, this is an executive action (or more aptly, inaction). Actions by probation officers, parole officers, and guards also are executive actions. The following example illustrates how an executive action will be reviewed to see if it meets the rule of law: Police Officer Jones arrests Baker without a warrant at Baker's home. While there, Jones conducts an extensive search of Baker's home believing it contains evidence of a crime. In fact, Jones finds evidence of a crime and seizes it. Baker files a motion to exclude the evidence Jones found at his home, claiming that

---

[45] See,
https://ballotpedia.org/Oregon_Measure_110,_Drug_Decriminalization_and_Addiction_Treatment_Initiative_(2020)#:~:text=Oregon%20Measure%20110%2C%20Drug%20Decriminalization%20and%20Addiction%20Treatment%20Initiative%20(2020),-From%20Ballotpedia&text=Oregon%20Measure%20110%2C%20the%20Drug,It%20was%20approved.
[46] Feldmeier and Schmalleger, *supra* at 2.
[47] *See*, Reichel, *supra*.

Jones violated the Fourth Amendment (the provision dealing with searches and seizures). At the hearing the judge is engaging in a judicial action by interpreting constitutional law and seeing whether Jones's actions violated a fundamental value (the right to be free from unreasonable searches and seizures found in the Fourth Amendment). No member of the executive branch (here, a police officer) is above the law, and no executive actions which conflict with our fundamental values should be allowed to go without remedy.

Legislative Actions and The Rule of Law

When Congress or state legislators enact laws, the laws may potentially conflict with the fundamental values in the Constitution. For example, consider a law that made it a capital offense (one in which the defendant may receive the death penalty) to write the word "shark" on a building. This is not only a silly law, but it may violate the Constitution since it is governmental action abridging speech which is prohibited by the First Amendment; the law allows for cruel and unusual punishment prohibited by the Eighth Amendment.[48]

Boumediene et. al v. Bush, 553 U.S. 723 (2008) provides an example of a legislative act being subject to the rule of law and judicial review. In that case, the Court ruled that prisoners held as enemy combatants at Guantanamo Bay could immediately challenge the legality of their confinement. The Court's majority ruled that the provision of the 2006 Military Commissions Act (MCA) (a legislative enactment) which stripped Guantanamo Bay prisoners of their habeas corpus rights (a mechanism by which prisoners could challenge their confinement) was unconstitutional.

Judicial Branch and The Rule of Law.

Since judicial review is one of their primary functions, courts play a pivotal role in fostering the rule of law in the United States. Courts review legislative and executive acts for their constitutionality and, when those laws and actions conflict with the Constitution, the courts declare them "null and void" (having no force or validity). Courts also engage in judicial review of judicial actions. Appellate courts invalidate erroneous judgments of trial court (this is the primary function of the appellate courts). Courts may also review actions (or inactions) by members of the judiciary or judicial branch to determine whether they violate the Constitution. For example, if it could be shown that a judge routinely refused to set bail for defendants based upon their race, the courts would review this action and find such action violates the Equal Protections Clause of the Constitution. As another example, a U.S. District Court ruled that a granite carving of the Ten Commandments installed in the Alabama Supreme Court was an unconstitutional endorsement of religion. The then Alabama Supreme Court Chief Justice, Roy Moore, refused to obey the federal court's order to remove it, and he was ultimately removed from office by a state judiciary ethics panel.

SPECIALIZED COURTS AND TRIBUNALS

MILITARY LAW AND TRIBUNALS

Military law and military tribunals make up a separate system of justice--one of the many systems of justice found in the United States. Article 1, Section 8 of the Constitution grants Congress the authority to regulate the armed forces. Under this authority, Congress enacted the Uniform Code of Military Justice (UCMJ). Under the UCMJ, military tribunals have courts-martial jurisdiction to try all offenses committed by military personnel.[49] The military trial

---

[48] The Court defines cruel and unusual punishment as punishment that is disproportionate to the severity of the offense.

[49] Military tribunals only have jurisdictions over civilians under conditions of martial law. *Ex parte Milligan,* 71 U.S. 2 (4 Wall.) (1866).

procedure and rules of evidence are similar to those of the federal district courts. A military judge presides at the courts-martial convened by the commanders of the various military units. Trial counsel, referred to as a "staff judge advocate," serves as a prosecutor, and the government provides the defendant with legal counsel (also a staff judge advocate) unless the defendant chooses to hire private defense counsel. Decisions of the courts-martial are reviewed by military courts of review in each branch of the armed forces. Appeals are heard by the United States Court of Appeals for the Armed Forces staffed by civilian judges appointed by the President, with the consent of Senate.

TRIBAL COURTS

The tribal courts and tribal laws make up another distinct system of justice in America. The law governing tribal courts is somewhat confusing because the Court has taken an inconsistent, patchwork approach in deciding when tribal courts have jurisdiction over matters. Generally speaking, crimes that occur on tribal reservations and on tribal lands are decided in tribal courts. Crimes committed by members of the tribe or against a tribal member are also generally handled in tribal courts. That said, Indian tribes are subject to Congressional legislation under Article I, Section 8 of the U.S. Constitution, and Congress gave federal courts jurisdiction over specified offenses committed by Native Americans on Indian reservations. Congress has also permitted certain states to exercise jurisdiction over certain offenses.

One landmark 5-4 Supreme Court opinion is *McGirt v. Oklahoma*, 591 U.S. ____ (2020). McGirt, an enrolled member of the Seminole tribe, was convicted in Oklahoma state courts for three sex crimes which took place on the Creek Indian Reservation. He argued that only the federal government had jurisdiction to prosecute him because, under the federal Major Crimes Act, exclusive jurisdiction belonged to the United States. The Major Crimes Act provides that

> Within "the Indian country," "[a]ny Indian who commits" certain enumerated offenses "shall be subject to the same law and penalties as all other persons committing any of [those] offenses, within the exclusive jurisdiction of the United States." 18 U. S. C. §1153(a). "Indian country" includes "all land within the limits of any Indian reservation under the jurisdiction of the United States Government." §1151.

The Court agreed with McGirt. Justice Gorsuch stated, "Today we are asked whether the land these treaties promised remains an Indian reservation for purposes of federal criminal law. Because Congress has not said otherwise, we hold the government to its word." The opinion further stated,

> By subjecting Indians to federal trials for crimes committed on tribal lands, Congress may have breached its promises to tribes like the Creek that they would be free to govern themselves. But this particular incursion has its limits—applying only to certain enumerated crimes and allowing only the federal government to try Indians. State courts generally have no jurisdiction to try Indians for conduct committed in "Indian country." . . . The key question Mr. McGirt faces concerns that last qualification: Did he commit his crimes in Indian country?

The majority held that he did. Thus, the Court held that when a crime falls under the Major Crimes Act, much of the eastern portion of the state of Oklahoma is not under state jurisdiction but rather under Tribal jurisdiction. These crimes are properly be prosecuted in federal courts, not in the state court as McGirt had been.

The McGirt decision left many questions unresolved. One thing that McGirt did not declare (contrary to news headlines) was that "half the land in Oklahoma would be returned to Native Americans." Nor did the decision hold that all the state court prosecutions in the eastern half of the state were invalid (just the ones involving tribal members).[50] Quickly many legal challenges were filed contesting the McGirt decision, and within two years the U.S. Supreme Court had accepted for review, heard oral arguments on, and decided the case of *Oklahoma v. Castro-Huerto*.[51] Justice Kavanaugh's majority opinion in Castro-Huerto seriously undermined the holding in McGirt by stating that the "Federal Government and State Governments have concurrent jurisdiction to prosecute crimes committed by non-Indians against Indians in Indian country."[52]

SOURCES OF CRIMINAL LAW

Where do you look to see if something you want to do violates some criminal law? Because criminal law originates from many sources, the answer is "in many places." Some criminal law is the result of constitutional conventions—so you would need to review federal and state constitutions. Other criminal laws result from the legislative or initiative process—so you will need to scan state statutes or congressional acts. Other criminal law results from the work of administrative agencies—so you need to review state and federal administrative rules. Other criminal law, called case law, originates from appellate court opinions. These court opinions, called "decisions," are published in both official and unofficial reporters (volumes of books, but now available on the internet as well). Much of the criminal law descended from the English common law—this law developed over time, through custom and tradition, and it is a bit more difficult to locate, but it is mentioned in treatises and legal "hornbooks" (like legal encyclopedias) and is often referred to in case decisions. Finally, criminal law has its roots in natural law-- considered law from a supreme being. Although Americans do not tend to refer to natural law to help us resolve our disputes today, principles of natural law were important to the foundation of our criminal law and remain important in many countries' legal systems.

FEDERAL AND STATE CONSTITUTIONS

As you have just read, the Constitution plays a significant role in the American criminal justice system: it establishes federalism, requires the separation of powers between the three branches of government, and limits Congress's ability to pass laws not directly related to either its enumerated or implied powers. The Constitution says other things about criminal law and procedure as well. Article I restricts Congress from passing any laws that are retroactively

---

[50] For a brief description of the historical context of the "Trail of Tears" and a factual context of McGirt's crimes, see, https://www.natlawreview.com/article/review-mcgirt-v-oklahoma-how-supreme-court-and-justice-gorsuch-s-revolutionary. For an article discussing the interplay between tribal courts and federal courts and the track record of the federal courts in prosecuting crimes against Indians see https://www.washingtonpost.com/politics/2020/07/22/oklahoma-decision-reveals-why-native-americans-have-hard-time-seeking-justice/.

[51] Castro-Huerta was charged, tried, convicted and sentenced to 35 years in state court for child neglect. While Castro-Huerta's state-court appeal was pending, the Court decided *McGirt v. Oklahoma* which recognized the eastern part of Oklahoma, including Tulsa, as Indian country. Following this development, Castro-Huerta argued that the Federal Government had exclusive jurisdiction to prosecute him (a non-Indian) for a crime committed against his stepdaughter (a Cherokee Indian) in Tulsa (Indian country), and that the State therefore lacked jurisdiction to prosecute him. The Oklahoma Court of Criminal Appeals agreed and vacated his conviction. The U.S. Supreme Court accepted review (by granting a petition for the writ of certiorari). See, https://www.supremecourt.gov/opinions/21pdf/21-429_8o6a.pdf.

[52] See, also https://news.bloomberglaw.com/us-law-week/oklahoma-wins-second-supreme-court-round-on-tribal-prosecutions; and https://cops.usdoj.gov/html/dispatch/01-2022/McGirt_decision.html

applied (the Ex Post Facto Clause), or that are directed at named individuals (Bills of Attainder). The First Amendment limits Congress's ability to pass laws that limit free speech, freedom of religion, freedom of assembly and association. The Second Amendment limits Congress's ability to outlaw the personal possession of firearms. The Fourth, Fifth, Sixth and Eighth Amendments have provisions that govern criminal procedure during the investigative, pretrial, and trial phases of the criminal justice process. The Eighth Amendment sets limits on the government's ability to impose certain punishments. The Due Process Clause of the Fifth and Fourteenth Amendment require that criminal justice procedures be fundamentally fair. The Fourteenth Amendment's Equal Protection Clause requires that, at a minimum, there be some rational reason for treating people differently.

States' constitutions, similar to the U.S. Constitution, set forth the general organization of state government and basic standards governing the use of governmental authority. Although the federal constitution is preeminent because of the Supremacy Clause, state constitutions are still significant. State constitutional rules are supreme as compared to any other rules coming from all other state legal sources (statutes, ordinances, administrative rules) and prevail over such laws in cases of conflict.

As indicated above, state constitutions can grant individuals in the state more personal protections than does the federal constitution. For example, on September 4, 2020. In *McKelvey v. State,* (Ak. Ct. of Ap., No. A-12419), the Alaska Court of Appeals held that under the Alaska Constitution an aerial surveillance constituted a search and seizure when the resident/property owner took steps to protect the ground-level privacy of the yard. The court held that police must obtain a warrant before conducting targeted surveillance of a residential backyard when using a telephoto lens to discern objects not otherwise visible from that height. McKelvey's greenhouse was a short distance from his house and in an area surrounded by a natural sight-barrier of tall woods. It could not be seen from the ground by anyone who had approached his front door by normal means and who otherwise heeded the no-trespassing sign McKelvey had posted. The U.S. Supreme Court considered the federal constitution's protections in very similar situations in other cases but concluded that the Fourth Amendment to the U.S. Constitution did *not* require a warrant because such aerial surveillance was not a search. (See, e.g., *California v. Ciraolo*, 476 U.S. 207 (1986) and *Florida v. Riley*, 488 U.S. 445 (1989).)

LEGISLATIVE LAW

Most substantive criminal law is legislative law. State legislatures and U.S. Congress enact laws which take the form of statutes or congressional acts. Statutes are written statements, enacted into law by an affirmative vote of both chambers of the legislature and accepted (or not vetoed) by the governor or President. State legislatures may also establish legal standards through interstate compacts (for example, the Uniform Extradition Act, or the Uniform Fresh Pursuit Act). Congress makes federal law through passing acts and approving treaties between the United States and other nation states. Local legislators, city and town councilors, and county commissioners also make laws through the enactment of local ordinances.

BALLOT MEASURES, INITIATIVES, AND REFERENDUMS

In several states, citizens have the power to enact laws through direct democracy by putting "ballot measures" or "propositions" up for a vote. This type of lawmaking by the people started primarily in the Western states around the turn of the 20th century. Initiatives, referendums, and referrals have some slight differences, but generally, these ballot measures ultimately find their way into either statutes or the constitution, and so they are included in this section on legislative law. For example, Oregon Ballot Measure 11, establishing minimum mandatory sentences for 17 person felonies, was voted on in November 1994 and took effect

April 1, 1995. It is now found in the Oregon Revised Statutes as ORS 137.700. Proposition 36, overwhelmingly approved by Californians in 2012, significantly amended the "three strikes" sentencing laws, they approved in 1994.[53] Initiatives, referendums and referrals can be effective in quickly changing the criminal law (for example, mandatory sentencing in the 1980s) and is a way to circumvent what could have been a contentious legislative process (for example, the decriminalization of marijuana).

ADMINISTRATIVE LAW

State and federal legislatures cannot keep up with the task of enacting legislation on all the myriad subjects that must be regulated by law. In each branch of government, various administrative agencies exist with authority to create administrative law. At the federal level, for example, the Environmental Protection Agency enacts regulations against environmental crimes. At the state level, the Department of Motor Vehicles enacts crimes and violations concerning drivers' license suspension. Administrative regulations are enforceable by the courts provided that the agency has acted within the scope of its delegated authority from the legislature.

COMMON LAW

One source of criminal law in the United States is common law.[54] Generally, the reference to common law means the laws brought over from England to the United States.[55] LaFave describes the process by which common law was derived in England.

---

[53] See, https://law.stanford.edu/stanford-justice-advocacy-project/three-strikes-basics/.

"Statistics from the California Department of Corrections show that the law disproportionately affects minority populations. Over 45 percent of inmates serving life sentences under the Three Strikes law are African American. The Three Strikes law is also applied disproportionately against mentally ill and physically disabled defendants. California's State Auditor estimates that the Three Strikes law adds over $19 billion to the state's prison budget. Criminologists agree that life sentences for non-violent repeat offenders does nothing to improve public safety.

Prop. 36 eliminated life sentences for non-serious, non-violent crimes and established a procedure for inmates sentenced to life in prison for minor third strike crimes to petition in court for a reduced sentence. In order to win a reduced sentence, a court must find that the prisoner no longer poses an unreasonable threat to public safety. Prop. 36 was the first voter initiative since the Civil War to reduce the sentences of inmates currently behind bars.

In the first eight months of its enactment, over 1,000 prisoners were released from custody under Prop. 36. Of these inmates released, the recidivism rate stands at less than 2 percent charged with a new crime, a number well below state and national averages. Proposition 36 has saved California taxpayers between $10 and $13 million; and if the reform is applied to all eligible inmates, it is estimated that Californians would save almost $1 billion over the next ten years."

See however, https://www.peninsuladailynews.com/news/lifers-stay-jailed-despite-3-strikes-law-change/ which indicates that, although eleven of the states which had enacted three strikes laws have eased these laws since 2009 by removing property crimes or restoring sentencing discretion to judges, only California has made these reforms retroactive.

[54] There are no federal common law crimes. If Congress has not enacted legislation to make certain conduct criminal, that conduct cannot constitute a federal crime.

[55] "When courts or commentators today speak of "common law rules," it is not always clear to which common law they are referring. At times, our concern is with common law as it was first brought to this country, i.e., the common law of England at the time of the revolution. When the United States Supreme Court contends that a provision of the federal constitution should be interpreted in light of its common law background, it is to this English common law that they usually refer." Kerper, *supra* at 27.

. . . Although there were some early criminal statutes [in England], in the main the criminal law was originally common law. Thus, by the 1600s the judges, not the legislature, had created and defined the felonies of murder, suicide, manslaughter, burglary, arson, robbery, larceny rape, sodomy and mayhem; and such misdemeanors as assault, battery, false imprisonment, libel, perjury, and intimidation of jurors. During the period from 1660 . . . to 1860 the process continued with the judges creating new crimes when the need arose and punishing those who committed them: blasphemy (1676), conspiracy (1664), sedition (18th century), forgery (1727), attempt (1784), solicitation (1801). From time to time the judges, when creating new misdemeanors, spoke of the court's power to declare criminal any conduct tending to "outrage decency" or "corrupt public morals". . . . : thus they found running naked in the streets, publishing an obscene book, and grave-snatching to be common law crimes.

Of course, sometimes the courts refused to denote as criminal some forms of anti-social conduct. At times their refusal seemed irrational, causing the legislature to step in and enact a statute: thus, false pretenses, embezzlement, incest and other matters became statutory crimes in England. ... Some immoral conduct, mostly of a sexual nature (such as private acts of adultery or fornication, and seduction without conspiracy) was punished by ecclesiastical courts in England. The common law courts never punished these activities as criminal, and thus, they never became English common law crimes.

At the same time that judges were developing new crimes, they were also developing new common law defenses to crime, such as self-defense, insanity, infancy, and coercion. ...

About the middle of the nineteenth century, the process of creating new crimes almost came to a standstill in England. …

The original colonists in American who emigrated from England brought with them the common law with its then existing statutory modifications . . . so far as applicable to the conditions in America." [56]

COMMON LAW TRADITION AND THE CIVIL LAW TRADITION

The United States and other countries that follow the English common law are described as having a common law legal tradition. This description is used to contrast our legal system/tradition with the European civil law legal system/tradition. The civil law system uses legislative codes as the primary source of law. In the civil law tradition, substantive law is "revolutionary"—meaning that new laws *replace* old ones rather than supplement them. Judges in the civil law tradition are not bound by prior interpretations of legislative codes, and all courts are free to interpret the codes according to generally accepted principles of legal interpretation. *Stare decisis*, discussed below, plays no persuasive or binding role in the civil law tradition.

Though the description of the Anglo-American system as a "common law legal system" notes an important distinction between it and the civil law system, that description should not lead one to ignore the fact that legislation also constitutes an important source of law in the Anglo-American system. That system is actually

---

[56] Wayne R. LaFave, *Criminal Law,* 70 (3d. ed., 2000).

a mixed system of common law rules and statutory rules. The common law rules established by American and English courts have always been subject to displacement by legislative enactments. Indeed, the courts have authority to develop common law standards only where the legislatures have not sought to provide legislative solutions. ... In our country, the common law also is subject to the legal limitations imposed by federal and state constitutions. The supremacy of the constitutions extends over all forms of law, including the common law. Just as legislation cannot violate a constitutional limitation, neither can a common law rule.[57]

JUDGE-MADE LAW--CASE LAW

The term "case law" refers to legal rules announced in opinions written by appellate judges when deciding appellate cases before them. Judicial decisions reflect the court's interpretation of constitutions, statutes, common law, or administrative regulations. When the court interprets a statute, the statute as well as its interpretation, controls how the law will be enforced and applied in the future. The same is true when a court interprets federal and state constitutions. When deciding cases and interpreting the law, judges are bound by precedent, a doctrine known as "stare decisis."

STARE DECISIS [58]

Under the doctrine of *stare decisis,* past appellate court decisions form precedent that judge "must" follow in similar subsequent cases.[59] Trial courts (and appellate courts) follow the controlling case law that has already been announced in appellate court decisions from their own jurisdiction. Trial courts rely upon precedent when they decide questions of law.[60] The doctrine of *stare decisis* comes from a Latin phrase that states, "to stand by the decisions and not disturb settled points." It tells the court that if the decisions in the past have held that a particular rule governs a certain fact situation, that rule should govern all later cases presenting the same fact situation. The advantages of *stare decisis* include: efficiency, equality, predictability, the wisdom of past experience, and the image of limited authority.[61]

Efficiency occurs because each trial judge and appellate judge does not have to work out a solution to every legal question.[62] Equality results when one rule of law is applied to all persons in the same setting. "Identical cases brought before different judges should, to the extent humanly possible, produce identical results. ... *Stare decisis* assists in providing uniform standards of law for similar cases decided in the same state. It provides a common grounding used by all

---

[57] Kerper, *supra* at 28-29, and note 6.

[58] The Court in *Vasquez v. Hillery*, 474 U.S. 254 (1986), held that *stare decisis* "permits society to presume that bedrock principles are founded in the law rather than in the proclivities of individuals, and thereby contribute to the integrity of our constitutional system of government, both in appearance and fact."

[59] For a discussion about the current members of the Court's view on the binding nature of *stare decisis* see, https://prawfsblawg.blogs.com/prawfsblawg/2020/03/is-stare-decisis-for-suckers.html#:~:text=The%20trope%20that%20%E2%80%9Cstare%20decisis,phrase%20is%20gaining%20wider%20attention or listen to the Strict Scrutiny podcast's inaugural cast on July 1, 2019.

[60] Questions of law include what a statute means, what the law states, how the constitution should be interpreted, whether a particular law even applies under the facts in the case before them. Questions of fact, on the other hand, are decided by jurors (or judges in bench trials) and include, for example: how fast was the defendant driving, what color hat the defendant was wearing, whether the gun went off accidentally?

[61] *See,* Kerper, *supra* at 47-49.

[62] *Id.* at 49.

judges throughout the jurisdiction."[63] *Stare decisis* provides stability in allowing individuals to count on the rules of law that have been applied in the past. Kerper cites as an example, a police officer's reliance on past decisions to help determine the legality of a pending arrest— "without regard to past decisions, the conduct of a wide variety of activities would take on an added hazard of unpredictable legality. Without stability, the law could well loose (sic) its effectiveness in maintaining social control."[64] *Stare decisis* also ensures proper recognition of the wisdom and experience of the past. Justice Cardozo observed that "no single judge is likely to have 'a vision at once so keen and so broad' as to ensure that his new ideas of wise policy are indeed the most beneficial for society."[65] Since *stare decisis* is not absolute, courts can still reject past precedent, but it requires a judge to "think long and hard before he departs from the findings of his predecessors over the years."[66] Finally, *stare decisis* enhances the image of the courts as the impartial interpreter of the law.

> *Stare decisis* decreases the leeway granted to the individual judge to settle controversies in accordance with his own personal desires. ... Indeed, the doctrine of *stare decisis* indirectly serves to restrict the law-making role of the judge even in those cases presenting "open issues" not resolved by past precedent. ... A sudden change in the composition of the judiciary, even at the highest level, should not present an equally sudden change in the substance of the law.[67]

In the federal system all federal courts must follow the decisions of the Supreme Court -- it is the final interpreter of the federal constitution and federal statutes. If, however, the Supreme Court has not ruled on an issue, then the federal trial courts (U.S. District Courts and U.S. Magistrate Courts) and federal appellate courts (Circuit Courts of Appeals) must follow decisions from their own circuit. Each circuit is treated, in effect, as its own jurisdiction, and the court of appeals for the various circuits are free to disagree with each other.[68]

Because *stare decisis* is not an absolute rule, courts may reject precedent by overruling earlier decisions. One factor that courts will consider before overruling earlier case law is the strength of the precedent. Another factor is the field of law involved. Courts are more reluctant to override precedents governing property or trade where commercial enterprises are more likely to have relied quite heavily on the precedent.[69] Courts also consider the initial source of precedent-- for example statutory interpretation. For example, if the courts decided in 1950 that the statute meant that individuals could graze their cattle on federal lands without being in violation of any trespass laws, and then the federal government did not subsequently change the law, the legislature's inaction indicates the interpretation was probably right. The most compelling basis upon which a court will overturn precedent is if it perceives the presence or absence of changed circumstances. For example, scientific or technological developments may warrant the application of new rules.[70] One final ground for overruling a prior decision is general changes in

---

[63] *Id.*

[64] *Id.*

[65] Benjamin Cardozo, *The Growth of Law,* 141 (1924).

[66] Kerper, *supra* at 49

[67] *Id.* at 50-51.

[68] Chapter Three discusses the structure of both federal and state trial and appellate courts in much greater detail.

[69] *See,* Kerper, *supra* at 52.

[70] Technological changes result in new rules. For example, at common law, in order to prove the crime of murder, the state had to prove that the victim died within one year and a day of the attack (in order to prove that it was the defendant's act that caused the victim's death). Medical science now makes it possible to trace the source of fatal blow, so generally, murder statutes no longer include the "year and a day rule."

the spirit of the times. In *Trop v. Dulles*, 356 U.S. 86 (1958), the Court looked to "evolving standards of decency."

If there are no binding precedents in its own state[71], a court may find persuasive case law from other states. In those cases, the court is not bound by *stare decisis* to follow those decisions. When there is no precedent or controlling case, the case or issue is referred to as "a matter of first impression." In cases of first impression, courts must decide what the relevant rule should be. Courts will look to relevant statutes, legislative history, and cases involving similar situations.[72]

> The situation may be a new one. ... Yet the judges do not throw up their hands and say the case may not be decided; they decide it. Maybe they can use some settled law in an analogous situation. ... Even if there is no available analogy, or if there are competing analogies, the judge will make (some prefer to say discover) the law to apply to the new situation. The new law will be decided according to the judges' ideas (ideas they acquire as members of society) of what is moral, right, just; of what will further sound public policy, in light of customs and traditions of the people of which the judges are members.[73]

JUDICIAL "LAW-MAKING" VERSUS "LAW-APPLYING"

At times, people criticize judges for being "judicial activists." At the heart of this criticism is the notion that judges have exceeded their authority to interpret and apply the law and have ventured into the realm of making law—a legislative function. It is not necessarily easy, however, to apply the law to the facts of a case. Facts can be messy, the law can be less than clear, and not everyone will agree on the appropriate meaning of the law's mandate. LaFave notes,

> There is something of a dispute among those who like to speculate on the workings of the judicial mind as to whether courts first decide how a defective statute ought to be interpreted and then display whatever canons of statutory construction will make this interpretation look inevitable, or whether the courts actually first use the applicable canons and second reach the result. Doubtless the truth lies somewhere in between--some judges are apt to do it one way, some the others; some cases lend themselves to one technique, some to the other. ... [M]ost of the rules are stated in a way which ends with the exception that the rule does not apply if the meaning of the statute is clear, but a good deal of discretion remains in the courts as to when a statute is clear and when it is ambiguous. (Footnotes omitted.) [74]

Judges rely on several tools or approaches when interpreting the language of a statute. First, judges may take a "strict constructionist approach" and look at the plain meaning of the statute. This approach suggests that the wording of a statute is central to the meaning to the law. The strict constructionist approach often relies on dictionary-like tools to discover the meaning of words. "Where the language is plain and admits of no more than one meaning, the duty of

---

[71] Trial judges are not required to follow the decisions of other trial judges within the state.

[72] For example, if a court had to decide whether a *private* citizen could lawfully use deadly force to apprehend a fleeing thief, it could point to an earlier case holding that police officers could not lawfully use deadly force to apprehend a fleeing thief. The court would observe that police officers have greater authority to apprehend criminals than do private citizens and would hold that the private citizen may not use deadly force to apprehend a fleeing thief.

[73] LaFave, *supra* at 69.

[74] *Id.* at 80.

interpretation does not arise."[75] Judges can, and do, still disagree whether the language of the statute is plain.

Second, judges may look at the intent of the framers or the legislators who wrote the law. Generally, this approach would require an examination of legislative history, including the record of legislative hearings and floor debates. More legislative history exists at the federal level (see, for example, the Congressional Record) than at the state level. Sometimes figuring out the framers' intent is easy, but sometimes their purpose is not readily apparent. Moreover, different lawmakers may have had different intentions when they voted to pass the law.

> When interpreting an ambiguous statute, the court will seek to find the intention of the legislature. At times it is clear that the legislature never thought of the particular fact situation now in question, in which case "intention of the legislature" may mean simply "intention the legislature would have had if it had thought of this problem," to be determined from a consideration of the general purpose the legislature had in mind in enacting the statute. In order to help solve the often difficult problem of the legislature's intention, the courts have a large assortment of rules and maxims at their disposal. (Footnotes omitted.)
>
> . . .
>
> The use of legislative history as an aid to statutory interpretation has its limits. While a good deal of legislative history can be mined for a federal statute, most state legislatures, although they may go through much the same motions a Congress, do not keep as good a written record of their work. Elaborate committee reports are seldom made, and it is rare for a record to be kept of legislative debates. ... (Footnotes omitted.)
>
> It should be noted also that not all judges are enamored of the use of legislative history in interpreting ambiguous statutes. And in any event, legislative history is less likely to be controlling in construing criminal statutes than civil statutes. If one purpose of a criminal statute is to warn the public of what conduct will get them into criminal trouble, that is, if prospective criminals are entitled to fair warning-- then the public should be able to ascertain the line between permitted and prohibited conduct from the statute itself. (Footnotes omitted.)[76]

Third, judges may look at the original understanding or original meaning of the law. The court focuses on how the law would have been understood by the common person in the period during which the law was first implemented. This approach might yield different interpretations because different people could have had different understandings of what the law meant.

Fourth, as discussed above, judges may interpret the law based on precedent. One drawback to this approach is that facts of the earlier cases will always differ somewhat from the facts in the new case the court is trying to interpret. Another difficulty occurs when the court is faced with a new situation or a new law and there is no precedent to guide the court. LaFave identified the difficulty in adhering too closely to precedent:

> Sometimes a court, having earlier construed a criminal statute strictly in favor of the defendant, later decides that its earlier construction was wrong. ... Obviously, other things being equal, courts should interpret statutes correctly, regardless of past mistakes. On the other hand, it may not be fair to . . . change the rule now.

---

[75] *Caminetti v. United States*, 242 U.S. 470 (1917).
[76] LaFave, *supra* at 86-89.

The choice, however, is not necessarily between following the precedent (thus letting a defendant off but perpetuating a bad decision) and retroactively overruling it (thus eliminating a bad precedent but putting the defendant behind bars). There are two techniques by which the defendant may go free even if the precedent is overruled. It is not impossible for the court to overrule for the future only, letting the defendant go but stating in the opinion that anyone who from now on conducts himself the way this defendant did will be guilty of the crime.[77]

Finally, there are common law doctrines that hep courts decide how to interpret a statute. These include:

> ➤ The "rule of lenity" : courts should interpret ambiguous terms in a light that is favorable to the defendant.
> ➤ The Latin maxim "expressio unius est exclusion alterius" (the inclusion of one is the exclusion of all others): when a legislative body includes specific items within a statute, the assumption is that it intends to exclude all other terms.
> ➤ The Latin maxim "in pari materia" (on the same matter or subject): the court should determine an ambiguous statute in light of other statutes on the same subject.
> ➤ The title of the statute: sometimes a statute's title throws some light on the meaning of an ambiguous statute.[78]
> ➤ The Latin maxim, ejusdem genaris: where criminal statutes list specific items followed by a general catch all phrase, usually introduced by the words "or other", the general phrase may be construed to be limited to things of the same kinds as the specific items.[79]
> ➤ Striking changes of expression (meaning the use of different language): when the legislature uses different language in two parts of the same statute, this can be an indication of different legislative intent.
> ➤ General rules of interpretation:
>> ➤ specific language controls over general language and
>> ➤ later statutes control over earlier statutes.

So, as you can see, there is a lot of guidance for judges to follow when determining how to best interpret other sources of law.

COURT RULES

The U.S. Supreme Court and state supreme courts make law that regulate the procedures followed in the lower courts in that jurisdiction.

[C]ourt rules . . . are adopted on the court's own initiative as . . . the administrative regulations for the court system. Court rules ordinarily are limited in scope to governing the procedure for presenting cases before the courts of a particular jurisdiction. ... Many key procedural rights of the defendant, such as the right to a prompt trial, may be governed by court rule rather than statute in a particular jurisdiction.[80,81]

---

[77] LaFave, *supra* at 96-97.
[78] *See*, LaFave, *supra* at 89.
[79] *Id*. at 90.
[80] Kerper, *supra* at 26.
[81] One example of a state court rule involves Oregon Chief Justice Martha Walter's order of July 21, 2020 allowing presiding judges in Oregon counties to conduct the criminal arraignment procedures remotely

Local courts may also pass local court rules that govern the day-to-day practice of law in these lower courts. For example, a local court rule may dictate when and how cases are to be filed in that jurisdiction. Generally, the local bar (all the attorneys in the jurisdiction) are consulted, and a work force consisting of judges, trial court administrators, and representatives from district attorney's office, the public defender's office, assigned counsel consortiums, and private attorneys will meet periodically to decide on the local rules.[82]

MOVEMENT TOWARDS CODIFICATION -- THE AMERICAN INSTITUTE AND THE MODEL PENAL CODE

In the 1960s and 1970s, states began codifying their criminal codes if they had not already done so. These codifications would likely not have taken place if not for the American Law Institute (ALI) and the publication of its Model Penal Code (MPC). Established in 1923, the ALI is an organization of judges, lawyers, and academics that draft model codes and laws. Its most important work in the criminal justice realm is the Model Penal Code. The ALI began working on the MPC in 1951, and it proposed several tentative drafts over the next decade. In 1962 the Model Penal Code was finally published. It consists of general provisions concerning criminal liability, definitions of specific crimes, defenses, and sentences. The MPC has had significant impact on legislative drafting of criminal statutes. Every state has adopted at least some provisions (or at least the approach) of the MPC; some states have adopted many of the provisions in the MPC (these are referred to as "code states"), but no state has adopted the MPC in its entirety.

WRAP UP

This chapter reviewed many of the foundational elements of the structure of the American system of government: federalism, the three branches of government and their functions, and the primacy (superiority) of the federal constitution. States have vast police power and authority to create laws that regulate behavior impacting the health and welfare of their citizens; on the other hand, the federal government must tie its authority to pass criminal laws to either enumerated or implied powers found in U.S. Constitution. Judicial review is critical in ensuring that police and other executive branch actions do not conflict with the values enshrined in our constitution. Similarly, judicial review is critical in guaranteeing that lawmakers do not enact laws that are repugnant to our fundamental values.

Criminal law--both substantive and procedural--has many sources: constitutions, legislative enactments, administrative rules, case law, and common law. Because of this, it is not necessarily an easy task to determine whether your behavior, or the way government responds to your behavior, is lawful. Because courts generally follow precedent due to the doctrine of *stare decisis*, one red flag that your behavior may be unlawful is that, in the past, the courts have found behavior similar to yours to be unlawful.

Codifying criminal law by enacting statutes has not historically been as important in the common law legal tradition as it is in the civil law legal tradition. Nevertheless, following the development of model codes (such as the MPC) states have increasingly moved towards

---

due to ongoing threat of covid-19 in the state's courthouses. *See*, https://www.courts.oregon.gov/rules/ORAP/CJO_2020-028.pdf

[82] One example of a local trial court rule is the Lane County Oregon Presiding Judge's order effective June 22, 2020 requiring all persons entering the courthouse to wear protective face coverings while in the courthouse. *See*, https://www.courts.oregon.gov/courts/lane/Documents/Lane_PJO_20-05_Face%20Coverings.pdf

codifying their criminal law. In interpreting these codes, judges rely on several tools to help them decide what the law means, but they still may be criticized for making, and not just applying, the law.

SOME THINGS TO THINK ABOUT OR EXPLORE

➢ Identify a recent executive order from the current administration.

➢ Identify a recent federal investigation into violation of federal law that has made the news.

➢ Should the Court follow precedent and stare decisis? Can you think of topics (for example, abortion (*Roe v. Wade, Dobbs v. Jackson Women's Health Organization*), or corporate political contributions (the *Citizens' United* case)) that make you want the Court to feel constrained by prior opinions but other cases where you wish it would "distinguish" the case from earlier precedent. (Distinguishing a case means pointing out the differences from a current controversy from the facts of earlier cases decided by the Court.)

➢ Much has been said about the importance of the "rule of law" in the past years. How effective have the courts been in holding the executive branch, the legislative branch, and itself (the judicial branch) accountable to the fundamental values found in our Constitution? Give examples in which the court has held that an executive or legislative action has not violated the Constitution and examples where the Court has held the executive or legislative branch accountable and struck down the enactment or practice as violating the Constitution.

➢ Consider the interplay of the federal charges facing individuals who stormed the capitol on January 6, 2021 with the possible criminal charges for crimes committed on that day on the streets of Washington D.C., which were not part of the capitol complex. A whole area of law exists determining whether D.C. prosecutors can file charges against individuals for actions done on federal property. Should there be concurrent jurisdiction, say for example, like there was in the Oklahoma City Bombing Case (Timothy McVeigh and Terry Nichols).

TERMINOLOGY

- administrative law
- affectation doctrine
- American Law Institute (ALI)
- ballot measure
- case law
- case of first impression
- civil law (legal) tradition
- codes, codification
- common law
- common law (legal) tradition
- constitutional law
- constitutional supremacy
- enumerated powers
- executive orders
- expansion clause
- federalism
- implied powers, implied powers doctrine
- initiatives
- Interstate Commerce Clause
- law applying
- law making
- judicial review
- Model Penal Code
- natural law
- Necessary and Proper Clause
- police powers
- precedent
- Rechtstaat
- separation of powers
- stare decisis
- statutory construction
- statutory law
- strict constructionist approach

Chapter Three: The Courts

OVERVIEW AND LEARNING OBJECTIVES

This chapter examines the structure and role of the courts and courtroom players in the American Criminal Justice system. As you read this text pay attention to the context when you encounter the word "court" because it is used in a variety of ways. "Court" can mean a building (for example, "He went to the court"), one judge (for example, "The trial court held in his favor"), a group of judges (for example, "The Supreme Court unanimously reversed his conviction"), or an institution/process generally (for example, "Courts hopefully resolve disputes in an evenhanded manner").

Courts determine both the facts surrounding a crime and also the legal sufficiency of the criminal charge. Did the defendant commit the crime (facts) and can the government prove it (legal sufficiency). Courts ensure that criminal defendants are provided "due process of law" meaning the procedures used to convict the defendant are fair.

After reading this chapter, you should be able to answer the following questions:

> What is jurisdiction? What types of jurisdiction do courts have?
> What is the structure of courts in America?
> What are the functions of state courts? What are the functions of federal courts?
> What are the roles, functions, and titles of people working in the judicial branch?
> What does a trial court do?
> What does an appellate court do?
> How do appellate court justices announce their decisions?
> What action does an appellate court take if it agrees with the lower court's ruling or when it disagrees with the lower court's ruling?
> What is meant by a "standard of review?" What standards of review are applied when deciding questions of fact, questions of law, mixed questions of fact and law, or matters of discretion?
> How are prosecutors selected and what are their functions?
> How are defense attorneys selected and what are their functions?
> When will courts appoint attorneys to represent indigent defendants?
> How are trial judges selected and what are their functions and duties
> How are appellate judges selected and what are their functions and duties?
> What are the functions of the following members of the courtroom workgroup: bailiff, jury clerk, law clerk, judicial assistant, trial court administrator, docketing (scheduling) clerk, indigency verification officer, release assistance officer?

This chapter begins by exploring "jurisdiction." Jurisdiction refers to the legal authority to hear and decide the case. Jurisdiction can be based upon geographical location--for example, the courts in Arkansas do not have jurisdiction over crimes committed in Maine. Jurisdiction also refers to the court's authority over the parties in the case--for example, a New York court does not have jurisdiction over the parties when Acme Car Company, a Nevada business, rents a defective car to Mr. Johnson, a Florida resident who drives the car only in Nevada. You will learn that jurisdiction is also tied to federalism--state courts have jurisdiction over state matters and federal courts have jurisdiction over federal matters. Both federal courts and state courts have a hierarchy that divides trial courts and appellate courts. Trial courts have jurisdiction over pretrial matters, trials, sentencing, and probation and parole violations. Trial courts deal with facts. Did the defendant stab the victim? Was the eyewitness able to clearly see the stabbing? Did the probationer willfully violate terms of probation? Trial courts determine legal guilt and impose punishments. Appellate courts, on the other hand, review the decisions of the trial courts. Appellate courts are primarily concerned with matters of law. Did the trial judge properly instruct the jury about the controlling law? Did the trial court properly suppress evidence in a pretrial hearing? Does the statute allow the defendant to raise a particular defense? Appellate courts correct legal errors made by trial courts and develop law when new legal questions arise. In some instances, appellate courts determine if there is legally sufficient evidence to uphold a conviction (that is, do the facts shown at trial support the verdict.)

The chapter then discusses how judges and juries determine the outcome of a case by applying the legal standards to the facts presented. It examines how appellate courts review the trial record for legal error and make their decisions known. In order to understand how appellate courts do their jobs in reviewing lower court decisions, one must understand the concept of "standards of review" — that level of scrutiny courts employ in deciding questions of law, questions of fact, and mixed questions of fact and law. Perhaps the best way to think about standard of review is to relate it to the deference an appellate court must give to the findings of the lower courts. In some instances, the appellate court gives great deference to the conclusions and findings made by the trial judge and jury; in other instances, the appellate court may substitute its own opinion and need not defer to the trial judge at all. From time to time, the appellate courts may recognize and correct "plain error" (error obvious on its face) that it sees when reviewing the record even though the parties have failed to mention it in their appellate briefs.

Finally, this chapter introduces the roles and training of the various individuals who work in the courts and are part of the "courtroom workgroup." Unlike civil disputes which may be "settled out of court" (resolved by the parties without resorting to the courts), all criminal prosecutions must be funneled through the courts. Thus, courts and court procedures are essential in the resolution of criminal matters.

JURISDICTION

Courts are generally classified according to their jurisdiction, a term which means the authority or power of a court to hear a particular type of case. If a court can deal with cases involving only a certain subject matter, such as only criminal law, it is described as a court with jurisdiction limited to that legal field. If a court has authority to conduct trials, its jurisdiction is described as "trial jurisdiction." The jurisdiction of each court ordinarily is set forth in the constitution or statute that creates that court. The jurisdictional divisions between courts tend to be based on four factors: (1) the distinction between trial and appellate authority, (2) the subject matter of the cases considered, (3) the seriousness of the cases considered, and (4) the type of parties involved.

The distinction between trial courts and appellate courts is recognized in all fifty-one judicial systems. The trial court holds the basic hearing on the evidence in the case, determines the applicable law, and either itself applies the law to the facts presented, or directs the jury in their performance of that function. The appellate court on the other hand reviews the trial court's decision to ensure that the trial court did not act erroneously. It does not hold an evidentiary hearing, but proceeds to review the case based on an official record (called a transcript) which relates all that occurred at the trial.[83] The most well-known example of a court with appellate jurisdiction is the United States Supreme Court. Trial court jurisdiction . . . is possessed by most local courts such as the typical state "County," "Circuit," or "Superior Court."

The second jurisdictional distinction—the subject matter of the case—tends to be utilized primarily in distinguishing between different trial courts. Appellate courts ordinarily can hear all types of cases, although there are several states that have separate appellate courts for criminal and civil appeals. At the trial level, most states have established one or more specialized courts to deal with particular legal fields. The most common areas delegated to specialized courts are wills and estates (assigned to courts commonly known as probate . . . courts), divorce, adoption or other aspects of family law (family or domestic relations courts). . . . The federal system also includes specialized courts for such areas as customs and patents. While significant, the specialized courts represent only a small portion of all trial courts. Most trial courts are not limited to a particular subject, but may deal with all fields. Such trial courts are commonly described as having general jurisdiction since they cover the general (i.e., non-specialized) areas of law. Criminal cases traditionally are assigned to courts with general jurisdiction.

The third level of division—based on the seriousness of the case—also is found at the trial level in almost all jurisdictions. Both civil and criminal cases of a minor nature commonly are assigned to one group of courts and more serious cases to another, higher-level court. Those trial courts limited to minor cases are commonly described as magistrate courts since their judges are in many respects successors to the English office of the magistrate. Their jurisdiction is described as "limited" or "inferior" as compared to that of the "general trial courts" the courts which try the more serious cases. The dividing line between minor and major cases will vary from state to state...

The fourth dividing line for allocating authority among courts—the special nature of the parties involved—is used far less frequently than the other three dividing lines. Perhaps the most common illustration of its use if found in the juvenile court. That court has jurisdiction over a variety of proscribed activities committed by persons under a specified age. ... Another illustration of a specialized court based on the special nature of one of the parties is the state court known as the "court of claims," which has jurisdiction over all suits against the state government for money damages. The federal court of military appeals is a specialized appellate court whose jurisdiction also is determined by a combination of specialized law and special parties. [84]

STRUCTURE OF THE COURTS

SEPARATE FEDERAL AND STATE COURT SYSTEMS

Each state has two complete, parallel court systems--a federal system, and the state's own system. Thus, there are more than 51 legal systems -- the fifty created under state laws and the

---

[83] See, Kerper, *supra* at 33, footnote 3. ("The record is a complete transcription of all that went on in the trial court, including the testimony of witnesses, rulings of the court, and of course, the final decision announced by the judge or jury. The transcription is made by a court reporter or a mechanical recording device.")

[84] Kerper, *supra* at 34-35.

federal system created under federal law. This arrangement is sometimes referred to as the "dual court system." State crimes, created by state legislatures generally, are prosecuted in state courts that are concerned primarily with the applying state law. Federal crimes, created by Congress, are prosecuted in the federal courts that are concerned primarily with applying federal law. It is, however, possible for a case to move from the state system to the federal system through either a "petition for writ of habeas corpus" or a "petition for writ of certiorari." (These terms will be discussed in greater detail in Chapter Twelve.)

THE FEDERAL COURT SYSTEM

Article III of the U.S. Constitution established a Supreme Court of the United States and granted Congress discretion in deciding whether to adopt a lower court system.[85] Fearing that the state courts might be hostile to congressional legislation, Congress immediately created a lower federal court system in 1789.[86] The lower federal court system has since been expanded over the years. Congress provided that when federal officers are charged with crimes under state law in connection with their federal activities, these prosecutions can also be transferred to federal courts to ensure that officers will receive a fair trial.

U.S. SUPREME COURT[87]

The United States Supreme Court, located in Washington, D.C., is the highest appellate court in the federal judicial system. Nine justices sitting *en banc* (as one panel), together with their clerks and administrative staff, make up the Supreme Court. "These nine individuals have the final word in determining what the U.S. Constitution requires, permits, and prohibits in the areas of law enforcement, prosecution, adjudication and punishment." [88]

The Court has discretionary review over most cases brought from the state supreme courts and federal appeals courts in a process called a petition for the writ of certiorari. Four justices must agree to accept and review a case (referred to as the "rule of four") and this happens in roughly 10% of the cases filed. Once accepted, the Court schedules and hears oral arguments on the case and then delivers written opinions.[89] Over the past ten years, approximately 8000 petitions for writ of certiorari have been filed yearly. It is difficult to guess which cases the court will accept for review, but one common reason the court accepts review a case is because the federal circuits courts have reached conflicting results on important issues presented in the case.

---

[85] Article III of the U.S. Constitution provides that the "judicial Power of the Unites States shall be vested in one supreme Court, and in such inferior Courts as the Congress may from time to time ordain and establish."

[86] The Judiciary Act of 1789 (Ch. 20, 1 Stat 73) created the federal court system, and in 1891 Congress created separate appellate courts.

[87] Volumes could be written about the current climate of the Court—what judges are on the Court and what their political leanings are; whether the U.S. Senate abdicated its constitutionally required duty in not calling for a vote on President Obama's selection, Merrick Garland, to replace Justice Scalia upon Scalia's unexpected death in 2016; whether Justice Kavanaugh should have been approved by the Senate in light of the allegations of sexual assault and black-out drinking when he was younger; whether the number of justices should be increased; whether President Trump should have appointed (and the U.S. Senate approved) Justice Coney Barrett to the Court on October 27, 2020 soon after the death of Justice Ginsberg with the presidential election of 2020 already in process (and completely inapposite to the position taken by the Senate after Justice Scalia's death). Those topics are more about the politics of the court (which is very important) and not about the function of the court in resolving criminal matters. Thus, these important questions and discussions they prompt, are beyond the scope of this text.

[88] Scheb, *supra* at 40.

[89] See, https://www.supremecourt.gov/opinions/info_opinions.aspx for information about the publication of the Court's opinions.

The U.S. Supreme Court's decisions have the broadest impact because they govern both the state and federal judicial system. The Court is influential when it is the final arbiter in interpreting the U.S. Constitution,[90] but the Court also supervises the activities of the lower federal courts within its judicial system.

Original (Trial Court) Jurisdiction of the Supreme Court

In a few important situations, for example, when one state sues another state, the U.S. Supreme Court acts as a trial court and considers the facts and law of a case without it first being heard by a lower court.[91] When the Court acts as a trial court, it is said to exercise "original jurisdiction." Original jurisdiction cases are rare—recently the Court has averaged only one or two cases per term[92] -- for several reasons. First, the Constitution prohibits Congress from increasing the types of cases over which the Supreme Court has original jurisdiction. Second, parties in an original jurisdiction suit must get permission (by petitioning the court) to file a complaint in the Supreme Court. In fact, there is no right to have a case heard by the Supreme Court--even though it may be the only venue in which the case may be brought.[93] Finally, except in suits or controversies between two states in which the court has exclusive jurisdiction (meaning, it is the only court that can here the dispute) the Court has increasingly permitted the lower federal courts to share its original jurisdiction.

In the event that the Court does hear an original jurisdiction case, the Court appoints a "special master" to hear arguments and gather facts and evidence and then report back to the Court with a recommendation. The Court then essentially reviews the findings of the special master which are submitted via a report. Parties in the dispute may also challenge the findings of the special master, and the Court may then determine whether or not to hear their challenges or accept the special master's recommendation. [94]

U.S. CIRCUIT COURTS OF APPEAL

The intermediate appellate courts in the federal system are the U.S. Courts of Appeals (also known as Circuit Courts.) There are twelve geographical circuits and one federal circuit. Figure 1 shows the geographical jurisdiction of the U.S. Courts of Appeals. The smallest circuit is the First Circuit with six judgeships, and the largest court is the Ninth Circuit, with 29 judgeships.[95] Appellate court panels generally consist of three judges, but occasionally, when the court decides to sit "en banc," all the judges on the court will comprise the panel.

The U.S. Courts of Appeal, like all federal appellate courts, trace their existence to Article III of the U.S. Constitution. Circuit Courts hear criminal and civil appeals from the U.S. District

---

[90] Justice Jackson stated about the U.S. Supreme Court, "[w]e are not final because we are infallible, but we are infallible only because we are final." *Brown v. Allen*, 344 U.S. 433, 450 (1953) (Jackson, J. concurring).

[91] *See*, U.S. Constitution. art III, §2, cl.2. For federal courts, original jurisdiction is granted in disputes involving maritime law, United States law, cases concerning citizens of different states, cases involving different state governments, disputes where the United States is a party, and in cases between foreign nations and ambassadors.

[92] See, https://ballotpedia.org/Original_jurisdiction

[93] *See,* Scheb, *supra at 45* ("Such petitions are frequently denied, sometimes because the Court believes that a matter between states is too trivial (e.g., whether state universities breached a contract to play football) or, conversely, when the Court considers that the matters sought to be reviewed are too broad or unmanageable (e.g., issues of interstate water or air pollution) or simply because the Court is not ready to hear the matter.")

[94] See, https://ballotpedia.org/Original_jurisdiction; See, e.g., https://ballotpedia.org/Florida_v._Georgia.

[95] http://www.uscourts.gov/statistics-reports/federal-judicial-caseload-statistics-2019

Courts and from quasi-judicial tribunals in the independent regulatory agencies (such as social security or bankruptcy courts). The Circuit Courts are busy, and there have been efforts to both fill vacancies and increase the number of judgeships to help deal with the caseloads. For example, the Federal Judgeship Act of 2013 would have created five permanent and one temporary circuit court judgeships in an attempt to keep up with increased case filings; the bill died in Congress.

Figure 1
U.S. Courts of Appeal by Circuit

U.S. District Courts — Trial Courts of General Jurisdiction

U.S. District Courts are also "Article III courts" created by Congress in the Judiciary Act of 1789. Now, ninety-four U.S. District Courts[96] handle prosecutions for violations of federal statutes. Each state has at least one district, and larger states have up to four districts. Each district court is described by reference to the state or geographical segment of the state in which it is located (for example, the U.S. District Court for the Northern District of California). The district courts have jurisdiction over all prosecutions brought under federal criminal law and all civil suits brought under federal statutes. A criminal trial in the district court is presided over by a judge who is appointed for life by the president with the consent of the Senate.

Although the U.S. District Courts are primarily trial courts, district court judges also exercise an appellate-type function in their review of petitions for writs of habeas corpus brought by state prisoners. (Writs of habeas corpus are civil suits by state and federal prisoners who allege that the government is illegally confining them in violation of the federal constitution.) The party who loses at the U.S. District Court can appeal the case in the U.S. Circuit Court (the court of appeals for the circuit) in which the district court is located. These first appeals must be reviewed--thus, they are referred to as "appeals of right."

U.S. Magistrate Courts- Courts of Limited Jurisdiction

U.S. Magistrate Courts are the courts of "limited jurisdiction" in the federal court system; they do not have full judicial power. These courts were created by Congress under their authority given in Article I of the Constitution. Congress first created U.S. Magistrate Courts with the Federal Magistrate Act of 1968. Under this Act, federal magistrate judges assist district court

---

[96] This includes 89 District Courts in the States and 5 in the territories.

judges by conducting pretrial proceedings, such as setting bail, issuing warrants, and conducting trials of federal misdemeanor crimes. There are more than 500 Magistrate Judges who dispose of over one million matters.[97] Magistrate Judges[98] are appointed for eight-year terms (unlike Article III judges who hold lifetime appointments.)

STATE COURT SYSTEMS

Each state has its own independent judicial system. State courts handle more than 90 percent of criminal prosecutions in the United States.[99] Although state court systems vary, there are some common features. Every state has one or more level of trial courts and at least one appellate court. Although there is no constitutional requirement that defendants be given the right to appeal their convictions,[100] every state has some provision (usually within its own constitution or statutes) that provides defendants at least one appeal (called an appeal of right). Most state courts have both trial courts of general jurisdiction and trial courts of limited jurisdiction. Courts of general jurisdiction conduct trials in felony and major misdemeanor cases and, in some states, also act like an appellate court for minor cases tried in the courts of limited jurisdiction. Trial courts of limited jurisdiction conduct trials for minor misdemeanor cases and for violations and infractions, and also handle pre-trial matters for felonies until they are moved into the general jurisdiction court. Most states have intermediate courts of appeals (some have more than one level of intermediate appellate courts); and all courts have some highest level, "court of last resort" court, generally referred to as the "Supreme Court." Some states court systems are streamlined, and some are complex—most states fall between the two extremes.

TRIAL COURTS AND THE PRINCIPLE OF ORALITY

The principle of orality is the idea that any evidence considered by the jury (or the judge in a bench trial) must have been developed, presented, and received during the trial. This principle would be violated if, for example, during deliberations the jury searched the Internet to find information on the defendant or witnesses and then considered that in its deliberations. Similarly, if the police questioned the defendant and wrote a report, the jury cannot consider the contents of the report unless it has been offered in a way that complies with the rules of evidence and the court has received information from it during the trial.

The principle of orality is one major difference between the adversarial system and the inquisitorial system. Frequently in countries following the civil law tradition and using the inquisitorial approach, the police, prosecutors or investigating magistrates question witnesses prior to trial and write summaries of their statements (called a _dossier_ or a protocol). In determining guilt, the trier of fact (sometimes a lone judge, sometimes a panel of professional judges, sometimes a panel of both professional and lay judges, sometimes a lay jury, sometimes a blue-ribbon jury) in those counties is presented with just the summaries of the witness statements, and it relies on those summarized reports as evidence upon which to base its verdict. (Note that the trial in civil law countries is generally less concerned with the presentation of evidence establishing the defendant's guilt and more concerned with determining an appropriate sentence and considering the defendant's presentation of mitigation evidence.)

---

[97] http://www.uscourts.gov/statistics-reports/us-magistrate-judges-judicial-business-2017
[98] "Magistrates" became "Magistrate Judges" on December 1, 1990 with the Judicial Improvement Act of 1990.
[99] Scheb, _supra,_ at 42.
[100] The right to appeal is, arguably, implicit in the Due Process Clauses of the Fifth and Fourteenth Amendments.

APPELLATE COURTS, THE APPELLATE FUNCTION, AND THE STANDARD OF REVIEW

Because the state cannot appeal when the jury *acquits* the defendant (finds him or her not guilty), almost all appeals involve defendants who have been found guilty at trial.[101] When the defendant appeals, he or she is now referred to as the "appellant," and the State is the "appellee." In routine appeals, the primary function of appellate courts is to review the record to discern if errors were made by the trial court before, during, or after the trial. No trial is perfect, so the goal is to ensure there was a fair, albeit imperfect, trial. Accordingly, the appellate courts review for errors they consider "fundamental" "prejudicial" or "harmful" meaning that they affected the outcome of the case. A lower court's judgment will not be reversed unless the appellant can show that some prejudice resulted from the error and that the outcome of the trial or sentence would have been different if there had been no error. Appellate review is designed to ensure that substantive justice (requiring fair laws) has been accomplished under constitutional standards of due process of law (requiring fair procedures). By reviewing for error and then writing opinions that become case law, appellate courts perform dual functions in the criminal process: error correction and lawmaking.

Appellate judges sit in panels of at least three judges. They read the written documents filed by the parties called "appellate briefs" and will listen to very short oral arguments by the parties—lasting no more than 30 minutes per side. In the appellate brief, the appellant will allege "assignments of error" -- these are list of allegations of everything that went wrong at trial. The brief must address every reason the appellant feels that the lower court erred, and failure to identify and argue a reason is a waiver of that basis for appeal. (The court will occasionally, but seldom, address "plain error" on the record not included in the assignments of error; see below.) When the appellate court finds that no prejudicial error was committed at trial, it will affirm the decision below. When the first appellate court finds there was prejudicial error(s) that deprived the defendant of a fair trial, it will issue an order of reversal. When the case is reversed the court will generally send the case back to the trial court ("reverse and remand") and require a new trial. Sometimes, but rarely, the appellate court may direct the lower court to dismiss the case if it finds there was insufficient evidence presented to demonstrate the defendant's guilt.

STANDARD OF REVIEW

Appellate courts do not consider each error in isolation, but instead they look at the cumulative effect of all the errors during the whole trial. Additionally, appellate court judges must sometimes let a decision of a lower court stand, even if they personally don't agree with it. We refer to this as an appellate court "showing deference" to the trial court's findings/holdings. How much deference to show the lower court's holdings or factual findings is the essence of "standards of review." The controlling standard of review may determine the outcome of the case. Sometimes the appellate court can substitute its judgment for that of the trial court and overturn a holding it does not agree with, but other times, it must uphold the lower court's decision even if it would have decided differently. How much latitude or deference an appellate court gives the trial court depends on whether the error involved a question of fact--in which case they defer greatly to the trial court and will overturn the conviction only if there was clear error on the record; a question of law--in which case they do not need to defer at all to the trial court,

---

[101] Although the defendant could appeal after entering a guilty plea, the only basis for his or her appeal is to challenge the legality of the sentence given.

and the error is reviewable *de novo* (anew); or a matter of discretion (for example, allowing a continuance in the trial)--in which case they will overturn the trial court only if they find that there was an abuse of discretion.[102]

QUESTIONS OF FACT: "ARBITRARY AND CAPRICIOUS" OR "CLEARLY ERRONEOUS"

When looking at whether the trial court got it wrong on a factual ruling, the courts will generally defer to the trial court. An appellate court will not overturn findings of fact unless it is firmly convinced that a mistake has been made and that the trial court's decision is clearly erroneous or "arbitrary and capricious." The arbitrary and capricious standard means the trial court's decision was completely unreasonable and it had no rational connection between the facts found and the decision made. The lower courts finding will be overturned only if it is completely implausible in light of all of the evidence. One court noted, "Where there are two permissible views of the evidence, the fact finder's choice between them cannot be clearly erroneous." [103] Sometimes the law requires, or the parties request, that a trial judge or jury make a special "finding of fact." Findings of fact are judicial statements and determinations based on evidentiary hearings which usually involve credibility determinations that are best made by the trial judge sitting in the courtroom listening to the evidence and observing the demeanor of the witnesses. Although appellate court judges may have weighed the evidence and themselves reached different conclusions; unless the trial court's findings of fact were clearly erroneous, the appellate court will defer to the trial judge.

QUESTIONS OF LAW: *"DE NOVO* REVIEW"

Questions of law include interpretation of statutes or contracts, the constitutionality of a statute, the interpretation of rules of criminal and civil procedure. Trial courts will presume that laws are valid and do not violate the constitution. The burden of proving otherwise falls on the defendant. Trial courts sometimes get it wrong. In these cases, the appellate courts employ a different standard of review--*de novo* (of new) review. *De novo* review allows the appellate court to use its own judgment about whether the trial court correctly applied the law. Appellate courts give little or no deference to the trial court decision when it concerns a question of law.

MIXED QUESTIONS OF LAW AND FACT

Sometimes the trial court must resolve a question in a case that presents both factual and legal issues. For example, if police stop and question a suspect there are legal questions -- for example, did the stop violate the Fourth Amendment because it was not based on reasonable suspicion for the stop) and factual questions (for example, did police read the suspect the required warnings). Mixed questions of law and fact are generally reviewed *de novo*. However, factual findings underlying the lower court's ruling are reviewed for clear error.

MATTERS OF DISCRETION: ABUSE OF DISCRETION

When the trial court makes a discretionary ruling--for example in granting a motion to continue or allowing a party to amend its pleadings--the decision will be reviewed for "abuse of discretion." Proving the trial court abused its discretion is difficult and the appellate court will find the action met that standard only if the judge failed to exercise sound, reasonable, and legal

---

[102] The selection of the appropriate standard of review depends on the context. For example, the *de novo* standard applies when issues of law tend to dominate in the lower court's decision. When a mixed question of law and fact is presented, the standard of review turns on whether factual matters or legal matters tend to dominate or control the court's decision.
[103] *United States v. Yellow Cab Co.*, 338 U.S. 338. 342 (1949).

decision-making skills. A trial court abuses its discretion, for example, when it does not apply the correct law, erroneously interprets a law, rests its decision on a clearly inaccurate view of the law, rests its decision on a clearly erroneous finding of a material fact, or rules in a completely irrational manner. Abuse of discretion also exists when the record contains no evidence to support trial court's decision.

PLAIN ERROR

Normally when an appellate court reviews an appeal, it limits its review to the record from the lower court and only addresses things griped about (claims of error) by the appellant and were objected to during the trial. If, for example, the defendant claims that the police conducted an illegal search and seizure, the appellate court will focus only on search and seizure issues—even if the court may itself spot what it believes is a illegal confession issue. The exception to this normal practice is when the record reveals "plain error." Plain error exists "[w]hen a trial court makes an error that is so obvious and substantial that the appellate court should address it, even though the parties failed to object to the error at the time it was made."[104] If the appellate court determines that the error was evident, obvious, clear and materially prejudiced a substantial right (meaning that it was likely that the mistake affected the outcome of the case below in a significant way), the court may correct the error. Usually, the court will not correct plain error unless it led to a miscarriage of justice. On January 8, 2021 the Court accepted review in *Greer v. United States*, a case which presents the question of whether a federal appellate court reviewing the decision of a lower court for plain error may review matters outside the trial record in order to determine whether the error affected a defendant's substantial rights or impacted the fairness, integrity, or public reputation of the trial.

APPELLATE DECISIONS

The appellate court will support its decisions with a written opinion setting forth the court's reasons for its order either affirming or reversing the lower court. This is the "majority opinion." Under Supreme Court protocol, when the chief justice is in the majority, he or she decides which justice will write the majority opinion. When the chief justice is not in the majority, then the most senior justice in the majority will decide who will write the opinion. Judges and justices[105] frequently disagree and may want to write their own opinions. If a particular judge agrees with the result reached in the court's opinion but not the reasoning, he or she may write a separate "concurring" opinion. If a judge disagrees with the result and votes against the majority's decision, hc or she will write a "dissenting" opinion. Sometimes opinions are unsigned, and these are referred to as "*per curiam*" opinions. Finally, if not enough justices agree on the result for the same reason to reach a majority, a "plurality opinion" will be written. The plurality opinion reflects a position that did not receive convince more than half of the justices' votes, but did garner more support than any other reason.

> The opinions of the appellate courts are very important in determining the law
> since they are the primary record of past decisions, and . . . past decisions serve as
> the controlling guidelines for rulings in future cases. The opinion for the majority
> is most significant, of course, because it expresses the prevailing view, but a
> dissenting opinion may also be important. There is always the possibility that, as
> times change, the ideas expressed in today's dissents will gain acceptance in
> tomorrow's opinions for the majority. [106]

---

[104] http://www.law.cornell.edu/wex/plain_error.
[105] Trial court and intermediate appellate court judges are called "judges" and supreme court judges are called "justices."
[106] Kerper, *supra* at 39.

FEDERAL COURT OVERSIGHT OVER STATE ACTIONS AND LAWS

Through petitions for writ of certiorari, the U.S. Supreme Court will be in a position to review cases coming to it from the state courts. Because review is discretionary, the Court will generally accept review only when these cases appear to involve a significant question involving the federal constitution. As a case works its way through the state appeals process, the state courts may have made rulings about both the federal constitution and its own state constitution. Depending on the case and how the state opinions were written, the U.S. Supreme Court may find it difficult to determine whether the state interpreted its own constitution (in which case the Court will not accept review) or whether it interpreted the federal constitution (in which case the Court may accept review). *Michigan v. Long*, 463 U.S. 1032 (1983), explains when the Court will "weigh in" on a state court matter. It held,

> When . . . a state court decision fairly appears to rest primarily on federal law, or to be interwoven with the federal law, and when the adequacy and independence of any possible state law ground is not clear from the face of the opinion, we will accept as the most reasonable explanation that the state court decided the case the way it did because it believed that federal law required it to do so. If a state court chooses merely to rely on federal precedents as it would on the precedents of all other jurisdictions, then it need only make clear by a plain statement in its judgment or opinion that the federal cases are being used only for the purpose of guidance, and do not themselves compel the result that the court has reached. In this way, both justice and judicial administration will be greatly improved. If the state court decision indicates clearly and expressly that it is alternatively based on bona fide separate, adequate, and independent grounds, we, of course, will not undertake to review the decision.
>
> This approach obviates [*does away with*] in most instances the need to examine state law in order to decide the nature of the state court decision, and will at the same time avoid the danger of our rendering advisory opinions. It also avoids the unsatisfactory and intrusive practice of requiring state courts to clarify their decisions to the satisfaction of this Court. We believe that such an approach will provide state judges with a clearer opportunity to develop state jurisprudence unimpeded by federal interference, and yet will preserve the integrity of federal law. It is fundamental that state courts be left free and unfettered by us in interpreting their state constitutions. But it is equally important that ambiguous or obscure adjudications by state courts do not stand as barriers to a determination by this Court of the validity under the federal constitution of state action. (Citations omitted).[107]

THE COURTROOM WORKGROUP

The criminal justice process can be broken down into five stages or phases: the investigatory phase, the accusatory phase, the adjudicatory phase, the sentencing phase and the appeals phase. The investigatory phase primarily involves law enforcement, but the prosecutor is frequently involved in directing the investigation, and judges are involved in issuing search and seizure warrants. The accusatory (pretrial) and adjudicatory (trial) phases involve all the various

---

[107] 463 U.S. at 1040-1041. (Citations omitted).

people working with or in the trial court system. The prosecutor files the accusatory instrument, the defense attorney represents the defendant from pretrial through sentencing (and maybe on the appeal as well), and judges, aided by several court personnel, conduct the pretrial, trial, and sentencing hearings.

Eisenstein and Jacob coined the term "courtroom workgroup" in 1977 to describe the prosecutors, criminal defense attorneys, and judges who routinely work together in the criminal trial courts.[108] This text considers the term "courtroom workgroup" more broadly and includes under its umbrella all the court staff who are responsible for getting cases filed, getting exhibits marked and entered, who process orders and warrants, and who are responsible for the day-to-day activity of the court within that term are also considered part of the court room workgroup.

Prosecutors, defense counsel and judges perform different roles, but all are concerned with the judicial process and the interpretation of the law. These lawyer-professionals are graduates of law schools and have passed the bar examination[109] establishing their knowledge of the law and their ability to utilize legal analysis. As persons admitted to the practice of law, they are subject to legal codes of professional responsibility, disciplinary rules, and ethical rules and opinions for lawyers.

JUDGES

TRIAL JUDGES

Trial court judges are responsible for presiding over pretrial, trial and sentencing hearings, and probation and parole revocation hearings. They issue search and arrest warrants, set bail or authorize release, sentence offenders, engage in pre-sentence conferences with attorneys, work with court clerks, bailiffs, jail staff, etc. Trial judges have considerable, but not unlimited, discretion. Trial judges are subject to judicial codes of conduct and are bound by the applicable rules of law when deciding cases and in their written opinions. Some rules governing judges are flexible guidelines; other rules are very precise.

During the pretrial phase, the judge makes rulings on the parties' motions such as motions to exclude certain physical or testimonial evidence, motions to compel discovery, etc. Because most cases are resolved prior to trial through plea-bargaining, one important judicial function is taking the defendant's guilty plea.

At trial, if the defendant elects to waive a jury, there is a "bench trial" in which the judge sits as the "trier of fact." Like jurors in a jury trial, the judge in a bench trial has considerable discretion when deciding what the facts of the case are. When the defendant elects for a jury trial, then the jury decides what the facts are, and the trial judge makes rulings concerning the admissibility of evidence (whether jury is entitled to hear certain testimony or look at physical

---

[108] James Eisenstein and Herbert Jacob, *Felony Justice: An Organizational Analysis of Criminal Courts* (1977).
[109] Beginning Spring 2020, the pandemic presented challenges to states in administering the bar examinations and resulted in law schools and state bars looking for novel ways to allow candidates who would normally sit for a bar exam to gain licensure without having taken the exam—a practice known as diploma privilege. Oregon, among other states, temporarily decided not to require graduates from Oregon's three law schools to take the exam in order to practice law within the state. For more information about how states have dealt with the July 2020 bar exam and the February 2021 bar exam, see: https://news.bloomberglaw.com/business-and-practice/states-pressured-to-waive-bar-exam-for-new-lawyers-in-pandemic; https://www.justia.com/covid-19/50-state-covid-19-resources/bar-exam-modifications-during-covid-19-50-state-resources/; https://www.ncbex.org/ncbe-covid-19-updates/july-2020-bar-exam-jurisdiction-information/

evidence). The judge also decides whether certain witnesses "qualify" as experts--meaning whether they have the necessary training and expertise. At the end of the trial, the judge will inform the jurors on the law that applies to the case they are deciding by reading "jury instructions."

If the defendant is convicted, then the judge will impose the sentence.[110] In their role imposing sentences Judges have perhaps the broadest discretion; but with more states enacting mandatory minimums and sentence guidelines, judicial discretion is being severely curtailed.

. . . Neutral or impartial judicial decision making requires only that the judge's rulings be based on legally relevant factors and that those factors be applied in an even-handed manner to all similar cases. This requires in many instances that the judge ignore his own personal views as to the desirable objectives of the law. ... It is clearly contrary to judicial ethics to let a decision rest on the judges' personal antagonism toward a person involved in a lawsuit. The judge may not consider the race, sex, or religion of the defendant or victim. ... In a case where he feels that he has a personal bias or prejudice or personal stake in the outcome of the case, the judge should disqualify himself. Indeed, most judges will disqualify themselves where there is a potential for an appearance of partiality in his decision. ...

[A]nother important aspect of principled decision-making is the judge's full recognition of the adversary process. Thus, a judge must rely essentially on information presented in the hearing before him. He cannot base his decisions on his personal knowledge of disputed evidentiary facts. He should not engage in discussions of the case with the lawyers on either side without the other side being present.[111] . . . Above all, the judge should never penalize a client for the misconduct of his counsel.[112]

SELECTION AND QUALIFICATIONS

The sole qualification to be a judge in most jurisdictions is graduating from a law school and membership in the state's bar association. Although the trend is for judges to be lawyers, a few jurisdictions still do not require justices of the peace or municipal judges to be members of the bar.

There are four primary methods used to select judges in the United States: appointment, with or without confirmation by another agency; partisan political election; non-partisan election; and a combination of nomination by commission, appointment and periodic reelection (the Missouri Plan). Within these four primary methods there are variations. States may use different methods to select their judiciary based on the level in the judicial hierarchy. For example, municipal judges may be appointed, while supreme court judges are elected. The length of time a judge will "sit" (called a "term in office" or "tenure") varies greatly--generally from four to sixteen years. Frequently the term for a trial judge is less than a term for an appellate judge. At the appellate level, six years is the shortest term, and many states use terms of ten years or more for their appellate judges. Only a few states have lifetime tenure for their judges.

---

[110] Jurors are generally not involved in sentencing except when the state seeks the death penalty.
[111] Attorneys are prohibited by the rules of professional conduct for *"ex parte"* (one-sided) contact with the judge in attempt to get evidence before, or make motions and requests of, the judge without the other side's presence.
[112] Kerper, *supra* at 442-443.

In the federal system, the President appoints Article III judges (U.S. District Court judges, U.S. Circuit Court of Appeals judges, and U.S. Supreme Court judges) with the advice and consent of the Senate. Federal judges are appointed to "hold their Offices during Good Behavior"[113] (meaning, in essence, life-time appointments under most circumstances). As noted above, district courts appoint federal magistrate judges to either four- or eight-year terms.

BAILIFFS

Bailiffs are the court staff responsible for courtroom security. Bailiffs are often local sheriff deputies or other law enforcement officers or former officers, but they can also be civilians hired by the court. Sometimes, courts will use volunteer bailiffs. Bailiffs work under the supervision of the trial court administrator. During court proceedings, bailiffs (or clerks) call the session to order, announce the entry of the judge, ensure that public spectators remain orderly, keep out witnesses who might testify later (if the judge orders them excluded upon request of either party), and attend to the jurors. As courtroom security becomes a bigger concern, law enforcement officers are increasingly used as bailiffs, and they are responsible for the safety of the court personnel, spectators, witnesses and any of the parties. In some communities, law enforcement bailiffs may transport in-custody defendants from the jail to the courthouse and back. Bailiffs may also screen people for weapons before allowing them to enter the courtroom, and require them to turn off cellphones.

LOCAL AND STATE TRIAL COURT ADMINISTRATORS

Local and state trial court administrators oversee the administration of the courts. These administrators' responsibilities include: hiring and training court personnel (clerks, judicial assistants, bailiffs), ensuring that the court caseloads are efficiently processed, keeping records, sending case files to the appellate courts for review courts, ensuring that local court rules are being implemented, and working with the local and state bar associations to establish effective communications to promote the expedient resolutions of civil and criminal cases.

COURT CLERKS AND STAFF

Court structure varies from courthouse to courthouse, but frequently court staff are divided into units. For example, staff may be assigned to work in the criminal unit, the civil unit, the traffic unit, the small claims unit, the juvenile unit, the family unit, or the probate unit. In smaller communities, there may be just a few court clerks who do it all. With the trend towards specialized courts (drug courts, mental health courts, domestic violence courts, veteran courts), staff may specialize in and/or rotate in and out of the various units. Court staff are expected to have a vast knowledge of myriad local court rules and protocols, statutes, and administrative rules that govern filing processes, filing fees, filing timelines, accounting, record maintenance, as well as a knowledge of general office practices such as ordering supplies, mastering office machinery, and ensuring that safety protocol are established and followed. Recently, many courts have transitioned to electronic filing of all documents--usually managed through a centralized state court system. This transition presents challenges to court staff as they learn the new filing software and all its glitches, keep up with new filings, and archive the past court documents.

JURY CLERK

The jury clerk sends out jury summons to potential jurors; works with jurors' requests for postponements of jury service; coordinates with the scheduling clerk to make sure enough potential jurors show up at the courthouse each day there is a trial; schedules enough grand

---

[113] U.S. Const. art. III.

jurors to fill all the necessary grand jury panels; arranges for payment to jurors for their jury service; and arranges for lodging and meals for jurors in the rare event of jury sequestration.

SCHEDULING CLERK

The scheduling clerk/docketing clerk sets all hearings and trials on the court docket. Part of scheduling or docketing is keeping track of judges' calendars (meaning, their vacation time, days where they will be in training, and the time they will need for resolving those cases "taken under advisement"[114]), law enforcement officers' scheduled vacations, and defense attorneys' scheduled vacations. The scheduling clerk notes how long a trial is expected to take (most trials are concluded within one day), speedy trial constraints, statutory and local court rule time frames, etc. The role of the scheduling clerk is extremely important--an experienced scheduling clerk contributes to the overall efficiency of the legal process. Ineffective or inefficient scheduling causes delay, frustration, and may impede the justice process.

JUDICIAL CLERK, LAW CLERK, AND JUDICIAL ASSISTANT

Generally, judges have one or two main assistants. These individuals are known as "judicial clerks," "clerks of court," "law clerks," or "judicial assistants." Of course, there may be several court clerks who interact each day with all the judges in the courthouse, but judges generally have only one or two judicial assistants who work directly with them. In some jurisdictions, the law clerks are lawyers who have just completed law school and may have already passed the bar exam. In other jurisdictions, the judicial assistants are not lawyers but may have specialized paralegal training or legal assistant training.

RELEASE ASSISTANCE OFFICERS AND INDIGENCY VERIFICATION OFFICERS

Release assistance officers are court employees who meet with defendants at the jail to gather information to pass on to the judges who will then make release decisions. Release assistance officers make their recommendations based on defendant's likelihood of reappearance and other considerations specified by statute or local rules. In determining whether the defendant is likely to reappear, the release assistance officer considers:

- the defendant's ties to the community,
- the defendant's prior record of failures to appear,
- the defendant's employment history
- whether the defendant lives in the community,
- the nature and seriousness of the charges, and
- any potential threat the defendant may present to the community.

The availability of space at the jail may also play a role in whether an individual is released. Court and jail staff may need to work together to establish release protocols when space is limited. The release assistance officer should have a significant voice in drafting those protocols. Whether this staff member recommends security (bail) or conditional release, the release officer will generally suggest to the judge the conditions that the defendant should abide by if he or she makes bail or is conditionally released. Defendants released prior to trial will sign release agreements indicating the conditions of release recommended by the release assistance officer and imposed by the judge. Release assistance officers may also investigate the defendant's

---

[114] Trial judges can either decide "from the bench" (meaning they will rule immediately on the issues before them during the hearing) or after "taking the case under advisement" (meaning they will rule through a written decision/opinion letter after spending time researching the law, reviewing the parties' written pleadings, and considering the oral arguments).

proposed living conditions upon release to make sure that they promote lawful activity and the ability for reappearance for all scheduled court appearances.

Indigency verification officers are court employees who interview defendants to see if they are eligible for court-appointed attorneys. They consider all aspects of the defendant's financial status (salary, unemployment benefits, lottery winnings, home ownership, etc.) in deciding whether they meet the statutory criteria for court-appointed counsel. How poor a defendant must be to qualify for a court-appointed attorney varies from place to place, and each indigency verification officer will be using a screening device that takes into consideration the cost of defense in the locality as well as defendant's financial circumstances.

PROSECUTING ATTORNEYS

Prosecutors play a pivotal role in the criminal justice and work closely with law enforcement officials, judges, defense attorneys, probation and parole officers, victims services, human services, and to a lesser extent, with jail and other corrections officers. The authority to prosecute is divided among various city, state and federal officials. City and state officials are responsible for prosecutions under local and state laws, and federal officials for prosecutions under federal law.

STATE PROSECUTING ATTORNEYS

Since criminal law is public law, prosecutors represent the citizens of the state, not necessarily a particular victim. States vary in how they organize the groups of attorneys hired to represent the state's interest. Ordinarily the official with the primary responsibility for prosecuting state violations is the local prosecutor who is referred to as "district attorney," "county attorney," or "state's attorney." Local prosecutors are usually elected from a single county or a group of counties combined into a prosecutorial district. In many states, the state attorney general's office has authority that supersedes local prosecutors' authority, but in practice the state attorney general rarely intervenes in local matters. The state attorney general's office will intervene, for example, if there is a conflict of interest or when requested by the district attorney. It is not uncommon for a small local prosecutor's office when faced with prosecution of a major, complex, time-consuming trial, to request the aid of the attorney general's office. In these smaller offices, there may be insufficient resources to handle complicated prosecutions and still keep up with the day-to-day filings and cases.

The prosecuting attorney and the attorney general ordinarily are the only officials with authority to prosecute violations of state law. City attorneys may be hired to prosecute city ordinances, but the trend is that these attorneys primarily specialize in civil matters. When city attorneys and prosecuting attorneys have different policies for treating minor offenses, the result may be disparate (different) treatment of similarly situated offenders. This raises concern of inconsistent application of law. Additionally, different county prosecutors may follow quite different policies on which matters they will charge, the use of diversion programs, the use of plea bargaining, and the use of certain trial tactics. To limit some of these differences, some states have used statewide trainings, and district attorneys' conferences. Still, the policies and practices are far from uniform.

Generally assistant prosecutors, also called deputy district attorneys, are hired as "at will" employees by the elected district attorney. Historically, the political party of the applicant was a key criterion, and newly elected prosecutors would make a virtual clean sweep of the office and hire outsiders from the former office. Now, most offices hire on a non-partisan, merit-oriented, basis.

Most states require that the prosecutor be a member of the state bar. Some states also require that he or she have several years in the practice of law. Deputy district attorneys, on the other hand, are frequently fresh out of law school. They may have limited knowledge of state criminal law, but law school is designed to teach lawyers to enter any new field and educate themselves.

FEDERAL PROSECUTING ATTORNEYS

Prosecutorial authority in the federal system rests with the Attorney General of the United States. The Attorney General does not supervise individual prosecutors, but relies on the 94 United States Attorneys (one for each of the federal districts). U.S. Attorneys are given considerable discretion, but they must operate within general guidelines prescribed by the Attorney General. The U.S. Attorneys have a cadre of Assistant U.S. Attorneys who do the day-to-day prosecution of federal crimes. For certain types of cases, approval is needed from the Attorney General or the Deputy Attorney General in charge of the Criminal Division of the Department of Justice. The Criminal Division of the Department of Justice (DOJ) operates as the arm of the Attorney General in coordinating the enforcement of federal laws by the U.S. Attorneys.

SELECTION AND QUALIFICATIONS OF PROSECUTORS

Most local prosecuting attorneys are elected in a partisan election in the district they serve. State attorneys general may also have significant prosecutorial authority. They are elected in forty-two states, appointed by the governor in six states, appointed by the legislature in one state, and appointed by the state supreme court in another. State attorneys general serve between two-to-six-year terms, which can be repeated. Federally, senators from each state recommend potential U.S. Attorney nominees who are then appointed by the President with the consent of the Senate. U.S. Attorneys tend to be of the same political party as the President and are usually replaced when a new President from another party takes office. In 2006 there was a scandal involving the U.S. Department of Justice and the Office of the Attorney General, which, it was later determined, improperly acted to dismiss 26 U.S. Attorneys for political reasons. Ultimately nine members of the Department of Justice (including Attorney General Ernesto Gonzales) resigned in the wake of the scandal and the senate investigation into the firings.

PROSECUTOR'S FUNCTION

Prosecutors arguably have more discretion than any other official in the criminal justice system.[115] They decide whether to charge an individual. If they choose not to prosecute this is referred to as *nolle prosequi,* and this decision is largely unreviewable. Prosecutor decide which charges to file. Prosecutors guide the investigation and work with law enforcement to procure search and arrest warrants. Following arrest, prosecutors continue to be involved with various aspects of the investigation and meet with the arresting officers, interview witnesses, may visit the crime scene, review the physical evidence, determine the offenders prior criminal history, make bail and release recommendations, appear on pretrial motions, initiate plea negotiations, initiate diversions, work with law enforcement officers from other states who seek to extradite offenders, prepare the accusation to present to grand jury (or call witnesses and present *prima facia* case at the preliminary hearing), appear at arraignments for the state, conduct the trial, and upon conviction, participate during the sentencing hearing.

---

[115] See https://www.brennancenter.org/our-work/analysis-opinion/prosecutor-problem for an former insider's view of the prosecutorial function and the recent impact of "progressive prosecutors" and their self-imposed limits on prosecutorial discretion.

In many communities the prosecutor is the spokesperson for the criminal justice system and appears before the legislature to recommend or oppose penal reform. Prosecutors make public speeches on crime and law enforcement, take positions on requests for clemency for cases they have prosecuted, work extensively with victims' services (which are by and large an arm of the prosecutor's office). In some communities, with decreasing frequency, the prosecutor is also responsible for representing the local government in civil matters and may represent the state in civil commitment proceedings and answer accident claims, contract claims, and labor relation matters for the county.[116]

It is often stated, "The prosecutor's [ethical] duty is to seek justice." This means that the state should not go forward with a prosecution if there is insufficient evidence of the defendant's guilt or if the state has "unclean hands" (for example, illegally conducted searches or seizures or illegally obtained confessions). Ethical and disciplinary rules of the state bar associations govern prosecutors who must also follow state and constitutional directives when they prosecute crimes.

DEFENSE ATTORNEYS

PRIVATELY RETAINED DEFENSE ATTORNEYS

Individuals accused of any infraction or crime, no matter how minor, have the right to *hire* counsel and have them appear with them at trial and put on a defense.[117] The attorney must be recognized as qualified to practice law within the state or jurisdiction, but generally, criminal defendants do well to hire an attorney who specializes in criminal defense work. The U.S. Supreme Court has held that a defendant has the right to be represented by an attorney at all criminal proceedings that may substantially affect the right of the accused (referred to a "critical stages"), but because most criminal defendants don't have enough money to hire an attorney to represent them, the court will need to appoint an attorney to represent them in criminal cases.

APPOINTED COUNSEL

Federal and state constitutions do not mention what should be done when the defendant wants, but cannot afford, an attorney's representation. Initially the Court interpreted the Sixth Amendment as just allowing defendants who wanted an attorney to hire one and that attorney could stand in and assist them during trial. Later the Court held that the Due Process Clause of the Fifth and Fourteenth Amendment included the right of a defendant being prosecuted in a state court to have the right to a fair trial, which includes the right to the assistance of counsel. In *Powell v. Alabama*, 287 U.S. 45 (1932), the Court concluded that the focus on trial was too narrow.

> [T]he most critical period of the proceeding[s] against the defendants might be that period from the time of their arraignment until the beginning of their trial, when consultation, thorough going investigation, and preparation are vitally important. Defendants are "as much entitled to . . . [counsel's] aid during that period as at the trial itself. [118]

Powell also dealt with the need for states to provide representation to defendants who could not afford to hire counsel in those cases where fundamental fairness required it. In a statement that led to the dramatic extensions to the right to counsel, the Court continued,

---

[116] U.S. Attorneys still have substantial responsibilities for representation of the U.S. government in civil litigation. (There is generally a division within the office of those attorneys who do primarily civil matters and those that do criminal matters).

[117] The Sixth Amendment provides, "The accused shall enjoy the right . . . to have the Assistance of Counsel for his defense." Most state constitutional provisions use quite similar language.

[118] 287 U.S. at 58.

The right to be heard would be, in many cases, of little avail if it did not comprehend the right to be heard by counsel. Even the intelligent and educated layman has a small and sometimes no skill in the science of law. If charged with crime, he is incapable, generally, of determining for himself whether the indictment is good or bad. He is unfamiliar with the rules of evidence. Left without the aid of counsel he may be put on trial without a proper charge, and convicted upon incompetent evidence, or evidence irrelevant to the issue or otherwise inadmissible. He lacks both the skill and knowledge adequately to prepare his defense, even though he may have a perfect one. He requires the guiding hand of counsel at every step in the proceedings against him. Without it, though he be not guilty, he faces the danger of conviction because he does not know how to establish his innocence.[119]

Powell was decided in 1932, and because of television and the multitude of crime drama programs, people probably know more about the criminal justice process than ever imagined by the *Powell* court. Nevertheless, the Court's admonitions still ring true. Not many people know how to conduct themselves at trial, challenge the state's evidence, make evidentiary objections, or file proper pretrial motions with the rudimentary knowledge gained from watching television. One could consult with the many great Internet sources that are easily accessible; however, many individuals charged with crimes have limited education and lack the training and sophistication to distinguish between those sources that are applicable to their case (jurisdiction, for example), and which are not.

Between *Powell* (1932) and *Gideon v. Wainwright*, 372 U.S. 335 (1963) the Court decided when the appointment of counsel was necessary for a fair trial in state prosecutions on a case-by-case basis. In *Gideon*, however, the Court held that this case-by case-approach was inappropriate. It held that the state had to provide poor defendant access to counsel in every state felony prosecution. Lawyers in serious criminal cases, it said, were "necessities, not luxuries." Since *Gideon*, the Court has extended the obligation to provide counsel to state misdemeanors prosecutions that result in the defendant receiving a jail term. The legal problems presented in a misdemeanor case often are just as complex as those in felonies. In two cases, *Argersinger v. Hamlin*, 407 U.S. 25 (1972) and *Scott v. Illinois*, 440 U.S. 367 (1979), the Court held that appointed counsel was necessary in misdemeanor cases, but tied the right to the defendant's actual incarceration. Because it is difficult to predict when a judge will want to incarcerate a person convicted of a misdemeanor, this standard or approach is difficult to implement. Many states instead appoint counsel to any indigent charged with a crime where a possible term of incarceration could be imposed.

The Court left it for the lower courts to decide when a person is indigent. Lower courts have generally held that the financial resources of a family member cannot be considered. Also, courts cannot merely conclude that because a college student is capable of financing his or her education that he or she is capable of hiring an attorney. A person does not have to become destitute in order to be classified as indigent. An indigent defendant may have to pay back the court-appointed attorney's fees if they are convicted or enter a plea. In practice, most courts collect court-appointed attorney's fees (at a standardized rate, much reduced from the actual costs of representation) as part of the fines that a convicted defendant must pay. When acquitted, defendants are not required to pay the attorney fees.

---

[119] *Id.* at 68-69.

PUBLIC DEFENDERS, ASSIGNED ATTORNEYS, AND DEFENSE ATTORNEY ASSOCIATIONS

Most states now have public defenders' offices. Because public defenders and assistant public defenders handle only criminal cases, they become the specialists and have considerable expertise in representing criminal defendants. Public defender offices frequently have investigators on staff to help the attorneys represent their clients. In some states, courts appoint or assign attorneys from the private bar (i.e., not from the public defender's office) to represent indigent defendants. The mixed system uses both assigned counsel (or associations of private attorneys who contract to do indigent criminal defense) and public defenders. For example, the public defenders' office may contract with the state to provide 80% of all indigent representations in a particular county. The remaining 20% of cases would be assigned to the association of individual attorneys who do criminal defense work (some retained clients, some indigent clients) or private attorneys willing to take indigent defense cases. In practice, there is no purely public defender system because of "conflict cases." Conflicts exist when one law firm tries to represent more than one party in a case. Assume, for example, that Defendant A conspired with Defendant B to rob a bank. One law firm could not represent both Defendant A and Defendant B. Public defender offices are generally considered one law firm, so attorneys from that office could not represent both A and B, and the court will have to assign a "conflict" attorney to one of the defendants.

THE RIGHT TO COUNSEL IN FEDERAL TRIALS

The Court in *Johnson v. Zerbst*, 304 U.S. 458 (1938), held that, in all federal felony trials, counsel must represent a defendant unless the defendant waives that right. The Court further held that the lack of counsel is a *jurisdictional error* and not just a *procedural error*. This is an important distinction. If an error is considered jurisdictional the conviction is deemed void. A court that allows a defendant to be convicted without an attorney's representation has no power or authority to deprive an accused of life or liberty.

Zerbst also established rules for a proper waiver of the Sixth Amendment right to counsel. The court said that it is presumed that the defendant has not waived her right to counsel. For a waiver to be constitutional, the court must find that the defendant knew he or she had a right to counsel and voluntarily gave up that right, knowing that he or she had the right to claim it. Therefore, if the defendant silently goes along with the court process without complaining about the lack of counsel, his or her silence does not amount to a waiver. The Court defined waiver as an "intelligent relinquishment or abandonment of a known right or privilege."

In 1945 Congress passed the Federal Rules of Criminal Procedure (FRCP). Rule 44 of the FRCP requires defendants to have counsel (or affirmatively waive counsel), either retained or appointed, at every stage of the proceedings from the initial appearance through appeal. This rule was difficult to implement because there was a lack of a federal defense bar available or willing to take on appointed cases. So, in 1964, Congress passed the Criminal Justice Act of 1964 that established a national system for providing counsel to indigent defendants in federal courts.

CRITICAL STAGES OF THE CRIMINAL JUSTICE PROCESS

In *White v. Maryland*, 373 US 59 (1963), the Court found that defendants are entitled to the right to counsel at any *critical stage* of the proceeding—defined as a stage in which he or she is compelled to make a decision which may later formally be used against him or her. The Court has found the following court procedures to be critical stages:

- The initial appearance in which the defendant entered a non-binding plea. (*White, supra.* White made statements while entering his initial guilty plea during arraignments. He later withdrew his guilty plea, but the state had used the statements against him at his trial.)
- A preliminary hearing. (*Coleman v. Alabama,* 399 U.S. 1 (1970).)
- A lineup that includes a previously indicted defendant. (*Wade v. United States,* 388 U.S. 218 (1967) and *Gilbert v. California,* 388 U.S. 263 (1967).)

THE RIGHT TO COUNSEL IN OTHER PROCEEDINGS

The Court has extended the right to counsel to psychiatric examinations, juvenile delinquency proceedings[120], civil commitments proceedings,[121] and probation and parole hearings. *Estelle v. Smith,* 451 U.S. 454 (1981), held that a defendant charged with a capital crime and ordered by the court to be examined by a psychiatrist (to evaluate possible future dangerousness) was entitled to consult with counsel. Similarly, the Court found prejudicial error occurred when defense counsel was not appointed to represent a defendant subjected to a psychiatric evaluation. Additionally, counsel must have knowledge of the projected examination before it occurs.[122]

Probation and Parole Revocation Hearings

In *Mempa v. Rhay,* 389 U.S. 128 (1967), 17-year-old Mempa was placed on probation for two years after he plead guilty to "joyriding." About four months later, the prosecutor moved to have petitioner's probation revoked alleging that Mempa had committed a burglary while on probation. Mempa, who was not represented by counsel at the probation revocation hearing. admitted being involved in the burglary. The court revoked his probation based on his admission to the burglary. The U.S. Supreme Court held that Mempa should have had counsel to assist him in his hearing.

Five years later, in *Gagnon v. Scarpelli,* 411 U.S. 778 (1973), the state sought to revoke defendant's probation. Originally, Gagnon was sentenced to fifteen years imprisonment for armed robbery, but the judge had suspended the imposition of sentence and placed him instead on seven years of probation. The Court found that the probation revocation hearing did not meet the standards of due process. Because a probation revocation does involve a loss of liberty, the probationer was entitled to due process. The Court did not adopt a *per se* rule that all probationers must have the assistance of counsel in every revocation hearing. Rather, it stated,

> We find no justification for a new, inflexible constitutional rule with respect to the requirement of counsel. We think rather, that the decision as to the need for counsel must be made on a case-by-case basis in the exercise of sound discretion by the state authority charged with responsibility for administering the probation and parole system. ... Presumptively, it may be said that counsel should be provided in cases where, after being informed of his right to request counsel, the probationer or parolee makes such a request based on a timely and colorable claim. ... In passing on a request for the appointment of counsel, the responsible agency should also consider, especially in doubtful cases, whether probationer appears to be capable of speaking effectively for himself. In every case in which a

---

[120] *See, In re Gault,* 387 U.S. 1 (1967).
[121] *See,* Susan Stefan, "The Right to Counsel in Civil Commitment Proceedings." http://www.bazelon.org/LinkClick.aspx?fileticket=s4KpfNJBXEo%3D&tabid=222.
[122] *Satterwhite v. Texas,* 486 U.S. 249 (1988).

request for counsel at a preliminary or final hearing is refused, the grounds for refusal shall be stated succinctly in the record.[123]

Post-Trial Proceedings

When an out-of-custody defendant is found guilty at the end of a trial, the judge generally remands the defendant to custody and revokes conditions of bail if there had been any. The attorney representing the defendant has the legal obligation to make post-trial motions to preserve the defendant's rights. The Sixth Amendment's right to the assistance of counsel does not stop when the jury finds the defendant guilty. Counsel must assist the defendant through the end of the sentencing hearing.

The Court has distinguished between the defendant's right to the assistance of counsel on "appeals of right" and the defendant's right to the assistance of counsel for "discretionary appeals" (known as petitions for writ of certiorari.) In *Douglas v. California*, 372 U.S. 353 (1963), the Court found that indigent counsel should be provided to individuals for their first appeal as a matter of right. Once the first appeal has been dismissed or resolved, *Ross v. Moffitt*, 417 U.S. 600 (1974), holds that indigent defendants do not have a right to appointed counsel for discretionary review in either the state supreme court or the U.S. Supreme Court. The *Ross* majority reasoned that the defendant did not need an attorney to have "meaningful access" to the higher appellate courts because all the legal issues will have already been fully briefed in the intermediate appellate court (the initial appeal of right). Additionally, the Court noted that the concept of equal protection does not require absolute equality, so that "the fact that a particular service might be of benefit to an indigent does not mean that the service is constitutionally required."

Prisoners have a limited right to legal assistance for the purpose of filing writs of habeas corpus. In *Bounds v. Smith*, 430 U.S. 817 (1977), the Court held that "the fundamental constitutional right of access to the courts requires prison authorities to assist inmates in the preparation and filing of meaningful legal papers by providing prisoners with adequate law libraries or adequate assistance from persons trained in the law." Prisons can meet this obligation by training prisoners to be paralegal assistants to work under a lawyer's supervision or by using law students, paralegals, and volunteer lawyers. Again, it may seem inconsistent that the court requires more for habeas corpus relief than it does for discretionary review on appeals. The difference lies in the nature of habeas corpus as a collateral attack (side attack) where the claim is often being advanced for the first time and therefore the need for legal assistance may be greater.

FUNCTIONS OF DEFENSE ATTORNEYS

Defense lawyers investigate the circumstances of the case, keep clients informed of any developments in the case, and take action to preserve the legal rights of the accused. Some decisions, such as which witnesses to call, when to object to evidence, what questions to ask on cross-examination, are considered to be strategic ones and may be decided by the attorney. Other decisions must be made by the defendant (after getting advice from the attorney about the options and their likely consequences). Defendants' decisions include whether to plead guilty and forego a trial, whether to waive a jury trial, and whether to testify in their own behalf.

In *McCoy v. Louisiana*, 584 U.S. ___ (2018), McCoy was charged with murdering his ex-wife and her family members, and the state sought the death penalty. McCoy, an indigent defendant, consistently and continuously maintained his innocence. He was initially represented by a public defender who was removed from the case when refused to present McCoy's innocence claim. McCoy's new attorney encouraged McCoy to take the plea deal, but McCoy

---

[123] 411 U.S. at 790.

refused. At trial and despite McCoy's objections, McCoy's second attorney conceded McCoy's guilt but argued against the death penalty during the sentencing phase. McCoy was convicted and the jury recommended the death penalty. The Supreme Court held that a defendant's Sixth Amendment right to counsel is violated when counsel admits defendant's guilt to the jury when the defendant expressly told him not to do so. The Court noted that the decision to assert innocence as a defense is one of those decisions reserved exclusively to the client.

The ABA Standards relating to the Defense Function established basic guidelines for defense counsel in fulfilling obligations to the client. The primary duty is to zealously represent the defendant within the bounds of law. Defense counsel is to avoid unnecessary delay, to refrain from misrepresentations of law and fact, and to avoid personal publicity connected with the case. Fees are set on the basis of the time and effort required by counsel, the responsibility assumed, the novelty and difficulty of the question involved, the gravity of the charge, and the experience, reputation and ability of the lawyer.

Standard 4- 1.2, The Function of Defense Counsel, states:

(a) Counsel for the accused is an essential component of the administration of criminal justice. A court properly constituted to hear a criminal case must be viewed as a tripartite entity consisting of the judge (and jury, where appropriate), counsel for the prosecution, and counsel for the accused.

(b) The basic duty defense counsel owes to the administration of justice and as an officer of the court is to serve as the accused's counselor and advocate with courage and devotion and to render effective, quality representation.

(c) Since the death penalty differs from other criminal penalties in its finality, defense counsel in a capital case should respond to this difference by making extraordinary efforts on behalf of the accused. Defense counsel should comply with the ABA Guidelines for the Appointment and Performance of Counsel in Death Penalty Cases.

(d) Defense counsel should seek to reform and improve the administration of criminal justice. When inadequacies or injustices in the substantive or procedural law come to defense counsel's attention, he or she should stimulate efforts for remedial action.

(e) Defense counsel, in common with all members of the bar, is subject to standards of conduct stated in statutes, rules, decisions of courts, and codes, canons, or other standards of professional conduct. Defense counsel has no duty to execute any directive of the accused which does not comport with law or such standards. Defense counsel is the professional representative of the accused, not the accused's alter ego.

(f) Defense counsel should not intentionally misrepresent matters of fact or law to the court.

(g) Defense counsel should disclose to the tribunal legal authority in the controlling jurisdiction known to defense counsel to be directly adverse to the position of the accused and not disclosed by the prosecutor.

(h) It is the duty of defense counsel to know and be guided by the standards of professional conduct as defined in codes and canons of the legal profession applicable in defense counsel's jurisdiction. Once representation has been undertaken, the functions and duties of defense counsel are the same whether defense counsel is assigned, privately retained, or serving in a legal aid or defender program.

TRICKY ISSUES IN REPRESENTATION

Defendants sometimes want to have a friend or family member speak up for them. But, unless that friend or family member is an attorney, the Court will not permit that. The right to counsel means the right to be represented by an attorney--someone legally trained and recognized as a member of the bar association. Similarly, defendants may not necessarily get the attorney their choice. For example, in *Wheat v. United States*, 486 U.S. 153 (1988), one defendant wanted to be represented by the same attorney who was representing his accomplice/co-conspirator in a complex drug distribution conspiracy. Another of the co-defendants, represented by this attorney, had already pled guilty to one count of the indictment. Wheat and his co-defendants were willing to waive the Sixth Amendment rights to the counsel of his choice and to waive their rights to conflict-free counsel (the rules of professional ethics say attorneys cannot represent clients who may have conflicts of interest). Nevertheless, the Supreme Court denied the application for the counsel indicating that irreconcilable and unwaivable conflicts of interest would be created (there was a likelihood that one defendant would be called to testify against his co-defendant.) On the other hand, the Court in *U.S. v. Gonzalez-Lopez*, 553 U.S. 285 (2008), reversed the defendant's conviction because the trial court erroneously deprived defendant of his choice of counsel. Gonzales-Lopez had hired counsel from a different state; during pretrial proceedings, the judge and the counsel had some disagreements, and the judge ultimately prohibited the attorney from taking part in the defendant's trial. The Court found that trial judge violated defendant's Sixth Amendment rights.

Defendants cannot repeatedly "fire" their appointed counsel as a stall tactic, and, at some point, courts will not allow the defendant to substitute attorneys and will require the defendant work with whatever attorney is currently assigned. Although a defendant may not force an unwilling attorney to represent him or her, the court does have the discretion to deny an attorney's motion to withdraw from representation after inquiring about counsel's reasons for wishing to withdraw. This may present an ethical dilemma for the attorney because professional rules of responsibility require that even when an attorney withdraws from a case, he or she must still maintain attorney-client confidences. If the attorney knows that the defendant insists on taking the stand and presenting perjured testimony, the attorney must withdraw. But, at the same time, the attorney cannot disclose to the court the reason he or she needs to withdraw. At some point in the inquiry, after the judge has asked and the attorney has done a little verbal dance around the subject, the judge hopefully catches on, and the judges removes the attorney from the case.

"EFFECTIVE ASSISTANCE" OF COUNSEL

McMann v. Richardson, 397 U.S. 759 (1970), held that the right to counsel means the right to effective assistance of counsel. The constitutional standard for evaluating effective assistance was determined in *Strickland v. Washington*, 466 U.S. 688 (1984). *Strickland* enunciated a two-prong inquiry about the attorney's performance in determining whether there was ineffective assistance of counsel. In essence, the attorney's performance must meet minimal attorney performance standards and it must not have prejudiced the defendant (which means that what the defense attorney did or did not do must not have adversely affected the outcome of the case). If it did, the defendant may be entitled to a new trial.

The right to effective assistance of counsel does not mean that the defendant has the right to a lawyer who will knowingly present perjured testimony. In *Nix v. Whiteside*, 475 U.S. 157 (1986), Whiteside wanted to lie about seeing something metallic in the victim's hand as a means of raising a claim of self-defense. The lawyer, who knew this to be false and not consistent with defendant's other stories, refused to allow the Whiteside to testify. Whiteside claimed that his lawyer's refusal to put on his testimony violated his right to counsel. The court held that the rules of professional ethics prohibited the lawyer from putting on defendant's testimony, and that it could not be a violation of the defendant's Sixth Amendment rights for his counsel to act in accordance with professional rules.

Courts may be more inclined to find ineffective assistance of counsel in a case in which the defendant received the death penalty. (See, e.g., *Buck v. Davis*, 580 U.S. ___ (2017) discussed further in Chapter Ten in the section on expert witnesses.) The court will be quick to find ineffective assistance if defense counsel does not conduct an adequate social history or family history investigation that would demonstrate mitigating evidence or mitigating factors favoring the defendant. For example, in *Wiggins v. Smith*, 539 U.S. 510 (2003), the court found that Wiggins' defense attorneys provided ineffective assistance of counsel in the sentencing portion of his trial for the capital murder of a 77-year-old woman because they failed to investigate and present evidence they had showing that he had been subject to regular sexual abuse as a child. The Court stated,

> In finding that . . . [Wiggin's attorneys'] . . . investigation did not meet *Strickland*'s performance standards, we emphasize that *Strickland* does not require counsel to investigate every conceivable line of mitigating evidence no matter how unlikely the effort would be to assist the defendant at sentencing. Nor does *Strickland* require defense counsel to present mitigating evidence at sentencing in every case. Both conclusions would interfere with the "constitutionally protected independence of counsel" at the heart of *Strickland*. We base our conclusion on the much more limited principle that "strategic choices made after less than complete investigation are reasonable" only to the extent that reasonable professional judgments support the limitations on investigation. ... A decision not to investigate thus must be directly assessed for reasonableness in all the circumstances.
>
> Counsels' investigation into Wiggins' background did not reflect reasonable professional judgment. Their decision to end their investigation when they did was neither consistent with the professional standards that prevailed in 1989, nor reasonable in light of the evidence counsel uncovered in the social services records--evidence that would have led a reasonably competent attorney to investigate further. Counsels' pursuit of bifurcation until the eve of sentencing and their partial presentation of a mitigation case suggest that their incomplete investigation was the result of inattention, not reasoned strategic judgment. In deferring to counsels' decision not to pursue a mitigation case despite their unreasonable investigation, the Maryland Court of Appeals unreasonably applied *Strickland*.[124]

In *Garza v. Idaho*, 586 U.S. ___ (2019), Garza's attorney did not file a notice of appeal even though Garza requested he do so. (The attorney believed that in defendant's plea pursuant to negotiations, he had waived his right to appeal.) The Court held that the attorney's decision to not

---

[124] 539 U.S. at 531.

file an appeal for the defendant triggered the "presumption of prejudice" and indicated ineffective assistance of counsel. The Court, citing an earlier case, stated that "prejudice is presumed . . . when counsel's constitutionally deficient performance deprives a defendant of an appeal that he would have otherwise taken." The Court noted that the filing of a notice of appeal (something Garza asked his attorney do) is "a purely ministerial task that imposes no great burden on counsel." The Court held that Garza's attorney's choice to override Garza's instructions to file an appeal was 1) not a strategic one, 2) was a decision for the defendant himself to make, and 3) was a decision made at a critical stage of the process. Thus, the requirements of *Strickland* were met.

WAIVER OF COUNSEL

Sometimes, a defendant wishes to waive counsel and represent him or herself at trial (referred to as appearing *pro se*). The Court, in *Faretta v. California,* 422 U.S. 806 (1975), held that the Sixth Amendment includes defendant's right to represent himself or herself. The *Faretta* Court found that, where a defendant is adamantly opposed to having an attorney's representation, there is little value in forcing him or her to have a lawyer. The Court stressed that it was important for the trial court to make certain and establish a record that the defendant knowingly and intelligently gave up his or her rights. This means the defendant must be informed of the dangers of appearing without a legally trained advocate.

> Although a defendant need not himself have the skill and experience of a lawyer in order competently and intelligently to choose self-representation, he should be made aware of the dangers and disadvantages of self-representation, so that the record will establish he knows what he is doing and his choice is made with eyes open. (Citation omitted).[125]

In *McKaskle v. Wiggins,* 465 U.S. 168 (1984), the Court held that a "defendant does not have a constitutional right to receive personal instruction from the trial judge on courtroom procedure. Nor does the constitution require judges to take over chores for a *pro se* defendant that would normally be attended to by trained counsel as a matter of course."[126] The constitutional right to self-representation does not mean that the defendant is free to obstruct the trial, and a judge may terminate self-representation by a defendant who is obstructing the process.[127] Frequently, judges will assign a "stand-by counsel" to assist defendants. Stand-by counsel can be available to answer questions by a pro se defendant, and if necessary, stand-by counsel can step in if the defendant is engaging in misconduct.

---

[125] 422 U.S. at 835.

[126] 465 U.S. at 174.

[127] For a YouTube video of a trial in which the defendant, on the second day of the trial asked the judge to allow him to represent himself and assign his attorney as standby counsel see, https://www.youtube.com/watch?v=t6g9eL2R1vQ. For a good example of why it is probably not a good idea to allow a defendant to represent him or herself (or for the defendant to request to do so), see https://www.youtube.com/watch?v=L0wNPsxlD0w. (defendant was screaming at the jury in his opening statements!) For pictures of defendants who were allowed to represent themselves, see, https://abcnews.go.com/US/slideshow/photos-infamous-defendants-represented-17376177/image-17376208. And finally, consider the October 26, 2022 convictions for several counts of first-degree intentional homicide connected with Darrell Brook's driving his vehicle at high rates of speed into the Waukesha Christmas parade on November 21, 2021 killing six and injuring 62. See, https://www.cnn.com/2022/10/26/us/waukesha-christmas-parade- and https://apnews.com/article/wisconsin-milwaukee-homicide-c7d48654ac60d1b7c0d2087b97b4d4da

WRAP UP

More than 51 court systems operate in the United States. We have a dual court system comprised of federal trial and appellate courts and state trial and appellate courts. Federal and state courts have similar hierarchical structures with cases flowing from lower trial courts through intermediate courts of appeals and up to the supreme courts. Courts also can be classified according to their subject matter jurisdiction or geographical jurisdiction.

Judges, prosecutors, defense attorneys work together along with court clerks, bailiffs, and other court staff to process tens of thousands of cases daily in trial courts across the nation. Together they comprise the "courtroom workgroup." Defense attorneys play an important role in the criminal justice process, and at critical stages in the process defendants must be represented by an attorney (at the government's expense if they cannot afford to hire an attorney) unless they have voluntarily waived the right and wish to represent themselves. Few cases actually go to trial, and the vast majority of criminal cases are resolved in the trial courts at the pre-trial stage.

Defendants who wish to appeal their convictions are entitled to have their cases reviewed at least once--a mandatory appeal of right in the intermediate courts of appeal. After that, review is discretionary (and rare). Appellate courts generally affirm the decision of the trial courts, but may also reverse and remand the case back to the trial court if they determine that prejudicial error occurred. At the intermediate appellate court level, judges most frequently affirm the trial court's decision without writing an opinion, but sometimes the judges will write opinions informing the parties of their decision and the reasons for holding as they did. Judges don't always agree, and at times, judges will write dissenting opinions or concurring opinions. Appellate court opinions become precedent that must be followed in the trial courts.

SOME THINGS TO THINK ABOUT OR EXPLORE

➢ Explore the U.S. Supreme Court building at https://www.supremecourt.gov/

➢ Read Ruth Marcus' November 4, 2022 article in the Washington Post https://www.washingtonpost.com/opinions/2022/11/04/supreme-court-john-roberts-tragedy-ruth-marcus/. Do you think that Chief Justice is getting a raw deal and deserves any sympathy for his failures to unify the Court and keep its reputation intact?

➢ Peruse the following website and write (and answer) 10 questions about the U.S. Supreme Court and its justices. https://www.uscourts.gov/; https://www.uscourts.gov/news/2020/03/17/annual-report-and-judicial-business-2019-now-available#:~:text=The%202019%20Judicial%20Business%20section,than%201%20percent%20to%20776%2C674.

➢ Peruse the following website and write (and answer) 10 questions about the U.S. Circuit Courts of Appeals, their caseloads, their judges, their pay, etc. https://www.uscourts.gov/ ; https://www.uscourts.gov/news/2020/03/17/annual-report-and-judicial-business-2019-now-available#:~:text=The%202019%20Judicial%20Business%20section,than%201%20percent%20to%20776%2C674.

➢ Peruse the following website and write (and answer) 10 questions about the U.S. District Courts and their members, caseloads, pay, etc. https://www.uscourts.gov/; https://www.uscourts.gov/news/2020/03/17/annual-report-and-judicial-business-2019-now-available#:~:text=The%202019%20Judicial%20Business%20section,than%201%20percent%20to%20776%2C674.

➢ Peruse the following website and write (and answer) 10 questions about the U.S. Magistrate Courts, magistrate courts, their caseloads, and pay, etc. https://www.uscourts.gov.

➢ Consider the Court's "shadow docket" and recent critique that much of the work of the Court is less than transparent because of it (https://www.abajournal.com/web/article/scotus-shadow-docket-draws-increasing-scrutiny). Note that on February 18, 2021 the House Judiciary Committee held hearings on the shadow docket. (https://www.youtube.com/watch?v=oC1Vo-MJ9IQ)(go to 20 minute mark to listen to testimony by experts about the court's shadow docket).

➢ Consider the February 2021 letter from Senators Sheldon Whitehouse and Lindsay Graham to Chief Justice Roberts and Clerk of the U.S. Supreme Court, Scott S. Harris calling for greater financial transparency and accountability of Supreme Court Justices (see, https://www.whitehouse.senate.gov/news/release/whitehouse-graham-call-on-federal-judiciary-to-strengthen-judicial-ethics-standards-). Do you agree that the justices should be held to the same standards as the executive and legislative branch with regard to financial transparency and ethics?

➢ There was much discussion during the nomination and confirmation of Justice Amy Coney Barrett to the U.S. Supreme Court about whether, in response, the new administration should consider "stacking (or packing) the court." Discuss the various arguments surrounding those discussions. See, https://www.nytimes.com/2020/09/19/us/politics/what-is-court-packing.html ; https://www.politico.com/news/magazine/2020/10/26/amy-coney-barrett-confirmation-court-packing-jursidiction-stripping-432566; https://www.vox.com/21514454/supreme-court-amy-coney-barrett-packing-voting-rights

TERMINOLOGY

- abuse of discretion standard of review
- appeal
- appellate court
- appeal of right (mandatory review)
- appointed counsel
- arbitrary and capricious
- Article I court
- Article III court
- assigned counsel system
- bailiff
- burden of persuasion
- burden of production
- burden of proof
- clearly erroneous
- concurring opinion
- court appointed attorney
- courtroom workgroup
- courts of general jurisdiction
- courts of limited jurisdiction
- critical stage of the criminal justice system
- *de novo* review
- discretionary appeal
- dissenting opinion
- dual court system
- effective assistance of counsel
- geographical jurisdiction
- harmless error
- indigency
- indigency verification officer
- judicial assistant
- judicial clerk
- jurisdiction
- jurisdictional error
- jury clerk
- majority opinion
- nolle prosequi
- plain error
- plurality opinion
- prejudicial error
- prima facie case
- principle of orality
- privately retained attorney
- procedural error
- *pro se* defendant
- *pro se* appearance
- public defender
- question of law
- question of fact
- original jurisdiction
- release assistance officer
- retained counsel
- standard of review
- subject matter jurisdiction
- trial court
- waiver of counsel
- writ of certiorari
- writ of habeas corpus

Chapter Four: Constitutional Limits on Criminal Law

OVERVIEW AND LEARNING OBJECTIVES

This chapter explores the role of the Constitution in the making and enforcement of criminal laws. After reading this chapter, you should be able to answer the following questions:

➤ How does the Constitution limit the ability of Congress to pass ex post facto laws?
➤ How does the Constitution limit the ability of Congress to pass laws that are overly vague?
➤ What is the rule of legality?
➤ What is the Bill of Rights?
➤ What is the Due Process Clause and what impact did it have on both state and national government?
➤ When will a law violate the ex post facto prohibition?
➤ Why do laws that are written too broadly violate the Constitution?
➤ When will a law violate the Equal Protections Clause?
➤ When, if ever, may government limit free speech, expressive conduct, symbolic speech, or commercial speech?
➤ When, if ever, may government place restrictions on the right of assembly?
➤ Do criminal laws that impact the right to practice one's religion necessarily violate the Constitution?
➤ What makes a punishment cruel and unusual?

States and federal constitutions limit the ability of the legislative and executive branch to pass certain types of criminal laws. The drafters of the federal Constitution were so concerned about two historic abuses by English Parliament--ex post facto laws and bills of attainder--that they prohibited Congress from passing these types of laws in original body of the Constitution.[128] Most of the other limitations discussed in this chapter are found within the Bill of Rights--the first ten amendments to the U.S. Constitution. The states adopted the Bill of Rights in 1791.[129] These amendments added several constraints on Congress that had not yet been worked out yet at the

---

[128] See, U.S. Const. art. I, § 9.

[129] There is a rich history about the political squabbles and compromises that existed when the federal constitution took effect, but it is beyond the scope of this text. Essentially, the statesmen had opposing viewpoints concerning how strong the national government should be and how strong state governments should be. Even as the original federal constitution was being circulated and ratified, the framers were thinking about the provisions that became known as the Bill of Rights. In his acclaimed Broadway Musical, *Hamilton*, Lin-Manuel Miranda explores this dispute between Thomas Jefferson (a strong state's rights politician and Alexander Hamilton (a strong federal rights proponent).

time of the Constitutional Convention. The impact of the Bill of Rights was to place substantial checks on the federal government's ability to define crimes.

This chapter explores the First, Second, and Eighth Amendments' impact on federal substantive law, and the Fourth, Fifth, Sixth, and Eighth Amendments' impact on federal procedural law. When drafted and passed, the U.S. Constitution and the Bill of Rights applied only to the federal government. Individual states each had their own guarantees and protections of individuals' rights found in the state constitutions. Since 1868, the Fourteenth Amendment has become an important tool for making states also follow the provisions of the Bill of the Rights. It was drafted to enforce the Civil Rights Act passed in 1866 in post-Civil War states. Section 1 of the Fourteenth Amendment enjoins the states from depriving any person of life, liberty, or property, without due process of law. It prohibits states from adopting any laws that abridge the privileges and immunities of the citizens of the United States and requires that states not deny any person equal protection under the law.[130]

The practice of making the states follow provisions of the Bill of Rights is known as "incorporation." Over decades, the Supreme Court debated whether the Bill of Rights should be incorporated all together, in one-fell swoop (called "total incorporation") or piece-by-piece (called "selective incorporation"). The case-by-case, bit-by-bit approach won out. In a series of decisions, the Supreme Court has held that the Due Process Clause of the Fourteenth Amendment makes enforceable against the states those provisions of the Bill of Rights that are "implicit in the concept of ordered liberty."[131] For example, in 1925 the Court recognized that the First Amendment protections of free speech and free press apply to states as well as to the federal government.[132] In the 1960s, the Court selectively incorporated many of the procedural guarantees of the Bill of Rights. The Court also used the Fourteenth Amendment to extend substantive guarantees of the Bill of Rights to the states. More recently, the Court, in *McDonald v. City of Chicago*, 561 U.S. 742 (2010), held that the Second Amendment's right to bear arms also applied to the states. Scheb noted,

> McDonald was the latest, and quite possibly the last, in a series of decisions incorporating provisions of the Bill of Rights into the Fourteenth Amendment. With the exception of the Fifth Amendment's Grand Jury Clause and the Eighth Amendment's prohibitions of excessive bail and excessive fines, all the provisions of the Bill of Rights have been incorporated into the Fourteenth Amendment making them applicable to state and local governments. Thus, the U.S. Constitution and the Bill of Rights, now stands as a barrier to unreasonable or oppressive criminal laws, whether they are enacted by Congress, a state's legislature, or a local governing body.[133]

Notwithstanding Scheb's prediction about *McDonald*, the Court in 2019 incorporated the Excessive Fines Clause's prohibition found in the Eighth Amendment to the states under the Fourteenth Amendment's Due Process Clause. *Timbs v. Indiana*, 586 U.S. ___ (2019). Timbs plead guilty to dealing in a controlled substance and conspiracy to commit theft, and at the time of his arrest, the police seized a Land Rover SUV that Timbs had recently purchased for $42,000 with money received from his deceased father's life insurance policy. The maximum fine that Timbs could have been ordered to pay for his convictions was $10,000. The Court concluded the

---

[130] U.S. Const. amend. XIV, § 2.
[131] *Palko v. Connecticut* 302 U.S. 319 (1937).
[132] *Gitlow v. New York* 268 U.S. 652 (1925).
[133] Scheb, *supra* at 65-66.

seizure constituted an excessive fine. The Court stated,

> The Fourteenth Amendment's Due Process Clause incorporates and renders applicable to the States Bill of Rights protections "fundamental to our scheme of ordered liberty" or "deeply rooted in this Nation's history and tradition. . . . Protection against excessive fines has been a constant shield throughout the Anglo-American history for good reason: Such fines undermine other liberties. They can be used to retaliate against or chill the speech of political enemies. They can also be employed, not in the service of penal purposes, but as a source of revenue. The historical and logical case for concluding that the Fourteenth Amendment incorporates the Excessive Fines Clause is indeed overwhelming.

EX POST FACTO LAWS

Ex post facto laws are ones that are applied retroactively. For example, assume that Cheryl catches and squashes a centipede on January 1st; in response, city council on January 2nd, passes a law that makes centipede-squashing a misdemeanor. The prohibition against ex post facto laws protects Cheryl from being prosecuted under this new law. Any attempt by the state to prosecute Cheryl using the new law applied retroactively would violate the provision against ex post facto laws. One of the reasons that ex post facto laws are problematic is because they violate the principle of legality that holds that individuals are entitled to know, in advance, what the law prohibits. Without the protection against ex post facto laws, Cheryl would only be able to guess at what types of laws could ensnare her at any time in the future.

According to the Court four types of laws that violate this principle. Justice Chase wrote,

> 1st. Every law that makes an action done before the passing of the law, and which was innocent when done, criminal, and punishes such action. 2d. Every law that aggravates a crime, or makes it greater than it was when committed. 3d. Every law that changes the punishment, and inflicts greater punishment, than the law annexed to the crime when committed. 4th. Every law that alters the legal rules of evidence and receives less or different testimony than the law required at the time of the commission of the offense in order to convict the offender.[134]

Modern legislatures are generally careful not to draft statutes that violate ex post facto prohibitions. However, courts occasionally find a law to be retroactive in ways that the legislature failed to consider. When that happens, the court will strike down the law. For example, the Court struck down Florida sentencing guidelines in 1987 to the extent they reduced time off for an inmate's good behavior because it had the effect of increasing the punishment for those who committed crimes before the enactment of the guidelines.[135] In another case, the Court found that the state had retroactively applied a law that altered the requirement that victim's testimony be corroborated. In that case the Court held that when a law changes the rules of evidence in a way that is detrimental to the defendant, the law cannot be applied retroactively.[136,]

---

[134] *Calder v. Bull*, 3 U.S. 386 (1798).

[135] *Miller v. Florida*, 482 U.S. 423 (1987). *See also, Lynce v. Mathis*, 519 U.S. 433 (1997) in which Lynce was released after serving his sentence minus "good time" and "provisional credits" applied by the state to reduce its overcrowding. The Attorney General subsequently decided that provisional credits should not be awarded to those convicted of murder and attempted murder, and so Lynce was rearrested. He challenged his release and the Court unanimously agreed that this violated the ban against ex post facto laws.

[136] *Carmell v. Texas*, 529 U.S. 513 (2000).

[137] On the other hand, the Court found that the ex post facto rules were not violated when the state increased the amount of time a prisoner would have to wait before reapplying for parole.[138] Finally, the Court found that Alaska's sexual offender registration law did not violate ex post facto when applied to previously convicted sex offenders because the law imposed no physical restraint and did not resemble imprisonment (the Court distinguished between punitive and regulatory impact).[139]

BILLS OF ATTAINDER

Article I, Section 9 of the Constitution bans bills of attainder. A bill of attainder is a legislative act that criminalizes conduct without the benefit of a judicial trial. Bills of attainder are laws directed at a specific person or group of easily identifiable individuals in such a way as to inflict punishment without the benefit of a trial. When reviewing a law challenged as a bill of attainder, the court must consider: (1) whether the statute falls within the historic meaning of legislative punishment, (2) whether the statute, viewed in terms of the type and severity of the burdens imposed, reasonably can be said to further non-punitive legislative purposes, and (3) whether the legislative record evinces a legislative intent to punish. [140] In other words, it is unconstitutional for Congress to hold "trial by legislature." Justice Black stated, "When our Constitution and Bill of Rights were written, our ancestors had ample reason to know that legislative trials and punishments were too dangerous to liberty to exist in the nation of free men they envisioned. And so they proscribed bills of attainder."[141],[142]

In one case, the U.S. Court of Appeals for the District of Columbia struck down the Elizabeth Morgan Act of 1996. Dr. Elizabeth Morgan spent two years in jail in the 1980s for defying a District of Columbia court order requiring her to allow her ex-husband, Dr. Foretich, to visit their daughter, Hilary Foretich, whom she claimed he had sexually abused. Her legislator took up her cause, and after her release from custody under the 1989 District of Columbia Civil Contempt Imprisonment Limitation Act which he sponsored, she moved to New Zealand to be with her daughter. Dr. Morgan and her daughter would not be able to return back to the United States without having to still abide by the initial visitation ruling, so again at her representative's bidding, Congress passed the Elizabeth Morgan Act of 1996 which allowed Hilary to decide whether to see her father or not. Dr. Foretich sued, claiming the law was unconstitutional because it was a bill of attainder. The Court of Appeals, in striking down the Act stated that "Congress singled out Dr. Foretich on the basis of a judgement that he committed criminal acts . . . and inflicted extraordinary reputational injuries upon Dr. Foretich." The Court noted that the law

---

[137] In 1994 California enacted a law that removed the statute of limitations for child molestation. Stogner was charged with, and convicted of, molesting his daughters fifty years earlier. Before the law, Stogner's crimes would have been barred from prosecution due to the expired statute of limitations. The Court held that California's new law extending the statute of limitations could not be constitutionally applied in these cases. *Stogner v. California*, 539 U.S. 607 (2003).

[138] *Garner v. Jones*, 529 U.S. 244 (2000).

[139] *Smith v. Doe*, 538 U.S. 84 (2003)

[140] *Nixon v. Administrator of General Services*, 433 U.S. 425 (1977).

[141] *United States v. Lovett*, 328 U.S. 303, 318 (1946).

[142] Other examples of impermissible bills of attainder include a law barring Communist Party members from holding positions as officers in labor unions (*United States v. Brown*, 381 U.S. 437 (1965)), the denial of the right to practice one's profession (*Ex Parte v. Garland*, 71 U.S. (4 Wall) 333 (1867)), and a federal statute which deprived individuals of the right to seek government employment (*United States v. Lovett*, 328 U.S. 303, 318 (1946)).

imposed unconstitutional punishment, and it was clear that the goal of Congress "was to assume the role of judicial tribunal and impose its own determination who was a fit parent."[143]

The legal defense team in the second impeachment trial of Donald Trump claimed that if the U.S. Senate were to convict him for inciting insurrection/riot this would be tantamount to a bill of attainder. Harvard Law Professor Noel Feldman wrote:

> But there is something new in the brief: the astonishing assertion that if the Senate tries Trump, it will have violated the constitutional rule against bills of attainder.
>
> What's a bill of attainder? Funny you should ask! A bill of attainder, prohibited explicitly by the Constitution in Article 1, section 9, is a law adopted by the legislature that singles out a particular individual or class of people for punishment without trial. The category has been analyzed and defined by the Supreme Court over the years, starting in the aftermath of the Civil War and most recently in a 1977 case involving Richard Nixon's papers.
>
> To start with, a bill of attainder is, as its name suggests, a bill — the kind of legislative act that only has effect when it is adopted by both houses of Congress and signed into law by the president. Impeachment and removal, by contrast, can be accomplished by Congress alone. So it's legally wrong for Trump's lawyers to say that conviction by the Senate counts as a bill of attainder. The Senate isn't voting on any such bill; it's trying Trump. And President Joe Biden has no role whatsoever in the process.
>
> The takeaway is that the bill of attainder argument in Trump's defense is a classic red herring. It's an attempt to distract from the case against Trump by invoking legal-sounding constitutional language that no specialist has ever contemplated for more than a moment or two.[144]

FREEDOM OF RELIGION

The First Amendment states, "Congress Shall make no law respecting an establishment of religion, or prohibiting the free exercise thereof. . . ." Religious freedom was particularly important to the new colonists, and it is the first right set forth in the Bill of Rights. As you can see, the it comprises two separate guarantees: that Congress won't establish a national religion (the "Establishment Clause") and Congress won't pass laws that interfere with an individual's right to exercise their own religion beliefs (the "Exercise Clause").

THE ESTABLISHMENT CLAUSE

Congress cannot create a national church or prescribe a religion. It is, however, impossible to completely separate the church and the state. For example, even church buildings have to conform to building codes. Nevertheless, the First Amendment tries to ensure that government neither favors, nor is hostile toward, one religion over another. In *Hamilton v. Regents of the University of California*, 293 U.S. 245 (1934), a state university required all freshmen and sophomores to complete six credits of military training to attain full academic standing as juniors.

---

143 *See,*
https://web.archive.org/web/20071203173505/http://www.cnn.com/2003/LAW/12/16/jailed.mother.ap/
144 *See,* https://www.bloomberg.com/opinion/articles/2021-02-02/trump-s-impeachment-filing-contains-a-bizarre-legal-argument

The students petitioned the university to exempt them as conscientious objectors, but their petition was denied. The students refused to take the classes and were suspended. They filed suit claiming their suspension violated their constitutional rights. They lost at trial and appealed. The Court held that the regents' order to take the prescribed courses did not obligate the students to serve in or in any way become a part of the U.S. military establishment. It found that the regents were entitled to include military courses in the required curriculum and that the petitioning students' suspension for failure to take the classes involved no violation of their rights.

In 1947, the Court held that the Establishment Clause of the Constitution was applicable to the states through the Fourteenth Amendment and found that a state statute allowing reimbursement to parents for money spent to transport their children to parochial schools on the public bus system did not constitute the establishment of religion. The Court noted that the reimbursement policy applied to parents of both public and parochial school students and conformed to the intent of the clause. It likened the statute to general public welfare legislation. [145]

In 1962, the Court held that prayer, compulsory or voluntary, in public schools was unconstitutional. Similarly, a school reserving a moment of silence for meditation or voluntary prayer to encourage religious values was held unconstitutional in 1985. The Court also invalidated a state's attempt to subsidize costs of parochial schools' education—finding that, at that time (1971), secular and religious education were so tightly intertwined that to support one without supporting the other would be virtually impossible and that separating the two would involve the state so deeply in the religious institution's administration as to impair its independence. The Court concluded that the scheme violated the Establishment Clause. In another case, the Court struck down a Kentucky law requiring the posting of the Ten Commandments in all classrooms.[146] It also barred the City of New York from sending public school teachers into parochial schools to provide remedial education to disadvantaged children pursuant to a congressionally mandated program.[147] However, the Court did allow a program that involved federally funded remedial education in New York City that was aimed at disadvantaged and educationally deprived children, most of whom attended parochial schools.[148] In 2014, the Court upheld a town's practice of beginning the monthly town board meetings with a prayer given by clergy selected from the congregations listed in a local directory. It found that this practice did not violate the First Amendment's Establishment Clause where 1) legislative prayer is not required to be nonsectarian; 2) absent a pattern of prayers that over time denigrate, proselytize, or betray an impermissible government purpose, a challenge based solely on the content of particular prayer will not likely establish a constitutional violation; and 3) so long as the town maintains a policy of nondiscrimination, the Constitution does not require it to search beyond its borders for non-Christian prayer givers in an effort to achieve religious balancing.[149]

In order to survive an Establishment-Clause-challenge the state law must: (1) have a primary secular (non-religious) purpose; (2) have a principal effect that neither advances nor inhibits religion; and (3) not generate excessive entanglement between government and religion. The cases in the Establishment Clause area show the struggle between changing norms and constitutional interpretations. In the most recent case, The *American Legion v. American Humanist Association*, 588 U.S. ___ (2019), the Court held that when a local government displays and maintains a large memorial cross, it does not violate the Establishment Clause. Although these

---

[145] *Everson v. Board of Education*, 330 U.S. 1 (1947).
[146] *Stone v. Graham*, 449 U.S. 39 (1980).
[147] *Aguilar v. Felton*, 473 U.S. 402 (1985).
[148] Public funds were used to purchase materials and supplies and to pay instructors, including those teaching in private schools. *Agostini v Felton*, 521 U.S. 203 (1977).
[149] *Town of Greece v. Galloway*, 572 U.S. ____ (2014).

cases are interesting reads in constitutional law, most Establishment Clause cases have little bearing on the criminal justice system.[150]

THE FREE EXERCISE OF RELIGION CLAUSE

The second guarantee, the free exercise of religion, has a much clearer connection to the criminal law. This connection is seen when the government impacts a person's exercise of religious beliefs as part of some court-imposed punishment for criminal behavior. It also is seen when people, motivated by religious sentiments, engage in behavior which violates the criminal law.

Under the Religious Land Use and Institutionalized Persons Act of 2000 (RLUIPA) no government shall impose a substantial burden on the religious exercise of an institutionalized person unless the government demonstrates that the burden is the least restrictive means of furthering a compelling governmental interest.[151] In January 2015 the Court decided *Holt v. Hobbs*, 574 U.S. ___ (2015), in which a devout Muslim inmate wished to grow a 1/2-inch beard in accordance with his religious beliefs but against prison policy. Holding that the policy substantially burdened Holt's religious exercise, Justice Alito wrote,

> Although we do not question the importance of the Department's interests in stopping the flow of contraband and facilitating prisoner identification, we do doubt whether the prohibition against petitioner's beard furthers its compelling interest about contraband. And we conclude that the Department has failed to show that its policy is the least restrictive means of furthering its compelling interest.[152]

WHEN FREE EXERCISE OF RELIGION CONFLICTS WITH CRIMINAL LAW

Although the freedom to believe is absolute, the freedom to act is not.[153]

> Freedom of conscience and freedom to adhere to such religious organizations or form of worship as the individual may choose cannot be restricted by law. ... Thus, the Amendment embraces two concepts—freedom to believe and freedom to act. The first is an absolute, but in the nature of things, the second cannot be. Conduct remains subject to regulation of the protection of society. The freedom to act must have appropriate definition to preserve the enforcement of that protection.[154]

Courts balance the Free Exercise Clause against society's legal and social needs. In *Cantwell v. Connecticut*, 310 U.S. 296 (1940), the Court struck down a state statute that made it a misdemeanor to solicit door-to-door without having approval from the local officials tasked with deciding if the solicitors represented *bona fide* religions. More recently, lower appellate courts have struck down sentences that mandated participation in Alcoholics Anonymous or Narcotics

---

[150] *But see*, https://www.aclu.org/aclu-defense-religious-practice-and-expression, for a list of cases in which the ACLU represented individuals who have been charged, lost jobs, been denied membership, been denied housing, etc. because of their religious beliefs.

[151] 42 U.S. C. Section 2000cc-1(a)

[152] *Holt v. Hobbs*, 574 U.S. _____, at _____ (2015).

[153] *Cantwell v. Connecticut*, 310 U.S. 296 (1940).

[154] *Id*. at 302.

Anonymous, saying these sentences violate the Establishment Clause because of the religious components of the 12-step programs.[155]

When religion and criminal law conflict, the courts will generally look at whether the criminal statute is one of general applicability (for example, criminally negligent homicide) or whether it is more inclined to target religious practices. The Constitution permits the former but not the latter. For example, sometimes parents get charged with crimes when they refuse, on religious grounds, to seek medical treatment for their children. Courts recognize the right of adults to refuse medical treatment for themselves based on their personal religious beliefs, but when adults make similar decisions for their children, they may violate the criminal law. "Parents may be free to become martyrs themselves. But it does not follow that they are free in identical circumstances to make martyrs of their children before they have reached the age of full legal discretion when they can make that choice for themselves."[156]

One free exercise case involved the convictions of several members of the Native American Church for possession of peyote.[157] The California Supreme Court reversed the convictions, finding that the defendants' sacramental use of peyote was central for the members of that church and thus was protected by the First Amendment. In another case, *Employment Division v. Smith*, 492 U.S. 872 (1990), two American Indian drug counselors in Oregon lost their jobs because they used peyote as part of a religious ritual in their church. They sought unemployment benefits, but Oregon refused to pay. The Court upheld the Employment Division's refusal. It reasoned that because respondents' ingestion of peyote was constitutionally prohibited under Oregon law, Oregon could deny respondents unemployment compensation when they were dismissed from their jobs because of their drug use. The Court tried to make clear in *Smith* that the Free Exercise Clause does not allow individuals to avoid the responsibilities and consequences of a generally applicable criminal statute.[158]

Three years after the *Smith* case, the Court unanimously struck down a statute that made it an offense to "unnecessarily kill, torment, torture, or mutilate an animal in a public or private ritual or ceremony not for the primary purpose of food consumption." The Court found that the "laws in question were enacted by officials who did not understand, failed to perceive or chose to ignore the fact that their official actions violated the Nation's essential commitment to religious freedom." The Court specifically noted that the City of Hialeah had criminalized and targeted activity practiced by a religious group and was not enacting a general criminal prohibition against the slaughter of animals.[159]

In *Fulton v. City of Philadelphia*, ___ U.S. ____ (2021) one question presented was whether the *Smith* should be overturned. In *Fulton*, the City of Philadelphia had barred the Catholic Social Services (CSS) from placing children in foster homes because CSS had adopted a policy that prohibited licensing same-sex couples as foster parents. CSS sued Philadelphia asking the court to renew its contract arguing that its right to free exercise of religion and free speech allowed it to

---

[155] *See, Griffin v. Coughlin*, 88 N.Y.2d 674, 673 N.E.2d 98, 649 N.Y.S.2d 903 (1996), *Kerr v. Farrey* 95 F.3d 472 (1996), *Warner v. Orange County Department of Probation*, 115 F.3d 1068 (1996). The Supreme Court has, to date, declined to review cases contesting court-mandated participation in AA or NA.
[156] *Prince v. Massachusetts*, 321 U.S. 158 (1944).
[157] *People v. Woody*, 394 P.2d 813 (Cal. 1964).
[158] Congress passed, and President Clinton signed, the Religious Freedom Restoration Act of 1993 (Pub. L. No. 103-141, 107 Stat 1488 (November 16, 1993); its explicit purpose was to overturn the holding in the *Employment Division v. Smith* case. Congress intended to limit government's interference with religious practices, but the Court struck down this act in *City of Boerne, Texas v. Flores*, 521 U.S. 507 (1997) holding that it was a legislative encroachment on the judicial right of the courts to interpret the U.S. Constitution.
[159] *Church of the Lukimi Babalu Aye, Inc. v. City of Hialeah*, 508 U.S. 520 (1993).

reject qualified same-sex couples simply because they were same-sex couples (rather than any reason related to their qualifications for child care). The Court, in a surprisingly unanimous opinion, held in favor of CSS. Chief Justice Robert's opined for the court that Philadelphia violated CSS's free exercise of religion by requiring it to "curtail its mission" or to certify same-sex couples as foster parents, in violation of its stated religious beliefs." The Court's opinion noted that according to the Smith decision, a neutral, generally applicable law may incidentally burden religion, but held that the Philadelphia law was not neutral and generally applicable because it allowed for exceptions to the anti-discrimination requirement at the sole discretion of the Commissioner. Although unanimous in the holding, there were several concurring opinions written: Justice Barrett acknowledged several arguments for overruling *Smith,* but agreed with the majority that the facts of the case did not trigger *Smith;* Justice Alito noted he would overrule *Smith,* and replace it with a rule that any law that burdens religious exercise must be subject to strict scrutiny; and Justice Gorsuch's opinion criticized the majority's circumvention of *Smith.*

THE INTERSECTION OF EXERCISE AND ESTABLISHMENT CLAUSES

The case of *Kennedy v. Bremerton School District,* 597 U.S. ___ (June, 2022) involved both claims of free exercise of religion (by Kennedy) and the Establishment Clause's prohibition against the government for sponsoring a religion (by the school district). The school had attempted to avoid violating the First Amendment's Establishment Clause by forbidding Coach Kennedy from praying with students during and after school games. Coach Kennedy claimed that his ultimate firing for his refusal to stop doing so (publicly kneeling and praying with students at the 50-yard line in right after a football game-- a time where he should have been supervising players) violated his First Amendment rights to free speech and to the free exercise of his religion.

How the case was resolved largely was determined by how the factions of the court viewed the facts and what legal standard to apply. Justice Gorsuch's 6-3 majority opinion construed the prayer as a brief, quiet prayer by himself, that Kennedy's prayer was not trying to convey a government-created message, and that Kennedy did not require others to join him. Gorsuch analyzed the three prongs of the *Lemon* Test (used to analyze Establishment Clause cases it holds that the Establishment Clause is violated when laws lack a clear secular legislative purpose, have the primary effect of advancing or inhibiting religion, or promote excessive entanglement between church and state) but then rejected the *Lemon* test, choosing instead to look at Establishment Clause cases through the lens of "original meaning and history." Importantly, Justice Gorsuch did not find that Kennedy had coerced anyone to join him and that those who heard the prayers would need to be more tolerant. He opined that rules forbidding teachers from engaging in religious speech would signal that the Establishment Clause "had gone off the track and was suppressing religious liberty rather than protecting it."

Justice Sotomayor, in dissent, noted that 1) the evidence did not support the assertion that these were quiet private prayers, that 2) Kennedy had encouraged other to join him, and that 3) there were statements from students who felt coerced to join in the prayers lest they be in some way sanctioned for not participating (reduced field time for example). She expressed concern that the majority had abandoned the *Lemon* Test and substituted a history and tradition test. She found that Kennedy's prayer took him from his responsibilities as a public-school coach and that the controversy over his activities created hostile environment for those who may have refused to join. Ultimately, she concluded the prayers were his attempt to incorporate his own religious beliefs into a school event, and as such violated the principle of governmental neutrality in religious matters. [160]

FREEDOM OF ASSOCIATION AND ASSEMBLY

Maintaining public order is one of the primary purposes of the criminal law. The First Amendment specifically protects the right of people to peacefully assemble. Sometimes public demonstration is an essential element of a political movement. The #BlackLivesMatter, a national organization founded in the wake of the Trayvon Martin killing, has galvanized local protests across the nation in response to police shootings in areas rife with racial strife. Another, and somewhat less volatile example, is the Occupy Wall Street movement which began in September 2011 and other subsequent occupy movements which relied on the assembly of large groups of people to draw attention to the disparate income between the very wealthy few and the rest of the population. The Civil Rights Movement of the 1960s provides another example of when the "exercise of basic constitutional rights in their most pristine and classic form"[161] looked like a breach of the peace.

The right of association is not specifically mentioned in the Constitution; but it is considered a natural right and thus protected by the Constitution. Chief Justice Warrant Burger wrote in *Richmond Newspapers, Inc. v. Virginia* (1980):

> Notwithstanding the appropriate caution against reading into the Constitution rights not explicitly defined, this Court has acknowledged that certain unarticulated rights are implicit in enumerated guarantees. For example, the rights of association and of privacy, the right to be presumed innocent, and the right to be judged by a standard of proof beyond a reasonable doubt in a criminal trial, as well as the right to travel, appear nowhere in the Constitution or Bill of Rights. Yet these important but unarticulated rights have nonetheless been found to share constitutional protection in common with explicit guarantees. ... Fundamental rights, even though not expressly guaranteed, have been recognized by the Court as indispensable to the enjoyment of rights explicitly defined.[162]

TIME, MANNER, AND PLACE RESTRICTIONS

The right of assembly is not absolute. The government may impose reasonable time, place, and manner regulations on public assemblies. Governments may not ban assemblies in the public forum so long as they are peaceful and do not impede the operations of government or the activities of other citizens.

In *Wood et al. v. Moss et al.,* 572 U.S. ____ (2014), the Court held that anti-Bush protestors could not claim monetary damages against Secret Service Officers for viewpoint discrimination and violating their First Amendment rights. While campaigning for a second term, President George W. Bush visited Jacksonville, Oregon and supporters and protestors were lined along the street from his motorcade route. President Bush made a last-minute decision to dine at the Jacksonville Inn, and the protestors had moved to that location. Secret Service officials then

---

[160] See, https://www.aclu.org/press-releases/aclu-comment-supreme-court-decision-kennedy-v-bremerton-school-district. See also, https://www.seattletimes.com/seattle-news/politics/supreme-court-sides-with-bremertons-praying-coach/. See also, https://www.mtsu.edu/first-amendment/article/2137/kennedy-v-bremerton-school-district

[161] See, *Edwards v. South Carolina,* 372 U.S. 229 (1963).

[162] *Richmond Newspapers, Inc. v. Virginia,* 488 U.S. 555, 579 (1980).

moved the protestors from that area to an area two blocks away and beyond "weapons reach" of the President. The agents did not require the guests already inside the Inn to leave, stay clear of the patio, or even go through a security screening. After the President finished dining, his motorcade passed by where the supporters were lined up, but did not pass the protestors because they had been moved two blocks away. The Court held that the Secret Service agents were entitled to qualified immunity (they did not have to pay damages) noting,

> Government officials may not exclude from public places persons engaged in peaceful expressive activity solely because the government actor fears, dislikes, or disagrees with the views expressed. ... The fundamental right to speak, however, does not leave people at liberty to publicize their views "whenever and however and wherever they please." [163]

PUBLIC FORUMS, QUASI PUBLIC FORUMS, NON-PUBLIC FORUMS

The courts evaluate the constitutionality of laws regulating public assemblies in terms of the forum in which the assembly occurred.

- Public forums — property generally used for purposes of public assembly, communicating thoughts between citizens and discussing public questions;
- quasi-public forums — areas such as shopping stores and other privately owned building or property to which the public has general access; and
- non-public forums — privately owned property.

Courts will be more likely to strike down ordinances and laws that limit the right to assemble in public forums and less likely to strike down regulations of assemblies in quasi-public and non-public forums.

FREEDOM OF SPEECH

One of the most fervently-held but misunderstood "rights" is that of freedom of speech. The First Amendment couches the "freedom of speech" not as an affirmative right ("I have the right to say what I want") but rather a limit on government's ability to pass laws that affect speech. It says, "Congress Shall make no law . . . abridging the freedom of speech." In general, the government may neither require, nor substantially interfere with, individual expression. For example, a student may not be compelled to pledge allegiance to the American Flag. Justice Jackson observed,

> If there is any fixed star in our constitutional constellation, it is that no official, high or petty, can prescribe what shall be orthodox in politics, nationalism, religion, or other matters of opinion or force citizens to confess by word or act their faith therein. If there are any circumstances which permit an exception, they do not now occur to us.

> We think the action of the local authorities in compelling the flag salute and pledge transcends constitutional limitations on their power, and invades the sphere of intellect and spirit which it is the purpose of the First Amendment to our Constitution to reserve from all official control.[164]

---

[163] _Wood et al. v. Moss et al.,_ 572 U.S. at ___ (2014).
[164] _West Virginia State Board of Education v. Barnette,_ 319 U.S. 624, 642 (1943).

Most First Amendment cases do not involve the government compelling expression, but rather involve challenges to a statute or ordinance because it in some way unlawfully limits a person's speech or expression. Although the First Amendment's protection of free speech is broad, it is not absolute.

UNPROTECTED SPEECH

The Court has said that certain types of speech are so inherently lacking in value as not to merit any First Amendment protection:

> There are certain well-defined and narrowly limited classes of speech, the prevention and punishment of which have never been thought to raise any constitutional problem. These include the lewd and obscene, the profane, the libelous, and the insulting or "fighting words" — those which by their very utterance inflict injury or tend to incite an immediate breach of peace. It has been well observed that such utterances are no essential part of any exposition of ideas, and are of such a slight societal value as a step to truth that any benefit that may be derived from them is clearly outweighed by the societal interest in order and morality.[165]

LIBEL AND SLANDER[166]

One major limitation to the freedom of speech guaranteed by the First Amendment is the civil causes of action known as libel and slander. Libel and slander involve defamatory speech (oral or written) that harms another person's reputation. People can sue others who say something that injures their reputation. Public officials must have a thicker skin, however. In order for public officials to recover damages for slander or liable, the statement made against them must have been made with actual malice (with knowledge that it was false or with reckless disregard whether it was false or not). *New York Times v. Sullivan*, 376 U.S. 254 (1964). Lippman notes that, " [T]his reckless disregard or actual knowledge standard only applied to public figures and states [are] free to apply a more relaxed, simple negligence (lack of reasonable care in verifying the facts) standards in suits for libel brought by private individuals."[167]

PROFANITY

In 1942, the Court held that profanity is speech not worthy of protection,[168] but today courts generally hold that profanity is protected speech. For example, in *Cohen v. California*, 403 U.S. 15, 25 (1971), the defendant entered a courthouse with a jacket bearing the slogan "F**k the Draft." Justice Harlan stated,

> While the particular four-letter-word being litigated here is perhaps more distasteful than others of its genre, it is nevertheless often true that one man's vulgarity is another man's lyric. Indeed, we think it is largely because government officials cannot make principled distinctions in this area that the Constitution leaves matters of taste and style so largely to the individual.

Many states' laws and local ordinances still prohibit public profanity, but these provisions are largely unenforced and are likely to be struck down if challenged.

---

[165] *Chaplinsky v. New Hampshire*, 315 U.S. 568, 571 (1942).
[166] Libel and slander are both forms of defamation--the use of words to harm someone's reputation or livelihood. Libel is a written defamatory statement, and slander is a spoken defamatory statement.
[167] Lippman, *Contemporary Criminal Law*, supra at 38.
[168] *Chaplinsky*, 315 U.S. 568 (1942).

In two recent cases, the Court has reviewed the Lanham Act's prohibition on the registration of "immoral" and "scandalous" trademarks. In *Matal v. Tam*, 582 U.S. ___ (2017), the Court held that a prohibition of trademarks based on their viewpoint violates the First Amendment and that a provision of the Lanham Act prohibiting registration of "disparaging marks" was viewpoint based. In June 2019, the Court issued its ruling in *Iancu v. Brunetti*, 588 U.S. ___ (2019). Eric Brunetti owned the clothing brand "fuct." In 2011, Brunetti applied for the mark FUCT. The government refused to register the mark under Section 2(a) of the Lanham Act finding that it comprised "immoral" or "scandalous" matter. The Court held in a unanimous opinion with some concurring opinions filed that the Lanham Act prohibition on the registration of "immoral" or "scandalous" trademarks infringes the First Amendment. The Court noted that the section's prohibition distinguishes between ideas aligned with conventional moral standards and those hostile to them, which is the epitome of viewpoint-based discrimination (which it had struck down in the *Tam* case).

OBSCENITY

Obscene materials are considered to lack "redeeming social importance" and are not constitutionally protected. Distinguishing between obscenity and protected speech is not easy, and the Court has conceded that obscenity cannot be defined with "God-like precision." Justice Stewart pronounced with frustration, that the only viable test seemed to be that he "knew obscenity when...[he]...saw it."[169] In 1973 the Court finally defined obscenity, holding that it was limited to works that, when "taken as a whole, in light of contemporary community standards, appeal to the prurient interest in sex; are patently offensive; and lack serious literary, artistic, political, or scientific value." [170] Still, the concept remains somewhat vague. Under this definition, for example, a medical textbook portraying individuals engaged in sexual intercourse would probably not constitute obscenity because the book could have scientific value.[171] The Court has found that obscenity refers only to "hard-core" pornography.[172]

The growth of Internet pornography has led to national and international child pornography rings. Police and prosecutors no longer target violators of traditional obscenity laws, but rather are directing their resources to aggressively fighting child pornography. Legislatures, however, have found it difficult to draft child pornography statutes that survive First Amendment challenges as these laws have been successfully challenged on grounds that they violate the doctrine of overbreadth discussed below.

FIGHTING WORDS: FREE EXPRESSION OR DISRUPTION OF PUBLIC ORDER?

Saying something that threatens public peace and order, considered "fighting words," may violate the law and may not be protected speech. "Fighting words" are words directed at another individual that an ordinary reasonable person should be aware are likely to cause a fight or breach of the peace. Fighting words are "those personally abusive epithets which, when addressed to ordinary citizen, are as a matter of common knowledge, inherently likely to provoke violent reaction."[173] They are prohibited under the fighting words doctrine, established in *Chaplinsky v. New Hampshire*, 315 U.S. 568 (1942). There, the Court upheld the conviction of a Jehovah's Witness who, when distributing religious pamphlets, attacked a local marshal with the

---

[169] *Jacobellis v. Ohio*, 378 U.S. 184 (1974).
[170] *Miller v. California*, 413 U.S. 15 (1973).
[171] *Id.* at 25.
[172] *Jenkins v. Georgia*, 418 U.S. 153 (1974).
[173] *Cohen v. California*, 403 U.S. 15, 20 (1971).

accusation that "you are a God damned racketeer" and "a damned Fascist and the whole government of Rochester are Fascists or agents of Fascists." These words, according to the Court, would be likely to provoke a violent reaction and were not deserving of First Amendment protection.

CLEAR AND PRESENT DANGER

Some words are so potentially dangerous that they are not protected by the First Amendment. The clear and present danger test, first enunciated in the *Gitlow* case in *1925*, determined that "a state in the exercise of its police power may punish those who abuse this freedom by utterances inimical to the public welfare, tending to corrupt public morals, and incite to crime, or disturbing the public peace."[174] Being able to speak against the government has always been recognized as an important right; however, it is not an absolute right. Gitlow had been indicted under a New York law that prohibited the advocacy of the overthrow of the government by force or violence. In 1940 Congress enacted the Alien Registration Act of 1940 (the Smith Act)[175] that made advocating the overthrow of the government by force or violence to be unlawful.

INCITEMENT TO VIOLENT ACTION

Saying something that incites others to imminent violent action is also considered unprotected speech. In *Terminello v. Chicago*, 337 U.S. 1, 4 (1947), the Supreme Court held that a speaker could not be punished for speech that merely "stirs to anger, invites dispute, brings about a condition of unrest, or creates a disturbance." But, in *Feiner v. New York*, 340 U S 315, 320 (1951), the Court ruled, "when clear and present danger of riot, disorder, interference with traffic upon the public streets, or other immediate threat to public safety, peace, or order, appears, the power of the State to prevent or punish is obvious."

IMMINENT LAWLESS ACTION TEST

In the 1969 opinion in *Brandenburg v. Ohio*, 395 U.S. 444 (1969), the Court refined the "clear and present danger" doctrine and enunciated an "imminent lawless action test."

It is a three-part test that the government must meet if certain communication is not to be protected by the First Amendment: (1) the speaker subjectively intended incitement, (2) in context, the words used were likely to produce imminent, lawless action, and (3) the words used by the speaker objectively encouraged and urged incitement.

Before the *Brandenburg* Court was a statute prohibiting criminal syndicalism (Ohio courts had said syndicalism meant advocating violence to achieve political change). The Court reversed the conviction of a Ku Klux Klan leader saying that the constitutional guarantees of free speech and free press do not permit a state to forbid advocacy. People cannot be prosecuted merely for advocating violence; there must be "imminent lawless action" to justify a criminal penalty on public expression.

The *Brandenburg* approach (frequently cited in the Senate's second impeachment trial of former president Trump), has been termed "the balancing test," a position taken by the appellate courts to balance society's need for law and order and for effective law enforcement against the rights of individuals. "When applying the balancing approach to First Amendment free speech

---

[174] *Gitlow v. People of the State of New York*, 268 U.S. 652, 667 (1925)
[175] Pub. Law 54 Stat. 670, 18 U.S.C. § 2385. The Act was ultimately overturned by the Court in 1957.

cases, the Supreme Court strives to strike a balance between the value of liberty of expression and the demands of ordering a free society."[176]

COMMERCIAL SPEECH

The Court has ruled that commercial speech is not protected under the First Amendment. In *Valentine v. Chrestensen, 316* U.S. 52, 54 (1942), the Court stated,

> This Court has unequivocally held that the streets are proper places for the exercise of the freedom of communicating information and disseminating opinion and that, though the states and municipalities may appropriately regulate the privilege in the public interest, they may not unduly burden or proscribe its employment in these public thoroughfares. We are equally clear that the Constitution imposes no such restraint on government as respects purely commercial advertising. Whether, and to what extent, one may promote or pursue a gainful occupation in the streets, to what extent such activity shall be adjudged a derogation of the public right of user, are matters for legislative judgment. The question is not whether the legislative body may interfere with the harmless pursuit of a lawful business, but whether it must permit such pursuit by what it deems an undesirable invasion of, or interference with, the full and free use of the highways by the people in fulfillment of the public use to which streets are dedicated. If the respondent was attempting to use the streets of New York by distributing commercial advertising, the prohibition of the code provision was lawfully invoked against his conduct.

The court explained that advertising was not afforded the same protection as "political speech" under the First Amendment because: 1) advertising is not as important as political speech, 2) it is harder to chill advertising, which has a strong profit motive, and 3) it is easier to verify ad claims than political claims, and therefore we have no need to tolerate false advertising. Courts usually review freedom of speech cases using a strict scrutiny review, but regulations on commercial speech must withstand only intermediate scrutiny.[177] Thus, it is less likely that laws impacting or regulating commercial speech will be found unconstitutional. Additionally, commercial speech that is false or misleading is not entitled to any protection under the First Amendment, and therefore can be prohibited entirely.

PROTECTED SPEECH

SYMBOLIC SPEECH AND EXPRESSIVE CONDUCT

According to Scheb, "Freedom of expression is a broad concept embracing speech, publication, performances, and demonstrations. Even wearing symbols is considered to be constitutionally protected symbolic speech."[178] Expressive conduct includes: "sit-ins" to protest racial segregation, civilians wearing American military uniforms to protest the Vietnam War, and "picketing" over a variety of issues.

---

[176] J. Scott Harr and Kren M. Hess, *Constitutional Law and the Criminal Justice* System, 131 (4th ed., 2007).
[177] To survive a strict scrutiny challenge, a law must further a "compelling governmental interest," and must be narrowly tailored to achieve that interest. To survive intermediate scrutiny, a law must further an "important government interest" by means that are substantially related to that interest.
[178] See, *Tinker v. Des Moines Independent Community School District,* 393 U.S. 503 (1969).

Flag Burning

Without question, the most controversial application of the concept of expressive conduct have been the Supreme Court's decisions holding that public burning of the American flag is protected by the First Amendment. In *Texas v. Johnson,* . . . the Court invalidated a Texas statute banning flag desecration. The Supreme Court's decision to reverse Mr. Johnson's conviction and strike down the Texas law resulted in a firestorm of public criticism on the Court as well as the enactment of a new federal statute. The Flag Protection Act of 1989 . . . imposed criminal penalties on anyone who knowingly "mutilates, defaces, physically defiles, burns, maintains upon the floor or ground, or tramples upon" the American flag. In *United States v. Eichman* . . . the Supreme Court invalidated this federal statute as well, saying that "punishing desecration of the flag dilutes the very freedom that makes this emblem so revered, and worth revering." . . . On several occasions, Congress has attempted to pass a constitutional amendment to overturn the Supreme Court's flag burning decisions, but in every instance the measure has failed to receive the necessary two thirds vote in the Senate. (Citations omitted.)[179]

Nude Dancing

The Court upheld a Chicago ordinance requiring dancers to wear at least pasties and a G-string saying that the requirement was a modest imposition and the minimum to achieve the state's purpose. Chief Justice Rehnquist's found that while nude dancing enjoyed some marginal First Amendment protection, it must be balanced against the state's interest in promoting order and morality — thus, nude dancing could be prohibited just as could other forms of public nudity.[180]

POLITICAL SPEECH AND FORUMS

Similar to the right to assembly discussed above, the amount of protection afforded to political speech depends, in large part, on the location from which the person is speaking. The Court refers to forums, and has identified three types of forums: traditional public forum, designated public forums, and non-public forums. Some places are not considered forums.

Traditional public forums include public parks, sidewalks, and areas that have been traditionally open to political speech and debate. Speakers in these areas enjoy the strongest First Amendment protections. In traditional public forums, the government may not discriminate against speakers based on their views. This is called "viewpoint discrimination." The government may, however, subject speech to reasonable, content-neutral restrictions on its time, place, and manner. When considering government restrictions of speech in traditional public forums, courts use "strict scrutiny." Under strict scrutiny, restrictions are allowed only if they serve a compelling state interest and are narrowly tailored to meet the needs of that interest.

Sometimes, the government opens public property for public expression even though the public property is not a traditional public forum. These [types of properties] are designated public forums. After opening a designated public forum, the government is not obligated to keep it open. However, so long as the government does keep the forum open, speech in the forum receives the same First Amendment protections as speech in traditional public forums. Examples of

---

[179] Scheb, *supra* at 68-69.
[180] *Barnes v Glen Theatre*, 501 U.S. 560 (1991).

designated public forums include municipal theatres and meeting rooms at state universities.

The government may limit access to a designated public forum to certain classes or types of speech. In these "limited forums," although the government may discriminate against classes of speakers or types of speech, it may not exercise viewpoint discrimination. For example, the government may limit access to public school meeting rooms by only allowing speakers conducting school-related activities. It may not, however, exclude speakers from a religious group simply because they intend to express religious views. ...

Nonpublic forums are forums for public speech that are neither traditional public forums nor designated public forums. Government restrictions on speech in nonpublic forums must be reasonable, and may not discriminate based on speakers' viewpoints. Examples of nonpublic forums include airport terminals and a public school's internal mail system. . . . .

Finally, some public property is not a forum at all, and thus is not subject to this forum analysis. For example, public television broadcasters are not subject to forum analysis when they decide what shows to air.[181]

In *Citizens United v. Federal Election Commission*, 558 U.S. 310 (2010), the Court eased restrictions on political and campaign spending by corporations and labor unions, ruling that such restrictions infringe on the organizations' First Amendment free speech rights. In essence, the Court held that for the purposes of speech, a corporation is an "individual." This decision drew sharp criticism across the political spectrum. Thereafter, *McCutcheon v. Federal Election Commission*, 572 U.S. ___ (2014) held that campaign aggregate spending limits are invalid under the First Amendment.[182]

In *Morse v. Frederick*, 551 U.S. 393 (2007), the Court explored the limitations of the freedom of speech for students at school-related events. Joseph Frederick, a high school senior at Juneau-Douglas High School (Alaska) was standing across the street from a school-related event (watching the Olympic Torch Run) and held up a banner reading, "Bong Hits 4 Jesus." Morse, the school principal, told him put away the banner. He refused, so she suspended him for ten days. He sued under 42 U.S.C. 1983 claiming she violated his constitutional rights. The U.S. District Court ruled in favor of Morse, saying that Frederick had no constitutionally protected right of free speech during a student event. The U.S. Court of Appeals for the Ninth Circuit reversed, finding that his speech was protected. The U.S. Supreme Court in a 5-4 decision, found in favor of Morse saying that the Constitution does not prevent a school administrator from restricting student expression which reasonably is viewed as promoting illegal marijuana use. The Court determined that the Constitution provides fewer protections to certain types of student speech at school or school-supervised events. In finding that Frederick's speech was not political, the Court distinguished this case from the 1969 case of *Tinker v. Des Moines*, 393 U.S. 503 (1969) which held that students' political speech (wearing arm bands to protest against the Viet

---

[181] http://www.law.cornell.edu/wex/forums.

[182] "The right to participate in democracy through political contributions is protected by the First Amendment, but that right is not absolute. Our cases have held that Congress may regulate campaign contributions to protect against corruption or the appearance of corruption. ... At the same time, we have made clear that Congress may not regulate contributions simply to reduce the amount of money in politics, or to restrict the political participation of some in order to enhance the relative influence of others." *McCutcheon v. Federal Election Commission*, 572 U.S. ___ , ___ (2014).

Nam War) could only be limited if it substantially disrupted the educational process. In its 7-2 holding, the Tinker Court held that "students do not shed their constitutional rights to freedom of speech or expression at the schoolhouse gate."

In *Mahanoy Area School District v. B.L*, 593 U.S. ___ (2021) the Court again addressed the issue of whether the First Amendment prohibits school officials from regulating off-campus student speech. In this case a high school student (B.L.) posted a Snapchat message to about 250 people which was critical of her school and the varsity cheerleading team (she had tried out for varsity cheer, but had made only the junior varsity team). B.L. posted her picture with the caption" Fuck school fuck softball fuck cheer fuck everything." The post was visible to MAHS students, among them MAHS cheerleaders. A fellow student showed the message to the coaches who decided that the snap violated the team and school rules that B.L. had previously agreed to when joining the junior varsity team. She was suspended from the junior varsity cheer team for one year. B.L. then sued the school for violating her civil rights arguing that her suspension violated the First Amendment, the rules were overbroad and viewpoint discriminatory, and that the rules were unconstitutionally vague (see the void-for-vagueness doctrine below). The trial court and the intermediate appellate court agreed with B.L. (that the suspension violated her First Amendment rights) and the school appealed to the U.S. Supreme Court. In an 8-1 majority decision, the Court agreed with B.L. The court recognized that, though schools may regulate speech in some specific circumstances, because B.L.'s snap was not sent while she was in the care of the school (in loco parentis) and was not particularly disruptive to school activities, and because she had not threatened harm to others, her speech was protected.

HATE SPEECH

Hate speech raises interesting First Amendment concerns. Hate speech is defined as speech that denigrates, humiliates, and attacks individuals on account of some race, religion, ethnicity, nationality, gender, sexual orientation, or other personal characteristics and preferences (hate crimes target categories of people named specifically in the statute). Hate speech can be verbal, written or symbolic. Because it constitutes expression, it is generally protected by the Constitution unless it falls within one of the recognized exceptions to the First Amendment.

Hate speech must be distinguished from hate crimes or criminal offenses directed against a member of a specific groups. Hate crime statutes have been upheld because they target conduct rather than expression. The most important two rulings from the Court that highlight the distinction between hate speech and hate crimes are *R.A.V. v. St. Paul*, 505 U.S. 377 (1992), and *Wisconsin v. Mitchell*, 508 U.S. 475 (1993). In *R.A.V.* several Caucasian juveniles burned a cross inside the fenced-in yard of an African-American family. They were charged under a statute that provided that "[w]hoever places on public or private property a symbol, object, including and not limited to, a burning cross or Nazi swastika, which one knows or has reasonable grounds to know arouses anger, alarm or resentment. ... on the basis of race, color, creed, religion or gender commits disorderly conduct . . . shall be guilty of a misdemeanor." The Supreme Court held that this ordinance was unconstitutional, noting, "Let there be no mistake about our belief that burning a cross in someone's front yard is reprehensible. But St. Paul has sufficient means at its disposal to prevent such behavior without adding the First Amendment to the fire."[183] (For example, St Paul could have prosecuted the juveniles for trespass, menacing, reckless burning or arson, or criminal mischief).

---

[183] 505 U.S. at 396.

In *Mitchell* the Court ruled that a Wisconsin statute that enhanced the punishment of individuals convicted of hate crimes did not violate the defendant's First Amendment rights. Todd Mitchell challenged a group of other young African-American males by asking whether they were hyped up to move on white people?" As a young Caucasian male approached the group, Mitchell exclaimed "there goes a white boy, go and get him. He then led a group assault on the victim. The Wisconsin trial court increased his sentence because of his "intentional selection of the person against whom the crime is committed because of the race, . . . of that person." Mitchell claimed that he was being punished more severely for harboring and acting on racially discriminatory views in violation of the First Amendment. The Supreme Court ruled that Mitchell was being punished for a harmful act rather than for the fact that his act was motivated by racist views. It noted that acts based on discriminatory motives are likely to provoke retaliatory crimes, inflict distinct emotional harms on their victims and incite community unrest.

In 2003 the Court upheld a law banning cross burning with "an intent to intimidate a person or group of persons."[184] Justice O'Connor wrote the plurality decision concluding that "the First Amendment permits Virginia to outlaw cross burnings done with intent to intimidate because burning a cross is a particularly virulent form of intimidation." [185]

RETALIATORY ACTION

The Court has generally held that the First Amendment protections of free speech prohibit retaliatory action by the government in response to an employee or citizen's speech or expression. This protection against retaliatory action is enforced by bringing a 42 U.S.C. § 1983 (violation of civil rights) action against the government. In *Tanzin v. Tanvir*, 592 U.S. ____ (2020) two Muslim men, lawful permanent residents who lived and worked in the United States, sued the FBI. The FBI had approached them and requested they act as spies on fellow Muslims. When they declined, citing religious reasons, the F.B.I. agents pressured them and placed them on no-fly lists, despite the fact that they posed no threat. One man booked various flights to visit his ill mother in Pakistan, but was unable to board; another flew regularly for his employment, and ended up giving up his job. The men sought monetary damages by suing the F.B.I. agents both personally and officially. The Court held that the Religious Freedom Restoration Act of 1993 did permit the men to seek monetary damages.

One year earlier, the Court examined whether a claim of retaliation (retaliatory arrest) is defeated when the government can prove that police had probable cause to make the arrest. The Court's majority in *Nieves v. Bartlett*, 587 U.S. ___ (2019), found that it is (that probable cause to arrest does defeat a claim of retaliation). The case arose in the context of Arctic Man, a multiday ski and snowmobile race event in a remote part of Alaska. The defendant, Russell Bartlett was one of about 10,000 people who attended the event in 2014. An officer approached Bartlett, but Bartlett declined to talk to the officer and walked away. Later, Bartlett saw officers questioning a teenager and approached them. Nieves, the officer, shoved Bartlett, pinned him to the ground, and arrested him for disorderly conduct (Bartlett was intoxicated and belligerent) and resisting arrest. Charges against Bartlett were dropped, but Bartlett later sued claiming he was arrested in retaliation for exercising his First Amendment rights by refusing to speak to the officers and for his challenging their attempt to question the teenager. (He also claimed that the arrest violated his Fourth Amendment rights). Typically, to prevail in this type of suit, Bartlett had to demonstrate that 1) he was engaged in protected conduct (that is, that his speech or expression was the type traditionally covered under the First Amendment); 2) that the action taken by the police against him would deter a "person of ordinary firmness" from continuing to engage in that

---

[184] *Virginia v. Black*, 538 U.S. 343 (2003).
[185] *Id.*

speech or conduct; and 3) that there was a cause and effect relationship between the two elements (meaning the police/governmental action was at least in part motivated by the plaintiff (Bartlett's) protected conduct. In this case, the Court held that the existence of probable cause to arrest, prompted the arrest (the adverse governmental action), and Bartlett lost.

THE DOCTRINE OF VOID-FOR-VAGUENESS

No specific constitutional provision bans overly vague laws. Instead, the Due Process Clauses of the Fifth and Fourteenth Amendments require clarity in criminal statutes. The Court has repeatedly struck down laws that are so vague that a person of ordinary intelligence could not reasonably understand them or determine when they applied. Due process requires that individuals receive notice of criminal conduct, and vaguely written laws result in individuals having to guess at whether their behavior is allowed or prohibited. The Court will strike down laws that give excessive discretion to law enforcement officials to decide who can be arrested or prosecuted.[186] Police, prosecutors, judges, and jurors must have a reasonably clear statement of what is prohibited behavior. The "definite standard" requirement ensures the uniform and nondiscriminatory enforcement of law.

Void-for-vagueness cases have historically fallen into two categories — those dealing with obscenity laws and those dealing with loitering and vagrancy statutes. In a landmark decision, the Court struck down a Jacksonville, Florida ordinance that prohibited various forms of vagrancy, including loitering and "prowling by auto."[187] Justice Douglas objected to the unfettered discretion the ordinance placed in the hands of the police, saying it allowed for "arbitrary and discriminatory enforcement of the law."

In *Kolender v. Lawson*, 461 U.S. 352 (1983), the Court struck down a statute criminalizing any person who "loiters or wanders upon the streets or from place to place without apparent reason or business and who refuses to identify himself and to account for his presence when requested to do so." The Court held that,

> As presently drafted and as construed by the state courts, [the statute] contains no standard for determining what a suspect has to do in order to satisfy the requirement to provide a "credible and reliable" identification. As such, the statute vests virtually complete discretion in the hands of police to determine whether the suspect has satisfied the statute and must be permitted to go on his way in the absence of probable cause to arrest. An individual, whom police may think is suspicious, but do not have probable cause to believe has committed a crime, is entitled to walk the public streets 'only at the whim of any police officer' who happens to stop that individual under [the statute].[188]

Recall that the court presumes laws are constitutional. The burden of proving otherwise falls on the defendant. In the context of claiming void-for-vagueness, the defendant,

---

[186] The "vagueness doctrine" is "designed more to limit the discretion of police and prosecutors than to ensure that statutes are intelligible to persons pondering criminal activity." *U.S. v. White*, 882 F.2d. 250, 252 (7th Circuit, 1989). When dealing with statutes that may be too vague, the Court throws the statute a lifeline by upholding them if, through judicial interpretation, they can be construed with sufficient specificity. *See, Rose v. Locke*, 423 U.S. 48 (1975).

[187] *Papachristou v. City of Jacksonville*, 405 U.S. 156 (1972).

[188] *Kolender*, 461 at 358.

[M]ust show that upon examining the statute, an individual of ordinary intelligence would not understand what he is required to do under the law. Thus, to escape responsibility . . . [the defendant] must prove that he could not reasonably understand that . . . [the law in question] prohibited the acts in which he is engaged. ... The party alleging that a statute is unconstitutional must prove this assertion beyond a reasonable doubt. [189]

In a recent case, *United States. v. Davis*, 588 U.S. ___ (2019) the Court held that the term "crime of violence" used in the federal crime for possessing, using, or carrying a firearm in connections with actions comprising a crime of violence[190] is unconstitutionally vague.

THE DOCTRINE OF OVERBREADTH (DUE PROCESS)

Closely related to the void-for-vagueness doctrine is the doctrine of overbreadth. The Court first discussed the overbreadth doctrine in *Thornhill v. Alabama*, 310 U.S. 88 (1940), and it is relatively new to American jurisprudence.[191] Under this doctrine, the Court should strike down criminal laws that are written so broadly that they infringe on a person's constitutionally protected right, generally, free speech. "The overbreadth doctrine encourages legislators to consider free speech issues when drafting legislation because these statutes will be especially vulnerable to constitutional challenges. The threat of a court invalidating a statute as overbroad incentivizes the legislatures to narrowly tailor their statutes."[192]

A law is overbroad when it prohibits what the constitution protects. In *Coates v. City of Cincinnati*, 402 U.S. 611 (1971), the Court examined a statute that was both vague and overbroad. The ordinance made it unlawful for "three or more persons to assemble. . . on any sidewalks and there conduct themselves in a manner annoying to persons passing by." The Court found the ordinance to be vague because men of common intelligence must guess at its meaning. The Court also found that the ordinance was overly broad because it criminalized speech and assembly that are protected by the First Amendment.

Because statutes that are overbroad have a "chilling effect" on people's behavior, they may be challenged even by persons not charged with violating the law.[193] This runs contrary to the general holding that a person must have "standing" (a specific personal interest in the outcome of the case) before he or she can challenge a statute. "The overbreadth doctrine creates a distinct exception to the standing requirement, which, in effect, allows any litigant willing to challenge an allegedly overbroad statute to bring suit." [194]

When applying the overbreadth doctrine, a court considers the constitutionality of a statute on its face (rather than as it is applied under these facts). However, the Court will not necessarily declare a statute automatically void when it is overbroad. For example, the Court

---

[189] *State v. Anderson*, 566 N.E. 2d 1224 (Ohio, 1991).

[190] 18 U.S.C. §924 (c)(3)(8)

[191] Christopher A. Pierce, The "Strong Medicine" of the Overbreadth Doctrine: When Statutory Exceptions Are No More than a Placebo. 64(1) *Fed. Comm. L. J.* 182 (2011).

[192] *Id.*

[193] "Normally, a party seeking to challenge a statute's constitutionality must demonstrate that his or her personal rights were violated in order to have standing. However, the overbreadth doctrine is a "narrow exception to [the] general [standing] rule" because an 'overly broad law may deter constitutionally protected speech. ...' In more colorful language, the overbreadth doctrine has been described as 'strong medicine . . . a potion that generally should be administered only as a last resort.'" *Id.* at 181-182.

[194] *Id.* at 182.

refused to strike down a child pornography statute that defendant argued was overbroad in *New York v. Ferber*, 458 U.S. 747 (1982). The court believed the statute might possibly be applied to punish constitutionally protected artistic expression but held that a statute should not be invalidated for overbreadth if its legitimate reach "dwarfs its arguably impermissible applications."[195] Fifteen years later, however, the Court struck down the Communications Decency Act of 1996[196] finding that Congress had attempted to ban "indecent" as well as "obscene" speech from the Internet and thus swept within its ambit constitutionally protected speech as well as obscenity. [197]

THE RIGHT TO PRIVACY

The U.S. Constitution does not explicitly guarantee the "right to privacy." *Griswold v. Connecticut*, 381 U.S. 479 (1965), however, noted that the Ninth Amendment means that rights not spelled out in the in the Constitution (enumerated rights), nevertheless exist. Similarly, *Richmond Newspapers, Inc. v. Virginia*, 448 U.S. 555 (1980), held that "certain unarticulated rights . . . {including the right to privacy] . . . are implicit in the enumerated guarantees." Courts have found the important, but unarticulated right to privacy in the following circumstances:

- A married couple's use of contraceptives.[198]
- A single person's use of contraceptives.[199]
- The right of a minor over the age of fifteen to get contraceptives.[200]
- A woman's right to terminate an unwanted pregnancy.[201]
- The right of adults to engage in consensual homosexual conduct.[202]
- The right of an adult with a terminal illness to refuse medical treatment that would unnaturally prolong life.[203]
- The right of an adult to possess pornographic movies.[204]
- The right of family members of a comatose woman to remove extraordinary means of life support.[205]

---

[195] *Ferber*, 458 U.S. at 773.

[196] This Act bans computer-generated or "virtual" child pornography.

[197] *Reno v. American Civil Liberties Union*, 521 U.S. 844 (1997). In response to this decision, Congress passed the Child Online Protection Act in 1998, but it never took effect due to a series of permanent injunctions granted by the Third Circuit Court of Appeals. In *Ashcroft v. Free Speech Coalition*, 535 U.S. 234 (2002), the U.S. Supreme Court rejected the federal child pornography law because it intruded on free speech rights. In 2004, the Supreme Court upheld the injunctions against implementation of the law, finding that the Act would likely be found unconstitutional. *Ashcroft v. American Civil Liberties Union*, 542 U.S. 656 (2004). Litigation continued, and since a 2009 ruling, it appears that this Act is now "dead."

[198] *Griswold v. Connecticut*, 381 U.S. 479 (1965).

[199] *Eisenstadt v. Baird*, 405 U.S. 438, 453 (1972). (The right to privacy "is the right of the individual, married or single, to be free from unwarranted governmental intrusion into matters so fundamentally affecting a person as the decision whether or not to beget a child").

[200] Carey v. Population Services International, 431 U.S. 678 (1977).

[201] *Roe v. Wade*, 410 U.S. 113 (1973). *Stenberg v. Carhart*, 530 U.S. 914 (2000); *Gonzales v. Carhart*, 550 U.S. 124 (2007).

[202] *Lawrence v. Texas*, 539 U.S. 558 (2003).

[203] *Satz v. Perlmutter*, 379 So.2d 359 (Fla.1980).

[204] *Stanley v. Georgia*, 394 U.S. 557 (1969).

[205] *In re Quinlan* 355 A.2d 647 (N.J. 1976).

The Court has not extended the right to privacy as a justification for euthanasia[206] or doctor-assisted suicide.[207]

Legislatures must be careful not to criminalize behavior that intrudes on an individual's right to privacy. Privacy interests are also implicated when police conduct searches of a person or a person's property under the Fourth Amendment. Since 1967 the litmus test for whether the Fourth Amendment has been violated is whether the government in some way violated an individual's reasonable expectation of privacy.[208]

RIGHT TO BEAR ARMS

There are thousands of local, state, and federal prohibitions against the sale, possession, and use of certain firearms and ammunition. Arguably, these laws seem to conflict with the Second Amendment's "right to keep and bear arms." The poorly drafted Second Amendment[209] has left courts and commentators debating its reach and application to modern circumstances.

In *United States v. Miller,* 307 U.S. 174 (1939), the Court upheld a federal law criminalizing the interstate shipment of sawed-off shotguns. The Court held that phrase "to keep and bear arms shall not be infringed" had to be interpreted in relation to the phrase "a well-regulated militia." Since possession of sawed-off shotguns had no reasonable relationship to serving the militia, the statute (regulating shotguns) was not unconstitutional. In 1980 the Court reaffirmed this reasoning in *Lewis v. United States*, 445 U.S. 55, 58 (1980) stating, "The Second Amendment guarantees no right to keep and bear a firearm that does not have some reasonable relationship to the preservation of efficiency of a well-regulated militia."

In *District of Columbia v. Heller,* 554 U.S. 570 (2008), however, the Court declared the right to keep and bear arms was a personal right tied to a natural right of self-defense that had nothing to do with being part of a militia. Washington, D.C. had enacted an ordinance that created a complete ban on handguns and required that any weapons kept at home must be unloaded and non-functional. Heller, a special police officer in D.C., was authorized to carry a handgun at his job at the Federal Judicial Center. He applied to register his personal gun, but the government refused. He sued to enjoin the District of Columbia from enforcing the ordinance, arguing that he (and others) had a constitutional right to possess a weapon in his home for his personal safety. The Court did not define the scope of the right to keep and bear arms, nor did it indicate whether the Second Amendment was applicable to the states through the Fourteenth Amendment, but it did hold that the D.C. ordinance was too restrictive, nevertheless noting that the right to bear arms was subject to reasonable government regulations.

Several suits were filed in state courts after *Heller* was decided. In Chicago, gun owners challenged Chicago ordinances which were virtually identical to the ordinance in *Heller*. They asked the Court to hold that the Second Amendment applied to the states through the Fourteenth Amendment. In a five-four decision, the U.S. Supreme Court held that an individual's right to keep and bear arms is incorporated and applicable to the states through the 14th Amendment's Due Process Clause. Writing for the majority in *McDonald v. City of Chicago*, Justice Alito observed: "It is clear that the Framers and ratifiers of the Fourteenth Amendment counted the right to keep and bear arms among those fundamental rights necessary to our system of ordered

---

[206] *Gilbert v. State*, 487 So. 2d 1185 (Fla. App. 1986).
[207] *Washington v. Glucksberg*, 521 U.S. 702 (1997).
[208] See, *Katz v. United States*, 389 U.S. 347 (1967).
[209] "A well regulated Militia, being necessary to the security of a free state, the right of the people to keep and bear arms shall not be infringed." U.S. Const. amend. II.

liberty. ... The Fourteenth Amendment makes the Second Amendment right to keep and bear arms fully applicable to the States."

The Court majority did not ultimately rule on the constitutionality of this gun ban; however, the Court made it clear that such restrictive bans are unconstitutional. The *McDonald* Court reiterated what it said in Heller -- the Second Amendment only protects a right to possess a firearm in the home for lawful uses such as self-defense. It stressed that some firearm regulation is constitutionally permissible and the Second Amendment right to possess firearms is not unlimited. The Second Amendment does not guarantee a right to possess any firearm, anywhere, and for any purpose.[210] The dissent argued that the right to own guns was not "fundamental" and therefore states and localities should be free to regulate, or even ban, them. Dissenting justices maintained that *Heller* was incorrectly decided, and--even if correct--they would not have extended its applicability to states.

On June 23, 2022 the Court issued its opinion in *New York State and Rifle Association v. Bruen*, 587 U.S. ___ (2022). At issue in that case was whether a New York State law which regulated concealed carry licenses violated the Second and Fourteenth Amendment. New York made it a crime to possess a firearm without a license, whether inside or outside the home, but an individual could obtain an unrestricted license to carry a concealed pistol or revolver if he or she could prove that proper cause existed for doing so — which under the statute meant that he or she could demonstrate a special need for self-protection distinguishable from that of the general community. Two individuals applied for these unrestricted licenses, and the State denied both of their applications, so they sued the state officer who oversaw the processing of the applications. Justice Thomas's majority opinion struck down the New York's law. After the *Bruen* case, New York passed the Concealed Carry Improvement Act, which enacts a strict permitting process for concealed-carry licenses, requires background checks for ammunition sales, and restricts the concealed carry of firearms in locations such as government buildings; the Act was immediately challenged, and this case and others "gun" cases across the nation which arose in response to the *Bruen* holding are currently wending their way through the various courts.

EQUAL PROTECTION UNDER THE LAW

The Equal Protections Clause of the Fourteenth Amendment forbids states from denying citizens equal protection of the laws. Although there is no equal protections provision found in the Bill of Rights (which applies to the federal government not the states), the Court has said this limitation of the Fourteenth applies equally to the federal government as it does to state governments. Basically, equal protection of laws means legislators cannot write laws that treat people differently. But obviously, in some circumstances, they do. Consider laws that limit sales to and consumption of alcohol to those over 21 years of age. Such laws treat 19-year-olds differently than 21-year-olds. According to case law, it is one thing to treat people differently based on age or employment or educational level, but it is quite another to treat people differently because of their sex or race.[211]

---

[210] *See*, Vernon Rose, *OLR Research Report: Summary of McDonald Recent Gun Control Case*, August 20, 2010 at http://cga.ct.gov/2010/rpt/2010-R-0314.htm.

[211] The Court struck down a law criminalizing interracial marriage in *Loving v. Virginia*, 388 U.S. 1 (1967). It found that the statute criminalized conduct solely on the basis of race of the parties and thus was rendered null and void. In *Eisenstadt, supra,* the Court struck down a law that criminalized the use of birth control devises by a single person but not married couples. In *Craig v. Boren*, 429 U.S. 190 (1976) the Court invalidated a law that forbade the sale of beer containing 3.2 percent alcohol to females under the age of 18 and males under the age of 21. The Court concluded that the state lacked a sufficient justification for discriminating between the sexes regarding the legal availability of the beer.

STANDARD OF JUDICIAL REVIEW IN EQUAL PROTECTION CHALLENGES

Generally, the Court evaluates and reviews legislation based on whether it has a reasonable relationship to a legitimate state interest. This is called "rational basis" review. Criminal laws that have any impact on a constitutionally protected interest must at least be rationally related to furthering a legitimate government interest. A statute that prohibits sales of alcohol to minors will probably survive rational basis review because the law protects the health of a minor--a legitimate state objective. Under the Equal Protection Clause, when a law targets a "quasi-suspect" classification, such as gender, the courts apply "intermediate scrutiny." To pass constitutional muster under this level of review, the law must be substantially related to an "important government interest." If the statute targets a suspect classification (such as race) or impacts a fundamental right (such as the freedom of speech, freedom of religion, or the right to due process), then the court will apply "strict scrutiny." This means the statute must be narrowly tailored to address a compelling state interest.[212] This is a very heavy, but not impossible, burden for the government to carry as it is presumed that laws limiting fundamental rights are unconstitutional.

CRUEL AND UNUSUAL PUNISHMENT

The Eighth Amendment tells the government that it cannot make punishment cruel or unusual. The Eighth Amendment was written to prohibit torture and other forms of punishment practiced in England but seen as reprehensible. The Court has interpreted the term "cruel and unusual" in several cases. The terms cruel and unusual, according to the Court, "may acquire meaning as public opinion becomes enlightened by a humane justice."[213] For example, corporal punishment was acceptable when the Eighth Amendment was passed in 1791, but was abolished in 1972.[214] Cruel and unusual punishment encompasses not only certain forms of punishment (those considered barbaric, see below) but also punishment which is grossly disproportionate in severity to the seriousness of the crime. Additionally, the case of *Robinson v. California*, 370 U.S. 660 (1962), illustrates that the Supreme Court the prohibition in the Eighth Amendment against cruel and unusual punishment also limits the legislative authority to make some conduct criminal. In that case, the Court invalidated a California statute, holding that although a state may make it a crime to possess or use drugs, it may not make it a crime to be addicted to narcotics. Professor LaFave lists these three approaches the Court has used in interpreting the clause:

1) limiting the methods employed to inflict punishment,
2) restricting the "amount of punishment" that may be imposed, and
3) prohibiting the criminal punishment of certain acts.[215]

In *Trop v. Dulles*, 356 U.S. 86 (1958), Chief Justice Warren wrote that the Cruel and Unusual Punishments Clause "must draw its meaning from the evolving standards of decency that mark the progress of a maturing society." *Trop* involved removing a soldier's citizenship after he had been found guilty of desertion. The Court found the penalty too extreme. This "evolving standards of decency" language has been quoted in more recent cases in which the Court has found to be cruel and unusual laws which authorize the death penalty for a crime of

---

[212] *Shapiro v. Thompson*, 394 U.S. 618 (1969).

[213] *Id.*

[214] Delaware, the last state to allow corporal punishment, repealed its statute that allowed whipping in 1972.

[215] LaFave, *supra* at 187.

child rape, [216] for individuals who have become insane,[217] for those individuals who are mentally retarded,[218] and for crimes committed the crimes by juveniles.[219]

Sometimes conditions of incarceration are said to violate the Cruel and Unusual Punishment Clause. Recently, in *Taylor v. Riojas*, 592 U.S. ____ (2020) the Court held that correctional officers were not entitled to qualified immunity because they should reasonably have known that the prison conditions they subjected Taylor, an inmate, to violated his Eighth Amendment right. Taylor, the inmate, was held for six days in September 2013 in a Texas correctional facility where the cell walls were nearly covered in feces, and he was unable to eat or drink for days out of food safety concerns. He was later moved to a second cell that was cold, without a bed, and with a clogged open sewage drain on the floor. He was not given clothing, and was made to sleep on the floor. Similarly, in two joined cases, (*Coleman v. Brown* and *Brown v. Plata*) the Court examined the effect of prison conditions on prisoners with serious mental disorders (*Coleman*) and those with serious medical conditions (*Brown*). After monitoring prison conditions for several years, the Court noted that without reducing the prison population, the constitutional violations could not be remedied. The Court found that the courts had the authority to order release of prisoners as a remedy to cure a systemic violation of the Eighth Amendment. The Court discussed the overcrowding prevalent and persistent (over decades) in California prisons and found that it created unsanitary and unsafe conditions and that it was the "primary cause of the violation of a Federal right … specifically the severe and unlawful mistreatment of prisoners through grossly inadequate provision of medical and mental health care." Overcrowding caused unnecessary and wanton infliction of pain in violation of the Eighth Amendment. Consequently, the Court approved the remedy of requiring California to release a significant portion of its prison population. [220]

Using the Cruel and Unusual Punishment Clause, the Court in 2010 (*Graham v. Florida*, 560 U.S. 48 (2010)) held that a juvenile offender could not be sentenced to life without the possibility of parole for non-homicide offenses. Two years later, the Court extended this ruling in *Miller v. Alabama*, 567 U.S. ____ (2012), invalidating mandatory life sentences with no possibility of parole for any juvenile offenders (even if the charge was murder). Recently, the Court in *Jones v. Mississippi*, 593 U.S. ____ (2021) held that juvenile offenders may be sentenced to life without the possibility of parole without requiring a finding of incorrigibility first. Brett Jones stabbed his grandfather to death when he was 15 years old and was convicted of murder in Mississippi. In accordance with Mississippi's sentencing guidelines, Jones received life without parole. Jones argued that this sentence was cruel and unusual punishment since there had not be a prior determination that he was "permanently incorrigible." In a 6-3 majority, the Court sided with the state of Mississippi, referencing previous decisions. Although a sentencer must consider the offender's youth when determining his or her sentence, and a finding on incorrigibility is not required.

The Court frequently examines death penalty claims. For example, in *Bucklew v. Precythe*, 587 U.S. ____ (2019) Russell Bucklew was convicted by a state court jury of murder, kidnapping, and rape, and was sentenced to death. Bucklew was scheduled to be executed on May 21, 2014. He then filed an action in federal district court alleging that execution by Missouri's lethal injection protocol would constitute cruel and unusual punishment in violation of the Eighth Amendment as applied to him because of his unique congenital medical condition. According to

---

[216] *Kennedy v. Louisiana*, 554 U.S. 407 (2008).
[217] *Ford v. Wainwright*, 477 U.W. 399 (1986).
[218] *Atkins v. Virginia*, 536 U.S. 304 (2002)
[219] *Roper v. Simmons*, 543 U.S. 551 (2005)
[220] See, *Brown v. Plata*, 563 U.S. 493 (2011).

Bucklew, lethal injection would likely cause him to hemorrhage during the execution, potentially choking on his own blood." As an alternative method, Bucklew proposed execution by nitrogen hypoxia. The Court never actually reached the defendant's claim that he should be entitled to an alternative method of execution because under existing Supreme Court case law, a death row inmate who alleges that the state's method of execution constitutes cruel and unusual punishment must show there is a feasible and readily implemented alternative method that would significantly reduce a substantial risk of pain, and that the state had refused to adopt the method without a legitimate penological reason. In a 5-4 opinion, the Court held that Bucklew had not met this burden to prove that nitrogen hypoxia was viable and that it could be readily implemented. The Court further noted that Bucklew failed to show that the state lacked a legitimate reason for declining to switch from its current method of execution. Finally, the Court noted that even if he had proven that nitrogen hypoxia was a viable alternative, he failed to show that the alternative would significantly reduce a substantial risk of severe pain.

In another case,[221] the Court concluded that the Texas Court of Criminal Appeals erred by its use of an outdated analysis of mental and intellectual disability when deciding that Bobby James Moore was eligible for the death penalty. The Court held that the outdated standards regarding intellectual disability to determine whether a person was exempt from execution violated the Eighth Amendment's Cruel and Unusual Punishment Clause as well as precedent established in *Adkins v. Virginia* (the case where the Court held that the death penalty could not be used as punishment for individuals who, at the time of their crimes, were legally insane.)

In 2019 Vernon Madison who had been on death row for 30 years for killing a police officer in Alabama. While awaiting his execution, Madison suffered a series of strokes and was diagnosed with vascular dementia, and he cannot remember killing the officer. Madison sought review of his proposed execution[222] , and the Court revisited cases[223] it previously decided. In the earlier *Ford* case, the Court held that the Eighth Amendment ban on cruel and unusual punishment prevents the state from executing a prisoner who has "lost his sanity" after sentencing. In the *Panetti* case, the Court held that the state may not execute a prisoner "whose mental state is so distorted by a mental illness that he lacks a rational understanding of the State's rationale for his execution or when a prisoner's concept of reality is so impaired that he cannot grasp the execution's meaning and purpose or the link between his crime and punishment." (Quotations and citations omitted). The Court had to decide whether the Eighth Amendment prohibits a state from executing a prisoner who due to mental disability cannot remember committing his crime. The Court held that it does not. The second question before the Court was whether the Eighth Amendment prohibits a state from executing a prisoner who cannot rationally understand the reasons for his execution whether that inability is due to psychosis or dementia. The Court held that it does. Justice Kagan's opinion noted the distinction:

> First, a person lacking memory of his crime may yet rationally understand why the State seeks to execute him; if so, the Eighth Amendment poses no bar to his execution. Second, a person suffering from dementia may be unable to rationally understand the reasons for his sentence; if so, the Eighth Amendment does not allow his execution. What matters is whether a person has the "rational understanding" *Panetti* requires—not whether he has any particular memory or any particular mental illness.

---

[221] *Moore v. Texas*, 586 U.S. ___ (2019)
[222] *Madison v. Alabama*, 586 U.S. ___ (2019)
[223] *Ford v. Wainwright*, 477 U.S. 399 (1986) and *Panetti v. Quarterman*. 551 U.S. 930 (2007).

BARBARIC PUNISHMENT

Punishment that is "barbaric" is cruel and unusual punishment. Barbaric punishment describes the form of punishment. When the Eighth Amendment passed, barbaric punishment included: burning at the stake, crucifixion, breaking on the wheel, drawing and quartering, the rack and the thumbscrew. Now most courts are willing to consider that some punishments that were not included in that original list may be cruel and unusual. The death penalty has historically been viewed as a constitutionally acceptable form of punishment, and the Court has noted that punishments are "cruel when they involve torture or lingering death; but the punishment of death is not cruel within the meaning of that word or as used in the constitution. Cruelty implies there is something inhuman or barbarous—something more than the mere extinguishment of life."[224]

In *Coker v. Georgia*, 433 U.S. 584 (1977), the Court held that a punishment is unconstitutional if it (1) makes no measurable contribution to acceptable goals of punishment and hence is nothing more than the purposeless and needless imposition of pain and suffering, or (2) is grossly out of proportion to the severity of the crime. The five methods of execution used in the United States (hanging, firing squad, electrocution, the gas chamber, and lethal injection) have all been found by the Court to not be inherently cruel and unusual.

Lippman notes that judges have intervened to prevent barbarous methods of discipline in prison. In *Hope v. Pelzer*, 536 U.S. 730 (2002), the Court ruled that Alabama's use of the "hitching post" to discipline inmates constituted "wanton and unnecessary pain." During Hope's seven-hour ordeal on the hitching post in the hot sun, he was painfully handcuffed at shoulder level to a horizontal bar without a shirt, taunted, and provided with water only once or twice and denied bathroom breaks. There was no effort to monitor his condition despite the risks of dehydration and sun damage. The Supreme Court held that the use of the hitching post was painful and punitive retribution that served no legitimate and necessary penal purpose.[225]

DISPROPORTIONATE PUNISHMENT

A punishment will also be considered cruel and unusual if it is disproportionate to the severity of the crime. In striking down the death penalty for rape of an adult victim, Justice White wrote in *Coker*, "The death penalty, which is unique in its severity and its irrevocability, is an excessive penalty for a rapist who does not take a human life."[226]

The proportionality requirement also may be raised if punishment is being imposed in an uneven manner. The 1970s' death penalty cases before the Court highlight this. In *Furman v. Georgia*, 408 U.S. 238 (1972), the Court ultimately struck down capital punishment laws across the nation, finding they were applied in an uneven, arbitrary and capricious manner. The states immediately reacted by enacting mandatory death penalty laws that required capital punishment for *all* defendants convicted of intentional homicide. The Court responded that mandatory laws were similarly unconstitutional--mandatory death for all homicides may not be arbitrary punishment, but these statutes may result in death being inflicted on undeserving defendants. Instead, the Court held, the jury must fit the punishment to the circumstances of the particular offense and the character and record of the individual offender.[227]

---

[224] *In re Kemmler*, 136 U.S. 436, at 436 (1897). (The Court held that electrocution was unusual, but not cruel.)
[225] See, Lippman, *Criminal Law*, at 65.
[226] 433 U.S. at 598 (1977).
[227] *Woodson v. North Carolina*, 438 U.S.280 (1976).

After several states attempted to pass constitutional death penalty laws in response to *Furman*, the Court ultimately approved of the Georgia's death penalty statute.[228] It required the jury to find that the murder was committed with aggravating factors, required a bifurcated (separate) guilt-innocence and sentencing phase, required jurors to consider mitigating factors in determining whether to impose death, and mandated automatic review of death sentences by the state supreme court.

Some federal appellate judges believe that it is perfectly acceptable for federal courts to evaluate state non-death penalty statutes to determine if they impose disproportionate punishment. Others disagree, believing that the length of a criminal sentence is the province of the elected state legislators and that judicial intervention should be extremely rare. These justices hold that proportionality review should be limited to those challenges arguing that the sentence is grossly disproportionate to the seriousness of the offense. Ewing made that claim in *Ewing v. California*, 538 U.S. 11 (2003), when he was sentenced to twenty-five years of imprisonment for stealing $1200.00 of merchandise (after several prior offenses); he argued that California's "three strikes laws" were grossly disproportionate and thus, cruel and unusual punishment. Justice O'Connor, writing for the Court, disagreed. The Court, she said, was required to respect California's desire to incapacitate and deter recidivist felons like Ewing.

CONSTITUTIONAL LIMITS ON PROCEDURAL ACTIONS [229]

FOURTH AMENDMENT LIMITATIONS

The Fourth Amendment limits the government's ability to engage in searches and seizures. Under the least restrictive interpretation, the Amendment requires that, at a minimum, searches and seizures be reasonable. Under the most restrictive interpretation, the Amendment requires that government officers need a warrant any time they do a search or a seizure. The Court has interpreted the Fourth Amendment in many cases and, the doctrine of *stare decisis* notwithstanding, search and seizure law is subject to the Court's constant refinement and revision. One thing is clear, the Court has never embraced the most restrictive interpretation of the Fourth requiring a warrant for every search and seizure conducted.

FIFTH AMENDMENT LIMITATIONS

The Fifth Amendment protects against self-incrimination in that it states that no person "shall be compelled in a criminal case to be a witness against himself." Defendants have the right to not testify at trial and the right to remain silent during a custodial interrogation. Additionally, this clause prohibits laws that require individuals to report information that may later be used against them in a criminal case. Statutory reporting requirements violate the freedom from compulsory self-incrimination when they 1) apply to an area of activity that is permeated with criminal statutes, 2) are directed at a highly selective group of persons that is inherently suspect of criminal activities, and 3) poses a substantial hazard or direct likelihood of self-incrimination.[230] The Fifth Amendment also provides for a grand jury in federal criminal prosecutions, prohibits double jeopardy, demands due process of law, and prohibits taking private property for public use (a civil action). The Court has incorporated the double jeopardy

---

[228] *Gregg v. Georgia*, 428 U.S. 153 (1976)

[229] Constitutional limitations on criminal procedures are covered more in depth beginning in Chapter Seven.

[230] *See* Scheb, *supra* at 79-80.

provision of the Fifth Amendment, but it has not held that states must provide grand jury review. Many states, however, do use the grand jury.[231]

SIXTH AMENDMENT LIMITATIONS

The Sixth Amendment guarantees a criminal defendant the right to a speedy trial, the right to a public trial, the right to a jury trial, the right to have the trial in the district where the crime took place, the right to notice of charges, the right to confront witnesses at trial, the right to compel witnesses to testify, and the right to assistance of counsel. This Amendment governs the federal court process, but because of the Fourteenth Amendment's Due Process Clause these rights also apply to defendants in state criminal cases.

EIGHTH AMENDMENT LIMITATIONS

In addition to the prohibition against cruel and unusual punishment, the Eighth Amendment also prohibits the imposition of excessive bail and excessive fines. To the extent that the Court has dealt with excessive fines (which it did recently in *Timbs*, see above), it has done so in the context of disproportionality review of punishment as part of the cruel and unusual punishments. The limitation on excessive bail does not mean that courts must set bail in every case, but rather, when courts do set bail, it must not be excessive. Bail is excessive when it is an amount more than necessary to assure the defendant's reappearance.

WRAP UP

Legislators must be very careful when making new laws. They cannot make laws that are so poorly drafted such that a person of ordinary intelligence would not understand the law or that would allow police too much discretion in how they will interpret and apply the law because such a law would be considered void for vagueness. They cannot make laws that apply retroactively (ex post facto laws) or target certain named individuals or groups of individuals (bills of attainder). Legislatures cannot create laws that limit individuals' speech--although some speech is deemed not worthy of protection. Legislatures cannot make laws that create a religion or laws that target and interfere with a person's exercise of their own religion. Legislatures cannot make laws that allow the government to invade people's privacy. Legislatures cannot make laws that completely limit people's ability to gather together peaceably, but they can place reasonable time and manner limitations based on the location in which the gathering is to take place. Generally, legislatures cannot make laws that treat people differently unless the laws are rationally related to a legitimate government interest. Legislatures can place restrictions on weapons and ammunitions purchase and possession, but they cannot completely restrict people's ability to possess guns for the purpose of self-defense. When legislatures attempt to pass laws that treat people differently based upon their sex or race, then they have to have even a more compelling reason to do so, and even then, the courts, employing "strict scrutiny" are likely to declare such laws unconstitutional. Legislatures cannot make laws that make the punishment for a crime "cruel or unusual." This means that punishments cannot be too severe to fit the crime or ones that are "barbaric" and cause needless pain.

This chapter merely introduces constitutional limits on police and court procedure. In this chapter, we learn that police are entitled to conduct only reasonable searches and seizures and are generally required to have a warrant authorizing the search and seizure. Similarly, police can investigate criminal behavior and get statements from suspects only in ways that do not violate the suspect's right to be free from self-incrimination. When sufficient evidence exists to charge a

---

[231] The states that do not provide a grand jury use a preliminary hearing instead. This process is discussed more fully in Chapter Ten. The Fifth Amendment's grand jury provision is now one of only two clauses of the Bill of Rights that has not been incorporated to the states through the Fourteenth Amendment.

particular suspect with a crime, the Constitution governs many pretrial, trial, sentencing, and post-trial procedures. For example, defendants are guaranteed the right to a speedy trial, a jury trial, and the right to have an attorney assist in their defense. What constitutions say about these rights is generally worded in broad statements (i.e., the right to be free from unreasonable search and seizure), but hundreds of court cases interpret what those broad statements mean and, thus, dictate the behavior of police and courts as cases progress through the criminal justice process.

SOME THINGS TO THINK ABOUT OR EXPLORE

➢ Examine the multimillion dollar libel and defamation cases filed by Dominion and Smartmatic (voting machine makers) against Rudolph Guiliani, Sidney Powell, Fox News Media, and MyPillow CEO Mike Lindell (see, https://www.cnbc.com/2021/02/24/dominion-smartmatic-defamation-cases-credible-experts.html) and contrast these with the libel case filed by California Representative Devin Nunes against CNN (see, https://www.politico.com/news/2021/02/19/judge-nunes-libel-suit-cnn-470275).

➢ Identify your school's policy on free speech forums. Can anybody make a speech anywhere on campus at any time?

➢ Identify your school's policy on hate crimes committed against students or by students.

➢ Explore the Death Penalty Information Center. See, https://deathpenaltyinfo.org/. What states currently allow the death penalty? What states currently have moratoriums against the death penalty even though it is a sanctioned punishment? What did Virginia voters do in 2021 about their death penalty and why is it a big deal? (See, https://time.com/5937804/virginia-death-penalty-abolished).

TERMINOLOGY

- barbaric punishment
- Bill of Attainder
- Bill of Rights
- Due Process Clause of the Fifth Amendment and Fourteenth Amendment
- chilling effect
- clear and present danger
- commercial speech
- cruel and unusual punishment
- designated public forum
- disproportionate punishment
- enumerated rights
- Equal Protections Clause
- Establishment Clause
- Exercise Clause
- ex post facto law
- expressive conduct
- fighting words
- fundamental right
- generally applicable criminal statute
- hate speech
- imminent lawless action test
- libel
- non-public forum
- obscenity
- overbreadth doctrine
- political speech
- public forum
- quasi-public forum
- quasi-suspect classification
- selective incorporation approach
- slander
- standard of review-strict scrutiny
- standard of review-intermediate scrutiny
- standard of review-rational basis scrutiny
- suspect classification
- symbolic speech
- time, manner, and place restrictions
- total incorporation approach
- unarticulated rights
- unfettered discretion
- void for vagueness doctrine

Chapter Five: General Principles and Elements of Criminal Law

OVERVIEW AND LEARNING OBJECTIVES

This chapter discusses the elements of a crime--those specific components of a criminal charge. After reading this chapter, you should be able to answer the following questions:

➢ What types of laws are found in the general part of a criminal code and what types of laws are found in the special part of a criminal code?
➢ What are the seven "elements of a crime?
➢ What type of behavior constitutes a "voluntary act?"
➢ When do failures to act constitute the *actus reus* element of the crime?
➢ When will possession of an object constitute the *actus reus* element of the crime?
➢ What are the MPC levels of criminal intent, and how are they defined?
➢ What factors will courts consider when deciding whether a statute that fails to mention a particular mental state is a strict liability crime or just a poorly drafted statute?
➢ What factors will jurors consider when deciding whether a defendant is the proximate cause or legal cause of the harm done?
➢ What are the *actus reus* and *mens rea* elements for attempt, conspiracy, and solicitation?
➢ Why are courts reluctant to uphold vicarious liability statutes and when will they do so?

SUBSTANTIVE CRIMINAL LAW DEFINES CRIMES

This chapter examines what the government must prove to convict someone for a crime. As discussed in Chapter One, substantive law is the law that defines crimes, identifies permissible defenses, and indicates the maximum penalties for crimes. Today, the great majority of substantive law has been codified (the writing down of enacted laws or codes) and is found in the state's particular criminal code[232] or in the federal code. Criminal codes are generally separated into two parts. The general part is the section of the code that defines terms that are used throughout the code, indicates all possible defenses, and provides the general scheme of punishments. The special part of the code is the section that defines each specific crime.

---

[232] Laws created through the initiative and referendum process are typically adopted into these codes.

THE ELEMENTS OF CRIMINAL LAW

There are seven elements of a crime. Generally, the first two elements (legality and punishment) are presumed and the state need not prove these at trial. If the defendant wants to challenge whether a criminal statute is lawfully enacted or that it contains a punishment, then that challenge is done prior to trial. The remaining five elements (*actus reus*, *mens rea*, concurrence of the *actus reus* and *mens rea*, causation, and harm) must be proven by the government beyond a reasonable doubt during the criminal trial or must be admitted to through an entry of a guilty plea. Even if the state is able to prove each of these elements, the defendant may nonetheless raise defenses that may keep him or her from being convicted. The seven elements of a crime are discussed in this chapter, and defenses to criminal liability are discussed in the next chapter.

LEGALITY AND PUNISHMENT

The first element of a crime is known as the legality requirement. Before any act can be treated as a crime the legislature must lawfully create the crime. This involves the legislature jumping through all the hoops required of law-making in the particular jurisdiction--for example, was there a quorum when the bill was passed? Was the vote properly recorded? The legality requirement stems from the legal maxim "no crime without law."

The legality principle, the void for vagueness doctrine, and prohibition against ex post facto laws are intertwined and based on the belief that before we blame an individual for bad behavior, they must be put on notice of what counts as bad behavior. Fair warning requires that the individual is able to determine whether his or her behavior will be illegal and the maximum punishment that may be imposed for such behavior.

Generally, there is a "presumption of legality" (meaning we presume that the law was legally enacted), and any challenges concerning the legality of the law (such as vagueness, or due process, or ex post facto) must be raised by the defendant in advance of the trial.

The second element or requirement of a crime is "punishment" -- the law must contain a statement of how a violation of the law will be punished. This requirement stems from the legal maxim, "no punishment without law." A law that forbids certain behavior but does not have a specified punishment is properly considered as just a guideline since there can be no crime without a punishment. When looking at a statute to see if it actually provides a punishment for the criminal behavior, half the states, specify the punishment in the statute that defines the crime. For example, the statute might read:

> A person commits the crime of harassment when he or she intentionally subjects another to offensive physical contact. Harassment is punishable by up to 6 months incarceration and a fine in the amount of $2500.

The other half of the states follows Model Penal Code approach which divides felonies and misdemeanors into several classes, each carrying a specific maximum penalty, and then refers to the definitional section to the particular category applicable to that crime. Thus, the statute might read:

> A person commits Harassment when he or she intentionally subjects another to offensive physical contact. Harassment is a Class B misdemeanor.

And another part of the code would state the punishment scheme for felonies and misdemeanors. For example, that section might read:

> Misdemeanors: Class A, punishable by up to one year incarceration and a fine in the amount of $5000.00; Class B, punishable by up to six months incarceration and a fine in the amount of $2500.00; Class C, punishable by up to 30 days incarceration and a fine in the amount of $1250.00.

Any challenge to a lack of specified punishment would also be addressed in advance of the trial.

ACTUS REUS

In order to prove a person has committed a crime, the state must prove that he or she satisfied the *actus reus* requirement. *"Actus reus"* means the act of a criminal.

> [A] person will not be punished on the basis of thoughts alone; he must have engaged in some harmful or potentially harmful behavior. To wish that an enemy were dead, to think about taking another's wallet, to contemplate burning another's property—such thoughts, though wrongful, cannot be made into crimes.[233]

VOLUNTARINESS

Most acts are voluntary. For example, when you move your hand to put your pencil on the desk, it is a voluntary act. Sometimes acts are not voluntary, however. For example, if you move your hand because of a muscle spasm or someone bumping you, then your act is not voluntary. The MPC defines an "act" as a "bodily movement whether voluntary or involuntary." MPC § 2.01(1) states, however, "a person is not guilty of an offense unless his liability is based on conduct that includes a voluntary act or the omission to perform an act of which he is capable."

Frequently people think of voluntariness as meaning wishing something to occur. But, when dealing with *actus reus*, voluntariness looks only at whether the action is a product of a reflex. Consider this example: Kirk sees a group of children walking on the sidewalk and decides it would be fun to drive his car toward them to scare them, but he does nothing. Seconds later, the passenger in his car grabs his arm causing him to drive into the children. Kirk has not committed a voluntary act.

However, in an oft-cited case, *People v. Decina*, 2 NY 2d 133 (1956), the defendant suffered an epileptic seizure while driving, his hands jerked the steering wheel, and his automobile jumped a curb killing four children. Decina was convicted for negligent homicide. The appellate court affirmed Decina's conviction, reasoning that the statute "does not necessarily contemplate that the driver be conscious at the time of the accident" and that it was sufficient that the defendant knew of his medical disability and knew that it would interfere with the operation of a motor vehicle. The dissenting judge pointed out that he was being punished for merely driving, something his driver's license allowed him to do.

Whether the defendant knew he or she was prone to seizures, should not matter one iota in determining the voluntariness of the act. If the act is a product of a reflex, there is nothing the defendant's awareness about his situation can do to change that. That said, the trend has been to hold people responsible for getting themselves in positions where things can go wrong—particularly if they know in advance that something bad could happen. Courts have embraced the theory that these are "voluntarily induced involuntary acts," and may find that the *actus reus*

---

[233] *Id.*

requirement is satisfied--this is particularly true when defendant's action results from voluntary consumption of an intoxicating substance.

The Model Penal Code provides that the following are all involuntary:

- a reflex or a convulsion,
- a bodily movement during unconsciousness or sleep, and
- conduct during hypnosis or resulting from hypnotic suggestion.[234]

The MPC also notes that an act is not involuntary just because the individual acted out of the habit and therefore was not conscious of what he or she was doing. In such a case, the act clearly was within the actor's physical control if more attention had been paid.

An act performed during a state of "unconsciousness" does not meet the *actus reus* requirement. But what is unconsciousness? What if the defendant testifies that he "blacked out?" Most courts agree that amnesia itself doesn't constitute a defense, but if the defendant can show that he or she was "on automatic pilot" and not conscious of what he or she was doing, then there is a chance that his act will be held to be involuntary. [The difference between being on automatic pilot and not conscious and doing something out of habit may be a matter of degree).

Although the MPC holds that acts performed under hypnosis are involuntary, some states hold that defendants who are hypnotized are nevertheless liable for their voluntary acts because of the view that nobody will perform acts under hypnosis that are deeply repugnant to them.

OMISSION TO ACT WHEN THERE IS A LEGAL DUTY

Sometimes not doing something counts as a voluntary act and can be the actus reus of a crime. When this is the case, we call this an act of omission. An act of omission is only criminal when a person has a legal duty to do some act that they failed to do. The Model Penal Code holds that liability may not be based on an omission unless that omission violates a "legal duty" that is imposed either in the penal code itself or in another source of law, such as a civil statute.[235]

Legal duties arise when a statute imposes a duty to do an affirmative act (for example, pay taxes or register as a sex offender). Some statutes are phrased in a way that implies an affirmative act but the harm comes about because of a failure to act. In those situations, it may be more difficult to prove liability. For example, if a homicide statute states that it is a crime to kill someone unlawfully, then it is hard to apply that statute when the death comes about because of the defendant's failure to prevent someone's death--even where there was a clear duty to protect the individual victim.

Legal duties arise when there is a special relationship between the defendant and the victim. For example, parents have a duty to care for their children. When they fail to provide food, clothing, or shelter that result in the child's harm, they may be charged with a crime. Similarly, a parent who fails to protect a child from harm from another person may be held criminal liable.

Legal duties also arise out of contracts--even ones that are not between the defendant and the victim. For example, if the city hires a lifeguard to guard a city pool, the lifeguard has a contractual duty to protect all the swimmers. When the lifeguard does nothing for a drowning

---

[234] MPC §2.01(2)
[235] *Id.*

victim, he has satisfied the *actus reus* requirement for failure to act where there is a legal duty. When the duty arises because of a contract, the contract's terms govern whether a legal duty exists or not.

Legal duties may also arise when a person assumes a duty to care for another. For example, if the defendant found a person lying unconscious and bleeding on the sidewalk, and instead of taking the injured person to the hospital, took him home and let him bleed to death, the defendant has assumed a duty of care and the failure to act is an unlawful omission to act.

Legal duties can arise when the defendant creates the peril that ultimately harms the victim -- a person who intentionally or negligently places another in danger has a duty to rescue them. For example, in the case of *Jones v. State*, 220 Ind. 384, 387 (Ind. 1942), the defendant raped a twelve-year-old girl who then fell off a bridge (or maybe jumped off the bridge) into a stream. Jones went into the water, but did not rescue the girl. The court stated, "Can it be doubted that one who by his own overpowering criminal act has put another in danger of drowning has the duty to preserve her life."

Property owners have a legal duty to others they invite onto their lands. For example, in one case, the defendant invited the victim over to barbeque out on his deck which hung out 100 feet above the canyon. The defendant knew the deck unstable and was liable when the deck collapsed because he failed to take precautions to prevent the harm to the victim.

Why is it that an omission constitutes the *actus reus* for a crime only when the actor has a legal duty to act? The answer lies in the basic function of the criminal law to hold liable those who are most directly responsible for causing harm. A person who performs an affirmative act that directly causes harm (as, for example, the person who poisons another) clearly establishes his primary responsibility for the act. On the other hand, acts of omissions are commonly shared by many persons. When an individual who could have been saved by emergency medical care dies, it often is true that there are a number of persons who could have called for an ambulance or otherwise provided that care. It is only the person with the legal obligation to provide the care who can be said to be responsible for legally causing the death. He is the only person as to whom the law can say, "You should have acted and your failure to do so makes you as responsible as a person who caused the same harm by an affirmative act.[236]

Duty to intervene: The Good Samaritan Rule and The American Bystander Rule.

In the United States an individual is generally not legally required to assist a person who is in peril. This is referred to as the American Bystander Rule. Even though it may be morally reprehensible not to render assistance, the law does not create a legal duty to intervene to help another person. Lippman identified some of the reasons justifying the American Bystander Rule:

- Individuals intervening may be placed in jeopardy.
- Bystanders also may misperceive a situation, unnecessarily interfere, and create needless complications.
- Individuals may lack the physical capacity and expertise to subdue an assailant or to rescue a hostage and place themselves in danger.
- The circumstances in which individuals should intervene and the acts required to satisfy the obligation to assist another would be difficult to clearly define.

---

[236] Kerper, *supra* at 98.

- Criminal prosecutions for a failure to intervene would burden the criminal justice system.
- Individuals in a capitalistic society are responsible for their own welfare and should not expect assistance of others.
- Most people will assist others out of a sense of moral responsibility and there is no need for the law to require intervention.[237]

"Good Samaritan" statutes, common in Europe, require individuals to intervene to assist those who may be in peril. The Good Samaritan Rule is said to promote a sense of community and regard for others. Proponents of the Good Samaritan Rule argue that there is no difference between pushing a child on the railroad tracks and failing to intervene to ensure the child's safety. They contend that criminal liability should extend to both acts and omissions.[238]

At common law certain individuals were required to render aid to another. For example, parents, spouses, and employers had a duty to provide aid to their children, spouses, and employees. Similarly, state statutes now create a duty to intervene. For example, doctors must report cases of suspected child abuse, and other professions have similar reporting requirements for child and elder abuse.

POSSESSION

Although possessing something doesn't seem like much action, there are several crimes for which the *actus reus* is possessing some forbidden object (e.g., guns, illegal drugs, or burglars' tools.) The overwhelming majority of states hold that for possession to be criminal, it must be "knowing possession." Knowing possession occurs when individuals are aware that they are in possession of the object--even if they do not know whether possessing the item is legal. "Mere possession" occurs when a person has actual possession of something, but is not aware that she possesses it. Only two states, Washington and North Dakota, criminalize mere possession, but, in practice, both states impose a knowing requirement to insure fair results. The Model Penal Code provides that possession can be a criminal act only if the defendant knew he had possession of the object, and "was aware of his control thereof for a sufficient period to have been able to terminate the possession."[239]

"Actual possession" exists when a person has something under his or her direct physical control. For example, if Mike has a bindle of heroin in his pocket, he has actual possession of the drugs. "Constructive possession" occurs when a person has the ability to control something that is not in their actual possession. If Mike gave Jamie the bindle of heroin to hold for him temporarily, Mike is in constructive possession of the drugs as long as he can direct what happens to them. (Since Jamie knew that she was holding something for Mike, she would be in actual, knowing possession of the drugs.)

Sometimes it is difficult to prove possession when several people have access to, or joint possession of, an object—for example, drugs on a table in the living room of a house shared by several people. Most courts hold that anyone in the room can be found to have been in possession of the drugs as long as there is some specific proof connecting each person to the object. In one case the Court held that police had probable cause to arrest all occupants in a car where drugs were found in the back sear and a large amount of cash was found in the glove compartment. (See, *Maryland v. Pringle*, 540 U.S. 366 (2003).)

---

[237] Lippman, *Criminal Law,* at 99.
[238] *Id.*
[239] MPC §2.01 (4)

STATUS

"Status" under the criminal law means a person's condition over which he or she has no control (it does not have the same everyday meaning about how a person is viewed by other people.) The Court held in *Robinson v. California*, 370 U.S. 660 (1962), that it is cruel and unusual punishment to convict a person for a status offense. In *Robinson*, the statute criminalized the act of being addicted to narcotics. The Court, reversing Robinson's conviction stated,

> We deal with a statute which makes the "status" of narcotic addiction a criminal offense, for which the offender may be prosecuted "at any time before he reforms.
> . . . " We hold that a state law which imprisons a person thus afflicted as a criminal, even though he has never touched any narcotic drug within the State or been guilty of any irregular behavior there, inflicts a cruel and unusual punishment in violation of the Fourteenth Amendment. Even one day in prison would be cruel and unusual punishment for the 'crime' of having a common cold.[240]

Powell v. Texas, 392 U.S. 514 (1968), shows that it is not always easy to distinguish between what is a status and what is an action. Powell, an alcoholic, was arrested and charged with public intoxication after officers found him drunk and in a public place. He appealed his conviction, arguing that he had been unlawfully prosecuted for his status as an alcoholic--something over which he had no control. The Court upheld his conviction though, finding that he was being punished, not for his status, but for his action in placing himself in a public place on a particular occasion while intoxicated.

One persistent concern in most communities today is how to best deal with homeless, transient individuals. Many have substance abuse and mental health issues and are often caught up in the criminal justice system when charged with some form of criminal trespass after entering on public or businesses' property after being told not to come back ("trespassed"). Because they lack a permanent local residence, these defendants are less likely to be conditionally released while awaiting resolution of their cases. Since many are poor, they are unlikely to be able to post security for their release and end up spending short, but frequent, stays in the local jail--repeatedly pleading guilty to the charges and hoping to get released before they do "dead time" (continued incarceration after the recommended, negotiated sentence for a guilty plea). Mental health and veteran's courts are trying to respond to mitigate the harshness of the criminal justice system which essentially criminalizes the status of homelessness. Still, this complicated problem will be difficult to solve as there are no easy solutions.

MENS REA

One of fundamental principles in criminal law is that we punish only blameworthy individuals. What a person was thinking at the time they committed an act plays a key role in deciding our response. As Oliver Wendell Holmes Jr. remarked, "Even a dog distinguishes between being stumbled over and being kicked."[241] If, while standing in a crowded subway, someone touched your leg, your response (say, pulling away) would be similar regardless of what the person intended, but how you view the act and the type of consequence you want would likely be different if the person accidentally touched you than if they intentionally groped you. In this manner, the criminal law differentiates punishment based upon an actor's intent. Thus, the state must prove that, in addition to a voluntary act or omission to act, the defendant acted with the level of criminal intent required by the statute. This element is called the *mens rea*

---

[240] 370 U.S. at 666-667.
[241] "Early Forms of Liability," Lecture I from *The Common Law.* (1909)

of the crime. The Latin, *mens rea*, means "guilty mind," and another Latin phrase, *scienter*, means "guilty knowledge." Both have been used to refer to the mental element of the crime.

COMMON LAW *MENS REA*

The common law spoke of two categories of *mens rea*: general intent and specific intent.[242] General intent is the intent to commit the criminal act. For example, if the crime is assault and battery, the state must prove that the defendant intended to strike the victim but is not required to prove that the defendant intended to violate the law, that the defendant knew that the act was a crime, nor that the defendant knew the act would result in any specific type of harm. Since defendants rarely announce their intentions, proof that the defendant intended to strike the victim must be inferred from the circumstances surrounding the behavior.

Specific intent is the intent to engage in the criminal act and cause the particular result. For example, murder is considered a specific intent crime. In order to convict a defendant of murder, the state must show not only that the defendant wished to take out a gun and shoot it (the act), but also that the defendant wished that the bullet would strike the victim and that the victim would die (the act and the result).

The common law also recognized "transferred intent." Transferred intent applies in situations where an individual intends to harm one victim, but instead injures another. When Kendall throws a rock at Barb but the rock misses Barb and strikes Dawn, then the law "transfers" Kendall's criminal intent from Barb (intended victim) to Dawn (actual victim). The common law doctrine of transferred intent states that Kendall's guilt is exactly what it would have been had she hit Barb with the rock. Some states limit the transferred intent doctrine to situations in which the type of harm done is similar to the type of harm intended. In those states, Kendall would be not be guilty of striking Dawn with the rock if she had intended to break a window with the rock but instead accidentally hit Dawn (since the intent to injure property is different than the intent to injure a person.)

The final type of common law intent was "constructive intent." Constructive intent is used in situations in which an offender is particularly reckless. Individuals who are grossly and wantonly reckless are said to intend the natural consequences of their actions (even if they really don't). The law infers their intent from the recklessness of their actions. For example, if James dropped a big cement block from a freeway overpass and it hit Kelly's car causing her to swerve and fatally crash into the barrier, the state could prove the *mens rea* requirement through his constructive intent.

MODEL PENAL CODE *MENS REA*

Common law distinctions between *scienter*, general intent, specific intent became confused and incorrectly applied over time, and the Model Penal Code tried to clarify the criminal intent by limiting it to four distinct mental states. Except in the rare case of a strict liability crime (discussed below), all crimes require a mental element. Under the MPC all crimes requiring a mental element must include one of these four mental states: purposely, knowingly, recklessly, and negligently.

MPC §2,02

---

[242] The trend in modern statutes is to abandon these distinctions, but these terms continue to exist in some criminal statutes.

(1) Minimum Requirements of Culpability. ... A person is not guilty of an offense unless he acted purposely, knowingly, recklessly or negligently . . . with respect to each material element of the offense.

(2) Kinds of Culpability Defined.
  (a) Purposely.

A person acts purposely with respect to material elements of an offense when: (i) . . . It is his conscious object to engage in conduct of that nature or to cause such a result.

  (b) Knowingly.

A person acts knowingly . . . when: (i) If the element involves the nature of his conduct . . . he is aware of the existence of such circumstances or he believes or hope that they exist; and (ii) If the element involves a result of his conduct, he is aware that it is practically certain that his conduct will cause such a result.

  (c) Recklessly.

A person acts recklessly with respect to a material element of an offense when he consciously disregards a substantial and unjustifiable risk that the material element exists or will result from his conduct. The risk must be of such a nature and degree that, considering the nature and purpose of the actor's conduct and the circumstances known to him, its disregard involves a gross deviation from the standard of conduct that a law-abiding person would observe in the actor's situation

d) Negligently.

A person acts negligently with respect to a material element of an offense when he should be aware of a substantial and unjustifiable risk that the material element exists or will result from his conduct. The risk must be of such a nature and degree that the actor's failure to perceive it, considering the nature and purpose of his conduct and the circumstances known to him, involves a gross deviation from the standard of care that a reasonable person would observe in the actor's situation.

MATERIAL ELEMENTS OF A CRIME--APPLYING THE LEVELS OF INTENT

The four basic mental states (purposefully, knowingly, recklessly, and negligently) may be applied to different "material elements of a crime." Criminal statutes can be tricky to interpret, and this is particularly so in deciding what criminal mindset the statute requires. For example, if Bob took a bat and hit Tom's car with it and was charged with a statute that read: "a person commits the crime of criminal mischief when the person recklessly, knowingly or purposefully damages the property of another," there are several questions about criminal intent that the jury may need to answer when deciding if Bob is guilty of criminal mischief. For example, is the state required to prove that Bob recklessly, knowingly, or purposefully swung the bat at Tim's car (the act)? Or, is the state required to prove that Bob recklessly, knowingly, or purposefully damaged the car (the result)? Or, is the state required to prove that the Bob recklessly, knowingly, or purposefully damaged the car *of another* (the attendant circumstance)? The material elements include:

1. <u>The actor's physical conduct.</u> The *mens rea* required about the physical conduct relates to the actor's awareness of his physical conduct. In the example above, this would require that Bob recklessly, knowingly, or purposefully swung the bat.

2. <u>The result produced by the conduct.</u> The *mens rea* required about the result relates to the actor's awareness of the harm that is or may be caused. Many crimes require that defendant cause a particular harm. In the example above, the crime of criminal mischief requires that Bob damage (the result-harm) Tim's property. If Bob knowingly swung the bat but had taken great precautions not to be anywhere near Tim's car and there is no evidence that Bob intended to damage the car, the state may not be able to prove the *mens rea* required in the statute concerning the material element of result.

3. <u>The surrounding or "attendant" circumstances that exist apart from the individual's conduct.</u> Certain crimes specify particular circumstances that must exist for the crime to be committed. In our example, the attendant circumstance is that the property must be the property of another. If Bob thought he was damaging his own car, then he would not be guilty of the crime. Another example of a crime involving an attendance circumstance is that of providing alcohol to a minor. If the statute requires the defendant provide alcohol to a person knowing that person to be under age, then the defendant would not be convicted if he believed the person was not a minor. If, however, the statute required only that the state prove the defendant was negligent as to the recipient's age, the defendant may be convicted.

The Court grappled with this dilemma in *Rehaif v. United States*, 588 U.S. ___ (2019). Rehaif was in the United States on a nonimmigrant student visa studying at the Florida Institute of Technology. In December 2014 he was dismissed from the university and his immigration status was terminated in February 2015. Rehaif, however, remained in States and in December 2015 purchased ammunition and rented a firearm at a shooting range for one hour. Six days later, an employee at the hotel where Rehaif was staying called the police to report that Rehaif had been acting suspiciously. When an FBI agent investigating the report spoke with Rehaif, Rehaif admitted he had fired two firearms at the shooting range and that he was aware his student visa was no longer any good. Rehaif consented to a search of his room where agents found the remaining ammunition he had purchased at the range. A federal grand jury indicted him with violating a federal law which prohibits a person who is illegally or unlawfully in the United States from possessing any firearm or ammunition. In his opinion, Justice Breyer wrote:

> The question here concerns the scope of the word "knowingly." Does it mean that the Government must prove that a defendant knew both that he engaged in the relevant conduct (that he possessed a firearm) and also that he fell within the relevant status (that he was a felon, an alien unlawfully in this country, or the like)? We hold that the word "knowingly" applies both to the defendant's conduct and to the defendant's status. To convict a defendant, the Government therefore must show that the defendant knew he possessed a firearm and also that he knew he had the relevant status when he possessed it. . . . Whether a criminal statute requires the Government to prove that the defendant acted knowingly is a question of congressional intent.

Justice Breyer again wrote on this issue in 2022. *Ruan v. United States*, 597 U.S. ___ (2022) held that held that to be guilty of violating the federal statute involving dispensing a controlled substance, the physicians, Ruan and Kahn—both medical doctors licensed to prescribe controlled substances, must be proven beyond a reasonable doubt to not only intentionally prescribe the medicine but intentionally dispense it knowing that they were unauthorized to do so (the statute, 21 U. S. C. §841, makes it a federal crime, "[e]xcept as authorized[,] . . . for any person knowingly or intentionally . . . to manufacture, distribute, or dispense . . . a controlled substance.") The court stated,

> Section 841's "knowingly or intentionally" mens rea applies to the statute's "except as authorized" clause. Once a defendant meets the burden of producing evidence that his or her conduct was "authorized," the Government must prove beyond a reasonable doubt that the defendant knowingly or intentionally acted in an unauthorized manner.
>
> …
>
> In general, criminal law seeks to punish conscious wrongdoing. Thus, when a criminal statute is silent as to the mental state required, courts infer a requirement of knowledge or intent. When it is not silent, the general mental state provision applies to each term of the provision. Thus, the "knowingly or intentionally" requirement of 21 U.S.C. § 841 applies to the phrase "except as authorized." As such, once the defendant proves their conduct was "authorized," the prosecution must prove beyond a reasonable doubt that the defendant acted in an unauthorized manner.[243]

MOTIVE

The *mens rea* of a criminal statute is not the same thing as motive. Motive refers to a person's reasons or motivations for committing a crime. For example, a person may commit a theft or robbery in order to further buy drugs or pay off a gambling debt. Generally, the state must prove the defendant's *mens rea*, but it does not have to prove the defendant's motive. That said, it is much easier for the jury to convict the defendant if jurors can understand the defendant's motivations for committing the crime.

STRICT LIABILITY

A strict liability crime is one in which defendant's mental state is immaterial. Strict liability statutes do not mention or state a mental element that the state must prove. Strict liability offenses came into being around the time of the industrial revolution and the rise of public welfare or *mala prohibita* crimes. These crimes were written to protect society against unsafe working conditions, defective drugs and impure food, pollution, trucks, and unsafe railroads. Requiring prosecutors to establish criminal intent for these relatively minor cases consumes time and energy and diverts resources from other cases.

Although initially limited to crimes with minor punishments, the trend is toward expanding strict liability into non-public welfare crimes that carry relatively severe punishment. The Supreme Court has, nevertheless, shown willingness to strike down putative (so called) strict liability statutes and require *mens rea* when the penalty is severe and the nature of the crime is one that traditionally would require the defendant to possess criminal intent. Model Penal Code §1.04(5) adopts strict liability offenses but limits the crimes to "violations" that are not subject to imprisonment and are only punishable by a fine, forfeiture or other civil penalty.

---

[243] https://www.oyez.org/cases/2021/20-1410

Legislatures indicate that they are creating a strict liability crime by omitting the *mens rea* language (like "knowingly," "recklessly," "purposefully," etc.). Sometimes legislatures do not intend to create a strict liability crime but through inattention or poor draftsmanship they inadvertently omit reference to *mens rea*. In determining whether a crime is a strict liability offense or just a poorly drafted or improperly enacted crime, the court determines whether the legislature intended to impose strict liability. In addition to the missing *mens rea* requirement, the courts will consider the following factors in deciding whether the legislature intended to create a strict liability crime:

- Was the offense a crime at common law?
- Would a single violation of the statute pose danger to a large number of people?
- Is the risk of conviction of an "innocent" individual (one without moral culpability) outweighed by the public interest in preventing harm to society?
- Is the penalty relatively minor?
- Does a conviction harm the defendant's reputation?
- Does the law significantly impede the rights of individuals or impose a heavy burden.
- Are these acts ones that most people avoid?
- Do individuals who engage in such acts generally possess criminal intent?

Sometimes legislatures intend for strict liability to exist with regard to a specific material element of a crime, but not for another material element. And, as you can imagine, this is where it gets really tricky. For example, the crime of statutory rape prohibits even consensual sexual conduct with an individual under a certain age. In many jurisdictions, the state must prove that the defendant had the *mens rea* to commit the sexual act (i.e., he knowingly had intercourse), but it does not have to prove that the defendant had the mens rea regarding the victim's age (i.e, that he knew his partner was 15 years old). In this respect, the crime is strict liability with respect to the circumstance of age.

Another example of a strict liability crime is driving while intoxicated (DWI) or driving under the influence of an intoxicant (DUII). Prosecutors must prove that the defendant drove while intoxicated, but do not have to prove that the defendant intended to drive while intoxicated. In a sense, felony murder statutes also impose strict liability. When someone dies during the course of an inherently dangerous felony, the defendant will be held liable for the death, even if the defendant never intended to hurt anyone and took reasonable steps to make sure no one got hurt. The state must prove that the defendant had the *mens rea* for the underlying felony, but need not prove that the defendant's mental state with regard to the death.

CONCURRENCE OF *ACTUS REUS* AND *MENS REA*

To be a crime, the criminal act must be triggered by the criminal intent. This is called the concurrence requirement of *actus reus* and *mens rea*. For example, assume that on day one Jack decides to run over Jill because he is angry that she tumbled down the hill and spilled the pale of water. Assume also that Jack does nothing, cools off, and later decides he could never harm anyone-- even Jill. On day two, Jack accidentally runs Jill over as he backs out of his driveway. His criminal intent on day one does not trigger his running over Jill on day two, so Jack cannot be found guilty of a crime. (This example also illustrates the difficulty in proving intent. How would anyone know that Jack had decided to run Jill over when he did nothing to act upon it?)

CAUSATION

Some crimes – crimes of causation – require that the criminal act cause a particular harm or result. Causation is a material element of these "criminal causation crimes," and the state must prove beyond a reasonable doubt that the defendant caused the harm. Since the criminal law is based on personal responsibility, the causation requirement connects the person's acts to the resulting harm. The causation element of the crime limits liability to people whose actions produce the prohibited harm. When individuals cause harm, then it is fair for society to hold them responsible and blameworthy. When individuals do not cause the harm, then it is not fair to hold them responsible.

Lippman observed,

> Establishing that a defendant's criminal act caused harm to the victim can be more complicated than you might imagine. Should an individual who commits a rape be held responsible for the victim's subsequent suicide? What if the victim attempted suicide a week before the rape and then killed herself following the rape? Would your answer be the same if the stress induced by the rape appears to have contributed to the victim contracting cancer and dying a year later? What if the doctors determine that the murder victim who was hospitalized would have died an hour later of natural causes in any event?[244]

In order to prove the element of causation, the state must prove that the defendant is the actual cause of the victim's harm and the legal or proximate cause of the harm.

ACTUAL, CAUSE IN FACT, "BUT FOR" CAUSATION

Actual cause, also known as "cause in fact" or "but for causation," occurs when the defendant's actions lead to the harm. The defendant is actual cause of the harm when, but for the defendant's act, the victim would not have been harmed. Generally, actual causation is fairly easy to establish. If the defendant set into motion a chain of events that resulted in the victim's harm, then he or she is said to be the actual cause of the harm. If not for the defendant's shooting the victim, would the victim have died? If not for the fact that the defendant struck the victim, would the victim have a welt over his eye? If not for the fact that the defendant drove carelessly and ran into a tree, would the victim have sustained the injuries in the crash? If the answer is, "yes," then the defendant is the actual cause of the harm.

"LEGAL CAUSE" OR "PROXIMATE CAUSE"--A MATTER OF FAIRNESS

The defendant is said to be the legal cause, or proximate cause, of the harm when, under the circumstances, he or she is not only the actual cause of the harm, but it is also fair to hold the him or her responsible. The linchpin of whether it is fair to hold defendant responsible, according to court decisions, is whether the harm was a foreseeable result of defendant's conduct. In most cases, the defendant is clearly both the actual cause and legal cause of the harm. But sometimes circumstances exist which make the question of legal or proximate cause not so clear. Consider the following: Chris drank several beers before getting into his car and driving the wrong way down the highway. He swerved to miss an oncoming car, and instead hit a tree. Shawn his passenger, sustained a broken foot in the crash. So far, it should be pretty obvious that Chris is the cause in fact of the Shawn's harm. If charged with an assault or battery, Chris should be convicted. (But for his driving into a tree, Shawn would not have been injured). But, what if Shawn after being raced to the hospital was shot by a crazed gunman on a rampage at the hospital? Chris is still the cause in fact of the Shawn's death. (But for the fact that Chris ran into a tree, Shawn would not have been at the hospital and been killed. Chris set into motion a chain of events that ultimately resulted in the Shawn's death.) But, is it fair to charge Chris with Shawn's murder? Assault? Sure. But murder?

---

[244] Lippman, *Criminal Law, supra* at 122.

To find proximate cause, the jury must find that not only is the harm a foreseeable result of the defendant's actions, but also that the manner in which the harm occurred was foreseeable. For example, a jury may find that it is very foreseeable that a person who drives drunk will cause a crash in which someone will die. What is not foreseeable is the existence of the crazed gunman at the hospital. The crazed hospital gunman is considered an intervening act. And, in this case the gunman is considered a "superseding intervening" cause. It is fair to hold the gunman liable for Shawn's death. What if the gunman's shot only grazed Shawn and the hospital doctors failed to properly treat Shawn, will Chris still "be off the hook" for Shawn's death? Probably not. Generally, a third party's failure to act, unlike an affirmative act, will not be considered a superseding cause that cuts off defendant's liability.

For the most part, a defendant who commits a crime is responsible for the natural and probable consequences of his or her actions. In most instances the defendant will be liable for the harm that occurs from the victim's response to the situation they were placed in by the defendant's actions. The issue is whether the victim's response is foreseeable, not whether the victim's response is reasonable. In *People v. Armitage,* 194 Cal.App.3d 405 (1987), the defendant, who had been drinking heavily, drove his speedboat extremely fast and was zigzagging along the Sacramento River when he flipped the boat over. Armitage and Maskovich (the victim) clung to the capsized boat. Maskovich decided to swim to shore (although Armitage told him to "hang on"). Maskovich drowned. The California appellate court ruled that the Maskovich's decision to swim for it did not break the chain of causation started by Armitage. The "fact that the panic-stricken victim recklessly abandoned the boat and tried to swim ashore was not a wholly abnormal reaction to the peril of drowning" and "Armitage cannot exonerate himself by claiming that the 'victim should have reacted differently or more prudently.'"[245]

Courts looked to a variety of factors in determining whether the necessary proximate causation existed. Such factors include:

- whether the actor intended to inflict serious harm,
- whether the actor did inflict serious harm,
- whether the intervening event was a product of "natural events" (e.g., the infection of the wound) or the action of a third person (e.g., the sloppy doctor),
- whether the final result was foreseeable.

At least where the final result could have been anticipated from the dangerous nature of the defendant's conduct, the ultimate test may be whether the result was "too remote or accidental in its occurrence to have a just bearing on the actor's liability."[246]

HARM, FUTURE HARM, AND INCHOATE OFFENSES

Some statutes specify an element of harm. When specific harm is listed in the statute (for example, "substantial pain"), the prosecution must prove beyond a reasonable doubt that the harm occurred and that defendant caused it. Many statutes do not list a specific harm, and in prosecuting those crimes, the state need not prove that harm occurred. Some people argue that every crime causes harm (or possible harm) even though it may be difficult to quantify or describe harm specifically--they contend there is no such thing as a "victimless" crime.

---

[245] 194 Cal.App.3d at 410, 412.
[246] Kerper, *supra* at 110-111.

Ordinarily, a crime involves the infliction of an injury by the offender upon a protected subject matter. That protected subject matter usually is the body or property of another person. However, it also may be the government and its operations, as in the crimes of treason or bribery of a public official. The protected subject also may be the offender himself, as in the case of victimless crimes, such as drug abuse, where the offender is viewed as hurting himself. For some crimes, such as the distribution of obscene literature to adults, it has been suggested that the injury extends to a less tangible subject protected by the law, the moral fiber of the community and its attitudes toward sex and marriage.

Offenses commonly are classified according to the subject matter protected (crimes against the person, crimes against property, etc.). The offenses within each of these categories then often are ranked according to the degree of harm caused of the protected subject matter. Consider, for example, a crime against the person of another. If an individual intentionally assaults another and kills him, the crime is murder. If he inflicts serious bodily harm, the crime is aggravated assault. If the injury is minor, the crime is simple assault. ...[247]

INCHOATE OFFENSES

Sometimes the law seeks to prevent harm that may happen in the future. When we know that individuals present a threat, but yet the threat they pose has yet to take shape and cause the harm, society is justified in acting to protect itself from this future harm. To do so, each state has passed laws dealing with "inchoate offenses."

Inchoate means underdeveloped, unripened, incomplete, or only partly begun. Inchoate crimes often involve preparation to commit some harm, and they are sometimes referred to as preparatory crimes. By criminalizing inchoate offenses police are able to intercept suspects before they can inflict the injury involved in the intended crimes. The three inchoate offenses are attempt, solicitation, and conspiracy. Attempt, solicitation, and conspiracy are not crimes in themselves, and must be tied to an intended offense. That said, inchoate offenses are separate and distinct crimes and charges from the intended crime. For example, a person may be charged with attempted rape, solicitation to commit murder, or conspiracy to commit fraud. With solicitation and conspiracy, the defendant may be charged both with the inchoate offense as well as the intended offense (for example, Mike could be charged with solicitation to commit perjury as well as perjury), but with an attempt charge, if the defendant is successful, he or she is only charged with the completed offense (for example, Mike could not be charged with both attempted theft and theft if he actually was successful in taking someone's property without permission).

The *mens rea* element for inchoate offenses is purposefully or intentionally. To convict for an inchoate offense, the state must prove defendant had the specific intent or purpose to accomplish the intended crime. The *actus reus* element for inchoate offenses varies among jurisdictions, but generally, the state must prove defendant engaged in some act to carry out the purpose of the intended crime. Inchoate offenses are generally punished less severely than the intended crime.

THE INCHOATE OFFENSE OF ATTEMPT

Attempts occur in two ways. First a person fails to complete an act after making every effort to complete it but failing to succeed – called a complete attempt. For example, an individual fires a weapon and misses the intended target. Second, a person abandons, or is

---

[247] *Id.* at 108.

prevented from completing an act because of some factor outside his or her control – called an incomplete attempt. For example, an individual who is about to rob a bank is interrupted from doing so because of the arrival of the police.

Elements of Attempt

The *mens rea* for attempt is the specific intent to complete the intended crime. So if the charge is attempted theft, the state must prove that the defendant intended to steal someone's property.

The *actus reus* of attempt is far more complicated, and legislatures, judges, and lawyers have long disagreed how far individuals must progress toward completing the intended crime before the individual can be held liable for attempt. At one end of the spectrum is mere preparation, and all agree that mere preparation is not sufficient to constitute the *actus reus* of attempt. At the other end of the spectrum is the commission of the last act necessary, although most states don't require the defendant have gone that far in order to be liable for attempt. At the very least, the defendant needs to have committed some act or acts toward the commission of the crime. The Model Penal Code and many states require that the defendant take a substantial step toward the completion of the crime. This "substantial step test" provides a fairly simple and easily applied test for attempt. An individual must take a clear step toward the commission of a crime and the step must be strongly corroborative of the actor's criminal purpose. The Code gives examples of steps that would constitute a clear step:

- Lying in wait, search for, or following the contemplated victim of a crime
- Enticing the victim of the crime to go to the place contemplated for its commission
- Surveillance of the site of the contemplated crime
- Unlawful entry of a building or vehicle that is the site of the contemplated crime
- Possession of materials specifically designed for the commission of the crime
- Soliciting an individual to engage in conduct constituting a crime.

The last element of attempt is the failure to commit the crime. If the crime is completed, the attempt "merges into" the intended, completed crime and only the intended crime is charged.

Defenses to Attempt

Abandonment or Voluntary Renunciation

What about defendants who intend to commit crimes and do some act towards committing them but change their minds and decide not to go through with it? Are they still liable for attempt? The answer is, "it depends." Individuals who abandon their attempts to commit crimes because of some outside or extraneous factor (say the unexpected presence of the police at the location where he intended to commit the crime) remain criminally liable. But, those who voluntarily renounce their criminal schemes and manifest changes of heart may have a defense to a charge of attempt. The Model Penal Code recognizes the defense of abandonment in those instances in which an individual commits an attempt and "abandoned his effort . . . under circumstances manifesting a complete and voluntary manifestation of criminal purpose." The important point is that an individual can commit an attempt and then relieve himself of liability by voluntarily abandoning the criminal enterprise. A renunciation is not voluntary when (1) it is motivated by a desire to avoid apprehension, (2) it is provoked by the realization that the crime is too difficult to accomplish, or (3) the offender decides to postpone the crime or to focus on another victim. Abandonment is a defense to attempt when an individual freely and voluntarily undergoes a change of heart and abandons the criminal activity. The defense of abandonment recognizes that an individual who abandons a criminal enterprise lacks firm commitment to complete the crime and should be permitted to avoid punishment. The defense also provides incentive for individuals to renounce their criminal conduct before completing the crime.[248]

Legal Impossibility v. Factual Impossibility

Suppose a person attempts to commit an act which, it turns out, was impossible to complete. That person may have may have a defense to criminal liability for a charge of attempt to commit the crime. The success of the defense depends on whether it was factually impossible to commit the crime or it was legally impossible to commit the crime. Factual impossibilities (which do not provide a defense to the charge of attempt) occur when defendants do everything possible to complete the crime but, for some reason, are prevented from completing the event by some extraneous factor beyond their control. Consider the defendant, Frank, who goes to the hospital thinking it is a good time to shoot his enemy Victor. Frank sneaks into Victor's room and shoots into Victor's bed. Frank's bullet strikes Victor's heart which had stopped beating ten minutes ago. Frank has no defense to attempted murder. It is factually impossible to murder a corpse, but that doesn't make the Frank any less dangerous. He did everything he could to kill Victor, but because of the extraneous fact (that Victor had died minutes before), his attempt was factually impossible.

A legal impossibility (which does provide a defense to a charge of attempt) occurs when an individual mistakenly believes that he or she is acting illegally. A commonly cited example is that of a people who take a tax deduction, thinking they are not entitled to it and believing they are breaking the law, when in fact, the law allows the deduction. The real issue about the defense of legal impossibility is that it will practically never be raised because prosecutors do not spend valuable time and energy prosecuting someone for behavior that is not criminal.

INCHOATE OFFENSE: SOLICITATION

Solicitation is defined as commanding, hiring, or encouraging another person to commit a crime. Many states do not have solicitation statutes and rely instead on the common law of solicitation. States that do have solicitation statutes have adopted various approaches. Some punish the solicitation of all crimes, while others limit solicitation charges to intended felonies. Solicitation convictions, like attempt convictions, generally result in punishment that is slightly less severe or the equivalent punishment to the intended crime. Solicitation can be a form of accomplice liability if the person solicited agrees to render aid in the completion of the crime. Solicitation, however, is complete, even when the person solicited refuses to help commit the target crime. Unlike attempt, a charge of solicitation does not merge or fold into the completed crime. A person can be charged both with solicitation to commit murder (by asking another to complete the crime) and also charged with the crime of murder (on an aiding and abetting theory) when the solicited person agrees and kills the victim.

The crime of solicitation involves a written or spoken statement in which an individual intentionally advises, requests, counsels, commands, hires, encourages, or incites another person to commit a crime (*actus reus*) with the intent that the other individual commit the crime (*mens rea*). Solicitation is complete the moment the statement requesting another to commit a crime is made.

Is it solicitation when a person makes a comment intended as a joke or uttered out of frustration? No, because the person lacks the specific intent or purpose that the other person commit the crime. Similarly, merely making a statement about hoping that the crime is committed is not enough to be liable for solicitation--some effort must be made to get another

---

[248] *See,* LaFave, *supra* at 612-614.

person to commit the crime. Under the Model Penal Code, an individual is guilty of solicitation when he or she writes a letter asking another to commit a crime even if the letter is intercepted and does not reach its intended recipient ("It is immaterial that the actor fails to communicate with the person he solicits to commit a crime if his conduct was designed to effect such communication." MPC §5.02 (2).) California takes the opposite approach, and an appellate court reversed the conviction of a gang member who sent a letter (intercepted by authorities) asking another gang member to cause his girlfriend to miscarry their child. The court found that the words "solicits another" in the California statue required proof that the intended recipient received the defendant's message. (The court did uphold the conviction for attempted solicitation to commit murder.) [249]

Defenses to Solicitation

Solicitation occurs when the words are uttered making the request, not when the intended crime is completed. In fact, solicitation occurs even if the defendant never could convince anyone to agree to commit the crime. Thus, it is difficult for a person to successfully claim a defense to solicitation. Nevertheless, a person charged with solicitation may have an affirmative defense of voluntary renunciation if he "after soliciting another person to commit a crime, persuaded him not to do so or otherwise prevented the commission of the crime, under circumstances manifesting a complete and voluntary renunciation of his criminal purpose." (MPC §5.02 (3)). Because solicitation involves getting another on board to complete the crime, it is not enough for the individual to simply change his or her mind. The person must take every action necessary to prevent the recipient of the solicitation from completing the crime to have a defense to solicitation. As with attempt, it is not a defense to solicitation that the defendant abandoned the criminal purpose based on the intervention of outside or extraneous factors.

INCHOATE OFFENSE: CONSPIRACY

Conspiracy is among the most commonly charged federal offenses. It is construed broadly by courts and applied by prosecutors to a variety of situations. At common law, conspiracy was an agreement by two or more persons to accomplish a criminal act or to use unlawful means to accomplish a non-criminal objective. Today all jurisdictions have statutes that generally define conspiracy as an agreement between two or more persons to commit a criminal act. At common law the charge of conspiracy merged into the completed crime, but defendants can now be convicted of the conspiracy to commit the intended crime and the intended crime.

Mens Rea Of Conspiracy

In all states, the *mens rea* of conspiracy is the intent and purpose to complete a crime. In general, the government must prove that at least two people intended to commit some target crime (sometimes called the predicate offense). Some intent may be inferred from the conduct of the parties. But, what if one party does not truly intend to go through with the crime? For example, if Kelly and Julie are sitting around in a bar, drinking, and Kelly suggests, "Hey, let's kill Shorty," and Julie says, "Yea, I hate that guy…let's get him." Is there an agreement when Kelly is just joking, but Julie is serious? Under the common law plurality requirement, a conspiracy exists only when there is a meeting of the minds of at least two people, and, under these facts, it does not appear that two people have the same mindset or agreement. Further, it would be difficult to prove a conspiracy existed, unless the state can show by circumstantial evidence that both were committed to killing Shorty. At common law, both Kelly and Julie would be acquitted although Julie was quite serious about killing Shorty. The plurality

---

[249] *See, People v. Saephanh*, 94 Cal. Rptr.2d 910 (Cal. Ct. App. 2000). *See also, State v. Cotton*, 790 P.S. 1050 (NM 1990) ("The mere writing and sending of letters by defendant to his wife, without proof of solicitation of a specific felony and proof of defendant's intent to induce another to commit such crime, is insufficient to establish proof of criminal solicitation.")

requirement presents particular problems in situations involving undercover officers who agree to participate in a crime in order to gain trust of the members of a drug ring. In this situation, the drug ring member is fully committed to the agreement and to committing the intended crime, so he or she presents danger of future harm (what conspiracy law was intending to prevent) even if the officer does not. Because of this, the Model Penal Code and some jurisdictions have adopted a "unilateral approach to conspiracy", which would allow prosecution of individuals who believed they were agreeing to commit a crime, even though their "co-conspirators" did not have that same intent so technically, there was no meeting of the minds.

Actus Reus Of Conspiracy

The heart of conspiracy actus reus is the agreement between two or more people to commit a crime. In addition to proving the parties entered into an agreement, several states require proof that at least one conspirator did some overt act towards completing the intended crime. Federal law requires proof of an overt act by one or more persons to "effect the object of a conspiracy to commit an offense or to defraud the United States." 18 U.S.C.A. § 371. To establish conspiracy, "the government must prove beyond a reasonable doubt the existence of an agreement between two or more people to violate the law of the United States and that any one of the conspirators committed an overt act in furtherance of the agreement."

The agreement to commit the crime need not be in writing. A simple understanding is sufficient. In those states which require an overt act towards completing the intended crime, the act need not be a substantial—just any overt act (something observable) tending to implement the conspiracy. Even a single telephone conversation arranging a meeting has been found to be sufficient proof of an overt act.

Structure of Conspiracies

Conspiracies take two typical forms: a chain conspiracy or a wheel conspiracy. A chain conspiracy exists when the conspirators are linked together in a vertical chain to achieve a criminal objective. The classic example is an illegal drug distribution conspiracy. In *United States v. Bruno*, 105 F.2d 921 (1939), eighty-eight defendants were indicted for a conspiracy to import, sell, and possess narcotics. The case involved smugglers who brought the narcotics into New York and sold them to middlemen who, in turn, distributed the drugs to retailers who then sold them to operatives in Texas and Louisiana for distribution to purchasers and users. Bruno and Iacono appealed their convictions claiming there were three conspiracies rather than one large conspiracy. The court ruled that this was a single chain conspiracy in which the smugglers knew "that middlemen must purchase the drugs from smugglers. Even though the distributors didn't have an agreement with the smugglers, the conspirators at one end of the chain knew that the unlawful business would not and could not, stop with their buyers; and those at the other end knew that it had not begun with their sellers." Each member of the conspiracy knew that the success of that part with which he was immediately concerned, was dependent upon the success of the whole.

A wheel conspiracy involves a single person or group that serves as a hub or common core, connecting various independent individuals or spokes. The spokes typically interact with the hub rather than with one another. If each of the spokes shares a common purpose to succeed, then a single conspiracy exists. If one of the spokes has no interest in the success of the other spokes, then courts are likely to find multiple conspiracies rather than a single conspiracy. In *Kotteakos v. United States*, 328 U.S. 750 (1946), the Court held that although Simon Brown, the hub, helped thirty-one independent individuals obtain separate fraudulent loans from the government and all were engaged in the same type of illegal activity, there was no common purpose or overall plan so the defendants were not liable for a single conspiracy. Each loan was an end in itself, separate from all the others.

Pinkerton Rule: Acts and Statements Furthering a Conspiracy

You may be wondering why it matters whether the court views the arrangement as a single conspiracy or multiple conspiracies. It matters because of the Court's holding in *Pinkerton v. United States*, 328 U.S. 640 (1946). In that case, the Court held that Daniel Pinkerton was criminally responsible for his brother Walter's failure to pay taxes despite the fact that Daniel was in prison at the time that Walter submitted his fraudulent tax return. The Court held that every member of a conspiracy is liable for any act of any other member of the conspiracy if it is done in furtherance of that conspiracy. The Court reasoned that conspirators are each other's agents. The "Pinkerton Rule" has broad implications and has been rejected by some courts. Think about the *Kotteakos* case mentioned above. If the court had found only one conspiracy, then any crime committed by any of the 31 individuals to promote their venture would be considered a criminal action by each of the 30 co-conspirators. If the court found (as it did) that each was a separate conspiracy, only the hub (Simon Brown) and the one individual would be criminally liable for the acts of that one individual.

Under federal and states' rules of evidence, statements made by a co-conspirator during the course of a crime are akin to the defendant's own statements or admissions. Defendant's admissions are admissible and can be used against them at trial under the rules of evidence; thus, co-conspirators statements are similarly admissible against all other co-conspirators. "In the eyes of the law, conspirators are one man, they breathe one breath, they speak one voice, they wield one arm, and the law says the acts, words, and declarations of each, while in pursuit of the common design, are the words and declarations of all."[250]

Once formed, a conspiracy continues to exist until the target crime has been completed, abandoned, or otherwise terminated by some affirmative act.[251] If a person joins a conspiracy and does not withdraw, he or she is not insulated from the actions of his or her co-conspirators.

Defenses to Conspiracy

Some states statutes allow defendants to raise a withdrawal or renunciation defense when charged with conspiracy. But, in the absence of a statute specifically permitting this, courts have been reluctant to allow withdrawal as a defense--since even if one of the co-conspirators wants to withdraw, the conspiracy can still proceed. When the defendant raises renunciation as a defense, the courts have generally required the defendant to take steps necessary to thwart the objective of the conspiracy. At the very least, the defendant would have the burden of establishing his or her withdrawal from the conspiracy, but many states require that the defendant also notify law enforcement authorities about the pertinent details of the conspiracy (in a timely manner) in order they might prevent the crime.

SPECIAL ELEMENTS AND NON-ELEMENTS OF CRIMES

ATTENDANT CIRCUMSTANCES.

Although attendant circumstances are not technically "elements of a crime," the government may nevertheless have to prove them beyond a reasonable doubt. For example, the common law crime of burglary required that the defendant break and enter a dwelling of another at night with the intent to commit a felony in the dwelling. The "dwelling," "nighttime," and "of another" requirements are considered attendant circumstances. (Breaking and entering constitutes the *actus reus* element, and the intent to do the felony at entry is the *mens rea* element.)

---

[250] *Territory v. Goto*, 27 Hawaii 65 (1923).
[251] *Cline v. State*, 319 S.W.2d 227 (Tenn. 1958).

[S]ome criminal statutes may specify additional elements or circumstances that must be present in order to constitute a crime. These additional items are called necessary attendant circumstances and generally refer to the facts surrounding an event, such as the time or place of the conduct or the instrument used to facilitate the harmful act. The term necessary suggest that the existence of such statutorily identified circumstances is required in order to sustain a conviction.

. . .

Sometimes the inclusion of attendance circumstances is used to increase the degree, or level of seriousness of an offense.

. . .

Attendant circumstances surrounding a crime are often discussed in terms of aggravating circumstances (heightening a person's culpability) or mitigating circumstances (reducing a person's culpability). The presence of such factors can be used to increase or lessen the penalty that can be imposed on a convicted offender. In some jurisdictions, necessary attendant circumstances that increase potential criminal punishment are referred to as specifications. A specification is a separate factual allegation made in a charging instrument that serves as a supplement to the base criminal charge. This specification, if proven beyond a reasonable doubt, enhances the possible penalties for the underlying crime. For example, in an indictment for murder (the purposeful killing of another), the grand jury may also include a gun specification . . . that alleges that the defendant used a gun to commit the offense. This specification is written in addition to the primary charge of murder contained in an indictment

. . .

Other types of specifications include circumstances arising out of gang activity, sexual motivation, and repeat offenses. The idea behind these specifications and others is to distinguish between crimes committed under aggravating circumstances . . . from those committed under average circumstances, and to allow courts to punish aggravated activity accordingly.[252]

In *Stokeling v. United States*, 586 U.S. ___ (2019), the Court held that a state robbery offense that includes "as an element" the common law requirement of "overcoming the victim's resistance" was categorically a violent felony under the Armed Career Criminal Act even though the offense requires only slight force to overcome resistance.

CORPUS DELICTI:

The term *corpus delicti* literally means "body of a crime." Contrary to a frequent misconception, the rule does not mean that the state must produce a murder victim's body in order to prosecute a defendant for murder. Instead, the *corpus delicti* rule is a common law principle holding that a criminal conviction cannot be based solely on the uncorroborated confession or admission of the accused. Accordingly, under the *corpus delicti* rule, a prosecutor must prove (1) that a certain result or injury has occurred, and (2) that a person is criminally responsible for this injury.[253] Prosecutors must produce some substantive evidence, independent of the defendant's confession that shows that the confessed-to crime actually occurred. This rule is firmly implanted in American law, although several states have modified the rule in the last few decades. The purpose of the rule is to ensure that coerced and mentally unstable defendants who make false confessions are not convicted for crimes that have not occurred. For example, in in order to prove the *corpus delicti* in a murder case, the prosecution must show by direct or

---

[252] Feldmeier and Schmalleger, *supra* at 82-83.
[253] *Id.* at 84-85.

circumstantial evidence, independent of the accused's statements, that a victim died as a result of the defendant's criminal act.

PARTIES TO CRIME

COMMON LAW CLASSIFICATIONS

Common law judges were aware that people often worked together to complete a crime. Some individuals take a more active role in the crime, and others less so. Some planned and carried out the crime, others helped get the tools needed to commit the crime, and still others were involved with helping their friends evade arrest or dispose of the fruits of their crimes. Common law distinguished between principals in the first degree, principals in the second degree, accessories before the fact, and accessories after the fact. Principals in the first degree were the perpetrators of the crime. In the classic bank-robbing example, the principal in the first degree is the person who entered the bank, pointed the gun at the teller, and took the money. Principals in the second degree were physically present or constructively present at the scene of the crime and aided the principal in the first degree. (Constructive presence occurs when a person is not physically present at the scene, but is nevertheless an eyewitness and watching the crime.) A lookout or the get-away driver would be a principle in the second degree. Accessories before the fact are individuals who helped prepare for the crime but who were not present during the crime. Accessories before the fact in the bank robbery include individuals who bought the guns and masks, got the blueprints for the bank, or encouraged the robbers. Accessories after the fact were individuals who assisted the perpetrators, knowing that they had committed a crime in an effort to help them evade capture. In the bank-robbing example, the accessories after the fact were the people who helped the bank robbers "lie low" or helped them hide the stolen money.

Almost all crimes at common law were capital offenses, so a complicated set of rules developed to prevent individuals who were less involved, less culpable, or less blameworthy from being prosecuted, convicted, and executed when the more involved, more culpable, more blameworthy individuals escaped such punishment. At common law, for example, principals in the second degree could not be tried until the principal in the first degree had been tried and convicted and accessories before or after the fact could only be tried in the states where their actions took place.

MODERN CLASSIFICATIONS

Every jurisdiction has abandoned the common law classification and instead uses a simpler classification scheme. States distinguish between two types of parties to the crime: accomplices and accessories.

ACCOMPLICES: AIDERS AND ABETTORS

Federal law states that, "whoever commits an offense against the United States or aids, abets, counsel, commands, induces, or procures its commission, is punishable as a principal." (18 U.S.C.A. §2 (a).) Individuals who at common law were classified as principals in the first degree, principals in the second degree, or accessories before the fact are now called "accomplices." Accomplices are treated as if they were the primary actor. They are held to the same level of liability as the primary perpetrator. The law presumes that the individuals who assist in committing a crime implicitly consent to be bound by the conduct of the principal in the first degree. Individuals who were accessories after the fact at common law are referred to as simply "accessories" and are now charged with separate minor offenses such as hindering prosecution or obstruction of justice.

Actus Reus: Aiding and Abetting

Statutes and judicial decisions describe the *actus reus* of accomplice liability using many terms: aid, abet, encourage, and command. Whatever called, the *actus reus* is satisfied by one who gives even a relatively insignificant amount of aid or encouragement. The state must prove that the accomplice assisted in the commission of a crime, but that assistance does not have to be crucial to the outcome of the crime. That said, under the "mere presence rule" being present and watching the crime is not sufficient to satisfy the *actus reus* requirement. Mere presence is ambiguous; it doesn't necessarily support an inference that the person encourages or wishes to aid the criminal. Even when a person flees with the principal, it does not necessarily mean that they are accomplices. *United States v. Bailey*, 416 F.2d 1110 (D.C. Cir. 1969). The one exception to the general rule that people will not be found liable as accomplices if they are present and do nothing is when the person had a duty to intervene. In *State v. Walden*, 293 S.E. 2d 780 (1982), for example, a mother was convicted of aiding and abetting an assault with a deadly weapon when she failed to intervene to prevent an acquaintance from brutally beating her son.

Mens Rea: Aiding and Abetting

To convict a person as an accomplice requires the state to prove that the defendant assisted and intended to assist the commission of a crime. States differ on whether the accomplice needs to simply intend to assist the primary party or whether the accomplice needs to intend that the primary party commit the offense charged. Also, some states require the government to prove purposeful or intentional aiding and assisting, but others have held that knowingly aiding and assisting is enough.

> An accomplice, regardless of whether a "purposive" or "knowledge" standard is employed, is subject to the natural and probable consequences doctrine. This provides that a person encouraging or facilitating the commission of a crime will be liable as an accomplice for the crime he or she aided and abetted as well as for crimes that are the natural and probable outcome of the criminal conduct.[254]

A few courts have even imposed accomplice liability on individuals for acting in a reckless or negligent fashion. For example, in one case, Foster believed Middleton was the man who had recently raped and robbed his girlfriend. Accordingly, he hit him with his fist and a blunt instrument and knocked him to the ground. Foster then handed a knife to his friend, Cannon, and told him to guard Middleton until he could get back and confirm that Middleton was, indeed, her attacker. During his absence, Cannon fatally stabbed Middleton. The state successfully prosecuted Foster as an accessory for criminally negligent homicide. [255]

ACCESSORY AFTER THE FACT

At common law individuals could be convicted as an accessory after the fact only when they concealed or assisted an individual whom he or she knew had committed a felony for the purpose of hindering the perpetrator's arrest, prosecution or conviction. One interesting facet of common law held that a wife could not be held liable as an accessory the fact after her husband's acts because it was expected that she would assist her husband. Other states have also, at times, held that parents could not be held liable as accessories after the fact for the crimes of their children. (See, e.g., *State v. Ulvinen*, 313 NW 2d 425 (Minn. 1981).)

---

[254] Lippman, *Criminal Law, supra* at 162.
[255] *State v. Foster*, 202 Conn. 520, 522 A.2d. 277 (1987).

The modern view is that accessories after the fact get involved after the completion of the crime, and they should not be treated as harshly as the perpetrator of the crime or accomplices. Accessories are now prosecuted for "hindering prosecution" and are punished for frustrating the arrest, prosecution, or conviction of others who have committed felonies or misdemeanors. A spouse no longer is immune from prosecution in most states for accessory liability. Most states follow the Model Penal Code which provides:

MPC §242.3 Hindering Apprehension or Prosecution

A person commits an offense if, with purpose to hinder the apprehension, prosecution, conviction or punishment of another for crime, he:

- harbors or conceals the other
- provides or aides in providing a weapon, transportation, disguise or other means of avoiding apprehension or effecting escape; or
- conceals or destroys evidence of the crime, or tampers with a witness, informant, document or other source of information, regardless of its admissibility in evidence; or
- warns the others of impending discovery or apprehension.
- volunteers false information to a law enforcement officer.

VICARIOUS LIABILITY

Accomplice liability involves imposing criminal responsibility based upon a person's intentionally aiding another to complete a crime. Vicarious liability, on the other hand, involves imposing criminal responsibility on one person for the acts of another. Vicarious liability runs counter to the core principle that individuals should be held responsible and liable for their own conduct. In vicarious liability, the defendant committed no voluntary act or omission and may have had no criminal intent (or even know that the other person was committing the crime). Instead, the law imputes the wrongful acts of one person to the other because of a special relationship. Because vicarious liabilities crimes are easily susceptible to constitutional challenges on due process grounds, courts are reluctant to find that a statute imposes vicarious liability unless there is clear statutory intent. Connecticut, Louisiana, Oregon, and Wyoming have found these vicarious liability statutes to be unconstitutional.

The most common form of vicarious liability involves holding an employer liable for the acts of an employee. The justification for allowing vicarious liability in employee/employer situations is to encourage employers to control and monitor employees to ensure that the public is protected from potential dangers. For example, in *U.S. v. Dotterweich,* 320 U.S. 277 (1943), the Court held that corporations, along with corporate executives and employees, could be held liable under the Food and Drug Act when the company introduced adulterated or misbranded drugs into interstate commerce. Corporations may be held liable under criminal statutes under the doctrine of *respondeat superior.* Under this test/doctrine, employers may be held liable for the conduct of an employee who commits a crime if the act was committed within the scope of his or her employment and if the employee possessed the intent to benefit the company. *Respondeat superior* also extends vicarious liability to corporations for the acts of employees even when such acts are contrary to corporate policy.

The Model Penal Code adopts a different test for corporate vicarious liability. It holds that criminal liability may be imposed in those instances that the criminal conduct is authorized, requested, commanded, performed, or recklessly tolerated by the board of directors or by a high managerial official acting on behalf of the corporation within the scope of his or her employment.

Car owners have been found vicariously liable for parking violations when others have, with their permission, driven their cars and parked illegally. For example, courts have upheld parking statutes that hold the owner of the vehicle to be *prima facia* (on its face) responsible for paying parking tickets. Unless the owner can show he or she wasn't responsible, he is presumed liable for the ticket.

Finally, vicarious liability has been used to hold parents liable for crimes committed by their children. Cities and states have passed parental responsibility laws holding parents strictly and vicariously liable for the criminal acts of their children. Legislatures, presuming that parents have a duty to control their children, pass statutes geared at holding parents responsible for their failure to take reasonable steps to prevent their children from engaging in serious or persistent criminal behaviors. Somewhat different, but frequently confused with vicarious liability statutes are social host civil statutes which hold individuals liable for injuries caused by others (generally minors) who have consumed alcohol at the adult's home. The point of social host laws is to hold adults responsible for their act of allowing (or failure to prevent) their homes to be used as a venue for under-age drinking. There are similarly criminal statutes which penalize providing alcohol to minors or providing a venue to minors; these statutes aren't vicarious liability statutes because they do not impute punishment for the actions of another but rather punishing the adult for their part in making alcohol available or knowingly allowing it to be consumed.

WRAP UP

Criminal statutes specify elements of a crime that the prosecution must prove beyond a reasonable doubt in order to convict a defendant of a crime. Some statutes include only the elements of *actus reus* (a voluntary act, voluntary commission to act where there is a legal duty to act, or possession), the *mens rea,* any attendant circumstances, and punishments. Other criminal statutes also specify a particular harm and require the state prove that defendant caused the harm. Statutes are generally silent on the other elements of a crime: legality and concurrence. The legality element is met when a law is validly enacted and puts people on notice that certain behavior is illegal. Laws are presumed to be valid, and state generally does not have to begin each case by proving that proper procedure was followed in the enactment of the law. Although not generally specified in statute, the state must also prove the concurrence element--that the criminal intent triggered the criminal act.

In order to prevent future harm, state and federal governments have enacted statutes that criminalize attempts to commit crimes, solicitations to commit crimes, and conspiracies to commit crimes. With each of the inchoate crimes, the state must prove that the defendant intended to commit some other crime--the highest level of criminal intent. State laws vary in the approaches and tests of whether the defendant has taken enough steps to be charged with attempt, but all agree that mere preparation does not constitute an attempt. Conspiracies involve an agreement between the parties to commit some crime; agreements require a meeting of minds. Solicitations do not even require an agreement, and a defendant is guilty of solicitation by simply asking another to commit a crime. Defendants may raise defenses when charged with attempt (impossibility and abandonment/renunciation), conspiracy (renunciation) and solicitation (renunciation).

Strict liability crimes are ones where the government does not have to prove criminal intent. Courts are disinclined to find in favor of strict liability statutes unless there is clear indication that the legislature intended to create strict liability. The courts will examine legislative history, the seriousness of crime, whether the crime is *male in se* or *mala prohibitum,* and the seriousness of the punishment in deciding whether the state should be relieved of its obligation to prove criminal intent of the defendant.

People who commit crimes frequently do so with assistance. Common law recognized four parties to a crime: principal in the first degree, principal in the second degree, accessory before the fact, and accessory after the fact. Many complicated legal rules developed to offset the harsh common law treatment of most crimes as capital offenses. The modern trend has been to recognize accomplices--people who render assistance before and during the crime--and accessories after the fact. Accomplices as equally liable as the main perpetrator--"the hand of one is the hand of them all." Under the modern trend, hindering prosecution or obstructing justice after the crime are punished to a lesser extent.

Vicarious liability statutes violate our belief in individual responsibility. Only people who do something wrong should be blamed for the crime, but vicarious liability imputes (transfers) both the criminal intent and the criminal act of one person (for example an employee or child) to another (for example to the employer or parent). Courts generally invalidate these statutes.

SOME THINGS TO THINK ABOUT OR EXPLORE

➤ Explore the criminal code in. your state. What are the punishments set out in the statutory scheme? Does your state follow the MPC approach?

➤ Think about the laws concerning accomplice liability in your state; can you think of a case where it would not be "fair" to hold an accomplice to the same degree of culpability as the primary actor?

➤ Explore your state's laws on attempt, conspiracy, and solicitation liability.

➤ Consider the two-tiered approach to causation (requiring a finding of actual/but for causation, then a finding of proximate causation). Does "foreseeability" seem to be the appropriate benchmark for whether it is "fair" to hold a person responsible for the harm? Should the courts adopt some sort of per se rule about when intervening causes cut off liability, or is it appropriate to leave that determination to the fact-finder/jury?

➤ Explore your state's substantive criminal codes. For example, look at how murder and manslaughter are defined; look at crimes against public order (riot, rout, disorderly conduct, for example); examine rape and sexual assault laws; explore the robbery, burglary, and any arson statutes (or any type of crime that intrigues you).

➤ If you were a lawmaker in your state, would you enact vicarious liability crimes?

TERMINOLOGY

- abandonment
- accessory after the fact
- accessory before the fact
- accomplice
- actual cause
- actual possession
- *actus reus* (element)
- aiding and abetting
- attempt
- attendant circumstances
- American Bystander Rule
- but-for causation
- cause in fact
- chain conspiracy
- concurrence requirement
- conspiracy
- constructive possession
- *corpus delecti*
- elements of a crime
- factual impossibility
- general part of the criminal code
- Good Samaritan Rule
- harm
- knowing possession

- inchoate offense
- intervening cause
- legal cause
- legal impossibility
- legality (element)
- *mens rea* (element)
- mere possession
- mere presence rule
- omission to act
- parental responsibility statutes
- *Pinkerton* rule
- Plurality requirement
- possession
- *prima facia*
- principle in the first degree
- principle in the second degree
- proximate cause
- punishment element
- solicitation
- special part of the criminal code
- status
- strict liability
- substantive law
- transferred intent

Chapter Six: Defenses to Criminal Liability

OVERVIEW AND LEARNING OBJECTIVES

This chapter discusses the defenses that allow the defendant to escape conviction even though the prosecution could prove all the elements of the crimes. Defenses can be described as: perfect or imperfect defenses; negative or affirmative defenses; and excuses, justifications, or procedural defenses. After reading this chapter, you should be able to answer the following questions:

> ➤ What are the differences between perfect, imperfect, affirmative, and negative defenses?
> ➤ How do justifications differ from excuses?
> ➤ What must the defendant show to successfully raise an affirmative defense?
> ➤ What must the defendant show to successfully raise the following justification defenses: self-defense, defense of others, defense of habitation, defense of property, consent, and necessity?
> ➤ How do current "stand your ground laws" change the doctrine of retreat and the "castle exception" rules from common law?
> ➤ What must the defendant show to successfully raise the following excuse defenses: insanity, diminished capacity, age, mistake, intoxication, and duress?
> ➤ How does the necessity defense differ from the claim of duress?
> ➤ What are syndrome defenses, how do defendants raise these defenses, and how successful are they?
> ➤ What are procedural defenses and what must the defendant show to successfully claim entrapment, a speedy trial violation, double jeopardy, or immunity?
> ➤ How does the subjective test of entrapment differ from the objective test of entrapment?
> ➤ How do statutes of limitations work? How do statutes of limitation differ from speedy trial protections?

PERFECT AND IMPERFECT DEFENSES

A perfect defense is one that completely exonerates the defendant. If the defendant is successful in raising this defense (meaning the jury believes him or her), the jury should find the defendant not guilty. An imperfect defense is one that reduces the defendant's liability to that of a lesser crime. If the jury believes the defendant, it should find the defendant guilty of a lesser charge.

NEGATIVE AND AFFIRMATIVE DEFENSES

Sometimes the government is unable to prove all the elements of the crime charged. When this happens, the defendant may raise a negative defense claim. The defendant doesn't have to prove anything; instead, he or she just argues that something is missing in the state's case and therefore the jury should find him or her not guilty. For example, when charging a defendant with theft, the state must prove that the defendant intentionally took the property of another. If the jury finds that the defendant didn't intend to take the property, or took property that that was rightfully his or hers, then it should find the defendant not guilty. Negative defenses are just claims that there are "proof problems" with the state's case. The defendant's claim that the state failed to prove its case does not depend on whether the defendant has put on any evidence or not.

An affirmative defense, on the other hand, requires the defendant to put on evidence that will persuade the jury that he or she should either be completely exonerated (for a perfect defense) or be convicted only of a lesser crime (for an imperfect defense). The defendant can meet this requirement by calling witnesses to testify or by introducing physical evidence. Because of the presumption of innocence, the burden of proof[256] cannot switch completely to the defendant, however. The state ultimately bears the burden of proving defendant's guilt by putting on enough evidence that defendant has committed the crime by proving each and every material element of the crime. And it must convince the jury of this guilt beyond a reasonable doubt. But when the defendant raises an affirmative defense, the burden of production or persuasion switches, at least in part and temporarily, to the defendant. The defendant's burden is limited, however, to proving the elements the defense he or she asserts. Affirmative defenses are the focus of this chapter.

Note the interplay of negative defenses and affirmative defenses. Even if a defendant is unsuccessful in raising an affirmative defense, the jury could nevertheless find him or her not guilty based upon the state's failure to prove some other material element of the crime.

JUSTIFICATIONS

Sometimes doing the right thing results in harm. Society recognizes the utility of doing some acts in certain circumstances that unfortunately result in harm. In those situations, the defendant can raise a justification defense. Justification defenses allow criminal acts to go unpunished because they preserve an important social value or because the resulting harm is outweighed by the benefit to society. For example, if a surgeon cuts someone with a knife to remove a cancerous growth, the act is a beneficial one even though it results in pain and a scar. In raising a justification defense, the defendant admits he did a wrongful act (such as taking someone's life), but argues that the act was the right thing to do under the circumstances. At times, the state's view differs from the defendant's view of whether the act was, in fact, the right thing to do. In those cases, the state files charges to which the defendant raises a justification defense.

Justifications are affirmative defenses. The defendant must produce some evidence in support of these defenses. In most cases, the defendant must also convince the jury that it was more likely than not (a preponderance of the evidence standard) that his or her conduct was justified. For example, the defendant may claim that he or she acted in self-defense and at trial would need to call witnesses or introduce physical evidence that supports the claim of self-defense and make jurors believe that it was more likely that his actions were done in self-defense than his actions were not done in self-defense. State laws vary about how convinced the jury must be (called the standard of proof) or when the burden of putting on evidence switches to the defendant, but all states generally require the defendant to carry at least some of the burden of proof in raising justification defenses.

EXECUTION OF PUBLIC DUTIES

Police officers, soldiers and public executioners often have to use physical force in the course of their jobs. Arrests involve physical force. Even in the least confrontational of arrests, police officers must use a certain amount of force to place the defendant in handcuffs. During war, some soldiers must kill or wound the enemy in a premeditated fashion. In order to carry out a death sentence in states that use the death penalty, some person or persons deliberately and

---

[256] Recall that the burden of proof is made up of the burden of production (the requirement that evidence be presented) and the burden of persuasion (the requirement that the fact-finder be convinced to some degree of certainty about the existence of a fact.)

intentionally act to take the life of the condemned. All of these situations involve individuals who harm or kill others, yet none of these individuals are routinely charged with crimes. Even if they were charged, they would generally escape conviction by raising the execution of public duties defense. Prosecutors rarely spend resources prosecuting cases that are easily defensible so we don't often hear about this defense being raised.

Recent charges of police use of excessive force in arresting individuals have spotlighted the limits on permissible use of force in execution of one's duties. When police use too much force in arresting a suspect or soldiers act outside the rules of war, the execution of public duties defense may not be successful. The Model Penal Code §3.07 (1) (a) provides that "The use of force upon or toward the person of another is justifiable when the actor is making or assisting in making an arrest and the actor believes that such force is immediately necessary to effect a lawful arrest." §3.07 (2) limits police use of deadly force against fleeing felons to circumstances in which the felon presents substantial risk of death or serious bodily harm and only when the use of force presents no substantial risk of injury to innocent persons. The MPC is far more restrictive than the common law that allowed the use of deadly force against any fleeing felony suspect. Today, police officers who use excessive force in arresting a suspect may be subject to both civil and criminal liability.

RESISTING ARREST

English common law recognized the right to resist an unlawful arrest by reasonable force except in cases in which the defendant was charged with murder of the officer.[257] The U.S. Supreme Court recognized that the right to resist unlawful arrest had been incorporated into the common law of the United States. In 1963, 45 states still recognized the right of an individual to resist an unlawful arrest with force since imprisonment, even for brief periods, subjected individuals to a "death trap characterized by disease, hunger and violence."[258] As jail conditions improved, approval of the defense dwindled. Currently, only 12 states allow individuals to

---

[257] At common law, any citizen could arrest a felon, and citizens could also use deadly force where needed to stop a fleeing felon. When that force resulted in the death of the felon, the homicide was nevertheless considered justified (that is, not criminal). The citizen took his chances as to the accuracy of his judgment, however. If it turned out that the person killed was not engaged in committing a felony, then his use of deadly force (and any resulting homicide) was not justified -- even when it was reasonable to believe that the person being arrested had committed a felony. With the development of the Metropolitan Police Force in the nineteenth century, the law governing citizen's arrest gradually changed, restricting the general authority of citizens to arrest and use deadly force. *See*, Kerper, *supra* at 133.

[258] Arnold Lowey observed,

- Incarcerated individuals are no longer subjected to harsh, inhuman, and disease-ridden prison conditions that result in illness and death.
- An arrest does not necessarily lead to a lengthy period of incarceration. Individuals have access to bail and are represented by hired or appointed attorneys at virtually every stage of the criminal justice process.
- The complexity of the law often makes it difficult to determine whether an arrest is illegal. An officer might, in good faith, engage in what is later determined to be an illegal search, discover drugs, and arrest a suspect. The legality of the search and resulting arrest may not be apparent until tan appeals court decides the issue.
- The development of sophisticated weaponry means that confrontations between the police and citizens are likely to rapidly escalate and result in severe harm and injury to citizens and to the police.
- Individuals have access to a sophisticated process of criminal appeal and may bring civil actions for damages.
- The common law rule promotes an unacceptable degree of social conflict and undermines the rule of law.

Criminal law in a Nutshell, 82-83 (4th ed. 2003).

forcefully resist an unlawful arrest by a law enforcement officer. In other states, a person who is unaware that the aggressor is a police officer may possibly be successful in raising this defense. Also, a person may use force to resist arrest when faced with an officer's use of excessive force. (Generally, the defense raised under those circumstances is self-defense.)

SELF-DEFENSE

State laws governing the use of force in self-defense vary. The general rule concerning self-defense is that a person may use reasonable force, including deadly force, to defend against the unlawful use of imminent force. The law traditionally looked at three factors in determining whether the defendant's acts were justified by self-defense: (1) whether defender's belief that he had to use force to save himself was reasonable, (2) whether the defender had an opportunity to retreat in safety, and (3) whether the defender was the initial aggressor in the circumstances that lead to the use of deadly force. Scheb notes that the use of deadly force also requires that the person using such force is in a place where he or she has a right to be, acts without fault, and acts in reasonable fear or apprehension of death or great bodily harm.[259]

The defense applies only when the defendant resists unlawful force. In general, this means that the aggressor must be attempting to commit a crime or a tort against the defendant. If the aggressor is entitled to act, then the defense may not be raised. If the aggressor is entitled to use some force but exceeds the force he or she is allowed to use, then the defendant may resist by also using force. If the defendant makes a reasonable mistake about whether the force being used against him is legal or not, he will nonetheless be protected by the defense.[260]

When acting in self-defense the defendant may use only the degree of force necessary to repel the unlawful force; this requirement is called the proportionate force requirement. The defense allows the use of deadly force, when necessary, but "[a] minor attack not dangerous to life or limb should not be met with an annihilating response."[261] For example, if Bob came at Tom with a plastic knife, Tom could only use non-deadly force to protect himself. People may use non-deadly force to resist virtually any kind of unlawful force, and the common law retreat rule (discussed below) is not applicable when a defender only uses non-deadly force. Deadly force is usually defined as force that is intended or likely to cause death or serious bodily harm. The actual amount of harm that occurs is irrelevant to determining whether a particular force qualifies as deadly force. If defendant used a gun and points it at his assailant and shoots, this is deadly force – even though he missed or inflicted merely a flesh wound. If, on the other hand, the defender used force that would not necessarily cause death or serious bodily injury, but in this instance it did, the force will be treated as non-deadly even if death or serious bodily harm results.

Because one may use self-defense only to repel against an unlawful imminent use of force being used against him or her, an "initial aggressor" cannot generally raise the defense. The first exception to this rule is when the defendant provoked the exchange but did not use force or only used non-deadly force which was then met by deadly force from the other. In that case, the defendant is allowed to use force, including deadly force, to repel the disproportionate attack. The second exception is when the defendant, who was the initial aggressor, retreats and withdraws from the conflict and is then faced with unlawful force by the other party who has initiated a second conflict.

---

[259] Scheb, *supra* at 433.
[260] Emanuel, *supra* at 110.
[261] *Id.*

When the defendant is charged with homicide and raises a claim of self-defense, the defendant, to be successful, must show that he or she had a reasonable belief of unlawful harm being used, that the force used was in response to imminent harm, and that the deadly force used was proportionate to the force used by the murder victim. In some states, the defendant must also show that he or she was not required to, or was unable to, safely retreat.

In determining whether a defender's belief as to the need for deadly force was reasonable, a fact-finder (usually the jury) must consider a variety of factors. These include the comparative size of the defender and the attacker, whether the attacker was armed, whether the attacker had a reputation as a vicious fighter etc. The fact-finder must also recognize that the defender is under extreme emotional stress in responding to an attack. He cannot be expected to draw fine lines as to the degree of force needed to repel a threat of serious bodily harm. As Justice Holmes once noted, "detached reflection cannot be demanded in the presence of an uplifted knife." The law does, however, place certain limits on what can be deemed reasonable. For example, the defender's belief must have related to immediate harm. One cannot respond with . . . force presently because he believes his assailant intends to ambush him several hours from now. The law also requires that the defender be in reasonable fear of possible death or serious bodily injury [to use deadly force.] If he fears no more than minor injuries, he cannot use deadly force. One who feels that the attacker will do no more than knock him to the ground cannot respond with deadly force simply because he does not want to suffer any kind of humiliation or injury. On the other hand, if he reasonably fears that the attacker will break his bones or disfigure him, this is sufficient without actually fearing death. Deadly force (i.e., force readily capable of causing death) can be used to respond to a serious bodily injury as well as loss of life.

The second factor in evaluating a self-defense claim--the opportunity to retreat in safety--is given somewhat different treatment in different states. In some jurisdictions, there is no special rule on retreat. On the one hand, the courts have said that there is no absolute duty to escape danger by retreating; the law will not require a non-aggressor to act in a humiliating or cowardly way. On the other hand, the judge or jury is not barred from considering the possibility of retreat as one of the many factors examined in determining the reasonableness of the defender's decision to use deadly force. Thus, under this approach, the significance of opportunity to retreat will vary with the facts of the particular case and the weight of the other circumstances supporting the reasonable use of deadly force, but the failure to retreat will not, by itself, automatically negate a claim of self-defense. Moreover, the possibility of retreat is given no weight whatsoever unless the retreat clearly could be accomplished with complete safety. Thus, retreat rarely is a factor when the attacker threatens the defender with a weapon such as a gun. No matter how fast the defender can flee, he is unlikely to be able to escape from such a threat with complete safety.

If the defender in a particular case originally was an aggressor — the initiator of the fight that resulted in the homicide — then a duty of withdrawal may make the availability of self-defense even more complex. To be an aggressor, a person ordinarily must deliver the first blow or directly challenge his opponent to fight. Simply using foul language or otherwise starting a verbal dispute is not sufficient. If the aggressor initiates the dispute with deadly force, then he ordinarily cannot reclaim a right of self-defense unless he effectively withdraws from his original position as an aggressor. In some jurisdictions, he can do this only by getting across to his opponent the message that he no longer desires to fight. In others, a reasonable attempt to communicate such a message is sufficient even if the other party refuses to recognize it. Once withdrawal is achieved, if the other party persists in the battle, the former aggressor now has a restored right of self-defense. If the aggressor began the battle using non-deadly force, then he may not have to communicate his withdrawal although he may bear some special burdens in claiming self-defense. Since he limited his aggression to non-deadly force, his opponent should not have escalated to the use of deadly force. Both he and his opponent are at fault, and a completed withdrawal therefore may not be needed to restore the right of self-defense. However, the defender still has a special responsibility as the person who started it all, and he therefore may be required to retreat (when physically possible) even in a state that ordinarily does not require retreat. Moreover, in the case of the aggressor, that duty to retreat may include retreat from the home.[262]

The trend has been for states to reject the common law doctrine requiring persons to retreat before meeting force with force. Instead, laws now permit individuals to stand their ground and use any force reasonably necessary to prevent harm. Many courts adopted the retreat rule but recognize a "castle exception" to the rule. The castle exception allows individuals to stand their ground (and not retreat) when they are faced with imminent, unlawful force in their homes--even when they could retreat safely. Domestic assault scenarios where both parties are "at home" and neither party has a duty to retreat raise interesting questions for the courts. A few courts have held that the castle exception is inapplicable in domestic violence situations where the assailant and defendant were both residents of the dwelling. However, the majority position (in states with a retreat rule) is to require retreat even in those cases.

NEW STAND YOUR GROUND LAWS

Although, Arizona, Colorado, and Texas had previously enacted, "Make My Day" statutes allowing the use of deadly force in defense of habitation, in 2005, Florida enacted a new law which significantly expanded the right of self-defense for individuals.[263] This law allows individuals to use deadly force in public places without any duty to retreat. The difference between the Florida "stand your ground" statute and the common law "castle exception" is that

---

[262] Kerper, *supra* at 135.
[263] Florida Statutes § 776.013
(1) A person is presumed to have held a reasonable fear of imminent peril of death or great bodily harm to himself or herself or another when using defensive force that is intended tor likely to cause death or great bodily harm to another if
(a) The person against whom the defensive force was used was in the process of unlawfully and forcefully entering, or had unlawfully and forcibly entered, a dwelling, residence or occupied vehicle, or if that person had removed or was attempting to remove another against the person's will from the dwelling, residence, or occupied vehicle: and
(b) the person who uses defensive force knew or had reason to believe than an unlawful forcible entry or unlawful and forcible act was occurring or had occurred.
. . .
(3) A person who is not engaged in an unlawful activity and who is attacked in any other place where he or she has a right to be has no duty to retreat and has the right to stand his or her ground and meet force with force, including deadly force if he or she reasonably believes it is necessary to do so to prevent death or great bodily harm to himself or herself or another or to prevent the commission of a forcible felony.
(4) A person who unlawfully and by force enters or attempts to enter a person's dwelling, residence, or occupied vehicle is presumed to be doing so with the intent to commit an unlawful act involving force or violence.

the Florida law does away with the need to retreat not just in one's home but also in public. [264] Significantly, and problematically, Florida's law states that when a person claims to have used force in self-defense, the police may not arrest, detain, or initiate prosecution against them. Additionally, the person against whom they used force is prohibited from suing them civilly. Critics of the new law dubbed it the "shoot first" law and predicted it would lead to preemptive shootings. This law has been controversial and presents difficulty for law enforcement officers. Nevertheless, by 2009 twenty-five states had adopted some form of "stand your ground" laws. By 2020, it appears that 34 states have some form of stand your ground laws.[265] Some research suggests that these laws do nothing to deter violent crime and may, in fact, contribute to a higher homicide rate.[266]

BATTERED WOMAN'S SYNDROME AND SELF-DEFENSE

Self-defense claims frequently arise in cases where a woman kills her partner or spouse after ongoing battering and abuse. Increasingly, same-sex partners have been raising this defense. When relationships involve constant, ongoing abuse with high levels of violence, victims are in "present danger" but may not necessarily be in imminent danger. Because the offender may strike out at any time, the victim lives in constant fear of unlawful harm. Courts generally apply the same rules of self-defense requiring proof of imminent harm in these situations, but they have increasingly attempted to allow defendants a fair chance to assert self-defense claims by presenting evidence on battered woman's syndrome. Still, even almost forty years since the first use of the battered woman syndrome defense, only two states have relaxed the requirement that the threat must be imminent and not just ever-present. Although most courts now admit expert testimony concerning battered woman syndrome, they limit the testimony to showing why the defendant, as the victim of ongoing assaults, simply did not leave the abuser rather than resort to using violence. The court may allow the syndrome evidence to explain why the defendant had a genuine and reasonable fear of imminent danger. But courts have not allowed evidence of ongoing violence to substitute for proof that the defendant was faced with an attack that required an immediate use of force to repel. Emanuel notes, "In these clearly non-confrontational

---

[264] One case that received a lot of media attention involved the February 2012 shooting of Trayvon Martin by George Zimmerman in Sanford, Florida. The Zimmerman case increased racial tensions and ignited a debate about these laws. There were no witnesses to what happened, but when police arrived, they found Martin dead from a single shot to the chest at close range. Zimmerman told police he fired in self-defense after Martin attacked him. After questioning Zimmerman for five hours, police released him without charging him.

Zimmerman was later charged with second-degree murder in April 2012, and although the 2005 Florida law would have provided Zimmerman immunity from prosecution if he could show, to a preponderance of the evidence, that he thought he would be killed or seriously injured by Martin, Zimmerman did not rely on Florida 2005 laws. Instead, he relied on general principles of self-defense. He elected to be tried by a jury in his trial in June 2013. The jury began deliberating on July 12th, 2013 and found Zimmerman not guilty after only one day.

About three weeks after the shooting, Florida Governor Rick Scott created a task force to review Florida's laws concerning justifiable use of force. Public hearings followed, and the task force ultimately suggested the repeal of the 2005 statute, increased training and public education on use of force, but it rejected a recommendation by County State Attorney to limit the provision providing prosecutorial immunity. The Florida legislature introduced bills to repeal the stand your ground laws, but these died without hearings.
[265] See, https://www.rand.org/research/gun-policy/analysis/stand-your-ground.html.
[266] See, https://www.rand.org/blog/2019/09/stand-your-ground-laws-increase-violence.html.

situations, the defendant generally loses."[267] Typically, trial judges either do not give the jury a self-defense instruction or they give one that makes it clear that the defense only applied if physical danger was imminent. These trial courts' refusals to give instructions are rarely reversed by the appellate courts.[268]

DEFENSE OF OTHERS

At common law a person had the right to use reasonable force to either prevent the commission of a felony or to protect members of his or her household. Many jurisdictions have codified this "defense of others" defense.

States have adopted one of two approaches to this defense: the reasonable perception approach or the alter ego approach. The reasonable perception approach allows a person to use force to defend another from what he or she reasonably believes is the unlawful and imminent use of force by a third person. Under this approach, the defendant should be found not guilty if the defendant erroneously, but reasonably, believed that the person they were protecting was justified in using force. The alter ego approach places the defender in the shoes of the person they are seeking to protect. Under this approach, the defendant should be found not guilty only if the person being aided or protected could lawfully use force to defend him or herself — the defendant's reasonable belief that the other is in danger is not sufficient. If the defender is wrong in believing the person being defended was entitled to use force, there is no defense.

An example highlights how these approaches result in different verdicts. Assume that Sally encounters her friend Sam in a standoff against Joe on the main square in front of city hall. She hears Joe shouting threats and sees him pull out a knife and quickly plunge toward Sam. Sally pulls her revolver out of her purse and shoots Joe dead, believing he was using deadly, imminent force against Sam. Unbeknownst to Sally, Sam and Joe were enacting a theatrical performance and Sam could not lawfully use force to repel Joe's fake attack. In a state that follows the alter-ego approach Sally will not prevail because Sam could not lawfully use deadly force against Joe. In a state that follows the reasonable perception approach, Sally should prevail because she reasonably believed Sam needed to be protected and reasonably believed Sam could lawfully have use deadly force to protect himself from Joe.

Some states had limited the defendant's right to use deadly force to defend another to those cases where the defendant came to the defense of a person with whom he or she had a special protective relationship (e.g., spouse, child, relative, employee). The trend has been to permit the use of deadly force to protect any other person. As with self-defense, the degree of force must be proportional--a person defending the other can use deadly force only when he reasonably believes the other is in immediate danger of serious bodily harm. A person is not justified in using more force than is necessary to repel the unlawful force.

---

[267] According to the court in *Jahnke v. State*, 682 P.S. 991 (Wyo. 1984),

> It is difficult enough to justify capital punishment as an appropriate response of society to criminal acts even after the circumstances have been carefully evaluated by a number of people. To permit capital punishment to be imposed upon the subjective conclusion of the individual that prior acts and conduct of the deceased justify the killing would amount to a leap into the abyss of anarchy.

[268] In *North Carolina v. Norman* (1989) the defendant shot and killed her husband while he was asleep. She showed at trial that he had tormented, physically abused, and humiliated her for years. The Court held that she was not entitled to a self-defense instruction.

> The imminence requirement ensures that deadly force will be used only where it is necessary as a last resort in the exercise of the of the inherent right of self-preservation. . . The evidence in this case did not tend to show that the defendant reasonably believed that she was confronted by a threat of imminent death or great bodily harm. ... The defendant was not faced with an instantaneous choice between killing her husband or being killed or seriously injured.

DEFENSE OF PROPERTY AND HABITATION

The general rule concerning defense of property is that a person may use force, but not deadly force, to protect his or her property. The rules concerning the defense of habitation (one's home) are less clear.

> Deadly force cannot be used against a mere trespasser. Neither may it be used against a thief. If a thief steals a car, the owner cannot use deadly force to stop him even if there is no other way to gain the immediate return of his property. Simply put, the law values the protection of life, including that of a thief, over the protection of property. There are, however, various other avenues through which property can be indirectly protected with the use of deadly force. Thus, . . . the law authorizes the use of deadly force to prevent some dangerous felonies, including several involving the taking of property.[269]

Today, states vary in how much force they allow a person to use in defending his or her home. The common law placed great emphasis on the security of a person's dwelling and permitted the use of deadly force against an intruder. The castle doctrine allowed the inhabitant to use all the force necessary to repel any invasion of the home when it appeared that people were in danger, but did not justify the use of deadly force to repel a mere trespass. Some courts permit the use of deadly force to prevent a forcible entry into the habitation in circumstances where the occupant is threatened, or reasonably fears death or great bodily harm to self or other occupants, or reasonably believes the assailant intends to commit a felony. But many states treat the home like property and hold that deadly force may not be used to defend it. When the occupants feel threatened, then the general rules of self-defense apply, and deadly force may be justified.

CONSENT

Unless lack of consent is a material element of the crime (for example, in the case of rape), the fact that a victim may have consented to the act or harm does not provide a defense. Recall that crimes are harms against society and not specific individuals. Thus, it makes sense that consent by the specific individual does not mean that the state has no interest in denouncing and deterring certain conduct. Still, there may be limited circumstances in which the defendant may successfully raise consent as an affirmative defense. In these cases, the defendant must show that the person giving consent is legally competent and voluntarily gives consent.

Three situations where the law recognizes consent as a defense to criminal conduct include:

- Incidental contact. Acts that do not cause serious injury or harm and customarily are not subject to criminal prosecution and punishment. For example, being bumped or pushed on a crowded bus.
- Sporting events. Ordinary physical contact or blows that are a part of sports such as football, boxing, wrestling. The defense of consent does not extend to all harms caused during the sport, however. For example, although it is appropriate to punch another in boxing, it is not appropriate to tackle the opponent—or bite off the opponent's ear.
- Socially beneficial activity. Individuals often benefit from activities such as medical procedures and surgery.

---

[269] Kerper, *supra* at 132.

CHOICE OF EVILS (NECESSITY)

Sometimes breaking the law is necessary or, at least, the better option. In those situations, the defendant may raise the justification known as either "necessity" or "choice of evils." Necessity defenses are found either in state statutes or state common law. The central elements of the necessity defense are: the defendant was faced with immediate or imminent harm; the defendant was not substantially at fault in creating the emergency; the harm created by defendant's criminal act is less than the harm he or she confronted; the defendant had no legal alternatives to violating the law; and the legislature had not already identified and chosen the lesser evil.

The test of necessity (whether the choice was the right one) is an objective test, and it is up to the court, not the defendant, to make the final determination on whether the harm sought to be avoided was greater than that committed by the defendant's criminal act. Most courts refuse to allow the necessity defense in intentional homicide cases, reasoning that one life cannot be weighed against another. Courts will examine the text or legislative history of a statute in order to determine whether the legislature disallows the necessity defense and will not give a jury instruction on the defense of necessity when it is clear that the legislature has already weighed the evils. For example, if the legislature had debated whether to enact a medicinal marijuana statute, but chosen not to, then a defendant charged with possession of marijuana could not claim medical necessity when charged with possession.

Prisoners, threatened with assaults or homosexual rape by other prisoners or guards have raised the necessity defense when charged with escape. The necessity defense may be successful in these cases, but only if defendants are able to prove:

- They were faced with a specific threat of death, forcible sexual attack, or substantial bodily injury in the immediate future.
- They had no time to complain to the authorities or there exists a history of futile complaints.
- They had no time or opportunity to resort to the courts,
- They did not use force or violence toward prison personnel or other innocent persons during their escapes.
- They immediately reported to proper authorities.

Perhaps the most well-known and cited case of necessity is the English case of *Queen v. Dudley and Stephens*:

> The three crew members of the yacht, the Mignoenette, along with the seventeen-year-old cabin boy were forced to abandon ship when a wave smashed into the stern. The four managed to launch a thirteen-foot dinghy with only two tins of turnips to sustain them while they drifted sixteen hundred miles from shore. On the fourth day, they managed to catch a turtle that they lived on for a week; they quenched their thirst by drinking their own urine and, at times, by drinking seawater. On the nineteenth day, Captain Thomas Dudley murdered young Richard Parker with the agreement of Edwin Stephens and over the objection of Edmund Brooks. The three only survived by eating Parker's flesh and drinking his blood until rescued four days later. The English court rejected the defense of necessity and the proposition that the members of the crew were justified in taking

the life of Parker in order to survive. [T]he facts . . . are no legal justification of the homicide.[270]

Ultimately defendants received a pardon from the Queen after sixth-months of incarceration.

Although earlier cases of necessity presented choices demanded by "forces of nature," the law gradually changed, and most modern cases now arise in response to pressures exerted by social conditions and events. The Model Penal Code permits a "choice of evils" defense that is similar to necessity. MPC §3.02 Choice of Evils provides:

> (1) Conduct that the actor believes to be necessary to avoid a harm or evil to himself or another is justifiable, provided that:
> (a) the harm or evil sought to be avoided by such conduct is greater than that sought to be prevented by the law defining the offense charged; and
> (b) neither the Code nor other law defining the offense provides exceptions or defenses dealing with the specific situation involved; and
> (c) a legislative purpose to exclude the justification claimed does not otherwise plainly appear.
>
> (2) When the actor was reckless or negligent in bringing about the situation requiring a choice of harms or evil or in appraising the necessity for his conduct, the justification afforded by this Section is unavailable in a prosecution for any offense for which recklessness or negligence, as is the case may be, suffices to establish culpability.

Unlike the common law, the MPC choice of evils defense is also available where the source of the emergency is coercion by another person rather than an event. The MPC also does not rule out the this defense in intentional homicide cases.

Not everyone agrees that necessity should be a defense. Some argue that individuals should obey the law and should not be encouraged to violate legal rules. They note that society suffers when individuals make the wrong choice.

EXCUSES

Excuses are defenses to criminal behavior that focus on some characteristic of the defendant. With excuses, the defendant is essentially saying, "I did the crime, but I am not responsible because I was . . . insane (or too young, intoxicated, mistaken, or under duress)."

INSANITY

Inanity is a legal determination that, at the time of the crime, the individual had a mental disease or defect that warrants either a finding of not guilty, a finding of guilty but insane, or a finding of not guilty by reason of insanity. Insanity is not a term used by psychiatrists or psychologists who, instead, discuss mental diseases or disorders.

Mens Rea and Insanity

The interplay between *mens rea* and insanity is complex. Someone who is legally insane, may very well have the ability to form the mens rea required by the criminal statute. Conversely, a defendant who has a mental impairment not rising to the level of legal insanity may still not

---

[270] *Regina v. Dudley and Stephens*, (1884) 14 QBD 273 DC.

have the requisite *mens rea* required by the statute (and thus should be found not guilty). Kerper wrote,

> Whenever a certain state of mind is an element of the offense, a mental condition which would render the accused incapable of that state of mind will negate the presence of the necessary *mens rea*. This is true even though the defendant's mental condition is not so severe as to relieve him from general criminal responsibility. Thus, an unsoundness of mind which would not meet the test of legal insanity may nevertheless establish the absence of the *mens rea* for a particular crime. This possibility is especially significant for the crime of murder, where first degree murder requires the element of premeditation. Very often the kind of deliberate decision-making required for premeditation will not be possible due to a mental illness that falls short of establishing legal insanity. The mentally ill (but not legally insane) accused will not be liable for first degree murder, although he will still be liable for second degree murder, which requires a lesser *mens rea*.[271]

TESTS OF INSANITY

The law has always struggled to provide an acceptable definition of insanity or unsoundness of mind that relieves a defendant of criminal responsibility for a criminal act. States have developed and adopted several tests--or definitions--of insanity. Three main tests of insanity exist today, one test is still used only in one state,[272] and one eighteenth-century test has been abandoned.[273] Idaho, Kansas, Montana, and Utah have abolished the defense of insanity, a practice approved of by the Court in 2020.[274]

The M'Naghten Rule

In 1843 Daniel M'Naghten shot and killed Sir Robert Peel's secretary Edward Drummond.[275] M'Naghten suffered from a delusional psychosis and thought he was being persecuted by certain King's ministers (including Peel). In fact, M'Naghten believed he was shooting at Peel when he shot Drummond. M'Naghten was tried and acquitted of the offense when the jury found him not guilty by reason of insanity. Because Drummond and Peel were

---

[271] Kerper, *supra* at 117.

[272] The *Durham* test arose in the D.C Circuit (*Durham v. United States*, 214 F.2d 862 (1954)) and held that an accused is not criminally responsible if his or her unlawful act was the product of mental disease or defect. This test never gained support and is currently only used in New Hampshire. It is also referred to as the "product test." The test required psychiatrists to determine whether defendant's acts were the product of a mental disease or defect. It was criticized as giving too much deference to expert witnesses (the psychiatrists) and not enough to the jury.

[273] The "wild beast test" was developed by the English courts by the middle of the eighteenth century, the courts said, "a man . . . totally deprived of his understanding and memory, . . . and doth not know what he is doing, no more than an infant, than a brute, or a wild beast is never the object of punishment. (*Rex v. Arnold*, 16 Howell's State Trials 695 (Engl. 1724). Persons excused by this rule were the so called, "raving maniacs." Lesser states of mental illness were not deemed sufficient to excuse criminal responsibility. In the case of mental defect, the test was whether the person was so retarded as to be an idiot — one who could not county twenty pence, identify his parents, or know his age.

[274] In *Kahler v. Kansas*, ____ U.S. ____ (2020), the Court upheld a state's right to not provide a defense of insanity to criminal charges. Kahler, a Kansas death row inmate, argued that failure to allow him to raise an insanity defense violated his Eighth and Fourteenth Amendment rights. The Court disagreed. (See, https://www.americanbar.org/groups/committees/death_penalty_representation/project_press/2020/summer/us-supreme-court-sides-with-kansas/#:~:text=On%20March%2023%2C%202020%2C%20in%20Kahler%20v.&text=In%20its%20ruling%2C%20the%20Court,his%20crime%20was%20morally%20wrong.

[275] Peel established the first modern police system in England, known as "Bobbies."

popular figures in government of that day, and because an attempt on the Queen's life had been made shortly before Drummond's killing, M'Naghten's acquittal raised a public furor. The House of Lords (the upper house of the Parliament of the United Kingdom) posed a question to Queen's Bench judges (the equivalency of American felony trial court judges) concerning the nature and extent of the unsoundness of mind that would excuse the commission of a murder. Their response to the House of Lords is now known as the *M'Naghten* Rule.

The judges stated that, in order to excuse a defendant from criminal responsibility,

> It must be clearly proved that, at the times of committing the act, the party accused was laboring under such a defect of reason, from disease of the mind, as not to know the nature and quality of the act he was doing, or if he did know it, that he did not know it was wrong.

While the *M'Naghten* case itself dealt only with mental illness, the *M'Naghten* test soon was applied to defects of reason arising from intellectual developmental disabilities (formerly referred to in case law as mental retardation) as well as mental illness. This test has become known as the "right or wrong test," and it was adopted in both federal and state courts in the United States. As psychiatry and psychology developed, the test became criticized for its sole focus on cognition (intellect) and ignoring a person's emotions. In response, some states accepted the irresistible impulse test first enunciated in *Parsons v. Alabama,* 81 Ala. 577 (1887).

The Irresistible Impulse Test

The irresistible impulse test applies to a person who, because of "reason of the duress of his mental disease, . . . had so far lost the power to choose between right and wrong and to avoid doing the act in question, that his free agency was at the time destroyed." Thus, a sane person under *M'Naghten* (someone who knows that his acts were wrong) may be found insane under the irresistible impulse test (someone who cannot control those acts). The irresistible impulse test is limited to cases of mental illness (not intellectual developmental disability/retardation). While M'Naghten stressed the lack of "cognitive capacity," the irresistible impulse test stressed the lack of "volitional capacity" (i.e., self-control). This test is premised on the belief that a person acting under an irresistible impulse was not really committing a voluntary act.

The Model Penal Code/Substantial Capacity Test

The Model Penal Code combines the elements of cognitive capacity with volitional capacity in its test of legal insanity. Under the MPC test, impairment of either capacity need not be total -- substantial impairment suffices. The test extended cognitive capacity to understanding as well as simple awareness (the term "appreciate" is used instead of "know"). Also, the lack of volitional capacity need not be the product of a sudden impulse; it refers to the lack of ability to "conform" behavior rather than control it. The drafters also wanted a standard that precluded a person from claiming legal insanity based only on his or her criminal or anti-social acts.

The MPC Substantial Capacity Test states,

(1) A person is not responsible for criminal conduct if at the time of such conduct as a result of mental disease or defect he lacks substantial capacity either to appreciate the criminality [wrongfulness] of his conduct or to conform his conduct to the requirements of law.
(2) As used in this Article, the terms "mental disease or defect" do not include an abnormality manifested only by repeated criminal or otherwise anti-social conduct.

The MPC test was adopted by most federal courts and some state courts. The jurisdictions that did not adopt the MPC test chose to retain their versions of the M'Naghten rule.

THE FEDERAL APPROACH TO INSANITY

The federal government was following the MPC approach when John Hinkley, Jr. attempted to assassinate U.S. President Ronald Reagan in March 1981. Hinkley's motivation for shooting at President Reagan, his press secretary, and two law enforcement officers was to impress actress Jodie Foster. At trial, he successfully claimed insanity and pointed to his obsessional fixation on her. The public outcry following the verdict of not guilty by reason of insanity in Hinckley's federal trial resulted in a change of the test of insanity in the federal court system. In 1984 Congress enacted the Insanity Defense Reform Act of 1984[276] which eliminated the volitional prong of the federal test of insanity and essentially embraced the M'Naghten test. In addition to re-adopting the M'Naghten test, the Act changed the burden of proof in asserting insanity. The federal standard now requires the defendant to prove the defense of insanity by clear and convincing evidence.[277] There has been some controversy in placing the burden of proof of insanity on the defendant, but the Court has held that this burden-shifting does not violate the defendant's right to due process under the constitution.[278]

The Act also limited psychiatrists' ability to present evidence concerning the defendant's inability to control his or her behavior. It was unclear whether the Act prohibited the use of psychiatric evidence concerning the defendant's lack of specific intent to commit an offense. But, the Eleventh Circuit Court of Appeals noted in 1990, "Both Congress and the courts have recognized the crucial distinction between evidence of psychological impairment that supports an "affirmative defense," and psychological evidence that negates an element of the offense charged." It ruled that the language of the Act does not bar the use of psychiatric evidence to negate specific intent where that level of intent is an element of the offense charged by the government. [279]

STATE DEVELOPMENTS[280]

Some states classify insanity as an affirmative defense and require the defendant to bear the burden of persuasion on insanity--generally using the 'preponderance of the evidence' standard. Some states have adopted the higher, 'clear and convincing' standard. In some states, when the defendant raises the defense of insanity and presents some evidence of insanity, the burden of production and persuasion then reverts to the state that must then prove defendant is not insane—usually beyond a reasonable doubt.

A defendant who claims insanity may be found "not guilty." In these cases, the defendant is like any other defendant who has been acquitted. In some states, the defendant may be found "not guilty by reason of insanity." In these cases, the defendant is institutionalized indefinitely in a mental institution. In some states, the defendant is found "guilty but mentally ill." In these states the defendant is generally sentenced in the criminal courts as other guilty defendants are, but there may be provisions for institutionalization in a mental institution or a special ward or wing in a criminal institution (prison).

---

[276] 18 U.S.C. §4241 (1984).

[277] The clear and convincing evidence standard is higher than the usual civil evidentiary standard of preponderance of the evidence, but lower than that of beyond a reasonable doubt.

[278] *Patterson v. New York*, 432 U.S. 197 (1977).

[279] *U.S. v. Cameron*, 907 F.2d 1051 (1990).

[280] For a state-by-state analysis, see, "*The Insanity Defense Among the States*" at criminal.findlaw.com/criminal-procedure/the-insanity-defense-among-the-states.html.

INSANITY VERSUS FITNESS-TO-PROCEED

Some individuals are so mentally disturbed that they may not be able to stand trial at which they would raise an insanity claim. The defendant's attorney may, after interviewing his or her client, determine that the defendant has a mental defect or is of such limited intelligence or understanding that he or she is not able to aid in his or her legal defense. In these cases, the attorney must inform the court that the defendant is incompetent or not fit to proceed. Unlike the insanity defense, which looks at the defendant's mental condition at the time of the offense, the fitness-to-proceed inquiry looks at defendant's mental condition at the time he or she is charged and prosecution commences. Courts will generally order a "competency" or "aid and assist" evaluation be done. If evaluators determine that the defendant is able to aid and assist, then the prosecution continues; if defendant is unable to aid and assist, then due process prohibits the states from continuing the criminal prosecution. State statutes control the fitness-to-proceed process and determine who has jurisdiction over a defendant who is unable to proceed. Often, if the defendant is found not fit to proceed, he or she will be institutionalized for treatment. Prosecution may continue, if and when the defendant, through medical or mental treatment, regains the ability to aid and assist in his or her own defense.

EXTREME EMOTIONAL DISTURBANCE (DIMINISHED CAPACITY)

The excuse of diminished capacity (also called extreme emotional disturbance) is recognized in approximately fifteen states. This defense allows experts to testify that the defendant suffered from a mental disturbance that diminished his or her capacity to form the required criminal intent necessary to commit the crime. Diminished capacity is a compromise between finding the defendant not guilty by reason of insanity and finding the defendant fully liable. In some states, defendants may only raise diminished capacity/EED defenses when they are charged with intentional murder. When the defense is successful, the accused may still be convicted of second-degree murder. For example, Dan White claimed diminished capacity when he was charged with killing Harvey Milk, his co-worker, and San Francisco Mayor, George Moscone. The jury found White guilty of manslaughter (instead of murder) after he claimed he could not form the specific intent to murder because his depression was exaggerated by junk food--Twinkies, in particular.[281] California voters responded by adopting abolishing the defense

---

[281] In October, 1985, Dan White committed suicide.

"Mr White, who had been released from prison January 6, 1984, after serving five years, one month and nine days in jail for the killings, had been troubled since his release, his lawyer said.

...

He said Mr. White's suicide vindicated his controversial plea of "diminished capacity" at the 1979 trial.

Mr. White's layer argued that his client was mentally unstable and hada diminished capacity at the time of the shooting, in part, he argued, because Mr. White had an addiction for sugary junk foods.

Although critics deplored what they called the "Twinkie defense," it succeeded with jurors.

When they convicted Mr. White of voluntary manslaughter rather than murder, thousands of protesters, including many members of the homosexual community here, marched to City hall where they met the police in a violent confrontation."
Robert Lindsay, "*Dan White, Killer of San Francisco Mayor, a Suicide*," New York Times, October 22, 1985.

of diminished capacity. Many states reject diminished capacity as a defense feeling it places too much reliance on psychiatrist testimony or may be too confusing for jurors.

The Model Penal Code allows a diminished capacity defense--although not labeling it as such. The MPC admits evidence that a defendant suffers from a mental disease or defect whenever relevant to prove defendant did or did not have a state of mind that is an element of the offense. Under the MPC, the defendant may introduce psychiatric evidence that refutes the state's evidence that he had the required *mens rea*--the crux of the diminished capacity defense.

AUTOMATISM

The criminal law requires the state prove that defendant committed a voluntary act (or omission to act). Certain mental or physical conditions may prevent a defendant's act from being considered voluntary. When the defendant argues that some physical condition prevented his act from being voluntary, he is asserting the defense of automatism. Automatism is a negative defense (the defendant asserts that the state failed to prove something it was required to prove). But it also qualifies as an excuse because the defendant is, in essence, saying, "I did the act, but I am not responsible because some physical condition (such as a seizure) made my act involuntary."

Some courts have refused to allow the defense of automatism on the grounds that this defense is superseded by the insanity defense. They reason that if a condition affects the defendant's mind to the extent that the defendant's conduct is involuntary, it constitutes a mental disease or defect; and any defense involving mental disease or defect may be asserted only by the use of an insanity defense.[282] The majority of American courts and the MPC,[283] however, do allow the automatism defense as distinct from the insanity defense. [284]

AGE / INFANCY

At early common law, young and old alike could be found guilty of committing a crime. "Neither age, sex, nor unsoundness of mind could be offered as an excuse, and neither were these factors generally considered in mitigation of punishment."[285] Once the Church declared that a child under the age of seven could not be guilty of sin, it followed that ecclesiastic (church) courts would find that a child under seven years old could not be guilty of a crime. The church rule found its way to the king's courts and into common law. If the child was under the age of seven it was presumed (an irrebuttable presumption) that the child was not responsible. No matter how much evidence the prosecutor had about the sophistication of the child, if the child hadn't yet reached his or her seventh birthday, he or she could not be found guilty of a crime. If the child was between the age of seven and fourteen it was still presumed that the child was not criminally responsible, but the government could rebut the presumption by putting on evidence that child

---

[282] *But see, Regina v. Quick*, 3 W.L.R. 26 (Engl. 1973). The automatism defense was allowed when the defendant attacked another person and lapsed into unconsciousness because of low blood sugar (hypoglycemia). The court noted that the attack could have been prevented if the patient had eaten a lump of sugar beforehand, and that the case was "not the sort of disease for which a person should be detained in a hospital rather than be given an unqualified acquittal. Insanity is only applicable where there is a malfunctioning of the mind caused by disease. A mental malfunctioning of transitory effect caused by the application to the body of some external factor such as violence, drugs . . . cannot be said to be due to the disease."

[283] MPC §2.01(1) and (2) precludes liability for involuntary acts and excludes reflexes, convulsion, movement during unconsciousness from its definition of what constitutes a voluntary act.

[284] Emanuel, *supra* at 85-86.

[285] Kerper, *supra* at 112.

understood the nature and quality of the act and knew that it was wrong. Once a child reached the age of fourteen, no presumption existed, and defendants could not raise an "infancy" defense.

Although the common law rules about age were originally adopted by all of the states, today many states have discarded them. Some states have adopted an absolute minimum age for responsibility whereas some states have no minimum age of responsibility. All states have developed juvenile court systems to balance the desire to hold children responsible and yet treat them differently than adults. Some states allow juveniles to be "waived" or "transferred" into the adult system. Some states have "legislative exclusions" (statutes) that exclude the juvenile court from having jurisdiction over some children or some offenses. The question of juvenile court jurisdiction is a different question than whether a child of a certain age can be responsible for his or her actions. But, because the discussion stems from the same concern (not wanting to treat children as adults) these issues frequently get lumped together.

INTOXICATION

VOLUNTARY INTOXICATION

Generally, defendants cannot escape liability for the crimes they commit after voluntarily becoming intoxicated with alcohol or some other substance. However, when a person is so intoxicated that he does not know what he was doing at the time of the crime, he may raise the imperfect defense of voluntary intoxication.

Where a crime requires an intention to cause a certain result and the defendant lacked that intention due to intoxication, he will not be liable for that crime. A person who killed another but was so intoxicated that he did not realize what he was doing would not be liable for the level of homicide (usually first-degree murder) that requires an intent to kill. He would, however be liable for lesser degrees of homicide that do not require such an intent (unless the intoxication was involuntary and met the applicable standard for total excuse from responsibility). Intoxication may also negate a *mens rea* of knowledge. Thus, if a person is so intoxicated that he does not realize he is taking the property of another, he will not be liable for theft since that crime requires knowledge.

The two levels of *mens rea* not negated by intoxication are negligence and recklessness. Since negligence does not require awareness of an unjustifiable risk, the intoxicated person may be negligent even though he was so intoxicated that he could not appreciate the presence or nature of the risk taken. Recklessness, on the other hand, does require an awareness of the risk, at least as defined by the Model Penal Code. Yet the law will not recognize voluntary intoxication as a defense to a crime requiring recklessness even if the defendant was so intoxicated he did not know what he was doing. Using intoxicating substances is considered, in itself, a very risky business, automatically establishing the presence of recklessness on the part of the actor.[286]

State legislatures have limited the defendant's ability to raise the defense of voluntary intoxication. In 1996, for example, the Court upheld a Montana law that did not allow the jury to consider the defendant's voluntary intoxication in determining whether defendant possessed the mental state necessary for the commission of a crime.[287] In 1996 the Florida Legislature enacted a statute that eliminated the defense, specifying that evidence of voluntary intoxication is not

---

[286] Kerper, *supra* at 117.
[287] *Montana v. Egelhoff*, 518 U.S. 37 (1996).

admissible to show a lack of specific intent or to show insanity at the time of the offense.[288] The trend is for states to disallow the defense on the theory that a defendant who voluntarily deprives herself of the ability to distinguish between right or wrong should be criminally responsible for her actions.

INVOLUNTARY INTOXICATION

Society expects people to be aware that alcohol and various drugs can cause intoxication. But when intoxication is not self-induced, the person should not be blamed. People who commit crimes after becoming intoxicated contrary to their own will or actions may raise the defense of involuntary intoxication. These defendants must show either that they were coerced by others into consuming an intoxicating substance or were tricked into taking such a substance by misrepresentation. Defendants may also raise the involuntary intoxication defense after mistakenly consuming a narcotic different than their prescribed medicine. Finally, some courts have allowed individuals who have had an extreme and unanticipated reaction to medication prescribed by a doctor to raise this defense. Acts committed by defendants who ingest intoxicating (non-prescribed) substances knowing what they are, but unaware of their full intoxicating capacity--for example, unwittingly smoking marijuana laced with LSD-are generally viewed as committing voluntary acts and the defense is unlikely to succeed. Similarly addicts who claim they cannot keep themselves from drinking or ingesting drugs are generally unsuccessful in raising the defense of involuntary intoxication.

The Model Penal Code recognizes involuntary intoxication as a defense where "by reason of such intoxication the actor at the time of his conduct lacks substantial capacity either to appreciate its criminality or to conform his conduct to the requirements of law." Thus, the involuntary intoxication defense excuses responsibility with a standard quite similar to that applied with the insanity defense.

DURESS

People who commit crimes because they have been threatened with death or harm claim the excuse of duress (also referred to as coercion or compulsion). Duress is a defense when the defendant could only escape the threatened harm by committing a crime. Defendants must show that they exhausted all reasonable and available alternatives to violating the law. To successfully raise the defense, four further requirements must be met. First, the defendant must be threatened with serious bodily injury or death. Second, the threat must have been so substantial that a person of "reasonable firmness" would have been unable to resist it. The jury will decide what a reasonable person would have done under the circumstances and not necessarily what the defendant, ideally, could have done. Third, the threat must have been immediate or imminent. If there was ample time or opportunity to avoid the threatened harm, the defendant should have avoided it. Fourth, the defendant must not have placed himself in a situation where it was probable that he would be subjected to a threat.

Prisoners who escape and claim their lives were in danger due to threats from other prisoners frequently raise the duress defense. In these cases, the defendant must show that he or she had taken reasonable, but unsuccessful steps to report the threats, that he or she did not use force or violence toward prison personnel or other innocent people, and that he or she surrendered or return to custody as soon as the claimed duress had ended or lost its coercive force.

---

[288] The statute, makes an exception for controlled substances taken as prescribed by a doctor.

As with most defenses, state statutes vary in their requirements and approaches to the defense of duress. Some states permit the defendant to raise the defense when he or she negligently (rather than recklessly or purposely) placed himself or herself in a potentially threatening situation. Some states follow the common law approach and limit the defense to defendants who have responded only to threats against themselves or members of their immediate families; other states permit the defense only when the defendant was threatened. Most states do not permit the defense to be raised in cases of intentional homicide. Some states do not require that the threat involve serious bodily injury if the offense committed is only a misdemeanor.

Some courts look to duress as negating the element of the offense charged and classify it as a negative defense (the defendant raised a reasonable doubt as to whether he acted in the exercise of free will). Most courts, however, classify duress as an affirmative defense and require the defendant prove the defense by the preponderance of the evidence.

The Model Penal Code §2.09 provides:

It is an affirmative defense that the actor engaged in the conduct charged to constitute an offense because he was coerced to do so by the use of, or a threat to use, unlawful force against his person or the person of another, that a person of reasonable firmness in his situation would have been unable to resist.

The defense . . .is unavailable if the actor recklessly . . . [or negligently] placed himself I such a situation . . .

It is not a defense that a woman acted on the command of her husband. [289]

The MPC significantly extended the common law standard in the following ways:

- It does not require threats of death or serious injury.
- It does not require imminent threats.
- It permits the defense even in cases of intentional homicide.
- It extends to situations in which the threats were made to people other than the defendant or the defendant's immediate family members.

Necessity and Duress

The excuse of duress and the justification of necessity are similar but distinct. The necessity defense applies to situations in which an actor, to avoid significant harm, must commit a less significant crime. The need to commit a crime may arise because of a situation, and the defense is not limited to circumstances involving threats from other people. The duress excuse applies to situations in which the threat is from a person or persons and the threat is serious-- involving serious physical injury or death to the defendant unless the defendant commits a crime. With the necessity defense, the harm the defendant seeks to avoid must be greater than, not merely equal to, the harm caused by the defendant's conduct. The duress excuse does not require that the defendant prove that the harm from the threat was greater than the harm of the crime committed.

---

[289] The common law held that married women were exempted from liability if she committed a crime in the presence of her husband under the assumption that she acted under his direction.

MISTAKE OF FACT/ MISTAKE OF LAW

With strict liability and vicarious liability crimes being the exception, criminal responsibility is always tied to culpable, blameworthy conduct. Sometimes people make mistakes and end up violating the law. But, since only morally blameworthy individuals should be punished, the law excuses individuals whose mistakes demonstrate a lack of intent, blameworthiness, or culpability. The Model Penal Code §2.04 (1) states that "ignorance or mistake is a defense when it negatives the existence of a state of mind that is essential to the commission of an offense."

Some courts require that the defendant's mistake of fact must be objectively reasonable – meaning a reasonable person would have made the same mistake. For example, Sam walks into an office and drops his wet umbrella off at the door. Upon leaving, Sam takes Frank's umbrella, believing it to be his. Sam would have made a mistake about the fact of the umbrella's true owner. Because the law excuses only reasonable mistakes, the jury will want to consider what Frank and Sam's umbrellas looked like when deciding whether Sam stole Frank's umbrella. Was Frank's umbrella the same size, color, and shape as Sam's? Was it in the same general location that Sam had left his umbrella? Was Frank's umbrella colorful and unique while Sam's umbrella was a generic looking black umbrella? Other facts may also be important. Was Sam color blind? What if Sam took Frank's umbrella without really paying much attention to color because he was in a hurry?

States must grapple with policy questions in determining whether mistake of fact should be permissible defense. Should an honest and good faith mistake of fact, however misguided, negate criminal intent? Should the law insist that the mistake be a reasonable one? If Sam can show that he truly believed he was taking his own umbrella (even if that belief was unreasonable), shouldn't that be enough to show he didn't have the type of guilty mind that we require before punishing people?

If Sam knew that he was taking Frank's umbrella but thought that the law allowed him to take other people's property he found preferable to his own, Sam would assert a mistake of law defense. Courts generally do not excuse these types of mistakes. Society is prepared to condemn people who willfully ignore of the law or those who try to understand the law but are mistaken as to what it says. The common saying, "ignorance of law is no defense," is generally, but not one hundred percent, accurate. Ordinarily, a mistake of law arises in a setting in which defendants intend to do an act that is prohibited, but claim that they should not be held liable because they honestly believed that they were not committing a crime. There are several problems with excusing defendants' behavior in these cases. First people are expected to know the law. Second, defendants may falsely claim that they were unaware of the law, and this claim would be difficult for the prosecution to overcome. Third, enforcing the laws promotes the public policy of social stability. (Consider a society where people avoid learning the law so they can honestly state that they were ignorant of it, and will thus have an excuse if ever brought to court.) Finally, individuals should not be permitted to define for themselves the legal rules that govern society. Because of these considerations, the common law rule, "ignorance of the law is not an excuse" developed.

Critics of the "mistake of law is no defense" approach note that because of the complexities of modern society, some people who violate some laws should not be considered morally blameworthy. The courts have, in fact, begun to relax the rigid application of the general mistake of law rule when (1) the law is one which would not have come to the defendant's notice and application of the law would violate the due process requirement of notice, (2) when the law required a showing of willful intent but the average person might not know all the laws because of how vast, complex, and highly technical they are (for example certain provisions of the tax code), and (3) when an individual relied to their detriment on the advice of a person, such as a chief of police, concerning the legality of their action.

In *Lambert v. California* 355 U.S. 225 (1957), for example, the Supreme Court reviewed a case where the defendant, a convicted felon, was charged with failing to register with authorities as required by a Los Angeles city ordinance. The Court held that

> [A]s applied to one who has no actual knowledge of a duty to register and where no showing is made of the probability of such knowledge, the ordinance violates the Due Process Clause of the Fourteenth Amendment. The public welfare offenses punish failure to act only in "circumstances that should alert the doer to the consequences of his deed."

Justice Frankfurter dissented, stating, "*Lambert* is an isolated deviation from the strong current of precedents—a derelict on the waters of the law."

The Model Penal Code recognizes an ignorance of the law defense where the defendant does not know the law and the law has not been published or made reasonably available to the public. The MPC defense also applies where the defendant relies on official statements of the law (reliance).

NONTRADITIONAL DEFENSES

Defendants have raised novel and innovative defenses that, for the most part, have been unsuccessful. These include:

- road rage,
- cultural defense,[290]
- compulsive gambling,
- victim negligence,
- television intoxication,[291]
- pornography addiction or intoxication,
- postpartum depression,[292]

---

[290] The cultural defense asserts that a foreign-born defendant was understandably unaware of the requirements of American law. Lippman observed,
> Multiculturalism may be in conflict with important American values regarding respect for women and children. Various Laotian American tribal groups continue the practice of "marriage by capture," in which a prospective bride is expected to protest sexual advances and the male is required to compel the woman to submit in order to establish his courage and ability to be strong and suitable husband. In one California case, a young woman who did not accept her parents' Hmong cultural practice alleged that she had been raped by her new husband who invoked the cultural defense. *Law and Society*, *supra* at 327-328.

One problem with the acceptance of this defense is that judges and juries don't have the expertise to determine authentic customs and traditions of the various immigrant groups and will be forced to rely on expert witnesses.

[291] *See, Id.* at 326. Ronald Howard unsuccessfully argued in mitigation of a death sentence that he had killed a police officer while listening to rap music.

[292] Postpartum depression refers to a group of symptoms a new mother may experience after giving birth. It involves severe depression, and it has been raised as a defense in cases involving infanticide in an effort to mitigate punishment.

- chromosome abnormality,[293]
- premenstrual syndrome defense,[294]
- multiple personality defense,[295]
- urban survival defense,[296]
- black rage,[297] and
- environmental defense.[298]

Some nontraditional defenses that have been successfully raised in court include posttraumatic stress disorder, battered woman syndrome, and battered child syndrome.

POSTTRAUMATIC STRESS DISORDER

Posttraumatic stress disorder (PTSD) refers to the unique stresses suffered during combat[299] (or more recently, any exceptionally traumatic experience). PTSD often manifests itself in flashbacks, outbursts of anger, blocked-out memories. PTSD is not a legal defense in itself, but

---

[293] XYY chromosome defense is based on research that indicates that a large percentage of male prison inmates possess an extra Y chromosome that results in enhanced "maleness." In *Millard v. State*, 261 A.2d 227 (Md. Ct. Spec. App. 1970) a Maryland appeals court dismissed a defendant's claim that his robbery should be excused based on the presence of an extra Y masculine chromosome that allegedly made it impossible for him to control his aggressive, antisocial, and aggressive behavior. *Id. at 325*.

[294] Premenstrual syndrome refers to certain physiological changes that occur in some women, usually in the days close to the onset of menstruation. This results from a hormonal imbalance and can cause serious depression and irritability. In certain cases, medical treatment is required. Women have raised the PMS defense to show they were unable to control their actions at the time of crime. It is argued as a automatism type of defense. No American court has allowed the defense, but an English case, *Regina v. Craddock*, 1 C.L. 49 (Engl. 1981) has allowed evidence of the defendant's PMS as a mitigating factor for sentencing purposes.

[295] This defense asserts that one of the defendant's alternate personalities (of which defendant has no memory) committed the crime. Multiple Personality Disorder would generally be raised as part of an insanity defense. In 2000, a Kansas City woman was found guilty of murdering her sons and several additional child abuse charges. She unsuccessfully claimed that her multiple personalities were responsible for the deaths of her two sons. Trial testimony indicated she had severe psychosis and an alternate personality named Sharon controlled her actions. *See,* Scheb, *supra* at 454.

[296] Urban survival syndrome defense is based upon defendants having lived under substandard environmental conditions in deteriorated urban neighborhoods plagued with drug dealers and acts of violence.

[297] Black defendants have sometimes raised the defense of black rage in attempt to absolve or mitigate their liability on the basis of years of oppression and racist hostility. Proponents contend that as a result of racism, substandard education, inadequate employment opportunities, substandard housing and medical care, black defendants can justify retaliatory action against white citizens. In a well-publicized case from December 1993, Colin Ferguson boarded a Long Island Railroad train and as it approached the last station, he began a shooting spree that left six dead and nineteen wounded passengers. The police found notes in which Ferguson expressed hatred for Caucasian and Asians (those passengers he targeted). Initially Ferguson's lawyer indicated that he would offer the defense of extreme racial stress precipitated by the destructive racial treatment of blacks. Ferguson ultimately represented himself and never raised the claim. He was convicted in 1995 and is now serving multiple life sentences.

[298] One Massachusetts defendant raised an environmental defense claiming that the chemicals he used in his lawn care work resulted in involuntary intoxication and led him to violently respond to a customer's complaint. *Commonwealth v. Garabedian*, 503 N.E.2s 1290 (Mass. 1987).

[299] Following World War II, "combat fatigue" was used to describe these anxiety disorders. Present generations have heard these conditions described as PTSD. Because of the bizarre type of warfare that service personnel endured in Vietnam, the unpopularity of the war, the availability of drugs, and the difficulties encountered in adjusting to civilian life, many veterans suffered severe psychological reactions. To a lesser extent, the stress of combat in Operation Desert storm also caused delayed traumatic stress disorder. Military operations in Afghanistan, Iraq, and elsewhere can be expected to cause similar results.

in some instances, PTSD may affect a defendant's understanding so severely that is allows him or her to raise an insanity defense. Courts may allow defendants to introduce PTSD evidence for its bearing on defendant's intent or during sentencing hearing to mitigate punishment.

BATTERED WOMAN SYNDROME (BWS) AND BATTERED CHILD SYNDROME (BCS)

Defendants frequently raise a battered woman syndrome or a battered child syndrome excuse with their claims of self-defense in cases involving domestic violence. Self-defense, as noted above, is a justification defense in which the defendant argues that what he or she did was the right thing to do under the circumstances. Some states now admit battered spouse syndrome evidence on the issue of whether the actor lawfully acted in self-defense or defense of another. As an excuse, BWS or BCS are defenses in which the defendant asserts that even though what they did was the wrong thing to do, that he or she is not responsible because of something particular to them (i.e., "Yes, I shot him, but I am not responsible because . . . I am a battered woman acting in a manner typical of other battered women.")

Psychologists have identified a battered woman syndrome--a series of common characteristics that appear in women who have been abused physically and psychologically over a long time by their mate or other dominant person in their lives. Experts who have studied BWS say that most domestic violence occurs in a series of three-phase cycles: phase 1 is the "tension-building stage," during which the male engages in minor battering incidents and verbal abuse while the woman tries to placate him; phase 2 is the "acute battering incident," during which the more serious violence occurs; and in phase 3, the male becomes extremely contrite and loving. Proponents of the BWS say that women stay in abusive relationships because the male's loving behavior during phase 3 leads the woman to believe that the male will reform. The woman also frequently sinks into a state of psychological paralysis believing that she cannot prevent or escape from the violence. Also, she may come to believe, with good reason, that if she attempts to escape, the male will find her and beat her even worse.

Most cases in which the woman kills her abusing mate turn on the reasonableness of the defendant's conduct. Assuming that the defendant's belief that the danger was genuine, was that belief objectively reasonable? In many domestic violence cases the issue is whether the danger to the woman was imminent. The defendant cannot kill today to avoid an extremely great likelihood of serious bodily harm or death tomorrow. The courts allow BWS testimony to explain to the jury that the battered woman typically has a better sense of the degree of danger and why the danger is greater, and likely imminent on this particular occasion, than an outside observer would believe.[300]

Some defendants assert the Battered Child Syndrome (BCS) as a defense when charged with killing or assaulting the abusive parents arguing that the victims had abused them repeatedly during their childhood. Many prosecutors claim that this defense undermines the law of self-defense, yet there are experts who claim that a child's perception of the need to use force are shaped by his or her experience of constant abuse by a parent. These experts argue that when juries hear such evidence, they may be persuaded that a child acted in self-defense and not out of retribution.

Since the 1990s scholars have studied and written extensively about BWS and BCS. Courts have received and considered the social science literature about these syndromes, and defense attorneys now make convincing arguments to the court about why juries should be instructed

---

[300] *See, Emanuel, supra* at 120-122.

and allowed to hear how living in the perpetual fear of ever-present violence skew a reasonable belief that an attack may be imminent. However, the dynamics of family violence, the lingering assumptions underlying the common law rules of self-defense (two equally able-bodied unrelated strangers), and the court's reluctance to allow a carte blanche for individuals to retaliate rather than act upon immediate harm have all contributed to the complexities of this area of law. There are few, and no easy, solutions.

PROCEDURAL DEFENSES

When defendants raise "procedural defenses" they are claiming that, in some way, the government had done something wrong or failed to do something that was required and, because of this, they should not be held responsible. When defendants claim entrapment, they assert that the government wrongly caused them to commit their crimes. When defendants assert the defense of double jeopardy, they assert that the government is wrongly prosecuting them because it has already done so. When defendants assert the speedy trial defense, they assert that the government took too long to bring its case to trial. Finally, when defendants claim immunity, they assert that the government cannot prosecute because it has agreed, either contractually or though policy, not to do so.

ENTRAPMENT

Is it "okay" for the police to hide somewhere on the roadway, wait for drivers to come speeding by, and then pull them over for speeding? The short answer is "Yes." But sometimes police go too far in enticing a person to commit a crime.

The entrapment defense developed in the United States in the 1930s. In *Sorrells v. United States* (1932), an undercover agent posed as a thirsty tourist and ultimately overcame Sorrell's resistance and persuaded him to locate some illegally manufactured alcohol. The Court reversed Sorrells' conviction, finding that the officer's inducement by trickery, persuasion, or fraud to get Sorrells--a person who otherwise would not have committed the crime--caused Sorrells to commit the crime. The Court held that entrapment occurs when criminal conduct is the product of "creative activity of law enforcement officers."

Since *Sorrells* the courts have adopted one of two approaches in deciding whether police have gone too far--both of which were discussed in *Sherman v. United States*, 356 U.S. 369 (1958). In *Sherman* a government informant (facing criminal charges) befriended the defendant, and confided to him his addiction to narcotics and the difficulty in overcoming it. The government agent eventually convinced Sherman to obtain and split the cost of illegal narcotics. Although the entire Court found Sherman was entrapped, five justices supported what is now known as the "subjective test of entrapment," and four justices supported what is now known as the "objective test of entrapment."

SUBJECTIVE TEST OF ENTRAPMENT

The subjective test of entrapment focuses on the defendant and asks whether he or she was predisposed to commit the crime. Did the government created the intent to commit the crime in someone who would otherwise not intend to commit a crime, or did the government do no more than plant a trap for the unwary criminal? If it is the former, then the defendant was entrapped under the subjective approach. This approach, embraced by the federal courts and majority of the states, excuses the defendant from criminal liability because it is wrong for the government to punish the defendant when it was the state that prompted the defendant to act in the first place. With this approach, the jury must first decide whether the idea of committing the crime originated with the government agent, and if so, did the agent use tactics that induced the defendant to commit the crime. Merely providing an opportunity to commit a crime does not constitute an inducement. Rather, inducement involves appeals to friendship, promises of sexual favors, promises of economic or material gain, appeals to compassion, or requesting assistance in carrying out the crime. A person who is predisposed to commit the crime is someone who is ready and willing to engage in conduct in the absence of government inducements. Factors the court considers in determining whether the defendant was induced include:

- The character or reputation of the defendant, including prior criminal arrests and convictions for the type of crime involved.
- Whether the accused suggested the criminal activity.
- Whether the defendant was already engaged in criminal activity for profit.
- Whether the defendant was reluctant to commit the offense.
- Whether the defendant seemed to be familiar with the culture surrounding the criminal endeavor.
- The attractiveness of the inducement.

One critique of the subjective test of entrapment is that it fails to provide police with any bright line rules since it is factually specific and focuses on characteristics of the individual defendant.

OBJECTIVE TEST OF ENTRAPMENT

The objective test, followed by a substantial minority of the states, focuses on keeping police from engaging in inappropriate activities designed to manufacture crime. "The crucial question" according to Justice Frankfurter's opinion in *Sherman*, "is whether the police conduct revealed in the particular case falls below standards to which common feelings respond, for the proper use of governmental power." Frankfurter noted that the government agent in *Sherman* took advantage of Sherman's susceptibility to narcotics and manufactured Sherman's response by his repeated requests to get him drugs. One question courts ask in applying the objective test of entrapment is whether police activity went beyond judicial tolerance--is this something we want police to be doing?

ENTRAPMENT AND DUE PROCESS

Defendants sometimes argue that entrapment tactics violate the Due Process Clause of the Constitution claiming that the government's conduct was so unfair and outrageous that it would be unjust to convict them. The Court has rejected this argument in several cases finding that due process is violated only when law enforcement tactics violate fundamental fairness or were shocking to the universal sense of justice.

DOUBLE JEOPARDY

Double jeopardy is the successive (repeated) prosecution of a defendant for the same offense by the same jurisdiction. The Fifth Amendment provides that "no person shall be subject for the same offense to be twice put in jeopardy of life or limb." This Amendment and similar state double jeopardy provisions protect against "a second prosecutions for the same offense after acquittal. It protects against a second prosecution for the same offense after conviction. And it protects against multiple punishments for the same offense."[301]

Double jeopardy protections have significant limitations. First, they do not bar a civil trial after a criminal trial. Second, double jeopardy is limited to re-prosecution of the "same offense,"

---

[301] *North Carolina v. Pearce*, 395 U.S. 711, 717 (1969).

(if the elements of crimes charged differ, there is no double jeopardy). Third, double jeopardy bars prosecution by the same jurisdiction; it does not stop one jurisdiction (state, federal, tribal) from prosecuting the defendant after another jurisdiction has already prosecuted the crime.

SAME OFFENSE

Double jeopardy only applies to prosecutions for the same *criminal* offense. The government may prosecute the defendant for behavior even if he or she has already been sued civilly for that same harm. The defendant may likewise be sued civilly even though he or she has been successfully or unsuccessfully prosecuted. For example, the families of Nicole Brown Simpson and Ronald Goldman sued O.J. Simpson for killing the two even though California had unsuccessfully prosecuted Simpson for their murders.

Assuming the government seeks to begin a subsequent criminal proceeding, there is still the question of whether the first prosecution and the second prosecution involve the *same* offense. *Blockburger v. United States,* 284 U.S. 299 (1932), sets forth the test to determine when behavior constitutes the same offense.

> Where the same act or transaction constitutes a violation of two distinct statutory provisions, the test to be applied to determine whether there are two offenses or only one, is whether each provision requires proof of a fact which the other does not.[302]

Under *Blockburger*, double jeopardy bars two prosecutions for crimes with identical statutory elements or when one crime is a lesser-included offense of the other. A lesser-included offense is an offense that has some, but not all, of the elements of the greater crime, and it does not have any elements that the greater offense does not have.

For example, in *Brown v. Ohio,* 432 U.S. 161 (1977), Brown stole a 1965 Chevrolet from a parking lot in East Cleveland, Ohio on November 29, 1973. Nine days later, police caught Brown driving the car in Wickliffe Ohio on December 8, 1973. Brown was charged and plead guilty to joy riding (taking and operating a vehicle without the owner's consent) in the car on December 8, 1973. He was sentenced to 30 days in jail and a $100.00 fine. When released from jail, he returned to East Cleveland where he was indicted for stealing the car "on or about the 29th day of November 1973." Brown objected, claiming that the Double Jeopardy Clause prohibited the state from prosecuting him. The Court agreed, finding that auto theft and joyriding are the same offense within the meaning of the Double Jeopardy Clause.

> As is invariably true of a greater and lesser included offense, the lesser offense-- joyriding--requires no proof beyond that which is required for conviction of the greater--auto theft. The greater offense is therefore by definition the "same" for purposes of double jeopardy as any lesser offense included in it.[303]

Defendants have argued that the Double Jeopardy Clause bars their prosecution under repeat offender or "three strikes" type of sentencing. They claim that the sentence for their current crime is longer because of their past conviction and that they are being subjected to multiple punishments for the earlier crime. The Court, unconvinced, found that persistent offender statutes do not violate the bar against double jeopardy.

---

[302] 284 U.S. at 304 (1932)
[303] *Brown*, 432 U.S. at 168.

An enhanced sentence imposed on a persistent offender . . . 'is not to be viewed as either a new jeopardy or additional penalty for the earlier crimes' but as a 'stiffened penalty for the latest crime which is considered to be an aggravated offense because a repetitive one.'[304]

SAME JURISDICTION — DUAL SOVEREIGNTY DOCTRINE

The double jeopardy bar does not limit successive prosecutions by different jurisdictions. The federal government can prosecute the defendant for a crime for which the defendant was already convicted or acquitted in a state court. Similarly, a state prosecutor may bring state charges against a defendant who has already been prosecuted in federal court. For example, the federal government prosecuted Terry Nichols for his role in the Oklahoma City bombing. He was convicted of conspiracy and several counts of criminal homicide and was sentenced to life imprisonment without the possibility of parole (the jury had deadlocked on the death penalty.) The State of Oklahoma then successfully prosecuted him for first-degree murder for the killings connected to the bombing. A state is, similarly, not barred from prosecuting a defendant who has already been prosecuted in another state. *United States. v. Lara, 541 U.S. 193 (2004)*, held that double jeopardy does not bar prosecution by a sovereign Indian court after a federal or state court proceeding of vice versa. The court reasoned that the Tribe acted in its capacity as a sovereign authority, and that the Double Jeopardy Clause does not prohibit the Federal Government from proceeding with the present prosecution for a discrete federal offense. Similarly, in *Denezpi v. United States*, 596 U.S. ___ (2022) the Court held that an individual can be prosecuted in the Court of Indian Offenses and also in federal court for the same offense without violating the Double Jeopardy Clause.

Gamble v. United States, 587 U.S. ____ (2019), discussed the "separate sovereign's exception" to the Double Jeopardy Clause. The Court stated,

> The dual-sovereignty doctrine is not an exception to the double jeopardy right but follows from the Fifth Amendment's text. The Double Jeopardy Clause protects individuals from being "twice put in jeopardy" "for the same offence." As originally understood, an "offence" is defined by a law, and each law is defined by a sovereign. Thus, where there are two sovereigns, there are two laws and two "offences." [305]

---

[304] *Monge v. California*, 524 U.S. 721 (1998).

[305] Note that although the Court upheld the dual sovereignty doctrine in the context of a federal prosecution, state double jeopardy laws may be more limiting. Such was the case involving former President Trump's friend and advisor, Paul Manafort. In that case, New York state's double jeopardy law acted as a limitation to the "dual sovereignty doctrine." Manafort was convicted of federal charges and sentenced to more than seven years of federal custody. (See, https://apnews.com/article/e15da42b6f7f250fd0be9ca49f25d4c2). Immediately, thereafter, New York prosecutors filed charges of mortgage fraud against him. (It was suspected that former President Trump would likely pardon Mr. Manafort -- which he, in fact, did.) Manafort's attorney successfully filed a motion to dismiss those New York charges based on state double jeopardy law arguing that the facts and circumstances underlying the mortgage fraud crimes were substantially the same as those which had been dismissed as part of the federal prosecution. State prosecutors had argued that the elements were different and they were not barred by double jeopardy. The trial court disagreed and dismissed the charges. One legal analyst wrote,

> This decision markedly narrows the separate sovereignty doctrine in New York. . . . [F]or state and federal charges to be sufficiently different for purposes of N.Y. CPL §40.20(2)(b), the evil or harm sought to be outlawed must be substantially different. Following Mr. Manafort's motion it is that much harder for state law enforcement to bring charges related to a prior federal action."

WHEN DOUBLE JEOPARDY "ATTACHES"

Double jeopardy "attaches" or starts in a jury trial when the jury is sworn in or, in a bench trial, when the first witness has been called and sworn in.[306] Defendants generally raise the claim of double jeopardy issues pre-trial in motions to dismiss, but it may be possible to raise them after the defendant has been convicted.

In *Martinez v. Illinois*, 572 U.S. ___ (2014), the state was not ready on the day of trial. Prosecutors declined to present evidence because they wanted the court to grant a continuance, which the court refused to do. The court used several delay tactics before empaneling a jury, but ultimately the trial judge told the government that it would either have to dismiss the case or begin presenting its case. Prosecutors neither made an opening statement, nor called any witnesses stating instead "the state is not participating in this case." The defendant moved for a directed verdict of not guilty (see Chapter Ten), and the trial court granted that motion. The state appealed, arguing that the trial court should have granted its motion for continuance. The Illinois courts found that double jeopardy did not attach, but the U.S. Supreme Court disagreed. The Court noted that this was an easy case and that precedent was clearly established that jeopardy attaches when the jury is empaneled; it found that that jeopardy did attach to Martinez and that double jeopardy barred his retrial.

WAIVING DOUBLE JEOPARDY

Double jeopardy is "waived" under certain circumstances: when a mistrial is declared, when defendant appeals, and when defendant files a writ of habeas corpus. In *Currier v. Virginia*, 585 U.S. ___ (2018), for example, the Court found that double jeopardy rights were waived when Currier consented to the severance of multiple charges against him. He was convicted at trial on the first of the charges, and when the state sought to try him for the additional charges, he claimed the case was barred by the Fifth Amendment double jeopardy provision. The Court disagreed.

Mistrials

If defendant requests a mistrial--even based on prosecutorial misconduct[307]--and the court grants the request, then the defendant waives his or her right to protection against double jeopardy and the case can be tried again. When the court grants a mistrial over the defendant's

---

https://www.thsh.com/criminal-justice-insider/double-trouble-paul-manafort-and-the-state-of-double-jeopardy-in-new-york

The state appealed, but in February 2021, the New York appellate court let stand the lower court ruling that the mortgage fraud charges were barred by New York's then-existing double jeopardy statute. That said, the New York legislature enacted legislation in October 2019 which specifically was directed at reaffirming the dual sovereignty doctrine/exception in New York. This law allows state prosecutors to pursue charges against individuals who have been granted presidential pardons for similar crimes.

[306] In 2005 the Court held that a trial judge could not reconsidering his earlier acquittal on one charge midtrial after he heard additional evidence. *Smith v. Massachusetts*, 543 U.S. 462 (2005).

[307] When prosecutors engage in misconduct intending to cause a mistrial or are indifferent to the possibility of a mistrial this may result in double jeopardy. *See, e.g., State v. Worth*, 274 Or App 1 (2015). ("Under Article 1, Section 12 of the Oregon Constitution, prosecutorial misconduct bars retrial of a defendant only when (1) the misconduct is so prejudicial it cannot be cured by means short of a mistrial; (2) the prosecutor knew that the conduct was improper and prejudicial; and (3) the prosecutor either intended or was indifferent to the resulting mistrial.") Under the federal standard, the prosecutor must intend to provoke the mistrial.

objection, double jeopardy may not bar a subsequent prosecution if the court finds there was "manifest necessity" in declaring the mistrial. Although the doctrine of "manifest necessity" is a vague concept, courts have held that a deadlocked or "hung" jury creates manifest necessity to declare a mistrial, and sets up the state's ability to re-prosecute. For example, in *Renico v. Lett*, 559 U.S. 766 (2010), the Court held that the trial judge had exercised sound discretion in declaring a mistrial. The case was a first-degree murder prosecution that took only nine hours for the entire trial (from jury selection through jury instruction). After four hours of deliberation, the court received a note that questioned what would happen if the jurors could not agree. Based on that note, the judge declared a mistrial. The defendant argued that the judge had declared a mistrial without manifest necessity. The Court, citing *U.S. v. Perez*,[308] found that clearly established federal law holds that when a judge discharges a jury on the grounds that the jury cannot reach a verdict, the Double Jeopardy Clause does not bar a new trial for the defendant before a new jury.

> Trial judges may declare a mistrial when, in their opinion, taking all the circumstances into consideration, there is a manifest necessity for doing so . . . i.e., a high degree of necessity. ... The decision to declare a mistrial is left to the sound discretion of the judge, but the power ought to be used with the greatest caution, under urgent circumstances, and for plain and obvious cases. . . .[309]

There is no "rigid formula to determining when declaring a mistrial is appropriate. Nor must the judge make explicit findings concerning manifest necessity to do so."[310] Appellate courts generally defer to the trial judge as long as his or her discretion was sound.

Appealing Convictions

Defendants waive the protection against double jeopardy when they appeal their convictions or ask for their convictions to be set aside. The general view is that, by seeking an appeal, defendants are asking for a new trial and thus implicitly waive their double jeopardy rights. For example, consider *Miranda v. Arizona*, 384 U.S. 436 (1966). The Court reversed Miranda's conviction because police obtained his confession violation of his right against self-incrimination. Arizona tried him again (under an assumed name) and he was reconvicted on the basis of other evidence that did not include his illegally-obtained confession. No double jeopardy right was violated because, by appealing his conviction, he waived this right.[311]

Writs of Habeas Corpus

Finally, when defendants file writs of habeas corpus, they can be retried if their habeas corpus petition is successful. Filing a petition for a writ of habeas corpus is another way the defendant can attack his or her conviction, and for purposes of analyzing the bar of double jeopardy, it works like an appeal. The defendant is deemed to have waived double jeopardy when he or she files and is successful on habeas corpus grounds.

The rule that a defendant may be re-prosecuted if the verdict is set aside on appeal or habeas corpus has important exceptions. First, if the appellate court reverses the defendant's conviction finding the trial evidence was insufficient to support the verdict (meaning that no reasonable jury could have found the defendant guilty), re-prosecution is not allowed. Second, the Double Jeopardy Clause limits the sentence that can be imposed after a retrial. The Constitution requires that the defendant be given credit for the time served on the first conviction

---

[308] 9 Wheat 579 (1824).
[309] *Renico*, 559 U.S. at ___.
[310] *Id.*
[311] See, Del Carmen, R., *Criminal Procedure: Law and Practice* (7th ed., 2007).

before it was overturned.[312] Nevertheless, the trial judge hearing the second trial may impose a longer sentence than was imposed on the first conviction. "A corollary of the power to retry a defendant is the power, upon the defendant's reconviction, is to impose whatever sentence may be legally authorized, whether or not it is greater than the sentence imposed after the first conviction."[313] But, if the case involves the death penalty, and the first jury voted against the death penalty, then the Double Jeopardy Clause usually bars the court from sentencing the defendant to death if convicted on retrial.[314]

In *Bobby v. Bies, 556 U.S. 825 (2009)*, Bies raised the issue of double jeopardy after he was convicted in 1992 of murder, kidnap, and rape of a young boy and had received the death penalty. At his trial, the jury was told to consider evidence of his mental retardation as a mitigating factor when determining whether to impose death. On appeal, the Ohio Supreme Court in 1996 remarked that Bies' mild to borderline mental retardation merited some weight in mitigation. In a 2002 case the Court held the Eighth Amendment bars execution of mentally retarded offenders. Later Bies sued to vacate his death sentence based on retardation. The state requested a hearing to determine whether Bies lacked mental retardation. Bies argued that, since the Ohio appellate court had already found him mentally ill, such a hearing would violate double jeopardy. The Court disagreed,

> First, Bies was not "twice put in jeopardy." He was sentenced to death, and Ohio sought no further prosecution or punishment. Instead of "serial prosecutions by the government, this case involves serial efforts by the defendant to vacate his capital sentence." . . . Further, mental retardation for purposes of Atkins, and mental retardation as one mitigator to be weighed against aggravators, are discrete issues.[315]

STATUTE OF LIMITATIONS

It is in both society's and the accused's interest to hold criminal trials promptly and get them over with. A person should not have to live too long under the threat of criminal prosecution. Also, if trials are delayed too long, witnesses die or disappear, evidence is lost, parties move away, and many other things happen that make getting at the truth difficult. Because of this, legislatures have passed speedy trial statutes setting forth time limits in which the state must file charges. These statutes are referred to as "statutes of limitations." Neither common law nor the federal constitutional place limits on the time in which criminal actions can be filed.

State and federal statutes of limitation vary widely. Generally, the time clock starts running the date the crime was committed and then runs through the date the state filed formal charges, issued an arrest warrant, or when an indictment was returned. In cases involving deception, the clock starts on the date the crime was discovered. Usually, the time limit for felonies is longer than for misdemeanors. The time period is often longer when the victim is under-aged or may not even realize for some time that they have been victimized. States generally do not have statutes of limitations for very serious offenses, like murder. For example, Byron de la Beckwith was charged and convicted in 1997 for the 1963 murder of Mississippi civil rights activist Medgar Evers.

---

[312] See, *North Carolina v. Pearce*, 395 U.S. 711 (1969).
[313] *Id.* at 720.
[314] See, *Bullington v. Missouri*, 451 U.S. 430 (1981).
[315] *Bies*, 556 U.S. at 827.

Statutes of limitations generally specify periods of time when the clock stops running--this is referred to as a "tolling of the statutory period." The statutes describe when, and under what circumstances, the statute will toll. One reason the statute may toll, for example, is when the defendant leaves the jurisdiction.

Statutes differ in how the defense is to be raised. Some states view the statute of limitations as an affirmative defense that defendant must raise or it will be considered waived. Other states view the defense as "jurisdictional" (meaning the court will not have authority to hear the case) and bar the continued prosecution if the state's information or indictment reveals prosecution was initiated beyond the period allowed.[316]

In *McDonough v. Smith*, 588 U.S. ___ (2019) the Court examined when the statute of limitations for a 42 U.S.C. §1983 civil rights action begins to run. Defendant claimed that the government had presented fabricated evidence in his fraud trial. Youel Smith was the prosecutor who charged McDonough, a former election official, for fraud arising from a primary election. McDonough was indicted and tried twice (the first trial ended in a mistrial and the second trial ended in an acquittal.) Less than three years after his acquittal, McDonough sued Smith, stating that Smith fabricated evidence before the grand jury and at both of the trials in violation of his Fourth, Fifth, Sixth, and Fourteenth Amendments. The appellate court dismissed the claim, finding that the statute of limitations period began to run as soon as McDonough became aware of the use of fabricated evidence. The Court, however, held that the limitations period runs from the point at which the plaintiff has a complete cause of action. It noted that not all claims may be brought while the violation is ongoing, thus allowing for a later accrual date. Although the Court couldn't point to a specific constitutional or right alleged by McDonough to have been violated, the Court felt his gripe was similar to a common law claim of malicious prosecution and that these claims accrue only on favorable termination of the underlying criminal proceeding. Thus, McDonough's claims against Smith did not begin until his acquittal at the second trial (and within the period of limitations).

> This favorable-termination requirement is rooted in pragmatic concerns about avoiding parallel criminal and civil litigation over the same subject matter and the related possibility of conflicting civil and criminal judgments, and about precluding the use of Section 1983 to collaterally attack state convictions. Because a successful Section 1983 claim would "necessarily imply" the invalidity of the criminal proceedings against him, although he had not been convicted, a plaintiff must show that the proceedings were not valid. The majority also focused on the practical problems that a different rule would create, in putting criminal defendants to the Hobson's choice of allowing constitutional claims to lapse or filing civil actions against the government officials who are prosecuting them

---

[316] *United. States v. Briggs*, 592 U.S. ____ (2021) presents a complicated statutes of limitations issue. In 2014, Michael Briggs was found guilty in a military court for a rape that he committed nine years earlier, in 2005. Most crimes, according to the Uniform Code of Military Justice, must be charged within five years, unless they are punishable by death. According to the military code at the time, rape was punishable by death. In 2006, the code was updated to clarify that rape could be prosecuted without a time restriction. Briggs appealed his conviction arguing that the applicable statute of limitations in his case should be governed by the U.S. Supreme Court case (a civilian legal precedent) *Coker v. Georgia*, 433 US 584 (1977) in which the Court held that it would be "cruel and unusual punishment" to impose the death penalty for the rape of an adult woman. Thus, rape was not a death-penalty crime, and therefore it must be subject to the five-year statute of limitations. The Court, in a unanimous decision, held that the Uniform Code of Military Justice is a "uniform code that refers only to other provisions within the UCMJ itself," and not to other, outside legal sources. Thus, the statute of limitations had not run when he was prosecuted.

while the prosecution is ongoing; the former is undesirable, the latter "fraught with peril." In all, the majority argued, "the accrual rule we adopt today, by contrast, respects the autonomy of state courts and avoids these costs to litigants and federal courts."

SPEEDY TRIAL

Defendants are guaranteed the right to a speedy trial in both federal and state prosecutions.[317] The Sixth Amendment states, "In all criminal prosecutions, the accused shall enjoy the right to a speedy . . . trial." The Court has said that the Due Process Clause of the Fourteenth Amendment means that states must also provide speedy trials under the federal constitution. State legislatures and Congress have also enacted speedy trial statutes.

The Court has recognized that the speedy trial is one of our basic rights.[318] But, how quickly must the defendant be brought to trial? According to the courts, delay itself does not necessarily mean a constitutional violation. The Court has been concerned with unnecessary and unwanted delay. For example, *Barker v. Wingo*, 407 U.S. 514 (1972), the seminal case on speedy trial, held that the right to a speedy trial is a "vague concept" and that it is impossible to determine with precision when the right was denied."[319] The courts must decide based on the totality of the circumstances. The courts will look at the behavior of the prosecution and the defense and will consider: (1) the length of delay, (2) the reason for delay, (3) the defendant's assertion of the rights, and (4) any prejudice to the defendant. In *Barker v. Wingo* The Court found that an eighteen-month delay in filing an indictment did not violate the Speedy Trial Clause noting that prosecutors have an interest in delaying an indictment until they are persuaded that there is sufficient evidence to believe that the Government will be able to establish an individual's guilt beyond a reasonable doubt and that there is a societal interest in pursuing prosecutions. [320] The Court stressed that the remedy for a violation of the right to a speedy trial is a dismissal of the charge. Because of the severity of the remedy, courts may be reluctant to find that the right to speedy trial has been violated. The defendant may also have an interest in having the trial delayed, and may waive a speedy trial. A speedy trial claim generally must be raised at least by the trial phase or else the claim is waived. [321]

FEDERAL SPEEDY TRIALS

In federal prosecutions, the speedy trial provision of the Sixth Amendment has been essentially superseded by very elaborate legislation, the Speedy Trial Act. The Act sets out two separate time limits, one for the period from arrest to charge, and the other from the period from charge to trial. Under the Speedy Trial Act, the time between arrest and indictment must be no more than 30 days. The time between indictment or information and the commencement of trial must normally be no more than 70 days. There are, however, several periods of delay that do not count, and some which are very elastic. For instance, delay due to the unavailability of essential witness does not count. Similarly, delay due to a continuance granted at the prosecution's request does not count if the judge puts findings on the record as to why the "ends of justice served by granting such a continuance outweigh the best interests of the public and the defendant in a

---

[317] The speedy trial clock starts to run once the defendant has been formally charged with the commission of a crime; it does not start at the time the crime was committed. The period of time from commission of the offense to the arrest or filing of criminal charges is covered by pertinent statutes of limitations.
[318] *Klopfer v. North Carolina*, 386 U.S. 213 (1967).
[319] *Id.*
[320] See, *United Staes v. Lovasca*, 431 U.S. 783 (1977).
[321] See, *United States v. Strunk*, 412 U.S. 434 (1973).

speed trial."[322] The remedy for a speedy trial violation is dismissal of the charges. But, there is no requirement that the dismissal be "with prejudice," and so the prosecutor could re-file or re-indictment and restart the speedy trial clock--assuming no statute of limitation prevents this.

STATE SPEEDY TRIAL

State speedy trial guarantees are governed either by the state constitution, state statutes or both. For example, Oregon provides a constitutional right to a speedy trial in Article I Section 10 of the Oregon Constitution and also has a statutory right to a speedy trial. Before 2014, the court in reviewing speedy trial challenges examined whether the delay was reasonable, but a new statute (SB 1550-8 Amended, Adopted April 2014) established bright-line rules. Cases must now be brought to trial within two years for any misdemeanor from the date of filing of a charging instrument, and three years for any felony. The Department of Justice in concert with the Oregon Criminal Defense Lawyers Association structured the new statutory speedy trial provision,

> Having a statutory speedy trial provision is important because it protects societal and institutional interests beyond those recognized in constitutional guarantees. Constitutional guarantees recognized in the federal and state constitution are personal to the accused. A statutory right, by contrast, protects the rights of the public, including victims and witnesses, to the prompt adjudication of criminal charges, and helps assure that the judicial system will make wise use of its limited resources by ferreting out state allegations (Citing ABA Standard on Speedy Trial, Standard 12-1.2)

> Forty-eight states have a statutory speedy trial provision. ... [The Oregon statute] employs the template recommended by the ABA standards, and used in the federal system and in most other states. That template is to state a bright-line rule in bringing cases to trial, with clearly defined periods of excluded delay, and a remedy that affords finality but allows relief in exceptional circumstances.[323]

CONSTITUTIONAL AND CONTRACTUAL IMMUNITY

A grant of immunity makes a person immune from prosecution or civil suit. There are several types of immunity.

Defendants have constitutional immunity from testifying against themselves. The Fifth Amendment states that, "No person . . . shall be compelled in any criminal case to be a witness against himself." The defendant has an absolute privilege not to testify in his or her own trial, and they cannot be asked to take the stand.[324] Witnesses who are not the defendant may be called to give testimony that may possibly incriminate them. These witnesses are called, sworn in, and take the witness seat. When asked an incriminating question these witnesses may then "claim the Fifth." Individuals may refuse "to answer official questions put to him in any proceeding, civil or criminal, formal or informal, where the answers might incriminate him in further criminal proceedings."[325]

Sometimes the government wishes to compel the testimony of these essential witnesses and is willing to provide them immunity in exchange for their testimony. The type of immunity

---

[322] Emanuel, *supra* at 362-363.
[323] Gail Meyer, Legislative Representative, OCDLA, letter to Oregon Senate Judiciary Committee dated February 13, 2014.
[324] *See, Lefkowitz v. Turley*, 414 U.S. 70 (1973).
[325] *Kastigar v. U.S.*, 406 U.S. 441 (1972).

most likely to arise in the criminal justice realm is this immunity granted to a witness in exchange for his or her testimony at trial, grand jury, or some other proceeding. This grant of immunity comes in two forms--"use immunity" and "transactional immunity." Use immunity is the more limited of the two. With use immunity, prosecutors cannot use the immunized testimony in a subsequent criminal prosecution against the witness. But, the state could still prosecute and use other evidence it might have against that witness. Transactional immunity is broader and protects the witness from prosecution for any activity mentioned in the witness's testimony. Many states require a grant of transactional immunity before compelling a witness' testimony, but according to the Court, federal prosecutors only have to grant use immunity to compel an unwilling witness to testify.[326]

Governmental entities have immunity and cannot be sued unless they agree to be. State and federal tort claim laws are concessions made by the government to allow it, and its agent, to be sued under very limited circumstances. Generally, an agent of the state has immunity from suit to the extent that he or she was acting within the scope of his or her employment. Several cases mentioned in this book arose when someone sued a police officer for violating his or her civil liberties. In these cases, the question is not whether the defendant committed the crime, but rather whether the officer should have to pay monetary damages. For example, *Safford Unified School District v. Redding*, 557 U.S. 364 (2009), involved the search of a student at school. Although the Fourth Amendment was at issue, the case hinged not on whether the search violated Redding's rights (the Court found that it did), but whether the school officials had immunity (the Court found that they did) and if that had to pay Redding (the Court held they did not.) In *Scott v. Harris*, 550 U.S. 372 (2007), the question was whether the police had violated Scott's right by violating the Fourth Amendment's protection against reasonable searches and seizures by engaging in a high speed chased that left Scott paralyzed (the Court held that they did not and that the stop was reasonable).

Under international law, persons who have diplomatic status and serve as part of a diplomatic mission (including members of their staff and households) are immune from arrest and prosecution and enjoy diplomatic immunity. *Diplomatic immunity* attaches to the foreign state, not the individual diplomat. If a diplomat has really acted heinously, the foreign state may be asked to, and may agree to, waive the diplomat's immunity.

Legislative immunity is constitutionally based. Article I, Section 6 of the U.S. Constitution provides that members of Congress, in all cases except treason, felony, and breach of the peace, are privileged from arrest during attendance at and in going to and returning from legislative sessions. State constitutions have similar provisions.

WRAP UP

Assuming the government has proven all the elements of a crime, defendants may nevertheless raise defenses that may result in their exoneration. "Defense" is a general term that includes perfect and imperfect defenses, justifications and excuses, and procedural defenses. Justifications are defenses that assert, "I did the act, but I am not guilty because what I did was the right thing to do under the circumstances." Self-defense, defense of others, defense of property, defense of habitation, necessity, consent, and execution of public duties are justifications. Excuses are defenses that assert, "Although I did the act, I am not responsible because I was (fill in the excuse). Insanity, extreme emotional distress, age, intoxication, mistake, PTSD, PMS, and other syndromes are excuses. Procedural defenses, at their core, are attacks on the government's handling of the case or authority to prosecute the case. Double jeopardy,

---

[326] *Id.*

speedy trial violations, entrapment, statute of limitations, and several types of immunity are types of procedural defenses.

SOME THINGS TO THINK ABOUT OR EXPLORE

> - Identify the law on self-defense in your state. Does it have a "stand your ground rule?" What, if any requirements of retreat are there before a person can use force in defending against unlawful use of force?
> - Identify which approach your state has adopted for the defense of others defense (alter ego approach? Reasonable perception approach?)
> - What is your opinion about the defense of insanity? Do you agree with the Court that states should be free to limit this as a defense? Do you think that insanity claims are too frequently made? (See, Samuel Walker's book, *Sense and Nonsense about Crime, Drugs, and Communities*, in which he discusses how infrequently insanity claims are made.)
> - Are you aware of any local cases currently pending trial in which the defendant has raised a justification, excuse, or procedural defense? How likely is he or she to prevail given what you know about the case and the laws surrounding these defenses?
> - What justifications defenses are allowed in your state? What excuse defenses are allowed to be raised?
> - Investigate what the burden of persuasion is in your state concerning affirmative defenses (to what level must the defendant convince the jury that he or she was acting with a justification or with an excuse?)
> - Explore your state's statutes of limitation and speedy trial statutes.

TERMINOLOGY

- affirmative defense
- alter-ego approach (defense of others)
- automatism
- battered child syndrome
- battered woman syndrome
- Blockburger Test
- castle exception
- choice of evils
- deadly force
- diminished capacity
- diplomatic immunity
- double jeopardy attaches
- duress
- Durham Rule
- excuse
- extreme emotional disturbance
- fitness to proceed/aid and assist evaluation
- imminent danger
- imperfect defense
- incidental contact
- initial aggressor rule
- Insanity Defense Reform Act
- involuntary intoxication
- irresistible impulse test
- justification
- legislative immunity

- manifest necessity
- mistake of law
- mistake of fact
- M'Naghten Rule
- necessity
- negative defense
- non-deadly force
- objectively reasonable
- objective approach to entrapment
- perfect defense
- post-traumatic stress disorder (PTSD)
- present danger
- reasonable perception approach (defense of others)
- retreat rule
- socially beneficial activity
- stand-your-ground laws
- subjectively reasonable
- subjective approach to entrapment
- Substantial Capacity Test
- testimonial immunity
- tolling the speedy trial clock
- tolling the statute of limitations
- transactional immunity
- use immunity
- voluntary intoxication

Chapter Seven: Search and Seizure

OVERVIEW AND LEARNING OBJECTIVES

This chapter examines the constraints of the Fourth Amendment on police search and seizure procedures. After reading this chapter, you should be able to answer the following questions:

> ➤ What are the requirements of the Fourth Amendment?
> ➤ How does the Court define "search" in the context of the Fourth Amendment?
> ➤ What types of government action fall outside the definition of "search"?
> ➤ When will the following warrantless searches be allowed by the Court: automobile searches, exigent circumstance searches, hot pursuit searches, searches incident to arrest, community caretaking searches, school searches, jail and prison searches, administrative searches, inventory searches?
> ➤ How is probable cause different than reasonable suspicion, and what types of searches and seizures can the police engage in based on reasonable suspicion?
> ➤ How do arrests differ from stops? What objective basis is required for each?
> ➤ How does the Court define a "stop"?
> ➤ What are the requirements for a valid arrest?
> ➤ When will the Court permit a suspicionless checkpoint, roving patrol, or roadblock?
> ➤ What personal interests are involved when police search a person? Seize a person? Search a person's property? Seize a person's property?

THE FOURTH AMENDMENT AND THE WARRANT REQUIREMENT

The Fourth Amendment prohibits "unreasonable searches and seizures." Searches and seizures conducted by the government without a warrant are *per se* unreasonable unless they fall within one of the few specifically established and carefully delineated exceptions to the warrant requirement.[327] In addition to requiring a warrant, the Fourth Amendment specifies requirements for issuing a search warrant. It states: ". . . no Warrants shall issue, but upon probable cause, supported by Oath or affirmation, and particularly describing the place to be searched, and the persons or things to be seized."

---

[327] *See, Katz v. United States* 389 U.S. 347 (1967).

REQUIREMENTS FOR A WARRANT

OATH OR AFFIRMATION

In seeking a search warrant, the officer ("the affiant") must swear out a warrant application. The Fourth Amendment requires warrants be supported by statements made under oath or affirmation. Thus, the officer must 1) present a written affidavit to a magistrate that requests that a warrant be issued, 2) swear under oath or affirmation that the information in the affidavit is truthful, and 3) convince the magistrate that the information sworn to establishes probable cause. The officer will generally appear *ex parte* (a hearing with only one party present) and be questioned by the judge. Sometimes, a telephonic warrant is appropriate, and in those cases the judge will place the officer under oath, and later have the officer reaffirm what was said on the phone as soon as the officer can be physically present before the judge.

PROBABLE CAUSE

The Fourth Amendment states that warrants must be based on probable cause. Judges may issue warrants only if they find the evidence is sufficient to establish probable cause to arrest an individual, search an individual, search or seize property. Probable cause must be determined from the "four corners" of the affidavit. This means that every fact that the judge considers is in some way mentioned on the warrant affidavit. For an arrest warrant the judge must find there is probable cause to believe that a crime was committed and that the person to be arrested is the one who committed the crime. For a search warrant the judge must find that there is probable cause to believe that a crime has been committed and the search will discover things specified in the application associated with the crime. Probable cause must be based on information known to police before they make an arrest or conduct a search. What they police discover conducting the search cannot retroactively provide probable cause to a search that initially lacked probable cause.

<u>*Probable Cause is Different than Beyond a Reasonable Doubt, Clear Convincing Evidence or Preponderance of the Evidence.*</u>

Probable cause is a level of "objective basis." It is a standard of how much evidence exists and how certain we are of its existence. The Court remarked,

> In dealing with probable cause . . . as the very name implies, we deal with probabilities. These are not technical; they are the factual and practical considerations of everyday life on which reasonable and prudent men, not legal technicians, act.[328]

Sufficient evidence to constitute probable cause is less than that needed for the beyond a reasonable doubt standard, less than that needed for the clear and convincing evidence standard, and less than that required for preponderance of the evidence.[329] The Court has said that

---

[328] *Brinegar v. United States*, 338 U.S. 160, 175 (1949)

[329] In a criminal trial, the government must put on evidence and convince a jury beyond a reasonable doubt of defendant's guilt. It is the highest objective basis the law requires. The clear and convincing standard is used with some criminal defenses and is higher than the preponderance of the evidence standard but less than beyond a reasonable doubt standard. The clear and convincing standard is used with some criminal defenses and is higher than the preponderance of the evidence standard but less than beyond a reasonable doubt standard.

[329] The preponderance of the evidence standard, means there is proof that something is more likely than not. This standard is used as a standard for raising some criminal defenses, but is more frequently used in civil trials as the standard of proof

probable cause to search exists when "there is a fair probability that contraband or evidence of a crime will be found in a particular place."[330] The probable cause determination is a "practical, common sense" decision based upon the totality of the circumstances."[331] Probable cause exists where the known facts and circumstances are sufficient to warrant a man of reasonable prudence in the belief that contraband or evidence of a crime will be found."[332] Probable cause, for the purpose of arrest, appears to mean the same "fair probability" standard established by the Court for searches. Arrests require a fair probability that an offense has been or is being committed by the person who is to be arrested. Probable cause under the Fourth Amendment is generally determined by an essentially *objective standard* (what a reasonable person would think) as opposed to a *subjective standard* (what the arresting officer thought).

Probable Cause Is More Than Reasonable Suspicion

The Court will sometimes allow interferences with liberty, property, and privacy rights based on less than probable cause. "In a series of decisions, * * * the Supreme Court has held that reasonable articulable suspicion of criminal activity justifies searches and seizures when the intrusion on individual privacy is minimal and outweighed by an important government interest."[333] These decisions, however, do not allow the issuance of an arrest warrant or a search warrant, but do allow the police to do a limited seizure, called a "stop," and a limited search, called a "frisk" The Court in *Terry v. Ohio,* 392 U.S. 1 (1968), first held that government officers can interfere with a person's Fourth Amendment liberty without having probable cause as long as the interference is "reasonable." Although the phrase "reasonable suspicion" wasn't even used in *Terry,* this phrase has become known as the . . .

> standard of evidence that police must have to detain a person for a brief field interrogation. The reasonable suspicion standard is also the basis of certain other warrantless searches. . . A definition of reasonable suspicion is the existence of articulable facts that support an officer's reasonable interference with a person's Fourth Amendment liberty, which facts do not rise to the level of probable cause. In contrast to probable cause, in which evidence creates an inference that a crime has been committed, reasonable suspicion is a lower standard of evidence. Reasonable suspicion exists only when evidence creates a suspicion that criminal activity 'may be afoot'.[334]

Probable Cause Is More Than A Hunch or "No Particularized Suspicion"

Another standard of evidence is "no particularized suspicion." This standard means that the police don't necessarily have any reason (or good reason) to think that a person is involved in criminal activity. The officer's interest could be peaked by a "hunch" or general curiosity and the inquisitiveness that goes along with being a police officer.

> When no Fourth Amendment interests are at stake, the police may perform certain law enforcement or investigative functions, without having to have any level of evidence to support their action. At the most basic level, a patrol officer can observe anyone walking or driving about and can be on the lookout for suspicious activity even though there was nothing suspicious about a person that drew the officer's attention to that particular person. A person walking or driving in a public place has no constitutional right not to be observed by members of the

---

[330] *Illinois v. Gates,* 462 U.S. 213, 238 (1983).
[331] *Id. at* 462 U.S. at 235.
[332] *Ornelas v. United States,* 517 U.S. 690 (1996).
[333] *Thirty-Fifth Annual Review of Criminal Procedure,* 35 Geo.L.J. Ann. Rev. Crim. Proc., 18 (2006).
[334] Zalman, *supra* at *86.*

public, including police officers. A patrol officer in a police car can follow a particular car driven on the public highway for the distance without having to justify this with any level of suspicion. [335]

To the extent that police do not either seize citizens or their property or search where a person has a legitimate privacy interest, police do not need any articulable suspicion to approach them on the street and ask them questions. A seizure does not occur simply because an officer walks up to an individual and asks a few questions -- so long as a reasonable person would feel free to disregard the officer and go about his or her business. Such encounters are consensual and need not be supported by reasonable suspicion of criminal activity.[336] Based on these encounters, police may develop "escalating probable cause." For example, Officer Andrews nonchalantly contacts Beth—a person he knows to be a meth user and asks, "How you doing Beth, when's the last time you used meth?" And Beth honestly replies, "Well, Officer Andrews, it has probably been a couple hours ago." And Officer Andrews asks, "do you have any on you right now?" and Beth replies, "Yes, as a matter of fact, I do." Officer Andrews now has at least reasonable suspicion to do a more significant field interrogation. Is it probable cause? More facts would be needed to determine that. For example, does Andrews know Beth to be an honest, (but rather naïve) individual? Has Beth possessed meth on her person in the past?

Not all judges think alike and agree whether the facts presented rise to the level of reasonable suspicion or probable cause. Maybe the officer just has a hunch. Who decides when it is a close call? In *Ornelas v. United States*, 517 U.S. 690 (1996), the Court established a standard of review to apply to a magistrate's determination of reasonable suspicion or probable cause. The Court found that determining probable cause or reasonable suspicion involved "mixed questions of law and facts," and therefore, the de *novo* standard of review is warranted. This means that the appellate court judges get to decide for themselves whether probable cause or reasonable suspicion existed, and they do not have to defer to the trial judge's findings. In drawing conclusions, however, the appellate court should evaluate the facts from the perspective of an "objectively reasonable police officer."

The Test Of Probable Cause May Depend On The Source Of Information

Probable cause is established on the affidavit by referring to information known by the officer based upon personal observations. Additionally, warrant applications frequently spell out the officer's special training and experience to show why seemingly meaningless information may be indicative of criminal behavior. Police officers may also rely on the collective knowledge and observations of other officers in their affidavit supporting the warrant.[337] Finally, police officers frequently rely on second hand information from non-police sources. These sources are referred to as "informants" and they are generally categorized as either named or unnamed informants.

To establish probable cause on the basis of informant's statements, the court will require an adequate foundation be established. In the past the court relied on the "Aguilar/Spinelli" test that required sufficient information to show that the informant was both reliable and had an adequate basis of knowledge. In 1983, however, the court abandoned that two-pronged test and adopted instead a "totality of the circumstances test."[338] For example, in *Navarette v. California*, 572 U.S. _____ (April 22, 2014), the court found that, under the totality of the circumstances, police had a probable cause to stop the defendant after they received an anonymous tip that a silver

---

[335] *Id.*

[336] *United States v. Drayton*, 536 U.S. 194 (2002).

[337] United States v. Hensley, 469 U.S. 221 (1985)

[338] *Illinois v. Gates*, supra.

Ford F150 pickup truck, with a specific license plate number, had forced the caller off the road, that he was weaving and driving erratically. The Court, in a 5-4 decision, held that the officer had a reasonable suspicion that the driver was intoxicated which justified the stop. "Because the reasonable suspicion standard allows an officer to rely on information beyond what that officer personally observed, a stop based on an anonymous tip does not violate the Fourth Amendment as long as the officer had reason to believe the information contained in the tip was reliable."

Some states still maintain the dual- pronged approach from the Aguilar and Spinelli cases, so you should be familiar with it. The first prong examines the informant's reliability.

The informant's reliability is described as the veracity prong. The affidavit must demonstrate that the informant is believable or that the information is reliable. Fine distinctions may be drawn between establishing reliability by showing that the informant is credible and establishing reliability by showing that the information comes from circumstances assuring that the particular information is indeed trustworthy on a specific occasion.[339]

In deciding whether the informant is reliable a magistrate will consider the following:

- Did law enforcement provide enough data to allow an independent judgment (by the magistrate) of the informant's trustworthiness?
- Did the informant make statements against their own interest? (Generally, such statements would not be made unless they were true.)
- Did the informant make previous statements that were reliable?
- Was there a controlled buy where the police searched the informant before sending them off to the target location, and did the police immediately thereafter recover drugs from the informant?
- Was there independent police corroboration supporting the informant's statements?
- Was the corroboration by police only about easily identifiable and innocent information? (Standing alone such information does not establish reliability.)
- Was there any cross-corroboration with other informants?
- How detailed was the information? (The more detailed the more indicative of reliability.)
- Is there any information that suggests that the informant has a reason to lie?
- Does the informant have a criminal history or background?
- Is the informant a disinterested citizen? (A disinterested citizen, even if unnamed, will be considered more reliable than an interested citizen. [340])

The second prong of the Aguilar/Spinelli test requires that the affiant establish the informant has a basis of knowledge for the information he or she is providing. Some statutes and cases require that the affidavit set forth facts justifying the inference that the informant was in a position to perceive the events the informant reported to the police.[341] In deciding whether the informant has an adequate basis of knowledge the magistrate will consider the following:

- Did the affidavit set forth the informant's basis of knowledge? (If not, the information should be disregarded.)
- Was the officer able to answer how the informant (or officer) knows that each specific assertion of fact is true?

---

[339] Oregon Department of Justice, Oregon Search and Seizure Manual, 2008.
[340] See, *id.*
[341] *Id.*

- Did the informant personally observe the facts that were conveyed to the officer?
- Did the officer include sufficient detail from the informant's account to convey that a law was being broken (balancing that with the need to keep the informant's identity secret)?
- What is the weight of the detail? Is it important or simply superficial?
- Did the informant have knowledge about contraband?[342]
-

Some states use the Aguilar/Spinelli test with unnamed informants, but the totality of the circumstance test with named informants. Named informants are subject to both civil and criminal liability for filing false reports, which is why courts generally find them to be more credible than unnamed informants. Informants also include those who are unnamed but identifiable. For example, a person may make an "anonymous" tip, but still be identified by the police. These unnamed-but-not-confidential informants may be given credence to the same extent as a named informant if they are not criminally involved. Some states require that named informants who are criminally involved must have their information corroborated.[343]

Negative Information About An Informant May Affect Whether Probable Cause Exists.

In applying for a warrant, the officer should tell the judge everything--except information unlawfully obtained--including information that may reflect negatively on the informant or the investigating officers. This includes negative information about informants' backgrounds, informants' motivations to tell the truth or exaggerate or fabricate evidence. Information that led to an earlier illegal search may be used to lay the foundation for an informant even thought the fruits of the earlier search cannot be used in the warrant affidavit. Police affiants need to disclose negative information about any prior unlawful searches and improper conduct of the officers.

Probable Cause And Anticipatory Warrants.

Sometimes police have reason to believe that at some time in the future there will be evidence of a crime in a certain location. They may obtain an "anticipatory" search warrant based on an affidavit that demonstrates probable cause will exist at some future time after a triggering event occurs. These anticipatory warrants are permissible under the Fourth Amendment.[344] An affidavit for an anticipatory warrant satisfies the probable cause requirement if it establishes that: (1) if the triggering condition occurs, there is a fair probability that contraband or evidence of a crime will be found in a particular place; and (2) there is probable cause to believe that the triggering condition will occur.[345]

Probable Cause Cannot Be Based on Stale Information

To satisfy the Fourth Amendment, information used to form the basis of probable cause should not be "stale." If, for example, a police officer has information that the suspect murdered someone and stashed the body in his apartment, the officer should not wait one or two weeks before going to apply for a warrant to search the apartment for evidence of a crime. Why? Well, it is highly likely that in the intervening week or two, the body will be moved from the residence. Waiting two weeks to apply for the warrant makes the information stale. This no-staleness requirement is particularly important when the location to be searched is the suspect's residence. To get a warrant to search a residence, the police must establish probable cause to believe that the suspect committed the crime and *still has* evidence of the crime in his or her possession, and the affidavit must establish probable cause that the evidence is *currently* located in the suspect's

---

[342] *Id.*

[343] *State v. Arnold*, 115 Or App. 258 (1992), rev. den 315 Or 312 (1993).

[344] *United States v. Grubbs*, 547 U.S. 90 (2006).

[345] *Id.*

residence — the mere fact that the suspect resides there is not necessarily sufficient to establish the nexus.

Probable Cause and Profiles

Courts may consider the special expertise of trained investigators to evaluate otherwise ambiguous conduct, and conduct, innocent in itself, may serve as part of the foundation for reasonable suspicion or probable cause. Just because some fact observed by an officer also fits some generic criminal profile of the general characteristics of a class of offenders this does not detract from their evidentiary significance as seen by a trained agent.[346] Such observations are properly included in the determination of whether there was probable cause. But, officers may not rely solely upon general statistics regarding profiles of offenders to develop a basis for an investigative stop or for probable cause.[347] Officers do not have probable cause simply because they see someone with a certain characteristic or trait associated with a general profile of criminal behavior. Particularly concerning is racial and ethnic profiling which suggests that certain individuals are more likely to have committed crimes simply because of their race. For example, a nationwide study by the United States Customs Service revealed that while over 43 percent of those subjected to searches as part of the Service's drug interdiction efforts were black or Hispanic, the "hit rates" for those groups per capita were lower than for white Americans. And according to the congressional General Accounting Office, while black female U.S. citizens were *nine times* more likely to be subjected to x-ray searches by U.S. Customs Officials than white female U.S. citizens, these black women were less than half as likely to be found carrying contraband as white females.[348] Although the Court has permitted "pretext stops" in *Whren v. United States,* it specifically noted,

> We of course agree with petitioners that the Constitution prohibits selective enforcement of the law based on considerations such as race. But the constitutional basis for objecting to intentionally discriminatory application of laws is the Equal Protection Clause, not the Fourth Amendment. Subjective intentions play no role in ordinary, probable cause Fourth Amendment analysis.

PARTICULARITY REQUIREMENT

Under the Fourth Amendment, a warrant must "particularly describe the place to be searched, and the persons or things to be seized." Technical errors (or "scrivener's errors") do not invalidate a search and seizure so long as the place to be searched is adequately described and the mistakes are reasonable. *Marron v. United States,* 275 U.S. 192 (1927), indicates that the goal of the particularity requirement is that nothing is left to the discretion of the police.[349] In *Groh v. Ramirez,* 540 U.S. 551 (2004), the Court found that a search conducted under a warrant that completely failed to state the things to be seized was unconstitutional. In *Grubbs* (supra), the court emphasized that the particularity requirement has only two components: that the warrant particularly describe the place to be searched, and (2) that the warrant particularly describe the persons or things to be seized.

---

[346] United States v. Sokolow, 490 U.S. 1 (1989).

[347] *Reid v. Georgia,* 448 U.S. 438 (1980).

[348] *See,* http://www.civilrights.org/publications/justice-on-trial/race.html?referrer=https://www.google.com/.

[349] *Marron, 275 U.S.* at 196. ("The requirement that warrants shall particularly describe the things to be seized makes general searches under them impossible and prevents the seizure of one thing under a warrant describing another. As to what is to be taken, nothing is left to the discretion of the officer executing the warrant.")

The Particularity Requirement and Residences

The general rule regarding the requirement for a particular description of the place to be searched is that it "is enough if the description is such that the officer with a search warrant can, with reasonable effort, ascertain and identify the place intended."[350] This typically requires a street address and where relevant an apartment number. The police are not required to be technically accurate in every detail. An accurate physical description of the structure and the surrounding area likely will be determined to be reasonable. In *Maryland v. Garrison*, 480 U.S. 79 (1987), a search was conducted based on a warrant that authorized the search of a third-floor apartment of 2036 Park Avenue. Following the search, the police discovered that there were two apartments rather than a single apartment on the third floor and that they had seized illegal drugs from the wrong unit. The Court upheld the constitutionality of the search and explained that the police had taken a number of steps before applying for the warrant to determine the layout of the building. The Court held that the constitutionality of the police conduct must be evaluated "in light of the information available to them at the time they acted. Facts that emerge after the warrant is issued have no bearing on whether or not a warrant was validly issued." [351]

The Particularity Requirement and Persons

The particularity requirement applies equally to search warrants involving persons. If the person to be searched is named or described in the supporting affidavit, the warrant must contain a similar description to comply with requirements. In *Ybarra v. Illinois*, 444 U.S. 85 (1979), the Court found that a warrant that permitted the police to search a tavern and the bartender "Greg" did not allow police to search each patron at the tavern, notwithstanding a state statute that permitted law enforcement officers to detain and search any person found on the premises during the execution of a warrant. The Court found that Ybarra's rights under the Fourth and Fourteenth Amendment had been violated. When police entered the bar, the Court reasoned, they had no probable cause to believe that any person, aside from the bartender would be violating the law. There was nothing noted in the warrant that would have given the police any authority to search all people who were present.

NEUTRAL AND DETACHED MAGISTRATE

Although the Fourth Amendment doesn't specifically mention that the warrant be issued by a neutral and detached magistrate, case law makes clear that the magistrate must be neutral and detached. "Neutral" means that the magistrate must be unbiased in the case. "Detached" means that the magistrate should not be part of the executive branch nor closely intertwined, nor be overly interested in the outcome of the case.

The Court examined whether the magistrate was neutral and detached in several cases. In *Coolidge v. New Hampshire*, 403 U.S. 43 (1971), for example, a statute made the state's attorney general a justice of the peace. The attorney general took charge of a murder investigation and issued a search warrant to search the suspect's home and automobile. The Court found that this violated the Fourth Amendment because the attorney general was not part of the judicial branch but rather part of the executive branch of government.

In *Connally v. Georgia*, 429 U.S. 245 (1977), the magistrate received five dollars for each warrant issued, but no money if the warrant was denied. The Court held that the mere possibility of financial gain was sufficient to violate due process and the Fourth Amendment rights of suspects. In *Lo-Ji Sales, Inc. v. New York*, 442 U.S. 319 (1979), the Court found that an overly helpful town judge who joined in on the search and raid of an adult bookstore and was there on

---

[350] *Steele v. United States*, 267 U.S. 498 (1925).
[351] *Maryland v. Garrison*, 480 U.S. 79, 85 (1987).

hand to determine whether there was probable cause to seize various materials was not a detached magistrate. The Court stated, "The Town Justice did not manifest that neutrality and detachment demanded of a judicial officer when presented with a warrant application for a search and seizure." The loss of detachment could be inferred from the objective fact that the town justice "allowed himself to become a member, if not the leader, of the search party which was essentially a police operation."

In judging whether the warrant was issued by a "neutral and detached magistrate" the person's position in government is, however, not controlling. The Court, in *Shadwick v. City of Tampa*, 429 U.S. 245 (1972), upheld a law that allowed a municipal court clerk to issue arrest warrants for municipal ordinance violations. The Court found that the clerk, under this law, was not subject to the authority of the prosecutor or police but worked for the judicial branch and was under the supervision of a municipal judge and that the clerk was charged with determining and was capable of determining whether probable cause existed to believe a municipal ordinance had been violated.

SPECIAL WARRANTS FOR ELECTRONIC EAVESDROPPING

Omnibus Crime Control and Safe Street Act of 1968

If police are interested in doing a wiretap or electronic surveillance of an individual, they must apply for a special warrant. Title III of the Omnibus Crime Control and Safe Streets Act of 1968[352] relating to wiretapping and electronic surveillance sets forth the special application process and limitations of a wiretap order. This act provided the most protection for individual privacy by placing a general ban on the interception of "wire, oral, or electronic communications" while they were taking place (§2511). However, the ban contained a serious crime exception. Serious crimes were those punishable by death or more than one year in prison. Under the Act, the U.S. Attorney General or other senior Department of Justice official had to approve a law enforcement officer's application for a court order from a federal judge to allow the officer to secretly intercept and capture conversations. The application had to include how long the interception was going to last.

Patriot Act

The U.S. Patriot Act[353] reduced the constrictions upon electronic surveillance and provided more government power and less privacy protection for individuals. The Act significantly expanded government surveillance power beyond the Crime Control and Safe Streets Act of 1968. It allows the government to access stored "wire and electronic communications," such as voice and e-mail. Second, the power applies to "any criminal investigation," not just to serious crimes. Officers still have to get a warrant based on probable cause. But, if the information has been stored for more than six months, the government doesn't have to tell subscribers about the warrant for 90 days if doing so would jeopardize the investigation. The Patriot Act also allows "trap and trace" devices and pen registers which can be used to investigate any crime without court approval and without officers' ever notifying subscribers they have it or what they learn from it. Officers are limited in getting and using the secret caller IDs only by having to get approval of a department senior official. Finally, the Patriot Act has expanded governmental authority by allowing sneak and peek warrants (§ 213). Sneak and peek warrants allow officers to enter private places without the owner or occupant consenting or even knowing about it. In order to issue a sneak and peek warrant the judge must

---

[352] Pub L. 90-351, 82 Stat 197, 42 U.S.C. § 3711 (1968).

[353] Uniting and Strengthening America by Providing Appropriate Tools Required to Intercept and Obstruct Terrorism (USA PATRIOT ACT) Act of 2001'. PUB L. 107 – 56 (2001).

find (1) reasonable cause to believe that providing immediate notification of the execution of the warrant may have an adverse effect, (2) that the warrant prohibits the seizure of tangible [personal] property . . . except where reasonable necessity for the seizure, and (3) the warrant requires giving notice within a reasonable time after its execution, which period may be extended by the court for good cause shown.

EXECUTING A WARRANT

NO-KNOCK WARRANTS--THE KNOCK AND ANNOUNCE REQUIREMENT

At the time the Constitution was adopted, there was a principle of the English common law that law enforcement officers should ordinarily announce their presence and authority before entering a residence to conduct a search or make an arrest pursuant to a warrant. Under federal law an officer is required to knock and announce on arrival at the place to be searched. 18 U.S.C.A. §3109. That section stipulates:

> An officer may break open any outer or inner door or window of a house, or any part of a house, or anything therein, to execute a search warrant, if, after notice of his authority and purpose, he is refused admittance or when necessary to liberate himself or a person aiding him in the execution of the warrant.[354]

In *Wilson v. Arkansas,* 514 U.S. 927, 936 (1995), the Court held that the knock-and-announce requirement is an element of the Fourth Amendment "reasonableness" inquiry and that the "search and seizure of a dwelling might be constitutionally defective if police officers entered without prior announcement." Nevertheless, the Supreme Court found that a violation of the knock-and-announce requirement does not necessarily trigger the exclusionary rule.[355] Moreover, the Fourth Amendment allows exceptions to the knock and announce rule.[356] The Fourth Amendment does not permit a blanket exception to the knock-and-announce requirement for all felony drug investigations; instead, the officers' actions must be evaluated based on the circumstances at the time of the entry. In *Richards v. Wisconsin,* 520 U.S. 385 (1997), the Court noted that, in appropriate circumstances, it would be reasonable under the Fourth Amendment for the issuing magistrate to authorize a no-knock entry on the face of the warrant. *Richards* indicated that police need not knock and announce their presence when doing so could enable the occupants to destroy the evidence.

PROTECTIVE SWEEPS DURING EXECUTION OF ARREST WARRANT

The Courts have allowed a protective sweep when officers, armed with an arrest warrant, went to the suspect's home and arrest him.[357] A "protective sweep" is a quick and limited search of premises, incident to an arrest of a suspect and conducted to protect the safety of police officers or others. It is narrowly confined to a cursory visual inspection of those places in which a person might be hiding.[358]

In *Maryland v. Buie,* 494 U.S. 325 (1990), two men committed the robbery of a Godfather's Pizza in Prince George County Maryland. One of the two men was wearing a red running suit at the time of the robbery. Police obtained a warrant for Buie and his accomplice and staked out Buie's home. Two days later seven police officers went to Buie's home to execute the arrest

---

[354] Scheb, *supra* at 484.
[355] *Hudson v. Michigan,* 547 U.S. 586 (2006).
[356] *Id.*
[357] *See, Maryland v. Buie,* 494 U.S. 435 (1990).
[358] *Id.* at 327.

warrant. The police officers spread out through the first and second floor of the home and then shouted down into the basement to see if anyone was down there. Buie responded, and the police ordered him to come upstairs with his hands up. Officers arrested and handcuffed Buie. One officer went to the basement in case someone else was down there. While down in the basement, that officer saw the red running suit that was believed to be worn at the Godfather's Pizza parlor lying in plain view on a stack of clothes. Officers seized the suit, and defendant moved to have it suppressed as the product of an illegal search of his basement.

> We should emphasize that such a protective sweep, aimed at protecting the arresting officers, if justified by the circumstances, is nevertheless not a full search of the premises, but may extend only to a cursory inspection of those spaces where a person may be found. The sweep lasts no longer than is necessary to dispel the reasonable suspicion of danger and in any event no longer than it takes to complete the arrest and depart the premises.
>
> . . .
>
> We conclude that by requiring a protective sweep to be justified by probable cause to believe that a serious and demonstrable potentiality for danger existed, the Court of Appeals of Maryland applied an unnecessarily strict Fourth Amendment standard. The Fourth Amendment permits a properly limited protective sweep in conjunction with an in-home arrest when the searching officer possesses a reasonable belief based on specific and articulable facts that the area to be swept harbors an individual posing a danger to those on the arrest scene.[359]

DETAINING AND SEARCHING PERSONS AT THE SEARCH SCENE

Absent probable cause or reasonable officer-safety concerns, police cannot search and frisk persons not named in a search warrant who just happen to be present during the execution of a warrant unless they have reasonable suspicion to believe the particular person is armed or dangerous.[360] But, according to *Michigan v. Summers*, 452 US 692 (1981), a warrant to search the premises for contraband implicitly carries with it the limited authority to detain occupants of the premise while a proper search is conducted. Police may conduct an officer-safety search of the immediate area around an individual when the officer has reason to believe that the individual may gain immediate control of a weapon. The court has also approved of handcuffing individuals during warrant executions under some circumstances.[361]

In *Bailey v. United States*, 568 U.S. 186 (2013) the Court held that police could not search Bailey's home when they arrested him, without a warrant, about one mile from his apartment. The Court reasoned that *Summers* did not apply because Bailey was not in or immediately outside the residence being searched when he was detained. Arrests incident to the execution of a search warrant are lawful under the Fourth Amendment, but once an individual leaves the premises being searched, any detention must be justified by another means.[362]

In *Los Angeles County v. Rettele*, 550 U.S. 609 (2007), the Retteles sued the police under 42 U.S.C. § 1983 when, during an execution of a warrant of their home, police ordered them out of bed and had them stand for a brief period of time while still naked. The Retteles were of a different race than the suspects indicated on the warrant. The court, nevertheless, determined that the police orders to the occupants, in the context of the lawful search in this case, were

---

[359] *Id.* at 325-326, 326-327.
[360] *Ybarra v. Illinois*, 444 U.S. 85 (1979).
[361] *Muehler v. Mena*, 544 US 93 (2005).
[362] http://www.oyez.org/cases/2010-2019/2012/2012_11_770

permissible, and perhaps necessary, to protect the safety of the deputies and the residents' detention was not unreasonable either.

NIGHTTIME WARRANTS

The judge may authorize execution of the warrant at any time of the day or night under state laws, but generally, the search warrant affidavit must specify the special circumstances justifying a nighttime search. For example, Rule 41 (e) of Federal Rule of Criminal Procedure provides, "the warrant shall command the officer to search, within a specified period of time not to exceed 10 days, the person or place named or the property or person specified. The warrant shall be served in the daytime, unless the issuing authority . . .authorizes its execution at times other than daytime." Section (a) (2) (B) defines daytime as the period between 6:00 a.m. and 10:00 p.m. State laws vary as to the period of time in which a warrant should be executed. California, for example, limits warrant service from 7 a.m. to 10 p.m. unless there is specific direction in the warrant; Texas does not impose restrictions on the hours when a warrant may be executed.

TIMELINESS/LACK OF STALENESS

Officers should execute the warrant within a short time period. States generally have statutes governing the time period within which the warrant must be executed. If not, the judge may also set the time period within which it must be executed on the face of the warrant. Failure to execute the warrant within a statutory time requirement or within the period set forth on the face of the warrant puts the officers in the same position as if they did not have a warrant.[363]

Assuming there is no statutory period, nor a time set by the magistrate, police should nevertheless make sure they execute the warrant in a timely fashion or the defendant can claim it was stale. Information contained in an affidavit must justify the conclusion that the seizable evidence is still present at the location to be searched at the time that application for the warrant is made. In determining whether a warrant is stale, courts consider:

- The totality of the circumstances
- The length of time
- The character of the crime and the thing to be seized
- The commercial quantity of the drugs (for example, seeing three pounds of marijuana at the house two days before the warrant issued was not stale)
- The durable quality of the items sought (things not readily discarded or consumed are more likely to be there longer and thus the warrant is less likely to be stale.)
- Whether the item is contraband (things criminally possessed)
- Whether there is evidence of ongoing criminal activity — this increases the likelihood that even after the passage of time, items subject to seizure will remain in the location to be searched.
- Any admissions regarding expectation of continuing presence of seizable evidence
- Any prior criminal activity.

THIRD PARTIES PARTICIPATING IN THE EXECUTION OF THE WARRANT

The Court addressed the issue of law enforcement inviting the media or "ride-alongs" into a home while executing a warrant it the case of *Wilson v. Layne*, 526 U.S. 603 (1999).

> While executing a warrant to arrest petitioners' son in their home, respondents, deputy federal marshals and local sheriff's deputies, invited a newspaper reporter

---

[363] *See, e.g., United States v. Jones*, 565 US 400 (2012).

and a photographer to accompany them. The warrant made no mention of such a media "ride-along." The officers' early morning entry into the home prompted a confrontation with petitioners, and a protective sweep revealed that the son was not in the house. The reporters observed and photographed the incident but were not involved in the execution of the warrant. Their newspaper never published the photographs they took of the incident. Petitioners sued the officers in their personal capacities for money damages under *Bivens* v. *Six Unknown Fed. Narcotics Agents,* (the federal marshals) and 42 U.S.C. § 1983 (the sheriff's deputies), contending that the officers' actions in bringing the media to observe and record the attempted execution of the arrest warrant violated their Fourth Amendment rights.

The Court held, "It is a violation of the Fourth Amendment for police officers to bring members of the media or other third parties into a home during the execution of a search warrant when the presence of the third parties is not in aid of the execution of the warrant.[364]

SECURING A PREMISE OR AUTOMOBILE WHILE A WARRANT IS OBTAINED

Under the Fourth Amendment, "securing a dwelling, on the basis of probable cause, to prevent the destruction or removal of evidence while a search warrant is being sought is not itself an unreasonable seizure of either the dwelling or its contents."[365] In *Illinois v. McArthur*, 531 U.S. 326 (2001), the actions of police officers in securing defendant's residence for two hours while seeking a search warrant, based upon probable cause to believe that the residence contained illegal drugs, did not violate the Fourth Amendment.

[U]nder the circumstances of this case, which included the officer's reasonable fear that defendant might destroy evidence inside the house if not restrained, the seizure was not unreasonable. However, a warrantless entry into a dwelling without exigent circumstances is an illegal search under the Fourth Amendment.[366]

Similarly, courts have found it is reasonable to seize and impound an automobile, on the basis of probable cause, for whatever period is necessary to obtain a warrant for the search.[367]

SCOPE OF SEARCH WITH A WARRANT

Police may search only those areas that could contain the items listed in the warrant. For example, if the warrant allows the police to seize a three-foot-long shotgun, then they will not be able to look in the nightstand drawer (because of its size, the shot gun would not fit in a nightstand drawer). Also, the character of the things specified in the warrant defines the areas that may be searched. For example, police could not move a stereo to examine serial numbers when the basis for their search was the investigation of a shooting.[368]

Items Subject To Search And Seizure With A Warrant

The court will generally find that items seized were within the scope of the warrant when they are reasonably consistent with the warrant's description. For example, in one case, the court

---

[364] *Wilson v. Layne*, 526 U.S. 603 (1999).
[365] *Segura v. United States*, 468 U.S. 796 (1984).
[366] *Id.*
[367] *See, e.g., Chambers v. Maroney*, 399 U.S. 42, 51 (1970).
[368] *Arizona v. Hicks*, 480 U.S. 321 (1987).

held that a search was not fatally compromised when officers seized a letter on motel stationary when the search warrant affidavit described the item to be seized as a newspaper in an envelope with no return address. [369]

Things Seen In Plain View During A Search

When officers enter to execute a warrant and they see something that is in plain view and obviously criminal, they can seize the objects (under the plain view doctrine) even though there were not listed on the warrant. Officers, for example, do not need to ignore a pile of cocaine on a living room table when they enter on a warrant directing them to seize money stolen in a bank robbery.

AFTER EXECUTING THE WARRANT

Police must generally give a receipt to the person from whom they seized items, listing the things that were seized, the time and date of the warrant execution, and the officer in charge of executing the warrant. If the owner of the property is unknown or not present, the police can give the receipt to the person in apparent control of the premises or vehicle. Police also file that list with the court. This is called a warrant return.

THE WARRANT RETURN

State laws generally require that the officer who has executed the search return the warrant, the original affidavit, and a list of things seized and the date and time of the search to the issuing judge as soon as reasonably possible. Some states specify a time frame for which the return must be filed.[370] Defects in returning the warrant do not lead to suppression of seized evidence unless the failure to comply results in the state being unable to prove they searched according to a lawful search warrant.

SEALING THE WARRANT AND APPLICATION

State and federal law requires search warrant proceedings to be conducted with secrecy appropriate to the circumstances. After the warrant is executed, no secrecy is required. Federal courts hold that trial courts have inherent authority to issue orders to seal search warrants in appropriate cases. [371] Courts have rejected claims that the sealing of a search warrant material violates the public's First Amendment right of access or the common law right of access.

DEFINING SEARCHES

The Fourth Amendment protects against unreasonable searches and seizures. To be protected by the Fourth Amendment, a suspect must be impacted by a government action that qualify as "searches" or "seizures" as defined by the Court. The Court, has not been necessarily consistent in its definitions, however. It has, however, consistently maintained that the Fourth Amendment applies only to searches and seizures that are the product of government action. [372] A suspect cannot complain of action by a private party. The Fourth Amendment is "wholly inapplicable to a search or seizure, even an unreasonable one, effected by a private individual not acting as an agent of the government or with the participation or knowledge of a government official."[373] That said, the Fourth Amendment's restrictions to "government" actions have been

---

[369] *State v. Eisman*, 21 Or App 92 (1975),

[370] Under federal rules, the warrant must be returned in ten days.

[371] Although there is no statutory law or controlling precedent, Oregon prosecutors have asked for and received orders sealing search warrants and search warrant affidavits.

[372] Thirty-Fifth Annual Review, *supra* at 3 (2006).

[373] *United States v. Jacobsen*, 466 U.S. 109, 113 (1984).

read to broadly encompass any governmental actor—not just the police.[374] Also, if the police initiate or participate in an otherwise private search, that search may constitute government action. A private-party search becomes a government search if "the government coerces, dominates or directs the actions" of the person conducting the search.[375]

OLMSTEAD: SEARCHES TRESPASS ON A PERSON'S PROPERTY INTEREST.

The Court reviewed search and seizure cases from the 1920s through 1967 using the "trespass doctrine" established in *Olmstead v. United States*, 277 US. 438 (1928). In *Olmstead*, courts considered whether police had physically trespassed in order to see what they saw. If police physically intruded upon a constitutionally protected area without a warrant, this qualified as an unreasonable search under the Fourth Amendment. In *Olmstead* the Court reviewed whether police had illegally obtained evidence by placing a wiretap on telephone wires outside of Olmstead's home. Because the police did not physically intrude into Olmstead's home, the Court upheld the police action. Justice Brandeis dissented and urged that the proper question in defining a search is not whether police had trespassed, but rather whether their action invaded a person's expectation of privacy and the right to be left alone.

KATZ: SEARCHES INVOLVE A PERSON'S REASONABLE EXPECTATION OF PRIVACY

Forty years and several cases later, the Court in *Katz v. United States*, 389 U.S. 347 (1967), ostensibly abandoned the trespass doctrine and opted instead to define a search in terms consistent with Brandeis' *Olmstead* dissent. Under the Fourth Amendment, a search occurs when government officials invade a defendant's legitimate expectation of privacy.[376] "Official conduct that does not compromise a legitimate interest in privacy is not a search subject to the Fourth Amendment." In *Katz* the Court set forth a two-part test to determine if a person's expectation of privacy is a legitimate one. "First, the individual must have an actual subjective expectation of privacy. Second, society must be prepared to recognize that expectation as objectively reasonable."[377] For example, areas in which the Court has found no objectively reasonable expectation of privacy include: open fields,[378] inside a car[379] and in the areas outside a business.[380] "What a person knowingly exposes to the public, even in his own home or office, is not a subject of Fourth Amendment protection."[381] For example, a person has no legitimate expectation of privacy in garbage bags left at the curb,[382] or in a telephone number dialed on a phone,[383] or in the odor of controlled substances that may be detected by trained dogs from outside a vehicle.[384] On the other hand, the Fourth Amendment does protect activities conducted privately within a home. "In the home . . . all details are intimate details, because the entire area is held safe from prying eyes."[385] In one case the Court held that "any interest in possessing contraband is not be deemed legitimate, and thus, governmental conduct that only reveals possession of contraband compromises no legitimate privacy interest."[386] A defendant is not entitled to suppression of

---

[374] *See e.g., Dow Chemical v. United States*, 476 U.S. 227 (1986) and New Jersey v. TLO, 469 U.S. 325 (1985).
[375] *United States v. Smythe*, 84 F3d 1240, 1242 (10th Cir 1996).
[376] *Oliver v. United States* 466 U.S. 170 (1984); *Katz v. United States*, 389 U.S. 347 (1967).
[377] Thirty-Fifth Annual Review, supra at 3 (2006).
[378] *Oliver*, 466 U.S. at 177-178 (1984).
[379] *United States v. Knotts*, 460 U.S. 276 (1983).
[380] *Dow Chemical Co. v. United States*, supra.
[381] *Katz v. United States*, 389 U.S. at 351.
[382] *California v. Greenwood*, 486 U.S. 35 (1988).
[383] *Smith v. Maryland*, 442 U.S. 735 (1979).
[384] *Illinois v. Caballes*, 543 U.S. at 407-408
[385] *Kyllo v. United States*, 533 U.S. 27 (2001).
[386] *Illinois v. Caballes*, supra.

evidence discovered in a search unless the defendant demonstrates that the search violated his or her *own* personal Fourth Amendment right to a legitimate expectation of privacy.[387]

"The degree of intrusiveness involved in the government action is also relevant to determining whether a search has occurred."[388] A government agent's minimal intrusion into an area in which the defendant has a reasonable expectation of privacy may not violate the Fourth Amendment.[389] But when "the Government uses a device that is not in general public use [e.g., a thermal imaging device], to explore details of the home that would previously have been unknowable without physical intrusion, the surveillance is a "search" and is presumptively unreasonable without a warrant."[390]

FROM *KATZ* TO *OLMSTEAD*: *UNITED STATES V. JONES* AND *FLORIDA V. JARDINES*

Although the dust really hasn't settled on two relatively new cases—and it is hard to say for sure if this is a momentary "blip" or an approach that will get traction--the Court's decisions in *United States v. Jones*, 565 U.S. 400 (2012), and *Florida v. Jardines*, 569 U.S. 1 (2012) seem to breathe a bit of life into the *Olmstead* trespass doctrine that was long considered dead.[391] In *Jones* the Court unanimously decided that the government conducted an unreasonable search and seizure when it placed a GPS tracker on the defendant's wife's car. Justice Scalia wrote that in placing the tracker on the car, the police had violated the trespass doctrine which was a *per se* violation of the defendant's privacy. Justice Sotomayor agreed that *Katz* supplemented (not replaced) the common law trespass doctrine that still remains, and also noted that she would have found an unreasonable search and seizure in this case based solely on the government's violation of Jones' expectation of privacy. Justice Alito wrote a concurring opinion suggesting that the trespass doctrine in the context of GPS technology was neither necessary nor sufficient to establish a constitutional violation.

In *Jardines* the police brought a trained drug-detection dog to Jardines' home. The dog "alerted," a warrant was obtained, and ultimately Jardines was arrested and charged. He claimed that the police conducted an unreasonable search of his home, and in a 5-4 decision, the Court agreed. Justice Scalia authored the majority opinion and, citing precedent from his *Jones* decision, found the police action to be an unreasonable search based on Jardines' property rights. Finding the search unconstitutional, he opined that it was unnecessary to examine whether it was also a violation of their privacy rights. Justice Kagan filed a concurring opinion (joined by Justice Ginsberg and Justice Sotomayor) finding that the search violated both privacy rights and property rights.

How controlling the *Jones* and *Jardines* decisions are is still unclear, but it is something to consider in reading cases which were, by in large, decided on the basis of a *Katz* (privacy) not *Olmstead* (trespass). The fun and challenging thing about criminal law is its constantly changing landscape. Although the court has seemingly been on stable ground equating searches with invasions of privacy for fifty years, perhaps the sands have started to shift. This may call into question whether privacy is still the lynchpin of reasonableness. In *Byrd v. United States*, 584 U.S. ___ (2018), the Court seemed to revert to the privacy as the test of the Fourth Amendment by

---

[387] *Minnesota v. Carter*, 525 U.S. 83 (1978).

[388] Thirty-Fifth Annual Review, supra at 3 (2006).

[389] *Maryland v. Wilson*, 519 U.S. 408 (1997).

[390] *Kyllo v. United States*, 533 U.S. at 40.

[391] *See, Jones (supra)* in which the court said that the Katz doctrine merely added to, but did not replace, the trespass doctrine.

holding that a driver of a rental car who has permission to drive the car but was not listed as an authorized drive had a reasonable expectation of privacy in the car.

"SEARCHES" THAT, BY DEFINITION, ARE NOT FOURTH AMENDMENT SEARCHES

PLAIN VIEW

People who expose things to public view do not have a reasonable expectation of privacy; thus, what the government sees in open view is not a search. The "plain view" doctrine, established in *Coolidge v. New Hampshire,* 403 U.S. 433 (1971), applies when government agents are lawfully inside a private space looking inside—for example when police execute a warrant and come upon evidence of a crime not expected nor listed in the warrant. The plain view rule obviates (does away with) the officer's need to obtain a warrant to seize. For example, when an officer, who is lawfully inside private premises executing a warrant allowing her to search for and seize a gun used in a homicide, finds unrelated contraband in plain view while looking for the gun, she may seize the contraband without stopping and getting a warrant. Her entry and observation are lawful, and she does not need either an additional search warrant or an exception to the warrant requirement before seizing the contraband. In sum, an officer who is in a place where he or she has a right to be may seize evidence seen in plain view without the necessity of first securing a search warrant. Generally, plain view applies to broaden the scope of what an officer may seize, but does not broaden the perimeter within which the officer may search.

Neither the plain view doctrine nor the open fields doctrine technically apply when officers observe something from an area that is not protected by a privacy interest. In those circumstances, under the *Katz* definition, it is no search. Still, some refer to these as "plain view searches."

In the *Coolidge* plurality's view, the "plain view doctrine permits the warrantless seizure by police of private possessions where three requirements are satisfied. First, the police officer must lawfully make an "initial intrusion" or otherwise properly be in a position from which he can view a particular area. Second, the officer must discover incriminating evidence "inadvertently," which is to say, he or she may not "know in advance the location of certain evidence' and intend to seize it," relying on the plain view doctrine only as a pretext. Finally, it must be "immediately apparent" to the police that the items they observe may be evidence of a crime, contraband, or otherwise subject to seizure.[392]

In the case of *Texas v. Brown,* 460 U.S. 730 (1983), the court discussed at length the intended meaning of the "immediately apparent" requirement. In *Brown,* the officer, while doing a license check, looked inside a car with his flashlight and saw defendant holding a green balloon. The entire Court concluded that the search was lawful, but grappled with whether the officer had to immediately know that the balloon held drugs. The Court seemed to back off the requirement of "immediately apparent" as part of the plain view analysis, and agreed that at least under those circumstances, the officers had probable cause to believe the balloon contained contraband. But, in *Arizona v. Hicks,* 480 U.S. 321 (1987), the Court overturned defendant's conviction when police officers moved a stereo system around to see the serial number to ascertain whether it was stolen. It held that police officers cannot move things around in order to get to a vantage point where they can see something in plain view.

---

[392] *See, Texas v. Brown,* 460 U.S. 730 (1983).

The Court has relaxed the "inadvertent discovery" prong of the plain view doctrine. In *Horton v. California*, 496 U.S. 128 (1990), it concluded that the Fourth Amendment does not prohibit a warrantless seizure of an item an officer finds in plain view during a lawful search of premises for different items, even though the officer's discovery of the seized item was not inadvertent. As long as the officer's presence on the premises was otherwise lawful, the Court determined that no logical reason justified suppression simply because the officer expected to find the items that were seized in plain view.

Illinois v. Andreas, 463 U.S. 765 (1983), held that after a customs officer lawfully opened a container and identified its contents as illegal, the contents were then in "plain view" and owner's privacy interest in the item was lost. Resealing the package for a controlled delivery did not violate the Fourth Amendment. *Washington v. Chrisman*, 455 US 1 (1982), held that an officer had the right to accompany a student he was arresting into the student's dorm room to get identification, and he was entitled to enter the room to seize contraband that he observed while standing in the doorway of the room.

PLAIN VIEW AND OTHER SENSES DOCTRINES

In *Minnesota v. Dickerson*, 58 US 366 (1993), the Court extended the plain view doctrine to include objects felt, in addition to those seen. Thus, when an officer lawfully pats down a suspect and feels an object whose contour or mass makes its identity immediately apparent to the officer as contraband, the officer may seize it without a warrant. Although the Court found the inspection of the package in *Dickerson* to be unlawful (because of officer did not immediately recognize the package as contraband), the Court clearly announced an extension of the "plain view" doctrine.

TECHNOLOGY AND SENSORY ENHANCEMENTS

One of the requirements of the plain view doctrine is that the observation is made with unaided senses. The Court has had to determine in a series of cases what types of devices would "aid" the government to the extent that the plain view doctrine would no longer be applicable. For example, using regular eyeglasses does not turn a plain view scenario into a search. The Court found that the use of a sophisticated aerial camera that enhanced human vision somewhat to take aerial photographs did not constitute a search,[393] but suggested that "surveillance of private property using highly sophisticated surveillance equipment not generally available to the public, such as satellite technology, might be constitutionally proscribed absent a warrant." The Court of Appeals for the Ninth Circuit found that the use of binoculars without a warrant did not violate the Fourth Amendment.[394] Similarly, the Court has found that the "use of artificial means to illuminate a darkened area does not constitute a search, and thus triggers no Fourth Amendment protection." Monitoring an electronic beeper on a public highway and in the 'open fields' of private property does not constitute a search or seizure under the Fourth Amendment.[395] But, the Fourth Amendment is violated when officers, without a warrant, monitor a beeper in a private residence.[396]

State courts have also had to examine how much technology their constitutions allow under comparable state plain view doctrines. For example, an Oregon court found that when police used a night-vision scope and camcorder to observe the defendant's activities in a lighted car in a tavern parking lot, this did not invade a privacy interest protected by the Fourth

---

[393] See, *Dow Chemical Co.*, supra.
[394] *United States v. Dubrofsky*, 581 F2d 208 (1978),
[395] *United States v. Knotts*, 460 U.S. 276 (1973).
[396] *United States v. Karo*, 468 U.S. 705 (1984).

Amendment or state constitution.[397] But other uses of technology have been found to violate states' constitutions. This is an area of law in which state constitutional protections may be greater than those required by the Fourth Amendment.

The two key cases from the Supreme Court that deal with technological enhancements are *Kyllo v. United States*, 533 U.S. 27 (2001) and *Jones* (2012) (discussed above). Justice Scalia wrote both majority opinions. In *Kyllo,* federal agents suspected that Danny Kyllo was growing marijuana in his home in Florence, Oregon (before medicinal and recreational use were allowed). Agents parked in a car across the street from Kyllo's home and used a thermal imaging device to scan the home. The scan showed the roof over the garage and part of the home were significantly hotter than others in the neighborhood. Based on the scans and utility bills showing inordinate use of electricity, agents concluded that Kyllo was using high-intensity lamps to grow marijuana. They got the federal magistrate to issue a warrant, and upon executing the warrant they found an indoor growing operation with more than one hundred marijuana plants. Kyllo was indicted for manufacturing marijuana and challenged the use of the thermal imaging devise claiming it was a unconstitutional search of his home. In a split decision (5-4) the Supreme Court found that "where . . . the Government uses a devise that is not in general public use, to explore details of the home that would previously have been unknowable without physical intrusion, the surveillance is a search and is presumptively unreasonable without a warrant.[398]

The technological enhancement used in *Jones* was a GPS tracking device attached to his wife's Jeep from which the government monitored his movements on public streets for over a month.[399]   Jones was the owner and operator of a nightclub in the District of Columbia who the FBI and Metropolitan Police suspected of trafficking in narcotics. Officers employed various investigative techniques, including visual surveillance of the nightclub, installation of a camera focused on the front door of the club, and a pen register and wiretap covering Jones's cellular phone. The government then obtained a warrant allowing it to place the GPS on Jones's wife's car, but they did not place the GPS on the vehicle until the day after the warrant allowed. The government used the GPS to track the vehicle's movements by tracking signals from multiple satellites. The GPS relayed 2,000 pages of data over the four-week period. Based on this data, the government obtained a multiple-count indictment charging Jones with conspiracy and cocaine possession. Jones unsuccessfully moved to suppress that evidence, was convicted at trial, and was sentenced to life imprisonment. As mentioned above, the Court held that police had illegally seized the evidence because they conducted an illegal search (based on the trespass doctrine) of *Jones's* vehicle.

Justice Sotomayor's concurring opinion noted some concerns of technological developments and the Fourth Amendment.

> [T]he *Katz* test rests on the assumption that this hypothetical reasonable person has a well-developed and stable set of privacy expectations. But technology can change those expectations. Dramatic technological change may lead to periods in which popular expectations are in flux and may ultimately produce significant changes in popular attitudes. New technology may provide increased convenience or security at the expense of privacy, and many people may find the tradeoff worthwhile. And even if the public does not welcome the diminution of privacy

---

[397] *State v. Wacker*, 317 Or 419 (1993).
[398] *Kyllo v. United States*, 533 U.S. at 40 (2001)

that new technology entails, they may eventually reconcile themselves to this development as inevitable.

. . .

Perhaps most significant, cell phones and other wireless devices now permit wireless carriers to track and record the location of users—and as of June 2011, it has been reported, there were more than 322 million wireless devices in use in the United States. ... Similarly, phone-location-tracking services are offered as "social" tools, allowing consumers to find (or to avoid) others who enroll in these services. The availability and use of these and other new devices will continue to shape the average person's expectations about the privacy of his or her daily movements.

In the pre-computer age, the greatest protections of privacy were neither constitutional nor statutory, but practical. Traditional surveillance for any extended period of time was difficult and costly and therefore rarely undertaken. The surveillance at issue in this case—constant monitoring of the location of a vehicle for four weeks—would have required a large team of agents, multiple vehicles, and perhaps aerial assistance. Only an investigation of unusual importance could have justified such an expenditure of law enforcement resources. Devices like the one used in the present case, however, make long-term monitoring relatively easy and cheap. In circumstances involving dramatic technological change, the best solution to privacy concerns may be legislative. A legislative body is well situated to gauge changing public attitudes, to draw detailed lines, and to balance privacy and public safety in a comprehensive way.

To date, however, Congress and most States have not enacted statutes regulating the use of GPS tracking technology for law enforcement purposes. The best that we can do in this case is to apply existing Fourth Amendment doctrine and to ask whether the use of GPS tracking in a particular case involved a degree of intrusion that a reasonable person would not have anticipated.

[T]he use of longer term GPS monitoring in investigations of most offenses impinges on expectations of privacy. For such offenses, society's expectation has been that law enforcement agents and others would not—and indeed, in the main, simply could not—secretly monitor and catalogue every single movement of an individual's car for a very long period. In this case, for four weeks, law enforcement agents tracked every movement that respondent made in the vehicle he was driving. We need not identify with precision the point at which the tracking of this vehicle became a search, for the line was surely crossed before the 4-week mark.

PEN REGISTERS, BANK ACCOUNTS, CELL PHONE RECORDS, E-MAILS

A pen register is a device that records the phone numbers that are dialed from a particular phone number. This common feature on every cell phone today used to be something that only the telephone company had access to. In *Smith v. Maryland*, 442 U.S. 735 (1979), the court held using a pen register is not a search under the meaning of the Fourth Amendment. Justice Blackman held that "merely by using the phone, the defendant voluntarily conveyed numerical information to the telephone company and exposed that information to its equipment in the ordinary course of business….[in doing so, the defendant] . . . assumed the risk that the company would reveal to the police the numbers he dialed.[400] In a dissent, Justice Marshall wrote, "[p]rivacy in placing calls is of value not only to those engaged in criminal activity and . . . the prospect of unregulated governmental monitoring will undoubtedly prove disturbing even to those with nothing illicit to hide."[401]

The court's reasoning in *Smith* was extended to bank records, utility records, cell phone records, etc. The information we may assume is private (like our bank records) may not be. The court reasons that since bank employees, utility company employees, etc. see those records that we no reasonable expectation of privacy.

Federal courts have held that users of cordless phones have no reasonable expectation of privacy, so when police intercepted their calls, there was no Fourth Amendment search.[402] The Florida Supreme Court, however, deciding on the basis of a Florida statute, held that a non-consensual interception of cordless phone calls without prior judicial approval violated the privacy of communications protected by the statute. In 1994 Congress provided legislation to protect individual privacy for cordless phones following up on legislation to protect against eavesdropping on cellular phones. The Communications Assistance for Law Enforcement Act of 1994 did, however, require telecommunications carriers ensure that their equipment and services were complying with electronic surveillance by law enforcement. Scheb notes that Congress was providing through legislation protection to individual privacy that federal courts were unwilling to provide via the Fourth Amendment. Indeed, Justice Sotomayor's concurring opinion in *Jones* (above) indicated that this might be the way we will need to deal with the current infringements on privacy by drones, national security monitoring of e-mails, etc.

The Court has held that a warrantless search and seizure of cell phone records which revealed the location and movements of the phone use over several months violated the Fourth Amendment.[403] *Carpenter* presented the question whether a Fourth Amendment search occurs when the Government accesses historical cell phone records that provide a comprehensive chronicle of the user's past movements.

> In 2011, police officers arrested four men suspected of robbing a series of Radio Shack and (ironically enough) T-Mobile stores in Detroit. One of the men confessed that, over the previous four months, the group (along with a rotating cast of getaway drivers and lookouts) had robbed nine different stores in Michigan and Ohio. The suspect identified 15 accomplices who had participated in the heists and gave the FBI some of their cell phone numbers; the FBI then reviewed his call records to identify additional numbers that he had called around the time of the robberies.

> Based on that information, the prosecutors applied for court orders under the Stored Communications Act to obtain cell phone records for petitioner Timothy Carpenter and several other suspects. That statute . . . permits the Government to compel the disclosure of certain telecommunications records when it "offers specific and articulable facts showing that there are reasonable grounds to believe" that the records sought "are relevant and material to an ongoing criminal

---

[400] 422 U.S. at 744.
[401] *Id.* at 751.
[402] *Tyler v. Berodt* (8th Cir. 1989) *rev. den.* 877 F.2d.705 (8th Cir. 1989). For a discussion on privacy with wireless and cordless communications see, www.privacyrights.org/wireless-communications-voice-and-data-privacy
[403] *Carpenter v. United States*, 585 U.S. at ___ (2018)

investigation." Federal Magistrate Judges issued two orders directing Carpenter's wireless carriers—MetroPCS and Sprint—to disclose "cell/site sector [information] for [Carpenter's] telephone[ ] at call origination and at call termination for incoming and outgoing calls" during the four-month period when the string of robberies occurred. . . . Altogether the Government obtained 12,898 location points cataloging Carpenter's movements—an average of 101 data points per day.

[Carpenter filed a pre-trial motion to suppress the cell-site data provided by the wireless carriers claiming that the Government's seizure of his records violated the Fourth Amendment because they had been obtained without a warrant supported by probable cause.. The court denied the motion.]

[At trial on six counts of robbery and an additional six counts of carrying a firearm during a federal crime of violence seven of Carpenter's confederates pegged him as the leader of the operation.]…In addition, FBI agent Christopher Hess offered expert testimony about the cell-site data. Hess explained that each time a cell phone taps into the wireless network, the carrier logs a time-stamped record of the cell site and particular sector that were used. With this information, Hess produced maps that placed Carpenter's phone near four of the charged robberies. In the Government's view, the location records clinched the case: They confirmed that Carpenter was "right where the . . . robbery was at the exact time of the robbery." Carpenter was convicted on all but one of the firearm counts and sentenced to more than 100 years in prison.

The Court of Appeals for the Sixth Circuit affirmed. The court held that Carpenter lacked a reasonable expectation of privacy in the location information collected by the FBI because he had shared that information with his wireless carriers. Given that cell phone users voluntarily convey cell-site data to their carriers as "a means of establishing communication," the court concluded that the resulting business records are not entitled to Fourth Amendment protection.[404]

Justice Roberts' Supreme Court majority opinion found that the acquisition of wireless carrier cell-site records which revealed the location of Carpenter's cell phone was digital data maintained by a third party and did not "fit neatly under existing precedents." He noted that the "requests for cell site recordings lie at the intersection of two lines of cases.

The first set of cases addresses a person's expectation of privacy in his physical location and movements. [The court then discusses *Knotts* (beeper tracing) and *Jones* (GPS tracking). . . . In a second set of decisions, the Court has drawn a line between what a person keeps to himself and what he shares with others. We have previously held that "a person has no legitimate expectation of privacy in information he voluntarily turns over to third parties." . . . That remains true "even if the information is revealed on the assumption that it will be used only for a limited purpose." . . . As a result, the Government is typically free to obtain such information from the recipient without triggering Fourth Amendment protections. [The Court then discusses the *Smith* (telephone/pen register), *Miller* (bank records), and the "third party doctrine'.]

---

[404] *Carpenter v. United States*, 585 U.S. at ___ (2018), (Chief Justice Roberts, majority opinion.)

The question we confront today is how to apply the Fourth Amendment to a new phenomenon: the ability to chronicle a person's past movements through the record of his cell phone signals. Such tracking partakes of many of the qualities of the GPS monitoring we considered in *Jones*. Much like GPS tracking of a vehicle, cell phone location information is detailed, encyclopedic, and effortlessly compiled.

At the same time, the fact that the individual continuously reveals his location to his wireless carrier implicates the third-party principle of *Smith* and *Miller*. But while the third-party doctrine applies to telephone numbers and bank records, it is not clear whether its logic extends to the qualitatively different category of cell-site records. After all, when *Smith* was decided in 1979, few could have imagined a society in which a phone goes wherever its owner goes, conveying to the wireless carrier not just dialed digits, but a detailed and comprehensive record of the person's movements.

We decline to extend *Smith* and *Miller* to cover these novel circumstances. Given the unique nature of cell phone location records, the fact that the information is held by a third party does not by itself overcome the user's claim to Fourth Amendment protection. Whether the Government employs its own surveillance technology as in *Jones* or leverages the technology of a wireless carrier, we hold that an individual maintains a legitimate expectation of privacy in the record of his physical movements as captured through CSLI. The location information obtained from Carpenter's wireless carriers was the product of a search.[405]

Perhaps a more familiar case involving cell tower records is that of Adnan Syed whose case was featured in the 2014 podcast, *Serial*. Syed was convicted in 2000 of killing his girlfriend Hae Min Lee, 18, who was found strangled in Baltimore's Leakin Park in February 1999. Syed's case was one of the first cases in which prosecutors relied on cell phone records to locate someone in connection with a crime. In 2000 the technology was nowhere near as developed as it is now. During the trial, a prosecution expert told the jury that cell phone records placed Syed at the time and place of the murder, in Baltimore's Leakin park. The expert based his findings on information from AT&T which had included a disclaimer that the location could not be considered reliable. Neither the expert witness nor Syed's attorney Christina Guttierez, mentioned the A T & T disclaimer at trial. Syed claimed in his post-conviction relief cases that his attorney was ineffective for failing to challenge the cell tower records that showed that incoming calls did not provide accurate location information.[406]

---

[405] Id. at ____.

[406] Although the appellate courts failed to grant Syed any relief on his post-conviction appeals, in September 2022 Maryland prosecutors asked a Maryland court to throw out his conviction because a year-long file review turned up evidence that showed the state had failed to disclose evidence in his case including two alternate (and viable) suspects and the office no longer had "confidence in the integrity of the verdict." The judge agreed and threw out Syed's conviction. The prosecutor's office then cleared Syed of all charges (part of the undisclosed evidence was that there was no DNA linking Syed to Ms. Lee), and Syed's attorneys are pursuing efforts to obtain an official exoneration.
https://www.bbc.com/news/world-us-canada-62964216

OPEN FIELDS

The Fourth Amendment's protection of "persons, houses, paper, and effects" does not protect open fields. Open fields include "any unoccupied or undeveloped area outside of the curtilage."[407] The curtilage is the area around the home "to which extends the intimate activity associated with the sanctity of a man's [or woman's] home and the privacies of life."[408] Whether an area fits within the curtilage turns on four factors: 1) proximity of the area to the home; 2) whether the area is within an enclosure surrounding the home[409]; 3) the nature of the uses to which they are put; and 4) the steps taken by the resident to protect the area from observation by a passerby.[410]

The Court in *Oliver* affirmed the open field doctrine. In that case, police went onto Oliver's property ignoring a "no trespassing" signs on his property and a locked gate. The police observed a field of marijuana and arrested Oliver for manufacturing contraband. The Court upheld the search concluding that the Fourth Amendment did not apply to the open fields around the owner's home, despite his attempt to protect it by posting signs.

Again, some state courts have provided greater protection under their state constitutions. New York and Oregon cases, for example, have found that when an individual posts "no trespassing" signs on private property, they have a reasonable expectation of privacy that must be respected. [411]

CONSENT SEARCHES

When a person tells the officer, "sure, go ahead and look" he or she no longer has a reasonable expectation of privacy. Thus, when the officer does look, it really isn't a search. Nevertheless, consent is frequently cited as an "exception" to the warrant requirement. A valid search may be made of the person (or the person's property) without a warrant and without probable cause because the person gave voluntary consent for the search.   Issues surrounding the "consent exception" concern whether consent was voluntarily given, whether the police exceeded the scope of consent given, and under what circumstances may a third person give consent for the police to search. More recently, the court has examined whether police may ask for consent to search in traffic stop situations.

The key case examining the voluntariness of consent is *Schneckloth v. Bustamonte* 412 U.S. 218 (1973). The Court focused on whether, under the totality of the circumstances, the suspect voluntarily consents to the search. Valid, voluntary, consent does not require the person to know that he or she has the right to refuse consent. Like other questions of voluntariness, it is a question of fact (for the jury) whether voluntary consent has been given. Even a person who is in custody may give valid, voluntary, consent to search.[412] The test for voluntariness is an objective one, and courts will consider the totality of the circumstances. Custody would be just one fact a court would consider. The Court has held that consent is involuntary when it is the product of

---

[407] *Oliver*, 466 U.S. at 170.

[408] *Id.* at 180.

[409] In *United States v. Cuevas-Sanchez*, 821 F.2d 248 (5th Cir. 1987) the court held that the use of a video-camera mounted on a utility pole surveilling a defendant's fenced-in backyard was a search entitled to Fourth Amendment protection.

[410] *United States v. Dunn*, 480 U.S. 294 (1987).

[411] *People v. Scott*, 593 N.E. 2d 1328 (N.Y. 1992).

[412] *United States v. Watson*, 423 US 411 (1976).

coercion or threat, express or implied. The court has also found involuntary consent when the police lied about having a warrant.[413]

SCOPE OF CONSENT

The scope of a consent search may not exceed the scope of the consent given (meaning, the police can only look where the individual consenting to the search says they can). The scope of consent is determined by asking how a reasonable person would have understood the conversation between the officer and the suspect or third party when consent was given. Generally, the expressed object of a search ("I want to search for drugs.") defines the scope of consent, unless the suspect or third-party giving consent expressly limits its scope.[414] A retail store does not consent to a general search just because it has invited the public to enter.[415] An unqualified consent to search ("Go ahead and look wherever, I don't care.") permits the officer to open closed containers that could contain objects that would be within the scope of the requested search.[416]

THIRD-PARTY CONSENT

When a third party (a person who is not the person charged with the crime) gives police consent to search a premise or a possession, the question arises whether they had authority to consent. Authority arises from shared access, use, and control, and is not based necessarily on ownership over the property or relationship between the third party and the defendant. For example, homeowners cannot consent to a police search of a home they have rented to a tenant simply because they own the home. Likewise, parents who allow their child to live in their home, does not, by itself, give them the authority to consent to a police search of their child's room.

In *U.S. v. Matlock*, 415 U.S. 164 (1974), the Court dealt with a roommate giving the police consent to search a common area. The Court stated,

> Consent of one who possesses common authority over premises or effects is valid as against the absent, nonconsenting person with whom that authority is shared." . . . "Common authority is, of course, not to be implied from the mere property interest a third party has in the property. The authority which justifies the third party consent does not rest upon the law of property, with its attendant historical and legal refinements, but rests rather on the mutual use of the property by persons generally having joint access or control for most purposes, so that it is reasonable to recognize that any of the cohabitants has the right to permit the inspection in his own right and that the others have assumed the risk that one of their number might permit the common area to be searched. [417]

What if it appears to the police that the third party shares authority, but in fact does not? This happened in *Illinois v. Rodriguez*, 497 I.S. 177 (1990). The *Rodriguez* Court distinguished between "actual authority" (one who, in fact, has the legal authority to consent for someone else) and "apparent authority" (one who the officers reasonably believed had authority, but in fact did not). It found, that apparent authority is sufficient to make the search reasonable under the

---

[413] *See, Bumper v. North Carolina*, 391 U.S. 543 (1968). ("The claim of a warrant, announces, in effect that the occupant has no right to resist the search.")
[414] Thirty-Fifth Annual Review, supra at 13 (2006).
[415] Lo-Ji Sales, Inc. v. New York, 442 U.S. 319 (1979).
[416] *Florida v. Jimeno*, 500 U.S. 248 (1991).
[417] *415 U.S. at 171, fn 7.*

Fourth Amendment's. Other states require actual authority to make the consent valid under their own constitutions

In 2006, the Court examined whether a husband who objected to the police's search of his home (he was there and told them they couldn't come in) could prevent a search when his wife, who shared authority, consented to the search (she was there and invited them in).[418] The Court found that the resident who is present and refuses to give consent controls, and his or her denial of consent trumps the third-party consent. The Court noted that the police can just wait until the resident is gone and then get consent from the third party. This is what essentially happened in a case the Court decided in 2014. Police believed that Fernandez was a suspect in a gang-related assault. They went to his home and heard screaming and fighting. Police knocked on the door and were met by the suspect's bloody girlfriend. Police separated Fernandez and his girlfriend, and Fernandez yelled, "You don't have a right to come in here, I know my rights." Police arrested Fernandez and then later returned to his home at which time his girlfriend consented to a search of the apartment, and police found evidence tying him to the gang-related assault. He unsuccessfully challenged the lawfulness of the third-party consent.[419]

In earlier third-party consent cases, the Court has held that a hotel clerk did not have authority to consent to a police search of a guest's room. The Court said, "It is important to bear in mind that it was the petitioner's constitutional right which was at stake here, and not the night clerk's or the hotel's."[420] Similarly, the Court found that a landlord may not give consent to a police search into a tenant's apartment or house, even though the landlord has a general right of entry for normal inspection purposes.[421]

WITHDRAWING CONSENT

The U.S. Supreme Court has not yet decided a case where the issue is whether a person who has given consent can turn around and withdraw consent. Federal circuit courts and state courts that have dealt with this question have unanimously held that people can withdraw their consent. In *U.S. v Sanders*, 424 F.3d 768, at 774 (8th Circuit, Iowa, 2005), for example, the court held that "any such withdrawal must be supported by unambiguous acts or unequivocal statements." In *U.S. v. Gray*, 369 F.3d 1024 (8th Circuit, Ark., 2004), the court similarly stated that, "Withdrawal of consent need not be effectuated through particular "magic words," but an intent to withdraw consent must be made by unequivocal act or statement."

OTHER CASES ON CONSENT

In *Florida v. Bostick*, 501 U.S. 429 (1991), two officers, with badges and insignia, boarded a bus. They explained their presence on the bus as "being on the lookout for illegal drugs." Without any suspicion, they approached Bostick and asked him for consent to search his bag and told him that he had the right to refuse consent. Bostick, instead, gave consent. The Court found Bostick's consent to be voluntary. In addition, the Court held that the officer's conduct in boarding buses, questioning passengers, and requesting consent to search luggage "was not a "seizure" that vitiated consent; under these circumstances, which included notice of the right to refuse consent, a reasonable person would have felt free to decline the request for consent or otherwise terminate the encounter." Furthermore, police do not need to tell bus passengers of their right to not cooperate.[422]

---

[418] *Georgia v. Randolph*, 547 U.S. 104 (2006).
[419] *Fernandez v. California*, 571 U.S. ____ (2014).
[420] *Stoner v. California*, 376 U.S. 483 (1964).
[421] *Chapman v. California*, 386 U.S. 18 (1967).
[422] *United States v. Drayton*, 536 U.S. 194 (2002).

The Court has rejected the suggestion that police officers must always inform citizens of their right to refuse when seeking permission to conduct a warrantless consent search. A person who is lawfully stopped for a traffic infraction need not be advised that he or she is free to leave before the officer can lawfully request consent to search for evidence of an unrelated offense. *Ohio v. Robinette*, 519 U.S. 33 (1996). In *Robinette,* A police officer stopped Robinette for speeding, issued him warning, and returned his driver's license. The officer then asked him if he was carrying any contraband. Robinette answered that he was not. The officer then asked if he could search the car, and Robinette gave consent. The officer did not inform him that he was "free to go." Contraband was found. The Court found that the search was constitutional and that the officer did not have to tell Robinette that he was free to go.

ABANDONED PROPERTY

Although "abandoned property" is frequently viewed as an exception to the search warrant requirement, abandoned property is more properly thought of as a category of property for which a warrant is not needed because no privacy interest is invaded. By "voluntarily abandoning property, an individual forfeits any reasonable expectation of privacy in that property, even if he or she retains an ownership interest in it."[423]

The Court has consistently held that warrantless searches of abandoned property do not violate the Fourth Amendment. For example, in *Abel v. United States,* 362 US 217 (1960), the warrantless seizure of items abandoned in a hotel wastepaper basket was found to not violate the Fourth Amendment. Likewise, in *Hodari D. v. California, 499 U.S. 621 (1991),* the Court found that the Fourth Amendment did not protect Hodari when he abandoned cocaine during a police pursuit.

To lose Fourth Amendment protections, the property must actually be abandoned, and not merely set aside or concealed. For example, in *Smith v. Ohio,* 494 U.S. 541 (1990), where the suspect threw a sack onto the hood of a car when approached by the police, he did not abandon the sack, but instead attempted to protect it.

California v. Greenwood, 486 U.S. 35 (1988), is the key decision on abandoned property. After receiving a tip, Laguna Beach Police began thinking that Greenwood was involved in drug trafficking. As part of their investigation, in addition to conducting surveillance of Greenwood's home, a detective asked the trash collector to pick up the plastic garbage bags that Greenwood had left on the curb in front of his home and turn them over without mixing them together with garbage from other houses. The garbage collector cleaned his truck bin, collected Greenwood's garbage and turned it over to the detective. The detective used the information she gleaned from the trash as the basis for a search warrant for Greenwood's home. Drugs found, Greenwood arrested, Greenwood charged and moves to suppress. Justice White wrote,

> The warrantless search and seizure of the garbage bags left at the curb outside the Greenwood house would violate the Fourth Amendment only if respondents manifested a subjective expectation of privacy in their garbage that society accepts as objectively reasonable. ... Here, we conclude that respondents exposed their garbage to the public sufficiently to defeat their claim to the Fourth Amendment protection.

---

[423] Thirty-Fifth Annual Review, *supra* at 121 (2006).

The court noted that precedent was against finding that people have a reasonable expectation of privacy in the property that they discard in public areas. Most Fourth Amendment cases do not recognize a continuing expectation of privacy in premises that have been abandoned.[424]

DOG SNIFFS[425]

The Court first held that the use of a dog to detect contraband is a "search" under the Fourth Amendment in *U.S. v. Place, 462 U.S. 696* (1983). It examined dog sniffs again in *Illinois v. Caballes*, 543 U.S. 405 (2005) holding that when police allowed a drug dog to sniff around a stopped car this did not violate the Fourth Amendment. In *Jardines* (discussed above), a police dog and handler approached Jardines' front door but never went in the home. The state argued that there was no reasonable expectation of privacy in narcotics or contraband. Jardines argued that this was not the type of dog sniff in *Caballes*, but rather this was a search of something in his home—an area that the Court has afforded the highest level of privacy. In a 5-4 decision, the Court held that the dog sniff at the front of a door of a house was a search and police needed a warrant.

In another 2013 case the Court examined whether the alert of a drug-sniffing dog alone could constitute probable cause.[426] The case involved a drug detection dog brought to sniff around a stopped car when the defendant seemed particularly nervous. The dog sniffed around the car and it alerted. The police searched further and found pseudoephedrine. The defendant filed a motion to suppress the drugs based on a lack of probable cause because the dog was not properly trained, but the trial court denied the motion. The Court, in a unanimous decision, did not concentrate on the training of the dog, and held that a probable cause hearing in dog alert cases should be like all others. Lower courts should look at the totality of the circumstances in that probable cause is to be a flexible common-sense decision. Under these circumstances the court found that the drug detection dog's alert to the exterior of the vehicle provided the officer with probable cause to allow a warrantless search.

INTERNATIONAL BORDERS

The Fourth Amendment does not require warrants for routine border and custom stops and searches because of national sovereignty.[427] The Court recognized the executive branch's plenary authority to conduct such searches "in order to regulate the collection of duties and to prevent the introduction of contraband into this country."[428] The Court found that a routine border inspection included the government's authority to remove, disassemble, and search a vehicle's fuel tank, because interference with the motorist's possessory interest is justified by the government's paramount interest in protecting the border.[429]

"International borders" include more than just physical, geographical borders between two countries, and the Court has extended the international border exception to the warrant requirement to searches conducted at the "functional equivalent" of the border.[430] The rationale for the border exception also applies to persons or objects leaving the country.[431]

---

[424] See, *Abel v. United States*, 362 U.S. 217 (1960); *California v. Greenwood*, 486 U.S. 35 (1988).
[425] See, http://www.scotusblog.com/?p=154569, for a blog about how the oral arguments went in *Harris* and *Jardines*.
[426] *Florida v. Harris*, 568 U.S. ___ (2013).
[427] See, e.g., *United States v. Ramsey*, 431 U.S. 606 (1977).
[428] *United States v. Montoya de Hernandez*, 473 U.S. 531 (1985).
[429] *United States v. Flores-Montano*, 541 U.S. 149 (2004).
[430] *Almeida-Sanches v. United States*, 413 U.S. 266 (1973).
[431] *California Bankers Association v. Schultz*, 416 U.S. 21 (1974).

SEARCHES THAT ARE PERMISSIBLE WITHOUT A WARRANT

SEARCHES INCIDENT TO ARREST

Police may conduct warrantless searches of individuals who they arrest. There are two historical rationales for the search-incident-to-arrest exception: (1) the need to disarm the suspect in order to take him into custody, and (2) the need to preserve evidence for later use at trial.[432] In a series of cases the Court examined the permissible scope of searches done incidental to an arrest; whether a search can be done when police are authorized to, but do not, arrest; whether a search done immediately prior to an arrest are "incidental" to it; how long after the arrest is conducted can the search take place and still be "incidental" to it; and whether a search incident to an arrest that turns out to be unlawful is still valid.

SCOPE OF SEARCHES INCIDENT TO ARREST

The scope of a search-incident-to-arrest is limited to the arrestee's person and the area within the arrestee's immediate control—the area from within which the arrestee might gain possession of a weapon or destructible evidence,[433] or closets or other places from which the officer could be attacked.[434] "Unlike a limited protective search for weapons conducted during an investigative stop, a full search of the arrestee for both weapons and evidence may be made during a search incident to arrest."[435] In general, an arrest does not justify a full-blown search of the arrestee's entire home. The Fourth Amendment, however, allows officers to conduct a limited protective sweep in the course of an in-home arrest if they have a "reasonable belief based on specific and articulable facts that the area to be swept harbors an individual posing a danger to those on the arrest scene."[436] A protective sweep is a "quick and limited search of premises, incident to an arrest and . . . narrowly confined to a cursory visual inspection of those places in which a person might be hiding."[437] Items in plain view may be seized during a protective sweep. The arrestee and everything the arrestee wears may be searched.

The court has decided a number of cases that have involved searches done incident to arrests occurring in and nearby a vehicle.[438] Searches of containers found on the arrestee or within the arrestee's reach are valid, but once police have gained exclusive control over the arrestee's personal property, a later search of that property is generally not valid as incident to arrest."[439] When the police make a valid arrest of the 'occupant" of a vehicle, they may search the passenger compartment and any containers within it.

In *Riley v. California*, 573 U.S. _____ (2014), the Court limited the scope of the search incident to a lawful arrest exception to the warrant requirement. It held that police may not search the cell phone of an individual incident to his or her arrest. The Court pointed to the volumes of private information that smart phones hold, and made a strong distinction between routine searches incident to arrest and the search of phones. The Court held that police may seize a phone and apply for a warrant to search its contents, but they are not allowed to search the phone contents simply because they seized it from a defendant.

---

[432] *United States v. Robinson*, 414 U.S. 218 (1973).

[433] *Chimel v. California*, 385 US 752 (1969).

[434] *Buie*, supra.

[435] Thirty-Fifth Annual Review, supra at 62 (2006).

[436] *Buie*, supra.

[437] *Id.* at 327.

[438] *See, e.g., New York v. Belton*, 454 US 454 (1981), *Thornton v. United States*, 541 US 615 (2004), and *Arizona v. Gant*, 536 US 322 (2009).

[439] Thirty-Fifth Annual Review, supra at 63 (2006).

Digital data stored on a cell phone cannot itself be used as a weapon to harm an arresting officer or to effectuate the arrestee's escape. Law enforcement officers remain free to examine the physical aspects of a phone to ensure that it will not be used as a weapon--say, to determine whether there is a razor blade hidden between the phone and its case. Once an officer has secured a phone and eliminated any potential physical threats, however, the data on the phone can endanger no one.

. . .

Modern cell phones are not just another technological convenience. With all they contain and all they may reveal, they hold for many Americans "the privacies of life". The fact that technology now allows an individual to carry such information in his hand does not make the information any less worthy of the protection for which the Founders fought.[440]

SEARCHES *INCIDENT TO* A LAWFUL ARREST

In order to search incident to arrest, police must have probable cause to arrest before the search is conducted. "Searches conducted immediately before formal arrest are valid if probable cause to arrest existed prior to the search."[441] Warrantless searches that provide probable cause to arrest where none existed previously are not justifiable as searches incident to arrest.[442] Police do not have to announce to the individual that they are under arrest for the search to be incident to arrest. Generally, searches incident to arrest are done immediately prior to or after taking the defendant into custody. However, the circumstances surrounding a particular arrest can justify substantial delay."[443]

SEARCHES INCIDENT TO A *LAWFUL* ARREST

The Court has examined whether police can conduct a valid search incident to a "lawful arrest" when state law does not permit the arrest.[444] Both state and federal courts had differed in their interpretation of this. A minority of courts that addressed the issue ruled that when state arrest law is violated, the federal Constitution requires suppression of any evidence that resulted from the arrest and a related search. A majority of courts, and the Supreme Court, by contrast, concluded that, if an officer has had probable cause to make an arrest, the Fourth Amendment is satisfied even if some provision of state law was violated in the process.

> We have treated additional protections exclusively as matters of state law. ... We . . . [conclude] that whether state law authorized the search was irrelevant. States, we said, remained free "to impose higher standards on searches and seizures than required by the Federal Constitution," but regardless of state rules, police could search a lawfully seized vehicle as a matter of federal constitutional law.

> In *California* v. *Greenwood*, we held that search of an individual's garbage forbidden by California's Constitution was not forbidden by the Fourth Amendment. "[W]hether or not a search is reasonable within the meaning of the Fourth Amendment," we said, has never "depend[ed] on the law of the particular State in which the search occurs." While "[i]ndividual States may surely construe their

---

[440] *Id.* at _____.

[441] Thirty-Fifth Annual Review, supra at 61, citing *Rawlings v. Kentucky*, 448 U.S. 98 (1980).

[442] Thirty-Fifth Annual Review, supra at 61, citing *Smith v. Ohio*, 494 U.S. 541 (1990).

[443] Thirty-Fifth Annual Review, supra at 61.

[444] *Virginia v. Moore*, 552 U.S. 164 (2008).

own constitutions as imposing more stringent constraints on police conduct than does the Federal Constitution," state law did not alter the content of the Fourth Amendment. . . .[445]

EXIGENT CIRCUMSTANCE SEARCHES

Emergency situations (known as exigent circumstances) have compelled the courts to relax the warrant requirement. In several cases the Court has held that the Fourth Amendment permits a warrantless entry and search "if exigent circumstances justify the intrusion." "Exigent circumstances exist when there is probable cause for a search or seizure and either the evidence sought is in imminent danger of destruction, the safety of law enforcement officers or the general public is threatened, the police are in hot pursuit of a suspect, or a suspect is likely to flee before the pursuing officer can obtain a warrant."[446] Nevertheless, to justify a warrantless search under the exigent circumstances exception, the government must demonstrate that the search was conducted in a reasonable manner.[447] The government should also be prepared to prove that a warrant, even a telephonic warrant, was unavailable or impractical. Under certain circumstances police may be able to "seize" a home without a warrant (secure the dwelling) but not enter and search it. Under the Fourth Amendment, securing a dwelling on the basis of probable cause, to prevent the destruction or removal of evidence while a search warrant is being sought is not itself an unreasonable seizure of either the dwelling or its contents."[448] For example, in *Illinois v. McArthur, 531 U.S. 326 (2001),* the court found that a two-hour seizure of the defendant's home while police obtained a warrant did not violate the Fourth Amendment because the police reasonably feared defendant would destroy evidence if allowed to enter the home unaccompanied by an officer. However, other circumstances allow police to enter the home if they believe that evidence is being destroyed.

Hot Pursuit

Hot pursuit is one form of exigent circumstance. Under the exigency exception commonly known as "hot pursuit" officers may conduct a warrantless search where: 1) the officer has probable cause to arrest the suspect; 2) the officer has probable cause to believe the suspect is in particular premises; and 3) there is an urgent need for immediate police action because delay would increase the risk of harm or escape.

In *Warden v. Hayden,* 387 U.S. 294 (1967), the police were in hot pursuit of an armed robber and followed him into a house where a gun, clothing, and other items relating to the robbery were discovered. The Court held that, in such a situation, it would be unreasonable to require the police to halt their investigation until a warrant was obtained. In *United States v. Santana,* 427 U.S. 38 (1976), the Court found that the fact that the pursuit ended almost as soon as it began did not make it less than a "hot pursuit." (The suspect attempted to avoid arrest by retreating from a doorway into the house as officers initiated an arrest.) In *Welsch v. Wisconsin,* 466 U.S. 740 (1984), however, the Court held that federal constitution did not allow a hot pursuit entry into a home for a minor traffic infraction where there was no immediacy and no continuous pursuit from the scene of the crime.[449]

---

[445] *Id.*
[446] Thirty-Fifth Annual Review, supra at 94.
[447] *Schmerber v. California*, 384 U.S. 757 (1966).
[448] *Segura v. United States*, 468 U.S. 796 (1984).
[449] Similarly, in *Oregon v. DeKuyper*, 74 Or App 534, (1985) the Oregon Court of Appeals held that a warrantless entry of a house to arrest for MIP was not permitted under Oregon statutes.

Zalman observed many legal principles of the hot pursuit exception could be seen in *Warden v. Hayden*:

- The hot pursuit exception must be based on probable cause to believe the person who has just entered the premises committed a felony or is dangerous to the safety of others.
- Hot pursuit may be based either on the officer's personal observations or on reliable hearsay.
- The pursuit need not be immediate; there may be a short time lapse between the suspect's entry into the house and the arrival of the police.
- The permissible scope of search must, . . . at the least, be as broad as may reasonably be necessary to prevent the dangers that the suspect at large in the house may resist or escape. In other words, until the offender is found, the police may search the entire premises for the suspects, weapons, and evidence of the crime. However, once the offender is apprehended, the police may not search beyond the limits of a search incident to a lawful arrest.
- The pursuit may begin on private property.
- Police may enter premises without a warrant in hot pursuit only for serious crimes. A minor offense does not create an exigency that overrides the Fourth Amendment rule that police must obtain an arrest warrant to arrest a suspect in his or her home.[450]

Lange v. California, 595 U.S. _____ (2021) presented the issue of whether the exigent circumstances exception to the Fourth Amendment's warrant requirement always applies when police are pursuing a suspect whom they believe committed a misdemeanor. There had been inconsistency in the intermediate appellate courts on this. Justice Kagan's opinion began,

The Fourth Amendment ordinarily requires that police officers get a warrant before entering a home without permission. But an officer may make a warrantless entry when "the exigencies of the situation" create a compelling law enforcement need. The question presented here is whether the pursuit of a fleeing misdemeanor suspect always—or more legally put, categorically—qualifies as an exigent circumstance. We hold it does not. A great many misdemeanor pursuits involve exigencies allowing warrantless entry. But whether a given one does so turns on the particular facts of the case.

This case began when petitioner Arthur Lange drove past a California highway patrol officer in Sonoma. Lange, it is fair to say, was asking for attention: He was listening to loud music with his windows down and repeatedly honking his horn. The officer began to tail Lange, and soon afterward turned on his overhead lights to signal that Lange should pull over. By that time, though, Lange was only about a hundred feet (some four-seconds drive) from his home. Rather than stopping, Lange continued to his driveway and entered his attached garage. The officer followed Lange in and began questioning him. Observing signs of intoxication, the officer put Lange through field sobriety tests. Lange did not do well, and a later blood test showed that his blood-alcohol content was more than three times the legal limit. The State charged Lange with the misdemeanor of driving under the influence of alcohol, plus a (lower-level) noise infraction. Lange moved to

---

[450] Zalman, *supra*, at 123.

suppress all evidence obtained after the officer entered his garage, arguing that the warrantless entry had violated the Fourth Amendment. The State contested the motion. It contended that the officer had probable cause to arrest Lange for the misdemeanor of failing to comply with a police signal.

Rather than allowing a per se rule that allowed police always to enter a home in hot pursuit of a fleeing misdemeanant (as the state requested), the Court adopted the approach that will require the trial court to decide on a case-by-case basis. "Under the usual case-specific view, an officer can follow the misdemeanant when, but only when, an exigency—for example, the need to prevent destruction of evidence—allows insufficient time to get a warrant." The Court concluded,

> The flight of a suspected misdemeanant does not always justify a warrantless entry into a home. An officer must consider all the circumstances in a pursuit case to determine whether there is a law enforcement emergency. On many occasions, the officer will have good reason to enter — to prevent imminent harms of violence, destruction of evidence, or escape from the home. But when the officer has time to get a warrant, he must do so—even though the misdemeanant fled.

PREVENTING ESCAPE

The risk of escape may also justify warrantless intrusions in other instances that differ in some respects from a typical hot pursuit. *Minnesota v. Olson*, 495 U.S. 91 (1990), held that simply being wanted for a serious felony does not in itself create an exigency. Police suspected that Olson, a murder suspect, was in a house, and then they entered without a warrant. The state's arguments that the warrantless entry was justified by hot pursuit were undermined by several factors including the fact that the police believed Olson was the driver of the getaway car not the shooter, that the police had already seized the murder weapon, there was no suggestion that the persons inside were in any harm from Olson, that the entry occurred a day after the murder, and that the house in which Olson was hiding was already surrounded by several squad cars.

DESTRUCTION OR LOSS OF EVIDENCE

A warrantless search may be conducted to preserve evidence when the police reasonably believe that, unless they immediately conduct a warrantless search, the sought after evidence is in imminent danger of being removed or destroyed."[451] For example, exigent circumstances justified warrantless search of fingernails for trace evidence related to a strangling when there was probable cause to arrest and there was danger that evidence would be destroyed.[452] Exigent circumstances justified warrantless entry of an apartment to search for drugs where police had probable cause to arrest and there was danger that evidence would be destroyed.[453] A warrantless search was not valid when there was merely a possibility that the evidence would be destroyed.[454] The threat of danger or destruction to the evidence must be real or imminent. In *Mincey v. Arizona*, 437 U.S. 385 (1978), the Court held that the fact that the place searched was the scene of a serious crime did not itself justify a warrantless search in the absence of any "indication that the evidence would be lost, destroyed, or removed during the time required to obtain a search warrant and there [was] no suggestion that a warrant could not easily and

---

[451] Thirty-Fifth Annual Review, supra at 94.
[452] *Cupp v. Murphy*, 412 U.S. 291 (1973).
[453] *Ker v. California* 374 U.S. 23 (1963).
[454] *Vale v. Louisiana*, 399 U.S. 30 (1970).

conveniently have been obtained." The Court has refused to adopt either a "murder scene exception"[455] or a "crime scene exception"[456] to the warrant requirement.

BLOOD ALCOHOL/ABSORPTION AND DISSIPATION

Because blood alcohol levels dissipate, courts have generally held that police may take a blood sample from an individual suspected of drunk driving without first obtaining a search warrant. Exigent circumstances exist because alcohol in the suspect's bloodstream might disappear in the time needed to obtain a warrant. The Court has not been consistent in either the way it analyzes breath and blood tests, nor in its holdings. For example, the Court ruled in *Missouri v. McNeely*, 569 U.S. 141 (2013), that a nonconsensual warrantless blood draw in a routine DWI investigation violated the Fourth Amendment, where no factors other than the natural dissipation of the suspect's blood-alcohol level suggested that there was an emergency. Three years later the Court ruled in *Birchfield v. North Dakota*,136 S. Ct. 2160 (2016) that a state's criminal penalty for declining to consent to a blood draw violated the Fourth Amendment. [457] But, three years after that, a plurality of the Court[458] held that when police directed the hospital staff to withdraw defendant's blood and test it for blood alcohol level they did not need a warrant to do so because of the exigent circumstance exception of the warrant requirement. [459]

---

[455] *Mincey*, supra.

[456] *Flippo v. West Virginia*, 528 U.S. 11 (1999).

[457] In *Birchfield v. North Dakota*,136 S. Ct. 2160 (2016) the Court analyzed breath and blood tests under state informed consent laws under the search incident to arrest rationale. They examined whether defendant's conviction for refusal to submit to a blood or intoxilyzer test when police could do a blood draw and/or a breath test as incident to the driver's arrest when suspects had refused to give consent. The Court held that a state statute may not criminalize the refusal to submit to a blood test in the absence of a warrant because, while the Fourth Amendment allows for warrantless breath tests incident to an arrest for drunk driving, warrantless blood tests incident to an arrest violate the Fourth Amendment. The *Birchfield* Court found warrantless breath tests are permissible under the search incident to arrest exception to the Fourth Amendment's warrant requirement because they do not implicate significant privacy concerns--they involve minimal physical intrusion to capture something that is routinely exposed to the public, reveal a limited amount of information, and do not enhance any embarrassment beyond what the arrest itself causes. On the other hand, blood tests, according to the Court, implicate privacy interests because they are much more physically invasive -- they require the piercing of the skin -- and they produce a sample that can be preserved and used to obtain further information beyond the subject's blood alcohol level at the time of the test. The Court also determined that criminalizing refusal to submit to a breath test is designed to serve the government's interest in preventing drunk driving, which is greater than merely keeping currently drunk drivers off the roads, and does so better than other alternatives. However, the same rationale did not apply to criminalizing refusal to submit to a blood test because of the greater degree of intrusion and the available alternative of the breath test.

[458] Recall that a plurality is less than a majority opinion and the result in this case only stands for this case and does not create a precedent. Note, too, the change of justices on the Court from 2016 and in 2019.

[459] *Mitchell v. Wisconsin*, 588 U.S. ___ (2019). Mitchell had been arrested for driving while intoxicated in Wisconsin which has an implied consent law. The issue before the Court was whether the warrantless blood draw of an unconscious individual allowed by that implied consent law violated the Fourth Amendment. (The Birchfield defendants had been conscious and had refused consent.) The Wisconsin implied-consent law imputes consent for a blood-alcohol test to any motorist on a public road, and allows an officer to order a blood draw of an unconscious person (who, by definition, cannot withdraw consent) without a warrant. The Court in examining the statute had to reconcile several aspects of Fourth Amendment jurisprudence. First, the key to the Fourth Amendment is the requirement of reasonableness. Prior case law holds that a warrantless search is unreasonable, unless it falls within one of the narrowly defined exceptions. The Court examined three recognized exceptions: exigent circumstances, search incident to a lawful arrest, and consent. Under the "exigent circumstances exception, an officer can engage in a warrantless search if there are exigent circumstances, for example, in order to preserve evidence from imminent destruction. Under the "search-incident-to-arrest exception," an officer can engage in a

AUTOMOBILE SEARCHES

Police may search cars without a warrant in a number of contexts. For example, police may search a car whenever the police get consent from someone with apparent authority over the car. Another example is the search of a car incident to the arrest of the driver or passenger from the car.[460] The officers' justification for searching the passenger compartment of the cars stemmed from the justifications inherent in allowing search within "arm's reach" of a person about to be placed in a patrol car and transported to the jail. Sometimes police may search a car even when they aren't arresting anyone.

In *Carroll v. United States,* 267 U.S. 132 (1925), the Supreme Court upheld a warrantless search of a motor vehicle when police had probable cause to believe it was carrying contraband. Thus began the so-called "automobile exception" to the Fourth Amendment warrant requirement. The "automobile exception" is a type of exigent circumstance search. It permits police officers to conduct a warrantless search of an automobile when they have probable cause to believe that it contains contraband or evidence of criminal activity. The Fourth Amendment automobile exception relies on the mobility of the car for the exigency. "If a car is readily mobile and probable cause exists to believe it contains contraband, the Fourth Amendment * * * permits police to search the vehicle without more."[461] Therefore, as with other exigent circumstance exceptions, there is probable cause and exigency. Because the exception recognizes that "the inherent mobility of vehicles . . . often creates exigent circumstances that make obtaining a warrant impractical," the exception includes parked and unattended cars that are readily capable of being moved.[462] The automobile exception has been extended to motor homes that are readily capable of being moved, as long as an objective observer would conclude that the motor home was being used as a vehicle rather than a residence.[463] (Be aware that states may impose additional requirements for an automobile search.)

In one case the Court upheld a search under the automobile exception even when the car was no longer mobile. This happened in *Chambers v. Maroney,* 399 U.S. 42 (1970), where police stopped a car at night because it, and its occupants, fit the description of a car recently involved in a gas station robbery. Police arrested the passengers and towed the car to the police station and then, without a warrant, searched it. They found incriminating evidence in the car. The Supreme Court upheld the search under the automobile exception even though the defendants could not move the car would once it was at the police station. The following year, the Supreme Court ruled that the search of an automobile conducted two-and-a-half weeks after it was seized and impounded by the police as part of a murder investigation—when done without a warrant—was unconstitutional.[464]

Through a series of cases, the Court has determined that the police can search anywhere in the car that they have probable cause to believe contains evidence of a crime. Originally, the Court did not extend the automobile search warrant exception to closed containers in the car, but ultimately recognized that a bright-line rule was important for efficient law enforcement ("A

---

warrantless search immediately after arresting a person Under the consent "exception," an officer can engage in a warrantless search if a suspect voluntarily consents to the search—and a suspect can generally (as discussed above) withdraw consent at any time. But, under Wisconsin's law consent was presumed and, since the suspects were unconscious, they obviously could not withdraw consent.

[460] See, *New York v. Belton,* supra; *Thornton v. United States,* supra; and *Arizona v. Gant,* supra.
[461] *Maryland v. Dyson,* 527 U.S. 465 (1999).
[462] Thirty-Fifth Annual Review, supra at 94.
[463] *See, California v. Carney,* 471 U.S. 386 (1985).
[464] *Coolidge v. New Hampshire,* 403 U.S. 443 (1971).

uniform rule avoids the need for police to guess where the probable cause lay. ...") and now allows police to open any closed container in a lawfully stopped vehicle if they have probable cause to believe that contraband is located in the container. [465] The Court reasoned that that since the motorist was lawfully stopped, a warrant (which could be obtained since police had probable cause) would offer little constitutional protection in that the container could just be held until police got the warrant. An officer may also open a container belonging to a passenger, regardless of individualized suspicion of criminal conduct by the passenger.

In *Collins v. Virginia*, 584 U.S. ___ (2018) the Court held that the Fourth Amendment's automobile exception does not permit a police officer without a warrant to enter private property to search a vehicle parked a few feet from the house. In an 8–1 opinion authored by Justice Sonia Sotomayor, the Court held that its own Fourth Amendment jurisprudence regarding the home and the "curtilage" of one's home (see above) clearly prevents officers from entering and searching without a warrant, even if the object searched is an automobile. The Court found that the area searched (the back of the driveway) was indeed the curtilage of the defendant's home, and thus the Fourth Amendment's highest degree of protection applies there. The Court intoned that privacy interests are at their highest in one's home and the curtilage of one's home are at. Although warrantless searches of automobiles are permissible in limited circumstances, the warrantless search of an automobile parked within the curtilage of one's home is not.

COMMUNITY CARETAKING SEARCHES

Police work is not limited to investigating crimes; sometimes it extends to "community caretaking." The concept of community caretaking was recognized in *Cady v. Dombrowski*, 413 U.S. 433, 441 (1973). The Court recognized that "local law enforcement officials frequently investigate motor vehicle accidents and engage in community caretaking functions, totally divorced from the detection, investigation, or acquisition of evidence relating to the violation of a criminal statute." Community caretaking searches differ from exigent circumstance circumstances in two regards. First, community caretaking searches are not necessarily "emergency" situations where the police are concerned with the destruction of evidence. In fact, community caretaking functions are those that have no criminal law enforcement purpose, for example, checking up on a report of a neighbor who hasn't been seen in some time. Police motivation is to render aid rather than investigate a crime. Second, police need no probable cause to perform these community caretaking functions as they do in exigent circumstance searches. It is likely that police don't even have reasonable suspicion about criminal activity when they engage in community caretaking functions. When police go into a residence to do a community caretaking check and find evidence of a crime, the Courts reason that the evidence of the crime is admissible under the plain view doctrine.

Although the U.S. Supreme Court has recognized "community caretaking" as an exception to the Fourth Amendment's warrant requirement in the context of a vehicle search, whether that concept applies in the context of a private home was a matter of first impression within the First Circuit where a recent case arose. In *Caniglia v. Strom*, ___ U.S. ___ (2021) Edward Canaglia and his wife Kim got into a heated argument, during which Canaglia displayed a gun and told Kim something to the effect of "shoot me now." Fearing for her husband's state of mind, Kim left the home for the night. The next morning, she asked an officer from the Cranston Police Department to accompany her back to the house because she was worried that her husband might have committed suicide or otherwise harmed himself. Kim and several police

---

[465] *See, California v. Acevedo,* 500 U.S. 565 (1991). In an earlier case, the Court had held that police who had probable cause to believe that somewhere in the car there was contraband but not in a specific container were not allowed to search the container. *Acevedo* changed that result.

officers went to the house, and while the encounter was non-confrontational, the ranking officer on the scene determined that Canaglia was imminently dangerous to himself and others and asked him to go to the hospital for a psychiatric evaluation, which Canaglia agreed to. While Canaglia was at the hospital, an officer entered Canaglia's home and seized two of Canaglia's guns, despite knowing that Canaglia did not consent to their seizure. Canaglia ultimately filed a lawsuit under Section 1983 alleging the seizure of his firearms constituted a violation of his rights under the Second and Fourth Amendments. The appellate court held that the emergency aid doctrine does apply in the context of a private home and found in favor of the officers. The Supreme Court, however, held that the warrantless seizure of handguns during the welfare check violated the Fourth Amendment. The Court's opinion emphasized the privacy the constitution guarantees for people inside their homes, even during community caretaking tasks that officers perform.

SPECIAL NEEDS SEARCHES

SCHOOL SEARCHES

The Supreme Court first decided a "school search case" in *New Jersey v. T.L.O*, 459 U.S. 325 (1985). *T.L.O.* is important for several reasons. First, it established the "special needs doctrine" which has been applied to several other cases in other contexts. Second, the court balanced the needs of schools against students' privacy interests. Third, it reaffirmed that, although schools act *in loco parentis* (school administrators are substitute parents while students are in school), students do enjoy the protections of the Bill of Rights — although perhaps not to the same degree — even while they are in school.

In *T.L.O*, a teacher had discovered T.L.O, a 14-year-old freshman, smoking in the bathroom in violation of a school rule. She was brought into the principal's office and questioned by an assistant vice principal. She denied that she had been smoking and claimed that she did not smoke. The assistant vice principal demanded to see her purse, opened the purse, found a package of cigarettes, removed the cigarettes and noticed a package of rolling papers. He searched the purse more thoroughly and found marijuana, a pipe, plastic bags, and a substantial quantity of money in one-dollar bills, an index card containing a list of those students who owed T.L.O. money and two letters that implicated her in marijuana dealing. The state brought delinquency charges, and the court found her to be a delinquent and imposed a one-year probation sentence. T.L.O. appealed.

The Court held that the Fourth Amendment applied to searches by school officials and that this particular search was reasonable. Justice White's opined that T.L.O. retained a Fourth Amendment privacy interest in her person and "there is no reason to conclude that students have necessarily waived all rights to privacy in such items. The court noted high school students may carry keys, money, necessaries of personal hygiene and grooming in purses and book bags and might also carry "highly personal items such as photographs, letters and diaries merely by bringing them onto school grounds." The Court disagreed with the state's argument that public school students have no reasonable expectation of privacy in school. It held that the Fourth Amendment's ban on unreasonable searches and seizures applies to searches conducted by public schools, and the school can't escape the commands of the Fourth Amendment because of their authority over school children. When schools search students, they aren't acting *in loco parentis*, and students have a reasonable expectation of privacy.

In analyzing whether the search of T.L.O. was reasonable, the Court observed that this search was conducted without a warrant and without probable cause to believe T.L.O. was carrying drugs. The Court, however, struck a balance between the student's reasonable expectation of privacy and the schools legitimate need to maintain a healthy learning environment by enforcing school rules such as the ban on smoking. The Court held that the "warrant requirement, in particular, is unsuited to the school environment: requiring a teacher to obtain a warrant before searching a child suspected of an infraction of school rules (or of the criminal law) would unduly interfere with the maintenance of the swift and informal disciplinary procedures needed in the schools."

The majority and dissent disagreed as to the standard of evidence needed for the warrantless school search by a teacher or administrator in a public-school setting. Because T.L.O. denied smoking after being caught, it was reasonable for the vice principal to resolve the dispute by inspecting her purse to determine if she carried cigarettes. When the vice principal saw rolling papers, he had some suspicion that she might be in possession of marijuana. The observation of the rolling papers did not give rise to probable cause, however. The majority decided the vice principal had reasonable suspicion and that was sufficient to justify the warrantless search. Although they agreed the school didn't need to get a warrant, the dissenters argued that for the search to be reasonable administrators needed probable cause. They believed that the facts in this case did not rise to such a level of seriousness as to tip the constitutional balance in favor of the school's interest when measured against the student's right to privacy.

Later cases have applied the reasoning of *T.L.O* and picked up on Justice Blackmun's formulation creating the "special needs doctrine." Until *T.L.O.* the Court had only allowed reasonable suspicion as a justification for Terry type of investigations. To justify a search for evidence that would be evidence of a crime, as well as a school rule violation, Justice White wrote that "the special needs of the school environment require assessment of the legality of such searches against a standard less exacting than that of probable cause." Justice Blackmun wrote, "Only in those exceptional circumstances in which *special needs*, beyond the normal need for law enforcement, make the warrant and probable-cause requirement impracticable, is a court entitled to substitute its balancing of interests for that of the Framers."

Stafford School District #1 v. Redding, 557 U.S. 364 (2009), also involved the search of a student at school. Savanna Redding sued school officials who had strip-searched her looking for ibuprofen. The Court found that school officials did not have reasonable suspicion to justify the search for the ibuprofin they believed Savanna possessed in violation of school policy, and eight justices decided that the search was unconstitutional under the Fourth Amendment. Still, a majority of the judges held that the school officials should receive qualified immunity (meaning that Savanna collected no money from the officials).

DRUG TESTS

The Court's second major "school case" involved drug testing of high school students involved in athletics. In *Vernonia School District 47J v. Acton, 515 U.S. 646 (1995)*, the high school in Vernonia, Oregon had enacted a mandatory, random urinalysis testing of all students involved in interscholastic athletic programs. James Acton, represented by the ACLU, sought a preliminary injunction against this policy. Whereas *T.L.O.* involved individualized suspicion, the search in *Vernonia* was suspicionless.

The *Vernonia* decision refers to two important drug-testing cases also decided under the "special needs doctrine" — *Skinner v. Railway Labor Executives' Association, 489 U.S. 602 (1989),* and *National Treasury Employees Union v. Von Raab*, 489 U.S. 656 (1989). In *Skinner* the court upheld a federal law that mandated drug testing of all on-site employees after a major train accident, whether the employees worked for a private railroad company line or a line run by the government. In *Van Raab*, U.S. Customs Service required automatic drug testing for the hiring or promotion of all officers who (1) are directly involved in drug law enforcement, (2) must carry firearms, or (3) handle classified material that drug smugglers could get by bribing or blackmailing drug-dependent employees. The program was not designed to prevent on-the-job impairment but to ensure that customs officers in drug enforcement would lead drug-free lives. The Court upheld drug testing for agents involved in drug law enforcement and those who carried firearms but could not agree on the reasonableness of testing agents handling classified information (and sent it back for further fact-finding).

In her dissent in *Vernonia*, Justice O'Connor criticized the lack of individual suspicion stating, "[b]y the reasoning of today's decision, the millions of these students who participate in interscholastic sports, an overwhelming majority of whom have given school officials no reason whatsoever to suspect they use drugs at school, are open to an intrusive bodily search."[466] She noted that the costs of failure to drug test school athletes simply did not put the lives and safety of many people at risk. Therefore, she concluded, the school district cannot decide to discard individualized suspicion without specific and compelling reasons to show that eliminating individualized suspicion is reasonable.

In *Board of Education of Independent School District No. 92 of Pottawatomie County v. Earls, 536 U.S. 822 (2002)*, the Court extended the rule of *Vernonia* to high school students engaged in any extracurricular activities. In *Earls*, however, there was no evidence of a widespread drug problem in the Tecumseh, Oklahoma schools--although there was some evidence that overall the drug problem had grown worse. In dissent, Ginsburg noted that the two reasons in *Acton* which justified the drug tests in the Vernonia school—drug use could be physically harmful for athletes, and athletes were leaders of an aggressive drug cult—did not apply to all extracurricular activities. She noted,

> At the margins, of course, no policy of *random* drug testing is perfectly tailored to the harms it seeks to address. The School District cites the dangers faced by members of the band, who must "perform extremely precise routines with heavy equipment and instruments in close proximity to other students," and by Future Farmers of America, who "are required to individually control and restrain animals as large as 1500 pounds." For its part, the United States acknowledges that "the linebacker faces a greater risk of serious injury if he takes the field under the influence of drugs than the drummer in the halftime band," but parries that "the risk of injury to a student who is under the influence of drugs while playing golf, cross country, or volleyball (sports covered by the policy in *Vernonia*) is scarcely any greater than the risk of injury to a student ... handling a 1500-pound steer (as [Future Farmers of America] members do) or working with cutlery or other sharp instruments (as [Future Homemakers of America] members do)." One can demur to the Government's view of the risks drug use poses to golfers . . . for golfers were surely as marginal among the linebackers, sprinters, and basketball players targeted for testing in Vernonia as steer-handlers are among the choristers, musicians, and academic-team members subject to urinalysis in Tecumseh. Notwithstanding nightmarish images of out-of-control flatware, livestock run amok, and colliding tubas disturbing the peace and quiet of Tecumseh, the great majority of students the School District seeks to test in truth are engaged in activities that are not safety sensitive to an unusual degree. There is a difference between imperfect tailoring and no tailoring at all.

---

[466] *Acton*, 515 U.S. at 667.

To summarize, this case resembles *Vernonia* only in that the School Districts in both cases conditioned engagement in activities outside the obligatory curriculum on random subjection to urinalysis. The defining characteristics of the two programs, however, are entirely dissimilar. The Vernonia district sought to test a subpopulation of students distinguished by their reduced expectation of privacy, their special susceptibility to drug-related injury, and their heavy involvement with drug use. The Tecumseh district seeks to test a much larger population associated with none of these factors. It does so, moreover, without carefully safeguarding student confidentiality and without regard to the program's untoward effects. A program so sweeping is not sheltered by *Vernonia;* its unreasonable reach renders it impermissible under the Fourth Amendment.[467]

COLLEGE DORMITORY SEARCHES

The Court has not yet decided a case that involves a search of college students on university premises. College students, as adults, should have greater expectations of privacy and the university would not be able to claim it was acting *in loco parentis*. Additionally, university personnel generally conduct these searches with local law enforcement. So, one could expect courts to find that a warrantless search of a dorm room violated the Fourth Amendment. On the other hand, universities and colleges generally have students sign residence contracts allowing consent to search to enforce college health and safety regulations. *Commonwealth v. Neilson, 423 Mass. 75 (1996),* is an example of a fairly typical state case.[468]

A maintenance worker heard a cat inside Neilson's dormitory suite. The worker reported the information to college officials, who visited the suite and told one of the residents to remove the cat because it violated university policy. That afternoon a university official posted a flyer notifying residents of the policy and advising them that a door-to-door check would be conducted. That night officials returned and while searching the room, officials noticed a light emanating from the closet. The defendant was not present, and fearing a fire hazard, they opened the closed door and discovered two four-foot-tall marijuana plants, fertilizer, grow lights, etc. School officials stopped their investigation at this point, and called in the local campus police who entered the room, observed the marijuana, took pictures, seized and removed all the contraband from the room—all without a warrant.

Neilson has signed a residence hall contract that provided, "residence life staff members will enter student rooms to inspect for hazards to health or personal safety." Accordingly, Neilson didn't argue that the initial entry by the residence hall staff was improper. He consented to reasonable searches to enforce college health and safety regulations and recognized that the search for the cat was within the scope of that consent. He argued instead that his constitutional rights were violated when the campus police searched the room and seized the evidence. The court agreed.

---

[467] *Board of Education of Independent School District No. 92 of Pottawatomie County v. Earls,* 536 U.S. 822, 852-853 (2002).

[468] *See also, Smyth v. Lubbers,* 398 F. Supp 777 (W.D. Mich 1975) (Fourth Amendment not limited to criminal prosecutions. This case involved a search for marijuana in an adult college student's dorm room by school officials and campus police who were also cross-designated sheriff deputies. The court found that defendant was protected by the Fourth Amendment even though the college handled the matter through a disciplinary procedure and not by means of a criminal prosecution. The court did not agree with the state that the search was only an administrative search pointing to the seriousness of the sanction (one term school suspension).

The police entered the room without a warrant, consent, or exigent circumstances. This search was unreasonable and violated the defendant's Fourth Amendment rights. ... First, there was no consent to the police entry and search of the room. The defendant's consent was given not to police officials, but to the University and the latter cannot fragmentize, share, or delegate it. ... Second, the plain view doctrine does not apply to the police seizure, where the officers were not lawfully present in the dormitory room when they made their plain view observations. While the college officials were legitimately present in the room to enforce a reasonable health and safety regulation, the sole purpose of the warrantless police entry into the dormitory room was to confiscate contraband for purposes of a criminal proceeding.[469]

JAIL AND PRISON SEARCHES

Historically, prisoners had no Fourth Amendment rights. *Lanza v. New York, 370 U.S. 139 (1962),* held that a "jail shares none of the attributes of privacy of a home, automobile, an office or hotel room, . . . and official surveillance had traditionally been the rule of the day in prisons," In *Hudson v. Palmer,* 468 U.S. 517 (1984), the court conceded that prisoners may have some expectation of privacy that society has recognized, and that "prisons are not beyond the reach of the Constitution. No 'iron curtain' separates one from the other," but "imprisonment carries with it the circumscription or loss of many significant rights."[470]

The reasonableness of prisoner searches depends on balancing the need to maintain prison and jail security, safety, and discipline against the invasion to prisoners' substantially reduced reasonable expectation of privacy. The court applying the balancing approach in *Hudson v. Palmer* found that an unannounced search of prisoners and their cells for weapons and contraband was not a search at all.

Notwithstanding our caution in approaching claims that the Fourth Amendment is inapplicable in a given context, we hold that society is not prepared to recognize a legitimate any . . . expectation of privacy that a prisoner might have in his prison cell and that, accordingly, the Fourth Amendment proscription against unreasonable searches does not apply within the confines of the prison cell. The recognition of privacy rights for prisoners in their individual cells simply cannot be reconciled with the concept of incarceration and the needs and objectives of the penal institutions.[471]

Justice Stevens wrote for a four-member dissent,

The view once held than at inmate is a mere slave is now totally rejected. The restraints and the punishment which a criminal conviction entails do not place the citizen beyond the ethical tradition that accords respect to the dignity and intrinsic worth of every individual. "Liberty" and "custody" are not mutually exclusive concept." By telling prisoners, that no aspect of their individuality, from a photo of a child to a letter from a wife, is entitled to constitutional protection, the Court breaks with the ethical tradition that I had thought was enshrined forever in our jurisprudence.[472]

---

[469] *Nielson,* 425 Mass at 80.
[470] 468 U.S. at 523.
[471] *Id.* at 525-526.
[472] 468 U.S. at 558.

Although the Court concluded that prison shakedowns are not searches, it found that full body searches, strip searches, and body cavity searches are Fourth Amendment searches. Nevertheless, they may be reasonable without warrants or probable cause if, in the particular situation, the need for security, safety or discipline outweigh prisoners' reasonable expectations of privacy. In *Bell v. Wolfish, 441 U.S 520 (1979)*, the U.S. Supreme Court held that it was reasonable to require jail inmates awaiting trial to expose their body cavities for visual inspection after every visit with a person from outside the jail. The court found these searches reasonable to maintain safety and order in the jail (and prevent contraband from coming into the facility). Courts have required reasonable suspicion to justify highly intrusive warrantless prisoner searches.[473] However, in 2012 the Court approved a strip search without reasonable suspicion as long as the person searched is being admitted into the general jail population.[474]

PROBATION AND PAROLE SEARCHES

Griffin v. Wisconsin, 438 U.S. 868 (1987), extended the special needs doctrine to warrantless entry and search of a probationer's home by probation officers who had reasonable grounds to believe that contraband was present. "Although a probationer had a Fourth Amendment reasonable expectation of privacy in his home, the existence of reasonable grounds to believe contraband is present creates a special need, beyond the normal need for law enforcement, to justify the warrantless search and seizure of the probationer's house. The Court found that a parolee does not have

> an expectation of privacy that society would recognize as legitimate. Parole allows convicted criminals out of prison before their sentence is completed. An inmate who chooses to complete his sentence outside of direct physical custody, however, remains in the Department of Correction's *legal* custody until the conclusion of his sentence, and therefore has significantly reduced privacy rights.[475]

The Court also reasoned that the parolee had given written consent through his parole contract to suspicionless searches, which "along with his already reduced privacy interests as a parolee, combined to make the search constitutional."[476]

ADMINISTRATIVE SEARCHES

The Fourth Amendment applies to every governmental agent who might violate a person's expectation of privacy including administrative agency employees. *Camera v. Municipal Court, 387 U.S. 523 (1967)*. The goal of most administrative agencies is not to enforce criminal law but rather to monitor compliance with regulations designed to promote health and safety. In order to enforce compliance with these regulations, agents must enter premises to conduct inspections. In *Camera*, the Court found it was not necessary for these agents to seek a warrant from a magistrate, but instead, they can use "area warrants."

---

[473] *See, e.g, Mary Beth G. v. City of Chicago*, 723 F.2d. 1263 (7th Cir. 1983) in which the U.S. Seventh Circuit Court of Appeals found Chicago's policy of strip-searching all women confined in the Cook County Jail was unreasonable and *Kennedy v. Hardiman*, 684 F. Supp, 540 (U.S. District Court, N.D., Illinois Eastern Division 1988) in which the court found that an extensive strip/body cavity search was unreasonable when based on an anonymous tip.

[474] *Florence v. Board of Chosen Freeholders of County of Burlington*, 566 U.S. 318 (2012).

[475] *Samson v. California*, 547 U.S. 843 (2006).

[476] *Id.*

By 1970, the Court held that regulatory agents did not even need to apply for area warrants to do inspections of businesses in "pervasively regulated industry" such as liquor stores or gun dealerships, as long as they did so during normal business hours and did not use force. Dealers who refused inspections, could lose their licenses. Safety inspections of mines was allowed without warrants under the Mine Safety and Health Act because all mine owners had to know of the law and it was a "constitutionally adequate substitute for the warrant requirement." The Court did not completely do away with the need for "area warrants" and still require them for worker safety inspections by OSHA (Occupational Safety and Health Authority) holding that simply requiring safety and health inspections of an industry does not make it a "pervasively regulated industry."

FIRE INSPECTIONS

When fire fighters enter a burning building or home, they are government agents who are intruding on a business or homeowner's expectation of privacy, but we certainly don't expect them to get a warrant before they can enter to put out the fire. Firefighters don't just put out fires though. They also look for the source of the fire and investigate possible arson—a crime. So, the Court in two Michigan cases[477] set forth a mix of administrative search and criminal search rules.

> Rule 1: A burning building creates an exigency that justifies a warrantless entry by fire officials to fight the blaze.
> Rule 2: [O]nce in the building, officials need no warrant to remain for a 'reasonable time to investigate the cause of the blaze after it has been extinguished.
> Rule 3: Where, however, reasonable expectations of privacy remain in the fire-damaged property, additional investigations begun after the fire has been extinguished and fire and police officials have left the scene, generally must be made pursuant to a warrant or the identification of some new exigency.
> Rule 4: If the primary object of a renewed search is to determine the cause and origin of a recent fire, and administrative warrant will suffice. To obtain such a warrant, fire officials need show only that a fire of undetermined origin has occurred on the premises, that the scope of the proposed search   is reasonable and will not intrude unnecessarily on the fire victim's privacy, and that the search will be executed at a reasonable and convenient time.
> Rule 5: If the primary object of the renewed search is to gather evidence of criminal activity, a criminal search warrant may be obtained only on a showing of probable cause to believe that relevant evidence will be found in the place to be searched.
> Rule 6: If evidence of criminal activity is discovered during the course of a valid administrative search (or during the initial firefighting), it may be seized under the plain view doctrine . . . This evidence them may be used to establish probable cause to obtain a criminal search warrant. [478]

INVENTORY SEARCHES

Local and state statutes and ordinances generally authorize police to impound vehicles for certain reasons—generally to remove vehicles in accidents, to permit the flow of traffic, to preserve evidence, to remove damaged vehicles from the highways, to tow vehicles which are unlawfully parked, to remove the vehicle after the driver has been arrested, etc. An inventory search of an impounded vehicle is an administrative search. Inventory searches of automobiles are reasonable under the Fourth Amendment and are part of routine caretaking functions. They

---

[477] *See, Michigan v. Tyler*, 436 US 499 (1978) and *Michigan v. Clifford*, 464 US 287 (1984)
[478] Zalman, *supra* at 171.

are not done for the purpose of obtaining evidence, and any evidence that is discovered in the inventory falls within the plain view doctrine. Thus, evidence found while conducting an inventory search is admissible despite the lack of a valid warrant. The Courts have put some constraints on inventory searches and require them to be conducted according to a well-delineated policy that leaves nothing to the discretion of the police officers. The key case on inventory searches is *South Dakota v. Opperman*, 428 U.S. 364 (1976). This case, involved police locating a marijuana cigarette in Opperman's glove box in his unlocked car that he left unattended and parked in the same spot on a street for three days. The police officers searched the car before having it towed.

Inventory searches also occur when an individual is lodged into the jail, and the unwarranted jail search is justified by the same rationales—the protection of property and the safety of individuals acting as custodians of the property. Jail inventory searches must be conducted under standardized rules and regulations so that each inventory search is as similar to all other searches as possible. The scope of jail inventory searches is broad, and the search can be very thorough due to the need to protect against contraband being brought into the facility.

SEIZING PEOPLE: ARRESTS, STOPS, AND ENCOUNTERS

The Fourth Amendment governs seizures as well as searches. Over the years, the Court has had several occasions to define what is a Fourth Amendment seizure. One would think it would be relatively straight-forward, but particular facts of particular cases have required the Court to tinker with exact meanings of the term "seizure." Police "seize" a person when, in view of all the circumstances surrounding the incident, a reasonable person would believe that he or she was not free to leave.[479] "Only when the officer, by means of physical force or show of authority, has in some way restrained the liberty of a citizen may we conclude that a 'seizure' has occurred."[480] No stop occurs under the Fourth Amendment even when police officers attempt to exert authority until the person actually submits to the officer's show of authority.[481]

In some cases, the Court has looked at the officer's intent in determining whether a stop has occurred.[482] In one case the Court concluded, "The primary law enforcement purpose was not to determine whether a vehicle's occupants were committing a crime, but to ask vehicle occupants, as members of the public, for their help in providing information about a crime in all likelihood committed by others. The police expected the information elicited to help them apprehend, not the vehicle's occupants, but other individuals."[483] But, in other cases the court has held that test is objective and the officer's underlying intent is immaterial.[484]

In *Michigan v. Chesternut, 486 U.S. 567 (1988)*, the defendant began running when he saw a police car approaching. Officers followed him to "see where he was going." As the officers drove alongside, they observed Chesternut pull a number of packets from his pocket and throw them away. The officers seized the packets and concluded they might be contraband. They then arrested Chesternut and conducted a subsequent search that revealed more drugs. Chesternut was charged with felony narcotics possession. The Court found that the offices' investigatory pursuit of Chesternut to "see where he was going" was not a seizure under the Fourth Amendment.

---

[479] *United States v. Mendenhall*, 446 U.S. 544 (1980).
[480] *Terry v. Ohio*, 392 U.S. 1 (1968).
[481] *California v. Hodari D.*, 499 U.S. 621 (1991).
[482] See, e.g., *Illinois v. Lidster*, 540 U.S. 419 (2003)
[483] *Id.*
[484] *See, e.g., Brendlin v. California* (officer stop of car is stop of both driver and passenger) and *Whren v. United States* (allowing pretext stops).

No bright-line rule applicable to all investigatory pursuits can be fashioned. Rather, the appropriate test is whether a reasonable man, viewing the particular police conduct as a whole and within the setting of all the surrounding circumstances, would have concluded that the police had in some manner restrained his liberty so that he was not free to leave. ... Under this test, respondent [Chesternut] was not 'seized' before he discarded the drug packets. ... The record does not reflect that the police activated a siren or flashers; commanded respondent to halt or displayed any weapons; or operated the car aggressively to block his course or to control his direction or speed. Thus, respondent could not reasonably have believed that he was not free to disregard the police presence and go about his business. The police, therefore, were not required to have a particularized and objective basis for suspecting him of criminal activity in order to pursue him.[485]

In another case, the Supreme Court stated, "Consistent with the language, history, and judicial construction of the Fourth Amendment, a seizure occurs when governmental termination of a person's movement is effected through means intentionally applied."[486] The most recent case on this matter is *Torres v. Madrid*, 592 U.S. ___ (2021).

Janice Madrid and Richard Williamson, officers with the New Mexico State Police, arrived at an Albuquerque apartment complex to execute an arrest warrant and approached Roxanne Torres, then standing near a Toyota FJ Cruiser. The officers attempted to speak with her as she got into the driver's seat. Believing the officers to be carjackers, Torres hit the gas to escape. The officers fired their service pistols 13 times to stop Torres, striking her twice. Torres managed to escape and drove to a hospital 75 miles away, only to be airlifted back to a hospital in Albuquerque, where the police arrested her the next day. (Case Syllabus)

Torres sued officers for violating her civil rights by using excessive force when they shot her in the back. The issue before the Court was whether the unsuccessful effort to stop Torres was a seizure. At the U.S. District Court (the trial court) the officers argued that Torres had not been "seized" under Fourth Amendment case law because her attempts to detain her were unsuccessful. They argued that people are only seized when they are stopped, and Torres kept going. The U.S. Court of Appeals for the 10th Circuit agreed and dismissed the civil suit against them finding, "a suspect's continued flight after being shot by police negates a Fourth Amendment excessive-force claim." The U.S. Supreme Court accepted review and reversed. Chief Justice Roberts in his majority opinion spent a good deal of paragraphs discussing the common law on arrest and placing *Hodari, D,* it this historical context before simply stating, "The application of physical force to the body of a person with intent to restrain is a seizure, even if the force does not succeed in subduing the person. ... This doesn't change even if someone escapes or if the physical force is by shooting with a gun rather than by grasping with a hand." The Court, refraining from deciding whether the seizure was reasaonble and whether the officers were entitled to qualified immunity, easily concluded that the officers "seized Torres by shooting her with the intent to restrain her movement."

ARRESTS

An arrest is something more than just a temporary or brief detention of a person. In order for an arrest to be lawful, officers must have probable cause to believe that a crime has been

---

[485] *Chesternut*, 486 U.S. at 574-576.
[486] *Brower v. County of Inyo*, 489 U.S. 593 (1989)

committed and that the person arrested committed it. The Fourth Amendment generally requires a warrant for seizures of persons as well as property. Through a series of cases, however, the Court has carved out significant exceptions that, for all practical purposes, allow most arrests to be made without a warrant.

WARRANTLESS ARRESTS

Under the hot pursuit exception police may go into a home and arrest a suspect without a warrant when there are exigent circumstances. In *United States v. Santana*, 427 U.S. 38 (1985) the court held that the police's warrantless arrest of Santana was valid because Santana was initially in a public place and then retreated to a private place. The undercover police officer in that case bought heroin from McCafferty and then drove her to Santana's house. McCafferty took the officer's money and then went into Santana's home; she later came out with several envelopes of said that Santana had the money. While the officer transported McCafferty to the police station, other officers went to Santana's home where they saw her standing in the doorway with a brown paper bag in her hand. They identified themselves as police officers, and Santana attempted to escape into her house. The officers chased and caught her. During the scuffle, two bundles of heroin fell to the floor. Police told Santana to empty her pockets, and she produced $135.00, of which $70.00 was the undercover officer's money. The court held that the warrantless arrest was not a violation of the Fourth Amendment because a warrantless arrest that begins in a public place is valid even if the suspect retreats into a private place and is arrested there.

> While it may be true under common law of property that the threshold of one's dwelling is 'private' place . . . not in an area where she had any expectation of privacy. ... She was not merely visible to the public but was exposed to public view, speech, hearing, and touch as if she had been standing completely outside her house. The police, therefore, had probable cause to arrest her and did so in the proper manner. Santana could not, furthermore, thwart her arrest by retreating into her private home. The District Court was correct in concluding that 'hot pursuit' means some sort of a chase but if need not be extended hue and cry 'in and about public streets.' The fact that the pursuit ended almost as soon as it began did not render it any less a 'hot pursuit' sufficient to justify the warrantless entry into Santana's house.

One year later, in *United States v. Watson, 423 U.S. 411 (1976)*, the Court found that the police could lawfully conduct a warrantless arrest in public, even when they had the opportunity to get a warrant but did not do so. In *Watson*, a reliable informant telephoned the postal inspector and informed him that he was in possession of a stolen credit card provided by Watson and that Watson had agreed to furnish the informant with additional cards. The informant agreed to meet with Watson and give a signal if he had additional stolen cards. When the signal was given, officers arrested Watson and took him from a restaurant where he was sitting to the street where he was *Mirandized*. When a search revealed no credit cards on Watson, the postal inspector asked if he could look inside Watson's car. The inspector told Watson "if I find anything, it is going to go against you." Watson agreed to the search. Using keys furnished by Watson, the car was searched and an envelope containing stolen credit cards was found. Watson was charged and convicted with possession of stolen credit cards.

Watson created a general "public place" exception to the warrant requirement regardless of the severity of the crime. The Court, however, drew the line between a public place and a private home four years later in *Payton v. New York*, 445 U.S. 573 (1980), stating, "In terms that apply equally to seizures of property and to seizures of persons, the Fourth Amendment has drawn a firm line at the entrance to the house. Absent exigent circumstances, that threshold may not reasonably be crossed without a warrant."

In *Payton* police officers conducted a two-day intensive investigation and assembled sufficient evidence to establish probable cause to believe that Payton had murdered the manager of a gas station. Although they had time to obtain a warrant, they went to Payton's apartment without a warrant to arrest him. The officers could see light and hear music from the apartment, but no one responded to their knock. They summoned emergency assistance and used crowbars to break open the door and enter the apartment. There was no one in the apartment, but in plain view was a .30-caliber shell casing that was seized and later admitted into evidence at Payton's trial. Payton later surrendered and was indicted for murder. Payton moved to suppress the evidence, but the lower court, although ruling that the search of the house was illegal, said that the shell casing was in plain view and thus admitted it into evidence. Payton was ultimately convicted.

The Court held that the Fourth Amendment requires police to get an arrest warrant when they enter a person's home to make a routine felony arrest when there is time to obtain a warrant. Police have lawful authority under the Fourth Amendment to enter the residence of a person for whom they have an arrest warrant, provided that the officers reasonably believe that the person named in the warrant is present.

> If there is sufficient evidence of a citizen's participation in a felony to persuade a judicial officer that his arrest is justified, it is constitutionally reasonable to require him to open his doors to the officers of the law. Thus, for Fourth Amendment purposes, an arrest warrant founded on probable cause implicitly carries with it the limited authority to enter a dwelling in which the suspect lives when there is reason to believe the suspect is within.[487]

In *Steagold v. New York, 451 U.S. 204 (1981)*, the Court held that an arrest warrant is not sufficient to let police enter the residence of a third person (not the person named in the warrant) and that they must seek a search warrant if they wish to arrest someone inside a third person's home. The Court was concerned with the privacy of the third person rather than the defendant's liberty. No Fourth Amendment right of the defendant is violated by an unlawful entry into a third person's home without a search warrant, but the homeowner has Fourth Amendment protections. These, however, cannot be claimed by the arrestee (since the arrestee would not have standing).

REASONABLE MANNER OF ARREST

Defendants can challenge their arrest on two grounds: 1) a lack of probable cause and 2) an unreasonable manner of arrest. The probable cause requirement was discussed above, so this section focuses on what is meant by "an unreasonable manner of arrest". It is not uncommon for a person who is being arrested to try to resist, so police often must use some degree of force in making an arrest. Reasonable force means that police use only the amount of force that is necessary to make the arrest. Historically, an officer was entitled to use whatever reasonable force was necessary, including deadly force, to make the arrest and to prevent the escape of the suspect. Generally, though, police officers had less discretion to use force in apprehending suspected misdemeanants than suspected felons.[488] Courts traditionally held that it was reasonable for a police officer to shoot a fleeing felon. But, in *Tennessee v. Garner, 471 U.S. 1 (1985)*,

---

[487] *Id.* at 602-03.
[488] Scheb, *supra* at 522.

the Court limited the use of deadly force by equating shooting a fleeing suspect with a Fourth Amendment seizure and requiring its reasonableness be tested under Fourth Amendment decisions. *Garner* narrowed the discretion of police officers in making arrests and broadened potential civil actions against the police for using excessive force.

Graham v. Connor, 490 U.S. 396 (1989) instructed the lower courts to analyze police use of force to arrest cases under the Fourth Amendment's reasonableness requirement not under the substantive due process test which focuses on officer's motivations. The facts in *Graham* are disturbing. Graham was a diabetic who needed to counteract the onset of an insulin reaction. Graham and his friend, Berry, went into a convenience store. Graham went into the store but saw many people ahead of him in line, so he hurried out and asked his friend to drive him instead to a friend's house. Officer Connor became suspicious after he saw Graham enter and hastily leave the store. He followed the car, made an investigative stop, and ordered Graham and Berry to wait while he determined what happened in the store. Other officers arrived, handcuffed Graham and ignored his attempt to explain his condition.

> In the ensuing confusion, a number of other Charlotte police officers arrived on the scene in response to Officer Connor's request for backup. One of the officers rolled Graham over on the sidewalk and cuffed his hands tightly behind his back, ignoring Berry's pleas to get him some sugar. Another officer said: "I've seen a lot of people with sugar diabetes that never acted like this. Ain't nothing wrong with the M. F. but drunk. Lock the S. B. up." Several officers then lifted Graham up from behind, carried him over to Berry's car, and placed him face down on its hood. Regaining consciousness, Graham asked the officers to check in his wallet for a diabetic decal that he carried. In response, one of the officers told him to "shut up" and shoved his face down against the hood of the car. Four officers grabbed Graham and threw him headfirst into the police car. A friend of Graham's brought some orange juice to the car, but the officers refused to let him have it. Finally, Officer Connor received a report that Graham had done nothing wrong at the convenience store, and the officers drove him home and released him.

> Graham sustained a broken foot, cuts on his wrists, a bruised forehead, and an injured shoulder; he also claims to have developed a loud ringing in his right ear that continues to this day."

Under the substantive due process analysis, the courts considered whether the officer acted in "good faith" or "maliciously and sadistically for the very purpose of causing harm." This meant the officer's subjective motivations were important in determining whether the force they used was unconstitutional. Under the *Graham* holding,

> The 'reasonableness of a particular use of force must be judged from the perspective of a reasonable officer on the scene, rather than with the 20/20 vision of hindsight. The Fourth Amendment is not violated by an arrest based on probable cause, even though the wrong person is arrested, nor by the mistaken execution of a valid search warrant on the wrong premises. With respect to a claim of excessive force, the same standard of reasonableness at the moment applies: 'Not every push or shove, even if it may later seem unnecessary in the peace of a judge's chamber,' violates the Fourth Amendment. The calculus of reasonableness must embody allowance for the fact that police officers are often forced to make split-second judgments—in circumstances that are tense, uncertain, and rapidly evolving—about the amount of force that is necessary in a particular situation.

The Court has evaluated excessive use of force cases where police officers use force to in police chase scenarios. *Scott v. Harris*, 550 U.S. 372 (2007), reviewed whether a deputy sheriff, Scott, could be sued for stopping Harris' car by ramming it with a police patrol car causing Harris to be permanently paralyzed. The outcome of the cases depended largely on the interpretation of a video taken by the patrol cruiser depicting Harris' driving and the high speed chase. The majority found Harris' driving to be reckless and that the officer's response was entitled to qualified immunity. The dissenting opinion found Scott's driving, although fast, did not warrant the officer's response that resulted in 19-year-old Scott's paralysis.[489]

In another car chase case[490] Brown and her husband approached a police checkpoint and then turned around to avoid it. Deputy Morrison and Reserve Deputy Burns pursued the vehicle for more than four miles at speeds of excess of 100 miles per hour. When the Browns stopped, Morrison pointed his gun at the truck and ordered them to raise their hands. Burns, who was unarmed, went to the passenger side of the truck and ordered Brown out of the vehicle. When Brown did not respond after the second request, Burns pulled Brown from the truck by the arm and swung her to the ground. The fall caused severe injuries to Brown's knees, possibly requiring knee replacement. Brown sued Burns, the county sheriff, and the county for her injuries claiming that they failed to adequately review Burn's background (he had a history of assault and battery, resisting arrest, driving while intoxicated, etc.) The Court held the county could not be liable for a case involving excessive use of force for a single hiring decision made by a county official.

Looking at these cases above (where a person claims that police used excessive for to arrest them), you can see that the remedy for the situation involving an unreasonable manner of arrest is to file a civil suit against the officers who used excessive force. Federal law (42 USC § 1983) allows private citizens to bring suits in federal courts when they claim their rights under the United States Constitution have been violated. But, Section 1983 currently doesn't allow citizens the right to sue *federal officers* for violating those rights, and Congress has never passed a statute authorizing these suits. However, in 1971 in *Bivens v. Six Unknown Named Agents*, 403 U.S. 388 (1971), the Court found the right to sue federal officers for damages should be presumed from the constitution.[491] Since the Court decided Bivens, it has been steadily rejecting and limiting suits against federal officers.[492] The 2021-2022 term was no exception, the Court "continu[ed] an unbroken decades-long run, . . . and refused to extend the right to sue a federal

---

[489] The case was a civil action, and the majority found that the officer had immunity. For a discussion of the videotape taken by the deputy's car in the high-speed chase of Harris that left Harris a paraplegic see, http://purplemotes.net/2008/02/10/editing.

[490] *County of Sacramento v. Lewis*, 520 U.S. 397 (1998).

[491] For more information about *Bivens* claims see, https://www.shouselaw.com/ca/civil-rights/bivens-claim/

[492] On December 8, 2021, House of Representatives Member Henry "Hank" Johnson introduced H.R. 6185 – known as the Bivens 2021 bill-- to the House Judiciary Committee." The Bill states that the purpose of the bill is "To provide a civil remedy for an individual whose rights have been violated by a person acting under Federal authority, and for other purposes." The bill would simply amend Section 1983 by inserting the words "of the United States" before "of any State"

(Every person who, under color of any statute, ordinance, regulation, custom, or usage, of [the United States or of] any State or Territory or the District of Columbia, subjects, or causes to be subjected, any citizen of the United States or other person within the jurisdiction thereof to the deprivation of any rights, privileges, or immunities secured by the Constitution and laws, shall be liable to the party injured in an action at law, suit in equity, or other proper proceeding for redress, except that in any action brought against a judicial officer for an act or omission taken in such officer's judicial capacity, injunctive relief shall not be granted unless a declaratory decree was violated or declaratory relief was unavailable. ...

officer for damages under Bivens."[493] The Court held in *Boule v. Egbert*, 596 U.S. ___ (2022) that a Washington State innkeeper (Boule) did not have an cause of action against Border Patrol Officer (Egbert) and other government agents for allegedly violating his First Amendment rights (based on retaliatory action for his exercising his right to free speech) or his Fourth Amendment rights.

> Robert Boule is a U.S. citizen who owns and runs the Smuggler's Inn, a bed-and-breakfast abutting the Canadian border in Blaine, Washington; drives a car with a "SMUGLER" license plate; and worked as a confidential informant for the Customs and Border Patrol. Erik Egbert, a Border Patrol agent, attempted to speak with a guest, newly arrived from Turkey via New York, outside the inn. When Boule asked Egbert to leave his property and attempted to intervene, Egbert shoved him to the ground; when Boule complained to Egbert's superiors, Egbert allegedly contacted the Internal Revenue Service and state agencies, resulting in a tax audit and investigations of Boule's activities.

> …Egbert brought an excessive-force claim under the Fourth Amendment and a First Amendment retaliation claim. The U.S. Court of Appeals for the 9th Circuit allowed both claims to go forward. … The Supreme Court reversed. It held both claims involved new contexts that differed from the limited Bivens claims the court has already recognized. The court has never recognized a Bivens claim for a First Amendment violation, and the immigration and border placed the Fourth Amendment claim in a new context."

> Justice Clarence Thomas wrote on behalf of the majority, "we have emphasized that recognizing a cause of action under *Bivens* is 'a disfavored judicial activity.'" Yet, while it kept *Bivens* alive, the Court make it clear that *Bivens* remains on thin ice, warning "that if we were called to decide *Bivens* today, we would decline to discover any implied causes of action in the Constitution."[494]

COURT JURISDICTION OVER UNLAWFULLY SEIZED DEFENDANTS

When police unlawfully seize property, courts will generally exclude the evidence when defendant files a motion to suppress. However, when police unlawfully seize the defendant, courts still retain jurisdiction over the defendant and the case. We don't exclude the defendant from trial as a "product of some police illegality." Is there any remedy for someone whom police arrest unlawfully? In *Frisbie v. Collins*, 342 U.S. 519 (1952), the unlawful arrest of an individual does not deprive the court of jurisdiction over the defendant. In that case, Collins claimed that Michigan officers came to Chicago where he was living, forcibly handcuffed, blackjacked, and abducted him and took him back to Michigan where he was tried and convicted of murder. While serving a life sentence for murder, he filed a writ of habeas corpus claiming his trial and conviction violated his due process rights and was therefore void. In deciding whether an unlawful arrest of a defendant affected the validity of the court's jurisdiction in a criminal proceeding, the Court held that it did not, stating:

> This Court has never departed from the rule announced in Ker v. Illinois, 119 U.S. 436 (1886) that the power of a court to try a person for a crime is not impaired by the fact that he had been brought within the court's jurisdiction by reason of a

---

[493] https://www.scotusblog.com/2022/06/court-again-rejects-extension-of-bivens-suits-against-federal-officials

[494] See, BIVENS IS BARELY ALIVE AFTER SUPREME COURT MAULING https://lisa-legalinfo.com/tag/bivens/#:~:text=BIVENS%20IS%20BARELY%20ALIVE%20AFTER,to%20the%20brink%20of%20extinction.

'forcible abduction.' No persuasive reasons are now presented to justify overruling this line of cases. They rest on sound basis that due process of law is satisfied when one present in court is convicted of crime after having been fairly apprised of the charges against him and after a fair trial in accordance with constitutional procedural safeguards.

STOPS

TERRY V. OHIO: STOPPING INDIVIDUALS WITH LESS THAN PROBABLE CAUSE

Terry v. Ohio, 392 U.S. 1 (1968), a landmark U.S. Supreme Court case, created an entirely "new" level of Fourth Amendment analysis. Although stops and frisks were not really new (officers had been doing these investigative stops that some states called "stops and frisk" for some time), *Terry v. Ohio* officially affirmed these practices. Recall that the Fourth Amendment demands that probable cause is needed for a search or seizure to be reasonable. The *Terry* Court held, however, that some seizures and searches were reasonable even with facts that didn't reach the probable cause standard of sufficiency of evidence. *Terry* created a rule allowing police officers to stop individuals and do a field investigation when the officer had reasonable suspicion to believe the person was either committing a crime or was about to commit a crime.

WHAT IS REASONABLE SUSPICION?

The Court did not define "reasonable suspicion" in *Terry v. Ohio*--in fact those words aren't even within the decision. In later cases, however, the Court has said that the reasonable suspicion means some minimal level of objective justification for making a stop--something more than an unparticularized suspicion or hunch, but less than the level of suspicion required for probably cause.[495] Every situation a police officer confronts will be different, and the facts that will give rise to reasonable suspicion cannot be "reduced to a neat set of legal rules." The determination of reasonable suspicion is a case-by-case determination. The police officer, in justifying the stop, must present specific and articulable facts that, together with rational inferences drawn from those facts, reasonably suggest that an individual has committed a crime or about to commit a crime. These facts are to be judged in accordance with a reasonable person standard and not based on what the officer subjectively believed. Police officers may not rely on a hunch, generalization, or stereotype. The officer can rely on his or her training and experience, as well as information from an informant. The court will review the legitimacy of the stop by looking at the totality of the circumstances—for example, whether the suspect is calm or nervous, whether the suspect is observed in a high crime area, the time of day, the arrests made in this vicinity by this officer in the past, the suspect's willingness to cooperate, whether the suspect's pattern of behavior suggests he or she may be engaged in criminal conduct.

That a suspect fits a criminal profile by itself does not mean the police have reasonable suspicion of criminal activity.[496] Neither can police justify a Terry stop based only on race, ethnicity, gender or other constitutionally-suspect personal characteristic.[497] In *United States v. Weaver*, 966 F.2d 391 (8th Cir. 1992), the Eighth Circuit Court of Appeals analyzed whether officers stopped Weaver based on a profile or based upon reasonable suspicion of criminal activity.

---

[495] See, e.g., *United States v. Sokolow*, 490 U.S. 1 (1989).
[496] See, *Reid v. Georgia*, 448 U.S. 438 (1980).
[497] *United States v. Weaver*, 966 F.2d 391 (8th Cir. 1992).

Our decision therefore turns on whether the officers had a reasonable, articulable suspicion that Weaver was engaged in criminal activity when they pursued him to detain his baggage after he attempted to leave.

Hicks testified that he took the following factors into consideration when he decided to detain Weaver's bags: (1) that Weaver got off a direct flight from Los Angeles, a source city for drugs; (2) that he was a roughly dressed young black male who might be a member of a Los Angeles street gang that had been bringing narcotics into the Kansas City area; (3) that he moved rapidly from the airplane toward a taxicab; (4) that he had two carry-on bags and no checked luggage; (5) that he had no identification on his person; (6) that he did not have a copy of his ticket; (7) that he appeared very nervous when he talked to Hicks; (8) and that he made no mention of visiting his mother until the last second before he tried to leave the consensual interview.[498]

In *Reid v. Georgia*, 448 U.S. 438 (1980), the Supreme Court concluded that a drug agent could not, as a matter of law, have reasonably suspected the defendant of criminal activity by relying on the following factors: (1) the defendant's arrival from a source city for cocaine; (2) the defendant's arrival early in the morning when "law enforcement activity is diminished;" (3) the defendant and his companion had no luggage other than shoulder bags; and (4) the apparent attempt of the defendant and his companion to conceal the fact that they were traveling together.

In *United States v. Sokolow*, 490 U.S. 1 (1989) the Court held that agents had a reasonable basis on which to suspect that the defendant was transporting illegal drugs where: (1) the defendant had paid more than $2,000 for two airline tickets in cash; (2) he traveled under a name which did not match the name listed for his telephone number; (3) his original destination was Miami, a source city for illicit drugs; (4) he stayed in Miami for only 48 hours; (5) he appeared nervous; and (6) he checked none of his luggage. Although "[a]ny one of these factors is not by itself proof of any illegal conduct and is quite consistent with innocent travel[,] ... together they amount to reasonable suspicion.[499]

The Court recently heard a case in which the defendant, Joshua Cooley, was parked in his pickup truck on the side of a road within the Crow Reservation in Montana when tribal Officer Saylor approached his truck.[500] During their exchange, Saylor assumed based on Cooley's appearance, that Cooley did not belong to a Native American tribe though Saylor did not ask Cooley or otherwise confirm his conclusion. During the conversation, Saylor began to suspect that Cooley was engaged in unlawful activity and detained him to conduct a search of his truck, where he found evidence of methamphetamine. Saylor called for assistance from county officers because Cooley "seemed to be non-Native." After Cooley was charged federally with weapons and drug offenses, he moved to suppress the evidence on the grounds that Saylor was acting outside the scope of his jurisdiction as a Crow Tribe law enforcement officer when he seized Cooley, in violation of the Indian Civil Rights Act of 1968 ("ICRA"). The Court unanimously held that a tribal police officer has the authority to detain temporarily and to search a non-tribe member traveling on a public right-of-way running through a reservation for potential violations of state or federal law. The Court analyzed this case as an issue of authority and jurisdiction and cited an earlier case which held that a tribe may "exercise civil authority over the conduct of non-

---

[498] *Id.* at 394.
[499] *Sokolow*, 490 U.S. at 9.
[500] *United States v. Cooley*, 593 U.S. ___(2021)

Indians on fee lands within its reservation when that conduct threatens or has some direct effect on the political integrity, the economic security, or the health or welfare of the tribe."

How Long Can A Stop Last?

Under the Fourth Amendment any investigatory detention must be temporary and last no longer than is necessary to accomplish the purpose of the stop. *Terry* noted that detentions must be brief, and in one case the Court held that whether a stop is too long depends not only on the length of time of the stop, but also on the surrounding circumstances. Was the length of time of detention reasonable? In assessing this, courts have imposed no rigid time limitations but have evaluated whether the police diligently pursued their investigation.[501]

Frisks

If, during the investigatory detention (the "stop") police have reasonable suspicion to believe that the person they have detained is armed with a weapon, they may conduct a pat-down of the suspect's outer clothing to locate weapons. This is called a "frisk." The Court ruled that where "nothing in the initial stages of the encounter serves to dispel [an officer's] reasonable fear for his own or other's safety, he is entitled for the protection of himself and others in the area to conduct a carefully limited search of the outer clothing of such persons in an attempt to discover weapons which might be used to assault him."[502] The carefully limited frisk is intended to protect the officer and others in the vicinity and must be "confined to an intrusion reasonably designed to discover guns, knives, clubs or other hidden instruments for assault of the police officer."

The officer need not be absolutely certain that the individual is armed and presently dangerous. The test is whether a reasonably prudent man or woman under the circumstances would believe that his or her safety or the safety of others is at risk. Reasonableness is to be determined based on the facts as interpreted in light of the officer's experience. This is an objective test. An officer may not base a frisk on the officer's subjective fear or apprehension or hunch. The opposite is also true. An officer who lacks fear that a suspect is armed and presently dangerous may conduct a frisk so long as an objective person would believe that the frisk is required.

The frisk must be directed at the discovery of guns, knives, and other weapons. The officer may reach inside the clothing only when he or she feels an object that is reasonably believed to be a weapon. An officer may remove a container or package and open it only if the officer reasonably believes that it may contain a weapon.

The frisk does not automatically follow from the stop. A suspect is to be afforded the opportunity to dispel the officer's fear that the suspect is armed and presently dangerous. The key fact is whether the suspect is reasonably believed to pose a threat. Courts have upheld frisks based on a combination of factors.

- A bulge in the suspect's pocket
- A suspect reaching into his or her pocket
- The suspect's movements
- The officer's knowledge that the suspect had been involved in violent activity
- The type of criminal activity

---

[501] *See, U.S. v. Sharpe*, 470 U.S. 675 (1985).
[502] *Terry*, 392 U.S. at 30-31 (1968).

- The suspect's presence in a high-crime neighborhood, particularly late at night
- The presence of another individual who is arrested by the police for a serious offense.

Extending Terry - Protective Sweeps

In 1983, in *Michigan v. Long*, 463 U.S. 1032 (1982), the Court extended *Terry* frisks to the passenger compartment of automobiles when police officers possess a reasonable fear for their safety. This "protective sweep of the automobile" is justified in those instances in which an officer possesses a reasonable belief that the suspect is potentially dangerous and may gain immediate control of weapons. The Court stressed that the search must be limited to those areas in which a "weapon may be placed or hidden." Seven years after *Long*, the Court decided *Buie's* (discussed above) and extended the right to do a protective sweep to a home when police have a reasonable suspicion that the sweep is necessary to locate any individuals (and Buie's co-conspirator in particular) who may pose a threat to the safety and security of the police officers.

Extending Frisks — Plain Feel Doctrine Established

In *Minnesota v. Dickerson* (supra), the Court extended *Terry* frisks to situations where officers stop an individual, conduct a frisk, and then feel something that, to the officer, is immediately apparent it is illegal narcotics. The officer's touch, not the visual observation (plain view), permits the officer to seize the object that the physical examination reveals is contraband. The Court held,

> If a police officer lawfully pats down a suspect's outer clothing and feels an object whose contour or mass makes its identity immediately apparent, there has been no invasion of a suspect's privacy beyond that already authorized by the officer's search for weapons; if the object is contraband, its warrantless seizure would be justified by the same practical considerations that inhere in the plain-view context."[503]

In this case, the Court found that the officer was not entitled to manipulate the squishy package he felt in Dickerson's pocket, concluding that the officer went beyond the permissible scope of the 'plain feel' doctrine it had just announced.

MERE ENCOUNTERS

The Court distinguishes between seizures of individuals, including stops and arrests, and non-seizures or "mere encounters." According to the Court, the police officer needs "no particularized suspicion" to approach an individual and question him. In *Florida v. Royer, 460 U.S. 491 (1983)*, the Court stated, "Law enforcement officials do not violate the Fourth Amendment by merely approaching an individual on the street or in another public place, by asking him if he is willing to answer some questions, by putting questions to him if the person is willing to listen, or by offering in evidence in a criminal prosecution his voluntary answers to such questions."

The Court highlighted the differences between seizures and mere encounters in *Florida v. Bostick, 501 U.S. 429 (1991)*. In that case two uniformed officers boarded a bus in Fort Lauderdale, Florida that was en route from Miami to Atlanta. The officers approached Bostick and asked him for identification and his bus ticket. The officers then asked him for consent to search his bag and told Bostick he could refuse consent. Bostick nevertheless consented to the search of his luggage that uncovered cocaine. Bostick moved to suppress the cocaine in court, arguing that it was

---

[503] *Dickerson*, 508 U.S. at 375-376.

illegally seized. The Court overruled the Florida Supreme Court which had found that "working the busses" was *per se* unconstitutional. Instead, it held,

> The appropriate test is whether, taking into account all of the circumstances surrounding the encounter, a reasonable person would feel free to decline the officers' request to otherwise terminate the encounter.

> . . . [A] seizure does not occur simply because a police officer approaches an individual and asks a few questions. So long as a reasonable person would feel free 'to disregard the police and go about his business,' the encounter is consensual and no reasonable suspicion is required. The encounter will not trigger Fourth Amendment scrutiny unless it loses its consensual nature.

> There is no doubt that if this same encounter had taken place before Bostick boarded the bus or in the lobby or the bus terminal, it would not rise to the level of a seizure. The Court has dealt with similar encounters in airports and has found them to be 'the sort of consensual encounters that implicate no Fourth Amendment interest.' We have stated that even when officers have no basis for suspecting a particular individual, they may generally ask questions of that individual and request consent to search his or her luggage—as long as the police do not convey a message that compliance with their requests is required. [504]

ACTIONS COMBINING SEARCHES AND SEIZURES

SEIZING CARS AND THEIR OCCUPANTS

The Court has decided a line of cases dealing with vehicle stops. In these cases, the Court explored the legality of pretext stops, ordering drivers and passengers out of a stopped car, seeking consent to search stopped drivers, and frisking the driver and passengers of a stopped car. In *Pennsylvania v. Mimms*, 434 US 106, 109-110 (1977), the Court stated,

> The touchstone of our analysis under the Fourth Amendment is always 'the reasonableness in all the circumstances of the particular governmental intrusion on a citizen's personal security' . . . and . . . that reasonableness depends on a 'a balance between the public's interest and the individual's right to personal security.

The Court ruled that a law enforcement officer may, as a matter of course, order the driver to exit the car upon making a valid traffic stop. The Court extended this holding to passengers twenty years later in *Maryland v. Wilson*, 519 U.S. 408 (1997). There, a state trooper attempted to stop a car in which Wilson was a passenger for speeding and an irregular license plate. After activating his blue lights, the trooper followed the car for more than a mile before it stopped. During this time, two of three passengers in the car kept looking back at the trooper, ducking below the line of sight and then reappearing. As the trooper approached the car after it stopped, the driver got out and met him halfway. The trooper reported that the driver was trembling and appeared very nervous, but did produce a valid driver's license. When the driver returned to the car to retrieve the rental papers, the trooper noticed that Wilson was sweating and appeared very nervous. When the trooper ordered Wilson out of the car, a quantity of crack

---

[504] 501 U.S. at 537-539.

cocaine fell to the ground. The court held that officers may order passengers, not just drivers, to exit the car after they make a traffic stop.

In *Ohio v. Robinette, 519 U.S. 33 (1996)*, the Court examined the circumstances in which an officer could ask for consent to search a car after he had lawfully stopped it. After stopping the defendant for speeding, the deputy asked him to step out of the car. The deputy issued a verbal warning and, after returning Robinette's license, he asked "One question before you get gone: are you carrying any illegal contraband in your car?" When Robinette replied "no," the deputy asked if he could search the car. After Robinette consented, the deputy searched the car and found a small amount of marijuana and a pill that turned out to be methamphetamine. Robinette claimed he should have been informed that he was "free to go" in order for the consent to search the car was valid. The Court found that the Fourth Amendment does not require police officers to inform motorists lawfully stopped for traffic violations that the legal detention has concluded before any subsequent interrogation or search will be found to be consensual. Chief Justice Rhenquist stated, "In light of the admitted probable cause to stop Robinette for speeding, the deputy was objectively justified in asking Robinette to get out of the car. . ." [505] The *Robinette* Court, citing past holdings, recalled that "voluntariness is a question of fact to be determined from all the circumstances," that "knowledge of the right to refuse consent is [just] one factor to be taken into account," and that "it would be unrealistic to require police officers to always inform detainees that they are free to go before a consent search may be deemed voluntary." (Citations omitted.)

In *Brendlin v. California*, 551 U.S. 249 (2007) the Court concluded that an officer's stop of a vehicle for the purpose of investigating the driver for an offense constitutes a seizure of other occupants as well. It noted that a reasonable person would understand the officer to be exercising control such that none of the occupants is free to leave. Two years later, a unanimous Court in *Arizona v. Johnson, 555 U.S. 323 (2009)*, upheld a police officer's right to conduct a Terry pat-down of a passenger who was riding in a car that was stopped for a vehicle infraction for which the officer could cite, but not arrest, the driver.

CHECKPOINTS ROVING PATROLS, CHECKPOINTS, AND ROADBLOCKS

In general, the court has drawn some limitations on suspicionless checkpoints and roadblocks that are used to simply ferret out general criminal activity[506] but has allowed criminal investigation roadblocks[507] used to investigate a specific crime and roadblocks designed to deter driving under the influence.[508] The Court has enunciated a three-step balancing test to judge the reasonableness of a suspicionless roadblock seizure.

> Consideration of the constitutionality of such seizures involves a weighing of the gravity of the public concerns served by the seizure, the degree to which the seizure advances the public interest, and the severity of the interference with, individual liberty. (Citation omitted.)

---

[505] *Ohio v. Robinette*, 519 U.S. 33, 38 (1996).
[506] *City of Indianapolis v. Edmond*, 531 U.S. 32, (2000).
[507] In *Illinois v. Lidster*, 540 U.S. 419 (2004) police officers investigating a fatal hit-and-run accident set up a checkpoint at that location a week after the accident in order to stop motorists briefly to hand out flyers and request any information concerning the accident, and the defendant was stopped at the checkpoint and eventually was arrested and convicted of DUII. The Court held that the brief and minimally intrusive checkpoint stop for the purpose of investigating the fatal accident did not violate the Fourth Amendment.
[508] *Michigan v. Sitz*, 496 U.S. 444 (1980)

A central concern in balancing these competing considerations in a variety of settings has been to assure than an individual's reasonable expectation of privacy is not subject to arbitrary invasions solely at the unfettered discretion of officers in the field. (Citation omitted.) [509]

Court has found that in the "absence of articulable facts justifying reasonable suspicion that the vehicle or the operator was unlicensed, a "random" stop of an automobile for the purpose of checking the vehicle registration and the operator's license violated the Fourth Amendment."[510] But, if all traffic is stopped in roadblock fashion, it is not a violation of the Fourth Amendment.[511] Thus, a roadblock set up to identify drunken drivers did not violate the Fourth Amendment as long as it was conducted pursuant to a consistently applied administrative scheme and the stop was brief.[512] Plain-view seizures following a stop at a driver-license checkpoint are similarly permissible.[513] The Court set some limits on roadblocks in *City of Indianapolis v. Edmond*, 531 US 32 (2000) by holding that a highway checkpoint program whose primary purpose is the discovery and interdiction of illegal narcotics violated the Fourth Amendment.

We decline to suspend the usual requirement of individualized suspicion where the police seek to employ a checkpoint primarily for the ordinary enterprise of investigating crimes. We cannot sanction stops justified only by the generalized and ever-present possibility that interrogation and inspection may reveal that any given motorist has committed some crime.[514]

MATERIAL WITNESS WARRANTS AND DETENTIONS

A material witness warrant allows prosecutors to arrest and detain (until trial) a person who has essential information needed to successfully prosecute another person accused of a crime. The justification for the detention is based on the need for the witness's testimony and the difficulty in getting them to appear at trial--it is not based upon any probable cause that the individual is somehow involved in the crime. Material witness warrants, because they involve the incarceration of a person not believed to have done anything wrong, are relatively rare. Recently, the Court examined the material witness warrant in *Ashcroft v. Al-Kidd*, 563 U.S. ___ (2011).

In 2003, the FBI arrested Abdullah al-Kidd as he was preparing to travel to Saudi Arabia to study Arabic and Islamic law. He was held for 16 days as a material witness in the terrorism trial of Sami Omar al-Hussayen. Al- Kidd argued the government classified him as a material witness because it lacked enough evidence to hold him as a suspect. He filed a lawsuit against then-Attorney General John Ashcroft claiming that he created and authorized a program that allegedly misused the material witness statute to detain suspected terrorists.

The lawsuit did not go to trial, and in September 2009, the U.S. Court of Appeals for the Ninth Circuit rejected Ashcroft's bid for absolute immunity, holding that it didn't apply because the government's motive for arresting al-Kidd allegedly had nothing to do with the al-Hussayen prosecution.

---

[509] *Brown v. Texas,* 443 U.S. 47, 50-51 (1979).
[510] *Delaware v. Prouse,* 440 U.S. 648 (1979).
[511] *Id.*
[512] *Sitz,* supra.
[513] *Texas v. Brown,* 460 U.S. 730 (1983).
[514] *Edmond,* 531 U.S. at 44 (2000).

In reviewing this decision, Justice Scalia wrote in the majority opinion, "Efficient and even-handed application of the law demands that we look to whether the arrest is objectively justified, rather than to the motive of the arresting officer." Ginsburg's concurred stating that Al-Kidd's "ordeal is a grim reminder of the need to install safeguards against disrespect for human dignity, constraints that will control officialdom even in perilous times."[515] Justice Sotomayor also wrote a concurring opinion and stated, "Whether the Fourth Amendment permits the pretextual use of a material witness warrant for preventive detention of an individual whom the Government has no intention of using at trial is. . . a closer question than the majority's opinion suggests."

SEIZING PROPERTY

Under the Fourth Amendment, "a property seizure occurs when a governmental intrusion meaningfully interferes with an individual's possessory interest."[516] The general principles set forth in *Terry* regarding stops of individuals are applicable to the temporary detention of property. Thus, it is sometimes lawful to temporarily detain a person's property to investigate its connection to a crime. The temporary detention of property often arises in the context of detaining a car for the purpose of allowing a drug-sniffing dog to arrive. Investigative detentions of personal property have been found to be constitutionally valid under the Fourth Amendment.

Investigatory detention of property, like that of a "stop" of an individual, must be temporary and last no longer than is necessary to effectuate the purpose of the stop. When officers seek to seize and detain the property for a prolonged period, the best course of action is to seek a warrant. In *Chambers v. Maroney (supra)*, for example, the court found it reasonable to seize and impound an automobile on the basis of probable cause, for whatever period is necessary to obtain a warrant for the search. The court has also held that "freezing a scene" (not allowing anyone to enter a house or move a car) until the officers can obtain a search warrant was not an unreasonable seizure.

WRAP UP

The Fourth Amendment establishes that law enforcement officers need to get a warrant based on probable cause before they may seize or search persons and their property. The police (the "affiants") will need to establish through their sworn affidavit that they have sufficient information to establish probable cause in an *ex parte* hearing in front of a neutral and detached magistrate. In the affidavit supporting the application for a warrant, police must describe who, where, or what they want to search and seize with particularity. Police may rely on evidence they know from personal observation, through past training and experience, through the observation of other officers, and through named or confidential informants or even anonymous tips.

In a long series of cases, the Court has recognized situations where a search is reasonable even when police do not have a warrant. Other case law defines what constitutes a search (e.g., the *Olmstead, Katz,* and *Jones* decisions) and probable cause (e.g, the *Ornelas decision*). According to the Court, sometimes police looking around is not even considered a "search" (e.g., plain view, open fields, abandoned property, and border "searches") so no warrant is needed as these situations fall outside the Fourth Amendment's protection. Where the Fourth Amendment does apply, the Court has allowed unwarranted searches in some situations where the police have probable cause to believe the suspect has committed a crime and that evidence of the crime will

---

[515] *See*, http://www.oyez.org/cases/2010-2019/2010/2010_10_98. (Note, this case highlights the various types of opinions written by Supreme Court Justices.)
[516] Thirty-Fifth Annual Review, *supra* at 3.

be found where police will be searching (e.g., the automobile, hot pursuit, and exigent circumstances searches). The Court has allowed unwarranted searches in some situations even when police do not have probable cause (e.g., searches incident to a lawful arrest, consent searches, some jail searches, some administrative searches, inventory searches). Finally, the Court has allowed unwarranted searches in some situations based on reasonable suspicion (e.g., special needs searches, frisks, school searches, probation and parole searches, some jail searches, and some administrative searches).

In another long series of cases, the Court has defined and identified what constitutes a stop (e.g., the *Terry, Mendenhall, Hodari D, and Torres* decisions) and reasonable suspicion (e.g., *Terry, Reid,* and *Sokolow*). A stop or arrest is a seizure protected by the Fourth Amendment. Until *Terry,* to justify any police seizure of an individual, the police were required to have probable cause. With *Terry,* the Court recognized the need for police to stop individuals to investigate upon a reasonable belief that a crime was just committed or was about to be committed. Police seize people when they stop for traffic violations, when they conduct roadblocks, checkpoints, and roving patrols. The Court has allowed unwarranted seizures of cars and their drivers and passengers under limited circumstances; generally, such stops are based upon probable cause that the driver has committed a traffic violation, but some unwarranted stops (such as DUII roadblocks) are suspicionless but justified by some compelling public policy.

SOME THINGS TO THINK ABOUT OR EXPLORE

- ➢ Consider the differences and similarities functionally and legally between using a dog for sniffs outside a home and modern advanced technology for remote surveillance and enhanced vision.
- ➢ Consider the policing reforms which are part of Illinois new criminal justice reform law (see, e.g., https://www.civicfed.org/iifs/blog/summary-provisions-illinois-house-bill-3653-criminal-justice-omnibus-bill). (Compare: https://www.chicagotribune.com/opinion/ct-opinion-police-reform-pritzker-illinois-20210326-t5htaqot2nc23p25hix2vx5e2q-story.html) and https://abc7chicago.com/police-and-criminal-justice-reform-bill-pritzker-house-3653-accountability/10361126/#) In the latter article there are several comments from police indicating they see the law as anti-police. In the earlier article there are several comments that this law does not go far enough to rein in the police. Do you think the reforms are necessary?
- ➢ Investigate whether your state constitution or state statutes provide any additional privacy protections when it comes to road blocks or other types of suspicion-less searches and stops.
- ➢ Research an instance from recent events where the amount of force used by police was legally or publicly contested. What were the facts surrounding the use of force? What were the results of this case?
- ➢ Did anything in this chapter surprise you? Discuss.

TERMINOLOGY

- abandoned property
- actual authority
- administrative search
- affiant
- affirmation
- Aguillar/Spinelli test
- anonymous tip
- anticipatory warrant
- apparent authority
- arrest warrant
- basis of knowledge prong
- bench warrant
- *Bivens* Action
- checkpoint
- community caretaking search
- confidential informant
- de novo review
- detached magistrate
- escalating probable cause
- evanescent evidence
- exigency
- ex parte appearance
- *Franks* Hearing
- frisk
- hot pursuit doctrine
- informant
- inventory search
- liberty interest
- material witness warrant
- mere encounter
- neutral magistrate
- nighttime warrant
- no knock warrant
- particularity requirement
- particularized suspicion
- Patriot Act
- pen register
- per se unreasonable
- plain feel doctrine
- plain view doctrine
- possessory interest
- pretext stop
- probable cause
- profile
- property interest
- protective sweep
- oath
- objective basis
- objective standard (of reasonableness)
- Omnibus Crime Control and Safe Streets Act of 1968
- open fields doctrine
- reasonable suspicion
- roadblock
- roving patrol
- search
- search incident to arrest
- seizure
- special needs search
- staleness
- stop
- subjective standard (of reasonableness)
- telephonic warrant
- third-party consent
- totality of the circumstance test
- trespass doctrine
- unparticularized suspicion
- veracity prong
- warrant return

Chapter Eight: Confessions, Interrogations and Identification Procedures

OVERVIEW AND LEARNING OBJECTIVES

This chapter examines additional legal constraints on the police when they investigate crime. It explores the investigative tactics of interrogating suspects, using lineups and other identification tools and examines the constitutional limits to these investigative techniques. After reading this chapter, you should be able to answer the following questions:

> What is the voluntariness test (of admissibility of confessions) and when does it apply?
> In what ways do the Fifth, Sixth, and Fourteenth Amendments govern police interrogations in state and federal investigations?
> What is the holding in *Miranda v. Arizona* and how has that case changed police investigations?
> How has the Court expanded or limited the *Miranda* holding from the 1960s until today?
> According to the U.S. Supreme Court, when is a suspect in "custody" and being "interrogated" under *Miranda*?
> What happens when a suspect invokes his or her rights under *Miranda?*
> How prevalent are false confessions and what factors may contribute to false confessions?
> What safeguards can be employed against false confessions
> Why are eyewitness identifications so problematic and what can police do to minimize faulty identifications? How have recent courts attempted to impose safeguards?
> What arguments can defendants make to challenge identification procedures?

COERCED CONFESSIONS AND DUE PROCESS

The Fifth, Sixth, and Fourteenth Amendments govern the law of confessions and interrogations. The Court has interpreted, but not necessarily consistently, how these Amendments limit the ability of police to get confessions from suspects. The due process guarantees of the Fifth Amendment (for the federal government) and Fourteenth Amendment (for states) prohibit confessions that are coerced and involuntary. The question before trial judges in pretrial motions to suppress is what is a voluntary confession and when are defendant's statements involuntary?

THE VOLUNTARINESS REQUIREMENT

The Court barred the use of coerced confessions in federal prosecutions in *Bram v. United States,* 168 U.S. 532 (1897), and in state prosecution beginning with *Brown v. Mississippi, 297 U.S. 278 (1936).* In *Brown* the Court reasoned that coerced or involuntary confessions violated the guaranty of fundamental fairness, and by admitting them in a state court trial, the state violated due process. In *Brown* African American males were convicted of murder in Mississippi solely based on their confessions. Defendant Ellington had been confronted by a deputy sheriff and by a mob of white men who accused him of murder. He denied the crime and was hanged by a rope from the limb of a tree, let down, and then strung up once again. Ellington continued to deny his guilt, and he was tied to a tree, whipped, and then released. He later was arrested and severely whipped while being transported to jail and, when threatened with additional beatings, signed a confession dictated by the sheriff. Defendants Brown and Shields were also arrested, stripped, and beaten with leather straps with inlaid metal buckles. In his opinion, Chief Justice of the U.S. Supreme Court Charles Evan Hughes observed that the trial transcript read "more like pages torn from some medieval account than a record made within the confines of a modern civilization which aspires to an enlightened and constitutional government."[517] The Court concluded that Mississippi authorities had conspired to extract a coerced and untruthful confession. It held that government authorities may not coerce individuals into involuntarily providing evidence of their own guilt.

Ten years later, in *Aschcraft v. Tennessee*, 322 U.S. 143 (1944), the Supreme Court found that psychological coercion similarly violated the suspect's rights to due process of law. Ashcraft confessed to soliciting the murder of his wife after teams of police and lawyers detained and subjected him to incommunicado interrogation for thirty-six straight hours. The Court concluded that Ashcraft's confession was the product of a coercive set of circumstances that overwhelmed his ability to exercise rational choice and, accordingly, overturned his conviction.

According to *Brown* and *Ashcraft*, coerced confessions violate due process. In addition, coerced confessions raise concerns about the reliability of the confession. The Court noted that, to ensure fundamental fairness, the methods used to obtain confessions must have resulted in voluntary confessions. In *Lisenba v. California*, 314 U.S. 219 (1941), Justice Owen Roberts wrote that it would be contrary to due process to employ threats, promises, or torture in the courtroom to induce an individual to testify against himself and, a "case can stand no better, if by resort to the same means, the defendant is induced to confess and his confession is given in evidence." According to Roberts, such abusive behavior undermines respect for the criminal justice system.

In 1949, the Court found that police violated the defendant's constitutional rights when they interrogated the defendant for five consecutive evenings and deprived him of sufficient sleep and food[518]. According to the Court, the Due Process Clause "bars police procedures which violate basic notions of our accusatorial mode of prosecuting crime."[519] In another case, the Court also found that involuntary confessions are inadmissible because the police practices by which there were obtained violated fundamental decency--even though, under the circumstances presented in this case, the confession was reliable.[520] The Court said that confessions obtained by subterfuge and force must be disallowed "not because such confessions are unlikely to be true but because the methods used to extract them offend an underlying principle in the enforcement of our criminal law: that ours is an accusatorial and not an inquisitorial system."[521]

Lippman noted that the due process voluntariness test is designed to achieve four interrelated purposes.

- Trustworthiness—confessions that result from physical or psychological coercion run the risk that the defendant confessed to avoid or to halt abuse.
- Fundamental fairness—the use of an involuntary confession against the defendant is fundamentally unfair and compromises the integrity of the courtroom.
- Offensive police methods—confessions obtained in violation of the Due Process Clause that are the product of police tactics are offensive to fundamental values

---

[517] Lippman, *Criminal Procedure*, 298 (3d ed. 2017).
[518] *Watts v. Indiana*, 338 U.S. 49 (1949).
[519] *Id.* at 54.
[520] In *Rogers v. Richmond*, 365 US 534 (1961), the police obtained the defendant's confession by pretending to arrest his sick wife. The state court held that the confession was probably reliable and allowed it in as evidence.
[521] *Id.*

- Free will and rational choice—confessions violate due process if they are the product of drugs administered by the police or of a suspect's psychological disabilities if they do not result from free will or rational choice. [522]

When police obtain an involuntary confession, they violate the defendant's rights, and the confessions are presumed to lack reliability. As such, they are not admissible for any purpose—even impeachment. Sometimes even non-coerced confessions are disallowed because they were not the product of the defendant's free choice -- even when the police practices weren't necessarily objectionable. For example, in *Townsend v. Sain*, 372 U.S. 293 (1963), the defendant, who was sick, was given some medication that had the effect of a truth serum. The police, unaware of the drug's effects, questioned the suspect and obtained a confession from him. Although reliable and not obtained through particularly coercive methods the Court held that "[a]ny questioning by police officers which in fact produces a confession which is not the product of free intellect renders that confession inadmissible."[523]

The voluntariness test was the only test used by courts to determine the admissibility of confessions in state prosecutions from 1936 (*Brown*) until 1964 (*Malloy v. Hogan*, 378 U.S. 1 (1964)). The test was criticized for not giving defendants enough protection. In determining whether a confession had been made voluntarily, courts examined the totality of the circumstances, giving judges tremendous discretion. Federally, the courts could have decided confession cases based on the Fifth Amendment's protection against self-incrimination, but they also relied on a voluntariness inquiry in the few cases they decided. The Court in two cases, *McNabb v. United States*, 318 U.S. 332 (1943), and *Mallory v. United States*, 354 U.S. 449 (1957), told lower federal courts they must exclude evidence from any confessions police obtained during any period of unnecessary delay in taking the defendant to a magistrate for arraignment.[524] Fifty-two years later, the Court limited this *McNabb-Mallory* rule by holding that a defendant's voluntary confession made within six hours of arrest is admissible—even if there were some unnecessary delays in taking the defendant before a magistrate. [525]

THE TEST OF VOLUNTARINESS: TOTALITY OF THE CIRCUMSTANCES

To be admissible a confession must have been made freely, voluntarily, and without compulsion or inducement of any sort. A confession that involves physical or psychological coercion or overcomes the will of an individual to resist violates due process and should be excluded from evidence. The test of voluntariness is evaluated by the "totality of the circumstances."[526] The prosecution bears the burden of proving voluntariness by a preponderance of the evidence.[527] In *Spano v. New York*, 360 U.S. 315 (1959),[528] the Court

---

[522] Lippman, *Procedure,* supra at 267-268.

[523] *Townsend v. Sain*, 372 U.S. 293, 298 (1963).

[524] *McNabb v. United States,* 318 U.S. 332 (1943), and *Mallory v. United States*, 354 U.S. 449 (1957).

[525] *Corley v. United States*, 556 U.S. 303 (2009).

[526] *Haynes v. Washington*, 373 U.S. 503 (1963).

[527] *Lego v. Twomey*, 404 U.S. 477 (1972).

[528] The Court found that Spano's will was overborne by official pressure, fatigue and sympathy falsely aroused. The Court noted:

- the police employed a childhood friend to play on the defendant's sympathies,
- the defendant was questioned for eight hours at night by fourteen officers and his confession was written down by a skilled and aggressive prosecutor,
- the police disregarded the defendant's refusal to speak on the advice of his counsel and ignored his request to contact his lawyer,

identified the following factors to be considered in evaluating whether a confession was voluntary.

- Physical abuse--was there physical abuse or threats of abuse by the police or angry crowds?
- Psychological abuse and manipulation--were there threats, rewards, or trickery used to induce a suspect to confess?
- Interrogation--what was the length, time, and place of questioning and the number of police officers involved.
- Attorney--was the suspect allowed to consult with an attorney, friends or family?
- Defendant's features--what is defendant's age, education, and mental and emotional development?
- Procedural regularity -- did the police follow proper legal procedures, including the *Miranda* warning?
- Necessity--were police trying to solve a crime or were they already in possession of evidence of defendant's guilt? (Police are generally provided greater flexibility in interrogation when they are attempting to solve a crime or exonerate the defendant.)

Later in this chapter you will read about the *Miranda* rule that requires police to warn a suspect who is in custody when they wish to interrogate him or her. But a confession may be involuntary and, thus inadmissible, even if police have *Mirandized* the defendant. Giving *Miranda* warnings does not transform an involuntary confession into an admissible confession if the statement was taken by coercion that overbore the person's will. Courts must still evaluate all the facts surrounding the taking of statements from a defendant and not just examine whether warnings were given and waived.

Two cases demonstrate that police still need to still be concerned about voluntariness of a confession. In *Mincey v. Arizona,* 437 U.S. 385 (1978), Mincey was in intensive care at the hospital, and was interrogated by a police detective who informed him that he was under arrest for murder. Mincey had to write down his answers because he could not talk due to a tube in his mouth. The Court found that he was "weakened by pain and shock, isolated from family, friends, and legal counsel, barely conscious, and his will was simply overborne. The Court forbade the use of his confession at trial for any purpose stating, "But *any* criminal trial use against a defendant of his *involuntary* statement is a denial of due process of law 'even though there is ample evidence aside from the confession to support the conviction.'" In *Arizona v. Fulminante,* 499 U.S. 279 (1991), the police placed a paid federal informant in the defendant's cell with instructions to get information about his involvement in the murder of his daughter.[529] To do so, the informant told the defendant that he would protect him from the other inmates who disliked child killers on the condition that Fulminante tell him what happened to his daughter. Fulminante confessed to sexually abusing and then shooting his daughter in the head. The informant testified about the confession at defendant's murder trial. The Court examined the totality of the circumstances and concluded that defendant's confession was involuntary (and inadmissible) because his fear of physical retaliation led him to confide in the informant. The Court noted that defendant was susceptible to physical retaliation because he had a slight build

- the defendant was only 25 years old and had never been in custodial arrest or police interrogation. He had not completed high school and had a psychological disability,
- the police failed to immediately bring the defendant before the judge as was required, and
- the police already possessed eyewitnesses to the shooting and were engaged in securing the evidence required to convict.

[529]In an earlier case, the Court held that use of informants placed in cells were not "custodial interrogations" for the purpose of Miranda, so no warnings needed to be given.

and couldn't cope with the pressures of incarceration during his earlier imprisonment and had also been housed in a psychiatric institution.

FALSE CONFESSIONS AND "VOLUNTARINESS"

PEOPLE CONFESS TO CRIMES THEY DID NOT COMMIT

Research on DNA exonerations over the past several decades has consistently revealed:

- People will confess to crimes they did not commit.
- Certain types of individuals (juveniles and mentally unstable individuals, in particular) are more likely to make false confessions than others.
- Many false confessions are police-induced, and police are far more confident about their ability to discern between lies and truth in pre-interrogation interviews than their accuracy (about the same as chance) would allow them to be.
- When a confession has been made, police, court personnel, and jurors are likely to believe it--despite independent evidence suggesting that the confessor is not the perpetrator.

Researchers have identified several well-known cases of false confessions, but these cases (which generally involve a DNA exoneration of a person who has been conclusively cleared of any involvement in the crime) are likely the tip of the iceberg. Research has revealed approximately 300 proven false confessions in recent decades. In approximately 25% of wrongful conviction cases, the individual has spent years in prison for a crime that he or she did not commit before the case is finally acknowledged or identified as a wrongful conviction and a miscarriage of justice. The injustice of punishing innocent individuals while letting the true offenders escape punishment, has prompted several scholars to delve into questions why individuals would confess to crimes they did not commit, what factors lead to false confessions, and how the system can prevent, or at least minimize the risk of, false confessions.

Richard Leo noted,

> False confessions raise important questions for social scientists, mental health professionals, policy makers, and the public. They are consistently one of the leading, yet most misunderstood, causes of error in the American legal system and thus remain one of the most prejudicial sources of false evidence that lead to wrongful convictions.
>
> . . .
>
> Despite substantial documentation and analysis by scholars, the phenomenon of police-induced false confessions remains counterintuitive to most people. Most lay people believe in what has been referred to as the myth of psychological interrogation; that an innocent person will not falsely confess to police unless he is physically tortured or mentally ill. ... The myth of psychological interrogation persists because most people do not know what occurs during police interrogations, and because they wrongly assume that individuals do not act against their self-interest or engage in self-destructive behavior, such as falsely confessing to a crime they did not commit.[530]

---

[530] Richard Leo, "False Confessions: Causes, Consequences, and Implications" 37 *J. Am. Acad. Psych. Law* 332-43 (2009).

Redlich and Meissner (2010) summarized the research on police's ability to detect when a person was being deceptive. Some key findings were:

- No one behavioral cue is definitely indicative of deception.
- People (including law enforcement) generally perform no better than chance at detecting deception.
- Although there are some cues that associate with deceit, these same cues also associate with anxiety and ambivalence.
- It is not yet possible to distinguish between behavioral cues that are the result of lying, the result of being accused of lying, or simply the result of speaking in public.
- Truth tellers were significantly more likely to provide evasive answers, to cross their legs, and shift posture, and were less likely to name someone who did not commit the crime than were liars.
- Truth tellers and liars shared many of the same behaviors, and in some instances, truth tellers exhibited behaviors that are attributed to liars.
- Vast majority of studies have found accuracy rates to approximate chance detection (about 50%) despite interrogation training claims of 85% levels of accuracy when evaluating the deception of suspects.
- Even professionals who have to make daily decisions of whether people are lying do not demonstrate high rates of accuracy when detecting deception.
- Training on typical interrogation deception techniques has been shown to have a deleterious effect on accuracy (studies with college students and police officers found that trained participants were less accurate than naïve participants, but were nevertheless significantly more confident in their abilities to detect deception).

They conclude, "In sum, most, if not all, of the available evidence suggests that interrogators who place weight on non-verbal and linguistic cues as indicators of deceit are prone to error. There are numerous examples of proven false confessions in which these supposed cues of deception were misread."[531]

ERRORS THAT LEAD TO FALSE CONFESSION

Leo identifies three errors that may lead to false confessions: misclassification, coercion, and contamination. The first error that leads to false confession is misclassification.

> Investigators first misclassify an innocent person as guilty; they next subject him to a guilt-presumptive, accusatory interrogation that invariably involves lies about evidence and often the repeated use of implicit and explicit promises and threats as well. Once they have elicited a false admission, they pressure the suspect to provide a post-admission narrative that they jointly shape, often supplying the innocent suspect with the (public and nonpublic) facts of the crime.[532]

The misclassification error occurs partly because police believe they are able to accurately identify when people are lying.

---

[531] Allison Redlich and Christian Meissner, "Techniques and Controversies in the Interrogation of Suspects: The Artful Practice versus the Scientific Study" in Jennifer L. Skeem, Kevin S. Douglas, & Scott O. Lilienfeld (Eds.), *Psychological Science in the Courtroom: Controversies and Consensus (2009)*.
[532] *Id.* at 334.

However, social scientific studies have repeatedly demonstrated across a variety of context that people are poor human lie detectors and thus are highly prone to error in their judgment about whether an individual is lying or telling the truth. Most people get it right at rates that are no better than chance (i.e., 50%) or the flip of a coin. More specific studies of police interrogators have found that they cannot reliably distinguish between truthful and false denials of guilt at levels greater than chance; indeed, they routinely make erroneous judgments. The method of behavior analysis taught by the police training firm Reid and Associates has been found empirically *to lower judgment accuracy.* (Emphasis added) ... As Kassin and Gudjonsson note, police detectives and other professional lie-catchers are accurate only 45 to 60 percent of the time.[533]

Leo identifies other reasons for misclassification,

The suspect may, for example, simply be the most readily noticed person who fits a very general description given by an eyewitness or others. ... [T]he target may be chosen simply because he happens to be noticed by the police, reported by someone who had seen a police sketch or falsely identified from a mug shot or lineup, or he fits an official profile of the perpetrator.

The second error Leo identified which leads to false confessions is coercion. He noted that:

Once detectives misclassify an innocent person as a guilty suspect, they often subject him to an accusatorial interrogation. Getting a confession becomes particularly important when there is no evidence against the suspect, especially in high-profile cases in which there is great pressure on police detectives to solve the crime, there is no other source of potential evidence to be discovered, and typically there is no credible evidence against an innocent but misclassified suspect.

Once interrogation commences, the primary cause of police-induced false confession is psychologically coercive police methods. Psychological coercion can be defined in two ways: police use of interrogation techniques that are regarded as inherently coercive in psychology and law, or police use of interrogation techniques that, cumulatively cause a suspect to perceive that he has no choice but to comply with the interrogator's demands. ... [W]hen today's police interrogators employ psychologically coercive techniques, they usually consist of (implicit or express) promises of leniency and threats of harsher treatment. ... Most documented false confessions in recent decades have been directly caused by or have involved promises or threats.

The second form of psychological coercion, causing a suspect to perceive he has no choice but to comply with the wishes of the interrogator, is not specific to any one technique but may be the cumulative result of the interrogation methods as a whole. ... Interrogation is designed to be stressful and unpleasant, and it is more stressful and unpleasant the more intense it becomes and the longer it lasts. Interrogation techniques are meant to cause the suspect to perceive that his guilt has been established beyond any conceivable doubt, that no one will believe his claims of innocence, and that by continuing to deny the detectives' accusations he will only make his situation (and the ultimate outcome of the case against him)

---

[533] *Id.* at 335.

much worse. The suspect may perceive that he has no choice but to comply with the detectives' wishes because he is fatigued, worn down, or simply sees no other way to escape an intolerably stressful experience. Some suspects come to believe that the only way they will be able to leave is if they do what the detectives say.[534]

Researchers have found that some individuals are more likely to confess falsely than others. For examples, individuals with little experience with, but with much faith in, the criminal justice system may confess due to beliefs that the truth will ultimately prevail and that confessing will be the most expedient course of action. Researchers consistently have identified that individuals who are "highly suggestible or compliant," juveniles, mentally ill, and developmentally disabled individuals are especially vulnerable to the coercive nature of interrogations.

All other things being equal, those who are highly suggestible or compliant are more likely to confess falsely. Individuals who are highly suggestible tend to have poor memories, high levels of anxiety, low self-esteem, and low assertiveness, personality factors that also make them more vulnerable to the pressures of interrogations and thus more likely to confess falsely. Interrogative suggestibility tends to be heightened by sleep deprivation, fatigue, and drug or alcohol withdrawal. Individuals who are highly compliant tend to be conflict avoidant, acquiescent, and eager to please others, especially authority figures.[535]

The third error identified by Leo is that of contamination. Contamination occurs when police disclose facts of the case to the innocent suspect and then attribute those facts as first being disclosed by the suspect. Garrett examined the substance of false confessions to see whether what was said during these interrogations could "shed any light" on the phenomenon of confession contamination.[536]   He found,

Police may, intentionally or not, prompt the suspect on how the crime happened so that the suspect can then parrot back an accurate-sounding narrative. ... Detectives sometimes specifically testified that they had assiduously avoided contaminating the confessions by not asking leading questions, but rather allowing the suspects to volunteer crucial facts.

The nonpublic facts contained in confession statements then became the centerpiece of the State's case. Although defense counsel moved to exclude almost all of these confessions from the trial, courts found each to be voluntary and admissible, often citing to the apparent reliability of the confessions.[537]

Garrett concluded from his study of forty known false confession cases that the majority of the confessions were contaminated. He found that in thirty-six of thirty-eight cases for which he had the transcripts, that the confessor had specific details about how the crime occurred. He noted,

---

[534] Leo, *supra,* at 335. Consider the case of Brendan Dassey, whose conviction was thrown out in August 2016 after a U.S. Magistrate Judge determined his confession to be involuntary and the product of police coercion. His story and video tapes of his confession can be seen in the Netflix documentary, Making a Murder. See, http://www.cbsnews.com/news/brendan-dassey-making-a-murderer-subject-conviction-tossed/ last visited, August 17, 2016.

[535] Leo, *supra,* at 335.

[536] Brandon L. Garrett, The Substance of False Confessions, *62 Stan. L. Rev. 1051* (2010).

[537] *Id.* at 1066.

The trials of these exonerees then centered on those facts. At trial, law enforcement testified that the suspect had volunteered specific details about how the crime occurred, typically details corroborated by expert evidence or crime scene evidence. In most, the innocent person did not merely guess or repeat one or two facts. Almost all exonerees were reported to have provided detailed statements that included facts likely to be known only by the culprit.[538]

Garrett described police training and noted that police are trained not to contaminate a confession by feeding or leaking crucial facts and recognize it "is important to keep certain facts confidential, because doing so later enhances the power of the confession in a subsequent prosecution or trial."[539] Nevertheless, "in all but two of these exonerees' cases, police claimed that the defendant had offered a litany of details that *we now know these innocent people could not plausibly have known independently.*"[540] His study revealed,

> In twenty-seven of the thirty-eight cases, the police officers testifying under oath at trial denied that they had disclosed facts to the suspect. Some were asked directly whether they had told the suspect key facts, others themselves noted they had not done so, and others carefully described an interrogation in which the suspect had volunteered each of the relevant facts. The question then arises whether officers were testifying falsely when they claimed that crucial facts were volunteered, where in fact they were disclosed by these police officers.
>
> . . . These officers most likely believed they were interrogating a guilty person. Officers may contaminate a confession unintentionally. During a complex interrogation, they might not later recall that as to important subjects they had in fact asked leading questions.[541]

Detective James Trainum described how he and his colleagues unintentionally secured a false confession:

> We believed so much in our suspect's guilt that we ignored all evidence to the contrary. To demonstrate the strength of our case, we showed the suspect our evidence, and unintentionally fed her details that she was able to parrot back to us at a later time. Contrary to our operating procedures at the time, my colleagues and I chose to videotape the interrogation. This is what saved me from making a horrible mistake in the long run. It was a classic false confession case and without the video we would never have known.[542]

SYSTEMS RESPONSE TO CONFESSIONS

One troubling problem with false confessions is that once an individual "confesses" the entire criminal justice system reacts more severely.

> Confessions are the most incriminating and persuasive evidence of guilt that the state can bring against a defendant. False confessions are therefore the most

---

[538] *Id.* at 1074.
[539] *Id.*
[540] *Id.*
[541] *Id.* at 1075.
[542] *Id.*

incriminating and persuasive false evidence of guilt that the state can bring against an innocent defendant. Former U.S. Supreme Court Justice William Brennan's observation that "no other class of evidence is so profoundly prejudicial" is amply supported by social science research. Confessions exert a strong biasing effect on the perceptions and decision-making of criminal justice officials and lay jurors alike because most people assume that a confession, especially a detailed confession, is by its very nature, true. Confession evidence therefore tends to define the case against a defendant, usually overriding any contradictory information or evidence of innocence.

A suspect's confession sets in motion a seemingly irrefutable presumption of guilt among justice officials, the media, the public, and lay jurors. (Footnote omitted.) This chain of events in effect leads each part of the system to be stacked against the individual who confesses, and as a result he is treated more harshly at every stage of the investigative and trial process. (Footnote omitted.) He is significantly more likely to be incarcerated before trial, charged, pressured to plead guilty and convicted. Moreover, the presence of a confession creates its own set of confirmatory and cross-contaminating biases (footnotes omitted) leading both officials and jurors to interpret all other case information in the worst possible light for the defendant. For example, a weak and ambiguous eyewitness identification that otherwise may have been quickly dismissed in the absence of a confession is treated instead as corroboration of the confession's underlying validity. As the case against an innocent false confessor moves from one stage to the next in the criminal justice system, it gathers more collective force, and the error becomes increasingly difficult to reverse.

This chain reaction starts with the police. Once they obtain a confession, they typically close their investigation, clear the case as solved, and make no effort to pursue any exculpatory evidence or other possible leads, even if the confession is internally inconsistent, contradicted by external evidence or the result of coercive interrogation. (Footnote omitted.) …

The presumption of guilt and the tendency to treat more harshly those who confess extends to prosecutors, defense attorneys, and judges as well. Like police, prosecutors rarely consider the possibility that an entirely innocent suspect has falsely confessed. … Once a suspect has confessed prosecutors tend to charge him with the highest number and types of offenses (footnote omitted) and set his bail at a higher amount (footnote omitted) and they are far less likely to initiate or accept a plea bargain to a reduced charge (footnote omitted). … Even defense attorneys treat suspects who confess more harshly, often pressuring them to accept a guilty plea to a lesser charge to avoid a higher sentence that will inevitably follow from a jury conviction. …

If the defendant's case goes to trial, the jury treats the confession as more probative of the defendant's guilt than any other type of evidence . . . especially if, as in virtually all high-profile cases, the confession receives pretrial publicity. (Footnotes omitted.) . . . [S]tudies demonstrate that a false confession is a dangerous piece of evidence to put before a judge or jury, because it profoundly biases their evaluation of the case in favor of conviction, so much so that they may allow it to outweigh even strong evidence of a suspect's factual innocence. (Footnote omitted). …

[A]s the U.S. Supreme Court stated in the case of *Arizona v. Fulimante*, "a confession is like no other evidence." It is "uniquely potent" (footnote omitted) in its ability to bias the trier of fact in favor of the prosecution, overwrite contradictory or exculpatory case evidence, and lead to the wrongful conviction of the innocent.[543]

According to Garrett, courts were willing to find that the confessions in his study were "corroborated" (the requirement for admissibility) even with the thinnest of evidence. Those courts found that the due process requirement of voluntariness was satisfied even though "many of these confessions raised significant indicia of involuntariness at the time."[544] In ninety-five percent of the cases in which the defendant went to trial, a pre-trial motion was made to exclude the confession--all were unsuccessful. Additionally, confession evidence adversely affected the appellate review of defendants' cases. Prior to the DNA evidence that ultimately exonerated the defendants in Garrett's study, the defendants had challenged their convictions either through direct appeal or through habeas corpus motions, and they were ultimately denied relief by the appellate courts — based in large part by the courts' reliance on the defendants' confessions.

PREVENTING FALSE CONFESSIONS

Researchers have suggested that one way to prevent police-induced false confessions is by requiring all custodial interviews and interrogations be videotaped in their entirety. Lassiter (2010) indicated that this single reform may not be sufficient to prevent confession-based wrongful confessions; however, Kassin et al. (2010) suggest that there are two reasons to believe that the videotaping may be effective. First, self-reports from police suggest the possibility that the recording of interrogations will alter the very process of interrogation by causing investigators, who are acutely aware that their sessions will later be scrutinized by prosecutors, defense lawyers, judges and juries, to limit their use of highly aggressive tactics. ... To the extent that the resulting process involves less egregious uses of the tactics that cause us great concern (e.g., the false evidence ploy and certain minimization tactics as well as explicit promises and threats), especially with regard to highly vulnerable suspect populations (i.e., juveniles and adults impaired by intellectual disability or psychological disorder, the net result should be a reduction in false confessions. Importantly for prosecutors, Sullivan et al (2008) found that police who have started to record interrogations also report a sharp reduction in the number of motions to suppress their custodial statements.

> The second basis for optimism is that videotaped interrogations, to the extent that they present an accurate and balanced account of the entire process, may well improve the fact-finding accuracy of judges (regarding voluntariness) and juries (regarding guilt). In a vast majority of confession-based wrongful convictions, the facts of what transpired were in dispute — such as whether or when the suspect was Mirandized; whether strong promises, threats or deceptions were used to elicit an admission; and most importantly, perhaps whether the crime details contained in the narrative confession originated with the suspect or the investigator.[545]

Garrett suggests additional precautions:

---

[543] Leo, *supra* at 340-41.
[544] Garrett, *supra* at 1094
[545] Saul Kassin, et. al., Police-Induced Confessions, Risk Factors, and Recommendations: Looking Ahead, 34 *Law of Human Behavior* 34, 50 (2010).

- Legislation requiring courts to conduct reliability reviews and exclude interrogations that display extensive feeding of facts; videotaping policies bolstered by clear policies and training regarding the nondisclosure of key investigative facts.
- Use of a "double blind" technique wherein a detective not familiar with the investigation does the initial interrogation.
- Requiring police to analyze and test the fit between the suspect's narrative and crime scene facts.
- A modification of current psychological interrogation techniques particularly with individuals vulnerable to suggestion and coercion.
- Barring lengthy interrogations when dealing with such vulnerable suspects.
- Abandoning the use of certain psychological techniques and conduct a hearing in which a judicial officer questions the suspect, at least in cases involving vulnerable individuals.[546]

The American Psychological Association's Council of Representative in 2014 adopted the Resolution on the Interrogation of Criminal Suspects -- largely based on research done by the many members of Division 41 of the APA, the American Psychology-Law Society.[547] It recommended that:

- all custodial interviews and interrogations of felony suspects be video recorded in their entirety and with a "neutral" camera angle that focuses equally on the suspect and interrogator;
- (in recognition of the risk of false confession is increased with extended interrogation times) law enforcement agencies consider placing limits on the length of time that suspects are interrogated;
- law enforcement agencies, prosecutors, and the courts recognize the risks of eliciting a false confession by interrogations that involve the presentation of false evidence;
- police, prosecutors, and the courts recognize the risks of eliciting a false confession that involve minimization "themes" that communicate promises of leniency;
- those who interrogate individuals who are young (with particular attention paid to developmental level and trauma history), cognitively impaired, those with impaired mental health functioning, or in other ways are vulnerable to manipulation receive special training regarding the risk of eliciting false confessions; and
- particularly vulnerable suspect populations, including youth, persons with developmental disabilities, and persons with mental illness, be provided special and professional protection during interrogations such as being accompanied and advised by an attorney or professional advocate.[548]

---

[546] Garrett, *supra* at 1116-1117.

[547] The American Psychology-Law Society promotes the contributions of psychology to the understanding of law and legal institutions, the education of psychologists in legal matters and law personnel in psychological matters, and the application of psychology in the legal system.
http://www.apa.org/about/division/div41.aspx (last visited, July 28, 2016).

[548] *See,* American Psychological Association Resolution on interrogations of criminal suspects. (2014).
http://www.apa.org/about/policy/interrogations.aspx (last visited, July 28, 2016)

THE FIFTH AMENDMENT'S SELF-INCRIMINATION PROHIBITION

The Fifth Amendment provides that no person shall be compelled in a criminal case to be a witness against himself. We refer to this as the right against self-incrimination—that a person cannot be forced to be "an instrument" in his or her own prosecution. According to case law, the Fifth Amendment covers only "natural persons" (meaning humans), and it does not protect corporations or their officers.[549] Like most of the Bill of Rights, the federal protection against self-incrimination found in the Fifth Amendment has been incorporated through the due process clause of the Fourteenth Amendment.[550]

CLAIMING THE FIFTH AMENDMENT

The mechanism by which a defendant charged with a crime and at trial for that crime claims the protection of against self-incrimination is by refusing to take the stand and testify. The state may not comment on the defendant's failure to testify, and courts will instruct jurors that defendants have an absolute right to not testify and that they may not draw any adverse inferences because the defendant asserted the right. Non-defendant witnesses claim the protections of the Fifth Amendment by taking the stand and refusing to answer questions asked of them. For example, in the O.J. Simpson case in which he was on trial for murder, Officer Mark Furman, a state's witness, repeatedly invoked the Fifth Amendment claiming something to the effect of: "I refuse to answer under the grounds that my answer might incriminate me." A person must claim the privilege by remaining silent (or asserting their right to remain silent) or the privilege is lost. A witness who makes an incriminatory statement cannot take back the statement once it has been made. And, accordingly, once a statement is made, it generally can be used as evidence against the person.

TYPES OF HEARINGS TO WHICH THE FIFTH AMENDMENT APPLIES

Although the privilege protects against the introduction of compelled incriminating statements specifically in a criminal trial, the privilege would offer little protection if incriminating statements could be compelled at other settings where a person is under subpoena to testify and then used against the person in a criminal trial. Courts have found the right to be free from self-incrimination in a variety of proceedings.[551] For example, although a delinquency hearing is not a "criminal prosecution," the Court has held that a juvenile, when facing delinquency adjudication, has the right to remain silent. Similarly, the defendant's statements to a state psychiatrist in a pretrial competency hearing are inadmissible in the defendant's sentencing hearing unless the defendant waives his or her rights.[552] The Court, however, allowed defendant's statements to a psychiatrist admissible in a civil commitment hearing in which the trial judge declared the defendant to be a sexually dangerous person and committed him to a maximum security institution.[553] Reasoning that the label "civil commitment" controlled, the Court found the Fifth Amendment's protections did not apply. Also, the Court held that inmates who must answer potentially incriminating questions to get into a treatment program were not protected by the privilege, because lost privileges and transfer to a maximum-security unit "are

---

[549] *U.S. v. Doe,* 465 U.S. 605 (1984).
[550] See, *Malloy v. Hogan,* supra.
[551] See, Zalman, *supra* at 211-212.
[552] *Estelle v. Smith,* 451 U.S. 454 (1981).
[553] *See, Allen v. Illinois* 478 U.S. 364 (1986).

not [consequences] that compel a prisoner to speak about his past crimes despite a desire to remain silent."[554]

In a 2018 case the petitioner, Vogt, a police officer with the City of Hays, Kansas applied for a new job at the Haysville Police Department. In his interview, he admitted keeping a knife that he obtained while a cop with the City of Hays. The Haysville Police Department conditioned its employment offer to Vogt on his disclosing this action to his current agency and returning the knife. Vogt did make the disclosure and returned the knife. The chief of police of the City of Hays police department ordered Vogt to issue a statement regarding the knife and then began an internal investigation. During the internal investigation, Vogt was required to issue a more detailed statement about the knife, and those statements were turned over to the Kansas Bureau of Investigation. As a result of the statements and the investigation, Vogt was charged criminally with two felonies. (The Haysville Police Department withdrew its offer of employment.) Ultimately the two felony charges against Vogt were dismissed at the probable cause hearing, and Vogt turned around and sued the City of Hays civilly for violating his Fifth Amendment right to be free from self-incrimination. The U.S. Supreme Court ultimately "punted the case" and held that the writ of certiorari about Vogt's civil suit against the City of Hays, Kansas was "improvidently granted," (meaning, they shouldn't have ever decided to review it). So, we don't know how they would have answered the question of whether Vogt's rights to be free from self-incrimination were violated — in any event, the criminal charges against him had been dismissed by the state district court — so perhaps the Court felt that Vogt got off good enough.[555]

TYPES OF EVIDENCE COVERED BY THE PRIVILEGE

The privilege against self-incrimination covers only testimonial evidence (statements by witnesses on the stand); physical evidence is not protected. For example, the suspect may be required to show his or her face to the court, jury or witnesses even over his or her objections.[556] The government can also compel a person to reenact a crime; shave his beard or mustache; try on clothing; dye his or her hair; demonstrate speech or other physical characteristics; furnish handwriting samples, hair samples, or fingerprints; have his or her gums examined; or submit to a blood alcohol, breathalyzer, or urine test. A suspect can be photographed and measured, have tattoos and scars examined, and be required to stand in a lineup. Police can require a person to provide blood samples taken by medical personnel where blood alcohol levels are relevant evidence.[557] The government can compel a defendant to provide writing samples[558] and voice exemplars[559] since these are not considered "testimony."

MIRANDA AND ITS PROGENY[560]

Miranda is the key case in confession and interrogations jurisprudence. Indeed, _Miranda_ is one of the most significant cases in criminal procedure.[561] Under _Miranda_, statements made by a

---

[554] _McKune v. Lile_, 536 U.S. 24 (2002).

[555] https://www.oyez.org/cases/2017/16-1495.

[556] _Holt v. United States_, 218 U.S. 245 (1910).

[557] _Schmerber v. California_, 384 U.S. 757 (1966).

[558] _Gilbert v. California_, 388 U.S. 263 (1967).

[559] _United States v. Wade_, 388 U.S. 218 (1967).

[560] "Progeny" is a word used frequently by courts to refer to cases that follow and further flesh-out a landmark case.

[561] Although most Americans would know their four "Miranda Rights" (e.g., the warnings that the case of Miranda requires police officers to give a suspect before a custodial interrogation), few know many facts about the case itself. Ernesto Miranda was described in the decision as an indigent Mexican defendant who

defendant in response to custodial interrogation by a government official cannot be used to prove the defendant's guilt at trial unless the defendant was advised of the appropriate Fifth and Sixth Amendment rights. The case raises four key questions:

- Were the warnings given?
- Is the defendant in custody?
- Were the defendant's statements made in response to interrogation?
- Did the defendant validly waive the protections of the Fifth and Sixth Amendments after receiving the required warnings?

Miranda was not narrowly confined to its facts. In fact, the *Miranda* decision was actually four companion cases — each with its own set of facts. In each of the cases (*Miranda v. Arizona*, *California v. Steward*, *Vignera v. New York*, and *Westover v. United States*), the defendants were questioned in interrogation rooms cut off from the outside world. All made oral admissions, and three of the four signed the confessions. In each of the cases, the defendants were not advised of the right to have counsel prior to being questioned. The *Miranda* decision broadened the right against self-incrimination holding that it covered virtually all custodial police interrogations. The Court found that police custodial interrogations are inherently compelling and pointed to the history of the "third degree" and the use of high-pressure psychological techniques to obtain confessions from arrested suspects. The Court did not rule that such techniques were a *per se* violation of the privilege against self-incrimination. Instead, the Court held that such confessions would be inadmissible if the police failed to warn suspects of their right to be free from self-incrimination. Although in colloquial terms, we talk about "*Miranda* rights," *Miranda* is rather a set of warnings about suspects' constitutional rights provided in the Fifth and Sixth Amendments.

CUSTODY

Miranda warnings are triggered by a custodial interrogation.[562] One question before the courts in every case then is whether the individual was in custody. When police officers arrest an individual, he or she is obviously in custody, but the Court has also held that the functional equivalent of a custodial arrest also triggers *Miranda*. The test of custody is whether a reasonable person, based on the totality of the circumstances, would believe that he or she was in police custody to a degree associated with a formal arrest. Factors that courts consider in deciding whether a reasonable person would feel free to leave include: 1) the number of police officers present, 2) whether the officer tells the individual that he or she is free to leave or not free to

---

was a seriously disturbed individual with pronounced sexual fantasies. At trial he was found guilty of kidnapping and rape and was sentenced to 20-30 years of incarceration. After the Supreme Court overturned his conviction, he was retried for the kidnapping and rape. The twenty-one-year-old victim testified against him, but on cross-examination, admitted that she was unable to positively identify Miranda as the perpetrator. Miranda's common law wife, however, came forward and testified that Miranda had confided in her that he had committed the kidnapping and rape and that he had asked her to tell the victim that he would marry her if she would drop the charges. Miranda asked his common law wife to show the victim their baby daughter and to ask her to drop the charges so that the baby could be with her father. Miranda was once again convicted and was sentenced to serve twenty to thirty years in prison. In 1972, at the age of thirty, Miranda was paroled. Shortly thereafter he was returned to prison after he was found with a gun and illegal drugs in violation of the terms of his parole. Miranda was released in 1975 and sold autographed "Miranda warning cards" to raise money. In January 1976, while drinking and playing cards, he got involved in a bar fight and was stabbed to death. Liva Baker, *Miranda: Crime, Law and Politics* (1983).

[562] *Miranda* warnings are not required when the police engage in general questioning at a crime scene or other general investigative questioning of a potential witness. *Miranda* warnings are not required in a roadside traffic stop. *See, Berkermer v. McCarty*. 468 U.S. 420 (1984).

leave, 3) the length and intensity of the questioning, 4) whether the officer employs physical force to restrain the individual, 5) whether the stop and location of the interrogation is in public or private, 6) whether a reasonable person would believe that the stop would be brief or whether the stop would result in a custodial arrest, 7) whether the individual is in familiar or unfamiliar surroundings, and 8) whether the suspect is permitted to leave following the interrogation.

In one case, the Court found that the defendant was in custody when four police officers entered his home at 4:00 a.m., surrounded him in his bed with guns drawn, and interrogated him regarding a shooting.[563] In another, the Court also found a defendant in custody (for purposes of *Miranda*) when police came to the prison where he was incarcerated but questioned him about a different crime.[564] On the other hand, the Court has held that a person is not in custody for the purposes of *Miranda* when a police-informant cellmate asked him questions about his crime — the Court reasoning that when a person is unaware they are talking to a police agent, the "third degree" coercive environment that the *Miranda* Court was concerned about just is not present.[565] The Court has also found that a probationer was not in custody when he met with his probation officer to talk about a treatment plan and ultimately confessed to a rape. The Court noted that the probationer was familiar with the office, was not physically restrained and could have left at any time.[566] Similarly, a parolee was not in custody when he voluntarily appeared at a police station at the request of the parole officer and then confessed to the parole officer when the officer said he believed the parolee was a suspect involved in a recent burglary. The Court reasoned that the defendant voluntarily came to the station, was told he was not under arrest, and left after the interview.[567]

In *Yarborough v. Alvarado*, 541 U.S. 652 (2004), the Court found Yarborough was not in custody when his parents brought to the station to be interviewed. Justice Kennedy opined,

> Fair-minded jurists could disagree over whether Alvarado was in custody. On one hand, certain facts weigh against a finding that Alvarado was in custody. The police did not transport Alvarado to the station or require him to appear at a particular time. They did not threaten him or suggest he would be placed under arrest. Alvarado's parents remained in the lobby during the interview, suggesting that the interview would be brief. In fact, according to trial counsel for Alvarado, he and his parents were told that the interview was "not going to be long." During the interview, Comstock focused on Soto's crimes rather than Alvarado's. Instead of pressuring Alvarado with the threat of arrest and prosecution, she appealed to his interest in telling the truth and being helpful to a police officer. In addition, Comstock twice asked Alvarado if he wanted to take a break. At the end of the interview, Alvarado went home. All of these objective facts are consistent with an interrogation environment in which a reasonable person would have felt free to terminate the interview and leave. (Footnotes omitted.)

> Other facts point in the opposite direction. Comstock interviewed Alvarado at a police station. The interview lasted two hours. … Comstock did not tell Alvarado that he was free to leave. Alvarado's legal guardians brought him to the police station rather than arriving on his own accord, making the extent of his control over his presence unclear. Counsel for Alvarado alleges that Alvarado's parents

---

[563] *Orozco v. Texas*, 394 U.S. 324 (1969)
[564] *Matthis v. United States*, 391 U.S. 1 (1968).
[565] *Illinois v. Perkins*, 496 U.S. 292 (1990)
[566] *Minnesota v. Murphy*, 465 U.S. 420 (1984).
[567] *Oregon v. Mathiason*, 429 U.S. 492 (1977).

asked to be present at the interview but were rebuffed, a fact that – if known to Alvarado – might reasonably have led someone in Alvarado's position to feel more restricted than otherwise. These facts weigh in favor of the view that Alvarado was in custody. (Footnotes omitted.)[568]

The majority of the Court felt that Alvarado was not in custody under the circumstances and that his confession was admissible even though the police failed to provide *Miranda* warnings. Justice Breyer dissented,

> … Would a reasonable person in Alvarado's position have felt free simply to get up and walk out of the small room in the station house at will during his two-hour police interrogation? I ask the reader to put himself, or herself, in Alvarado's circumstances and then answer that question. Alvarado hears from his parents that he is needed for police questioning. His parents take him to the station. On arrival, a police officer separates him from his parents. His parents ask to come along, but the officer says they may not. … (Footnotes omitted.)

> … The police take Alvarado to a small interrogation room, away from the station's public area. A single office begins to question him, making clear the process the police have evidence that he participated in an attempted carjacking connected with a murder. When he says that he never saw any shooting, the officer suggests that he is lying, while adding that she is "giving him the opportunity to tell the truth" and "take care of himself." … Toward the end of the questioning, the officer gives him permission to take a bathroom or water break. After two hours, by which time he has admitted he was involved in the attempted theft, knew about the gun, and helped to hide it, the questioning ends. … A reasonable person would not have thought he was free simply to pick up and leave in the middle of the interrogation.[569]

INTERROGATION

The second issue the court will need to address in determining whether *Miranda* warnings are required is whether the police "interrogated" the suspect. In *Rhode Island v. Innis,* 446 U.S. 291 (1980), the Court defined interrogation as "express questioning or its functional equivalent." Express questioning occurs when police direct questions at the suspect. The functional equivalent of express questioning comprises "words or actions on the part of the police that the police should know are reasonably likely to elicit an incriminating response.

WARNINGS

Miranda warnings must be given in a clear and unambiguous manner so that the individual understands his rights and feels free to exercise them. The police do not have to quote the exact words used in *Miranda*, but the warning must make clear that the person has the right to have an attorney present during the questioning, that the defendant has the right to remain silent and that if he does choose to speak anything he says can be used against him.[570] The Court has not required police to tell the defendant that their silence will not be used against him.

---

[568] *Yarborough v. Alvarado,* 541 U.S. at 653.

[569] *Id.* at 672. For an excellent analysis of the case and its implications for juvenile rights, *see,* Raynee Lumer, *Yarborough v. Alvarado: Why is the Supreme Court Pretending That a Child is an Adult or That a Blind Man Can See?* 38 Loy.L.A.,L. Rev 2297 (2005).

[570] *See, Commonwealth v. Singleton,* 266 A.2d 753 (Pa 1970) (The Court found inadequate warnings when police told the defendant only that anything he said could be used for or against him.)

In *Duckworth v. Eagan*, 492 U.S. 195 (1989), the police warned the defendant, "You have a right to talk to a lawyer for advice before we ask you any questions, and to have him with you during the questioning. You have the right to the advice and presence of a lawyer even if you cannot afford to hire one. We have no way of giving you a lawyer, but one will be appointed for you, if you wish, if and when you go to court." The defendant had argued that the statement was ambiguous whether he was entitled to a court-appointed lawyer before interrogation. Five members of the Court found this warning to be adequate albeit somewhat ambiguous. Four justices found that the warnings were clearly inadequate under *Miranda*. They believed that the "if and when you go to court" language led defendant to believe that he wouldn't be provided a lawyer until in the future after questioning.

The warnings must be given even if police believe that the suspect is already aware of his right to remain silent and to have a lawyer. If the police are absolutely sure that the defendant already has his own lawyer or has the money for one, then they do not have to tell him that one will be appointed for him. But this exception does not apply when there is any doubt or uncertainty at all concerning the suspect's financial ability.

If the suspect's lawyer is present during the interrogation, then police do not have to give the *Miranda* warnings. The Court stated, "The presence of counsel … would be adequate protective device necessary to make the process of police interrogation conform to the dictates of the privilege. His presence would ensure that statements made in the government-established atmosphere are not the product of compulsion."[571]

Miranda does not require that the police tell the suspect what he is charged with nor the seriousness of the crime. In *Colorado v. Spring*, 479 U.S. 564 (1987), for example, federal agents interrogated Spring about firearms violations, knowing that he was suspected of a murder. They asked him if he had ever shot anyone, and Spring made an incriminating statement that was later used in the state murder prosecution. The Court held that the statements were admissible and the failure of the police to inform the suspect on a minor offense that he would be questioned on much more serious murder charges did not negate his decision to waive his *Miranda* rights. That said, Emanuel suggests that the police may not intentionally trick the suspect into thinking his crime is less serious than it is in order to induce him to confess.[572] *Miranda* states, "any evidence that the accused was threatened, tricked, or cajoled into a wavier [of his right to silence or to a lawyer] will, of course, show that the defendant did not voluntarily waive his privilege."[573]

INVOKING (AND WAIVING) *MIRANDA*

When a defendant makes statements after police failed to heed the defendant's invocation of Miranda, the admissibility of those statements depends on 1) whether the defendant requested to remain silent, 2) whether the defendant requested an attorney ("lawyered up"), and 3) when defendant invoked the right. The Court has consistently held that the defendant must himself express some desire to invoke *Miranda*.[574]

INVOKING SILENCE

In *Michigan v. Mosley*, 523 U.S. 95 (1975), Mosley was interrogated about two robberies after receiving his *Miranda* warnings. Mosley declined to answer police questions and invoked only his right to remain silent; he did not assert during this time that he wanted counsel. The

---

[571] *Miranda*, 384 U.S. at 472
[572] *See*, Emanuel, *supra* at 213.
[573] *Miranda*, 384 U.S. at 476.
[574] *See*, *Moran v. Burbine*, 475 U.S. 412 (1986) and *Montejo v. Louisiana*, 556 U.S. 778 (2009).

police immediately ceased questioning Mosley. Several hours later, however, Mosley was taken to a different floor of a building where he was being held, and after again being given his *Miranda* warnings, he was questioned by a different police officer about a fatal shooting which had occurred in a third robbery. Mosley implicated himself. Mosley later moved to strike his statements on the ground that they were obtained in violation of his right not to be questioned after he invoked *Miranda*.

In a 7-2 decision, the Court held that Mosley's right not to be questioned had not been violated when police resumed questioning him. The Court emphasized that the second questioning was about a different crime, a significant time had passed between the two interrogations, the interrogations took place in different locations, and the defendant was given his *Miranda* warnings before each of the sessions.

The Supreme Court identified five *Mosley* factors that allow the use of an incriminating statement made in a second interrogation after a suspect has invoked the right of silence in a previous interrogation:

- Whether initial *Miranda* warnings were given.
- Whether police immediately ceased interrogating when the suspect invoked silence.
- Whether a significant time period had elapsed between the two interrogations.
- Whether a fresh *Miranda* warning was given before the second interrogation.
- Whether the second interrogation was for a different crime than that investigated in the first interrogation or was triggered by new circumstances (for example, the confession of a confederate).

INVOKING COUNSEL

The Court treats a defendant's invocation of his right to counsel differently than his invocation of his right to remain silent. *Edwards v. Arizona*, 451 U.S 477 (1981), the key case on invoking counsel, created a bright line rule: once a defendant invokes his right to an attorney, the police may not reapproach the suspect to question him or her-- regardless of how much time has passed.

Once a suspect requests counsel, that request must be heeded by all law enforcement officers not just the police officer who *Mirandized* the suspect.[575] If it were otherwise, officers could easily sidestep the Edwards rule by claiming ignorance of an initial invocation of the right to see an attorney. This bright line rule of Edwards applies even though the police want to question the suspect about a different crime than the one they were questioning him about when he first requested the lawyer.

Five years after *Edwards*, the Court decided the companion case in *Michigan v. Jackson, 475 U.S. 625 (1986)*. Both defendants, Bladel and Jackson, had spoken to police before their arraignments. At arraignment[576], both affirmatively requested counsel. The Court had earlier ruled that a suspect invokes counsel for interrogation purposes when he requests a lawyer at a formal arraignment. Police officers were present at arraignment and observed defendants request the appointment of counsel. The Court noted that in *Edwards* the defendants had requested counsel during interrogation, and in Jackson they requested counsel during arraignments. The

---

[575] *Arizona v. Roberson*, 486 U.S. 675 (1988.,

[576] Arraignments, a court procedure right after charges are filed against the defendant, are discussed in greater detail in Chapter Nine. At arraignments, the court informs the defendant of the charges that have been filed and determines release conditions (if any).

court held that defendants should have at least as much protection under the Sixth Amendment's right to counsel during a post-arraignment interrogation as they do under the Fifth Amendment's right to counsel during a custodial interrogation. Following *Jackson,* the Court decided *Minnick v. Mississippi, 498 U.S. 146 (1990),* in which Minnick invoked counsel during an interrogation and was allowed to consult with a lawyer. Police then interrogated Minnick without his counsel present. The Court found that this violated Minnick's rights and that the right to counsel meant the right to have counsel present during the subsequent questioning. After *Jackson* and *Minnick,* any desire on defendants' part to speak to police after invoking counsel must be initiated by the defendant.

In *Montejo v. Louisiana,* 556 U.S. 782 (2009) the Court modified its holding in *Edwards* and *Jackson.* The Louisiana courts automatically appoint counsel to indigent defendants. Defendant Montejo, unlike Bladel and Jackson, did nothing to affirmatively request an attorney during his mandatory preliminary hearing, but the court, per state policy, appointed counsel on his behalf. Later that day two detectives visited Montejo in custody before he met with his attorney. The detectives asked him to come with them to try to locate the murder weapon after he admitted throwing it in a lake. During this trip, police again read Montejo the Miranda warnings; nevertheless, he wrote a letter of apology to the victim's widow. Police returned the defendant to the prison, and he finally met with his court-appointed attorney (who was quite upset that the detectives had interrogated his client in his absence.). The Court held that *Edwards'* only purpose was to protect the defendant from repeated badgering by police, and since that scenario was not present here, police permissibly contacted the defendant. The court stated,

> The question in *Jackson,* however, was not whether respondents were entitled to counsel (they unquestionably were), but "whether respondents validly waived their right to counsel," and even if it is reasonable to presume from a defendant's request for counsel that any subsequent waiver of the right was coerced, no such presumption can seriously be entertained when a lawyer was merely "secured" on the defendant's behalf, by the State itself, as a matter of course. ...

> ... When a court appoints counsel for an indigent defendant in the absence of any request on his part, there is no basis for a presumption that any subsequent waiver of the right to counsel will be involuntary. There is no "initial election" to exercise the right that must be preserved through a prophylactic rule[577] against later waivers. No reason exists to assume that a defendant like Montejo, who has done nothing at all to express his intentions with respect to his Sixth Amendment rights, would not be perfectly amenable to speaking with the police without having counsel present. And no reason exists to prohibit the police from inquiring. *Edwards* and *Jackson* are meant to prevent police from badgering defendants into changing their minds about their rights, but a defendant who never asked for counsel has not yet made up his mind in the first instance.

> ... Under *Miranda's* prophylactic protection of the right against compelled self-incrimination, any suspect subject to custodial interrogation has the right to have a lawyer present if he so requests, and to be advised of that right. Under *Edwards'* prophylactic protection of the *Miranda* right, once such a defendant "has invoked his right to have counsel present," interrogation must stop. And under *Minnick's*

---

[577] A prophylactic rule is a judicially-crafted rule that overprotects a constitutional right, and gives more protection than such right might abstractly seem to require on its face, in order to safeguard that constitutional right or improve detection of violations of that right. (http://encyclopedia.thefreedictionary.com/Prophylactic+rule).

prophylactic protection of the *Edwards* right, no subsequent interrogation may take place until counsel is present, "whether or not the accused has consulted with his attorney."

These three layers of prophylaxis are sufficient. Under the *Miranda-Edwards-Minnick* line of cases (which is not in doubt), a defendant who does not want to speak to the police without counsel present need only say as much when he is first approached and given the *Miranda* warnings. At that point, not only must the immediate contact end, but "badgering" by later requests is prohibited. If that regime suffices to protect the integrity of "a suspect's voluntary choice not to speak outside his lawyer's presence" before his arraignment, it is hard to see why it would not also suffice to protect that same choice after arraignment, when Sixth Amendment rights have attached. And if so, then *Jackson* is simply superfluous.[578]

In *Maryland v. Shatzer*, 559 U.S. 98 (2010), the Court created a "break in custody" exception to *Miranda* and indicated that *Edwards* (that police could not reapproach once the suspect had requested counsel) was not a constitutional mandate, but rather a "judicially prescribed prophylaxis." According to this newly created "break in custody" rule, the police may reapproach a suspect who has invoked his or her right to counsel after a 14-day period has expired.

Representation by Counsel on Different Offenses

The interplay between the Fifth Amendment's right to have counsel during interrogation found in *Miranda* and the Sixth Amendment's right to assistance of counsel can be confusing. Sometimes a defendants Fifth Amendment rights are violated when his or her Sixth Amendment rights are not. Gilberts Law Summaries notes,

> There can be no violation of the Sixth Amendment right to counsel before formal proceedings have begun. Thus a defendant who is arrested but not yet charged does not have a Sixth Amendment right to counsel ... [b]ut ... he may have a Fifth Amendment right to counsel under *Miranda*. [579]

It is also possible that a statement made to an officer outside the presence of counsel would be admissible under the Fifth Amendment but nevertheless not be admissible as a violation of the Sixth Amendment right to counsel. For example, the Sixth Amendment can be violated, and even voluntary statements will be excluded from trial, if police violated the defendant's right to counsel by questioning the accused outside the presence of counsel or without a valid waiver of the right to counsel. This is true even if the defendant was not explicitly questioned, as long as police somehow obtained the incriminating information from the defendant when he or she was outside the presence of counsel. Courts consider whether the government knowingly circumvented the accused's right to have counsel present in a confrontation between the accused and a government agent. Recall the *Massiah* case in which Massiah who was represented by an attorney at the time was riding around in his co-defendant's car making incriminating statements that police were listening to via a listening device attached to the undercarriage of the car. Because Messiah was not in custody, there was no violation of his Fifth Amendment right to counsel, but since he had already requested counsel and police had deliberately elicited his statements when his attorney wasn't present (by surreptitiously attaching a listening device to a car), the Court concluded police had violated his Sixth Amendment rights.

---

[578] *Id. at* 787-790 (2009).
[579] Gilberts, *Criminal Procedure*, supra at 97.

The Sixth Amendment right to counsel is specific to critical stages in the criminal justice process and is "case specific." This means, that if the state is prosecuting a defendant for a burglary that occurred on New Year's Day, the defendant has a right to counsel to represent him on that burglary. If defendant also commits a battery against his wife two weeks later, that is a separate case. Defendant would have the right to counsel (the same or a different counsel) to represent him for the battery if, and when, he was prosecuted for it. Thus, it is important to know if the defendant has invoked his or her right to counsel during a custodial interrogation, or at some other court process. And it is important to know for which charges he or she has invoked counsel.

Since the Sixth Amendment right to counsel is offense specific, only statements relating to the charge for which the defendant has counsel will be inadmissible. Statements about other crimes for which the right has not attached (charges yet to be filed) are fully admissible. If a defendant requests counsel for the burglary charge, he must also make a request for counsel on the separate unrelated crime of domestic battery. The test for determining whether there are two different offenses under the Sixth Amendment is called the *Blockburger* test. Under that test, two crimes are considered different offenses when each requires proof of an additional element that the other crime does not require. (If the crimes happened at two distinct times, this is also a good indicator.)

Del Carmen highlights the differences between the *Miranda* warnings and the right to counsel as follows[580]:

Miranda Warnings	Right to Counsel
Comes under the 5th Amendment's right to counsel	Comes under the 6th Amendment
Applies only during custodial interrogation	Applies in any proceedings-before trial, during trial, and during an appeal
Given by the police	Lawyer is either retained by the suspect or assigned by the judge
Given in the absence of a lawyer	Once defendant has a lawyer, defendant cannot be questioned in the absence a lawyer unless the right is waived
Must be given every time there is a custodial interrogation	Once given, it is violated only if the interrogation deals with the same offense but not about other offenses

WAIVER OF MIRANDA

The *Miranda* opinion recognized that defendants may expressly waive their "*Miranda* rights." Individuals waive by making an express statement that he or she wishes to make a statement and does not want an attorney followed closely by a statement. The courts generally accept express waivers without much scrutiny. Implied waivers are more carefully scrutinized by the courts and are evaluated strictly on a case-by-case basis (there are no *per se* rules). The prosecution has a "heavy burden" to demonstrate that any waiver was intelligent (the suspect knows what he is giving up) and voluntary (uncoerced). Also, for a waiver to exist, the prosecution must show that defendant understood his *Miranda* rights and intended to relinquish them. Silence does not constitute a waiver of *Miranda,* but a nod or shrug followed by a statement

---

[580] Del Carmen, *supra* at 350.

does constitute a waiver. In *North Carolina v. Butler*, 441 U.S. 369 (1979), the Court ruled that a suspect's refusal to sign a written waiver form did not automatically negate his waiver. In that case the suspect stated, "I will talk to you, but I am not signing the form." He did not say anything at all when advised of his right to a lawyer's assistance. The Court held that "an express waiver of *Miranda* rights is not necessary," and that in some circumstances waivers can be "inferred from the actions and words of the person interrogated." The *Butler* case was remanded back to the state to determine whether a waiver could be inferred. The dissenters argued that *Miranda* should be interpreted to require an express waiver--otherwise ambiguous situations (like those in *Butler*) could arise in which it was not clear whether the suspect knowingly waived *Miranda*.

In *Connecticut v. Barrett*, 479 U.S. 523 (1987), a suspect expressed willingness to talk to police without a lawyer, but he wanted to consult with a lawyer to see whether he should make a written statement. The Supreme Court held that this was only a partial waiver of rights. It did not serve as an invocation of his right to attorney for all purposes. The court upheld the introduction of incriminating statements because Barrett's statement of his willingness to answer oral questions without a lawyer was unambiguous.

In *Davis v. United States*, 512 U.S. 452 (1994), the Court held that when a suspect who previously waived his rights subsequently invokes the right to counsel in an ambiguous way, the invocation does not count, and the police may proceed with an interrogation without supplying an attorney. The Court requires that an invocation be unequivocal in order for it to defeat a prior waiver. In *Berghuis v. Thompkins*, 560 U.S. 370 (2010), police arrested Thompkins in Ohio for murder, attempted murder, assault with intent to commit murder, and several firearms related charges. After taking him into custody, the officers read him *Miranda* warnings and asked whether he understood them. Thompkins indicated that he did, but he neither invoked his rights nor explicitly waived them. He refused to sign an acknowledgement that he had been informed of his rights. Detectives interrogated Thompkins for three hours about the suspected murder, and he rarely made eye contact with them but did respond with short verbal and nonverbal answers and without much elaboration. Eventually, police asked him whether he prayed to God for forgiveness for "shooting that boy down", and he responded, "Yes." The government later offered these statements into evidence at his trial.

The Sixth Circuit Court of Appeals found that Thompkins' statement to police should have been suppressed, because he had not waived his *Miranda* rights. The Supreme Court, however, reversed in a 5-4 decision and held that Thompkins had failed to invoke his Miranda rights because he failed to do so "unambiguously." The majority held that defendant had waived his right to remain silent when he knowingly and voluntarily made the statement to the police.

LIMITATIONS (EXCEPTION) TO MIRANDA

Many conservative justices were against the holding in *Miranda*, and, though they did not have enough votes to overrule the decision, they nevertheless weakened it through several case decisions in the 1970s. Beginning with *Michigan v. Tucker*, 417 U.S. 433 (1974), these justices implied *Miranda* did not have constitutional dimensions and that it was merely a prophylactic rule. Their sentiment that a violation of *Miranda* was not necessarily a violation of the Constitution, led the Court to identify "exceptions to the Miranda rule."

LIMITATIONS ON MIRANDA: STATEMENTS AT GRAND JURY

In *U.S. v. Dionisio*, 410 U.S. 1 (1973), the court held that a suspect has the right to be free from self-incrimination in a grand jury proceeding, but the grand jury witness does not have to be warned of his right to remain silent or to have an attorney present. Additionally, the un-*Mirandized* statements by a suspect are admissible during a grand jury hearing.

LIMITATIONS ON MIRANDA: IMPEACHMENT

Un-*Mirandized* statements may be admissible as impeachment evidence. In *Harris v. New York*, 401 U.S. 222, 226 (1971), the Court held that "*Miranda* cannot be "perverted into a shield that permits defendants to use perjury without the risk of confrontation with prior inconsistent utterances." More recently, the Supreme Court held that defendant's confessions obtained by a jailhouse informant in violation of the Sixth Amendment could also be used to impeach a defendant's testimony at trial.[581]

LIMITATIONS ON MIRANDA: THE PUBLIC SAFETY EXCEPTION

In 1984 the Court recognized a public safety exception to *Miranda* in the case of *New York v. Quarles*, 467 U.S. 649 (1984). This exception permits police to ask questions reasonably prompted by a concern with public safety without first advising a suspect of his or her Miranda rights. The exception makes sense in light of the facts of the case: police received information from a victim that a man had just raped her at gunpoint and had run into a grocery store with the gun. The patrol officers went to the store, surrounded Quarles and one asked, "where's the gun." Quarles told them, and he was arrested, transported, etc. The Court held that since the police officer's request for the location of the gun was prompted by an immediate interest in assuring that it did not injure an innocent bystander or fall into the hands of a potential accomplice to Quarles, his failure to read the *Miranda* warning did not violate the Constitution. Thus, the statement and gun did not need to be suppressed.

The *Quarles* Court emphasized that if police rely on the public safety exception, they must have a reasonable need to protect the police or the public, there must be a reasonable belief that the threat is imminent, that questions asked must be prompted by a reasonable concern for public safety and must be directed at public safety rather than guilt or innocence, and finally, that statements may not be the product of police compulsion that overcomes the suspect's will to resist.

The Court has held the public safety exception applied in a situation in which an officer arresting a narcotics dealer asked, "Do you have anything in your pocket that can harm me?" The defendant said he had a gun; the officer retrieved the gun and repeated the question, and the defendant said he had drugs in his car. The federal appeals court ruled that the officer's question was directed at public safety and that the drugs were properly admitted into evidence at trial, but the court warned of the "inherent risk that the public safety exception might be distorted into a general rule and the individuals arrested on narcotics charges could be questioned in every instance prior to reading Miranda rights.[582]

LIMITATIONS ON MIRANDA: THE ROUTINE BOOKING QUESTIONS EXCEPTION

In *Pennsylvania v. Munoz*, 496 U.S. 582 (1990), the Court held that routine questions asked by jail staff during the booking of a suspect do not require Miranda warnings, and that questions regarding defendant's name, address, height, weight, etc. did not require Miranda even though a

---

[581] *Kansas v. Ventris*, 556 U.S. 586 (2009). Recall that involuntary confessions are not admissible—even as impeachment.
[582] *United States v. Reyes*, 353 F. 3d 148, 155 (2d Cir. 2003).

video tape of the questions and defendant's answers was introduced at trial to show that defendant was drunk.

LIMITATIONS ON MIRANDA: QUESTION FIRST AND WARN LATER

In *Oregon v. Elstad* 470 U.S. 298 (1985), *Fellers v. United States,* 540 U.S. 519 (2004), and *Missouri v. Siebert,* 542 U.S. 600 (2004), the court dealt with the scenario where the defendant initially made voluntary, un-*Mirandized* statements, was later properly *Mirandized*, and then subsequently repeated essentially the same initial un-*Mirandized* statements. The Court in each case found the initial statements to be inadmissible, but noted that the real question was whether the proper reading of Miranda "cured" the problem and/or removed the taint from the subsequent statements.

In *Elstad*, the police visited the home of Elstad and briefly and casually interrogated him about a burglary. Elstad was not Mirandized, but did make voluntary incriminating statements. He was then arrested and taken to police headquarters. At the station, officers read Elstad his *Miranda* warnings and obtained a detailed confession. The Supreme Court found that the statements Elstad made at his home were inadmissible. But, the Court found that the unlawfully obtained voluntary confession did not automatically taint his second confession and ruled that "a suspect who has once responded to unwarned yet uncoercive questioning is not thereby disabled from waiving his rights and confessing after he has been given the requisite Miranda warnings." The Court held that the reading of Miranda cured the taint of the initial confession.

Police began exploiting the holding in *Elstad* and adopted the tactic of "question first, warn later" in order to obtain suspects' confessions. In *Siebert*, the Court stated, "the issue when the police question first and warn later is whether "it would be reasonable to find that in these circumstances the warnings could function "effectively" to advise the suspect that he or she "had a real choice about giving an admissible statement." The Court pointed out that in *Elstad*, the officer was confused as to whether the suspect was in custodial interrogation and committed the oversight of casually remarking that he believed that Elstad was involved in the burglary. Elstad then confirmed that he was at the crime scene. The living room conversation in Elstad was then corrected at the situation. The Court noted that a reasonable person would view the station-house interrogation as markedly different from the short conversation at home. Conversely, in *Siebert*, the plurality found that a reasonable person in the suspect's shoes would not have understood *Miranda* warnings after the initial confession to convey a message that she retained a choice about continuing to talk. *Siebert* involved a police strategy intended to undermine *Miranda*. Both interrogations took place at the station house; the same officer conducted both questionings. The first interrogation was systematic, exhaustive, and conducted with skill, and the officer did nothing to inform Siebert that the first confession could not be used against her. The officer gave the impression that the second interrogation was a continuation of the earlier questioning. The *Siebert* Court found that use of her statements at her trial violated her constitutional rights.

DICKERSON: MAKING MIRANDA "CONSTITUTIONAL"

In response to the *Miranda* holding, Congress immediately enacted legislation intended to overrule the Court's holding. The Act, 18 U.S.C., §3501[583], in essence, reverted back to the due

---

[583] 18 U.S.C. § 3501 Admissibility of Confessions:

> (a) In any criminal prosecution brought by the United States or by the District of Columbia, a confession, as defined in subsection (e) hereof, shall be admissible in evidence if it is voluntarily given. Before such confession is received in evidence, the trial judge shall, out of the presence of the jury, determine any issue as to voluntariness. If the trial judge determines that the confession

process--voluntariness analysis in determining whether the defendant's confessions in federal cases were to be admitted—without regard to whether *Miranda* warnings were given. Criminal justice practitioners did not rely on 18 U.S.C. §3501, suspecting the Act would not pass Court scrutiny in light of *Miranda;* they feared the trial courts would suppress the suspect's confession if the Act were found to be unconstitutional. When *Dickerson v. United States*, 530 U.S. 428 (2000), finally reached the U.S. Supreme Court, neither party addressed whether the Act was constitutional, and the Court had to assign an attorney to prepare written arguments why the Act was constitutional (to "brief the issue").

In *Dickerson* the Court faced squarely the question of whether *Miranda* should be overturned. Many scholars were very surprised when the Court, instead of laying *Miranda* to rest, held that *Miranda* had taken on constitutional dimensions. This is an important distinction. If a right is considered constitutional, then only a constitutional amendment can change it. If a right is considered a statutory right, then Congress or state legislatures may change it through legislation. The Court thus breathed new life into *Miranda* and disavowed Justice Rehnquist's interpretation of *Miranda* as merely a prophylactic rule. Since *Dickerson*, the Court has had to decide whether the exceptions created in the 1970s and 1980s still have any authority. The *Siebert* case, decided after *Dickerson*, may signify its willingness to put some teeth back into the Miranda guarantee.

In March 2014, Terence Tekoh, a nursing aid was accused of sexually assaulting a patient at the hospital where he worked. Los Angeles County Sheriff's Deputy Carlos Vega interrogated Tekoh at the medical center. Vega did not read Tekoh the Miranda warnings. According to Tekoh, Vega coerced him into making a confession in the small windowless room, blocked him from leaving, ignored his pleas to see an attorney, and threatened to deport Tekoh and his family. Eventually Tekoh confessed and provided a written statement apologizing for inappropriately touching the patient's genitals. That statement was offered against Tekoh when he was tried for unlawful sexual penetration. Tekoh was found not guilty by a jury. He then sued Vega under 42 U. S. C. §1983, seeking damages for alleged violations of his constitutional rights. The Ninth Circuit held that the use of an un-Mirandized statement against a defendant in a criminal proceeding violates the Fifth Amendment and may support a §1983 claim against the officer who obtained the statement. But the U.S. Supreme Court held that a violation of the Miranda rules does not provide a basis for a §1983 claim.[584]

---

was voluntarily made it shall be admitted in evidence and the trial judge shall permit the jury to hear relevant evidence on the issue of voluntariness and shall instruct the jury to give such weight to the confession as the jury feels it deserves under all the circumstances.

(b) The trial judge in determining the issue of voluntariness shall take into consideration all the circumstances surrounding the giving of the confession, including

(1) the time elapsing between arrest and arraignment of the defendant making the confession, if it was made after arrest and before arraignment,

(2) whether such defendant knew the nature of the offense with which he was charged or of which he was suspected at the time of making the confession,

(3) whether or not such defendant was advised or knew that he was not required to make any statement and that any such statement could be used against him,

(4) whether or not such defendant had been advised prior to questioning of his right to the assistance of counsel; and

(5) whether or not such defendant was without the assistance of counsel when questioned and when giving such confession.

The presence or absence of any of the above-mentioned factors to be taken into consideration by the judge need not be conclusive on the issue of voluntariness of the confession.

. . .

[584] See, *Vega v. Tekoh*, 597 U.S. ____ (2022)

In a decision that undermines almost 60 years of precedent, the U.S. Supreme Court last month declared that police officers who don't issue *Miranda* warnings before interrogations can't be sued for violating the Constitution. Named after the 1966 Supreme Court case decision, *Miranda v. Arizona*, law enforcement is generally required to issue *Miranda* warnings to inform criminal suspects that they have a right to remain silent and the right to an attorney. Without those now famous *Miranda* warnings, any evidence gained during an interrogation cannot be used against the defendant in a criminal case.

But the court's new decision in *Vega v. Tekoh* "strips individuals of the ability to seek a remedy for violations of the right recognized in *Miranda*," Justice Elena Kagan warned in a dissent. As a result, the Supreme Court has effectively created a new legal immunity for cops accused of infringing on the Fifth Amendment's protection against self-incrimination.

The High Court has previously ruled that *Miranda* was a "constitutional decision" and called *Miranda* warnings themselves a "constitutional rule." Nevertheless, by a vote of 6-3, the Supreme Court ruled in *Vega v. Tekoh* that "a violation of *Miranda* is not itself a violation of the Fifth Amendment." Writing for the majority, Justice Samuel Alito instead claimed that the *Miranda* decision merely "imposed a set of prophylactic rules" on law enforcement.

Although Alito hinted in a footnote that the Supreme Court may lack "the authority to create constitutionally based prophylactic rules," *Vega v. Tekoh* still allows defendants in criminal cases to suppress statements obtained from interrogations that weren't properly *Mirandized* (at least for now). But anyone who has been wrongfully convicted or imprisoned because they weren't properly informed of their constitutional rights can no longer sue the officers responsible in civil court.

As Justice Kagan noted in her dissent, "sometimes, such a statement will not be suppressed. And sometimes, as a result, a defendant will be wrongly convicted and spend years in prison…what remedy does he have for all the harm he has suffered?"

Kagan's concern is hardly hypothetical. An amicus brief by several scholars on wrongful convictions estimated that "false confessions have contributed to hundreds of wrongful convictions," while the proportion of "miscarriages of justice involving false confessions range from 14% to 60%."

To right this wrong, suing rogue officers for damages can both compensate victims and provide a powerful deterrent against future abuses, which is why Congress enacted Section 1983 in the first place. And a new database by the Institute for Justice identified multiple cases where federal courts from around the country have allowed civil lawsuits against officers who failed to issue *Miranda* warnings. But *Vega*, Kagan noted, "injures the right by denying the remedy."[585]

---

[585] https://www.forbes.com/sites/nicksibilla/2022/07/05/supreme-court-creates-new-immunity-for-cops-who-violate-the-fifth-amendment/?sh=6234889c468e

IDENFICATION PROCEDURES

FORMS OF IDENTIFICATION PROCEDURES

Police use identification procedures to both solve and prosecute crime. In most identification scenarios, police first ask witnesses to identify the suspect in an out-of-court procedure in order to identify the perpetrator; later, at trial, the prosecutor will ask the witness to identify the defendant as that perpetrator. When a witness identifies ("i.d.'s") the suspect, the witness is saying, "she did it, she's the one." When offered in court these pretrial statements and identifications are "hearsay" (a type of evidence frowned on, which will be discussed in Chapter Ten) and will be admitted into evidence only in limited circumstances. Police may also testify (both in pre-trial motions and at trial) about how the identification procedure was conducted. Evidentiary issues arise when a witness identifies a suspect before trial but is then unable to make an in-court identification. The converse problem also happens, and a witness may make a very tentative pretrial identification but then become very certain about the pretrial identification and the in-court identifications of the defendant.

Police use four different types of identification procedures in investigating crimes committed by unknown suspects: lineups, show-ups, photographic identification, and scientific identification. In a lineup, the victim or eyewitnesses view a group of individuals, typically six in number. They are then asked to identify the perpetrator for this group. Fillers, foils or distractors are people believed innocent of the particular offense who are recruited by the police to participate in the lineup. In a show-up, the police stage a confrontation between the victim or the eyewitness and a single subject. Photographic identification could either be a photo array, which is similar to the lineup but photos rather than live people are used, or a photo show-up in which only one picture is displayed to the witness. Scientific identification involves the use of fingerprints, DNA, hair analysis, handwriting analysis[586], and voice analysis. [587]

ERRORS IN EYEWITNESS IDENTIFICATION

Zallman noted,

Eyewitness identification is the most important source of truth in most criminal cases and, ironically, the leading source of error that results in the conviction of innocent persons. The necessity of eyewitness identification at every stage of the criminal process, from police investigation to trial, is self-evident. The risk of misidentification is as old as the trial, and ancient and medieval examples are known. Indeed, the common law trial and cross-examination are designed in part to sort out this kind of error.

Psychological experiments conducted for a century have demonstrated that human identification is fraught with error. … [M]ost miscarriages of justice were caused by sincere, yet woefully mistaken, eyewitness identification. Every year, newspaper accounts of such miscarriages of justice occur with regularity.[588]

---

[586] In *Gilbert v. California*, 388 U.S. 263 (1967), the Court held that a suspect could be compelled to provide a handwriting exemplar, explaining that it was not testimony but rather an identifying physical characteristic.

[587] In *United States v. Dionisio*, 410 U.S. 1 (1973), the Court held that a suspect could be compelled to provide a voice exemplar on the ground that the recording is being used only to measure the physical properties of the suspect's voice, as distinct from the content of what the suspect had said.

[588] Zalman, *supra* at 253-254.

Eyewitness identification relies on three aspects of human memory: intake of information at the time of the crime, retaining information from the time of the crime until the identification procedure (lineup, show-up, photo throw-down), and retrieving information from memory at time of lineup, show-up, or photo throw-down. Memory errors may occur during each of the phases. According to Wells and Olson (2003), the degree of accuracy of witness' first observation of strangers during a crime depends on the interaction of five circumstances: length of time to observe the stranger, distractions during the observation, focus of the observation, stress on the witness during the observation, race of the witness and the stranger. It is not difficult to understand why eyewitness identification is so unreliable when one recognizes that crimes are committed in brief time spans, they can be quick and chaotic, the victim is under considerable stress, and many crimes are cross-racial[589]

Faulty observation and acquisition of information is compounded by fading memories.

Memory fades most during the first few hours after an event (the very time when it's most important to keep it sharp); after that, it remains stable for several months. Curiously, at the same time witnesses' memory is fading their confidence in their memory is rising. Unfortunately, courts and juries place enormous weight on witnesses' confidence, even in the face of clear proof that confidence is not related to accuracy.[590]

Errors in eyewitness identification also occur when witnesses retrieve information from the crime at the time of the identification. Memory retrieval involves recalling and recognizing what the witness observed. Witnesses may fail to recall some details about the crime, or fail to recognize a suspect (retrieval errors of omission) or pick out the wrong person in the lineup, showup, or photo throw-down (retrieval errors of commission).[591] "Suggestion is a powerful contributor to mistaken identification during the retrieval phase of memory. ... Most mistaken identifications happen because of a combination of the natural imperfections of memory, and the normal susceptibility to innocent (and usually quite subtle) suggestion."[592]

Eyewitness expert Elizabeth Loftus (1996) found ... that witnesses add to their stories of crimes, and what they add depends on how *she* describes what happened. The power of Loftus's suggestions shapes what witnesses later take out of their memory "bin" and recall during the identification process.

The procedures used to identify strangers add to the problem created by the power of suggestion. Witnesses think of lineups and photo arrays as multiple-choice tests without a "none of the above" choice. And they think of show-ups and single pictures as true/false tests. So they feel that they have to choose the "best" likeness in the lineups and the right "true" or "false" likeness in the show-ups. They feel pressured by the suggestion, particularly in uncomfortable or threatening situations.

Suggestions by authority figures, such as the police, aggravate these tendencies. ... For example, the very fact that police have arranged an identification procedure puts pressure on witnesses. They believe the police must have found the culprit or

---

[589] Numerous studies show that people are less able to identify individuals of another race than their own.
[590] Joel Samaha, *Criminal Procedure 319* (7th ed. 2008)
[591] Wells 2002, at 665 cited in Samaha, *id.*
[592] Wells and Olson 2003, at 277, cited in Samaha, *id.*

they wouldn't have gone to the trouble of arranging the identification event. So they tell themselves, the culprit *has to be* in the lineup or the one person in the show-up or photo.[593]

LEGAL CHALLENGES TO IDENTIFICATION PROCEDURES

Defendants raise four types of constitutional challenges to the identification procedures used to identify them:

- The identification procedure violates their Fifth Amendment privilege against self-incrimination.
- The identification procedure constitutes an unreasonable search and seizure in violation of the Fourth Amendment.
- The identification procedure violates their Sixth Amendment right to counsel because it was conducted without a lawyer present.
- The identification procedure violates the general due process protections found in the Fifth and Fourteenth Amendments.

Defendants are generally unsuccessful with these challenges.

SELF-INCRIMINATION CHALLENGES

The Fifth Amendment protects against self-incrimination. The Court has held this means individuals do not have to testify against themselves. According to *Schmerber v. California*, 384 U.S. 747 (1966), physical identification procedures (for example, giving a voice sample or fingerprints) do not trigger the Fifth Amendment's privilege against self-incrimination. In subsequent cases the Court has extended *Schmerber* to fingerprints, photographs, measurements, physical movements, handwriting analysis, and examination by ultraviolet light. Suspects do not have a right to refuse to participate in these types of identification procedures since they are not within the privilege of self-incrimination. If they do refuse, the court may hold them in contempt of court and jail them indefinitely. To make things worse, prosecutors are not prohibited from commenting on the defendant's refusal to participate in these procedures at trial.

ILLEGAL SEARCH AND SEIZURE CHALLENGES.

Defendants sometimes claim that the state's attempt to identify them involves some seizure that, under the Fourth Amendment, must be reasonable (and generally supported by a warrant). In *Winston v. Lee*, 470 U.S. 753 (1985), the prosecution sought a court order requiring the suspect to have surgery to remove a bullet lodged in his chest. The prosecution believed that the ballistic test (scientific identification evidence) on the bullet would show that he was shot while involved in a robbery. The Court weighed the risks to the suspect against the government's need for evidence and disallowed the extraction surgery as not a reasonable seizure noting that the prosecutor had other evidence against the defendant that could be used instead.[594]

RIGHT TO COUNSEL CHALLENGES

Under some circumstances, the defendant is entitled to have the assistance of counsel during the identification procedure. *U.S. v. Wade*, 388 U.S. 218 (1967) and *Gilbert v. California*, 388 U.S. 263 (1967) announced a rule that a suspect who has already been indicted has the absolute right to have counsel present at any pretrial confrontation procedure (lineups and one-person

---

[593] Samaha, *Criminal Procedure, supra*, at 318-320.
[594] The Court had held *Rochin v. California*, 342 U.S. 165 (1952), held that police may not use methods that shock the conscience, such as pumping the suspect's stomach, to obtain physical evidence from suspects.

show-ups). *Wade-Gilbert* created a *per se* rule that any identification which occurs without the presence of counsel must be excluded as evidence at trial. If the lineup is improper, not only may the prosecution not introduce into trial the fact that the defendant was picked out of a lineup, but the prosecution will even have to make a special showing before the witness who made the lineup identification will be allowed to testify in court that the person sitting in the desk is the person observed by the witness at the scene of the crime. In order to make this independent, in-court identification, the states will have to show by clear and convincing evidence that the in-court identification is not the fruit of the poisonous tree.

Limitations of Wade-Gilbert:

Kirby v. Illinois, 406 U.S. 682 (1972), held that the defendant's right to counsel at lineups and show ups is triggered only after the state has initiated adversarial proceedings — whether by way of a formal charge, preliminary hearing, indictment, information or arraignment. Most lower courts have held that the issuance of an arrest warrant also triggers *Wade-Gilbert.* Where the police have only arrested defendant without a warrant, however, most courts have held the *Wade-Gilbert* right to counsel at lineup rule is not guaranteed.

In *U.S. v. Ash,* 413 U.S. 300 (1973) the Supreme Court ruled that the right to counsel does not apply where witnesses view still or moving pictures of the suspect. The Court reasoned that, unlike a lineup or show-up situation, the suspect is not present when the witness views the photographs. The major purpose of the right to counsel in the *Wade* lineup situation is to prevent the suspect from being penalized for his ignorance and inability to recognize and object to prejudicial conditions.

DUE PROCESS CHALLENGE

Defendants sometimes challenge an identification procedure as a violation of Due Process Clause claiming that "the confrontation was so unnecessarily suggestive and conducive to irreparable mistaken identification" as to deny a them due process of law."[595] Unnecessarily suggestive lineups are fundamentally unfair, but the Court has not established any bright-line rules for determining whether a procedure was so suggestive that it violates due process. Instead, due process is a general standard, and the courts look at the totality of the circumstances surrounding the identification procedure to decide whether due process was violated.

In 1972 the Court identified five factors to consider when analyzing whether a defendant's due process rights have been violated. *Neil v. Biggers,* 409 U.S. 188 (1972). The five factors are:

- The opportunity to view the suspect,
- The degree of attention,
- The accuracy of the witness's description,
- The witness's level of certainty,
- The time between the crime and the confrontation-identification.

Five years later, the Court, applying those five factors, concluded that an undercover police narcotics officer had ability to make an accurate identification based on a viewing of a single photograph. In *Manson v. Brathwaite,* 432 U.S. 98 (1977) a lower federal court opined that the photographic identification should have been excluded because the officer's examination of a single photograph was unnecessarily suggestive, and possibly unreliable. The Court, however, found that the identification procedure did not violate the defendant's due process rights. The

---

[595] *Stovall v. Denno,* 388 U.S. 293 (1967).

Court noted that, although a photographic array would have been preferable, even the inherently suggestive show-up did not require the *per se* exclusion of such identification.

Due process does not limit the introduction of possibly suggestive eyewitness identifications that occur but which were not staged or set up by the police. *Perry v. New Hampshire,* 565 U.S. 288 (2012). Justice Ginsburg wrote for the Court,

> In our system of justice, fair trial for persons charged with criminal offenses is secured by the Sixth Amendment, which guarantees to defendants the right to counsel, compulsory process to obtain defense witnesses, and the opportunity to cross-examine witnesses for the prosecution. Those safeguards apart, admission of evidence in state trials is ordinarily governed by state law, and the reliability of relevant testimony typically falls within the province of the jury to determine. This Court has recognized, in addition, a due process check on the admission of eyewitness identification, applicable when the police have arranged suggestive circumstances leading the witness to identify a particular person as the perpetrator of a crime.

> An identification infected by improper police influence, our case law holds, is not automatically excluded. Instead, the trial judge must screen the evidence for reliability pretrial. If there is "a very substantial likelihood of irreparable misidentification," *Simmons v. United States,* 390 U.S. 377, 384, 88 S.Ct. 967, 19 L.Ed.2d 1247 (1968), the judge must disallow presentation of the evidence at trial. But if the indicia of reliability are strong enough to outweigh the corrupting effect of the police-arranged suggestive circumstances, the identification evidence ordinarily will be admitted, and the jury will ultimately determine its worth.

> We have not extended pretrial screening for reliability to cases in which the suggestive circumstances were not arranged by law enforcement officers. Petitioner requests that we do so because of the grave risk that mistaken identification will yield a miscarriage of justice. [Footnote omitted.} Our decisions, however, turn on the presence of state action and aim to deter police from rigging identification procedures, for example, at a lineup, showup, or photograph array. When no improper law enforcement activity is involved, we hold, it suffices to test reliability through the rights and opportunities generally designed for that purpose, notably, the presence of counsel at postindictment lineups, vigorous cross-examination, protective rules of evidence, and jury instructions on both the fallibility of eyewitness identification and the requirement that guilt be proved beyond a reasonable doubt.[596]

ENSURING ACCURATE IDENTIFICATIONS

In order to protect against some of the inherent problems with eyewitness identification noted above, the U.S. Justice Department and the American Bar Association have suggested various modifications in the identification process to ensure greater accuracy. The goals of these procedures are to eliminate the possibility that the police officer conducting the identification will intentionally or unintentionally influence the eyewitness, to limit pressure on the witness to select one of the individuals in the lineup or photo array, and to increase the accuracy of the identification. These modifications include:

---

[596] *Perry v. New Hampshire,* 565 U.S. at 296 (2012).

- **Blind Administration** — the officer administering the identification procedures is not informed which individual in the lineup is the suspect. This prevents the administrator from unintentionally or intentionally influencing the selection. This is sometimes also referred to as "double blind" in that both the administrator and the eyewitness do not know who the suspect is.
- **Changes to Instructions** — the administrator should instruct the eyewitness that the administrator does not know the identity of the suspect and that the suspect may not be in the lineup. This eliminates the possibility that the eyewitness will look to the administrator to guide his or her selection or will feel compelled to single out an individual as the perpetrator. Following the identification, the police should not indicate that the witness has selected the "right" person as this may unduly influence the witness's future identification of suspect.
- **Single eyewitness** — only one individual at a time should view the lineup, showup, or photo array. The eyewitnesses should not be allowed to confer with one another. A witness should not be told whom other individuals identified. Witnesses, should not be shown photographs of the suspect or permitted to view the suspect prior to lineup.
- **Sequential presentation** — participants in the lineup or pictures in a photo array should be presented to the victim or eyewitness one at a time. The witness is asked to make a decision about each person immediately following the confrontation. This differs from the typical simultaneous lineup in which all lineup members are shown to the witness at the same time. The theory behind the sequential lineup is that the eyewitness will examine each suspect separately and determine whether he or she is the offender. This is thought to eliminate pressure on an eyewitness to select the person who most closely resembles the perpetrator.
- **Confident ranking** -- The witness is asked to rank his or her degree of confidence in the decision right after the lineup.

In 2003 the National Institute of Justice published a training manual for officers covering standards for identification procedures including the composition of a lineup or photographic array. The standards address: 1) the balance of the composition (participants should be similar age, height, weight, and race, dressed similarly), 2) the number of participants (at least five fillers in the photo array and at least four fillers in the lineup), 3) distinctive features (fillers should possess the distinctive features mentioned by the witness), 4) photographs (these should be uniform and neutral in appearance, there should not be a mix of color photos and black and white photos, there should be no visible identifying marks anywhere on the photo, and 5) preservation of the process (police should record the results on a standard form, noting the number of the lineup member who was selected, the name of the eyewitness, the date, the investigator, a statement describing the identification process). According to the NIJ manual, police should photograph or videotape the lineup or show-up.

Recognizing how powerful eyewitness identification is on juries and how "risky" eyewitness identification is with human limitations on the ability to perceive and recall, judges have started giving jury instructions advising jurors how to evaluate courtroom identification, and helping them understand how eyewitness identification can be mistaken. Jurors are instructed to evaluate whether the identification witness making the courtroom identification possessed the opportunity and ability to observe the offender at the crime scene and whether his or her identification was influenced by outside influences. Jurors are instructed to consider the length of time between the crime and the identification as well as any past failures by the eyewitness to identify the suspect. Judges have also permitted defense experts to testify about the psychological barriers to eyewitness identification.

The New Jersey and Oregon Supreme Courts have lead the way in recognizing the scientific research on the fallibility of eyewitness identification. In New Jersey, *State v. Henderson*, 27 A. 3d 872 (NJ 2011) examined social science research and determined that current tests (enunciated in *Neil v. Biggers*, supra) did not offer adequate measures of reliability. In Oregon, the unanimous decision in *State v. Lawson*, 352 Or 724 (2012), changed the way Oregon trial courts must evaluate identification evidence. In *Lawson*, the Court pointed to 2,000 scientific studies on the reliability of eyewitness identification published since the *Classen* decision in 1979 (*Classen* provided the test used by Oregon courts to determine the admissibility of eyewitness identification).

The Oregon Supreme Court concluded that the safeguards in *Classen* were inadequate to ensure that unreliable evidence would be excluded. After *Lawson*, when defendants file pretrial motions to exclude eyewitness identifications, the state must first demonstrate by a preponderance of the evidence that the witness perceived sufficient facts to support an inference of identification and that the identification was based on those perceptions. Second, when there are facts demonstrating that a witness could have relied on something other than his or her own perceptions to identify the defendant, the state must establish by a preponderance of the evidence that the identification was based on permissible basis rather than an impermissible one, such as suggestive police procedures. Third, the court must find that the identification must be helpful to the jury to form a clear understanding of the testimony of the witness. (The Oregon Supreme Court anticipated that the state will generally be able to easily meet this burden, but gave examples where witness's statements may be of little utility). Fourth, the court must weigh the prejudicial impact of the identifications with the probative value (helpfulness/utility) of the identification. Based on the results, the trial court may admit the identification, exclude the identification, or exclude parts of the identification testimony. Finally, the lower courts are to allow expert testimony to counteract juror misperceptions concerning eyewitness identification evidence since the normal process of cross-examination may not sufficiently apprise jurors and help them identify mistaken identification. The Oregon approach appears to be trailblazing, and provides the greatest protections against the inherent unreliability of eyewitness identification. According to the Innocence Project,

> The changes, designed to reduce the likelihood of wrongful convictions by taking into account more than 30 years of scientific research on eyewitness identification and memory, reject the balancing test that had been in place for 30 years and shifts the burden to the state to establish that the evidence is admissible. The decision comes after a 2011 landmark decision by the New Jersey Supreme Court mandating similar reforms.

> Relying on the robust body of scientific research concerning memory and perception, the court recognized that the reliability and accuracy of an identification can be affected by circumstances within the control of the criminal justice system as well as the characteristics of the witness, the alleged perpetrator and the environmental conditions of the event that cannot be controlled by the criminal justice system. The new legal framework requires Oregon courts to consider all of the factors that may affect an identification's reliability and instruct courts, where appropriate, to employ remedies, such as limiting the witness's testimony and permitting expert testimony to explain the scientific research on memory and identification. The Court is particularly concerned with the effects of suggestion (and in particular police suggestion) on memory and likened identification evidence to other forms of physical trace evidence, finding that "it is incumbent on courts and law enforcement personnel to treat eyewitness memory

just as carefully as they would other forms of trace evidence, like DNA, bloodstains, or fingerprints, the evidentiary value of which can be impaired or destroyed by Contamination.

The Oregon Supreme Court decision goes further than the recent New Jersey Supreme Court in *State v. Henderson* in protecting against wrongful convictions based on misidentification in several important respects. The new Oregon test shifts the burden to the state to establish that the evidence is admissible. If the state satisfies its initial burden, the court charges that judges may still need to impose remedies, including suppressing the evidence in some circumstances to prevent injustice if the defendant establishes that he or she would be unfairly prejudiced by the evidence.

A recent public records request that the Innocence Project sent to all Oregon law enforcement agencies showed that well under one fifth possessed written policies in the area of eyewitness identification. While these findings are not inconsistent with the findings of similar public records requests in other states, it does signal the need to address police practice in this area.

Boston attorney and Visiting Fellow at the National Institute of Justice, James Doyle commenting on the *Lawson* decision wrote,

Eyewitness memory evidence can be contaminated accidentally, just like blood or other trace evidence. The difference is that no memory can be sent back to the lab to be tested for contaminants. ... The only tests we can apply to memory evidence are the traditional thresholds that are embodied in evidence law. We haven't been using them. Now we can. The Oregon Supreme Court has shown us why we should. [597]

WRAP UP

Police routinely question witnesses and interrogate suspects as part of their criminal investigations. At times, the defendant's admissions are critical to the successful prosecution of the crime. Similarly, when strangers commit crimes, eyewitness identification may be crucial to solving and prosecuting the crime. Police interrogations and eyewitness identification, however, present myriad problems that may result in wrongful convictions. The Court, in the *Miranda* decision identified warnings that police must give that tell suspects of their constitutional rights in an attempt to mitigate what the Court observed in overzealous stationhouse interrogations. This landmark decision was followed with other important Court cases that have further defined the scope of Miranda and its limitations. The Court has been willing to exclude defendants' involuntary confessions and unwarned confessions. However, cases in which unreliable or suggestive identifications have, until recently, not been subject to much exacting scrutiny.

Wrongful convictions, resulting from false confessions and faulty eyewitness identifications, reflect the American criminal justice system at its worse. Innocent individuals may spend many years in prison before the injustice is revealed. Meanwhile, the actual perpetrators of the crime are allowed to go unpunished. Social science research has spotlighted the magnitude of wrongful convictions, identified factors contributing to false confessions and bad eyewitness identification, and suggested procedures to minimize the factors contributing to both. Police and court practices are beginning to change in response to these findings.

---

[597] James Doyle, *Oregon's Eyewitness Decision: Back to Basics*. www.thecrimereport.org/viewpoints

SOME THINGS TO EXPLORE OR THINK ABOUT

➢ Read Malcom Gladwell's book, *"Talking to Strangers: What we should know about the people we don't know."* Little Brown and Company, 2019. This book highlights the myriad reasons why people misinterpret others meanings and can be particularly bad at deciding whether others are lying or telling the truth.

➢ Investigate the legal test of admissibility for eyewitness testimony in your state (for example, Oregon's is now that one identified in State v. Lawson and New Jersey's is now that one identified in State v. Henderson. You may need to look at your state's statutes or code of evidence.

➢ Watch Part 2, Episode 2 of the Netflix series, "Making a Murderer" which explores whether Brandon Dassey's confession should have been admissible. Do you feel that his confession was coerced? What arguments made by his legal team suggest that his confession should have been excluded? If you really want to go the extra step, do further research to follow his appeals and see their results.

➢ Watch Part 1, Episode 1 of the Netflix series, "Making a Murderer" which explores the problems concerning the eyewitness identifications that lead to the initial conviction of Steven Avery resulting in his wrongful conviction and prolonged detention for rape.

TERMINOLOGY

- blind administration
- break in custody rule
- contamination of interrogation
- coerced confession
- custody
- Edwards rule
- express questioning
- eyewitness identification
- false confession
- filler, foil, or distractor
- functional equivalent (of express questioning)
- interrogation
- lineup
- photo array
- photo lineup
- photo throwdown
- prophylactic rule
- question first, warn later policy
- scientific identification
- sequential presentation lineup
- showup
- unequivocal invocation
- voluntariness test

Chapter Nine: Accusatory Phase—Pretrial Procedure

OVERVIEW AND LEARNING OBJECTIVES

This chapter examines the pretrial stage of the criminal justice system--after charges are filed against the defendant but before trial. Most cases (more than 95% of all cases that enter in the system) are resolved during this accusatory pretrial phase—primarily due to plea negotiations, but also because of successful pretrial motions. After reading this chapter, you should be able to answer the following questions:

> ➢ What is the purpose of a probable cause review and when must it occur?
> ➢ What happens when the defendant first appears before the court?
> ➢ When will a defendant be released or detained pretrial? What factors will the court consider in determining pretrial release?
> ➢ What are the three different processes by which felony charges can be filed against a defendant? How are they similar and how do they differ?
> ➢ How prevalent is plea-bargaining? What types of pleas result in the defendant's conviction without a trial?
> ➢ What is the exclusionary rule and its exceptions?
> ➢ What are the pretrial motions that a defendant may file?

PROBABLE CAUSE TO DETAIN HEARINGS

As discussed in Chapter Seven, police sometimes arrest suspects without a warrant. Because the arrest is made without a warrant, a neutral magistrate has not yet determined that probable cause exists to justify the arrest and detention (unlike the situation in which police arrest after obtaining a warrant). In *Gernstein v. Pugh,* 420 U.S. 103 (1975), the Court held that the magistrate must make a "prompt" determination of probable cause. The Court left "prompt" undefined, and many jurisdictions combined the probable cause determination with the defendant's initial appearance in court before the judge.

In 1991, in the case of *County of Riverside v. McLaughlin,* 500 U.S. 44 (1991), petitioner McLaughlin and other inmates, filed a suit against the County asking the Court to define "prompt." They argued for a *per se* rule and asked the Court to rule that anything over 24 hours was not prompt. Instead, the Court settled on 48 hours, noting that if a magistrate reviewed detention within 48 hours, it would be presumed that the government had acted promptly. A defendant could show that the government stalled, and that his or her detention was invalid, but the burden would be on the detainee show this. If a magistrate had not done a probable cause review within 48 hours of the detainee's arrest, the reviewing court would presume that the government did not act promptly. In those cases, the government carries the burden of showing a good reason why it could not present the defendant's case to the judge for a probable cause review. Normal sorts of delays, such as weekends and holidays, do not constitute a good reason why the defendant's case was not reviewed. On the other hand, the *McLaughlin* Court made allowances for true emergencies, such as the courthouse collapsing in an earthquake or a flood washing away the jail, and allowed the state to overcome the presumption that the detention was invalid even if made after 48 hours.

If the judge fails to make a probable cause determination within the 48 hours, the defendant should be released. Because probable cause determinations need not be made in open court, the general practice is that a judge will appear at the jail once or twice over the weekend and read all the probable cause statements written by the arresting officer, detailing the facts why the individual was arrested and is now being detained. If the judge finds probable cause exists justifying the detention, the case moves to the first appearance, which is a proceeding in open court on the record. Arrested individuals have no right to appear before the judge for these determinations, nor can they contest the facts in a hearing. If, after review of the probable cause statement prepared by the arresting officer, the judge finds insufficient evidence (i.e., no probable cause exists), the defendant is released. In those cases, the state is free to establish probable cause in an affidavit for an arrest warrant and get the defendant back before the court by arresting him or her on the warrant.

In *Manuel v. Joliet*, 580 U.S. ___ (2017), the defendant was detained on the basis of fabricated evidence and held for 48 days. After his release he sued the police officers in a §1983 civil suit claiming violation of his Fourth Amendment rights. The Court held that the Fourth Amendment covers not only arrest seizures but also any detentions noting that pretrial detention can violate the Fourth Amendment even when it follows the start of the legal process. The Fourth Amendment prohibits detaining persons absent probable cause. Here, probable cause was fabricated, thus there was no probable cause, and thus defendant can make a viable claim in the civil suit that his Fourth Amendment rights were violated.

FIRST APPEARANCES AND ARRAIGNMENTS

After a suspect is arrested or cited to appear, the police forward reports to the prosecuting attorney for determination of charges. The prosecutor will review the reports and file a complaint (a sworn statement by the prosecutor charging the defendant with a crime) or a charging document known as an "information" with the court. (The prosecutor has discretion to reject charges and not file anything with the court.). The defendant's presence in open court before a magistrate or judge, triggered by the filing of the complaint or information, is known as an initial appearance or first appearance. A police citation may trigger the first appearance when a defendant is charged with a traffic crime. Most state laws and the federal rules of criminal procedure require the defendant be brought before the magistrate or judge without unnecessary delay--especially if they are in custody.

At first appearance, the court will inform the defendant of what charges were filed, making sure the defendant is properly named on the charging document, and addressing the issue of release if the defendant is in custody. The judge will also inform the defendant of his or her right to counsel and inquire whether the defendant wishes to be represented by counsel. Frequently, the defendant will be arraigned during this first appearance. Arraignments are proceedings in open court, and the accused is generally required to be present at arraignments.

Arraignments are considered a "critical stage" of the criminal justice process, and as such the defendant has the right to the assistance of counsel during arraignments. The court may arraign the defendant during the first appearance if the defendant appears with counsel or decides to waive counsel. If, however, the defendant appears without an attorney and wants to consult with an attorney, then the court will not proceed with arraignment until an attorney can appear with the defendant. Holding over the arraignment process until an attorney "gets onboard" leads to inefficiency (multiple hearings). This inefficiency led many courts to implement a practice of temporarily appointing an attorney to represent the defendant only for that arraignment after which another attorney takes over the case. If the defendant wishes to hire counsel, then the court will delay the arraignment until that attorney can appear with the defendant.

Four important things happen during arraignments: first, the judge reads the charges filed by the prosecutor to the defendant and gives the defendant a printed copy of the charges; second, the judge assures that the defendant is correctly named on the charging document (either an information or an indictment); third, the judge decides whether to release the defendant or to set bail; and fourth, the defendant may enter a plea. Generally, the defendant will be expected to enter a not guilty plea that has the effect of starting the official criminal process against him, but in some jurisdictions a not guilty plea is automatically entered at first appearance.

If the state files felony charges, the first appearance or initial appearance is an opportunity for the defendant to request a preliminary hearing or grand jury. If the state filed only very minor charges, it is possible for the defendant to appear in court, be arraigned, enter a guilty plea, and be sentenced all during one court proceeding. For most cases, the first appearance and arraignment process begin a series of pre-trial hearings that lead to either a trial or an entry of a guilty plea followed by sentencing.

PRETRIAL RELEASE

BAIL—CONSTITUTIONAL PROVISIONS

The Eighth Amendment prohibits excessive bail. It does not, however, require courts set bail in every instance--only that, when set, bail may not be excessive.[598] The courts, for example, routinely deny bail for a charge of murder. *Stack v. Boyle* 342 U.S. 1 (1951), defined "excessive" bail as any amount of bail beyond that necessary to guarantee the defendant's appearance at trial. Setting bail is a critical stage of the criminal justice process, and therefore, the defendant is entitled the assistance of counsel when arguing for release or about terms of bail.

FORMS OF RELEASE

Cash bond has historically been the primary form of bail in the United States. Under the cash bail system, an individual pays a sum of money and is released from detention. If the defendant fails to show up for court appearances, the court keeps the money (and issues a bench warrant to get the defendant back to court.). If the defendant shows up for all court appearances, then the money is returned. Many people cannot afford to pay the full amount of bail, so in many states, these individuals can request a bail bondsman pay a surety bond. The general practice is that the defendant pays the bondsman 10% of the bail amount set by the court, and the bail bondsman pays the full amount set by the court. If the defendant makes all appearances, then the bondsman keeps the 10% paid by the defendant. If, however, the defendant fails to appear, the

---

[598] Despite the fundamental nature of individual access to bail, the Bail Clause has never been thought to accord a right to bail in all cases, but merely to provide that bail should not be excessive in those cases where it is proper to grant bail. *Carlson v. Landon*, 342 U.S. 524 (1952).

bondsman forfeits the entire amount to the court. Bail bondsman may hire "bounty hunters" to track down defendants who have failed to appear for trial.

Some states have abolished the private bail bond system. Instead, the system relies on recognizance release or a surety bond paid to the court. The court will set an amount of bail (for example, let's say $5,000), and the defendant will pay the court ten percent ($500.00) and sign a release agreement agreeing to pay the remaining 90% ($4500.00) in case of non-appearance. If defendant makes all court appearances, then the court will, upon resolution of the case, return the $500.00 posted by the defendant minus an administrative fee. If defendant fails to appear, the court will revoke the defendant's release, forfeit security, and enter a money judgment for $4500.00.

Release on Recognizance (ROR) is another form of release. Under this release the defendant pays no money but instead is released upon his or her promise to appear. One similar form of release is a conditional release[599] in which the court releases a defendant upon certain conditions that are tailored to the defendant's situation and designed to assure reappearance. Common conditions of release include:

- Do not move from current address.
- Do not contact victim.
- Maintain contact with attorney.
- Do not consume illegal substances or do not consume intoxicants (if there is some indication that the crime was committed under the influence of intoxicants).
- Submit to a UA or BA at the Release Assistance Officer's request
- Do not frequent places where illegal substances are kept.
- Maintain contact with the Release Assistance Officer.

Anecdotally, this author has noted that jail and pre-trial detention facilities that are overcrowded may, in practice, release offenders who are not great candidates for either security or conditional release and are very likely to fail to appear at their next scheduled court appearance. When the defendant fails to appear, the judge will issue a "bench warrant" for the offender's arrest and the prosecutor may potentially file new criminal failure to appear charges. When the jail has insufficient resources and releases individuals because of lack of bed space, this results in a cycle of arrest, release, failure to appear, arrest, release, failure to appear, etc. This further drains judicial and jail resources.

In *Jennings v. Rodriguez*, 583 U.S. ___ (2018) the Court held that a non-citizen subject to detention under the Immigration and Nationality Act are not entitled to periodic bail bond hearings (even if they are detained for longer than six months). The Act requires that noncitizens who the federal government determines to be inadmissible to the United States be detained during removal proceedings (some may be released on bond if they can demonstrate that they are not a flight risk or danger to the community.) Rodriguez, a lawful permanent resident alien, and other detained individuals filed suit claiming that prolonged detention without the possibility of hearings violated due process rights. Before the Court was whether a bond hearing was required and, if so, how long could the detention last before one was entitled to a hearing. Rodriguez and the others claimed if detention lasted six months, they should have a bond hearing and that they were entitled to release unless the government presented clear and

---

[599] Conditional release seems to be the predominant type of release in many states. Although judges frequently state, "I am releasing you on your own recognizance," most follow this "with the condition that you..." (turning the ROR release into a conditional release).

convincing evidence that the noncitizens were dangerous and a flight risk (i.e., putting the burden of proof on the government.) They also argued that if a detained person was denied bond, that there should automatically be a new hearing every six months. The 5-3 Court decision was split and only a plurality opinion was reached, but the plurality ruled against Rodriguez and the others.

PREVENTIVE DETENTION-FEDERAL BAIL REFORM ACT OF 1984

The Federal Bail Reform Act of 1984 was the model for modern bail reform efforts.[600] This Act allowed for preventive detention of offenders. Under this act, the judge is to order pretrial release of an individual on personal recognizance or a conditional release agreement (promise to pay in the event of non-appearance) "unless the judicial officer determines that such release will not reasonably assure the appearance of the individual . . . or will endanger the safety of any other person or the community."   In *U.S. v. Salerno,* 481 U.S. 739 (1987), two organized crime figures were prosecuted under the Federal Racketeer Influenced and Corrupt Organizations (RICO) Act. Prior to trial, the government successfully petitioned the federal district court to detain the defendants under the Federal Bail Reform Act of 1984. The defendants argued that detaining them without a trial under the Act violated their due process rights. The Supreme Court upheld the constitutionality of the preventive detention provisions of the Act allowing judges to deny bail in cases where releasing the defendant before trial threatens the safety of other persons or the community. Prior to this Act, the sole valid criterion upon which   judges could base release was defendants' likelihood of reappearance. After this Act, courts can now consider community safety as well.

GETTING TO THE COURT OF PROPER JURISDICTION

GRAND JURY

USE OF THE GRAND JURY

The Fifth Amendment provides that "no person shall be held to answer for a capital, or otherwise infamous crime, unless on a presentment or indictment of a Grand Jury." When the Bill of Rights passed, each state required a grand jury indictment for felonies. The grand jury was established to restrain governmental power and abuse. In 1859 Michigan decided that electing prosecutors was a sufficient constraint, and it moved away from requiring grand jury and allowed a preliminary hearing (or both). California and other states followed Michigan's lead, and allowed prosecutors to either file a charging document called an "information" after a preliminary hearing or a charging document called an "indictment" after a grand jury.

By 1884, the Court was faced with the question of whether the Grand Jury Clause of the Fifth Amendment was required by the Fourteenth Amendment's Due Process Clause. In *Hurtado*

---

[600] The report, "Challenge of Crime in a Free Society" published by the LEAA in 1967, concluded that the bail system discriminates against the poor who are unable to meet bail. Taxpayers also are also affected in that they must pay the cost of pretrial detention for those individuals unable to post bail.   The commission found that the amount of bail fixed by a schedule has little relationship with the offender's likelihood of reappearance. The report recommended pretrial release without financial conditions on most offenders. Only those who present a flight risk or who were charged with dangerous acts should be jailed pending trial, according to the report. Prior to this LEAA report, the Vera Institute, starting in 1961, sponsored the Manhattan Bail Project in which staff members interviewed indigent defendants to see what factors would influence their appearance at trial. The staff made recommendations to judges who would set conditions for release. Only 1.6% of the individuals recommended for release failed to appear for trial. Many jurisdictions modeled their own release programs in response to the success of the Manhattan Project (and the criticism found in the LEAA report).

v. California, 110 U.S. 516 (1883), the defendant claimed that his murder conviction should be set aside because it had been brought by way of preliminary hearing not a grand jury. The Court ruled that either a grand jury or a preliminary hearing adequately satisfied the fundamental fairness requirement of the Due Process Clause.

The United States is the only country that uses the grand jury. At common law the grand jury was composed of twenty-three individuals, and twelve grand jurors had to agree to support issuing an indictment. The federal grand jury is still comprised of 23 members, but states differ on the number of grand jurors, with the smallest panel being seven and the largest being 23 grand jurors. Although all states still have a grand jury, only about one-half of the states use grand juries, and only 22 states require grand juries to test the sufficiency of the state's evidence on felony charges. The trend is against reliance on the grand jury. Central criticisms include:

- The grand jury is an ineffective check on the prosecutor's power (a "rubber stamp").
- Grand jurors are unqualified lay people who lack the expertise to make the decision, so they follow the prosecutor rather than exercising independent judgment.
- The grand jury proceeding is non-adversarial.
- The grand jury is a resource-draining, lengthy process.

Lippman observed,

> The grand jury is in theory independent of prosecutors and judges and possesses significant powers that it exercises behind closed doors. The general rule is that the jury's decision to indict or refuse to indict may not be challenged by a prosecutor or by a defense attorney. … The grand jury remains a controversial institution, and there continues to be a debate over whether states and the federal government should continue to rely on this institution. Defenders of the grand jury argue that whatever its flaws, the jury is a mechanism for popular participation in deciding whether to prosecute an individual for a crime. This enhances public confidence in the criminal justice system and protects citizens against unfounded accusations. … The high percentage of cases in which the jury returns a true bill according to supporters of the grand jury does not necessarily mean that the jury is a "rubber stamp." The explanation may lie in the fact that prosecutors are aware that to obtain a true bill from the grand jury, a case must be thoroughly documented. The strength of the cases that are endorsed by the grand jury is indicted by the fact that a high percentage of those cases result in criminal convictions.[601]

FUNCTIONS OF THE GRAND JURY

In situations where police arrest a defendant right after a crime is committed, the prosecutor will file charges in the courts of limited jurisdiction. But, felonies must be brought and tried in general jurisdiction courts. So, when the charges are felonies, one function of the grand jury is to determine if there is enough evidence to proceed to trial in the court of general jurisdiction. The grand jury, after considering the evidence,[602] may charge the defendant with a greater offense or a lesser offense, with additional criminal charges, or no charges. Another function of the grand jury is to investigate the possibility of criminal activity. When the defendant

---

[601] Lippman, *Procedure, supra* at 533-534.
[602] In states that follow the Federal Rules of Evidence (43 states), grand juries may rely on evidence that would not be admissible during a criminal trial since the rules do not apply to grand jury proceedings.

is unaware that the grand jury is investigating him or her, this is called a "secret grand jury." In either the normal grand jury proceedings or the secret grand jury proceedings, the grand jury has power to compel witnesses to appear by issuing a subpoena and the power to compel documents be presented to it by issuing a *subpoena duces tecum*. Witnesses subpoenaed to testify before grand jury must appear and are not entitled to be assisted by attorneys during the grand jury investigation. In fact, only the grand jurors, the witness, and the prosecutor may be present during the process. Grand juries may compel witnesses to testify over their claims of self-incrimination by granting witnesses transactional or use immunity. Since there is no right to testify before the grand jury, the grand jury may refuse to hear from a witness.

BEING A GRAND JUROR

In most states, the grand jury pool is randomly selected from the list used to select the petit jury (trial jury); thus, the qualifications to be a grand juror are generally the same as for trial jurors[603]: one must generally be a resident in the jurisdiction, at least 18 years old, and not have been convicted of a felony. The list of grand jurors must comprise a fair cross-section of the community[604] and may be based on voters' lists, taxpayer lists, and DMV lists. Grand jurors cannot be excluded from service because of race, gender, or national origin. Prosecutors "purge the grand jury" (select the grand jurors from the names of the pool of all individuals selected to serve on jury duty) in the presence of a judge.

PRELIMINARY HEARINGS

In state felony cases where the grand jury is not used, the defendant is entitled to a preliminary hearing before a magistrate within a reasonably short time period after arrest. Preliminary hearings resemble adversarial trials, but their purpose is limited to the judge's deciding whether to "bind the defendant over for trial" (a term of art that means that the judge found sufficient evidence for the case to go forward.) The defendant and defense counsel, are entitled to be present at the preliminary hearing and may cross-examine the state's witnesses. However, the defense may not call witnesses or otherwise present evidence. Additionally, the state does not have to present all the evidence it has, but rather needs to show only a *prima facie* (on its face) case that sufficient evidence exists to go forward.

COMPARING GRAND JURY AND PRELIMINARY HEARINGS

Grand jury and preliminary hearings serve the same function: testing the sufficiency of the state's evidence to go forward in felony court. The grand jury differs from preliminary hearing in the following ways:

- Grand jurors decide whether the state has sufficient evidence in a grand jury hearing; the judge decides whether the state has sufficient evidence in a preliminary hearing.
- If the grand jury finds sufficient evidence it returns a "true bill" on an "indictment; if the judge finds sufficient evidence, he or she "binds the defendant over" and the prosecutor's office files an "information."

---

[603] The jurors who listen to the evidence presented at grand jury (grand jurors) will never be the same jurors who decide the defendant's guilt at his or her trial (petit jurors).

[604] After indictment, the defense attorney may challenge the composition of a grand jury, and if successful, the indictment will be dismissed.

- The grand jury is a closed hearing; a preliminary hearing is an open hearing.
- The defendant generally does not participate in grand jury; the defendant generally participates at the preliminary hearing by cross-examining the state's witnesses.
- The prosecutor is the legal advisor to the grand jury and the grand jury may add charges to the indictment as it sees fit; the prosecutor files the charges it believes are supported by the evidence and the judge may not add additional charges or suggest charges at the preliminary hearing.

Differences between Grand Jury and Preliminary Hearing

	GRAND JURY	PRELIMINARY HEARING
Who Decides sufficiency of evidence	Grand Jurors (7 – 23)	Judge (1)
Present at Hearing	State representative (prosecutor), witnesses (one at a time), no defendant	Judge, Defendant/Counsel, Prosecutor, Witnesses
Cross Examination of Witnesses	No	Yes
Decision (terms of art)	"Return a True Bill," "Return a Not True Bill"	"Bind the Defendant Over"
Title of Charging Document	Indictment	Information

WAIVER OF PRESENTMENT

Occasionally a defendant may wish to waive his or her right to have the sufficiency of the evidence in the case tested by the grand jury or judge in a preliminary hearing. In some states, the defendant is allowed to waive presentment of the case to the grand jury (or waive a preliminary hearing). Why would a defendant give up the opportunity to require the state to jump all possible hurdles in his or her prosecution? The defendant may wish to have the case handled as expediently as possible and may not wish for the delay in setting a grand jury or preliminary hearing. As part of plea negotiations, a defendant who is facing felony charges may be able to plead to a felony not currently listed on the indictment. Finally, the defendant may just be pragmatic and realize the state has more than enough evidence of felonious conduct (and perhaps is seeking to avoid the grand jury uncovering even more).

PLEA-BARGAINING

THE MAGNITUDE OF PLEA-BARGAINING AND ITS IMPLICATIONS

In the 1970s plea-bargaining was a hot topic. Nationwide, prosecutors and defendants engaged in plea-bargaining, but the courts had yet to specifically rule on the constitutionality of the practice. Strong sentiments about plea-bargaining existed, and as late as the 1980s, attempts to abolish plea-bargaining garnered support. Alaska, for example, instituted a ban on plea-bargaining in 1984 and 1985. Ultimately the Court approved the practice and resolved the debate,[605] and interest in plea-bargaining as a field for social science research waned. Over the

---

[605] In *Santabello v. New York*, 404 U.S. 257, 260 (1971), the Court stated, "The disposition of criminal charges by agreement between the prosecutor and the accused, sometimes loosely called, "plea bargaining" is an essential component of the administration of justice. Properly administered, it is to be encouraged. If every criminal charge were subjected to a full-scale trial, the States and the Federal Government would need to

past three decades, courts and researchers have been virtually silent on the topic. At the 2012 American Criminological Society Conference some social scientist called for a renewed examination of plea-bargaining practices noting that the number of cases now resolved by plea bargaining (96-98%), the advent of mandatory minimum sentencing schemes that push discretion to the prosecutors, and the establishment of specialized courts warrant further research.

CHARGE BARGAINING AND SENTENCE BARGAINING

Prosecutors' offices vary in how cases are assigned and which attorney is responsible for sending out "the offer," "the deal," or "the negotiation." Some offices have one assigned prosecutor who reviews all the incoming files and sends out offers; in other offices the individual attorney assigned to handle the case will send out offers in each of his or her cases. Ultimately, attorneys in the prosecutor's office will review the facts of the case, assess what the case is worth and send to the defendant's attorney a proposed offer stating what the state will recommend if the defendant enters a plea without going to trial. Because the decision to enter a plea of guilty or no contest involves waiving a significant constitutional right (i.e., to a trial by a jury), the Court has held that it is a critical stage of the criminal justice process and the defendant is entitled to have the representation of counsel during plea negotiations and the entering of a plea.

The state generally requires that the defendant accept the offer and enter his or her plea by a specific time, after which time the offer expires and "all deals are off." Also, in some fairly egregious cases--the offer is a "no deal, deal"--meaning that the defendant must "plead to everything" with "parties free to argue." Generally, however the prosecutor's offer will include a charge bargain, a sentence bargain, or both. With a charge bargain, the state agrees to dismiss certain "counts" (charges) filed against the defendant in exchange for a plea to other counts. With a sentence bargain, the state agrees to a particular sentence in exchange for defendant's plea on the charge. An example of a fairly typical deal might read,

> "State will dismiss counts 3 and 4 if defendant pleads to counts 1, 2, and 5. State will recommend 10 days jail (or other custodial programs) on counts 1 and 2 (to run concurrent), a $200 fine on each of Counts 1, 2, and 5; 18 months bench probation on each, court appointed attorney fees, restitution to the victim (amount pending). Deal expires at first status call."

FORMS OF PLEAS: GUILTY PLEAS, NO CONTEST PLEAS, AND ALFORD PLEAS

When defendants enter a guilty plea, a no contest plea (also called a nolo contendre plea), or an Alford plea, the court will sentence them and enter a judgment of convictions. Entering one of these three types of guilty pleas has the same effect of a jury or a judge (in a bench trial) finding the defendant guilty after trial. When defendants plead guilty, they admit they have committed the crime. When defendants plead no contest or an *Alford* plea, they acknowledge the truth of the accusation or recognize that the state has sufficient evidence to convict them.

NO CONTEST PLEA

A no contest plea is virtually identical to a guilty plea except in one respect. A no contest plea cannot be used as evidence in a subsequent civil case to prove the defendant's liability. Say,

---

multiply by many times the number of judges and court Facilities." In *Brady v. United States*, 397 U.S. 742, 753 (1970) the Court stated, "we cannot hold that it is unconstitutional for a State to extend a benefit to a defendant who in turn extends a substantial benefit to the State."

for example, Joe went into a fruit market and stole a kiwi. The state prosecutes Joe for theft; Joe is cited to appear; Joe shows up in court on the day he is supposed to; Joe is arraigned on the charge of theft, and he states that wants to "take care of this" and "no, I don't think I need an attorney for a lousy charge of theft of a kiwi." The proceeding continues and the judge makes sure that Joe knows his rights and voluntarily waives them on the record. Judge gets to the point where he asks Joe, "how do you plead?" and Joe states, "guilty." Judge accepts Joe's plea and imposes a hundred dollar fine and twenty hours of community service. Joe pays his fine, does his community service, and goes on his way. Two months later, fruit market sues Joe for theft of the kiwi in a civil action. Having decided he already "dealt with this," Joe decides to go to trial. At trial, fruit market will enter proof of defendant's guilty plea as pretty convincing (but not sufficient) evidence of his theft of the kiwi. If, however, Joe had entered a "no contest plea, " Joe's plea is not admissible to show that Joe stole the kiwi.

THE *ALFORD* PLEA

In order to accept a guilty plea (negotiated or otherwise), the judge must be satisfied that the defendant is competent to enter the plea and that the plea is made voluntarily.[606] The judge must determine that the defendant understands the charge to which he is pleading and the consequences of entering the plea (generally this means the judge will explain the maximum possible sentence that might be imposed, the minimum sentence that might be imposed, etc.) In many states and the federal system, the court must find that there is a factual basis for the plea. This means that the judge will not accept a guilty plea unless the defendant says something to the effect of "I did the acts I am charged with committing." Thus, if the defendant continues to protest his innocence, the court will not accept the guilty plea. The one exception to this is called an "*Alford* plea."

In *North Carolina v. Alford,* 400 U.S. 25 (1970), the defendant was charged with murder. He claimed that he did not commit the crime, but he nevertheless wanted to accept the prosecution's offer to allow him to plead guilty in exchange for a life sentence (rather than seeking the death penalty). The court ruled that Alford's plea was valid because all that is required for a valid guilty plea is a knowing waiver of rights, not an admission of guilt. In those jurisdictions requiring a factual basis be established, courts, in accepting an Alford plea, will ask the prosecutor to recite the facts rather than requiring the defendant to admit guilt. The Court also noted that a "criminal defendant does not have the absolute right under the Constitution to have his guilty plea accepted by the court."[607]

RATIFICATION OF THE PLEA—PRE-SENTENCING HEARING

Plea negotiations are subject to the approval of the trial court. Unless there has been a sentencing conference, judges generally tell the defendant as they take defendant's guilty plea that the sentencing judge is not required to follow the negotiations between the defendant and prosecutor. That said, judges do tend to defer to counsel and the sentencing recommendations. Why? Judge will have very little information about the events that resulted in the criminal charges and, apart from making sure there is a factual basis for the plea, will not know appropriate probationary conditions. If the court is unwilling to approve the plea bargain, the defendant must choose between attempting to withdraw his or her plea (an uphill battle) or accepting the plea bargain knowing that the judge may modify it.

Defense attorneys may wish to have greater assurances that the judge will follow the deal and will ask the court to ratify the plea and sentence prior to the defendant's entering his or her

---

[606] See *Brady*, 387 U.S. at 748.
[607] 400 U.S. 25, (1970), footnote 11.

guilty plea. If the judge ratifies the negotiated plea, but is later unwilling to follow the terms of the deal, the defendant is entitled to withdraw his or her plea. Similarly, if one judge is unwilling to follow the terms of a negotiated deal ratified by another judge, then the defendant may withdraw the plea or be sentenced by the judge who ratified the deal in the first place.

In some jurisdictions, judges participate directly in the plea-bargaining discussion in sentencing conferences. The advantage of sentencing conferences is that the judge can guide the parties to the equitable and expeditious resolution of the case. Additionally, defendants may have difficulty coming to terms with what is likely to happen to them after conviction. Hearing from a judge (rather than one's own attorney) what the likely sentence would be given the facts of the case may be a "wake up" call to the defendant who is overly optimistic about his or her chances at trial. On the other hand, some courts disfavor the participation of the trial judge in plea-bargaining discussions on the basis that the power and position of the judge may improperly influence the defendant to enter a guilty plea.

WITHDRAWING A PLEA

A defendant may withdraw a guilty plea prior to a judge's acceptance of the plea. Once a plea is accepted, however, the federal courts and most state courts provide that a defendant may withdraw a guilty plea prior to sentencing only if there is a fair and just reason. Judges are even more reluctant to allow the defendant to withdraw his or her plea after sentencing because this undermines the integrity of a defendant's decision to plead guilty.[608] In *Lee v. United States*, 582 U.S. ___ (2017), Lee moved to have his conviction vacated on the basis that his attorney provided ineffective assistance of counsel when he assured him that he was not eligible for mandatory deportation if he were to plea to the charge. In fact, he was as the crime for what he plead guilty to turned out to be considered an aggravated felony. The primary concern that Lee had expressed throughout the negotiations concerned deportation. The Court held that Lee demonstrated that he was prejudiced by his counsel's erroneous advice (even though the state had a "slam dunk" case if it went to trial.) The Court had to decide the standard to apply in assessing ineffective assistance of counsel in the context of a plea rather than trial. The court stated,

> When a defendant claims that his counsel's deficient performance deprived him of a trial by causing him to accept a plea, the defendant can show prejudice by demonstrating a reasonable probability that, but for counsel's errors, he would not have plead guilty and would have insisted on going to trial."

> Justice Roberts, rebuffed the state's arguments that it would have been irrational for Lee to insist on trial rather than accept the deal and risk a much lengthier sentence, stating, "Unlike the Government, we cannot say that it would be irrational for someone in Lee's position to risk additional prison time in exchange for holding on to some chance of avoiding deportation. "

In *Kernan v. Cuero*, 583 U.S. ___ (2017), the defendant pled guilty based on plea negotiations with the state. The state had incorrectly calculated defendant's prior criminal history (which subjected him to a 25-year mandatory minimum sentence rather than the 14 years it had agreed to.) At the sentencing hearing, the mistake was discovered, and the judge allowed defendant to withdraw his plea before sentencing. Instead of withdrawing his plea and demanding a trial, the defendant wanted to force the state to be bound by the 14-year agreement (even though his criminal history didn't' warrant it). He appealed his 25-year sentence, arguing

---

[608] See *Hyde. v United States*, 520 U.S. 670, 677 (1997).

that the state was bound and he was entitled to "specific performance." (requiring the state to honor the deal as agreed to). The Court filed a per curium opinion (unsigned opinion) holding there was no established federal law that, under the circumstances, required or allowed the remedy of specific performance.

DIVERSIONS AND CONDITIONAL DISCHARGES

State statutes may allow first-time offenders the option to informally resolve his or her case by entering a pretrial/pre-sentence agreement with the state.[609] Since these agreements allow the case to be diverted from the normal flow of criminal process, they are referred to as "diversions," "pre-sentence contracts", or "conditional discharges." Diversions for first time drunken driving are very common. A defendant charged with driving under the influence of intoxicants enters and agreement to complete treatment, pay fines, and attend classes. After successful completion of all the diversion contract's requirements, the case is dismissed (defendant's driving record will reflect that a diversion was completed to prevent the defendant from diverting over and over). If the defendant fails to complete the terms of the diversion agreement, the diversion is terminated (sometimes this is after a due process hearing resembling a probation violation hearing), and the defendant is brought back to court for sentencing. In some states, the defendant is not required to enter a guilty plea prior to "doing a diversion." If the defendant has not entered a plea, then it is possible that he or she can demand a trial after unsuccessfully attempting to complete the diversion.

Although drunk-driving cases are the most common forms of statutory diversions, other statutes allow for diversions for specific crimes (for example, those do not result in physical injury to a victim). These diversions allow the district attorney to reach an agreement with the defendant that if the defendant (usually a first-time offender) agrees to complete specific terms (for example, community service, attend AA/NA, go to classes, pay a fine, etc.) then, at the end of the diversionary period, the case will be dismissed and no conviction will appear on the defendant's record. Similar to the drunk-driving diversion, if the defendant fails to complete the terms, then the defendant is sentenced on the underlying charges.

PRETRIAL MOTIONS

Sometimes defendants file pretrial motions to get the case derailed, to discover what evidence the state has, to narrow the scope of evidence that can be presented at trial, to change the location of the trial, to force the case to be joined or severed, and/or to get pretrial rulings on whether the privileges exist. Although not an exhaustive list, many of the pretrial motions are discussed below.

AID AND ASSIST/COMPETENCY MOTION

Occasionally, it becomes apparent early on in a prosecution that the defendant is mentally disturbed and may not fully comprehend what is happening in court or during confinement. He or she may not be able to understand the arraignment process, what the state is claiming, or why he or she is being confined. In such circumstances, the defendant may need to have an attorney request the judge order that the defendant be evaluated to determine whether he or she is competent to stand trial and able to assist in his or her own defense.

The critical inquiry in a competency determination revolves around the defendant's current mental state, not his or her mental state when the crime was committed. The court must

---

[609] Diversions are becoming highly regulated, and it may no longer accurate to describe these as informal resolutions.

determine--with the assistance of defense counsel and mental health professionals--if the defendant understands the process well enough so as to be able to assist in his or her own defense. In federal cases the trial judge must determine whether the defendant has a rational and factual understanding of the pending proceedings and the ability to consult with his or her lawyer. State courts use varying standards to determine whether the accused is competent to stand trial. The burden of proving that defendant in unable to aid and assist and is therefore incompetent to stand trial rests with the defendant and the standard of proof is preponderance of the evidence. Generally, when an offender lacks capacity this is readily apparent to members of the courtroom work group and prosecutors may tend to stipulate to incompetency so long as proper documentation by mental health workers is filed. [610]

DISCOVERY MOTIONS

Discovery rules cover the exchange of information about the case between the state and the defense prior to trial. The requirement that the party's share information is based on the desire to avoid "trial by surprise." Discovery rules also facilitate the efficient resolution of cases (for example, if Bob knows the state will call fifteen eyewitnesses, who can accurately and positively identify him and will say that they saw him rob a bank, then Bob may be less likely to insist on going to trial and will be more inclined to accept plea offer from the state.) Statutes or court rules govern the requirements of discovery--there is no general constitutional duty on the part of the prosecutor to disclose material evidence to the defense.[611]

What has to be shared in discovery varies tremendously from state to state. Although the government generally has a larger discovery obligation, the defense must also produce certain information. The defense must, for example, disclose to the prosecution the names and addresses of witnesses it plans to call during the trial. The types of pretrial disclosure covered by a motion for discovery include:

- Defendant's statements. Nearly all states and the federal government require the prosecution to give the defense copies of prior recorded statements by the defendant if requested.
- Scientific reports. Federal prosecutors and most states prosecutors are required to turn over reports of medical and physical examinations and scientific tests made for the prosecution.
- Documents and tangible evidence. Generally, the defendant will have the right to inspect these.
- Witness lists. Many jurisdictions require the prosecution give the defense a list of the witnesses it intends to call at trial; some states require the disclosure of prior written and recorded statements of these witnesses.
- Police reports. Most jurisdictions do not require the prosecution to turn over police report viewing these as "work product," however, many prosecutors disclose official police reports but do not make copies of the police officer's notes.

The government is also entitled to receive information from the defense, but the types of information are much narrower. For example, defense must give the state notice that it intends to raise an affirmative defense (such as alibi or insanity), a list of witnesses it intends to call, and, in some states, a copy of witness statements.

---

[610] The clear and convincing standard was found to violate the Due Process Clause in *Cooper v. Oklahoma*, 517 U.S. 348 (1996).
[611] But see, *Brady v. Maryland*, 373 U.S. 83 (1963), and its progeny where the Court found that withholding information material and favorable to the defendant violates the Due Process Clause.

Failure to give discovery as required by law (or an order of the court in response to a motion to compel discovery) can result in dismissal of the case (very rare), continuances (more frequent), or simply a short postponement of the proceeding to allow the side to review the discovery given (very frequent). Violations of discovery rules can also result in a pretrial *Brady* motion (see below) and grounds to attack the conviction if the violation is discovered after the trial.

THE *BRADY* RULE [612]

In the seminal case of *Brady v. Maryland*, 373 U.S. 83 (1963), the defendant, Brady admitted at his trial to participating in a murder, but claimed that his companion, Bobbit, did the actual killing. He asked the jury to spare his life since he was not the actual killer, but the jury convicted him and voted in favor of the death penalty. Prior to trial, Brady's lawyer had requested that the prosecutor allow him to examine Bobbit's extrajudicial statements. The prosecutor showed these to Brady's lawyer but withheld Bobbit's statement in which he admitting doing the actual killing. Brady did not find out about this statement until after he had been tried and sentenced to death. The Court reversed Brady's conviction saying, "the suppression by the prosecution of evidence favorable to the accused upon request violates due process where the evidence is material either to guilt or to punishment, irrespective of good faith or bad faith of the prosecution."[613]

Brady held that the Due Process Clause requires prosecutors to disclose exonerating evidence within their possession that is relevant to innocence, guilt, or sentence of the accused. The purpose of the *Brady* rule is to prevent miscarriages of justice by requiring the disclosure of evidence that may prevent the conviction of an innocent individual or may result in a reduction of the defendant's sentence. Case law suggests that any impeachment evidence is subject to the *Brady* disclosure requirement. So, if the state has received inconsistent statements from its witnesses, even ones which do not necessarily "hurt" the defendant and which the state does not believe are exonerating, it must disclose those statements to the defense.

The *Brady* rule is not without limits. If the prosecution fails to turn over *Brady* material and the violation is not determined until after trial, the defendant will get a new trial—but only if the non-disclosure is found to have been "material." This means that there is a reasonable probability that had the disclosure been made, the result of the proceeding would have been different. Although the *Brady* case itself arose on direct appeal, frequently the defendant does not discover the failure of the state to disclose evidence until after the time period for filing an appeal has lapsed, and therefore, defendants must raise discovery issues as a collateral attack after the trial.

In *Turner v. United States*, 582 U.S. ___ (2017) the Court determined that though the state withheld evidence of witnesses who had seen a man, ((not the defendant), run into an alley after the murder and stop near where the victim's body was found, and other evidence which intended to impeach prosecution witnesses, it was not material evidence. The Court quoted from earlier decisions and stated, that

> [E]vidence is 'material' . . . when there is a reasonable probability that, had the evidence been disclosed, the result of the proceeding would have been different ... A reasonable probability of a different result is one in which the suppressed evidence 'undermines the outcome of the trial') . . . [The Court] "evaluates the withheld evidence in the context of the entire record. (Citations omitted.)

---

[612] *Brady v. Maryland*, 373 U.S. 83 (1963).
[613] Id.

Violations of the *Brady* rule can be costly to the state. For example, in March 2021, Fred Stees, who had been wrongfully convicted for a 1995 Nevada murder he did not commit and for which the state withheld evidence (including evidence that confirmed he was in a different state at the time the murder was committed), was awarded nearly 1.4 million dollars ($75,000 for each year he spent in prison and a certificate of exoneration.[614]

MOTIONS TO SUPPRESS — THE EXCLUSIONARY RULE

Defendants' motions to suppress evidence allege that police obtained evidence illegally because the search or seizure were "bad," the confession was involuntary or not given with warnings, or the pretrial identification violated due process standards. The Constitution does not explicitly require suppression for violations, but the Court has, in a series of cases, created exclusion as a remedy for many constitutional violations.

EXCLUSIONARY RULE AND THE FOURTH AMENDMENT

The Fourth Amendment protects against unreasonable searches and seizures done by federal law enforcement officers enforcing federal criminal law. It is silent on what should happen when its protections are violated. Between 1791 and 1914 very few federal cases involving the Fourth Amendment reached the Court due to the limited number of federal crimes.

The Court first suppressed evidence obtained illegally by federal officers in *Boyd v. United States*, 116 U.S. 616 (1886). [615] The Court found that police had violated the Fourth and Fifth Amendments. The Court ordered evidence excluded, but it did not actually create an "exclusionary rule." However, in *Weeks v. United States,* 232 U.S. 383 (1914), the Court first required the exclusion of evidence for any violation of defendants' rights in federal prosecutions. *Silverthorne Lumber v. United States,* 251 U.S. 385 (1920), extended the exclusion remedy to derivative evidence.

EXTENSIONS OF THE EXCLUSIONARY RULE--DERIVATIVE EVIDENCE RULE

Derivative evidence is evidence that "derives from" some other evidence obtained illegally by the police. The Court considers derivative evidence to be tainted and "fruit of the poisonous tree." *Silverthorne Lumber* involved federal officials illegally obtaining documents from the defendant and making copies of those documents. Although the government returned the originals, agents retained the copies and wanted to use them at trial against the defendant. The Court held that the copies were fruit of the initial illegal search and could not be used in the defendant's trial.

The Court later explored the limits of the derivative evidence doctrine, also known as the fruit of the poisonous tree doctrine, in *Wong Sun v. United States,* 371 U.S. 471 (1963). The Court found a "purged (or "dissipated") taint exception" to the derivative evidence rule in a case with a complicated set of facts: federal narcotics agents, acting on a tip, broke into Toy's apartment and handcuffed him. The entry was illegal because it was not supported by probable cause. During the police entry, Toy made statements implicating Yee of selling narcotics. The police then went to Yee's home. Yee gave the police some heroin and stated he had been sold the drugs by Toy and Wong Sun. The police then arrested Wong Sun. Wong Sun and Toy were arraigned on the drug charges and released on their own recognizance. Several days later, Wong Sun voluntarily went back to the offices of the Bureau of Narcotics. Police warned him of his right to remain silent and to have an attorney, but he nevertheless confessed.

---

[614] See https://www.propublica.org/article/fred-stees-wrongfully-convicted.
[615] *Boyd* didn't involve a search and seizure. The defendant challenged a law ordering him to turn over an invoice on cases of imported glass to determine whether customs taxes had been paid.

The Court held that Toy's statements were evidence derived from the illegal home entry, and the prosecution could not use them at trial. The Court also held that the government could not use evidence of the drugs seized from Yee since they were the direct result of Toy's statement. The Court, however found that the heroin was admissible against Wong Sun, even though its seizure had been the direct product of the illegal entry into Toy's house since Wong Sun lacked *standing* (discussed below) to complain of the illegality at Toy's house. The Court further held that even though police illegally arrested Wong Sun's (his arrest derived from Toy's tainted statements) his confession was, nevertheless, admissible because he had been out of custody on release for several days and the connection between his illegal arrest and his statements several days later had "become so attenuated as to dissipate the taint."

EXTENSIONS OF THE EXCLUSIONARY RULE--APPLYING IT TO STATES

In *Wolf v. Colorado,* 338 U.S. 25 (1949), the Court held that state law enforcement officers violated a citizens' rights to due process of law in violation of the Fourteenth Amendment when they conduct illegal searches and seizures. However, the Court did not initially extend the exclusionary rule to the states and, instead, allowed the state to use other remedies for such violations. It stated, "the practice the exclusion of evidence may be an effective way of deterring unreasonable searches, [but] it is not for this Court to condemn as falling below the minimal standards assured by the Due Process Clause a State's reliance upon other methods which, if consistently enforced would be equally effective."

By 1961 the Court recognized that an increasing number of states had adopted the exclusionary rule after they determined that other remedies were ineffective in deterring unreasonable searches and seizures. In *Mapp v. Ohio,* 367 U.S. 643, 646 (1961), the Court held that the Fourth Amendment right of privacy "is enforceable against [the states] by the same sanction of exclusion as is used against the Federal Government. Were it otherwise then . . . the assurance against unreasonable searches . . . and seizures would be a 'form of words'."

INDEPENDENT DISCOVERY, INEVITABLE DISCOVERY, AND GOOD FAITH

The Court has carved out several exceptions to the exclusionary rule in a series of cases. In *New York v. Quarles,* 467 U.S. 649 (1984), the Court recognized a public safety exception to *Miranda* and the exclusionary rule. *Quarles* was discussed in Chapter Eight and is the case where police cornered Quarles, a suspected rapist, in a grocery store, and asked "where's the gun." The Court held that Quarles' response should not be excluded even though police failed to warn him of his *Miranda* rights while he was "in custody" and "interrogated" as the Court has defined those terms. The Court cautioned that the public safety exception should be narrowly construed.

In *Nix v. Williams,* 467 U.S. 431 (1984), the court created an inevitable discovery exception to the rule. Williams kidnapped and murdered a ten-year-old girl in Des Moines, Iowa. Police *Mirandized* Williams who invoked his right to counsel. Police transported Williams from Davenport to Des Moines and during the trip made comments about needing to find the girl's body so her family could give her a Christian burial. Williams responded by making incriminating statements that ultimately led police to where he had disposed of the body. Although police violated *Miranda,* the Court held that the victim's body and related derivative evidence were admissible, reasoning that police would not have stopped searching until they located the body and would have inevitably discovered the evidence.

In *Murray v. United States,* 487 U.S. 533 (1988), the court enunciated an independent discovery exception. In this case federal agents illegally entered a warehouse without a warrant and saw bales of marijuana. They left the warehouse and continued surveillance of the defendant. They eventually obtained enough evidence to seek a warrant, and in the warrant application they did not mention anything they had seen during their illegal entry into the warehouse. The Court did not exclude the evidence seized with the warrant, finding that the exclusionary rule should not apply to evidence "initially discovered during, or as a consequence of, an unlawful search, but later obtained independently from activities untainted by the initial illegality."

In *United States v. Leon*, 468 U.S. 897 (1984), the Court declared that the primary purpose of the exclusionary rule is to deter police misconduct. It thereby created a good faith exception to the rule. The Court has found that the good faith exception also applies to evidence seized by police in a search incident to defendant's arrest after court personnel failed to clear an arrest warrant from the computer system[616]. According to the Court, the good faith exception enunciated in *Leon* also extended evidence discovered in a search incident to defendant's arrest after police negligently failed to clear a warrant from the system.[617] Chief Justice Roberts wrote,

To trigger the exclusionary rule, police conduct must be sufficiently deliberate that exclusion can meaningfully deter it, and sufficiently culpable that such deterrence is worth the price paid by the justice system. As laid out in our cases, the exclusionary rule serves to deter deliberate, reckless, or grossly negligent conduct, or in some circumstances recurring or systemic negligence. The error in this case does not rise to that level.[618]

STANDING

Only individuals who have personally suffered a violation of his or her own constitutional right may assert the exclusionary rule's protections. Individuals must have "standing" to move to suppress evidence. They cannot assert the remedy to bar evidence obtained through the violation of a right of some third party. For example, assume police illegally search Cat's home and discovery evidence that Pat committed a crime. Pat would not be able to successfully suppress the evidence because her own personal rights (to privacy) were not violated by the search of Cat's home.

The Court discussed standing in the 2020 case, *Carney v. Adams*, 592 U.S. _____ (2021). James Adams, a lawyer in Delaware, challenged a Delaware requirement that judgeship positions on certain courts could only be filled by Republican or Democrat judges. The state has a policy of balancing Republican and Democrat judges so that neither will have a clear majority. Adams himself had previously been a Democrat but, after retiring and reading a law review article about the Delaware policy, he registered as "unaffiliated," and filed a lawsuit, arguing that he wanted to apply for a judgeship but was unable to do so. The Court held unanimously that, since Adams was not actually "able and ready" to apply for a position, and he was not able to show "injury in fact" that was "concrete and particularized" and "actual or imminent," he did not have standing to raise the complaint. The opinion by Justice Breyer noted that Adams' suit suggested it was more of an "abstract, generalized grievance, not an actual desire to become a judge," and that there was no evidence that Adams had applied for any of numerous vacancies previously, when he was a registered Democrat.

---

[616] *Arizona v. Evans*, 514 U.S. 1 (1995). Court reasoned that since the purpose of the exclusionary rule was to deter police misconduct, that it should not apply to misconduct by court personnel.
[617] *Herring v. United States*, 555 U.S. 535 (2009)
[618] *Id.* at ____ (2009).

DEMURRERS

Defendants may challenge the constitutionality of the charges filed against them. This challenge is known as a "demurrer." A demurrer challenges the constitutionality of the statutory basis of the charge--for example, by claiming it violates the ex post facto prohibition, or the statute is impermissibly vague or overly broad. Defendants must generally file demurrers within a very short time period (ten days, for example) of their arraignment on the charges.[619] Because they challenge the constitutionality of a law, they are frequently filed right after legislators pass new laws that have yet to be reviewed and decided by the appellate courts.

SEVERANCE AND JOINDER

Prosecutors occasionally file charges in one information or indictment that could conceivably be charged separately. The state may believe that it is more efficient or advantageous to prosecute the offenses together. Procedural rules govern whether charges should be tried together (joinder) or separated (severance). Most state rules of criminal procedure follow the federal rule on joinder of charges. It states,

> The indictment or information may charge a defendant in separate counts with two or more offenses if the offenses charged — whether felonies or misdemeanors or both — are of the same or similar character, or are based on the same act or transaction, or are connected with or constitute parts of a common scheme or plan.[620]

Prosecutors sometimes wish to try co-defendants together in one trial. Federal rule of Criminal Procedure Rule 8 (b) authorizes joinder of two or more defendants in the same indictment "if they are alleged to have participated in the same act or transaction or the same series of acts or transactions constituting an offense or offenses."[621] The prosecution has a great deal of latitude in joining charges and defendants, which is why motions to join or sever are primarily filed by defendants. Defendants seeking severance bear the burden of showing that a joint trial would be so unfairly prejudicial that it would result in a miscarriage of justice.

Trial judges have considerable discretion when deciding to grant or deny a motion to join or sever. Constitutional considerations, such as the right to confrontation, will guide the court in these decisions, but in certain situations, severance is mandatory. For example, if the defendant wants to testify in one case but not in others, the judge should sever the cases. Similarly, the judge should separate the charges when not doing so would prejudice the defendant[622]--for example, if one charge requires proof that the defendant is a felon (for example, felon in possession of a weapon) and the other charge does not (for example, robbery). Evidence of a prior felony conviction is not relevant to the charge of robbery and will likely prejudice the jury against the defendant, but it is an element of the felon in possession charge that the state must prove. Thus, the judge may sever the two charges upon defendant's motion for severance.

---

[619] Recall that arraignment is a critical stage in the process requiring the assistance of counsel and that one common current practice is the use of "stand by" attorneys. Because demurrers need to be filed within days of the arraignment, it is important for attorneys to quickly become familiar with their new client, their charges, and possible defenses.

[620] Federal Rule of Criminal Procedure, Rule 8.

[621] Rule 8(b) also provides that "defendants may be charged in one or more counts together or separately. all defendants need not be charged in each count. "

[622] Rule 14(a) states that the court may grant a severance if the defendant or the government is prejudiced by a joinder of the offenses or of defendants.

When it comes to severing the cases of multiple defendants, the Court will grant a motion of severance if the prosecution intends to use one co-defendant's statements against another. Also, the Court is likely to sever the cases when defendants pursue inconsistent defenses or when their interests are antagonistic. Severance is required when one defendant's confession implicates another, non-testifying codefendant. [623]

CHANGE OF VENUE

Before trial, defendants may file motions for a change of venue. "Venue" describes the location of the trial. Generally, trials are held where the crimes occurred. A defendant may waive the right to proper venue[624] by issuing an express statement consenting to be tried in a judicial district having no connections to the crime. Federal and state statutes authorize trial courts to order case be moved from the original district to another district. Few states allow the government to file change of venue motion, but all states and the federal government allow the defendant to move for a venue change. Generally, policy considerations, such as the desire for a fair trial and a convenient forum, drive a change of venue.

Skilling v. United States, 561 U.S. 358 (2010), examined the trial court's refusal to allow the motion to change venue filed by CEO of Enron, Jeffery Skilling, and whether the venue resulted in an unfair trial due to potential juror bias based upon their familiarity with the case. The Court noted that a change of venue is required where the totality of the circumstances indicates that jurors are so influenced by pretrial publicity that they are not able to act in an impartial fashion and to decide the case based on the evidence to be presented in court. The factors considered by the court include:

- Whether there is a persistent and widespread publicity regarding the case immediately prior to the trial and during the selection of the jury.
- Whether the publicity describes the crime in detail and assumes the defendant's guilt.
- Whether a significant percentage of the community is exposed to the publicity.
- Whether a high percentage of the jury pool is aware of the case and possesses an opinion that the defendant is guilty.

In *Skilling*, the Court upheld the trial court's denial of the change of venue request.

OTHER PRETRIAL MOTIONS: MOTION TO DISMISS

Chapter Six discussed the procedural defenses of double jeopardy, speedy trial, statute of limitations, entrapment, and immunity. These pretrial motions could just as easily have been included in this chapter. Defendants file motions to dismiss their cases based upon these procedural defenses. Judges order dismissals either "with prejudice" (meaning the state cannot refile the charges) or "without prejudice" (meaning the state can refile the charges).

EXTRADITION

If a defendant commits a crime in one state and flees to another, the state where the crime was committed (known as the demanding state) may request that the state harboring the criminal (known as the asylum state) send him or her back to face charges. The Constitution specifically mentions the process of extradition in Article IV, Section 2. It provides,

> A person charged in any state with treason, felony or any other crime, who shall
> flee from Justice, and be found in another state, shall on demand of the executive

---

[623] *See, Bruton v. United States,* 391 U.S. 123 (1968).
[624] Venue is not said to be a fundamental right, and thus, can be waived.

Authority of the State from which he fled, be delivered, to be removed to the State having Jurisdiction of the Crime.

Most states have adopted the Uniform Criminal Extradition Law, enacted by U.S. Congress, which established procedural rules for handling interstate extradition. The governor of the demanding state issues a requisition warrant seeking return of the fugitive. This warrant is presented to the governor of the asylum state where the fugitive is currently located. The governor of the asylum state issues a warrant of arrest. The fugitive has the opportunity to contest the extradition in a court of law in the asylum state—generally challenging whether he or she is the person being sought.

Treaties regulate extradition between nations. Treaties generally limit international extradition to crimes considered serious in both nations and for which the penalty for the person extradited will not be disproportionate to the crime. Very few nations utilize the death penalty, and other nations frequently refuse to extradite an individual to the United States unless the state or federal government assures the other nation that the death penalty will not be sought.

Extraditions can be costly. Once the extradition process has taken its course and the asylum state/nation decides they have and will return the offender, the demand state must pay to go get him or her back. Recent budgetary constraints may force a jurisdiction to consider just how badly they want the offender back and how far they are willing to go (in miles) in order to gain custody of the offender if he or she should flee the jurisdiction. In requesting an arrest warrant for an offender, the prosecutor may indicate a zone on the warrant for which they are willing to send officers to go get a suspect. Another frustration for the demand state is arriving with officers in the asylum state to pick up the fugitive and bring him or her back, only to discover the fugitive has been released from custody (on bail, on a conditional release, or due to overcrowding) and has fled. In situations where the fugitive presents high risk of danger or has been particularly elusive, the state prosecutors communicate with each other to ensure that the asylum state recognizes the importance of not releasing the offender before the authorities from the demand state get there.

WRAP UP

At the accusatory stage of the criminal justice process, focus shifts from police and their investigations (although police may continue the investigation of crimes after charges are filed) to the courts (the attorneys and courtroom work group). Judges decide whether probable cause exists to justify the detention of individuals arrested without a warrant--generally within 48 hours. In-custody defendants make their initial appearances and are arraigned within a few days of arrest, but frequently police issue citations to defendants telling them when to appear in court and those suspects never see the jail. Prosecutors make charging decisions based upon police reports received in their offices daily. Misdemeanor charges are generally filed on a complaint or information, and the defendant can be arraigned immediately on those charges as soon as they are filed. When charging felonies prosecutors will either utilize a preliminary hearing or a grand jury--depending on state law in order to get the case into the felony courts. Occasionally, the defendant will waive the preliminary hearing or presentment of the case to the grand jury. Once the charges are filed in the felony court, the court will "arraign" the defendant on the charges. At arraignments, the court informs the defendant of the charges filed and will determine whether the accused will be released or detained pending the trial. Defense attorneys meet with their clients early on, file any appropriate demurrers, review police reports and discovery, file motions to suppress evidence, move to change venue, and review with their clients the prosecutor's plea offer. Most defendants decide to enter a guilty or no contest plea and forego their constitutional right to have a trial.

SOME THINGS TO EXPLORE OR THINK ABOUT

> ➤ What are the statutory discovery requirements in your state? What sanctions should prosecutors face when they intentionally violate their obligations under discovery statutes and under the *Brady* rule? Are there any cases you are familiar with in which a person spent considerable amount of time in custody because the prosecutors failed to turn over exculpatory evidence as required by *Brady*?
>
> ➤ What type of bail/release system is used in your state?
>
> ➤ Investigate whether your state uses grand jury or preliminary hearings and what those procedures look like in your state. What benefits are there for using a grand jury? A preliminary hearing? Do you think grand jury service benefits grand jurors?
>
> ➤ Research the statutory time frames used in your state for first appearances/arraignments/setting of bail.
>
> ➤ Consider the case of Scott Peterson, back in the news in Spring 2021. (See, https://www.kron4.com/news/california/scott-peterson-trial/scott-peterson-prepares-for-new-trial-in-2021/). His defense team was able to secure a change of venue for his trial for the murder of his wife, Laci Person, and their unborn child. (See, https://www.nbcnews.com/id/wbna3906362). His defense team successfully moved to change venue for his original sentencing as well. (See, https:www.sfgate.com/bayarea/article/THE PETERSON-TRIAL-High-court-to-rule-on-venue-2669592.php). Nonetheless, he was sentenced to death.

TERMINOLOGY

- _Alford_ plea
- aid and assist hearing/competency hearing
- arraignment
- asylum state
- bail
- bail bondsmen
- bench warrant
- "bind the defendant over"
- bond
- bounty hunter
- _Brady_ rule
- charge bargain
- conditional discharge
- conditional release
- demanding state
- demurrer
- derivative evidence
- discovery
- diversion
- exclusionary rule
- extradition
- Federal Bail Reform Act
- first appearance (initial appearance)
- fruit of the poisonous tree
- fugitive warrant
- good faith exception
- guilty plea
- grant jury
- independent discovery exception
- indictment
- inevitable discovery exception
- information
- joinder
- no contest/_nolo contendre_ plea
- petit jury
- plea bargaining
- plea ratification
- preliminary hearing
- preventive detention
- probable cause hearing
- probable cause statement requisition warrant
- public safety exception
- purging the grand jury
- release on own recognizance release ("OR")
- security bond
- security release
- sentence bargain
- sentencing conference
- severance
- standing
- _subpoena_
- _subpoena ducus tecum_
- true bill
- venue
- waiver of presentment
- work product

Chapter Ten: The Adjudicatory Phase — The Trial Process

OVERVIEW AND LEARNING OBJECTIVES

The role of the trial in the criminal justice process in the United States is very overrated. Television and movies show compelling courtroom drama. Fictional and non-fictional stories highlighting the criminal trial abound. But, in reality, a full adversarial trial resolves very few of the cases that flow through the criminal justice system. Still, trials are important, and courts across the country conduct hundreds of thousands of trials each year--most lasting less than a full day.

> More than 90 percent of felony charges and even a higher percentage of misdemeanor cases are disposed of before trial. Nevertheless, the criminal trial is the centerpiece of the criminal justice system for several reasons. First, trials are generally held before juries drawn from the community. Second, trials are the most visible aspect of the justice system and often attract widespread media coverage. Finally, cases disposed of by trial often have an important impact on the administration of justice.[625]

After reading this chapter, you should be able to answer the following questions about the trial process.

- ➤ What is the role of the judge, jury, prosecutor, defense attorney, defendant and victim at trial?
- ➤ Where are the rules of evidence found and what purpose do they serve?
- ➤ How do the rules of evidence influence what happens at trial?
- ➤ What is the process by which evidence is admitted or excluded from trial?
- ➤ What is a "privilege" and what are the most common privileges?
- ➤ Why is hearsay evidence generally not admitted in criminal trials? What are the most common exceptions to the hearsay rule?
- ➤ How does the right to confrontation limit the admissibility of evidence?
- ➤ What is the order of the stages of trial?
- ➤ How are jury members selected to be on a jury? What constitutional rights surround jury selection?
- ➤ What rights are essential to the right to have a fair trial?
- ➤ What are the substitutes for formally presenting evidence?
- ➤ What special rules are there for introducing scientific evidence?
- ➤ What special rules are there for expert witnesses?
- ➤ What special rules are there for death penalty cases?

ORDER OF THE AMERICAN CRIMINAL TRIAL

Kerper succinctly summarized the stages in the American trial:

---

[625] Scheb, _supra_ at 600.

The initial step in the trial process ordinarily is the selection of the jury (or the waiver of the jury if the case is to be tried to the judge alone). The court then gives the jury preliminary instructions[626] describing the trial procedure and advising them that they should not discuss the case until they are ready to deliberate. The court also will read to the jury the charge as stated in the information or indictment. ... The prosecution will then make an opening statement describing in general what the state intends to prove. The defense counsel may respond immediately with the defense's opening statement, or that statement may be postponed until the defense is ready to present its evidence. The opening statements are not evidence. They serve only to assist the jury in understanding the points that the prosecution and defense hope to establish at trial. Following the opening statements, the prosecution will present witnesses, who may be cross-examined by the defense counsel. The defense then will present its own witnesses, if it so desires. Those witnesses may be cross-examined by the prosecutor. The defendant may testify as a defense witness, but he need not do so. After the defense has presented its evidence, the prosecution may respond with additional witnesses (called rebuttal witnesses) to contradict the defense's case. The defense in turn may present its own rebuttal witnesses to contradict the prosecution's rebuttal. Ordinarily this would end the presentation of evidence. The order of the next few steps will vary from state to state. In most, the prosecution and defense will make their closing statements and the judge will then instruct the jury as to the law. In some states, the instructions will be given before the closing statements are made. In their closing statements, each side will present its own view of the evidence. Ordinarily, the prosecution will make an initial closing statement, the defense will respond, and then the prosecution may respond to the defense. The prosecution is given the final word because it bears the burden of proving the case beyond a reasonable doubt. [627]

At the end of the state's case, and when prosecutors are finished presenting all the evidence it wants the jury to consider, it will "rest." At this point, defendants frequently, but not always, move for a "directed verdict." This defense motion, made outside the jury's presence, challenges the sufficiency of the prosecution's case and asserts that there is no way that any reasonable jury could find the defendant guilty beyond a reasonable doubt based on the facts the state just presented. The prosecutor will obviously object to this motion and will argue to the court that various pieces of evidence, if believed, would convince a reasonable jury of defendant's guilt. Because a directed verdict is an extraordinary measure that takes the decision about defendant's guilt out of the jurors' hands and puts it into the judge's hands, the judge must consider the evidence in the "light most favorite to the state." If the judge does agree that there is simply too little evidence, he or she will grant the defendant's motion and direct a verdict of not guilty. On the rare occasion where this motion is granted, the judge reconvenes the jury in the courtroom and, perhaps without any explanation, dismisses them from further service.

THE JURY

The first thing that happens in a criminal jury trial is that a jury is selected. There are many aspects to the American system of jury trials.

---

[626] *See, e.g.*, Oregon Uniform Criminal Jury Instruction, 103.
[627] Kerper, *supra* at 306-307.

CONSTITUTIONAL RIGHT TO JURY TRIAL

The Sixth Amendment guarantees the accused in a criminal trial the right to an impartial jury. In *Duncan v. Louisiana*, 391 U.S. 145 (1968), the Court held that trial by jury is fundamental to the American scheme of justice and thus required by the Due Process Clause of the Fourteenth Amendment in state trials. The question unresolved by *Duncan*, is whether states had to provide a jury trial for even minor crimes. Two years after *Duncan*, in *Baldwin v. New York*, 399 U.S. 66 (1970), the Court held that a jury trial is not required for trials of petty crimes and held that trials for crimes with penalties of imprisonment of six months or less did not require a jury. The Court held that a crime was still a petty crime (and thus the state did not need to provide a jury) when a crime was punishable by six months in jail even when it carried additional penalties such as a minimum jail stay or community service. See, *Blanton v. City of North Las Vegas*, 489 U.S. 538 (1989). According to the Court (*McKeiver v. Pennsylvania*, 403 U.S. 528 (1971)) the state need not provide a jury trial in a juvenile delinquency proceeding. Because states are always free to provide more constitutional rights/protections than are required by the federal constitution, many state's constitutions or statutes require states provide jury trials for any charges which could result in incarceration.

JURY UNANIMITY

Almost fifty years ago the Court allowed for a non-unanimous, 10-2 jury verdict in *Apadoca v. Oregon*, 406 U.S. 404 (1972) and a 9-3 verdict in *Johnson v. Louisiana*, 406 U.S. 356 (1972). Decided the same day, these decisions involved non-death penalty charges. Despite the Court's holding, only Oregon and Louisiana embraced the Court's opinion and allowed non-unanimous verdicts. The Sixth Amendment right to a jury trial was held to require a unanimous jury verdict in federal trials, and if the Court meant what it stated in the 2010 case of *McDonald v. City of Chicago* about rejecting a two-track approach to constitutional rights, the Court would need to reconsider and overturn *Apodaca* and *Johnson*.[628] Indeed, in the case of *Timbs v. Indiana* (2019) *supra*, the Court again signaled that it did not see "any light of day" between the federal Bill of Rights and state's obligations under the due process clause. The *Timbs* court noted,

> The sole exception (to holding that the Bill of Rights are enforced against the state under the same standard as in the federal government) is our holding that the Sixth Amendment requires jury unanimity in federal, but not state, criminal proceedings. Apodaca v. Oregon, 406 U. S. 404 (1972). As we have explained, that "exception to th[e] general rule . . . was the result of an unusual division among the Justices, . . . "

In April 2020, the Court decided *Ramos v. Louisiana* 590 U.S. ___ (2020), and in a 6-3 complex decision, the Court laid *Apodaca* and *Johnson* to rest. Interestingly, by the time *Ramos* was decided, Louisiana's legislature had already required jury unanimity through a 2018 statute, and the Oregon courts and legislature had already "seen the writing on the wall" and, if the Court, had not so decided were prepared to amended the Oregon constitution to require jury unanimity. One issue argued by counsel in oral arguments before the Supreme Court and left unanswered by *Ramos* was that of reliance and retroactivity—meaning what should be done in those cases in which the defendant had previously been convicted by a non-unanimous jury.

---

[628] In 2010, it appeared that the Court might have been willing to revisit its rulings on jury unanimity, but it ultimately declined to hear review in two cases (one from Oregon and one from Louisiana). Scholars speculated for several years that the Court may be waiting for just the right case to revisit jury unanimity. *Ramos* was the case.

This issue was presented to the Court in its 2020-2021 term in *Edwards v. Vannoy*, 593 U.S.___ (2021). Thedrick Edwards was convicted and sentenced to life in prison for rape and robberies. At the time of his conviction in 2007, Louisiana law allowed for a 10-2 verdict. Edwards was tried by eleven white jurors and one black juror. The black juror voted to acquit, since because the jury did not have to be unanimous, he was convicted regardless. Justice Kavanaugh wrote the opinion for the majority, and noted that since *Ramos* was a new rule, and new rules have not historically been applied retroactively, the unanimity rule did not apply to Edwards. He also noted that Ramos decision was not a watershed rule of criminal procedure. In a dissent authored by Justice Kagan and joined by Justices Sotomayor and Breyer, Kagan noted that the majority was misapplying the "watershed" exception.

PETIT JURY DISTINGUISHED FROM GRAND JURY

Jurisdictions use a variety of approaches deciding who gets to be a juror. Jurors who ultimately are summoned and make up the large jury panel become either grand jurors or petit jurors. When a grand jury is utilized in the jurisdiction, grand jurors decide whether there is sufficient evidence for a case to go forward--they do not serve as trial jurors. Individuals chosen to be part of a trial jury (petit jurors) are chosen for a specific jury panel--called a jury venire. At trial, members of the jury venire are questioned and individuals are selected from the venire to sit on a particular case and deliberate on the defendant's guilt (in a criminal case) or the defendant's liability (in a civil case). Those individuals make up the trial jury.

CHALLENGING JURORS

The process for selecting the trial jury, called a "voir dire," involves questioning members of the jury venire. Some attorneys feel that a case is won or lost by what happens during voir dire. Some judges allow attorneys wide latitude in questioning the jury, and so the attorneys use this time of questioning to educate the jury on their theory of the case or the difficult issues that may arise (under the guise of exploring a juror's possible bias and ability to follow the law). Other judges severely limit the types of questions that the attorneys may ask. Attorneys sometimes push onto the judge the difficult task of asking the highly sensitive questions, claiming that if jurors are to be offended it is better to have them mad at the judge rather than at them. After each side questions potential jurors in the venire, the attorneys excuse the potential jurors through either a "challenge for cause" or a "peremptory challenge."[629]

CHALLENGES FOR CAUSE

A challenge for cause is the mechanism used to excuse potential jurors who have either express bias (prejudice against one side or person) or implied bias (bias assumed because of the relationship of the potential juror to one of the parties or participants in the trial.) Each party has an unlimited number of challenges for cause, and the judge can excuse for cause all potential jurors found to have express or implied bias.

PEREMPTORY CHALLENGES

A peremptory challenge is a mechanism used by attorneys to excuse jurors for whatever reason (for example, the juror's profession, hair style, criminal history) or no reason at all. The party need not demonstrate that the juror has either express or implied bias. As long as the challenge isn't based upon race, gender, or ethnicity, the parties may exercise these discretionary

---

[629] Nationwide, attorneys frequently spend lots of money hiring jury consultants to assist in the decision about who to excuse and who to keep on the jury.

challenges at will. Peremptory challenges are limited in number (generally, each party gets three or six challenges). Because peremptory challenges are made without regard to any particular quality of a juror, they became used as a tool to exclude certain segments of the citizenry from serving as jurors, but the Court has invalidated the improper use of peremptory challenges.[630]

Batson and Equal Protections

In the key case of _Batson v. Kentucky,_ 476 U.S. 79 (1986), the Court held that peremptory challenges may not be used to exclude a potential jury when the sole reason is race. The Court later extended the holding of _Batson_ to ethnicity[631] and gender.[632] The Court limited peremptory challenges based on these suspect classifications on two grounds: first, a party in the suit has the right to have a certain mix of jurors; and second, the Equal Protection Clause's ensures that a person may sit on a jury without regard for race or gender.[633] Through a series of cases since _Batson,_ the Court has established a three-step process by which a party may challenge the improper use of peremptory challenges resulting in a particular racial, ethnic, or gender composition of a jury.[634] First, the challenging party makes out a _prima facia_ case of impermissible exclusion. ("Hey look, that other side improperly excused all the women in the panel.") Second, the side exercising the suspect peremptory challenges must provide a race/gender/ethnicity neutral alternative explanation for why they exercised the challenge. ("No way, we did not excuse those jurors because they were women, we excused them because they scowled at the defendant and also because they said they were suspicious of people with long hair.") Finally, the court must examine the alternative explanation and see if, in fact, the side engaged in purposeful discrimination and the explanation is merely a pretext. ("Well, it appears that the defense team left on several men who similarly scowled and were similarly suspicious of people with long hair, so this appears to be a pretext.")

---

[630] _See, e.g., Strauder v. West Virginia,_ 100 U.S. 303 (1880) (State statute that explicitly excluded African Americans from jury service violated the Equal Protection Clause); _Norris v. Alabama,_ 294 U.S. 587 (1935) (Virtual exclusion of African Americans from grand juries violated the Equal Protections Clause); _Swain v. Alabama,_ 380 U.S. 202 (1965) (Exclusion of a prospective juror because of race violates the defendant's equal protection rights, but violations must be proven by a pattern of exclusions over a number of cases).

[631] _See, Hernandez v. New York,_ 500 U.S. 352 (1991). In _Hernandez_ the Court expanded _Batson_ to include peremptory challenges of Hispanic jurors since this ethnic category was akin to a cognizable racial group for purposes of exclusion from jury service during voir dire.

[632] _See, J.E.B v. Alabama ex rel. T.B.,_ 511 U.S. 127 (1994). _J.E.B._ involved a paternity suit by the state on behalf of T.B., the mother of a minor child. After challenges for cause, only ten of thirty-three jurors were male; the "State then used 9 of its 10 peremptory strikes to remove male jurors; petitioner used all but one of his strikes to remove female jurors. As a result, all the selected jurors were female." The Supreme Court upheld J.E.B.'s contention that the pattern of striking male jurors by the state, solely on the basis of gender, constituted the kind of purposeful discrimination that violated the Equal Protection Clause. To excuse male or female jurors by the use of peremptory challenges solely on the basis of their gender assumes men and women "hold particular views simply because of their gender." This stereotype reflects and reinforces patterns of historical discrimination that are contrary to the equal protection of laws

[633] In _Powers v. Ohio,_ 499 U.S. 400 (1991), the Court held that a defendant has standing to challenge a prosecutor's peremptory challenges to remove a juror from the jury on account of race, notwithstanding the fact that the juror is not of the same race as the defendant. In _Powers,_ the defendant was white, but the removed juror was African American. The Court stated, "A prosecutor's discriminatory use of peremptory challenges harms the excluded jurors and the community at large." In _Georgia v. McCollum,_ 505 U.S. 42 (1992), applied the ruling of _Batson_ to the defendant's exercise of a peremptory challenge by holding that the defense attorney who exercised a peremptory challenge was engaged in a state action. The Court reiterated that protection of the defendant was only one goal of Batson—the harm to the excluded juror and the community's confidence in a fair and impartial jury was at least as important.

[634] _See, Cateneda v. Partida,_ 430 U.S. 482 (1977); _Purkett v. Elem,_ 514 U.S. 765 (1995); _Miller-El v. Cockrell,_ 545 U.S. 231 (2005); _Yee v. Duncan,_ 563 F. 3rd 393 (2006).

Most cases coming before the Court for a *Batson* review have survived the challenge claiming the peremptory challenges were unconstitutionally made. However, in May, 2016 the Court held to the contrary in its opinion in *Foster v. Chatman*, ___ U.S. ___ (2016). Using Georgia's Open Records Law, Foster was able to get the prosecutor's trial file. The Court found that the race-neutral reasons offered by the state were contradicted by the notes in the file, and ultimately held that lower courts' determinations that "Foster failed to show purposeful discrimination" was clearly erroneous.

In *Flowers v. Mississippi*, 588 U.S. ___ (2019), the Court held that the trial court had committed clear error at Flower' sixth trial by concluding that the state's peremptory strike of a particular black prospective juror was not motivated in substantial part by discriminatory intent. Justice Kavanaugh wrote for a 7-2 majority, stating:

> In 1996, Curtis Flowers allegedly murdered four people in Winona, Mississippi. Flowers is black. He has been tried six separate times before a jury for murder. The same lead prosecutor represented the State in all six trials.
>
> In the initial three trials, Flowers was convicted, but the Mississippi Supreme Court reversed each conviction. In the first trial, Flowers was convicted, but the Mississippi Supreme Court reversed the conviction due to "numerous instances of prosecutorial misconduct." (Citation omitted.) In the second trial, the trial court found that the prosecutor discriminated on the basis of race in the peremptory challenge of a black juror. The trial court seated the black juror. Flowers was then convicted, but the Mississippi Supreme Court again reversed the conviction because of prosecutorial misconduct at trial. In the third trial, Flowers was convicted, but the Mississippi Supreme Court yet again reversed the conviction, this time because the court concluded that the prosecutor had again discriminated against black prospective jurors in the jury selection process. The court's lead opinion stated: "The instant case presents us with as strong a prima facie case of racial discrimination as we have ever seen in the context of a *Batson* challenge." (Citation omitted.) The opinion further stated that the "State engaged in racially discriminatory practices during the jury selection process" and that the "case evinces an effort by the State to exclude African-Americans from jury service."
>
> The fourth and fifth trials of Flowers ended in mistrials due to hung juries.
>
> In his sixth trial, which is the one at issue here, Flowers was convicted. The State struck five of the six black prospective jurors. On appeal, Flowers argued that the State again violated *Batson* in exercising peremptory strikes against black prospective jurors. . . .
>
> Four critical facts, taken together, require reversal. *First*, in the six trials combined, the State employed its peremptory challenges to strike 41 of the 42 black prospective jurors that it could have struck. ... *Second*, in the most recent trial, the sixth trial, the State exercised peremptory strikes against five of the six black prospective jurors. *Third*, at the sixth trial, in an apparent effort to find pretextual reasons to strike black prospective jurors, the State engaged in dramatically disparate questioning of black and white prospective jurors. *Fourth*, the State then struck at least one black prospective juror, Carolyn Wright, who was similarly situated to white prospective jurors who were not struck by the State.

We need not and do not decide that any one of those four facts alone would require reversal. All that we need to decide, and all that we do decide, is that all of the relevant facts and circumstances taken together establish that the trial court committed clear error in concluding that the State's peremptory strike of black prospective juror Carolyn Wright was not "motivated in substantial part by discriminatory intent." *Foster* v. *Chatman*, 578 U. S. ___, ___ (2016). … In reaching that conclusion, we break no new legal ground. We simply enforce and reinforce *Batson* by applying it to the extraordinary facts of this case.

ROLE OF JURIES IN SENTENCING: DEATH QUALIFIED JURIES

Defendants are entitled to be tried by a jury of their peers, but this does not mean that the actual composition of the jury in any given case must be specifically representative of the defendant nor of the demographics of the community from which it is chosen. For example, if a community is comprised of 53% women and 47% men, 80% Caucasian, 10% African American and 10% Hispanic, defendants in this community cannot insist their jury demographic match this distribution. Similarly, when it comes to cases involving the death penalty, the defendant cannot insist that the jury be made up of individuals whose opinions about the death penalty match the public opinion polls about capital punishment. Twenty-two states do not have the death penalty, and approximately 45% of individuals surveyed nationwide are against the death penalty. In those states having the death penalty, the defendant cannot insist that at least five of twelve jurors (42%) are against the death penalty. Why? Because death sentences must be unanimous! Consider, for example, potential-juror Smith. Smith is adamantly opposed to the death penalty and is part of the jury venire. His number is selected and during voir dire he states that, although he could impartially weigh the evidence in determining whether defendant Jones committed the murder, he could not, under any circumstance impose the death penalty--even assuming Jones did the most horrendous crime. Under these circumstances, it would be a colossal waste of time and energy to put on the sentencing hearing because one could predict the outcome from the beginning. Mr. Smith would not vote for death, the jury would not be unanimous, and it would "hang" as to the sentence.[635]

To get around this predicament, the Court allows "death-qualified juries." A death-qualified jury is one comprised of jurors, all of whom indicate that they can follow judge instructions, and, where warranted, could impose the death penalty. In *Witherspoon v. Illinois,* 391 US 510 (1968), the Court overturned Witherspoon's death sentence and declared void a state statute that allowed dismissal of any juror with conscientious scruples against the death penalty. During Witherspoon's trial, the prosecutor, using this statute, had excused half of the jurors that had mentioned having qualms about the death penalty (he did not inquire whether they could actually impose a death sentence). Witherspoon was convicted and appealed his death sentence saying the statute violated his Sixth Amendment right to an impartial jury and the Fourteenth Amendment's right to due process. The Court held that jurors who say they will not impose a death sentence could be dismissed (now known as "*Witherspoon* excludables"), but those jurors who simply oppose the death penalty as a personal belief may not, for that reason alone, be dismissed.

In *Lockhart v. McCree,* 476 U.S. 162 (1986), Lockhart was on trial for capital murder, and the judge excused for cause all prospective jurors who stated that they could not vote for the imposition of the death penalty under any circumstances. The jury convicted Lockhart, but it did not impose the death penalty as the state had requested. The Court held that a death-qualified

---

[635] In death penalty cases the same jurors who decided that defendant was guilty also decide what sentence to impose.

jury did not violate the "fair cross section" requirement of the Sixth Amendment so long as the jury reflected the composition of the community at large. Justice Rehnquist argued that the state has a legitimate interest in impaneling jurors who "can properly and impartially apply the law to the facts of the case at both the guilt and sentencing phases of a capital trial." Thus, as long as a jury is selected from a fair cross-section of the community, is impartial, and can properly apply the law to the circumstances of the case, a defendant's constitutional right to a fair trial has been protected.

One concern that arises after the *Witherspon* and *Lockhart* decisions is the potential that a death qualified jury may be more "prosecution prone" (meaning they are more likely to return a guilty verdict on lesser evidence.) Are folks who say they can impose the death penalty more likely from the get-go to be pro-state or pro-prosecution? If so, then they may not be impartial nor well-suited to determine guilt or innocence of the particular defendant.

WAIVING A JURY

The Sixth Amendment guarantees the defendant the right to have a jury trial for non-petty crimes. But what if the defendant does not want to have a jury decide? Some states allow the defendant to waive a jury and have the judge decide whether he or she is guilty or not guilty. This is called a "bench trial." In other states, the prosecution may insist on a jury trial even if the defendant wishes to waive a jury. The Court has determined that the criminal defendant has no right under the federal constitution to be tried by a judge alone.[636] When the defendant does waive jury, he or she may only do so if the waiver is both express and intelligent. Most jurisdictions require a written waiver.

JURY SIZE

The Sixth Amendment does not require a particular number of jurors.[637] Justice White noted that "the fact that the jury at common law was composed of precisely 12 is a historical accident, unnecessary to effect the purposes of the jury system and wholly without significance 'except to mystics.'"[638] A six-person jury is permissible,[639] but five-member juries are unacceptable.[640] All states require twelve-member juries in capital cases. Most require twelve-member juries for felonies. Many states use fewer than twelve-member juries for misdemeanors.

JURY INSTRUCTIONS

Towards the end of the trial, the judge reads to the jury a set of statements known as "jury instructions." Recall that the jury gets to decide what facts it believes, but it must follow the applicable laws and apply those laws to the facts. Thus, the court must communicate with the jury what the law is, and how they are to apply it to the facts they have considered. For example, if the defense is self-defense the judge must instruct the jury as to the relevant rules about self-defense. Generally, attorneys prepare and propose the jury instructions this wish to have read to the jury. The judge chooses from these offered instructions and may also prepare his or her own statements. Many states have adopted uniform criminal jury instructions which are usually drafted by the state bar association.[641] Often, the attorneys' proposed instructions are taken

---

[636] *Singer v. United States*, 380 U.S. 24 (1965).

[637] *Williams v. Florida*, 399 U.S. 78 (1970).

[638] *Id.*

[639] *Id.*

[640] *Ballew v. Georgia*, 435 U.S. 323 (1978).

[641] For example, Oregon Uniform Criminal Jury Instruction 104: FUNCTIONS OF THE COURT AND JURY states,

directly from these uniform instructions. After all the evidence is introduced, the judge will read the instructions to the jury before they leave to deliberate. In some states, the jury can take the set of written instructions into the jury room with them to guide them in their deliberations. In other places, the judge just reads these instructions. At times, jurors may have questions about the law that arise as they deliberate. They will submit their questions to the judge, and the judge will frequently re-read the instructions without further comment. When jurors present these questions, the judge generally calls the attorneys together and there may be arguments made (on or off the record) on how to proceed. Ultimately the judge will decide whether clarifications need to be made or just a re-reading of the instruction is needed.

CHARGING THE JURY

Before releasing the jury to deliberate the judge will "charge the jury" which is essentially telling the jurors that they have received all the evidence and that now they are to deliberate and consider the testimonial evidence they have heard, the physical evidence they have received, and the instructions about the pertinent law they just received. The judge will also provide the jurors with the verdict forms, instruct them to pick a foreman, and instruct them to return the verdicts to the bailiff after they have reached a decision. Finally, the judge's clerk will administer an oath to the jury as part of this process.

JURY DELIBERATION

Juries discuss the evidence and make a factual finding about the defendant's guilt on each of the charges submitted during the phase of the trial called "jury deliberations." Jury deliberations, at least in theory, are secret.

It is your sole responsibility to make all the decisions about the facts in this case. You must evaluate the evidence to determine how reliable or how believable that evidence is. When you make your decision about the facts, you must then apply the legal rules to those facts and reach your verdict.

Remember, however, that your power to reach a verdict is not arbitrary. When I tell you what the law is on a particular subject or tell you how to evaluate certain evidence, you must follow these instructions.

Do not allow anything I have said or done during the course of this trial to suggest that I have formed any opinion about this case.

Keep in mind that a judge is required by law to give certain instructions in every criminal case.

When I have sustained objections to evidence, or ordered that evidence be stricken or excluded from your consideration, you must follow these rulings. Do not consider such matters during your deliberations. Base your verdict on the evidence and these instructions. The lawyers' statements and arguments are not evidence. If your recollection of the evidence is different from the lawyers' recollection, you must rely on your own memory.

In deciding this case, you are to consider all the evidence you find worthy of belief. It is your duty to weigh the evidence calmly and dispassionately and to decide this case on its merits. Do not allow bias, sympathy, or prejudice any place in your deliberations. Do not decide this case on guesswork, conjecture, or speculation.

Do not consider what sentence might be imposed by the court if the defendant is found guilty.

Generally, the testimony of any witness whom you believe is sufficient to prove any fact in dispute. You are not simply to count the witnesses, but you are to weigh the evidence.

After the judge has charged the jury, the jurors are put into custody of the bailiff, and will remain sequestered (isolated from other people) until they reach a verdict, or until it becomes apparent that they are not able to reach a verdict and are discharged by the court. ... The jurors "retire" under the custody of the bailiff to a jury room to deliberate on their verdict. They take with them the pleadings in the case, the instructions to the jury, and usually any exhibits admitted into evidence. ... [642]

The duty of the jury is to consider the facts and the law of the case and arrive at a verdict. The foreman of the jury, chosen by the jurors (or sometimes automatically the first juror accepted by both the state and the defense during voir dire), frequently begins the deliberation by taking an initial vote by each juror. On rare occasions this initial vote reveals an immediate unanimous verdict. Typically, however, this first vote discloses that the jury is divided; some voting "guilty" and some voting "not guilty." Discussions then go back and forth between members of the jury, with votes being taken periodically, until the jury finally votes unanimously one way or another. Although we frequently speak of guilt and "innocence," whether defendant "did it" and is factually innocent of the charge is irrelevant. Jurors should consider only whether the state proved the charges beyond a reasonable doubt, warranting a "guilty" verdict, or did not prove the charges beyond a reasonable doubt, thus warranting a "not guilty" verdict.

If the jurors cannot reach agreement after prolonged deliberations, they report this fact to the court. The trial judge will usually instruct them to stay and keep trying.[643] If at the end of some time they still have not reached a verdict and have reached an impassible stale-mate, there is a "hung jury." If the jury "hangs," the judge may declare a mistrial and dismiss the jurors. If the state believes it still can

---

[642] Kerper, *supra* at 322-323.

[643] The court may give an "*Allen* charge" or "dynamite charge" to the jury that reports it is deadlocked. *See, Allen v. United States*, 164 U.S. 492 (1896). Some states prohibit the *Allen* charge because they deem it coercive. The *Allen* Court held that the trial court did not err when it instructed the trial jury after it had returned without reaching a decision that,

[i]t was their duty to decide the case if they could conscientiously do so; that they should listen, with a disposition to be convinced, to each other's arguments; that if much the larger number were for conviction, a dissenting juror should consider whether his doubt was a reasonable one which made no impression upon the minds of so many men, equally honest, equally intelligent with himself. If, upon the other hand, the majority were for acquittal, the minority ought to ask themselves whether they might not reasonably doubt the correctness of a judgment which was not concurred in by the majority. 164 U.S. at 501.

The Court noted,
While undoubtedly the verdict of the jury should represent the opinion of each individual juror, it by no means follows that opinions may not be changed by conference in the jury room. The very object of the jury system is to secure unanimity by a comparison of views, and by arguments among the jurors themselves. It certainly cannot be the law that each juror should not listen with deference to the arguments and with a distrust of his own judgment if he finds a large majority of the jury taking a different view of the case from what he does himself. It cannot be that each juror should go to the jury room with a blind determination that the verdict shall represent his opinion of the case at that moment, or that he should close his ears to the arguments of men who are equally honest and intelligent as himself. There was no error in these instructions. 164 U.S. at 501-502.

gain a conviction, it may retry the defendant. (See discussion on manifest necessity and double jeopardy in Chapter Six).

After *Apprendi* (see, Chapter Eleven), jurors will also decide if aggravating facts exist--for example, whether a weapon was used in the commission of the crime or whether the defendant displayed deliberate cruelty. In a criminal case, the jurors must find proof beyond a reasonable doubt that the defendant committed the crime in order to return a guilty verdict, and they must also determine whether the state has proved the aggravating factors beyond a reasonable doubt before the defendant can receive an enhanced sentence.

JURY SEQUESTRATION

Jurors are "sequestered" (kept from contacting the outside world) during deliberations. Occasionally, jurors are sequestered throughout the entire trial, but this is rare. Most juries are sequestered only after the close of the evidence. The bailiff ensures that jurors do not receive any material or communication that might influence their verdict. During the deliberation process the jury communicates with the judge and the court through the bailiff. When jurors are sequestered, they are not permitted to leave the jury room; meals are brought in, and, if necessary jurors may even be sent to a hotel if it gets very late and it appears deliberations will need another day. Generally, if the deliberation goes into multiple days, the jurors are sent home with instructions not to talk to anyone about the case, and not to read or listen to any news.

Trial judges are becoming increasingly concerned about jurors' use of smart phones. During breaks in the trial, jurors may want to tend to their business, communicate with their families and friends via text or e-mail, play games on their phone apps, and courts have tended to allow jurors to have their phones with them—generally giving instructions about proper and improper uses. The risk in allowing jurors access to their phones is that they may look things up to help them decide the case. Because jury verdicts are to be based on what is learned at trial, consulting outside information is improper. Jury verdicts may be "impeached" upon evidence of improper outside influence. Nevertheless, as courts are reluctant to inquire as to what was going on in the jury room, it may be difficult to prove that jurors are using their phones for these improper purposes.

ANNOUNCING THE VERDICT

After the jury reaches its verdict, it returns to the courtroom to find the judge, the attorneys, and the defendant waiting. The judge asks the jury foreperson whether the jurors have reached a verdict, to which the foreperson affirmatively responds, ("yes.") The judge asks the jury foreperson to give the bailiff the verdict forms. The bailiff hands the forms to the judge who reviews them. The judge either hands the form back to bailiff to give to the foreperson who then reads the verdict aloud in court or the judge reads the verdicts in court. The verdict will say something like, "We, the jury, duly impaneled and sworn, all of our number concurring, find the defendant as to Count I, "guilty/not guilty as charged." After *Apprendi*, the jury must also indicate whether they found beyond a reasonable doubt the alleged aggravating factors. The judge then typically thanks the jury for their service and tells them they are now free to go. The judge, the attorneys, and the defendant stay put.

If jury returns a verdict of "not guilty" on all of the charges, the judge will order that the defendant be immediately released from custody if he or she is being detained. Except for getting the physical evidence returned to the parties, the case is ended. If the jury finds the defendant guilty of any of the charges, the court will decide whether the defendant should be taken into custody pending sentencing (assuming that the defendant is free on release). The judge will listen to any comments the attorneys need to make for the record, and make appropriate arrangements for the physical evidence that was admitted during the trial. Frequently, the defense will make motions challenging the verdict that the court will rule upon prior to sentencing. In minor offenses, the court may immediately sentence the defendant at the conclusion of the trial, or it may also set sentencing for a block of time reserved for sentencing multiple offenders. If a pre-sentence investigation is ordered, sentencing will be delayed until it can be prepared. In some states, the defendant has the right to have a period of time (generally two or three days) between the verdict and imposition of sentence. This period is to allow the defendant, generally facing a lengthy period of incarceration, to make arrangements before reporting to jail or being transported to the penitentiary.

IMPEACHING JURY VERDICTS

Juries should reach their verdict based only on the evidence that they have heard or seen during the trial. Sometimes jurors notify the judge that other jurors may be basing their decisions on outside evidence that was not presented during the trial. Although our evidence rules developed largely because of our distrust and fear of the jury's ability to not be unduly persuaded by prejudicial or irrelevant evidence, we steadfastly hold that once the case "goes to the jury" its decisions should be trusted and accepted. Thus, a jury's verdict will stand unless it becomes apparent that there was some extraneous pressure brought to bear upon the jurors.

Challenging the validity of the jury's verdict is called "impeaching the verdict." Generally, whether a challenge will be successful depends on whether the alleged impropriety is based on something internal that happened as part of the jury deliberation (for example, a juror in a child abuse case discussing knowledge they may have about child abuse because he or she had been a victim or had known a victim) or something external (for example, someone trying to bribe a juror to vote in a certain way). Federal Rule of Evidence 606(b) states that a juror "may not testify as to any matter or statement occurring during the course of the jury's deliberations or to the effect of anything upon that or another juror's mind or emotions as influencing the juror . . . *except* that a juror may testify on the question whether extraneous prejudicial information was improperly brought to the jury's attention or whether any outside influence was improperly brought to bear upon any juror." Most states have identical, or nearly identical, rules against jury impeachment. Courts will impeach a jury verdict and consider evidence that something improper happened in jury deliberations only if the improper influence is external. This is exceedingly rare, but such was the case in *Pena-Rodriguez v. Colorado*, 580 U.S. ____ (2017). In that case, a Colorado jury convicted defendant of harassment and unlawful sexual contact. After the verdict, two jurors told defense counsel that during deliberation another juror had expressed anti-Hispanic bias toward the defendant and his alibi witness. The trial court acknowledges the bias, but denied a new trial citing Colorado's no jury impeachment rule. The Court held that where a juror makes a clear statement that he or she relied on racial stereotypes or animus to convict a criminal defendant, the no impeachment rule gives way to the Sixth Amendment's right to a jury trial. The Court set forth the way lower courts are to analyze such a claim.

> Before the no-impeachment bar can be set aside to allow further judicial inquiry, there must be a threshold showing that one or more jurors made statements exhibiting overt racial bias that cast serious doubt on the fairness and impartiality of the jury's deliberations and resulting verdict. To qualify, the statement must tend to show that racial animus was a significant motivating factor in the juror's vote to convict. Whether the threshold showing has been satisfied is committed to the substantial discretion of the trial court in light of all the circumstances, including the content and timing of the alleged statements and the reliability of the proffered evidence.

ROLE OF EVIDENCE IN AN AMERICAN TRIAL

The adversarial nature of the American trial requires a well-developed set of rules of evidence to govern the search for truth. Guilt or innocence should be based solely on the evidence produced at trial, and the rules of evidence control what evidence can be admitted and considered and what evidence should be excluded. The trial is a contest between opposing sides, with the judge acting as an impartial referee. The rules of evidence are rules of engagement in battle where, through the direct questioning and cross examination of witnesses, biases and infirmities of perception are revealed. Ultimately through this process the "truth" should emerge, and the jury should recognize and be persuasively convinced of it -- or so that's the idea.

> At trial, the judge's primary responsibility is to see that the defendant in a criminal case gets a fair trial. To accomplish this the judge has many duties, including deciding what law applies to the case; interpreting the law of the case for the jury; deciding what evidence is and is not admissible; ruling on objections made by attorneys; determining qualification of witnesses; protecting witnesses from overzealous cross-examinations; ensuring that the trial proceeds efficiently and effectively. … In some jurisdictions, the judge may comment on the credibility of the witnesses and the weight of the evidence. In a jury trial, the function of the judge is much like that of a referee. The judge keeps order in the court and sees that the trial progresses properly and smoothly.[644]

SOURCE OF RULES

Unfortunately, the rules of evidence are complex and not located in one place. In federal trials, the courts follow the Federal Rules of Evidence (FRE) (Title 28 of the U.S. Code Annotated). In some states, evidentiary rules are gleaned from common law and case law, but 43 states closely follow the FRE and have adopted similar codes of evidence (generally by statute). But the FRE and similar state codes are merely starting points. Attorneys must also consult statutes, ordinances, rules of civil and criminal procedure, local and state court rules, and state disciplinary and ethical rules from state bar associations in order to make the best arguments why some crucial piece of evidence should or should not be admitted. Finally, thousands of court decisions address various aspects and refinements of general rules, and common law rules still "fill in the gaps" left unaddressed by the FRE.

CLASSIFICATION OF RULES OF EVIDENCE

Evidence is classified as either "direct" or "circumstantial" and either "testimonial," "real," or "demonstrative." Direct evidence is based on eyewitness testimony that something did or did not occur. No inference is needed to be able to draw any conclusions about what happened based on the witness's statements. For example, Fiona's testimony, "I saw Frank hit Monika in the eye" is direct evidence. The jury does not need to draw any inferences from the statement in order to find that, if Fiona is to be believed, Frank hit the Monika in the eye. Circumstantial evidence, on the other hand, is evidence of certain facts from which the jury must draw an inference to establish other facts. For example, if Fiona states, "I heard a loud thump, I heard Monika cry out loudly in pain, I saw the Frank leave the house very quickly, and immediately afterwards I saw the Monika's right eye was red, puffy, and swollen," the jury might draw the inference from this testimony and conclude that the Frank hit the Monika in the eye.

Most trial evidence is in the form of testimony—that is, what the witness says while on the witness stand. Some evidence is physical evidence (you can pick it up, turn it over, and

---

[644] Norman Garland, *Criminal Evidence,* 35 (2006).

examine it). Physical evidence can be either real evidence which is connected to the crime--like the glove left at the home of murder victim Nicole Brown Simpson--or demonstrative evidence which is physical evidence that helps the jury understand something about the case but that isn't part of the crime--like a diagram of the skid marks in a reckless driving case. To classify a piece of evidence as either real evidence or demonstrative evidence requires context. Take, for example, a photograph. A photograph of the crime scene would be demonstrative evidence, but a photograph of a naked child in a child pornography case would be real evidence. Does it matter if it is real evidence connected to the trial or demonstrative evidence? It may. Unless parties stipulate to admissibility, physical evidence won't be admissible unless a chain of custody is established (thus "authenticating the evidence"). Without this chain of custody, the court will not allow witnesses to testify about the evidence. Additionally, real evidence may be more persuasive than demonstrative evidence. The gun seized at the crime scene (real evidence) may have more impact on the jury's consideration of the weight of the evidence than a gun that looks similar to the type of weapon the defendant was thought to be carrying (demonstrative evidence), but was not the actual gun used during the crime.

PURPOSE OF EVIDENTIARY RULES

Many of the rules of evidence grew out of our distrust of lay people (jurors) to elevate and weigh the evidence before them in a fair manner—for example, the rules concerning relevancy, hearsay, and character evidence. Some of our rules of evidence grew out of the intrinsic need to have a trial that is efficient and organized—for example, the rules concerning judicial notice, stipulations, and presumptions. Some of our rules of evidence grew out of public policy concerns such as our desire to protect some important relationship worthy of protection—for example, the rules concerning privilege. Some rules govern who can be a witness and what types of questions can be asked of witnesses--for example the rules concerning expert testimony. Finally, some of the rules reflect a preference for some types of evidence over others—for example, the best evidence rule which prefers the original document to copies of the document.

RELEVANT EVIDENCE

The most important evidence rule is the requirement of relevancy. In order to be admissible, evidence must, at a minimum, be relevant. Relevant evidence is evidence that has some logical connection[645] to the disputed issue. For example, assume that Alex slips and falls on a banana peel at his local grocery store. He sues Bart, the storeowner for negligence. At trial, Alex's attorney asks Bart "are you married?" Bart's attorney objects, claiming that the evidence is not relevant. The judge will sustain the objection (i.e., disallow the question and the answer) because Bart's marital status has nothing to do with whether he was negligent in not picking the peel up. Bart's marital status has no reasonable connection to the laws governing negligence. At a very minimum, evidence must be logically relevant to be admissible.

Some logically relevant evidence may still be excluded if it is not "legally relevant." The FRE allows the judge to exclude evidence that is logically relevant if its helpfulness is substantially outweighed by unfair prejudice, or if there is a danger that the evidence would confuse the issue or mislead the jury. Additionally, the court can exclude logically relevant evidence if it finds that allowing the evidence to be presented causes undue delay or a waste of time, or if it results in a "needless presentation of cumulative evidence." Evidence is legally

---

[645] Evidence laws define relevant evidence as evidence that "has a tendency to make the existence of any fact that is of consequence to the determination of the action more probable or less probable than it would be without the evidence."

relevant and admissible, if it is not unfairly prejudicial, too misleading, too confusing, too time-consuming to present, or too repetitious (cumulative).

CHARACTER EVIDENCE

Character evidence is evidence about how a person will generally respond to a wide variety of circumstances--for example, acting peacefully versus acting violently, or being dishonest or honest. Evidence rules are also concerned that a jury may be unduly swayed by evidence of the bad character of a witness, a victim, or a defendant. They may decide, "once a thief, always a thief" and convict a defendant on the basis of a prior criminal history as opposed to evidence that, on this occasion, he stole the hat.[646] Jurors may be willing to convict the defendant on very little evidence, using their assumptions based on bad character to fill in the gaps. The evidence rules restrict the use of character evidence -- traits of an individual about what kind of person they are. In the few, limited circumstances in which character evidence is allowed, it must be presented in the form of opinion or reputation. Evidence about prior bad behavior, like character evidence, is also generally not admissible. For example, if it is relevant, (both legally and logically relevant) a witness may be allowed to testify, "I think John is a violent person" or "John has a reputation in the neighborhood for being a violent person." The witness will not be allowed to testify, "John hit me regularly in the past. No doubt, he hit his brother this time too…that's just the kind of guy he is."

HEARSAY EVIDENCE

Many people use the term "hearsay" to mean secondhand information, but it has a much more precise definition in evidence law. The FRE define hearsay as "An out of court statement offered for the truth of the matter asserted." This definition may include second hand information, but it also includes much more. People who repeat in court what they themselves told their brother last week are as guilty of uttering hearsay as if they repeating gossip they heard from someone else. Most hearsay evidence is not admissible in court; there are, however, several exceptions to this general principle.

First, some statements made before the trial do not fit the hearsay definition. Statements that are not offered for the truth of what they assert do not fit the definition of hearsay. One common type of evidence not offered for "its truth" is impeachment evidence. (Impeachment is discussed in greater detail below). Other evidence not offered for the truth includes statements that have independent legal significance (for example, statements made to establish a contract). Second, the rules say that some statements that fit the definition are, nevertheless, not hearsay. These are referred to as "hearsay exemptions" or "hearsay exclusions." Two important examples of hearsay exclusions are the defendant's admissions or confession and co-conspirators' statements made during the course of a conspiracy. Third, the rules recognize several types of hearsay "exceptions." Exceptions are statements which are hearsay, but because of their general indicia of truthfulness or reliability, public policy suggests they should be admissible as evidence—Example include: excited utterances, evidence of a prior criminal conviction,[647] or statements in ancient documents. Finally, the rules recognize a few exceptions to the general rule excluding hearsay, but only when it can be shown that the person who made the statement is now unavailable (defined as being dead, beyond judicial process, protected by a privilege, or when the person refuses to testify).

---

[646] FRE 404 provides that "evidence of a person's character or trait of character is not admissible for the purpose of proving an action in conformity therewith on a particular occasion…" (This means that the fact that a person stole in the past is not admissible to prove that he stole on this occasion.)

[647] A prior criminal conviction is hearsay because it is, in essence, the jury's statement, "you are guilty." The statement was made outside of this court process (the earlier trial) and it is now being offered by the state to prove the truth of the statement (that defendant is guilty).

One important development in evidence law in the last decade is the interplay between the hearsay rule (and the admission of hearsay statements) and the defendant's right to confrontation in a criminal case. In *Crawford v. Washington*, 541 U.S. 36 (2004), the Court held that defendants' Sixth Amendment right to confrontation (the constitutional right to challenge any statements used against him or her made at trial) in criminal cases take precedence over any hearsay exception. The right to confrontation is discussed later in this chapter, but in essence the Court found that if defendant is denied the ability to cross examine a witness who made an out of court statement being used against him or her and the statement is "testimonial," then the statement should be excluded--regardless of whether it qualifies as some exception to the hearsay rule.

RULES RELATING TO WITNESSES

WITNESS COMPETENCY

To be admissible, evidence must be competent--that is, given by a competent witness. In determining competency, the court looks at the qualifications of the potential witness. Historically, many categories of people were not allowed to testify--for example, children, spouses, or persons who were mentally disturbed ("not of sound mind"). Some states also held that individuals convicted of crime were incompetent and could not testify. Today, witnesses are presumed competent and able to give testimony.[648] Under the FRE, an individual is competent to testify if they are able to provide relevant testimony--the FRE does not exclude any particular classes of people. Very young children may still be found to not be competent, but there is no specific rule limiting testimony by children under a particular age. Instead, courts consider whether the child is able to understand what he or she saw or heard, and whether the child knows the difference between right and wrong. The competency of a witness is a preliminary matter that the judge decides outside the presence of the jury. Parties opposing the testimony of particular witnesses, or judges *sua sponte* (on their own initiative), can raise the issue of witness competency. This requires the judge to then make a competency finding before the witness will be allowed to testify.

> The mere fact that evidence is competent does not, of course, mean that the jury must believe it. Some competent evidence may be almost worthless in terms of inducing belief. A wife's alibi for her husband may be competent, but the jury may dismiss her testimony as not worthy of belief. While competency of the evidence is for the judge to decide, the weight of the evidence is for the jury to decide.[649]

REQUIREMENT OF PERSONAL KNOWLEDGE—LAY AND EXPERT WITNESSES

Generally, witnesses can only testify about things they personally know, saw, heard, smelled, or felt. Lay witnesses (non-experts) cannot generally give their opinions--unless the opinions are ones that people commonly have and conclusions they commonly draw. For example, a lay witness can testify that the defendant was "drunk"—which is an opinion—but most people have enough experience seeing others who have been drunk to know the signs (i.e., bloodshot or watery eyes, slurred speech, unstable when walking, etc.). A lay witness could

---

[648] FRE 601 provides, "Every person is competent to be a witness except as otherwise provided in these rules. . . .." FRE 605 indicates that judge presiding over the trial may not testify as a witnesses (and so is not competent). FRE 606 similarly limits jurors from testifying.

[649] Kerper, *supra* at 319.

testify that a car was travelling "fast," but would not be permitted to testify it was travelling 83.5 miles an hour.

Experts are allowed to testify about their opinions and need not form their testimony on the basis of personal knowledge. For example, psychologists may be asked to testify about eyewitness perception and memories. If qualified as an expert, the court may permit the witness to give an opinion even though he or she was not present during the offense, and even if they have not examined or even met the witness. Attorneys can question experts and elicit their opinions by asking hypothetical questions, which must be based on facts in evidence. For example, "Dr. Jones, if you knew that a person was taking medication and had been sound asleep and awakened by a loud bang, would you expect them to be able to clearly identify the direction from which the loud bang came?" Handwriting and medical experts are frequently asked hypotheticals in court. Accident reconstruction experts frequently offer testimony about speed, braking, and other factors relevant in determining fault in car crashes. Experts may also testify based personal observation—for example, a psychiatrist who has examined the accused or a child victim.

Sometimes a party's own expert witness can backfire. This happened in *Buck v. Davis*, 580 U.S. ___ (2017), where the defense attorney called Dr. Quijano and introduced his report into evidence during the sentencing phase of a capital murder trial. Dr. Quijano testified that Buck was inherently more likely to commit future crimes because he was black.[650] Buck filed a petition for writ of habeas corpus claiming that his attorney rendered ineffective assistance of counsel by calling Dr. Quijana, not challenging his testimony, and by entering his report into the record for the jury to consider. The Court stated,

Buck has demonstrated ineffective assistance of counsel under *Strickland*.

(a) To satisfy *Strickland*, a defendant must first show that counsel performed deficiently. Buck's trial counsel knew that Dr. Quijano's report reflected the view that Buck's race predisposed him to violent conduct and that the principal point of dispute during the penalty phase was Buck's future dangerousness. Counsel nevertheless called Dr. Quijano to the stand, specifically elicited testimony about the connection between race and violence, and put Dr. Quijano's report into evidence. No competent defense attorney would introduce evidence that his client is liable to be a future danger because of his race.

(b) *Strickland* further requires a defendant to demonstrate prejudice—"a reasonable probability that, but for counsel's unprofessional errors, the result of the proceeding would have been different." It is reasonably probable that without Dr. Quijano's testimony on race and violence, at least one juror would have harbored a reasonable doubt on the question of Buck's future dangerousness. This issue required the jury to make a predictive judgment inevitably entailing a degree of speculation. But Buck's race was not subject to speculation, and according to Dr. Quijano, that immutable characteristic carried with it an increased probability of future violence. Dr. Quijano's testimony appealed to a powerful racial stereotype and might well have been valued by jurors as the opinion of a medical expert bearing the court's imprimatur. For these reasons, the District Court's conclusion that any mention of race during the penalty phase was *de*

---

[650] Dr. Quijano had testified in several similar cases in. Texas, this came to light, and all cases in which he was a witness were reviewed—Buck's was one of them. In the other cases, the state had confessed error and the defendant had been resentenced, but the state did not confess error in Buck's case.

minimis is rejected. So is the State's argument that Buck was not prejudiced by Dr. Quijano's testimony because it was introduced by his own counsel, rather than the prosecution. Jurors understand that prosecutors seek convictions and may reasonably be expected to evaluate the government's evidence in light of its motivations. When damaging evidence is introduced by a defendant's own lawyer, it is in the nature of an admission against interest, more likely to be taken at face value.

EXPERT WITNESSES AND SCIENTIFIC EVIDENCE

Scientific and technological innovations and methods can often provide both relevant and probative (helpful for the purposes it is offered) evidence. The courts have employed four primary tests over the years to determine the admissibility of scientific evidence—the *Frye* Test, the *Daubert* Test, the *Kumhoe Tire* Test, and FRE 702. In *Frye v. United States*, 293 F. 1013 (D.C. Cir. 1923), the court held "in admitting expert testimony deduced from a well-organized scientific principle or discovery, the thing from which the deduction is made must be sufficiently established to have gained general acceptance in the particular field in which it belongs."[651] The *Frye* test, because it requires well-established and generally-accepted methods, may limit evidence derived from emerging technology. That said, *Frye* was limited to scientific principles, and many areas of technology are not properly considered "scientific principle."

> For seventy years the *Frye* test, or general acceptance test, was commonly applied in federal courts and in most state courts faced with the issue of whether new or scientific tests should be admitted into evidence in criminal trials. In 1993, however, in *Daubert v. Merrell Dow Pharmaceuticals, Inc.*, 509 U.S. 579, the U.S. Supreme Court rejected the general acceptance test. Rather the Court ruled that the Federals of Evidence supersede *Frye*. The Court held that admissibility of scientific evidence must be based on several factors, including whether the evidence can be tested and whether it can be subjected to peer review. Under *Daubert*, the trial judge must make a preliminary assessment of whether the reasoning or methodology can be applied to the facts in issue. Once the court determines the admissibility, the jury determines the weight to give to such evidence. Because the Court's ruling in *Daubert* is not one of constitutional dimension, state courts are not required to follow it.

> In *Kumho Tire Co. v. Carmichael*, 526 U.S. 137 (1999), the Court extended its *Daubert* reliability requirement beyond scientific testimony to include technical and other specialized expert testimony. State courts are now divided on whether to accept the newer *Daubert* standard or remain with the classic standard announced in 1923 in *Frye v. United States*.[652]

Evidence resulting from modern technology may have a greater chance of being admissible under the *Daubert* standard that looks to several factors to determine admissibility. *Kumhoe Tire* covers testimony that requires expertise but not necessarily scientific evidence. Finally, FRE 702 is very broad (a combination of *Daubert* and *Kumhoe Tire* tests), and it generally favors the admission of testimony about generally reliable principles and methods by expert witnesses if the testimony will be helpful to the jury. It states,

---

[651] *Id.* at 1014.
[652] Scheb, *supra* at p. 623.

If scientific, technical, or other specialized knowledge will assist the trier of fact to understand the evidence or to determine a fact in issue, a witness qualified as an expert by knowledge, skill, experience, training or education, may testify thereto in the form of an opinion or otherwise, if (1) the testimony is based on sufficient facts or data, (2) the testimony is the product of reliable principles and methods, and (3) the witness has applied the principles and methods reliably to the facts of the case.

SEQUESTERING WITNESSES

In order to keep witnesses from adjusting their testimony to match other witnesses who have testified, the court may exclude witnesses from the courtroom and order them not to talk to each other about the case. This process is called "sequestering the witnesses." In addition to minimizing the effect that another witness's testimony will have on subsequent witnesses, sequestering also preserves order in the court because the testifying witness will not be subject to eye rolling, intimidating gestures, or loud sighs of courtroom spectators.

The process of sequestering a witness involves one party requesting the court exclude any possible witnesses. Courts generally grant that request, summarily. However, sometimes parties argue about who should be excluded. Any natural person (i.e., a human being) who is a party to the case may not be excluded, and if the party is not a natural person, the party's designated representative may not be excluded. Sometimes, experts are allowed to listen to the testimony of a witness in order to later form and testify about their opinion based upon that testimony. One controversial practice involves the prosecuting attorney designating a specific police officer (generally, the chief investigative officer) as the state's designated representative. Defense attorneys maintain that the prosecutor (not the officer) is the state's representative and is, thus, always present, but courts tend to allow one officer to sit at counsel table with the prosecutor during the trial. Because victims are not considered parties to a criminal case, they are subject to sequestration, but some states' victims' rights laws preclude the victim from being excluded during the trial.

IMPEACHING WITNESSES

Evidence is generally presented to prove some fact of the case. For example, when a witness states, "I saw the man in the blue hat in the white car run the red light." The purpose of this evidence is to show that it was the man in the blue hat in a white car who ran the light and not the woman in the purple hat in the green car who ran the red light. The statement is being offered for its truth and for a "substantive purpose." Sometimes, however, one side will offer evidence to call into question the believability of a witness's testimony. When that happens, they are said to be offering the evidence for an "impeachment purpose." Impeachment occurs when evidence suggests that the jury should not believe a particular witness. Sometimes evidence is both substantive evidence and impeachment evidence. If, for example, the prosecutor offers evidence that defendant has a prior felony conviction to prove that he is an "ex-con" in possession of a firearm, the prior conviction is offered for a substantive purpose. But, if the prosecutor offers the evidence of defendant's prior felony conviction for bribery to show he is not truthful or credible, it is offered for impeachment purposes.[653] Some rules allow evidence of a statement to be admissible as impeachment but not admissible if offered for their truth--for example, hearsay is defined as statements offered for their truth (and the general rule is that hearsay is not admissible--see above).

---

[653] Under the FRE, the use of a witnesses' prior misdemeanor conviction to impeach that witness is permitted only when the prior crime is one that involves dishonesty.

There are six major ways to impeach a witness:

1) Show witness bias—for example, information that the witness loves the defendant and therefore will say anything to "get him off."
2) Establish the witness made prior inconsistent statements—this shows that the witness changed his or her story and so obviously is either lying now or was lying then.
3) Demonstrate witness's inability to perceive/recall—this shows that the eyewitness's identification or story of events should not be trusted because he or she was unable to clearly see the activity, or now cannot remember what happened.
4) Introduce proof witness's prior criminal history—because the witness has been convicted of a felony or any crime of dishonesty, the jury can disregard or distrust the witness's testimony.
5) Put forth contradictory evidence—for example, if the party can show that an earlier witness says the hat was blue but this witness says the hat was red, it shows that the witness's testimony may be less than credible.
6) Show witness's bad character—show the witness is not to be believed because they have a character trait of dishonesty.

PRIVILEGES

Some special circumstances and relationships prevent individuals from being called as witnesses or prohibit them from testifying about certain matters. When these circumstances or relationships exist, the evidence or relationship is "privileged." Public policy considerations underlie most privileges. For example, the law seeks to protect the marital relationship and provides a privilege to allows spouses to refuse to testify against the other. Public policy also recognizes the importance of confidential communications between a person and his or her spouse, attorney, psychotherapist, clergy, and doctor. Some laws reflect this public policy by creating a confidential communication privilege. Finally, some privileges exist to protect national security, a government witness's identity, or the source of news to the media.

The FRE provides no specific federal privileges. Instead, the FRE defers to whatever state privilege law exists, either by statute or common law. State privilege law varies tremendously. Some states recognize certain privileges not recognized by other states. States laws vary with respect to who may claim the privilege (the "holder"). Finally, state laws vary with respect to whether the privilege ceases to exist when the holder of the privilege dies.

MARITAL PRIVILEGES

There are two types of privileges that may apply to married individuals. One of these privileges governs confidential communications during the course of the marriage. The second privilege (the spousal immunity privilege) disqualifies one spouse from testifying against the other spouse if they are married at the time of the trial.[654]

In *Trammel v. United States*, 445 U.S. 40 (1980), the Court examined the spousal immunity privilege recognized in 1980 by 33 states. It noted that the states either 1) treated both spouses as incompetent (the historical approach), 2) allowed either spouse or the defendant spouse to assert the privilege, or 3) allowed only the witness spouse to assert the privilege. *Trammel* adopted the latter approach and found that the witness spouse is the "holder" of the privilege. The Court reasoned, "[w]hen one spouse is willing to testify against the other in a criminal proceeding—

---

[654] This privilege was historically a rule of competency finding that a spouse was incompetent to give evidence against the other.

whatever the motivation—their relationship is almost certainly in disrepair."[655] In those circumstances, the Court noted, the justification for the privilege (marital harmony) no longer exists.

The spousal confidential communication covers only communications between spouses that were made in confidence during the marriage. It does not cover observations made by one spouse about the other. The privilege lasts after the marriage and continues after divorce or death of the other spouse. The spousal immunity privilege covers any matters seen or learned either prior to, or during, the course of the marriage; it covers not only confidential communications, but anything a spouse might have reason to know about the other. The spousal immunity privilege lasts during the course of the marriage, but does not continue upon divorce or death of the spouse. One frequent exception to the spousal immunity privilege is in cases where one spouse has committed a crime against the other or against the children of either spouse.

OTHER CONFIDENTIAL COMMUNICATIONS

All states recognize the attorney-client, husband-wife, psychotherapist-client, and clergy (priest)-penitent privileges. Some states recognize a doctor-patient privilege, a parent-child privilege, an accountant-client privilege,[656] a nurse-patient privilege, and a school counselor-student privilege. These privileges have several things in common. First, what is privileged is a communication made between the parties in confidence. Thus, if a third-party was present during the communication, no privilege exists. Second, the holder of the privilege is generally the client or patient. Third, if the holder wishes to waive the privilege, he or she may do so. Fourth, the attorney, clergy, therapist or doctor must assert the privilege on behalf of the holder and may not waive the privilege. Additionally, there may be professional or disciplinary constraints on the attorney, therapist, clergy, or doctor that supplement the privilege. Fifth, the privilege covers any confidential communication made between the parties, even after the relationship ceases to exist. For example, the marital communication privilege covers any confidential communication between spouses during their marriage even after they divorce.

OTHER PRIVILEGES: STATE SECRET PRIVILEGE, INFORMER IDENTITY, NEWS SOURCE IDENTITY.

The state secret privilege is a common law privilege, embraced and, at times, expanded by state statutes to allow the state to refuse to disclose matters that may impact national security. The privilege protects the government against compulsory disclosure of military, diplomatic, or other state secrets when it is in its best interest to do so. The government is the holder of the privilege and it can refuse to give evidence and may prevent another person from giving evidence if it can show there is a reasonable likelihood of danger that the evidence will disclose a state secret. The judge may order an *in camera* (in chambers, for judge's-eyes-only) inspection of documents to determine whether there is a valid state secret being protected. If the judge decides the evidence is not privileged, and if the state still refuses to turn the documents over, the court may order the case dismissed. The defendant's rights to confrontation under the Sixth Amendment trump the government's ability to keep the secret, but the government can keep the secret if it is willing to dismiss the complaint against the defendant.

---

[655] 445 U.S. at 46.

[656] The common law did not recognize a testimonial privilege covering confidential communications between a person and his or her accountant. Communications to accountants are now privileged in 28 states. Most states have crime-fraud provisions and do not allow the privilege to interfere with bankruptcy proceedings.

Similar to the state secret privilege is the government-informant privilege. The government is the holder of this privilege, and prosecutors may decide to disclose the identity of an informant, even against the informant's wishes. Generally, the state does not want to disclose the informant's identity, and it has a privilege to refuse to do so. Statutes or state rules of evidence permit law enforcement officers to withhold the identity of an informer unless disclosure is necessary for a defendant's fair trial.[657] Similar to the state secret privilege, if the judge orders the government to disclose the informant's identity, the state may end up dismissing the case if it wants to preserve the informant's identity.

One well-known, but frequently misunderstood, privilege is the one that allows journalists to refuse to name their source of information. Not all states recognize this privilege, and even states that do recognize the journalist-source privilege place stringent limitations on it. Indeed, journalists have been charged with contempt for failure to turn over the identification of a source. The privilege, when it exists, is governed by statutes that grant news reporters, publishers, editors, reporters, or other persons connected with or employed by a newspaper, magazine, or other periodical publication, or by a radio or television station protection against revealing a source. Usually just the source of the information is protected and not the information itself. (Thus, a news reporter may not refuse to appear in a judicial proceeding and furnish the requested information when commanded to do so without being held in contempt.)[658]

MAKING OBJECTIONS AND OFFERS OF PROOF

One of the trial judge's primary tasks is to make rulings on evidentiary objections. At times, the judge will overrule an objection. In this case, the witness should answer the question. The judge will "admit the evidence" and the jury can base its decision on that evidence--although they need not give the evidence much weight or even believe it at all. At other times, the judge will sustain an objection. In this case the witness should not answer the question. The judge will not admit the evidence, and the jury cannot base its decision on the evidence (to the extent that they have gleaned anything about that evidence). The party opposing the evidence must make a timely objection immediately after the question is asked. If a witness sneaks an answer in before the judge rules, the opposing attorney must immediately object upon hearing the witness's response. If the judge sustains the objection, the opposing attorney may ask the judge to strike the response. If the statements were particularly damaging, the attorney may also request the judge to specifically instruct the jury that they must not consider the evidence.

When making objections, parties (through their attorneys) must state the reason for the objection. Sometimes the party objects because of the nature of the evidence--for example, the question was irrelevant, the evidence is impermissible character evidence, the evidence is not proper impeachment evidence, or the evidence is impermissible hearsay evidence. Sometimes the party objects because of the form of the question--for example, the question was already asked and answered, the question is a compound question, the question badgers the witness, the question was impermissibly leading, the question calls for speculation, or the question goes beyond the scope of direct examination/cross-examination/rebuttal).

Sometimes attorneys make a tactical decision to not object to objectionable evidence. They may not want to highlight or call attention to the point that the witness just made or may not

---

[657] In *Roviaro v. United States*, 353 U.S. 53 (1957), the Court stated, "Where the disclosure of an informer's identity or the contents of his communication is relevant and helpful to the defense of the accused, or is essential to a fair determination of the cause, the privilege must give way. In these situations, the trial court may require disclosure and, if the government withholds the information, dismiss the action."
[658] *See, Branzburg v. Hayes*, 408 U.S. 665 (1968).

wish to waste the time or patience of the judge or jury to object to evidence that does only marginal damage. Sometimes, however, the failure to object to objectionable evidence is not strategic, and the attorney just fails to recognize the objection in time. Even if the attorney stays focused, things move very quickly at times during trial testimony.

Trial attorneys must keep in mind the need to create a record in case the defendant appeals. If the judge sustains an objection and keeps evidence out, the appellate court will have nothing to review. Therefore, if the excluded evidence is critical to the case, the attorney should make what is called an "offer of proof." Offers of proof allow the side to put into the record evidence that was excluded. For example, assume defense counsel asks the defendant to testify about a prior occasion when the victim reacted violently to show that the defendant had reason to fear the victim and was acting in self-defense. The prosecution objects and for whatever reason, the judge sustains the objection. On appeal, the court will never know about this prior event and whether it would have justified the defendant's belief and fear—a potentially crucial aspect of defendant's case--unless the attorney makes an offer of proof. The defense will make an offer of proof and establish that the victim has pummeled the defendant in the past and bragged that he can get away with it again.

Offers of proof take two forms and are done outside the presence of the jury. The first form of an offer of proof involves questions and answers by the attorney and witness as if the jury were actually present; the second form involves the attorney summarizing the proffered evidence and stating what the evidence would be if it had been allowed. In this way, a record is made for appellate review, but the jury doesn't hear the evidence and cannot consider it. When the judge excludes physical evidence, it will not "go into the jury box" and the jury will not be allowed to view it. If an offer of proof is made and a foundation has been laid,[659] the proffered physical evidence will be included with the case file and sent to the appellate court upon appeal.[660]

RULES GOVERNING THE SUBSTITUTION OF EVIDENCE

In American jury trials, jurors may only consider the evidence presented ("developed") at trial. Nevertheless, some evidence rules allow the parties to take shortcuts and offer substitutes for the full-blown presentation of evidence. These substitutes are presumptions and inferences, stipulations, or judicial notice.

PRESUMPTIONS AND INFERENCES

Presumptions allow a party to prove one thing (called a basic fact), and from that fact the jury is instructed to infer another non-proven fact (called the presumed fact). For example, many states have a presumption[661] that a person is dead if they have not been seen or heard from in over seven years. If a party in a civil case offered believable evidence that the last time anyone had heard from or had seen Kirk was more than seven years ago (the basic fact), the jury would be required to find that Kirk was dead (the presumed fact).

Presumed facts may not always be accurate. For example, Kirk may not be dead, but rather, living deep in the forest in some remote South American village. Still, presumptions are

---

[659] Before the court accepts any physical evidence, the party offering the evidence must lay a foundation that includes making a showing that the evidence is authentic (it is what it claims to be). In criminal cases, part of laying a foundation for physical evidence is to establish a chain of custody.
[660] The sheer size of what is sent to the appellate courts on appeal can be staggering. Not only are there volumes of transcript, but any physical evidence also gets boxed up and sent to the appellate court as well.
[661] Although state laws on presumption may be found in various sources, it is not uncommon for one state statute to set out multiple civil presumptions.

frequently warranted because they further some social policy--for example, one common presumption is that a child born to a married woman is the child of that woman and her husband. Presumptions also reflect common experience--for example, the presumption that an addressee receives a letter that was mailed properly. As with the presentation of other facts, the opposing party can always seek to introduce evidence that refutes the basic fact (i.e., that Kirk has been heard from, that the woman was not married, or that the person did not properly mail the letter.)

Civil cases require jurors to accept presumed facts as if they were proven. We call this a mandatory presumption. In criminal cases, however, jurors may draw "inferences" from basic facts, but they are not required to accept as proven presumed facts even if they believe the basic fact. The difference between presumptions and inferences is slight, presumptions are mandatory, and inferences are permissive. In a criminal trial, if the state party introduces evidence of a basic fact (the letter was properly mailed) then the judge will instruct the jury that they may believe that it was received by the addressee.

JUDICIAL NOTICE

Another shortcut to proving evidence at trial is to ask for and get the trial judge to "take judicial notice" of a certain, adjudicative, fact. Taking judicial notice promotes efficiency by paring the trial down to a contest over those matters that are really contested or disputed. Adjudicative facts are facts that would generally have to be proved to a jury. Judges may take judicial notice of adjudicative facts when the evidence is either well known in the relevant community or is easily verifiable. For example, in Southern Oregon a judge, when requested, could take judicial notice that Dutch Bros is primarily a drive-through coffee stand found in many communities throughout Oregon, but a New York judge would probably not take judicial notice of this fact because it may not be generally known in New York. [662] In New York, a judge may take judicial notice that Dunkin Donuts is a popular place for city dwellers to buy coffee, but judges in the west may be unwilling to take notice of that adjudicative fact. Once the judge takes notice of these facts, the judge instructs the jury to accept these as proven without any additional proof being offered.

The rules of evidence govern only taking judicial notice of adjudicative facts and are silent on "basic facts" and "legal or legislative facts." Basic facts are those facts that we can assume that most reasonable people know--for example, the meaning of common, everyday terms. Basic facts do not need to be proved at trial because we can assume that the jurors know basic facts. For example, we do not spend trial time proving what a cat is, or the function of a chair, or what a car is or how it works. Legal or legislative facts are the laws of the jurisdiction. All courts must take notice of the law, and parties are not required to prove to the court what the U.S. Constitution, state laws, federal laws, statutes, and judicial opinions all say. Thus, there is no need to request the court take judicial notice of these. Additionally, the court will instruct the jury concerning the law they need to follow.

STIPULATIONS

In order to streamline a trial, parties may sometimes stipulate that certain evidence exists. At trial, parties need not offer evidence that proves matters stipulated to if the judge has accepted the stipulation. For example, if the only issue in a case is whether the defendant was insane at the time she committed an assault on her neighbor, the parties may stipulate that she was present on

---

[662] Other examples of properly taken judicial notice include what day of the week a certain date was, historical facts, distances, that Chicago is a large metropolitan area in Illinois, or that Thanksgiving is on the fourth Thursday in the month of November.

the date, she was in the jurisdiction, she struck her neighbor, and she intended to strike her neighbor. The parties will then present evidence on the only issue that remains contested — did the defendant meet the test of insanity in this jurisdiction at the time she struck her neighbor.

CONSTITUTIONAL ISSUES AT TRIAL

RIGHT TO CONFRONTATION

One of the most important cases in recent history is *Crawford v. Washington*, 541 U.S. 36 (2004). The case examines the interplay between evidentiary rules (hearsay and privilege) and the Sixth Amendment's right to confrontation. The facts of the case are as follows: Michael Crawford was convicted for stabbing Kenneth Lee a man who had tried to rape Crawford's wife, Sylvia Crawford. At Michael's trial, Sylvia invoked the spousal testimony privilege and refused to testify against her husband. In lieu of Sylvia's testimony concerning the stabbing, the State played for the jury her tape-recorded statement to the police describing the stabbing. Crawford objected claiming this violated his right to confrontation. Although agreeing that the statements were hearsay, the trial judge allowed the statements to come in because they met the requirements of a well-established exception to the hearsay rule and had the indicia of reliability. At the time, if the court made those two findings, hearsay evidence could be admitted even if it did not come under any specific exception to the hearsay rule. The issue before the Court was whether Crawford's rights to confrontation were violated by the admission of the taped statements over his objections.

The Court found that Crawford's Sixth Amendment right to confrontation had indeed been violated. It held, "where testimonial statements are at issue, the only indicium of reliability sufficient to satisfy constitutional demands is confrontation."[663] The *Crawford* decision did not define the term "testimonial statements," but the Court did so two years later in the companion cases, *Hammond v. Indiana* and *Davis v. Washington,* 547 U.S. 813 (2006).

In *Davis* the defendant was charged with violating a domestic no-contact order after police responded to a 911 call from Michelle McCottrey. While on the telephone, McCottrey identified Davis as her assailant and told the operator that Davis had used his fists to beat her and that he had left her residence moments earlier. McCottrey did not testify at Davis' trial. The state submitted the recording of her 911-call as evidence linking Davis to McCottrey's injuries, over Davis' objections. The Washington Supreme Court affirmed Davis' conviction, finding that the 911-call was not a "testimonial" statement and that an emergency 911 call is not of the same nature as an in-custody interrogation by police. The Washington Court found the 911-call was not the functional equivalent of in-court, testimony. It reasoned that the purpose of a 911-call is generally not to "bear witness." If the purpose of the call was for help or rescue, it does not resemble the specific type of out-of-court statement with which *Crawford* is concerned. The Supreme Court upheld this holding.

In *Hammon* the defendant was charged with domestic battery after police responded to a call from the Hammon residence. Mrs. Hammon told the responding officer who came to her home that her husband, who was still present in the house, had thrown her to the ground and beaten her. Mrs. Hammon did not testify at Mr. Hammon's trial, but the officer testified as to what Mrs. Hammon told him that night. Mr. Hammon's attorney objected to this testimony, but the trial court admitted Mrs. Hammon's statements under the excited utterance exception to the hearsay rule. The Court found that Hammon's statements were, in fact, testimonial.The *Davis/Hammon* Court stated,

---

[663] 541 U.S. 36 (2004).

Without attempting to produce an exhaustive classification of all conceivable statements—or even all conceivable statements in response to police interrogation—as either testimonial or nontestimonial, it suffices to decide the present cases hold as follows: Statements are nontestimonial when made in the course of police interrogation under circumstances objectively indicating that the primary purpose of the interrogation is to enable police assistance to meet an ongoing emergency. They are testimonial when the circumstances objectively indicate that there is no such ongoing emergency, and that the primary purpose of the interrogation is to establish or prove past events potentially relevant to later criminal prosecution.[664]

Since *Crawford*, the Court has examined three cases[665] in which the state relied on lab analyst reports rather than calling the analyst to testify. In the first two cases, the Court concluded that the state's use of lab reports without testimony from the lab analysts violated the Sixth Amendment.[666] But, in a confusing 2012 case[667] the Court found no Confrontation Clause violation in what appears to be very similar circumstances.*[668]*

THE RIGHT TO CROSS-EXAMINE CO-DEFENDANT'S STATEMENTS

Co-defendants frequently make very incriminating statements against their crime partners that the state wishes to offer as evidence. The right to confrontation means the right to cross-examine statements of any witnesses--including partners in crime. Co-defendants have the absolute right to refuse to take the stand and testify thereby denying the defendant the opportunity to challenge the statement. The Court dealt with this situation in *Bruton v. United States*, 391 U.S. 123 (1968), in which Bruton and Evans were jointly tried. The trial judge allowed the Evans' confession to a postal inspector about their armed robbery with the limiting instruction to the jury that they could consider Evans' confession only against Evans. The trial judge admonished the jury that they must disregard Evans' statement when determining Bruton's guilt or innocence. The Court found a substantial risk that the jury, despite instructions to the contrary, would rely on Evans' confession in determining Bruton's guilt. It concluded that the admission of Evans' confession in the joint trial violated Bruton's right of cross-examination. After *Bruton*, the state will generally try co-defendants separately if there are confessions that are essential in proving its case.

RIGHT TO COMPEL WITNESSES—COMPULSORY PROCESS

The Sixth Amendment provides the accused the "right to compulsory process" for obtaining witnesses in his or her favor. The right to compulsory process includes the right to subpoena witnesses and to present a defense. Defense attorneys hire investigators to locate and interview essential witnesses; they identify and retain expert witnesses to evaluate the defendant and other crucial evidence and to testify at trial; they also hire process servers to subpoena

---

[664] 547 U.S. at 820

[665] For an analysis of these three cases, see http://www.aequitasresource.org/Williams-v-Illinois-and-Forensic-Evidence-The-Bleeding-Edge-of-Crawford-Issue-11.pdf

[666] *Melendez-Diaz v. Massachusetts*, 557 U.S. 305 (2009) and *Bullcoming v. New Mexico*, 564 U.S. ___(2011),

[667] *Williams v. Illinois,* 132 S.Ct. 2221 (2012).

[668] One commentator, David Boyd, responded to a Supreme Court case blog site:

> "I thought that the US Supreme Court, of all courts, should be giving litigants and the courts of appeal common sense guiding principles to apply to a broader set of cases. All they have done here is muddy the water for everyone (state and federal). They managed to do it on likely the most serious of cases, rape and murder. Nice work."

http://www.crimeandconsequences.com/crimblog/2012/06/making-sense-of-williams-v-ill.html.

essential witnesses. When representing indigent defendants, defense attorneys may petition the agency funding indigent defense for money for these services. Even though the defendant has this right to compulsory process and access to financial resources to make this right meaningful, this right often pales in comparison with the state's ability to access investigators (local, state, and federal law enforcement officers), process servers (the civil department of the sheriff's office), and expert witnesses (the myriad agents and employees of other state agencies).

In addition to guaranteeing the defendant the right to subpoena witnesses, the right to compulsory process may also include the right to present evidence helpful to the defendant. Trial courts may violate the defendant's right to compulsory process when they exclude substantially trustworthy evidence crucial to the defense. For example, in *Chambers v. Mississippi*, 410 US 284 (1973) the Court held that the trial court violated the defendant's rights by excluding evidence that another person had confession to the crime.

RIGHT TO A SPEEDY TRIAL

See, Chapter Six

RIGHT TO A FAIR TRIAL

JUDGE, JURY, PROSECUTORIAL, AND SPECTATOR MISCONDUCT

The defendant's rights to a fair trial may be violated if the judge or jury engages in misconduct during the case. In a bizarre 2010 case, the jury and bailiff had planned a reunion either during or after the penalty phase of the trial. Jury members had given the judge a penis-shaped chocolate and the bailiff a breast-shaped chocolate. Upon learning of this clearly improper *ex parte* contact between the judge and jury after his client had been convicted and sentenced to death, the defense attorney raised fair trial and discovery challenges to the verdict through a writ of habeas corpus (discussed in Chapter Twelve). The U.S. District Court (the first habeas corpus court) held that "the gifts given were inappropriate and represented an unusual display of poor taste in the context of a proceeding so grave as a capital trial."[669] The Eleventh Circuit Court of Appeals, however, denied habeas relief. The Supreme Court remanded, stating,

> [f]rom beginning to end, judicial proceedings conducted for the purpose of deciding whether a defendant shall be put to death must be conducted with dignity and respect. The disturbing facts of this case raise serious questions concerning the conduct of the trial, and this petition raises a serious question about whether the Court of Appeals carefully reviewed those facts before addressing petitioner's constitutional claims.

The state violates the defendant's rights to a fair trial when the prosecutor fails to "set the record straight." If, for example, a state witness lies at trial and the state fails to correct the information by disclosing *Brady* information (evidence that tends to exonerate the defendant), its failure to do so warrants a reversal of the conviction.[670] The state also violates the defendant's rights to a fair trial when the prosecutor misstates fact during defendant's trial.[671] A simple unintentional misstatement is probably not sufficient for the Court to overturn defendant's conviction, but where misconduct was "pronounced and persistent, with a probable cumulative

---

[669] *Wellons v. Hall*, 558 U.S. 220, at 224 (2010)
[670] *See, Banks v. Dretke*, 540 U.S. 668 (2004).
[671] *Berger v. United States*, 295 U.S. 78 (1935).

effect upon the jury which cannot be disregarded as inconsequential … a] new trial must be awarded.[672]

What happens in the courtroom during the trial may affect the defendant's right to a fair trial. Can the defendant get a fair trial when the victim's family and court spectators were wearing buttons with the victim's picture on them during his trial? The court, in *Carey v. Musladin*, 549 U.S. 70 (2006), said yes. It also noted that the button wearing was not a state-sponsored courtroom practice.

Making the defendant look guilty or dangerous violates the defendant's right to a fair trial. Forcing the defendant to appear before the jury in prison clothing violates the Fourteenth Amendment. [673] But, the presence of four uniformed state troopers seated immediately behind the defendant at trial was "not so inherently prejudicial that it denied the defendant a fair trial."[674] Forcing the defendant to appear in shackles during the guilt phase and penalty phases of trial violates the federal Constitution unless it is "justified by an essential state interest — such as the interest in courtroom security — specific to the defendant on trial.[675] The Court stated,

> We do not underestimate the need to restrain dangerous defendants to prevent courtroom attacks, or the need to give trial courts latitude in making individualized security determinations. We are mindful of the tragedy that can result if judges are not able to protect themselves and their courtrooms. But given their prejudicial effect, due process does not permit the use of visible restraints if the trial court has not taken account of the circumstances of the particular case.
> …
> The appearance of the offender during the penalty phase in shackles, however, almost inevitably implies to a jury, as a matter of common sense, that court

---

[672] *Id.* One gets an idea of how egregious the prosecutor's conduct was in the Court's recounting of the trial in that case:

> That the United States prosecuting attorney overstepped the bounds of that propriety and fairness which should characterize the conduct of such an officer in the prosecution of a criminal offense is clearly shown by the record. He was guilty of misstating the facts in his cross-examination of witnesses; of putting into the mouths of such witnesses things which they had not said; of suggesting by his questions that statements had been made to him personally out of court, in respect of which no proof was offered; of pretending to understand that a witness had said something which he had not said and persistently cross-examining the witness upon that basis; of assuming prejudicial facts not in question; of bullying and arguing with witnesses; and, in general, of conducting himself in a thoroughly indecorous and improper manner. . .

> The prosecuting attorney's argument to the jury was undignified and intemperate, containing improper insinuations and assertions calculated to mislead the jury.

> The United States Attorney is the representative not of an ordinary party to a controversy, but of a sovereignty whose obligation to govern impartially is as compelling as its obligation to govern at all; and whose interest, therefore, in a criminal prosecution is not that it shall win a case, but that justice shall be done. As such, he is in a peculiar and very definite sense the servant of the law, the twofold aim of which is that guilt shall not escape or innocence suffer. He may prosecute with earnestness and vigor--indeed, he should do so. But, while he may strike hard blows, he is not at liberty to strike foul ones. It is as much his duty to refrain from improper methods calculated to produce a wrongful conviction as it is to use every legitimate means to bring about a just one.

[673] *Estelle v. Williams*, 425 U.S. 501 (1976). The court found, however, that the defendant in that case had waived any objection to being tried in prison clothes by failing to object at trial.

[674] *Holbrook v. Flynn*, 475 U.S. 560 (1986).

[675] *Missouri v. Deck*, 544 U.S. 622 (2005).

authorities consider the offender a danger to the community—often a statutory aggravator and nearly always a relevant factor in jury decision-making. . . . It also almost inevitably affects adversely the jury's perception of the character of the defendant. And it thereby inevitably undermines the jury's ability to weigh accurately all relevant considerations—considerations that are often unquantifiable and elusive—when it determines whether a defendant deserves death. In these ways, the use of shackles can be a "thumb [on] death's side of the scale.[676]

RIGHT TO HAVE A PUBLIC TRIAL

The Sixth Amendment assures criminal defendants the right to a "public trial." The right to a public trial was well established at common law.

> The knowledge that every criminal trial was subject to contemporaneous review in the forum of public opinion was regarded as an effective restraint on possible abuse of judicial power. It was also thought that if trials were public they might come to the attention of important witnesses unknown to the parties who might voluntarily come forward to testify, and that the conduct of trials in public would enable the spectators to learn about their government and acquire confidence in their judicial remedies.[677]

The defendant's right to have the public present at trial is not unlimited. Kerper noted,

> While the right to a public trial has been construed broadly by the courts, all recognize that the defendant's right to have the public present is subject to certain limitations. The court may limit public attendance to avoid overcrowding, exclude disorderly persons, and bar youthful spectators where testimony involves subjects thought to be inappropriate for their ears.[678]

MEDIA'S RIGHT TO BE PRESENT

Do judges, attorneys, and witnesses posture for the camera? Are they shyer or more gregarious? Does the presence of cameras or coverage cause judges to act or rule in certain ways? Impose certain sentences? Make certain comments? The defendant's right to a public trial is not tantamount to (the same thing as the) media members' right to cover court proceedings. Media members' rights to attend a trial stems from the First Amendment whereas the defendant's right to a public trial stems from the Sixth Amendment.[679] Most state courts now permit cameras in the court if the presiding judge consents, and the judge has considerable discretion to control the coverage. Generally, the media may not photograph or video any jurors, juveniles, and victims of sex crimes. Although televised proceedings may enhance the public's awareness of the judicial process, televised coverage may negatively impact the courtroom work group. Back in 1965 the Court held that a defendant was denied due process because his criminal trial was televised over his objections.[680] At the time, most courts' practice was to ban cameras from the courtroom. In the 1970s, however, many state courts began to allow radio, television, and still-camera coverage of court proceedings subject to limitations to preserve the dignity of the trial. The current practice of

---

[676] 544 U.S. 622, at 628-630 (2005). (The Court ultimately found that defendant's rights to be free from shackles at sentencing is not an absolute constitutional right.)

[677] *United States v. Kobli*, 172 F.2d 919 (3d Cir. 1949).

[678] Kerper, *supra* at 307.

[679] *Garnett Co. v. DePasquale*, 443 U.S. 368 (1979).

[680] *Estes v. Texas*, 381 U.S. 532 (1965). There was significant pre-trial publicity in the *Estes* case, and defendant had moved for a change of venue that the trial court had denied. The Court held that the constitutional right to a public trial is to ensure that the defendant is fairly dealt with, not unjustly convicted.

television in the courtroom varies, and not all states allow proceedings to be televised. In the federal courts, the Federal Rules of Criminal Procedure prohibit the taking of photographs in courtrooms during the judicial proceedings. In March 1996, the U.S. Judicial Conference voted 14-12 to allow federal appeals courts to permit television and still photography coverage in civil but not criminal appeals.

The U.S. Supreme Court allows the recording of its oral arguments but has resisted the pressure to televise these proceedings.[681]

DEFENDANTS RIGHT TO BE PRESENT AT TRIAL.

Under most circumstances, the Sixth Amendment right to confrontation guarantees the physical presence of the defendant in the courtroom at the time any testimony is given against him and at every critical stage of the criminal proceeding.[682] This right may be waived by the defendant, who voluntarily chooses not to be present[683] or who engages in such disruptive behavior in the courtroom that the court chooses to remove him or her.[684] In *Illinois v. Allen*, 397 U.S. 337 (1970), the defendant was so disruptive that the trial court excluded him from the courtroom. The Court held,

> It is essential to the proper administration of criminal justice that dignity, order, and decorum be the hallmarks of all court proceedings in our country. The flagrant disregard in the courtroom of elementary standards of proper conduct should not and cannot be tolerated. We believe trial judges confronted with disruptive, contumacious, stubbornly defiant defendants must be given sufficient discretion to meet the circumstances of each case. No one formula for maintaining the appropriate courtroom atmosphere will be best in all situations. We think there are at least three constitutionally permissible ways for a trial judge to handle an obstreperous defendant like Allen: (1) bind and gag him, thereby keeping him present; (2) cite him for contempt; (3) take him out of the courtroom until he promises to conduct himself properly.[685]

The right to confrontation also includes the defendant's right to face witnesses at trial. In *Coy v. Iowa*, 487 U.S. 1012 (1988), the Court found that the use of a semi-transparent screen placed between the defendant and two youthful victims in a child sex abuse trial violated the defendant's rights. However, the Court later approved of the use of closed-circuit television "when preventing such confrontation is necessary to further important public policy and the reliability of the testimony is otherwise assured ... [stating that] ... although face-to-face confrontation forms the "core" of this constitutional right, it is not an indispensible element."[686]

---

[681] The Covid -19 pandemic necessitated the Court adapt and do things differently than history and customs have dictated; there are now younger justices on the court—many who have been used to an era of televised court proceedings, and so the Court will ultimately and in the near future, succumb to that pressure.

[682] *Snyder v. Massachusetts*, 291 U.S. 97 (1934).

[683] *Taylor v. United States*, 414 U.S. 17 (1973) (Taylor appeared for trial but then voluntarily left once the trial began. The court held that he could be tried *in absentia* (without being present).

[684] See, *Illinois v. Allen*, 397 U.S. 337 (1970)

[685] *Id.* at 339-340.

[686] *Maryland v. Craig*, 497 U.S. 836 (1990). Craig was a child sex abuse case in which the six-year-old victim was allowed to testify in a different room because courtroom testimony would result in the child's suffering such serious emotional distress that she could not reasonably communicate. The testimony was seen and heard via one-way, closed-circuit television.

RIGHT TO BE FREE FROM ADVERSE PRETRIAL PUBLICITY

A recurring theme in this text is that our criminal justice system embraces the principle of orality. In essence this principle holds that a person must be convicted solely on the basis of evidence admitted at trial. The underpinnings of this principle rests on the notion that we don't want the jury deciding guilt or innocence based on any outside information--this includes pretrial and trial publicity given to the case. The Court in *Sheppard v. Maxwell*, 384 U.S. 333 (1966), involved the trial of Sam Sheppard (the story upon which the movie "The Fugitive" was based). The case decision chronicled the intense pre-trial and trial publicity surrounding the case and found that this publicity prevented the defendant from getting a fair trial.

A judge can control publicity so as to ensure a fair trial through a variety of measures including a change of venue, sequestration of the jury, a gag order prohibiting parties in the trial from releasing information to the press or saying anything in public about the trial, and finally, excluding the media from the trial. Although the press has a right to attend a criminal trial, the media may be excluded if the court specifically finds that closure is necessary for a fair trial.

In *Skilling* (discussed above) the Court refused to find that trial publicity and community prejudice prevented Enron CEO, Jeffrey Skilling, from receiving a fair trial. Skilling had moved to change venue from Houston, claiming that adverse pre-trial publicity had poisoned potential jurors. The Court said *Skilling* was different than several earlier cases[687] in which the Court had overturned defendants' convictions because the trial atmosphere had been utterly corrupted by press coverage. The *Skilling* Court noted that pretrial publicity—even persuasive, adverse publicity does not inevitably lead to an unfair trial.[688] The Court found that Skilling neither established that a presumption of juror prejudice arose nor that actual bias infected the jury that had tried him. The trial court, it noted, had stressed impartiality at voir dire and had imposed adequate safeguards. The Court pointed to factors that courts should consider determining whether there was a presumption of prejudice.

- The size and character of the community in which the crime occurred. (Houston was the 4th most populous city in the United States at the time of the trial, and 4.5 million people qualified for jury duty.)
- Whether news story contained a confession by the defendant or blatantly prejudicial information of the type readers or viewers could not reasonably be expected to shut from sight.
- The time between the crime and the trial. (The Court noted that the level of media attention in Skilling's case diminished over time.)
- Evidence from the verdict that would undermine a finding of bias. (In this case, the jury acquitted Skilling of nine counts of insider trading.)

The Court deferred to the trial court's ability to assess through voir dire whether actual prejudice infected the jury. The Court reasoned that the news stories about Enron did not present information that was particularly likely to produce prejudice, particularly in light of Houston's size and diversity.

---

[687] *See, Sheppard v. Maxwell*, 384 U.S. 333 (1966), *Estes v. Texas*, 381 U.S. 532 (1965), and *Rideau v. Louisiana*, 373 U.S. 723 (1963).
[688] See, e.g., *Nebraska Press Assn. v. Stuart*, 427 U.S. 539 (1976).

COMMENTS ON DEFENDANT'S NOT TESTIFYING

The Fifth Amendment guarantees that the defendant has an absolute right to not take the stand and testify. Defendants can present evidence through other witnesses, or they can choose to offer no evidence whatsoever. Defendants often rely simply on cross-examination of the government's witnesses to present their side of the story and challenge the prosecution. The decision to testify or not rests with the defendant in consultation with defense counsel, and this decision is an important tactical decision. Two factors influence this decision. First, defense counsel may not knowingly present perjured testimony. So, if is clear that the defendant wants to take the stand in order to lie, defense counsel must do everything to convince the defendant that they should not do so. If defendant insists on taking the stand, counsel must withdraw from the case. It is a sticky situation, because in order to withdraw, counsel will need to convince the judge that there is a conflict between counsel and client, but counsel must also maintain client confidences and may not inform the judge that the reason they are withdrawing from the case is due to their belief that defendant insists on testifying and presenting false information.

The second factor influencing the defendant's decision whether to testify is the Court's holding in *Griffin v. California,* 380 U.S. 609 (1965), which prohibits a prosecutor from commenting upon defendant's refusal to take the stand.[689] Commenting on the defendant's failure to testify may be one surest and swiftest ways to get a judge to declare a mistrial. Even seemingly innocuous comments that do not even suggest that silence is indicative of defendant's guilt can incur the wrath of the judge. Moreover, prosecutorial comments about defendant's failure to testify are considered plain error, and the appellate courts will overturn verdicts upon those grounds--even when defense counsel fails to object during trial or raise the issue as an assignment of error on appeal.

VICTIMS' RIGHTS TO PARTICIPATE AT TRIAL

Historically, victims have had little right to participate in American criminal trials. Doak notes that victims were

> widely perceived as private parties whose role should be confined to that of witnesses, and participatory rights for such third parties are rejected as a threat to the objectives and public nature of the criminal justice system. However recent years have witnessed both a major shift in attitude in relation to the role of victims within the criminal justice system.[690]

---

[689] In *Griffin* the defendant had been seen with the deceased the evening of her death, and evidence placed him with her in the alley where her body was found. The Court noted that the prosecutor made much of the failure of petitioner to testify including the following statements:

> "The defendant certainly knows whether Essie Mae had this beat up appearance at the time he left her apartment and went down the alley with her. ... What kind of a man is it that would want to have sex with a woman that beat up is she was beat up at the time he left? . . . He would know that. He would know how she got down the alley. He would know how the blood got on the bottom of the concrete steps. He would know how long he was with her in that box. He would know how her wig got off. He would know whether he beat her or mistreated her. He would know whether he walked away from that place cool as a cucumber when he saw Mr. Villasenor, because he was conscious of his own guilt and wanted to get away from that damaged or injured woman. ... These things he has not seen fit to take the stand and deny or explain. ... And, in the whole world, if anybody would know, this defendant would know. ... Essie Mae is dead; she can't tell you her side of the story. ... The defendant won't." *Griffin v. California*, 380 U.S. 609 (1965).

[690] Jonathan Doak, Victims' Rights in Criminal Trials: Prospects for Participation 32(2) *J.L.Soc'y* 294-316 (2005).

Oregon is an example of a state that has seen significant increases in the rights of victims through ballot measures and legislation--particularly since 1985. Although victims have not yet obtained "party" status shared by the prosecution and defendant, victims' rights groups have expended significant effort toward that end. One result of such effort is that, like natural parties in civil cases, victims in Oregon may not be sequestered during the presentation of evidence as other witnesses may be (meaning, although witnesses can generally be kicked out of the courtroom unless they are actually on the stand testifying, a person designated as the victim cannot be kicked out—even though they will give testimony.)

WRAP UP

Although few defendants actually take their cases to trial, this adversarial stage of the criminal justice process is most frequently depicted in the media and, therefore, the most recognized by the public. In the United States the trial process places emphasis on the role of the prosecuting and defense attorneys and the questioning and cross examining of witnesses to present facts to the jury. In a jury trial, the judge plays a rather passive role, instructing the jurors on their obligations, ruling on evidentiary objections, and assuring that the trial keeps moving along. In a bench trial, the judge acts as the jury and must render a verdict of guilty or not guilty. The defendant may have no role in the trial whatsoever, and in many cases the defendant sits quietly throughout the entire trial never uttering a word to the jury--as he or she is constitutionally entitled to do.

The Sixth Amendment houses most of defendant's trial rights: the right to a speedy trial, the right to a jury trial, the right to the assistance of counsel, the right to confront the witnesses against him or her, the right to compel witnesses to testify on his or her behalf, the right to a public trial. Defendants have the right to a "fair trial" through the due process guarantee in the Fifth and Fourteenth Amendments. Defendants' rights to be free from self-incrimination come to fruition at the trial in that prosecutors may not in any manner comment upon defendant's exercise of their rights to remain silent during police interrogation or by refusal to take the stand to testify.

SOME THINGS TO EXPLORE OR THINK ABOUT

➤ Read CNN article from March 8, 2021 on the jury selection process in Derek Chauvin's trial for killing George Floyd in 2020. https://www.cnn.com/2021/03/08/us/derek-chauvin-trial-jury/index.html (last accessed March 9, 2021).

➤ Read about the gag order issued by Judge Amy Berman Jackson against former campaign advisor Roger Stone at https://www.rollingstone.com/politics/politics-news/roger-stone-gag-order-798827/. Read the actual gag order issued by Judge Amy Berman Jackson in the trial of Roger Stone at https://assets.documentcloud.org/documents/5746249/Transcript-Instagram-Post-Leads-ABJ-to-Broaden.pdf . Note, Roger Stone was convicted in November 2019 of lying to congress, witness tampering and obstruction of justice and sentenced in February 2020 to 40 months incarceration. He was pardoned by former president Trump in December 2020. He remains in the news for his potential involvement with the January 6, 2021 riot at the Capital and his association with the Oath Keepers.

➤ Do you think that the government should be able to try a criminal defendant who has voluntarily absented himself or herself from the trial? What dangers does the state face in going through a trial without the defendant's presence? How can those dangers be ameliorated?

- Go watch a criminal trial; how does it compare with your image of trials you have seen in the media? Was it as formal? As dramatic? As lengthy?
- Do you think that victims should be considered parties in a criminal prosecution? How would that change what happens at plea bargaining? Sentencing? The trial?

TERMINOLOGY

- _Allen_ charge
- attorney-client privilege
- _Baston_ challenge
- bench trial
- chain of custody
- challenge for cause
- character evidence
- charging the jury
- circumstantial evidence
- closing statement
- competency
- compulsory process
- confidential communications privileges
- cross examination
- Daubert test
- death-qualified jury
- demonstrative evidence
- direct evidence
- direct examination
- doctor-patient privilege
- expert witness
- eyewitness evidence
- fair cross section rule
- Federal Rules of Evidence
- _Frye_ Test
- government-informant privilege
- hearsay evidence
- hearsay exception
- hearsay exclusion (hearsay exemption)
- husband-wife privilege
- impeaching a jury verdict
- impeaching a witness
- impeachment evidence
- inference
- judicial misconduct
- judicial notice
- jury deliberation
- jury instruction
- jury poll
- lay witness
- offer of proof
- opening statement
- "overruled" ruling
- peremptory challenge
- petit jury
- physical evidence
- presumption
- privilege
- prosecutorial misconduct
- real evidence
- rebuttal
- relevant evidence--relevancy
- right to confrontation
- right to compulsory process
- sequestration
- scientific evidence
- spousal immunity (privilege)
- state secret privilege
- stipulation
- surrebuttal
- "sustained" ruling
- testimonial evidence
- venire
- voir dire
- vouching rule

Chapter Eleven: Sentencing

OVERVIEW AND LEARNING OBJECTIVES

This chapter examines the sentencing phase of the criminal justice system. It explores the role of the legislature in enacting sentencing statutes and schemes, the role of the judge in imposing particular sentences, and the limitations on judicial discretion in sentencing. This chapter also introduces sentencing approaches and philosophies adopted over time and examines the forms of punishment applied to convicted offenders. After reading this chapter, you should be able to answer the following questions:

> ➢ What is the role of legislators, judges, juries, correctional boards, and the voting public in determining appropriate sentences and punishments? How have those roles changed over time?
> ➢ What are the various approaches and philosophies of sentencing that have been identified and used over time? When were each employed?
> ➢ What is the significance of the decision in *Apprendi v. New Jersey*?
> ➢ What are the forms of monetary sanctions and how do they differ?
> ➢ What are the forms of confinement sanctions and how do they differ?
> ➢ What are the forms of community-based sanctions and how do they differ?

Once the defendant either enters a guilty plea or is found guilty by a jury, the case moves on to the sentencing phase. Judges are responsible for sentencing a convicted offender in all but death penalty cases. Sentencing is governed both by procedural and substantive laws. Procedural law governs whether the sentencing hearing should be bifurcated (separate) from the trial or entry of plea and the timing of such hearings; it guides judges in deciding whether the defendant can remain free on bail; it mandates that defendants have the right to be represented by an attorney at sentencing and have the right to make a statement to the judge before being sentence. In death penalty states, the procedures governing the jury's decision to impose capital punishment or not are complicated and specific. Substantive criminal law governs whether a particular sentence is impermissibly cruel and unusual--is it needlessly cruel or barbaric, is it disproportionate--or whether the sentence violates the Equal Protection Clause because it is imposed in a discriminatory manner. [691] One more "big picture" question is whether the legislature oversteps its authority and role by limiting judicial discretion enacting mandatory minimum sentences or mandatory sentencing guidelines.

---

[691] Sentences based on classifications involving a defendant's race, gender, ethnicity, or nationality violate the Equal Protection Clause. Sometimes, seemingly neutral laws have a discriminatory impact. The Court held in *McKlesky v. Kemp*, 481 U.S. 279 (1987), that, although statistical evidence may show that a neutral law has had discriminatory impact against one race generally, defendants must clearly establish that the decision makers in *his* case acted with discriminatory intent.

PROCEDURAL SENTENCING LAW

Every jurisdiction requires that adult sentencing hearings be conducted in open court. Some jurisdictions allow juvenile sentencing hearings to be conducted *in camera* (in the judge's chambers). In some states, when the defendant is charged only with misdemeanors the first appearance, arraignment, plea and sentence may take place all in one short hearing. But some state statutes require that the sentencing phase be "bifurcated"--meaning, separated by at least a few days. The defendant can generally waive the statutory period, but in felony cases, the court generally dockets the sentencing hearing a few weeks after the trial or entry of a guilty plea. This time allows presentence investigators, generally probation officers, to prepare a pre-sentence report and submit them to the court. If the judge allows the offender to remain out-of-custody on bail, this time also allows the offender, who is now possibly facing incarceration, to get his or her affairs in order before going to prison. All death penalty cases must be bifurcated. Unlike most sentencing hearings which are relatively informal and do not involve the jury, the penalty phase in a capital case involves an extensive, fact-finding process.

PRE-SENTENCE REPORTS

Pre-sentence investigations and reports (PSI) assist judges in determining the appropriate sentence to impose in serious felony cases and in all death penalty cases. As local criminal justice resources have dwindled, PSI's in state prosecutions have become increasingly rare, but federal judges continue to rely heavily on PSI's which are written by federal probation officers. Conducting a pre-sentence investigation and preparing the report can be very time consuming. These reports document the defendant's criminal or delinquency history, medical history, family background, economic status, education, employment history and other information. Most jurisdictions allow courts to order physical or mental examinations of defendants. The defendant has the constitutional right to inspect PSI in capital cases,[692] and most states and the federal government allow defendant to inspect PSI in all cases. In some states, judges have discretion to limit the defendant's access to the PSI. A judge may, for example, release factual materials from the PSI such as police reports, but then decline to disclose statements made in confidence to investigators. Other legal issues involving the use and preparation of pre-sentence investigation include whether hearsay should be included, whether the defendant has the right to have an attorney present during a pre-sentence interview, what should happen when the PSI contains significant factual errors/inaccuracies, and whether the court should consider information in the PSI that is the result of illegal search and seizure or an illegally obtained confession.

RIGHT OF ALLOCUTION

At the sentencing hearing, judges consider the terms of a negotiated plea or evidence received at trial, the pre-sentence report, evidence offered by either party that shows that this case or offender is more heinous or horrible than most (called "aggravating factors") or less serious or less culpable than most (called "mitigating factors"), and any statement the defendant may want to make. The defendant has the absolute right to make a statement to the court before being sentenced. This is called the right of allocution. The defendant's statements are generally the last comments the judge will hear before imposing sentence. If the defendant wants, he or she can also remain silent, and the judge cannot draw any negative inferences if the right to allocution is waived.

---

[692] *Gardner v. Florida*, 430 U.S. 349 (1977).

RIGHT TO COUNSEL AT SENTENCING

Because sentencing is considered a critical stage in the criminal justice process,[693] the defendant has the right to defense counsel's assistance during the sentencing hearing. Defense attorneys are expected to highlight the mitigating factors in the case and, to the extent possible, explain and minimize the aggravating factors. Since few cases go to trial, the sentencing will be the only time that most defendants have the opportunity to discuss their version of events. The presence of defense counsel at sentencing ensures that the plea bargain will be followed, and if there were any miscommunications, the plea can, under exceptional circumstances, be withdrawn before sentence is pronounced.

VICTIM AND VICTIM IMPACT STATEMENTS

Victim impact statements are testimony from the friends and family of a murder victim that demonstrate to the jury how they were impacted by the victim's death. These witnesses are allowed to include statements about the physical, economic, and psychological effects of the crime. Such testimony is often emotionally charged and can have a powerful impact on the jury. The Court initially disallowed these statements finding that they raised possibility that the death sentence would be based on irrelevant considerations.[694] But four years later it approved their use stating, "Just as the murderer should be considered as an individual, so to the victim is an individual whose death represents a unique loss to society."[695] The federal government and approximately twenty states authorize direct victim involvement in sentencing. All fifty states allow written submissions.[696] Prosecutors' offices generally have a victims' rights division that communicates with the victims to advise them of their rights and keep them notified as to sentencing dates. Even if victims do not wish to speak during the hearing or submit written testimony, they can participate in sentencing by providing the court restitution information.

SUBSTANTIVE SENTENCING LAW

The Constitution doesn't have much to say about sentencing specifically. Kerper described the interplay between judges', legislators', and jurors' roles in sentencing. She wrote,

> We tend to view sentencing as the responsibility of the judge since it is the judge who formally pronounces the sentence. Actually, the initial responsibility for sentencing lies with the legislature, which commonly shares that responsibility with the judge. How the responsibility is shared varies from state to state. In all states, the legislature will make the initial determination as to whether a particular form of punishment can be imposed for a particular crime. The legislature's refusal to authorize a certain punishment is binding on the judge. The court has no common law power to impose fines, for example, where the legislature has not provided for the use of fines in sentencing. Ordinarily, the legislature will authorize more than one punishment for a particular crime and will give the court some discretion in its selection of the appropriate punishment. The court will be given a choice, for example, between probation and imprisonment. Once that

---

[693] _Mempha v. Rhay,_ 389 US 128 (1967).

[694] _Booth v. Maryland,_ 482 U.S. 496 (1987).

[695] _Payne v. Tennessee,_ 501 U.S. 808 (1991). Payne stabbed the victim and her two-year-old daughter in front of her three-year-old son. The trial court admitted the victim's mother's testimony that the victim's son continued to cry for his mother. The Court held that disallowing victim impact statements "deprived the State of the full moral force of its evidence and may prevent the jury from having before it all the information necessary to determine the proper punishment for a first-degree murder." 501 U.S. at 825.

[696] Lippman, _Procedure, supra_ at 59.

choice is made, the court then will have further discretion in shaping the form of punishment (e.g., the length of imprisonment or the terms of probation.) That discretion will be subjected to at least some legislative control. For example, the legislature always will set a limit on the highest possible term of imprisonment for each offense.

The discretion granted to the judge in setting sentences usually varies with the type of sentence imposed. Legislatures tend to exercise different degrees of control over the imposition of capital punishment, imprisonment, probation, and fines. ...

We have assumed so far that the responsibility for sentencing is being shared only by the legislature and the court. In most jurisdictions, for fines and probation, these are the only two agencies involved in determining the sentence, Sentences of imprisonment, on the other hand, often involve another agency, the parole board. While the board does not set the term of imprisonment, it often has authority to determine the length of time actually served in a prison. ... The jury is another body that may be given sentencing responsibility. The authority to impose capital punishment commonly is divided between the legislature (which sets guidelines) and the trier of facts in the particular case. As a practical matter, since most defendants in capital cases prefer a jury trial to a bench trial, the responsibility for determining whether the death sentence is to be imposed usually lies with the jury. For most states, this is the sole area of juror sentencing responsibility.[697]

Kerper described the American criminal justice process in the 1970s--a time when indeterminate sentencing was common. The 1980s saw a dramatic change in sentencing philosophy, and cries for "truth in sentencing" resulted in a variety of measures aimed at reducing the range of judicial discretion and widespread enactment of sentencing guidelines. In the 1990s mandatory minimums and "three strikes" laws further limited judges' discretion, and with *Apprendi v. New Jersey*[698] in 2000, judges' role in sentencing has been further constrained. Today, Kerper would likely mention the diminished role of parole boards and the increased role of the voters through direct democracy in establishing mandatory minimum sentences through propositions, ballot measures, initiatives, and referendums. Scheb noted that judges still have discretion in sentencing.

Sharp disagreements exist regarding the roles that legislature, judges, and corrections officials should play in determining punishments. Generally, judges are required to impose sentences that fall within the parameters of appropriate punishments specified by statute, yet within these parameters, courts exercise substantial discretion.[699]

APPROACHES TO SENTENCING

State and federal approaches to sentencing have shifted in response to prevailing criminal justice thinking and philosophy. Over time, governments have embraced four different approaches to sentencing offenders to incarceration (indeterminate, indefinite, determinate, or definite). Criminal codes may incorporate more than one single approach. These approaches can be seen as a spectrum of judicial discretion. Indefinite and indeterminate sentences at one end are

---

[697] Kerper, *supra* at 157.
[698] 530 U.S. 466 (2000).
[699] Scheb, *supra* at 653.

those that allow judges and parole boards the most discretion and authority. Determinate and definite sentences, at the other end, allow little or no discretion. Currently, most states are following determinate sentencing coupled with sentencing guideline, mandatory minimums, habitual offender statutes, and penalty enhancement statutes.

INDETERMINATE SENTENCING APPROACH

For much of the twentieth century legislatures commonly allowed judges to sentence criminals to imprisonment for indeterminate periods. Under this system, judges sentenced the offender to prison (for no specific time frame) and release was contingent upon getting parole. Correctional officials were permitted to hold a criminal in custody until parole boards determined that he or she was rehabilitated. Because some criminals would quickly be reformed but other criminals would be resistant to change, indeterminate sentencing's open-ended time frame was deemed optimal for allowing treatment and reform to take its course--no matter how quickly or slowly. The decline of popular support for rehabilitation has led most jurisdictions to abandon the concept of indeterminate sentencing.

INDEFINITE SENTENCING APPROACH

Indefinite sentences give judges discretion, within defined limits, to set a minimum and maximum sentence length. The judge imposes a range of years to be served, and a parole board decides when offender will ultimately be released.[700]

DETERMINATE SENTENCING APPROACH

Under determinate sentencing judges have little discretion in sentencing. The legislature sets specific statutory parameters, and the judge sets a fixed term of years within that time frame. The sentencing laws allow the court to increase the term if it finds aggravating factors, and reduce the term if it finds mitigating factors. With determinate sentencing the defendant knows immediately when he or she will be released. In determinate sentencing, offenders may receive credit for time served while in pretrial detention and "good time" credits. The discretion that judges are allowed in initially setting the fixed term is what distinguishes determinate sentencing from definite sentencing.

DEFINITE SENTENCING APPROACH

Definite sentencing completely eliminates judicial discretion and ensures that offenders who commit the same crimes are punished equally. The definite sentence is set by the legislature with no leeway for judges or corrections officials to individualize punishment. Currently, no jurisdiction embraces this inflexible approach that prohibits any consideration of aggravating and mitigating factors in sentencing. Although mandatory minimum sentencing embraces some aspects of definite sentencing, judges may still impose longer than the minimum sentence and therefore retain some limited discretion.

PRESUMPTIVE SENTENCING GUIDELINES

In the 1980s state legislatures and Congress, responding to criticism that wide judicial discretion resulted in great sentence disparities, adopted sentencing guidelines drafted by legislatively-established commissions. These commissions proposed sentencing formulas based on variety of factors, but the two most important factors in any sentencing guideline scheme were the nature of the crime and the offenders' criminal history. Some states enacted advisory sentencing guidelines--suggestions to judges statewide of what was considered an appropriate sentence that should be followed in most cases. Some states enacted mandatory sentence

---

[700] *Id.* at 676.

guidelines that required judges to impose "presumptive" (presumed appropriate) sentences unless mitigating or aggravating factors were identified on the record.

Sentencing guidelines generally differentiate between presumptive prison sentences and presumptive probation sentences. Judges who "depart" (select a different sentence) from the presumptive sentences can do a dispositional departure in which they impose prison when probation was the presumptive sentence or do a dispositional departure in which they impose probation instead of prison. Judges may also do a durational departure in which they sentence the offender to a term length different than the presumptive term length--for example, giving a 18 month sentence rather than a 26 month sentence.

Guideline sentencing allows for judicial discretion, but at the same time limits that discretion. Judges must generally make findings when departing from a presumptive sentence that are tied to aggravating factors or mitigating factors.

FEDERAL SENTENCING GUIDELINES

The Sentencing Reform Act of 1984 first established federal sentencing guidelines. The Act applied to all crimes committed after November 1, 1987 and its purpose was "to establish sentencing policies and practices for the federal criminal justice system that will assure the ends of justice by promulgating detailed guidelines prescribing the appropriate sentences for offenders convicted of federal crimes."[701] It created the United States Sentencing Guideline Commission and gave it authority to create the guidelines. The Commission dramatically reduced the discretion of federal judges by establishing a narrow sentencing range and required that judges who departed from the ranges state in writing their reason for doing so. The Act also established for appellate review of federal sentences and abolished the U.S. Parole Commission.

STATE FELONY GUIDELINES

Most states have adopted some version of sentencing guidelines—from the very simple to the very complex. Many states restrict their guidelines to felonies. Although limiting judicial discretion, state sentencing guideline schemes all allow some wiggle room if the judge finds that the case differs from the run of the mill case.

There is still considerable uncertainty about the efficacy of sentencing guidelines. There is evidence that they have reduced sentencing disparities but they clearly have not eliminated this problem altogether. There is also concern that sentencing guidelines have promoted higher incarceration rates and have thus contributed to the problem of prison overcrowding. It is fair to say that to be successful, sentencing guidelines must be accompanied by policies designed to effectively manage prison populations. [702]

SENTENCING GUIDELINES — *APPRENDI* AND ITS PROGENY

In 2000 the Court called into question the validity of state and federal sentencing guidelines in those cases where a judge imposed harsher sentences than permitted under the guidelines. After a series of decisions, beginning with *Apprendi v. New Jersey*, if a judge wants to impose a sentence that is more severe than the presumptive guideline sentence for any reason

---

[701] Scheb, *supra* at 681; (18 U.S. C.A. §§ 3551 et. seq. 28 U.S.C.A. §§991-998.)
[702] *Id.* at 683.

other than the defendant's prior criminal history, that reason must be submitted to the jury, and the jury must find that this fact exists beyond a reasonable doubt.[703]

The facts of *Apprendi* were as follows:

Charles C. Apprendi, Jr. fired several shots into the home of an African- American family. While in custody, Apprendi made a statement, which he later retracted, that he did not want the family in his neighborhood because of their race. Apprendi was charged under New Jersey law with second-degree possession of a firearm for an unlawful purpose, which carries a prison term of 5 to 10 years. The count did not refer to the state's hate crime statute, which provides for an enhanced sentence if a trial judge finds, by a preponderance of the evidence, that the defendant committed the crime with a purpose to intimidate a person or group because of race. After Apprendi pleaded guilty, the prosecutor filed a motion to enhance the sentence. The court found, by a preponderance of the evidence, that the shooting was racially motivated and sentenced Apprendi to a 12-year term on the firearms count. In upholding the sentence, the appeals court rejected Apprendi's claim that the Due Process Clause requires that a bias finding be proved to a jury beyond a reasonable doubt.[704]

Apprendi, a 5-4 decision that has significantly impacted the criminal justice system, held that it was unconstitutional for a judge to justify a harsher sentence using facts proven only to the judge by a preponderance of the evidence. *Apprendi* ties the requirement that a jury make factual findings to the Sixth Amendment's jury trial guarantee. The right to a jury determination on sentencing factors is not absolute because *Apprendi's* holding does not extend to situations in which the judge imposes a sentence less severe than the presumptive guideline sentence.

Why *Apprendi's* holding was such a big deal became clear in 2004 when the Court applied its rationale to a state sentencing guideline scheme in *Blakely v. Washington*, 542 U.S. 296 (2004). The Washington sentencing guidelines used to sentence Blakely permitted the trial court to enhance his sentence based on the judge's determination that Blakely acted with deliberate cruelty. The Court held that the state trial court's sentencing of a defendant to a prison term longer than the guideline maximum on the basis of the judge's finding violated the defendant's Sixth Amendment right to a trial by jury.

Blakely called into question all sentencing guideline schemes across the nation, including the Federal Sentencing Guidelines. Federal judges wondered whether the federal guidelines would similarly be declared invalid (since their enhancement provisions were identical to those in *Blakely*.) Federal judges began to postpone sentencing offenders until they could get more guidance from the Court. Many Court watchers anticipated that the Court would immediately hear and decide the companion cases of *United States v. Booker/Fanfan*, 543 U.S. 220 (2005)[705] in order to prevent a backlog of federal cases waiting to be sentenced. But it did not. Although oral arguments on the case were held on Monday, October 4, 2004 (the first possible day of the new

---

[703] *Apprendi v. New Jersey*, 530 U.S. 466 (2000).
[704] http://www.oyez.org/cases/1990-1999/1999/1999_99_478
[705] Following U.S. Sentencing Guidelines, a federal district court judge enhanced Freddie Booker's sentence based on facts the judge determined. Booker appealed and the Seventh Circuit Court of Appeals ruled the guidelines violated the Sixth Amendment where they required sentences to be based on facts found by a judge. A federal judge sentenced Duncan Fanfan to 188-235 months in prison based on facts the judge determined. The judge decided *Blakely v. Washington* prevented him from enhancing the sentence and sentenced Fanfan to 78 months. The federal government appealed directly to the U.S. Supreme Court.

term), the decisions were not announced until January 12, 2005. Several justices wrote separate opinions. One majority of the Court determined that the federal sentencing guidelines were invalid, but a different majority held that the remedy was to declare the guidelines discretionary rather than mandatory. After *Booker/Fanfan* U.S. District Court judges have authority to determine sentencing factors by a preponderance of the evidence. But, if they wish to increase the defendant's sentence beyond the maximum in the guidelines, they must submit those facts to a jury who must be convinced beyond a reasonable doubt.

Because the federal guidelines are now advisory, judges can sentence outside the sentencing scheme, and federal judges who had been very critical of the scheme due to its disparate treatment of cocaine and crack possession are now free to ignore the guidelines and treat these cases more similarly. Since *Booker/Fanfan* the Court has held that federal trial judges' sentences which fall within the sentencing guideline are presumptively reasonable[706] and that appellate courts should give the sentencing courts due deference because they are in the best position to sentence the defendant.[707]

OTHER *APPRENDI* ISSUES

Although *Apprendi* had the potential of upsetting entire sentencing schemes (as it did in Blakely, an almost did in *Booker/Fanfan*), it applies, only in those cases in which a judge wants to enhance a penalty. The Court has not invalidated a defendant's sentence because it was too lenient. Notwithstanding *Apprendi*, trial judges, not jurors, decide whether to impose concurrent or consecutive sentences.[708] Jurors, however, are responsible for deciding whether to impose the death penalty. In a state death penalty case, *Arizona v. Ring*, 536 U.S. 584 (2002), the jury convicted Ring of murder, and during the bifurcated sentencing hearing the trial judge concluded that the murder was committed in an especially heinous manner and imposed death penalty even though the jury had only recommended a life sentence. The Court, relying on *Apprendi*, held that the jury should have made the factual determination that increased defendant's statutory maximum sentence from life to death. In light of *Ring*, five states that had similar sentencing schemes modified their death penalty laws. On January 12, 2016 the Court issued its opinion in *Hurst v. Florida*, 577 U.S. 92 (2016) and held that Florida's capital sentencing scheme violates the Sixth Amendment in light of Ring.

> A Florida jury convicted petitioner Timothy Hurst of first-degree murder for killing a co-worker and recommended the death penalty. The court sentenced Hurst to death, but he was granted a new sentencing hearing on appeal. At resentencing, the jury again recommended death, and the judge again found the facts necessary to sentence Hurst to death. The Florida Supreme Court affirmed, rejecting Hurst's argument that his sentence violated the Sixth Amendment in light of *Ring v. Arizona*, in which this Court found unconstitutional an Arizona

---

[706] *Rita v. United States*, 551 U.S. 338 (2007).

[707] *Gall v. United States*, 552 U.S. 38 (2007). While a student at University of Iowa, Gall was involved in a drug ring distributing ecstasy. He left "his life of crime," moved to Arizona, started a business, and when he found out the federal government had tracked him down, he turned himself in and plead guilty to the charge. The judge considered Gall's youth, his rehabilitation, and other mitigating circumstances and ordered 36 months of probation instead of following the 36-month prison term the "advised in" the guidelines. The appellate court rejected the sentence and held that even though the guidelines are advisory, trial courts should follow them and sentences outside the range must overcome a presumption of unreasonableness. The Supreme Court disagreed.

[708] *Oregon v. Ice*, 555 U.S. 160 (2009). *Ice* was a 5-4 split decision. Justice Scalia wrote for the four dissenting justices that because consecutive sentences increased the defendant's punishment based on judicial findings rather than jury findings, defendant's sentence violated the Sixth Amendment right to a jury trial.

capital sentencing scheme that permitted a judge rather than the jury to find the facts necessary to sentence a defendant to death.

. . . Applying *Apprendi* to the capital punishment context, the *Ring* Court had little difficulty concluding that an Arizona judge's independent factfinding exposed Ring to a punishment greater than the jury's guilty verdict authorized. *Ring's* analysis applies equally here. Florida requires not the jury but a judge to make the critical findings necessary to impose the death penalty. That Florida provides an advisory jury is immaterial. As with *Ring*, Hurst had the maximum authorized punishment he could receive increased by a judge's own factfinding. (Citations omitted.) [709]

Apprendi also impacts prosecutors' charging practices. Any potential enhancement factor must now be set out in the charging document (i.e., the information or indictment). If the case goes to a jury trial, the prosecution must prove the enhancement factor beyond a reasonable doubt as reflected in a special verdict form submitted to the jury.

The court dealt with *Apprendi* holding in a revocation of probation/release case. *United States v. Haymond*, 588 U.S. ___ (2019). Andre Ralph Haymond had been convicted by a jury of one count of possession and attempted possession of child pornography and was sentenced to 38-months' imprisonment followed by ten years of supervised release. Two years into his supervised release, probation officers conducted a surprise search of Haymond's apartment and seized several devices. After conducting a forensic examination of the devices, officers found evidence that the devices had recently contained child pornography. Based on these findings, Haymond's probation officer alleged that Haymond had committed five violations of his supervised release, the relevant one of which was the possession of child pornography, in violation of the mandatory condition that Haymond not commit another federal, state, or local crime. At a revocation hearing, a district judge, acting without a jury, found by a preponderance of the evidence that he knowingly downloaded and possessed child pornography.[710] Under 18 U. S. C. §3583(e)(3), the judge could have sentenced him to a prison term of between zero and two additional years. But because possession of child pornography is an enumerated offense under a section of that statute that requires a mandatory minimum, (§3583(k)), the judge, feeling bound by statute to do so, imposed that provision's 5-year mandatory minimum. Haymond appealed the new punishment and its constitutionality. The Tenth Circuit Court of Appeals observed that whereas a jury had convicted Haymond beyond a reasonable doubt of a crime carrying a prison term of zero to 10 years, this new prison term included a new and higher mandatory minimum resting on facts found only by a judge by a preponderance of the evidence. The Tenth Circuit therefore held that §3583(k) violated the right to trial by jury guaranteed by the Fifth and Sixth Amendments. The Supreme Court, in a split plurality opinion, found that,

Only a jury, acting on proof beyond a reasonable doubt, may take a person's liberty. That promise stands as one of the Constitution's most vital protections against arbitrary government. Yet in this case a congressional statute compelled a federal judge to send a man to prison for a minimum of five years without empaneling a jury of his peers or requiring the government to prove his guilt

---

[709] *Hurst v. Florida*, 577 U.S. 92 (2016).
[710] The judge decided in light of expert testimony regarding the manner in which cellphones can "cache" images without the user's knowledge there was insufficient evidence to show that Haymond knowingly possessed 46 of the images. At the same time, the judge found it more likely than not that Haymond knowingly downloaded and possessed the remaining 13 images.

beyond a reasonable doubt. As applied here, we do not hesitate to hold that the statute violates the Fifth and Sixth Amendments.

MANDATORY MINIMUM SENTENCES

Legislative enactments, ballot measures, initiatives, and referendums have resulted in mandatory minimum sentences schemes in which offenders who commit certain crimes must be sentenced to prison terms for minimum periods. Mandatory minimum sentences trump, but do not completely replace, whatever sentencing guidelines may be in place. It is possible for a judge to impose a sentence that exceeds the mandatory minimum on an offender who, because of his or her extensive criminal history or particular brutality of the crime, warrants a particularly harsh guideline sentence.

Mandatory minimum sentences are a type of determinate sentence. Most mandatory minimum sentences are for violent offenses or those involving the use of firearms. Federal law also mandates minimum prison terms for serious drug crimes prosecuted in federal courts. For example, a person charged with possession with the intent to distribute more than five kilograms of cocaine is subject to a mandatory minimum sentence of ten years in prison. See 21 U.S.C.A. §841 (b) (1)(A). In 1996 the Court held that federal courts have no authority to impose lesser sentences than those mandated by Congress unless prosecutors specifically request such departures. This, of course, provided federal prosecutors leverage in persuading defendants to turn against their co-defendants and provide evidence against other suspects--a particularly useful tool in prosecuting drug distribution conspiracies. Mandatory minimum sentences for federal drug crimes have contributed to prison overcrowding. Moreover, because federal drug laws treat crack cocaine and powder cocaine differently, these sentencing schemes have contributed to the racial imbalance in federal prisons. Crack cocaine, generally used more predominantly by minorities, was treated 100 times more severely than powder cocaine, generally used more predominately by Caucasians. The Fair Sentencing Act of 2012 removed some of the disparity by now treating crack use only 18 times more severely than powder cocaine use. This Act also eliminated the mandatory five-year minimum sentence that formerly applied to the simple possession of crack cocaine.[711]

In our attempts to limit judicial discretion, we may have perhaps gone too far. Judges must impose mandatory minimum sentences regardless of any compelling mitigating facts that warrant a lesser sentence--even when victims fervently request leniency for the defendant. Sentencing discretion resting with a neutral judge has been replaced by charging discretion resting with the prosecutor. Prosecutors, in filing certain charges, can now compel negotiated pleas, and they now hold "most of the cards." Critics argue that prosecutors wield this additional power in a coercive fashion to force defendants to give up going to trial on cases with "triable" issues out of fear of receiving a mandatory minimum sentence.

OTHER MANDATORY SENTENCES--PENALTY ENHANCEMENTS

Legislatures have also exercised their authority over sentencing by passing laws that enhance criminal penalties for crimes against certain victims, for crimes done with weapons, or for hate crimes. For example, Congress passed the Violent Crime Control and Law Enforcement

---

[711] Federal drug sentencing is an area in flux. In December 2015, President Obama, using his executive authority to deal with sentences outside of the judicial or legislative process, commuted the sentences of 95 more federal drug offenders and has called for an evaluation of federal drug sentences. His actions have called attention to federal drug sentencing laws which, at times, have been "draconian." See, https://www.washingtonpost.com/world/national-security/president-obama-commutes-sentences-of-about-100-drug-offenders/2015/12/18/9b62c91c-a5a3-11e5-9c4e-be37f66848bb_story.html

Act of 1994 that included several provisions for enhanced penalties for drug trafficking in prisons and drug free zones and illegal drug use in federal prisons. States have passed gun enhancements and hate crime enhancements.[712]

FEDERAL SENTENCING REFORMS

Federal drug sentencing is an area in flux. In December 2015, President Obama, using his executive authority to deal with sentences outside of the judicial or legislative process, commuted the sentences of 95 more federal drug offenders and has called for an evaluation of federal drug sentences. His actions have called attention to federal drug sentencing laws which, at times, have been "draconian."[713] Somewhat in response, Congress enacted the First Step Act in 2018-- described as one of the "most sweeping pieces of criminal justice reform in decades. The Act authorized defendants to file motions in federal court requesting reduced sentences and compassionate leave. It "made changes to the "safety valve," which relieves certain drug trafficking offenders from statutory mandatory minimum penalties. Additionally, it made the Fair Sentencing Act retroactive, applying the law to 3,000 people who were convicted of crack offenses before the law went into effect in 2010.[714] On September 29,2022 the United States Sentencing Commission[715] announced its tentative legislative policy priorities for the 2022-2023 "amendment year[716]" which were unanimously approved in October 2022[717]. Its top focus is on implementation of the First Step Act of 2018[718].

---

[712] *See, e.g.,* ORS 161.610 authorizing enhanced penalties for the use of firearm during commission of felony and *Wisconsin v. Mitchell*, 508 U.S. 486 (1993) authorizing enhanced penalties for hate crimes.

[713] See, https://www.washingtonpost.com/world/national-security/president-obama-commutes-sentences-of-about-100-drug-offenders/2015/12/18/9b62c91c-a5a3-11e5-9c4e-be37f66848bb_story.html

[714] https://www.nacdl.org/Landing/DrugLaw

[715] The United States Sentence Commission, an independent agency which is organized under the judicial branch and created by the Sentencing Reform Act of 1984, is tasked with establishing sentencing policies and practices of the federal courts. The Commission reviews and refines the guidelines in light of court of appeals decisions, congressional action, sentencing-related research and input from the criminal justice community. The Commission lost a voting quorum shortly after the enactment of the First Step Act in December 2018. This prevented the commission from setting priorities and amending the federal sentencing guidelines, but the Commission was newly reconstituted in late 2022.

[716] The amendment cycle begins in June and ends in April, but the recently confirmed commissioners are working on an expedited timetable to finalize priorities in October and adopt amendments by May 1, 2023. See, https://www.ussc.gov/about/news/press-releases/september-29-2022. See also, https://www.ussc.gov/policymaking/federal-register-notices/federal-register-notice-proposed-2022-2023-priorities

[717] https://www.ussc.gov/about/news/press-releases/october-28-2022

[718] In September, 2022 the Federal Bureau of Prisons (BOP) first announced its interpretations and calculations for "First Step Act" credits (reductions in sentences). It was not received well. To say it was "stingy" with how it calculated who would be eligible for reduced sentences is an understatement.

The BOP is known for narrowly interpreting policies that could lead to prisoners being taken out of their correctional institution custody. In fact, the BOP's initial interpretation how prisoner's earned FSA credits was so cumbersome and limiting that almost nobody would have realized a reduction in their sentence. Congressman Hakeem Jeffries (D–NY) comment in on the BOP's early interpretation of the type of participation needed to earn credits said that is, "...does not appear to be a good faith attempt to honor congressional intent." It is clear that Congress wanted fewer minimum security prisoners in prison.

There are already so many requirements that make even minimum and low security inmates ineligible. There are a total of 68 criminal offenses that exclude inmates from being eligible from

FORMS OF SENTENCES

Early forms of punishment included corporal punishment, fines, banishment, or execution. The primary forms of corporal punishment were branding, flogging, and mutilation. When the American colonies broke away from England, English law recognized over 200 different felonies--each subject to capital punishment. Many of the (felonies punishable by capital punishment) then, are just misdemeanors today. Eighty percent of executions were for property offenses, and some involved only petty theft. Executions were public affairs, attended by huge crowds, and often carried out as cruelly as possible. Gradually, people became dissatisfied with the heavy use of capital punishment, and judges and juries discovered various ways to get around imposing death sentences; for example, judges could reduce certain crimes to misdemeanors which did not require capital punishment.[719]

MONETARY SANCTIONS

FINES

Fines, a sum of money the offender has to pay as punishment for the crime, are generally viewed as the least severe of all possible punishments. Fines may either supplement imprisonment or probation, or they may be the sole punishment. Criminal codes generally authorize fines as punishment for most crimes, but some of the older criminal codes did not authorize fines for murder.

---

applying the FSA credits to reduce their sentence. Non-US citizens are not eligible. District of Columbia offenders are ineligible as are any offender who does not have a period of supervised release. According to the Department of Justice, approximately 65,000 out of 131,386 federal prisoners, would be ineligible to earn FSA Time Credits under the FSA due to the inmate's crime of conviction alone (as of August 27, 2020). This new 18-month requirement will further restrict those eligible for earlier release.

With this more restrictive condition, BOP is even going against the Department of Justice's intent of FSA which was to "transfer eligible inmates who satisfy the criteria in 3624(g) [awarding of FSA credits] to supervised release to the extent practicable, rather than prerelease custody [halfway house and home confinement]." The internal memorandum posted went on to state prisoners with "immigration issues" would not be eligible. One person who retired from the BOP said of the memorandum, "BOP is creating their own language and leaving the discretion in the hands of case managers to interpret who is eligible and who is not. They have completely disrespected the intent and FSA law states."

Thousands of prisoners will be affected by this unilateral decision by the BOP. For many prisoners, their date for returning to society has been prolonged by a memorandum that is both unfair and arbitrary. [T]the law allowed eligible inmates, those with an unlikely chance of recidivism and low or minimum security, to earn credits toward an earlier release from prison. Those credits were to be earned by prisoners participating in certain needs-based educational programs and actively participating in productive activities, like a prison job. For every 30 days of successful participation, the prisoner could earn up to 15 days off their sentence up to a maximum of 12 months (365 days).

That is what the law states, but the BOP added a new wrinkle stating that those with short sentences, who are also more likely to be minimum or low security, will get no benefit of an earlier release."

https://www.forbes.com/sites/walterpavlo/2022/09/09/bureau-of-prisons-interpretation-of-first-step-act-will-leave-thousands-of-inmates-incarcerated/?sh=762a6b552f94.

[719] *See,* Kerper, *supra* at 61.

The Model Penal Code proposed legislative guidelines on the use of fines, but states have generally rejected this provision. Instead, judges are given extremely broad discretion in setting the amount of the fines, and there are few limits on the judge's ability to impose a fine. Frequently, the criminal statute will specify the highest permissible fine. The Eighth Amendment's Cruel and Unusual Punishment Clause prohibits excessive fines, but courts rarely have found a fine to violate this provision. In *Tate v. Short*, 401 U.S. 395 (1971), the Court found that fines that punish poor people more harshly than rich people violate the Equal Protection Clause. Historically, magistrates had given offenders the option of paying a fine or serving a jail sentence. Sentences were frequently "thirty dollars or thirty days." If defendants were too poor to pay the fine, they went to jail. The *Tate* Court reasoned that the state could imprison Tate for committing the crime, but by requiring either time or a fine, the state was really incarcerating Tate because he was too poor to pay the fine. After *Tate*, courts began using installment plans that permit poor defendants to pay fines over a period of several months.[720]

CIVIL FORFEITURE

Federal law allows the government to confiscate or "forfeit" the proceeds (property or money) of criminal activities.[721] Laws that allow the state to forfeit the property used in illicit drug activity are particularly controversial. In deciding whether forfeiture is legal, state courts generally look to constitutional provisions dealing with excessive fines. In *Austin v. United States*, 509 US 602 (1993), the Supreme Court said that civil forfeiture "constitutes payment to a sovereign as punishment for some offense' . . . and, as such, is subject to the limitations of the Eighth Amendment's Excessive Fines Clause."[722] However the court left it to state and lower federal courts to determine the test of "excessiveness" in the context of forfeiture. The Illinois Supreme Court said that three factors should be considered in this regard: (1) the gravity of the offense relative to the value of the forfeiture, (2) whether the property was an integral part of the illicit activity, and (3) whether the illicit activity involving the property was extensive.[723] Federally, a $357,144 forfeiture for failing to report to U.S. Customs that more than $10,000 was being taken out of the country was found to be "grossly disproportionate" to the offense.[724] In one Pennsylvania case, the court found that forfeiture of a house used as a base of operations in an ongoing drug business was not excessive.[725]

Defendants, whose property has been taken through civil forfeiture, have argued that either the forfeiture hearing or the criminal trial (whichever happened last) violated their rights to be free from double jeopardy. But, the courts have not agreed. Instead, they hold that the double jeopardy prohibition is not triggered because forfeiture is a civil sanction and not considered a new criminal action.[726]

In order to satisfy due process, the owner is entitled to a hearing before property can be forfeited.[727] Courts have allowed forfeiture (and found it to be constitutional) even when the owner is not aware of the property's criminal use. For example, in *Bennis v. Michigan*, 516 U.S. 442 (1996), the Court upheld the government's seizure and forfeiture of Mrs. Bennis's car, even

---

[720] This practice may nonetheless subject the poor to an increased punishment if the court administration requires interest or some fee associated with a payment plan.
[721] *See,* 18 USCA §§981-982.
[722] 509 U.S. at 622 ((1993).
[723] *Waller v. 1989 Ford F350 Truck* (Kusumoto), 642 N.E. 2d 460 (Ill. 1994).
[724] *United States v. Bajakajian*, 524 U.S. 321 (1998).
[725] *In re King Properties*, 6235 A.2d 128 (Pa 1983).
[726] *United States v. Ursery* 518 U.S. 267 (1996).
[727] *United States v. James Daniel Good Real Property*, 510 U.S. 43 (1993).

though she claimed she did not know that her husband was using their car to engage in prostitution.

In 2000, Congress approved the Civil Asset Forfeiture Reform Act. This Act curbed the government's asset forfeiture authority and added additional due process guarantees to ensure that property is not unjustly taken from innocent owners. Under the Act, the government must show by a preponderance of the evidence that the property was used in some criminal venture. The Act also limited the statute of limitations to five years, and made it a crime to move or destroy property to prevent seizure for forfeiture. In a similar vein, Oregon voters passed Ballot Measure 3, the Oregon Property Protection Act of 2000 in the November election. This constitutional amendment imposed limits on government forfeiture, allowing forfeiture only if the person from whom the property was seized had been already convicted of the crime, and only if the government could prove by a clear and convincing evidence standard that the property was a proceed or instrument of the crime.[728]

RESTITUTION AND COMPENSATORY FINES

Restitution refers to the "return of a sum of money, an object, or the value of an object that the defendant wrongfully obtained in the course of committing the crime."[729] When judges order an offender to pay restitution, they require the offender pay enough money to place the victim in the same position they would have been had the crime not been committed. Restitution orders can include the actual cost of destroyed property, medical bills, counseling fees, and lost wages. Several state laws require offenders pay restitution as a condition of probation. Judges may order defendants to pay restitution for damages incurred during a criminal episode--even if the charge is dismissed through negotiations. Judges may also order the defendant to pay restitution to some party other than the victim.

Restitution is not practical in many criminal cases. Many offenders are not suited to probation, and even when they are, that does not guarantee that they will be able to make restitution payments. Because of this, several states have established victims' compensations commissions.[730] Statewide, defendants make their restitution payments to these commissions that then work with victims across the state to pay out their restitution claims. Through this statewide pot of money, victims can then get some, if not all, of what is needed to "make them whole." Also, these commissions make it possible for the victim to get compensated without having to maintain contact with the offender.

CONFINEMENT SANCTIONS

Confinement sanctions include incarceration in prisons and jails, incarceration in boot camps, house arrest, civil commitment for violent sexual offenders, short term shock incarceration, electronic monitoring, and split probation (when incarceration is imposed as a condition of probation). Most people believe that confinement is the only effective way to deal with violent offenders. Although people question the efficacy of prison, regarding it as little more than a factory for producing future criminals, incarceration does protect society outside the prison from dangerous offenders. Prison is effective at incapacitation, but rarely is it effective at rehabilitation. In fact, serving time in prison often reinforces criminal tendencies.[731]

---

[728] *See,* http://www.osbar.org/publications/bulletin/06nov/forfeiture.html, for a discussion of the recent history of asset forfeiture in Oregon and the debate about Ballot Measure 3 and subsequent forfeiture cases and statutes.

[729] John M. Scheb and John M. Scheb II, *Criminal Procedure* 268 (2012).

[730] Scheb, *supra* at 689.

[731] *Id.* at 655.

Frequently, judges sentence defendants for multiple crimes and multiple cases at the same sentencing hearing. Judges have the option of running terms of incarceration either concurrently (at the same time) or consecutively (back-to-back). States vary as to whether the default approach on multiple sentences is consecutive sentences or concurrent sentences. The Court has held that the decision to impose concurrent or consecutive sentences was a judicial determination not a jury determination (and thus not subject to *Apprendi*).[732] Justice Ginsberg wrote,

> Most States continue the common law-tradition: They entrust to judges' unfettered discretion the decision whether sentences for discrete offenses shall be served consecutively or concurrently. In some States, sentences for multiple offenses are presumed to run consecutively, but sentencing judges, may order concurrent sentences upon finding cause therefor. Other States, including Oregon, constrain judges' discretion by requiring them to find certain facts before imposing consecutive rather than concurrent sentences.[733]

CIVIL COMMITMENT OF VIOLENT SEXUAL OFFENDERS

Some sexual offenders may still be dangerous even after they serve their entire prison term. Both state and federal laws allow the continued confinement of violent sexual predators after the expiration of their criminal sentences. In 1997 the Court upheld a Kansas statute finding that such confinement did not violate the double jeopardy or *ex post facto* prohibitions.[734] In 2010 the Court decided that Congress had not exceeded its authority in enacting federal statute allowing civil commitment. Justice Breyer wrote, "the statute is a necessary and proper means of exercising the federal authority that permits Congress to create federal criminal laws, to punish their violation, to imprison violators, to provide appropriately for those imprisoned, and to maintain the security of those who are not imprisoned but who may be affected by the federal imprisonment of others."[735]

COMMUNITY BASED SANCTIONS

COMMUNITY SHAMING

Some judges -- seeking alternatives to jail or prison -- have imposed creative sentences such as requiring offenders to post billboards, make public apologies, place signs on the door reading, "Dangerous Sex Offender, No children Allowed," and attach bumper stickers proclaiming their crimes. These sentences are intended to shame or humiliate the offender and satisfy the need for retribution. Shame is part of the restorative justice movement, but for it to be effective it needs to "come from within the offender. ... Shame that is imposed without almost always hardens the offenders against reconciliation and restoration of the damage done." [736]

> At the heart of the current discussion of shaming offenders is the assumption that shame is a simple emotion that comes in only two sizes: shame or no shame. But actually shame is a complex emotion which comes in many shapes, sizes, and degrees of intensity. Legal scholars and judges who treat shame as merely binary are in a position of a skier who makes no distinction between the many kinds of snow. Just as lack of knowledge of types of snow may lead a skier to disaster, so the crude treatment of shame in current discussions could be a catastrophe. [737]

---

[732] *Oregon v. Ice*, 555 U.S. 160 (2009).
[733] *Id.* at 163-164.
[734] *Kansas v. Hendricks*, 521 U.S. 346 (1997).
[735] *United States v. Comstock*, 560 U.S. ____ (2010).
[736] http://www.critcrim.org/redfeather/journal-pomocrim/vol-8-shaming/scheff.html
[737] *Id.*

COMMUNITY SERVICE

Community service, as a penalty for a crime, is frequently imposed as a condition of probation. Generally, a probation officer or probation staff member will act as the community service coordinator. His or her job is to link the offender to the positions and verify the hours worked.

Ideally, it seems like an excellent way to instill in the offender a sense of responsibility to the community for having committed criminal actions, but community service also has its drawbacks. It is difficult for the community to reap any real benefit without providing a degree of training to and supervision of the offender. Training and supervision can be costly and can, in many instances, exceed the value of the service to be performed. [738]

PROBATION, PAROLE, AND POST-PRISON SUPERVISION

Suspended Sentences and Probation.

Any student of criminal justice will undoubtedly learn that John Augustus is the "father of probation." His efforts in the mid 1800s involved appearing in courts, urging the courts to release from prison or jail people whom he believed could be helped and reformed--particularly children.

The authority to grant probation probably grew out of the traditional practice of judges of "suspending sentences." The judge would simply fail to set a sentence or set the sentence and fail to direct that it be executed. The offender would then be released. If the offender's subsequent behavior was satisfactory, nothing more would be done. If he had further difficulty with the law, the judge, usually on request of the prosecutor, would revoke his freedom. This time the judge would set a sentence, or reinstate the previous sentence, and the sentence would be executed. The common law authority of a judge to spend a sentence was questionable, but many judges regularly exercised that authority.

Since the defendant released on a suspended sentence was not subject to formal supervisions, judges tended to suspend sentences only in minor cases. In the late 1800's, courts began to experiment with a combination of a suspended sentence and careful supervision that could be applied to more serious offenses. This new procedure, called probation, soon was authorized by statute and provision was made for the appointment of special probation officers. [739]

After embracing probation formally, many courts stopped using the mechanism of suspending imposition and suspending execution of sentences. The MPC recommended that states authorize both probation and suspended sentences, and about half of the states have statutes authorizing judges to impose suspended sentences in cases where they could still use probation. Provisions vary considerably. Some states follow the MPC proposal and distinguish probation (supervised) and suspended sentences (unsupervised). In other states suspension of sentence is conditioned on a single fact—the offender's non-violation of the law during the term of suspension—while probation is based on a variety of conditions. The length during which an offender must comply with a suspended sentence condition tends to be shorter than probation. Some states refer to this period as a "diversion" (note that other states use the term for diversion

---

[738] Scheb, *supra* at 659.
[739] Kerper, *supra* at 339.

as a pre-sentence contract as was discussed above). Finally, some courts use suspended sentences together with probation. Judges will "suspend the imposition of sentence" on specific terms (including incarceration and probation). If defendant violates the specific terms, then the offender is brought back and the judge can fashion the appropriate sentence. Occasionally, but much less frequently, the judge will "suspend the execution of sentence." When this happens, the judge announces the actual sentence, but then holds it in abeyance (does not execute or enforce it). If the defendant violates terms of probation, then defendant is brought back and sentence is executed (enforced). A suspended execution of sentence allows no discretion or leeway if the defendant violates the conditions of probation, and sometimes judges will use it as a last straw to send a strong message to the offender.

Defining Probation and Parole

Probation is one of the most common alternatives to incarceration. Both probation and parole involve supervision of the offender in a community setting rather than in jail or prison. The primary purpose of probation is to rehabilitate the defendant. Thus, the court releases the offender to the supervision of a probation officer[740] who then ensures that the offender abides by the conditions of probation. With parole, the offender is first incarcerated and is later released from prison to supervised control. Under both procedures, offenders who violate the terms of their supervision can be imprisoned to serve the remainder of their sentences.

Judicial Review of Probation and Conditions of Probation.

The appellate courts will reverse a judge's decision to grant probation only if "probation was denied for some arbitrary reason wholly unrelated to the statutory standard to be applied in determining whether to grant probation."[741] The Court has said little on probation since 1932 when it announced that probation conditions must serve "the ends of justice and the best interest of both the public and the defendant."[742] According to the Ninth Circuit Court of Appeals "The only factors which the trial judge should consider when deciding whether to grant probation are the appropriateness and attainability of rehabilitation and the need to protect the public by imposing conditions which control the probationer's activities."[743] The Court has fashioned a two-step process for reviewing conditions of probation: first, it determines whether the conditions are permissible, and, if so, it determines whether there is a reasonable relationship between the conditions imposed and the purpose of probation.

Many states follow California's standard for testing the reasonableness of probation conditions. This approach holds that probation conditions do not serve the ends of probation and are not valid if (1) the condition of probation has no relationship to the crime of which the offender was convicted, (2) the condition relates to conduct which is not in itself criminal, or (3) the condition requires or forbids conduct which is not reasonably related to future criminal act.[744]

Courts have invalidated the following probation conditions:

---

[740] In some cases, the court rather than a probation officer supervises probation; this is called "bench probation." Because judges do not actively supervise offenders, bench probation is used primarily when the only condition is the payment of fines.
[741] *Whitfield v. United States*, 401 F.2d, 480 (9th Cir. 1968).
[742] *Burnes v. United States*, 287 U.S. 216 (1932).
[743] *Higdon v. United States*, 627 F.2d 893 (9th Circ. 1980).
[744] *People v. Dominguez*, 64 Cal. Rptr. 290 (Cal. App. 1967). In *Dominguez*, the court struck down a condition that the "probationer not become pregnant without being married," saying it was unrelated to her offense or to future criminality and, thus, invalid.

- Requiring the offender refrain from using or possessing alcoholic beverages when nothing in the record showed any connection between alcohol consumption and the weapons violation of which the probationer had been convicted.[745]
- Requiring defendant to submit to a search of herself, her possessions, and any place where she may be with or without a search warrant, on request of a probation officer. (The court noted that a probation condition allowing a search of probationer, her property, her residence and any place where she may be living, with or without a warrant, based on reasonable suspicion by a probation officer or any law enforcement officer acting on the request of the probation department having reasonable suspicion that probationer violated the terms of probation would be valid.)[746]
- Prohibiting custody of children unless it had a clear relationship to the crime of child abuse.
- Prohibiting marriage and pregnancy.[747]
- Prohibiting the defendant from fathering any children during the probation period.[748]
- Requiring the defendant maintain a short haircut.[749]

Courts have upheld the following conditions:

- Prohibiting offenders convicted of child pornography from having access to the internet, possessing a computer, and requiring the offender to submit to polygraph testing.[750]
- Prohibiting the probationer from fathering any additional children unless he could demonstrate he had the financial ability to support them, and that he was supporting the nine children he had fathered.[751]
- Requiring probationers to pay all fees, fines and restitution, refrain from contacting the victim, undergo treatment for substance abuse, participate in alternatives to violence classes, stay in school, not leave the state without permission, abstain from alcohol, not drive. These conditions that apply to all probationers are referred to as "general conditions of probation."

Probation Revocation Hearings

Judges frequently revoke probation because the offender has committed technical violations of probation not because they have committed new crimes. Technical violations include, for example, failure to report, failure to complete treatment classes, failure to pay probation fees. In *Gagnon v. Scarpelli*, 411 U.S. 778 (1973), the Court held that, although the Sixth Amendment's guarantee applies specifically to criminal prosecutions (which technically do not include probation revocations), a probationer was entitled to a full hearing before probation could be revoked.[752] The Court reasoned that probationer or parolee suffers a grievous loss when liberty is withdrawn. Accordingly, the Court found that the Fourteenth Amendment's Due Process Clause requires the government provide a formal hearing whenever it seeks to revoke either probation or parole. According to *Scarpelli*,

[745] *Biller v. State*, 618 So. 2d 734 (Fla 1993).
[746] *Commonwealth v. LaFrance*, 525 N.E. 2d 379 (Mass. 1988).
[747] *Rodriguez v. State*, 378 So.2d 7 (Fla. App. 1979).
[748] *Burchell v. State*, 419 So.2d 358 (Fla. App. 1982).
[749] *Inman v. State*, 183 S.E.2d 413 (GA. App. 1971). (The court found this condition was an unconstitutional invasion of the right to self-expression).
[750] *See, United States v. Zinn*, 321 F.3d. 1084 (11th Cir. 2003), *United States v. Rearden*, 349 F.3d 608 (9th Cir. 2003), *State v. Ehli*, 681 N.W. 2d 808 (N.D. 2004), *People v. Harrisson*, 134 Cal.App.4th 637 (2005).
[751] *State v. Oakley*, 629 N.W. 2d 200 (Wis. 2001).
[752] The Court had recently found that parolees were entitled to full hearings when the state sought to revoke their parole in *Morrisey v. Brewer*, 408 U.S. 471 (1972).

- The probationer must be given written notice of the claimed violation in advance of the proceedings.
- The court cannot rely on information not disclosed to the probationer at the proceeding.
- The probationer must have an opportunity to be heard in person and to present witnesses and other evidence.
- The probationer must have the opportunity to confront and cross-examine the persons presenting information against him unless there is "good cause" justifying acceptance of their affidavits in lieu of their live testimony.
- The court must set forth the grounds for its decision.
- The court may not hold the probationer in custody awaiting a probation revocation proceeding without a reasonably prompt initial inquiry, similar to a preliminary hearing to determine whether there is probable cause to believe that he committed the alleged violation.
- The revocation hearing must be heard within a reasonably time after the probationer is taken into custody.

Parole Hearings

Because most states now use determinate sentencing, the use of parole is dwindling and is being replaced by "post-prison supervision" of offenders after their incarceration. However, for offenders sentenced in the 1970s and 1980s under indeterminate sentencing schemes, parole continues to be a very real hope--even if an unlikely possibility.[753]

[T]he states which have adopted determinate sentencing structures have either eliminated or drastically restricted parole. In states with indeterminate sentencing, however, parole remains an essential element of the sentencing structure. Parole involves the release of the prisoner subject to conditions similar to those imposed on the probationer. Parole may be granted by the responsible state agency (usually called a parole board) after the prisoner has served his minimum sentence. The parole board usually has several members, who are either interested citizens appointed by the governor or corrections department personnel selected by the head of that department. Frequently the board will be assisted by special hearing officers who hold hearings and make recommendations to the board. Most parole boards automatically schedule hearings for every inmate as soon as he become eligible for parole. If he is not released at that point, subsequent hearings will be scheduled at regular intervals.[754]

The procedures of parole hearings vary from state to state. Indeed, not all states regularly hold hearings. A few prefer simply to review the files in the case, permitting the prisoner to submit a statement on his own behalf. Ordinarily, hearings are rather informal affairs held before a hearing officer or one or more

---

[753] Consider the case of notorious California killer Charles Manson. Manson was found guilty in 1969 of the murder of five people. He was sentenced to death, but his sentence was converted in 1977 to "life with the possibility of parole" after the California Supreme Court invalidated its state death penalty statute. Manson applied for parole for the twentieth time in 2012--he was 78 years-old at the time. Under a change in parole release law, the next time Manson would be eligible for parole was in 2027. The board noted that if he were to complete programs designed to help deal with some of his issues, then he could petition for release sooner. Listen to the hearing at: http://abcnews.go.com/US/charles-manson-denied-parole-dangerous-man/story?id=16111128. (Charles Manson died in April 2017.)

[754] *See* Vincent O'Leary and Kathleen Hanrahan, *Law and Practice in Parole Proceedings*, 13 Crim. L. Bull. 181 (1977).

board members. The prisoner will be informed of the material in his parole file, which relates primarily to his offense, his prior criminal record, and his performance in prison. The prisoner also will be given the opportunity to state his own case for parole and to ask any questions about the parole process. In almost half of the states, he may be assisted by an attorney, and several states will appoint an attorney upon request of an indigent prisoner. The remaining states prohibit representation by an attorney on the ground that it interferes with the board's evaluation of the prisoner's statements and demeanor at the hearing. Shortly after the hearing, most boards will provide the prisoner with a written explanation of its decision. If the prisoner is not released on parole, he must be released after he has served his full sentence.[755]

Parolees are subject to a variety of conditions that are similar to probation conditions. They must contact ("report to") their parole officers on a regular basis and attend regular meetings. They may be released to half way houses, residential treatment programs, daytime work-release programs at the beginning of their parole in order to prepare for return into the community.

Even when states sentencing schemes utilize parole, not all inmates are eligible for parole. In some states, prisoners forfeit their eligibility for parole if they attempt to escape or if they engage in certain violent acts. Also, many states have "true life" sentences, and persons convicted of first-degree murder are frequently sentenced to life without the possibility of parole. Even a recommendation of parole by the parole board does not necessarily mean an individual will be paroled. On August 27,2021 for example, a California parole board recommended parole for 77-year-old Sirhan Sirhan who was convicted of murdering Senator Robert Kennedy on June 5th, 1968 and has spent 53 years in prison and had requested parole 16 times. Prosecutors who had long opposed his parole decided not to participate (either favor or oppose) the release decision. Governor Gavin Newsom denied his parole in January, 2022.[756]

Parole Revocation Hearings

Courts can revoke a parolee's release if the offender violates parole conditions. Under *Morrissey*, courts must hold a hearing within a reasonable time after the parolee is taken back into custody. The Court has stressed the informality of the hearing, saying that the "process should be flexible enough to consider evidence including letters, affidavits, and other material that would not be admissible in an adversary criminal trial.[757] In practice the courts generally admit any relevant evidence that is not privileged (i.e., not admissible because of an attorney client privilege, a spousal communication privilege, a psychotherapist-client privileged). Parole revocations cannot be based solely on hearsay evidence, and the state will call witnesses to testify at these revocation hearings. Parolees may have the right to counsel during a parole revocation hearing--depending on the complexity of issues involved. The judge or the parole board (it depends on state law) decides, based on a preponderance of the evidence standard, whether the state sufficiently proved that the parolee willfully violated his or her probation.

Post-Prison Supervision

Post-prison supervision stems from determinate sentencing schemes that states adopted beginning in the 1980s. Post-prison supervision boards are now often combined with parole boards, and they perform a similar function. Offenders do not apply for post-prison supervision,

---

[755] See, however, discussion about the civil commitment of violent sex offenders above.
[756] https://www.washingtonpost.com/nation/2022/01/13/sirhan-parole-denied/
[757] *Morrisey v. Brewer*, 408 U.S. 471, at 489 (1972).

since release is automatically given when the determinate sentence has been served. Generally, how long a person will be "on post-prison supervision" is set out in state sentencing guidelines. A post-prison supervision board will monitor whether the offender is abiding by the conditions of release while living in the community. If an offender violates conditions of release during post-prison supervision, he or she is entitled to a revocation hearing with the same due process protections given to parolees (notice, opportunity to challenge government's evidence, and the right to assistance of counsel).

PHYSICAL PUNISHMENT

CORPORAL PUNISHMENT

Up until 1978 the Supreme Court upheld the use of corporal (physical) punishment,[758] but it is no longer an approved sanction for a criminal offense in the United States. Nonlethal corporal punishment, such as flogging, was used extensively in English and American common law for non-felony offenses. The misdemeanant was taken to the public square, bound to the whipping post, and administered as many lashes as the law specified.

An American judge during the early American Republic was able to select from a wide array of punishments, most of which were intended to inflect intense pain and public shame. A Virginia statute of 1748 punished the stealing of a hog with twenty-five lashes and a fine. The second offense resulted in two hours of pillory (public ridicule) or public branding. A third theft resulted in a penalty of death. False testimony during a trial might result in mutilation of the ears or banishment from the colony. These penalties were often combined with imprisonment in a jail or workhouse and hard labor.

. . .

We have slowly moved away from most of these physically painful sanctions. The majority of states followed the example of the U.S. Congress, which in 1788 prohibited federal courts from imposing whipping and standing in the pillory. Maryland retained corporal punishments until 1953, and Delaware only repealed this punishment in 1972. Delaware, in fact, subjected more than 1600 individuals to whippings in the twentieth century. This practice was effectively ended in 1978 when the Eighth Circuit Court of Appeals ruled that the use of the strap, "offends contemporary standards of decency and human dignity and precepts of civilization which we profess to possess.[759]

CAPITAL PUNISHMENT--DEATH PENALTY

Capital punishment is a popular topic. Scholars have researched and written much about death penalty--most of which is outside the scope of this text.[760] Chapter Four examined whether the death penalty is cruel and unusual punishment, and this chapter examines the death penalty as a sanction for criminal behavior. The use of the death penalty as a response to crime in industrialized nations raises many questions:

---

[758] *Ingraham v. Wright* 430 U.S. 651 (1978). This case involved a school spanking a junior high school student with a paddle over 20 times causing him to need medical attention and to miss 11 days of school. The Court held that a school child had little need for the protection of the Eighth Amendment because of the openness of the public school and its supervision by the community.

[759] Lippman, *Criminal Law, supra* at 57.

[760] One excellent resource for learning about the death penalty is the death penalty information center (DPIC)--a nonprofit organization that publishes studies and analyzes trends in death penalty law and application. *See,* www.deathpenalty.org.

- Is the death penalty a deterrent?
- Is the death penalty justified by principles of retribution?
- Is the death penalty morally or ethically justified?
- Does it cost more to impose a death sentence or to impose a true-life sentence?
- Are factually innocent individuals erroneously executed (and if so, how often)?
- Is the death penalty, in itself, cruel and unusual punishment?
- Is any particular manner of execution cruel and unusual?

Courts answer only the last two questions, and, to date, the Court has upheld every manner of execution that is currently approved in the United States: firing squad, electrocution, gas chamber, hanging, and lethal injection. The Court appears willing to uphold capital punishment and has found it is not disproportionately cruel and unusual when the crime for which the defendant was convicted resulted in the death of another. It has reached an opposite result when the crime did not involve the victim's death--for example, when the defendant was convicted of rape of an adult woman[761] and a child rape.[762]

State Death Penalty

The Court, in the 1972 landmark case, *Furman v. Georgia,* 408 US 238 (1972), found that the death penalty was being applied in an arbitrary and capricious manner across the nation. Accordingly, it held that capital punishment, as it was being applied in the states, was unconstitutional.[763] After *Furman*, Georgia and other states, modified their death penalty statutes to reduce the problems the *Furman* Court identified. The Court approved three death penalty schemes and reaffirmed the constitutionality of the death penalty in *Gregg v. Georgia*, 428 U.S.153 (1976). Since *Gregg* over one thousand five hundred executions have taken place.[764] The most complete source of information on the death penalty (i.e., facts and figures) can be found at the Death Penalty Information Center.[765] This website is updated regularly and provides far more details in far more compelling charts and graphs that can be reproduced in this text, and it is strongly encouraged that the reader snoop around a bit on those pages.

Federal Death Penalty

Like state death penalty schemes, the federal death penalty was declared unconstitutional in *Furman*. Unlike the states, the federal government did not immediately reinstitute the death penalty. In fact, Congress did not enact a new death penalty statute until 1988. Currently, federal statutes allow for the execution of individuals for more than 40 crimes including crimes that do not involve murder (treason, espionage, trafficking in large quantities of drugs, and attempting, authorizing, or advising the killing of an officer, juror, or witness in a criminal

---

[761] *See, Coker v. Georgia*, 433 U.S. 584 (1977). In *Coker* the Supreme Court prohibited capital punishment for the crime of rape of an adult victim. *Coker* suggests that the death penalty is an inappropriate punishment for any crime that does not involve the taking of a human life."

[762] *See, Kennedy v. Louisiana*, 554 U.S. 407 (2008). In *Kennedy* the Court reaffirmed this stance by invalidating a Louisiana statute that allowed for the death penalty for rape of a child less than twelve years of age. Justice Kennedy (not the defendant, Kennedy) wrote, "the Eighth Amendment bars imposing the death penalty for the rape of a child where the crime did not result, and was not intended to result, in death of the victim."

[763] The courts will frequently analyze whether statutes or practices are unconstitutional "as applied" or "per se" (by itself--or by their very nature).

[764] 1503 executions have occurred since 1976. http://www.deathpenaltyinfo.org/. (Last visited, August 28, 2019.)

[765] (https://files.deathpenaltyinfo.org/documents/pdf/FactSheet.f1566566669.pdf).

enterprise case regardless of whether the killing actually occurs.) It is doubtful, however, that the federal courts would permit the death penalty for non-homicidal crimes.

As of November, 2022, federal death row houses 45 offenders[766] most in the Special Confinement Unit in the Terra Haute Complex that is part of the Federal Bureau of Prisons outside of Terra Haute, Indiana. The SCU was completed in 1996, and prior to its designation as the federal death row for adult males, all executions of federal prisoners had been carried out in the state where the defendant was sentenced--unless that state had no death penalty.[767]

In a July 2019 Attorney General Barr announced the federal government's intent to adopt a new federal execution using a single execution drug and has issued death warrants setting execution dates for five federal death-row prisoners. Barr had directed the Federal Bureau of Prisons (BOP) to adopt an addendum to the federal execution protocol specifying that federal executions will be carried out using the drug pentobarbital, in place of the prior three-drug protocol. Federal prosecutors also filed the proposed protocol in federal district court in Washington, as part of a pleading in the long-running lethal-injection lawsuit filed by federal death-row prisoners.[768]

After 17 years without a federal execution, the Trump Administration executed four prisoners on death row in July 2020.[769] Each had received the death penalty for murdering children. In Barr v. Lee, 591 U.S. __ (2020), the Court in a per curium opinion vacated a District Court's preliminary injunction on the executions. The Court found that, though the prisoners had argued that the use of the lethal drug pentobarbital sodium was cruel and unusual punishment since some experts believed it may cause a sensation of drowning and suffocation, the governments evidence to the contrary was compelling. The court, however, was divided; with Justices Sotomayor, Breyer, Kavanaugh and Ginsberg dissenting on various points. In their dissent, Justices Breyer and Ginsberg wrote, "In short, the resumption of federal executions

---

[766] https://deathpenaltyinfo.org/state-and-federal-info/federal-death-penalty/list-of-federal-death-row-prisoners. Note the number of 45 federal prisoners on death row in November 2022 is down from 62 offenders on death row in August 2019. The death penalty information center lists the following executions and stays for 2022 (as of November 9, 2022)

> 49 execution dates have been scheduled by 9 states for 2022.
> To date, there have been 13 executions by 5 states.
> 10 executions have been stayed.
> No executions have been halted by commutation.
> 17 executions have been halted by reprieve.
> 1 warrant has been withdrawn/removed/vacated/rescheduled.
> 1 failed execution was halted when execution personnel were unable to set an IV line.
> 1 prisoner has died on death row while his warrant was pending.
> 6 death warrants are pending.

[767] The federal government has executed 39 federal offenders since 1927, 36 of which occurred between 1927 and 1963. Since 1988, 79 federal offenders have been sentenced to death row. Three individuals have been executed, and twelve have been removed from death row. When the federal government executed Timothy McVay in 2001, it was the first execution since 1963. McVay was convicted and sentenced to death by lethal injection for twenty-eight counts of murder of a federal law enforcement agent on active duty for his role in the Oklahoma City bombings in 1997.

[768] https://deathpenaltyinfo.org/news/federal-government-announces-new-execution-protocol-sets-five-execution-dates (retrieved August 28, 2019)

[769] There were ten federal executions in 2020, three federal executions in 2021 (all in January during the Trump Administration) and no federal executions in 2022 under the Biden Administration. See, however, https://thehill.com/opinion/white-house/3695874-bidens-making-a-troubling-u-turn-on-the-death-penalty/.

promises to provide examples that illustrate the difficulties of administering the death penalty consistent with the Constitution. As I have previously written, the solution may be for this Court to directly examine the question whether the death penalty violates the Constitution."

Ruth Friedman, Director of the Federal Capital Habeas Project, called the notion that "the federal death penalty is 'the gold standard' of capital punishment systems" a "pervasive myth.

> Rather than being applied "only to the worst offenders for a narrow class of especially heinous crimes involving unique federal interests, with highly skilled and well-resourced lawyers on both sides," she said the federal death penalty "is arbitrary, racially-biased, and rife with poor lawyering and junk science. Problems unique to the federal death penalty include over-federalization of traditionally state crimes and restricted judicial review. These and other concerns, including troubling questions about the new execution protocol, are why there must be additional court review before the federal government can proceed with any execution."[770]

Critics of the federal death penalty argue that it is plagued by many of the same problems as state death-penalty systems, including racial bias (55% of defendants sentenced to death in the last decade were people of color), geographical arbitrariness (just three states – Virginia, Texas, and Missouri – are responsible for nearly half of all federal death-row prisoners), and disparities in the quality and funding of defense counsel.[771]

Mental Illness and the Death Penalty

The Constitution forbids the execution of someone who is legally insane.[772] In 2007, the Court ruled that a prisoner is entitled to a hearing to determine his mental condition upon making a preliminary showing that his current mental state would bar his execution.[773] The last federal death warrant was issued for Bruce Webster on April 16, 2007. Webster's execution was stayed and his death sentence was subsequently vacated on June 28, 2019 when a federal district court judge found that Webster is intellectually disabled, making him ineligible for the death penalty.

A different but related issue is the constitutionality of executing mentally retarded individuals who have committed capital offenses. In _Penry v. Lynaugh,_ 492 U.S. 302 (1989), the Court held that executions of mentally retarded prisoners does not necessarily violate the Cruel and Unusual Punishment Clause, but juries must be allowed to consider evidence of mental retardation as a mitigating factor in the sentencing phase of a capital trial. In _Atkins v. Virginia,_ 536 U.S. 304 (2002), the Court reconsidered the issue and held that there was a sufficient national consensus for the Court to prohibit the execution of mentally retarded persons via the Eighth Amendment. Justice Stevens, concluded,

> [M]entally retarded person who meet the law's requirement for criminal responsibility should be tried and punished when they commit crimes. Because of their disabilities in areas of reasoning, judgment and control of their impulses,

---

[770] Id.
[771] _Id._
[772] _Ford v. Wainwright,_ 477 US 399 (1986).
[773] _Panetti. v. Quarterman,_ 551 US 930 (2007).

however, they do not act with the level of moral culpability that characterizes the most serious adult criminal conduct.[774]

In *Hall v. Florida*, 572 U.S. 701 (2014), the Court held unconstitutional a Florida Supreme Court ruling that required defendants to prove that they had an IQ score of 70 or less before they could submit other evidence of their intellectual disability as a defense to the death penalty. The Court found that Florida's threshold requirement created an unacceptable risk that persons with intellectual disabilities will be executed. See, also the discussion about the cases of *Madison v. Alabama, supra* (examining the constitutionality of executing a death row inmate with dementia) *and Moore v. Texas, supra* (Texas erred in holding that Moore lacked intellectual disability) in Chapter Four.

Juvenile Offenders and the Death Penalty

Historically juveniles were treated no differently than adults in the criminal justice system, and so it follows that there is a long history of executing juveniles convicted of capital crimes. In the late 1980s the Court dealt with whether national sentiment had changed to the point where it would consider it cruel and unusual punishment to apply the death penalty to juveniles. The Court first held that the Constitution prohibits executing a juvenile who was fifteen years of age or younger at the time he or she committed the capital crime.[775] One year later, the Court, in a 5-4 decision, held that a juvenile sixteen years or older at the time of the crime could be sentenced to death.[776] Sixteen years later, in Roper v. Simmons, 543 U.S. 551 (2005), the Court forbade the execution of anyone who was under eighteen at the time of their offense. The *Simmons* decision pointed to the decreasing frequency with which juvenile offenders were being sentenced to death as evidence of an emerging national consensus against capital punishment for juveniles. The Court noted that only 20 of the 37 death penalty states allowed juveniles to be executed, and since 1995 only three states had actually executed inmates for crimes they had committed as juveniles (not surprisingly, Texas, Oklahoma, and Virginia).

WRAP UP

Judges do not single handedly decide what an offender's sentence will be. The legislature, in enacting criminal statutes generally expresses societal values in identifying crimes and specifying punishments. How much or how little judicial discretion there is in sentencing has changed over time. Prior to the 1980s, rehabilitation and indeterminate sentencing philosophy were popular, and judges had wide discretion in setting the conditions and terms of sentences. When it came to the length of imprisonment, parole boards worked in tandem with judges to decide when an offender was rehabilitated and when he or she could be released. Beginning in the 1980s, determinate sentencing became popular and judicial discretion was limited by sentencing guidelines and mandatory minimum sentencing. Special sentencing commissions drafted guidelines in the 1980s, and legislatures or initiative measures established mandatory minimum sentences throughout the 1990s.

In fashioning an appropriate sentence, judges can draw upon monetary sanctions in the form of fees, restitution, asset forfeiture, and compensatory fines. Judges may impose community-based sanctions (for example, probation, parole, and community service) and confinement sanctions (for example, jail, prison, transition centers, and boot camps). More controversial today is the use of physical sanctions (corporal and capital punishment).

---

[774] *Atkins v. Virginia*, 536 U.S. 304 (2002).
[775] *Thompson v. Oklahoma*, 487 U.S. 825 (1988).
[776] *Stanford v. Kentucky*, 492 U.S. 361 (1989).

Although an evolving area of law, the Court has recently interpreted that the defendant's Sixth Amendment right to a jury trial includes a much more vigorous role of the jury in sentencing. Until 2000, jurors were only involved with sentencing to the extent that, in death penalty states, they were involved with either deciding or recommending to the judge to impose or not impose the death penalty. After *Apprendi*, jurors must make specific findings about the existence of aggravating factors any time the judge imposes a sentence that is harsher than the norms. Most recently a death penalty schemes in which the jury only made a non-binding recommendation of death or life to the judge was held to violate the defendant's rights.

SOME THINGS TO EXPLORE OR THINK ABOUT

➤ What are the possible advantages to adopting mandatory minimum sentences? What are the disadvantages? Explore the "smart on crime" approach and its genesis from "tough on crime" policies. See e.g., https://www.americanprogress.org/issues/criminal-justice/news/2017/05/12/432238/smart-crime-alternative-tough-vs-soft-debate/. See also, https://www.americanbar.org/groups/litigation/publications/litigation_journal/2019-20/fall/prosecutors-and-voters-are-becoming-smart-crime/.

➤ What sentencing guideline scheme is in place in your state? Does your state use mandatory minimum sentences? Do you think judges should have some ability to use discretion and reject a mandatory minimum sentence if the circumstances are compelling? Do you think there should be some checks/guidelines/limits on prosecutors before they can charge cases that require mandatory minimum sanctions?

➤ Explore the death penalty generally. The most complete source of information on the death penalty (i.e., facts and figures) can be found at the Death Penalty Information Center. (See, https://files.deathpenaltyinfo.org/documents/pdf/FactSheet.f1566566669.pdf). This website is updated regularly and provides far more details in far more compelling charts and graphs that can be reproduced in this text, and it is strongly encouraged that the reader snoop around a bit on those pages.

➤ Explore the use of the death penalty federally. When the federal government executed Timothy McVeigh in 2001, it was the first execution since 1963. McVeigh was convicted and sentenced to death by lethal injection for twenty-eight counts of murder of 8 federal law enforcement agents on active duty for his role in the Oklahoma City bombings in 1997. Explore the use of the death penalty by the federal government. (See, https://deathpenaltyinfo.org/state-and-federal-info/federal-death-penalty/executions-under-the-federal-death-penalty.) In the last stages of the Trump Administration in a "spree of executions" 13 federal death row inmates were executed from July 2020 to January 13, 2021. The Associated Press reported strong evidence to suggest that the executions were covid-19 "super-spreader events." https://deathpenaltyinfo.org/news/associated-press-finds-federal-executions-were-likely-covid-superspreader-events The ACLU reported that each of the federal executions cost taxpayers nearly one million dollars. See, https://deathpenaltyinfo.org/news/records-disclose-taxpayers-picked-up-a-nearly-million-dollar-price-tag-for-each-federal-execution. Attorney General Merrick Garland expressed serious doubts about the federal death penalty in his confirmation hearings in March 2021.

➤ Explore trends in states' use of death penalty. Explore the trends in the popularity of, and historical development of the death penalty in your state. Which states currently allow the death penalty? In February 2021, the Virginia legislature voted to abolish the death penalty in Virginia (See, https://apnews.com/article/virginia-death-penalty-repeal-governor-c98c16a996037a4d1e1d497787b7e6f1). Virginia has been one of the top five states in the number of executions (second only to Texas) and percentage of executions (highest percentage of execution of death row inmates). Explore how the state, long a fan of death penalty, became a state which abolished its use. (See, https://time.com/5937804/virginia-death-penalty-abolished) .

➤ What sentencing guideline scheme is in place in your state? Does your state use mandatory minimum sentences?   Do you think judges should have some ability to use discretion and reject a mandatory minimum sentence if the circumstances are compelling? Do you think there should be some checks/guidelines/limits on prosecutors before they can charge cases that require mandatory minimum sanctions?

TERMINOLOGY

- aggravating factor
- Apprendi
- bifurcated/bifurcation
- capital punishment
- civil commitment
- civil forfeiture
- compensatory fine
- community shaming
- community service
- corporal punishment
- definite sentencing approach
- departure sentence
- determinate sentencing approach
- guideline sentencing
- indefinite sentencing approach
- indeterminate sentencing approach
- mandatory minimum sentencing
- mitigating factor
- parole
- parole hearing
- parole revocation hearing
- pre-sentence investigation-report (PSI)
- presumptive sentence
- probation
- probation revocation hearing
- restitution
- right of allocution
- split probation
- victim impact statement

Chapter Twelve: Challenges to Convictions-- Post-Trial Motions, Appeals, Habeas Corpus, Post-Conviction Relief Statutes, and Executive Relief

OVERVIEW AND LEARNING OBJECTIVES

After the defendant has either pleaded guilty or been found guilty at trial, there are still legal procedures that he or she can use to fight the conviction. After reading this chapter, you should be able to answer the following questions:

> ➢ What are the three motions that defendant can file after the trial and before the appeal? What must defendant show to win these motions?
> ➢ What is the difference between discretionary review/appeal and mandatory review/appeal?
> ➢ What is the difference between a direct appeal of a conviction and collateral attack of a conviction?
> ➢ What things may a defendant who has pleaded guilty appeal?
> ➢ When may the state appeal?
> ➢ What are the common assignments of error
> ➢ What effect has the AEDPA had on federal habeas corpus claims?
> ➢ When may persons convicted in state courts file habeas corpus claims in federal court?
> ➢ How are habeas corpus relief and statutory post-conviction relief different?
> ➢ What are the common grounds for filing habeas corpus or post-conviction relief claims?

POST-TRIAL MOTIONS FILED IN TRIAL COURT

The overwhelming majority of criminal convictions come about because the defendant has entered either a guilty or no contest plea. The only challenge the defendant can make in those circumstances is a motion to withdraw a plea. If a defendant is convicted at trial, there are additional post-trial motions a defendant can make (prior to sentencing) including a motion for judgment of acquittal and a motion for a new trial.

MOTION TO WITHDRAW A PLEA

Under federal law defendants can file a motion to withdraw a plea any time before they are sentenced, but they must show a "fair and just reason for requesting the withdrawal." [777] Successfully claiming that there is a fair and just reason is difficult. For example, defendants could claim that they misunderstood the plea agreement, that they were pressured to enter the plea, or that they were not aware what would happen after they entered their plea. But, remember that before the judge accepted the plea, he or she made specific findings that the defendant knowingly and intelligently entered the plea and ensured that a factual basis for the

---

[777] Federal Rule of Criminal Procedure (11) (d) provides,
  "A defendant may withdraw a plea of guilty or nolo contendere:
  (1) before the court accepts the plea, for any reason or no reason; or
  (2) after the court accepts the plea, but before it imposes sentence if:
      (A) the court rejects a plea agreement . . . ; or
      (B) the defendant can show a fair and just reason for requesting the withdrawal.

plea existed. To defend against a motion to withdraw the plea, the prosecutor need only rely on the transcript from the plea hearing demonstrating the intelligent and voluntary plea. The defendant's answers to the judge's question at the entry of plea will contradict defendant's current claims, and these motions generally fail. In most states and under the federal rules, defendants may not file motions to withdraw a plea after the court imposes sentence. Those pleas may be set aside only on direct appeal or on collateral attack--both of which will be discussed below.

MOTION FOR JUDGMENT OF ACQUITTAL (JNOV)

Even if the jury returns a guilty verdict, defendants may still ask the judge enter a verdict of not guilty by filing a motion for judgment of acquittal,[778] (also called a motion for an acquittal notwithstanding the verdict or a "JNOV"). The judgment of acquittal motion is similar to the motion for directed verdict of acquittal that defendant may raise at the end of the state's case in chief. Defendants must make JNOV motions prior to the imposition of sentence; thus, defendants generally make the motion right after the jury is excused after returning its verdict. In deciding the motion, judges are to view the facts in the light most favorable to the state and determine whether a reasonable juror could find, based on the evidence presented in trial, beyond a reasonable doubt that the defendant committed the crime.

MOTION FOR A NEW TRIAL

The defendant, after being found guilty, may seek a new trial based on extenuating circumstances (for example, newly discovered evidence), and he or she must show that the "interest of justice" warrants a new trial. If the court grants the motion, it will vacate the conviction and allow the second trial to proceed. Under the federal rules (Rule 33), if the defendant moves for a new trial on any grounds other than newly discovered evidence, the motion must be filed within 14 days after the verdict. If the original trial was a bench trial, and the judge rather than a jury found the defendant guilty, then the court, after granting a motion for a new trial, can simply take additional testimony and enter a new judgment without conducting a full-blown trial. (Federal Rule 33(a).)

DIRECT REVIEW: MANDATORY AND DISCRETIONARY APPEALS

APPEALING GUILTY PLEAS

Generally, when a defendant pleads guilty, there is not much left to appeal. Recall that appeals are essentially about reviewing the trial record to see if reversible error was committed at trial and when there is a plea, there isn't a trial record. A defendant who has entered a guilty plea may have the limited right to appeal three things: whether the trial court had jurisdiction of the case, whether the plea was entered voluntarily, and whether the sentence is a legal one (for example, if the judge sentences the defendant to a $10,000 fine and 5 years of incarceration when the maximum sentence allowed by law is a $5,000 fine and one year of incarceration). When a guilty plea is made as part of a plea bargain, there is an expectation that the defendant will not be filing an appeal—unless something went really wrong at sentencing.

Defendants who have filed unsuccessful pretrial motions prior to their entry of a guilty plea (for example a motion to suppress) may preserve their right to have the appellate court review those motions for error by entering a conditional *nolo contendere* (no contest) plea. If the

---

[778] The same holds true for a guilty finding by a judge, but it would be extremely rare for a judge to reverse himself or herself in this manner.

defendant's appeal is successful, then the plea may be withdrawn. States may also allow the defendant to plead no contest or guilty and reserve the right to appeal a specific ruling of the trial court.

In *Class v. United States*, 583 U.S. ___ (2018), Rodney Class entered a guilty plea for possessing weapons on U.S. Capitol Grounds (a violation of a federal statute) after plea negotiations with the government. Class, representing himself, entered his plea, at a plea hearing during which the District Court reviewed the terms of the plea agreement (Class was present and under oath) to ensure the validity of the plea (that is was made knowingly, intelligently, voluntarily, etc). The District Court provided required information and warnings and then accepted his plea and sentenced him to 24 days of imprisonment and 12 months of supervised release. Shortly thereafter filed an appeal challenging the constitutionality of the statute for which he was prosecuted. The Court of Appeals for the D.C. Circuit affirmed his conviction, and then Class filed a petition for writ of certiorari to the U.S. Supreme Court. The Court had to decide whether a guilty plea bars a federal criminal defendant from challenging the constitutionality of his or her conviction. In a 6-3 opinion, which examined prior case precedent, the Court held that it does not. The Court looked particularly at Class's plea petition, and found that Class had neither expressly nor implicitly waived his constitutional claims by pleading guilty.

APPEALS BY THE PROSECUTION

Because successive prosecutions violate the prohibition against double jeopardy, the government has no right to appeal when the defendant is found not guilty. The prosecution may, however, appeal certain aspects of the case, such as when it loses on a pre-trial motion.[779] For example, if the defendant won a motion to suppress evidence, the state could immediately file what is known as an "interlocutory appeal" on that ruling. The state can also appeal a sentence on the grounds that it is illegal. The state may appeal rulings on questions of law if the defendant is convicted and appeals. Finally, the state may appeal if the court grants relief when the defendant files a writ of habeas corpus or for post-conviction relief.

MANDATORY REVIEW--APPEALS OF RIGHT BY THE DEFENDANT

After sentence is imposed, defendants may appeal their convictions. Though there is no federal constitutional right to appeal, all states now provide for mandatory review of a conviction ("an appeal of right") through either a statutory or constitutional provision. Defendants may appeal their convictions from the magistrate court, a municipal court, or a justice of the peace court to a court of general jurisdiction, or from a court of general jurisdiction to an intermediate appellate court. The courts must accept review and consider these appeals. In the federal system, appeals go from the U.S. District Court to the U.S. Courts of Appeals.[780]

When appealing a criminal conviction, the defendant may challenge trial court rulings that he or she objected to during the pretrial, trial, or post-trial hearings. An appellate court considers only those legal points that were raised in the trial court. In an appeal, defendants must point out to the appeals court the grounds or basis for relief --the reasons they believe they did not get the right pretrial ruling, a proper trial, or a legal sentence. These grounds for appeal are called "assignments of error," and the appeals court tie any reversal of the trial court's judgment or sentence to any of the defendants' assignments of error which are clearly stated in the appeal.

---

[779] Double jeopardy does not apply ("attach") to cases prior to the impaneling of jurors or the questioning of the first witness in a bench trial, so it doesn't prevent the government from appealing pretrial rulings.
[780] Some appeals may go directly to the U.S. Supreme Court. Similarly, most states that allow the death penalty provide for automatic appeals of death sentences to their highest court. In such cases the defendant does not have to file an appeal; the process begins automatically.

Most commonly, defendants raise as assignments of error that the trial court erred in its ruling in one or more of the following areas:

- Pretrial violations of the defendant's rights, particularly those rights guaranteed by the Fourth, Fifth, and Sixth Amendments to the federal constitution.
- Procedural matters, especially trial court rulings admitting or excluding evidence.
- Irregularities in the impaneling or conduct of the jury.
- Trial court's failure to give jury instructions requested by the defendant or giving instructions objected to by the defendant.
- Prosecutorial misconduct such as improper remarks or arguments.
- Lack of sufficiency of the evidence to support a finding on the defendant's guilt beyond a reasonable doubt.
- Interpretations of statutes or ordinances.
- The legality, and in some jurisdictions, the reasonableness of the sentence imposed.
- Jury selection, deliberation, and misconduct.
- The voluntariness of a guilty plea.[781]

If the appeals court determines that no legal error was committed, it will "affirm" the result below. If the appeals court finds there was error, it must determine whether the error was harmless or prejudicial. Harmless errors are errors that do not affect the outcome of the case. Prejudicial errors or fundamental errors are errors that are significant and should not be disregarded; these errors do affect the outcome and warrant a reversal of the defendant's conviction. Prejudicial errors differ slightly from fundamental errors. Normally, defendants must object at trial to "preserve an error on appeal" and then raise those in the assignments of error on appeal. If the error is serious enough to have changed the result, then it is prejudicial. Fundamental errors are so bad that the appeals court will overturn the conviction even though the defendant failed to object at trial and failed to preserve the error for appeal. For example, if the trial court did not have jurisdiction over the defendant's case, that is considered a fundamental error. Essentially the courts find errors to be fundamental if they undermine confidence in the integrity of the criminal proceeding. When the defendant has been convicted of a capital crime, courts may be more liberal in reviewing errors first challenged at the appellate stage. Indeed, the U.S. Supreme Court has said that those fundamental errors not specifically challenged by the appellant should be corrected when a person's life is at stake.[782] Upon finding prejudicial or fundamental error the appellate court will reverse the conviction and remand the case (send it back) to the trial court. Ordinarily the case can be retried following the reversal, but a retrial is not permitted when the appellate court reversed on the basis of insufficient evidence-- i.e., not enough evidence upon which a jury could lawfully convict the defendant.[783]

The right of appeal must be available on an equal basis to all convicted persons--without regard to their financial resources. In *Griffin v. Illinois*, 351 U.S. 12 (1956), the Court held that the state must furnish a free transcript to indigent persons seeking to appeal their convictions. The state must also provide appointed counsel for an appeal of right filed by an indigent defendant.[784] The Court has held, however, that states are not required to appoint counsel for indigent defendants when they file discretionary appeals[785] reasoning that the attorneys in the first mandatory appeal of right would have already briefed any legal issue.

---

[781] Scheb, *supra* at 701.
[782] *Fisher v. United States*, 328 U.S. 463 (1946).
[783] *Burks v. United States*, 437 U.S. 1 (1978).
[784] *Douglas v. California*, 372 U.S. 353 (1963).
[785] *Ross v. Moffitt*, 417 U.S. 600 (1974).

DISCRETIONARY APPEALS BY THE DEFENDANT

WRITS OF CERTIORARI

If defendant loses his or her first appeal (the appeal of right) at the intermediate court of appeals, he or she may still have another opportunity for review by the highest state courts and in the U.S. Supreme Court. Defendants are not entitled to have the higher courts review their case again, but they can request discretionary review. To request discretionary review in federal courts, defendants file a petition for a writ of certiorari within 90 days after the entry of judgment of the lower court. For federal review the case must present a substantial federal question and at least four members of the U.S. Supreme Court must be interested in reviewing the case (called the "rule of four"). The Court almost always denies review and will grant the writ of certiorari only in a fraction of the cases where a petition is filed. One common theme in cases in which the Court "grants cert" is that the case involves an important federal question and there is opposite, conflicting, holdings within the federal circuits.

In the state court system, these petitions for discretionary review ("petition for review") must generally be filed within 30 days after the intermediate appellate court enters its ruling. In the state courts, the highest tribunal generally has unlimited discretion in deciding whether to grant the petition for review. Some states follow the "rule of four." Other states will consider whether the intermediate court of appeals decision conflicts with one of its (the highest tribunal's) holdings or a holding from another intermediate appellate court in that state if there is one.

COLLATERAL (INDIRECT) REVIEW OF CONVICTIONS

The Court distinguishes between direct attack on a conviction (an appeal) and an indirect attack on a conviction (either a writ of habeas corpus or a petition for post-conviction-relief). The following chart highlights the differences between appeals and writs of habeas corpus.

Appeal	Writ of Habeas Corpus
A direct attack upon the conviction	A collateral attack, meaning separate case from the criminal conviction
Part of the criminal proceeding	A civil proceeding
Purpose is to reverse the conviction	Purpose is to secure release from prison
Filed only after conviction	May be filed anytime a person is deprived of freedom illegally by a public officer, before or after conviction — with some exceptions
Accused has been convicted but may be free on bail	Person is serving time or is detained illegally, cannot be filed by a person who is not incarcerated
Based on any type of error made during the trial	Based on a violation of a constitutional right, usually during the trial
Must be undertaken within a certain period of time after conviction, otherwise the right of action lapses	Right of action does not lapse, must be filed while the person is serving time
All issues must be raised from the trial record	New testimony may be presented

WRITS OF HABEAS CORPUS

A defendant who is incarcerated may seek additional review of his or her conviction or sentence by applying for a writ of habeas corpus or seeking another form of post-conviction relief. The writ of habeas corpus (Latin for "you have the body") allows a court to review the legality of a prisoner's confinement. The writ of habeas corpus is referred to as the "Great Writ of Liberty." It was regarded as a great constitutional guarantee of personal liberty at the time of the adoption of the federal constitution. Article I, Section 9, Clause 2 of the United States Constitution guaranteed the availability of the writ in federal courts providing, "The Privilege of the Writ of Habeas Corpus shall not be suspended, unless when in Cases of Rebellion or Invasion the public Safety may require it." In the First Judiciary Act of 1789 Congress provided for use of the writ by persons "in custody under or by colour of the authority of the United States." After the Civil war, this Act was amended to include state prisoners because of the considerable concern that southern state courts may not give due respect to the federal constitutional guarantees.

The writ of habeas corpus permits prisoners to raise a variety of legal issues in attacking their convictions and sentences. Although the writ is a civil remedy, it is used by criminal defendants/convicts as a mechanism to ask the courts to commands prison and jail employees (usually the head of the corrections department) to bring that person into court and show that the detention is legal.

First, persons who are arrested and not promptly presented before a magistrate may use the writ to gain a hearing as to the legality of their detention. Ordinarily, an application for the writ is filed on behalf of the arrestee in the general trial court of the judicial district in which the arrestee is being held. The jailer is named as the defendant since he is the person holding the arrestee in custody. If the application sets forth facts suggesting the arrestee is being detained in violation of the prompt presentment requirement, the court will issue the writ directing the jailer to bring the arrestee forward. The writ was designed originally to prevent the Crown from taking a person into custody and holding him there without initiating prosecution. It still serves that purpose.

Once prosecution has been initiated, the defendant may challenge the legality of his detention through the regular criminal process. If his arrest was illegal, he may raise that issue before the magistrate. If the prosecution lacks probable cause to proceed, he may challenge its case at the preliminary hearing. If he is being detained because the magistrate denied his right to bail, that issue can be raised before the trial court. Since these other remedies are available, the writ of habeas corpus cannot be used. The writ is an extraordinary remedy, unavailable where other remedies may be used. Once the criminal proceedings are over and all appeal rights have been exhausted, the writ again becomes the only available remedy. If a convicted defendant believes that his conviction was invalid, he may use the writ to gain a reexamination of the legality of his conviction. The application will be filed with the general trial court in the district in which he is imprisoned, with the warden of the prison or the director of the state department of corrections as the defendant. Since the challenge is really to the conviction, the warden or director often will be represented by the prosecuting attorney who obtained the conviction. The writ at this point is serving as a means of gaining a post-appeal review of his conviction.

What kinds of issues are most likely to be viewed as appropriate for consideration in a habeas corpus application? One of the more common allegations is the prosecutor's violation of due process through the knowing use of perjured testimony at trial. A violation of this type commonly would not be discovered until well after the trial and could not be raised on appeal. Another claim commonly presented on habeas corpus is alleged coercion resulting in an involuntary guilty plea. Since the coercion existed at the time the plea was entered, the defendant could not reasonably have been expected to raise the issue before the trial judge. When an appropriate claim is raised in a habeas application, a hearing on the claim will be held. If the court concludes that there was a violation, it will order the defendant be released unless the state initiates a re-prosecution within a short period of time. Thus, the result is similar in practical impact to a reversal on appeal."

Federal Habeas Corpus for State Prisoners. Following the Civil War, Congress, doubtful of the southern states' willingness to adhere to constitutional safeguards, made the writ of habeas corpus in federal courts available to persons held in custody by state officials. The federal writ formerly applied only to persons held in custody by the federal government, but Congress made it applicable to any prisoner held in custody 'in violation of the Constitution or laws or treaties of the United States.' State prisoners raising valid federal claims were given the opportunity to eventually present those claims before federal courts . ... if they were ill-treated by state courts.

Over the years, a complicated body of law has developed as to the role of the federal courts in considering habeas corpus applications of state prisoners. The main thrust of the various decisions is that the federal writ, though expanded at times, still will be limited by traditional standards of habeas corpus relief. Thus, the state prisoner cannot seek habeas corpus until he first has exhausted his state remedies. Also, habeas corpus relief will be granted only where he shows that the state criminal proceeding was marred by a fundamental constitutional error. ...

Federal and State Court Conflict. State prisoner applications for federal habeas corpus relief have been a source of considerable conflict between federal and state courts in recent years. As we have seen, in the normal appellate process, the decisions of the highest state court will be subject to review only by the United States Supreme Court. Federal habeas corpus, however, permits a federal district court to order the release of a state prisoner after the highest state court has affirmed his conviction. After as many as three state courts. . . have held that the defendant's constitutional rights were not violated, a federal district court may hold otherwise and order the state to retry him (or release him if a retrial is impossible). Particularly irksome to some state courts is the fact that a single federal judge may reject an interpretation of the federal constitution adopted by a unanimous panel of several justices of the highest state court. ... [786]

The Court restricted federal habeas corpus relief to state prisoners during the 1970s, 1980s and 1990s — perhaps in response to the increasing professionalism of state judiciaries or because of criticism of federal court intervention. In *Stone v. Powell*, 428 U.S. 465 (1976) the Court barred state prisoners from filing habeas petitions in federal court when their only complaint was that police had violated search and seizure rights under the Fourth Amendment. The Court has also denied habeas corpus remedies to a state prisoner who challenged a jury instruction when the

---

[786] Kerper, *supra* at 325-328.

prisoner did not object to it during trial,[787] to a death row inmate when he had already filed a previous federal habeas corpus petition,[788] and to federal habeas corpus petitioners who failed to develop their claims in state court proceedings.[789] In *Brecht v. Abrahamson*, 507 U.S. 619 (1993), the Court held that federal district courts should not overturn state court convictions unless the petitioner showed actual prejudice from the errors cited in the habeas corpus petition. The Court in *Brecht* also held that it is the defendant's burden to show a prejudicial error and not the state's burden to prove that any error was harmless.

HABEAS CORPUS AND THE ANTI-TERRORISM AND EFFECTIVE DEATH PENALTY ACT

In addition to the Supreme Court's rulings limiting petitioners' access to federal habeas corpus relief, Congress also enacted the Antiterrorism and Effective Death Penalty Act of 1996 to limit state prisoners' opportunities to challenge their convictions in federal courts. President Clinton signed the AEDPA into law in April 1996. The Act implemented several strict procedures for habeas corpus petitioners. One of the provisions of the AEDPA requires petitions be filed within one year from the date on which the judgment of conviction becomes final.[790] In cases where the defendant fails to file an appeal, the one-year time period starts from the deadline date for filing the notice of appeal.

The AEDPA establishes three primary categories of federal habeas corpus filings: 28 U.S.C. § 2241 petitions are the mechanism for which pretrial detainees complain against their pretrial custody;[791] 28 U.S.C. § 2251 petitions are filed by federal prisoners in federal court; and 28 U.S.C. § 2254 petitions are filed by state court prisoners in federal court. In § 2254 cases, the Act requires federal courts to give substantial deference to the factual findings made by the state courts. To overcome this deference, petitioners must show that the state court findings were "objectively unreasonable." And with respect to conclusions of law, petitioners must demonstrate that state courts engaged in clear legal error. Section 2254(d) provides that the state court adjudication of the petitioner's claims must have "(1) resulted in a decision that was contrary to, or involved an unreasonable application of, clearly established Federal law, as determined by the Supreme Court of the United States or (2) resulted in a decision that was based on an unreasonable determination of the facts in light of the evidence presented in the State court proceeding."

---

[787] *Engle v. Isaac*, 456 U.S. 107 (1982).

[788] *McCleskey v. Zant*, 499 U.S. 467 (1991).

[789] *Keeney v. Tamayo-Reyes*, 504 U.S. 1 (1992).

[790] A conviction becomes final when the U.S. Supreme Court denies review on direct appeal or when a defendant terminates discretionary appeals on direct appeal.

[791] Under 28 U.S.C. 2241, a person in either state or federal custody who is not seeking to challenge the validity of his or her conviction or sentence and petition federal courts for a writ of habeas corpus in any of the following situations:

1) He is in custody under or by color of the authority of the United States or is committed for trial before some court thereof; or
2) He is in custody for an act done or omitted in pursuance of an Act of Congress, or an order, process, judgment or decree of a court or judge of the United States; or
3) He is in custody in violation of the Constitution or laws or treaties of the United States; or
4) He, being a citizen of a foreign state or domiciled therein is in custody for an act done or omitted under any alleged right, title, authority, privilege, protection or exemption claimed under the commission, order, or sanction of any foreign state, or under color thereof, the validity and effect of which depend upon the law of nations; or
5) It is necessary to bring him into court to testify or for trial.

The Act requires that § 2254 petitioners exhaust all state-provided remedies (for example, appeals and writs of habeas corpus or post-conviction relief under state law) before pursuing a federal writ, under the exhaustion of remedies requirement. Also, under the Act, federal courts may not consider claims when defendants failed to object to a violation of their rights in the trial court or failed to present an issue on direct appeal. This is known as the "procedural default rule", and although some exceptions to this rule exist, generally speaking, when a claim is procedurally defaulted, federal courts cannot provide habeas corpus relief even though the substance of the claim may have merit.

The AEDPA also curtails repeat filing by a state court prisoner in federal court. Generally, state court petitioners now only get only one shot at habeas relief. Any second or subsequent habeas petition must meet a high standard and pass the gatekeeping of the U.S. District Court. If the court of appeals denies the petitioner a request to file a second petition, that decision is not appealable as a writ of certiorari.

In *Felker v. Turpin* 518 U.S. 651 (1996), Ellis Felker, who was awaiting execution in Georgia, filed a petition for writ of habeas corpus, appellate or certiorari review, and a stay of execution after having his convictions for capital murder, rape, aggravated sodomy and false imprisonment affirmed on appeal. Felker's habeas petition challenged the constitutionality of Title I of the AEDPA arguing that the law was an unlawful suspension of the writ of habeas corpus.[792] Felker also argued that the prohibition against subsequent writs was an interference with the Supreme Court's Article III jurisdiction. The Court swiftly and unanimously rejected Felker's arguments and upheld the Act. The Court interpreted the Act to allow state death penalty prisoners to file habeas corpus petitions directly in the Supreme Court, and added that it would only exercise its jurisdiction in exceptional circumstances.

INEFFECTIVE ASSISTANCE OF COUNSEL AND HABEAS CORPUS

Congress has provided indigent federal prisoners seeking habeas relief in federal court the right to have appointed counsel. This right does not extend to state prisoners seeking federal habeas corpus review. Sometimes prisoners write their own petitions or get other inmates to assist them in filing these petitions. In some cases, lawyers provide *pro bono* (free) representation (for example, through the Legal Aid Society or the Innocence Project).

One of the most frequent claims for habeas or post-conviction relief (PCR) is "ineffective assistance of counsel." The Court has recognized that to be meaningful, representation means effective representation. Failure of trial counsel to be an effective advocate constitutes the basis for a new trial. Ineffective assistance of counsel claims cover situations like the defense attorney's failure to present favorable evidence during the death-penalty phase of the defendant's trial, the failure to challenge prosecutorial misconduct, or the failure to challenge the admissibility of the prosecution's evidence. Giving incorrect legal advice is also considered ineffective assistance of counsel. For example, in *Padilla v. Kentucky*, 559 U.S. 356 (2010), the Court said that Padilla had properly raised an ineffective assistance of counsel claim when his attorney had misadvised him saying he would not be deported because of his guilty plea. Claiming ineffective assistance of counsel on direct appeal is difficult since much of what an attorney does is not reflected in the trial record. Thus, this claim is an appropriate action for habeas or PCR.

---

[792] The framers of the Constitution had recognized the writ as a fundamental right of citizens and said that it should not be suspended unless public safety required it. Only one time, during the Civil War, has the writ been suspended throughout the federal courts, by an executive order issued by President Lincoln. In *Ex parte Mulligan*, 71 U.S. (4 Wall.) 2 (1866) the Court declared that this suspension was unconstitutional.

The Court set out the standard of ineffective assistance of counsel in the case of *Strickland v. Washington*, 466 U.S. 668 (1984). It stated,

> First, the defendant must show that counsel's performance was deficient. This requires showing that counsel made errors so serious that counsel was not functioning as the "counsel" guaranteed the defendant by the Sixth Amendment. Second, the defendant must show that the deficient performance prejudiced the defense. This requires showing that counsel's errors were so serious as to deprive the defendant of a fair trial, a trial whose result is reliable. Unless a defendant makes both showing, it cannot be said that the conviction . . . resulted from a breakdown in the adversary process that renders the results unreliable.[793]

DNA EVIDENCE AND HABEAS CORPUS

DNA evidence is a "two-edged sword." It is exceptionally helpful to prosecutors seeking convictions, but also extremely valuable to prove the actual innocence of persons convicted on the basis of flawed eyewitness testimony or coerced and false confessions. As of August 2019, the Innocence Project reports 365 post-conviction DNA exonerations since 1989.[794] Most states now recognize newly discovered evidence as a basis for post-conviction relief. In order to gain release due to DNA evidence, testing of genetic material is needed. In most cases, a convicted person needs to gain access to this evidence through a post-conviction discovery process. The requirements for seeking DNA testing are different under various state statutes and rules of courts. Many jurisdictions have not yet established standards or procedures to govern this discovery. In some states inmates have to argue that their due process rights have been violated and work through the courts for relief. In other states, prisoners must use executive clemency procedures to demonstrate their innocence. Some states also have rules that impose time limits for post-conviction DNA testing. In sum, this is an area in flux. Scheb notes,

> Advocates of expanding prisoners' access to post-conviction relief based on DNA evidence believe that prosecutors should be required to maintain biological evidence used to secure a conviction as long as that person is incarcerated. They also argue that statutes of limitations on convicted persons seeking post-conviction relief should be abolished (as Florida recently did) and that funding should be provided so that prisoners seeking post-conviction relief can have adequate legal representation throughout the process.

> Exonerations of convicted persons, especially those on death row, based on DNA testing have received enormous media coverage and have shocked the conscience of the public. While prosecutors often resist efforts to undo convictions through DNA testing, there is growing public sentiment that the need for finality in the judicial process must give way to the search for truth when such powerful scientific means of seeking the truth are now available. ...

> By allowing appeals based on newly discovered DNA and other technological developments, courts risk more extended processes with attendant delays and costs. But the risk of affirming convictions based on evidence that is proven to be scientifically unreliable forcefully argues for expansion of the appellate process to accommodate such developments. This is an issue that legislative bodies and

---

[793] *Id.* at 687.

[794] https://www.innocenceproject.org/dna-exonerations-in-the-united-states/

courts are now facing as new technologies are being developed and convicted defendants seek the right to ask expansion of the appellate process.[795]

The Court examined Maryland's DNA collection efforts in 2013.[796] Alonso King had been arrested for a felony assault for pointing a gun at several people. The police did not need his DNA to link him to the crime, but after his indictment under a new Maryland law, the police swabbed his cheek, and submitted his DNA to the crime lab. At the time, he had not yet been convicted of any crime. His DNA was sent to a national DNA database and ultimately King was linked to an unsolved rape for which he was found guilty. The opinion was very divided with dissenting justices noting, "because of today's decision, your DNA can be taken and entered into a national database if you are ever arrested, rightly or wrongly, and for whatever reason." The majority held that the DNA test, one which they found to be an informational administrative search, was justified because it is reasonable.[797]

> When officers make an arrest supported by probable cause to hold a suspect for a serious offense and bring him to the station to be detained in custody, taking and analyzing a cheek swab of the arrestee's DNA is, like fingerprinting and photographing, a legitimate police booking procedure that is reasonable under the Fourth Amendment.[798]

POST CONVICTION RELIEF (PCR): STATUTORY POST-CONVICTION REMEDIES

During the 1950s and 1960s courts (and legislators) began to realize that the writ of habeas corpus provided an awkward procedure for permitting post-appeal challenges to convictions. It makes far more sense for a person illegally convicted to bring an action against the prosecutor in the district of conviction rather than against the warden in the district of imprisonment. Moreover, since the convicted individual is challenging the process which lead to the conviction, it logically should be available to all convicted defendants, rather than just those held in custody. While recognizing these logical gaffes, states were nevertheless hesitant to completely alter the structure of the writ of habeas corpus since the writ served many functions aside from permitting post-appeal challenges to convictions. Still, about half of the states have adopted special statutes creating a simplified post-appeal procedure for challenging an illegal conviction. The legal actions created by these statutes commonly are referred to as "post-conviction remedies," "post-conviction relief," "PCR", or "collateral attack proceedings."

Post-conviction remedies are quite similar to the habeas corpus proceedings in those states that have adopted broad habeas corpus relief. Post-conviction statutory remedies are available only after the convicted defendant has exhausted his or her normal procedural remedies. If the defendant still has the opportunity for direct appeal, for example, the remedy is not available. The statutory remedies are also limited to claims based on jurisdictional defects and constitutional violations at trial. PCR claims ordinarily will not be considered if the defendant deliberately bypassed an opportunity to present these issues at trial or on appeal.[799]

---

[795] Scheb, *supra* at 720-721.

[796] *Maryland v. King*, 569 U.S. ____ (2013).

[797] For an interesting discussion of this case, see www.scotusblog.com/2013/01/scotus-for-law-students-sponsored-by-the-bloomberg-law-the-court-takes-on-DNA-sreening/

[798] *King*, 569 U.S. at ____.

[799] The ABA has published standards (a model for states) for post-conviction remedies (calling for a unified habeas corpus/post-conviction-relief procedure). See,

After the post-conviction civil suit is filed, a non-jury trial is held. The criminal defendant becomes the "petitioner" and the prosecution/state is the named "defendant." The losing party in this civil suit may appeal the judgment of the post-conviction court. This appeal follows the same procedures of any civil appeal and ultimately may find its way all the way to the U.S. Supreme Court.

NON-JUDICIAL RELIEF: CLEMENCY

Clemency relates back to the English tradition in which the king could forgive the perpetrator of a crime because all crimes were considered a breach of the king's peace. At common law, this appeal to the king was the remedy because there was no appeal to the higher court. America retained the common law extraordinary remedy of taking things outside of the judicial system, and under both the federal and all state systems individuals convicted of crimes can request that the president or governor grant relief. The basic forms of clemency granted today are full pardons, conditional pardons, and commutations. Moratoriums differ from pardons and commutations, as they do not focus on any specific individual.

PARDONS

 A full pardon releases an individual from the consequences of a conviction without any conditions. Conditional pardons are based on the condition that the prisoner complies with certain conditions relating to future behavior. If the pardoned person fails to comply, then the pardon may be lost. If the prisoner complies, then after a time, the conditional pardon is converted to a full pardon.

FEDERAL PARDONS

The Constitution grants the president power to pardon and issue reprieves. (*See*, Article II, Section 2, Clause 1). Pardon power includes the right to commute sentences, remit fines and penalties, and grant conditional pardons. A pardon may be issued even before conviction.[800] The Court has said that he "plain purpose of the broad power conferred . . . was to allow . . . the President to "forgive" the convicted person in part or entirely, to reduce a penalty in terms of a specified number of years, or to alter it with conditions which are in themselves constitutionally unobjectionable."[801] According to *Ex parte Garland*, 71 U.S. 333 (1866), a full presidential pardon completely restores any civil rights the offender may have lost because it results in the person being treated as if the offense had never been committed.

STATE PARDONS

Every state has either a statute or constitutional provision that establishes the power of pardon. The most common use of pardoning authority is the release of incarcerated defendants who are not eligible for release under a state's parole and sentencing provisions. Some people are pardoned because it turns out they are factually innocent and were unjustly convicted. For example, state prisoners have sought clemency in cases where they have been convicted of rape

---

http://www.americanbar.org/publications/criminal_justice_section_archive/crimjust_standards_postconviction_blk.html

[800] For example, see President Ford's pardon of former president Nixon for his actions in Watergate. See also, President George H.W. Bush's pardon of Casper Weinberger for his role in the trading of arms for hostages. See too, President Clinton's controversial pardon of Marc Rich for federal income tax evasion. See, also, https://en.wikipedia.org/wiki/List_of_people_granted_executive_clemency_by_Donald_Trump

[801] *Schick v. Reed*, 419 U.S. 256 (1974).

and murder, but subsequent DNA testing reveals they are innocent. Most pardons, however, are based simply on the grounds that further imprisonment would be unjust.

In most states, it is the governor who has the power to pardon,[802] but in several of these states the governor may grant clemency only upon the recommendation of special boards. Even when the governor has the sole discretion to grant clemency, he or she may adopt a policy of only granting pardons recommended by the parole board. In a few states, a special state board has pardoning power. In Connecticut, Georgia and Idaho, the governor cannot commute a death sentence imposed under state law or pardon a death row inmate. Rather, a board of clemency is responsible for those pardons.

COMMUTATIONS

Commutation of sentence consists of a reduction of the penalty. A commutation of sentence can be used to overturn a sentence without officially acknowledging that the individual was wrongfully convicted. A death penalty sentence may be commuted (converted) to one of life imprisonment, or a prisoner's term of imprisonment may be reduced.

One of the most dramatic uses of executive clemency in American history took place in January 2003, when Governor George Ryan commuted the death sentences of 156 inmates awaiting execution in Illinois. All but three of the inmates had their sentences commuted to life in prison without the possibility of parole; the other three were given life sentences with the possibility of seeking parole. Governor Ryan's dramatic and controversial order came three years after he announced a moratorium on the death penalty in Illinois and appointed a commission to study the issue. After receiving the commission's report, which identified various problems with trials, sentencing, and the appeals process, Governor Ryan concluded that the system was "haunted by the demon of error, error in determining guilty, and error in determining who among the guilty deserves to die. [803]

MORATORIUMS

A moratorium is different than a grant of clemency. A moratorium is defined as a suspension of a planned or ongoing activity. Governors who announce moratoriums can reverse their policy decision. Moratoriums are not technically pardons, but rather a notice of how the governor will act in certain cases. The governors of Colorado, Washington, Pennsylvania, and Oregon have announced moratoriums on the death penalty in recent years.

For example, in November 2011 Oregon's former governor, John Kitzhaber announced a moratorium on the death penalty for the remainder of his term. One death row inmate, Gary Haugen, sued Governor Kitzhaber and attempted to reject his grant of clemency and force his execution to go forward. The Oregon Supreme Court ruled in favor of the governor. At the time Kitzhaber announced the moratorium, he indicated he would not commute the sentences of all death row inmates even though the Oregon constitution allowed him to do so because "the policy on capital punishment is a matter for voters to decide." Successor Governor, Kate Brown, announced she was continuing the moratorium.

---

[802] As of July 2022, Governor Newsom, while in office, has granted a total of 129 pardons, 123 commutations, and 35 reprieves. https://www.gov.ca.gov/2022/07/01/governor-newsom-grants-executive-clemency-7-1-22/
[803] Scheb, *supra* at 722.

De facto moratoriums exist in California, North Carolina, Arkansas, Kentucky. A *de facto* moratorium exists when a court or legislature indefinitely stay executions pending the outcome of a review of a law, holding, or practice. Some states have *de facto* death penalty moratoriums through disuse of the death penalty.

In all states, the decision to grant a pardon, commute a sentence, or declare a moratorium is politically sensitive. Pardons are not subject to judicial review, and the executive officer wants to ensure that pardons are granted only for appropriate reasons. States rely upon "the glare of publicity as a restraining influence." [804] Where the governor is given exclusive pardoning power, most states require that a report to the legislator be made of each pardon noting the reasons for the pardon. About one half of the states require that the notice of each pending pardon be given to the prosecuting attorney, the sentencing judge, and other interested parties.[805]

WRAP UP

Sometimes things go wrong. Sometimes mistakes are made. This chapter focused on the remedies that people convicted of crimes can seek when they allege that things went wrong in their criminal cases. Individuals who have pleaded guilty to crimes may seek to withdraw their plea. Before being sentenced, individuals who have been found guilty at trial may file for a motion for judgment of acquittal notwithstanding the verdict, or ask for a new trial. Individuals can file direct appeals when they are convicted at trial and even when they enter guilty pleas. They must allege errors were committed at trial that were so serious that they warrant a reversal of conviction. Each state and the federal government have procedures that require at least one review of defendant's conviction by an appellate court when an appeal is filed. Subsequent appeals, however, are all discretionary, and the higher courts will only infrequently and very reluctantly review the holding of the lower courts.

Sometimes the things that go wrong aren't revealed on the trial record. Sometimes newly discovered evidence emerges long after the time clock for filing a direct appeal has run out. Individuals, in some of these cases, may file a petition for writ of habeas corpus or file a civil suit for post-conviction relief. Habeas corpus remedy is only available to individuals who are incarcerated, but post-conviction relief may be sought by anyone claiming they were illegally convicted.

Sometimes when things go wrong, the courts cannot fix it. For example, when the law is followed, but injustice results. In those cases, where it is just "not fair" to further punish someone, he or she may be able to get extrajudicial relief by seeking a clemency in the form of a pardon, a commutation, or amnesty. Sometimes governors or legislatures believe that certain punishments, in particular the death penalty, are so fraught with error in their implementation that they adopt policies, called moratoriums, that prevent those types of punishments in the future.

SOME THINGS TO EXPLORE OR THINK ABOUT

➢ Consider the use of presidential pardons. See, e.g., https://www.pewresearch.org/fact-tank/2021/01/22/trump-used-his-clemency-power-sparingly-despite-a-raft-of-late-pardons-and-commutations/;

---

[804] Kerper, *supra*, at 381.
[805] *Id.*

https://www.justice.gov/pardon/clemency-statistics;
https://ballotpedia.org/Executive_clemency_and_presidential_pardons.

- ➢ Look up your state's post-conviction relief statutes.
- ➢ Investigate the process by which a person appeals his or her conviction in your state; investigate the process by which a person files a writ of habeas corpus or post-conviction relief in your state.
- ➢ Investigate recent clemency (pardons, commutations, amnesty) granted by the governor in your state.
- ➢ Refer again to the death penalty information center (you were encouraged to do this in chapter four when considering cruel and unusual punishment) to see what the death penalty policy is in your state. Is it a possible punishment? Is there a moratorium? Is there a de facto moratorium? President Biden, the first president to admit opposition to the death penalty, has been encouraged to grant clemency (in the form of commutations) to federal death row inmates. (Following the federal execution spree of the former administration). Research the current state of those pressures. Do you think it likely that he will commute federal death row inmates' sentences?

TERMINOLOGY

- amnesty
- clemency
- collateral attack
- commutation
- conditional pardon
- de facto moratorium
- direct appeal
- discretionary review
- fundamental error
- harmless error
- JNOV
- mandatory review
- moratorium
- motion for a judgment of acquittal notwithstanding the verdict
- motion for a new trial
- motion to withdraw a plea
- pardon
- petition for review
- post-conviction relief
- prejudicial error
- writ of certiorari (petition for writ of certiorari)
- writ of habeas corpus (petition for habeas corpus)

Selected Sections of the United States Constitution

Preamble
We the People of the United States, in Order to form a more perfect Union, establish Justice, insure domestic Tranquility, provide for the common defence, promote the general Welfare, and secure the Blessings of Liberty to ourselves and our Posterity, do ordain and establish this Constitution for the United States of America.

Article I

Section 8. (1) The Congress shall have Power. . .

. . .

(3) To Regulate Commerce with foreign Nations, and among the several States, and with the Indian Tribes;

(4) To establish an uniform Rule of Naturalization. . .

. . .

(9) To constitute Tribunals inferior to the Supreme Court.

(10) To define and punish Piracies and Felonies committed on the high Seas and Offenses against the Law of Nations;

. . .

(18) To make all Laws which shall be necessary and proper for carrying into Execution the foregoing Powers, and all other Powers vested by this Constitution in the Government of the United States, or in any Department of Officer thereof.

Section 9. (2) The privilege of the Writ of Habeas Corpus shall not be suspended, unless when in Cases of Rebellion or Invasion the public Safety may require it.

(3) No Bill of Attainder or ex post facto Law shall be passed.

Article II

Section 2 (2)...[The President] shall have Power, by and with the Advice and consent of the Senate to make Treaties, provided two thirds of the Senators present concur; and he shall nominate, and by and with the Advice and Consent of the Senate, shall appoint — Ambassadors, other public Ministers and Consuls, Judges of the Supreme Court, and all other Officers of the United States, whose Appointments are not herein otherwise provided for, and which shall be established by Law; but the Congress may by Law vest the Appointment of such inferior Officers, as they think proper, in the President alone, in the Courts of Law, or in the Heads of Departments.

Article III

Section 1. The judicial power of the United States, shall be vested in one supreme Court, and in such inferior Courts as the Congress may from time to time ordain and establish. The Judges, both for the supreme and inferior Courts, shall hold their Offices during good Behavior, and shall, at stated Times, receive for their Services a Compensation which shall not be diminished during their Continuance in Office.

Section 2. (1) The judicial Power shall extend to all Cases, in Law and Equity, arising under this Constitution, the Laws of the United States, and Treaties made, or which shall be made, under their Authority;--to all Cases affecting Ambassadors, other public Ministers and Consuls;--to all Cases of admiralty and maritime Controversies between two or more states;--between a State and Citizens of another State;--between Citizens of different States;--between Citizens of the same State claiming Lands under Grants of different States, and between a State or the Citizens thereof, and foreign States, Citizens or Subjects.

(2) In all Cases affecting Ambassadors, other public Ministers and Consuls, and those in which a State shall be a Party, the supreme Court shall have original jurisdiction. In all other Cases before mentioned, the supreme Court shall have appellate Jurisdiction, both as to the Law and Fact, with such Exceptions and under such Regulations as the Congress shall make.

(3) The trial of all Crimes, except in Cases of Impeachment, shall be by Jury; and such Trial shall be held in the State where the said Crimes shall have been committed; but when not committed within any State, the Trial shall be at such Place or Places as the Congress may by law have directed.

Section 3. (1) Treason against the United States, shall consist only in levying War against them, or in adhering to their Enemies, giving them Aid and Comfort. No Person shall be convicted of Treason unless on the Testimony of two Witnesses to the same overt Act, or on Confession in open Court.
(2) The Congress shall have Power to declare the Punishment of Treason, but no Attainder of Treason shall work Corruption of Blood, or Forfeiture except during the Life of the Person attainted.

Article IV.

Section 2. (1) The Citizens of each State shall be entitled to all Privileges and Immunities of Citizens in the several States.

(2) A Person charged in any State with Treason, Felony, or other Crime, who shall flee from Justice, and be found in another State, shall on Demand of the executive Authority of the State from which he fled, be delivered up, to be removed to the State having Jurisdiction of the Crime.

Article VI.

Section 2. This Constitution, and the Laws of the United States which shall be made in Pursuance thereof; and all Treaties made, or which shall be made, under the Authority of the United States, shall be the supreme Law of the Land, and the Judges in every State shall be bound thereby, and Thing in the Constitution or Laws of any State to the Contrary notwithstanding.

The Bill of Rights

Amendment I. (1791)

Congress Shall make no law respecting an establishment of religion, or prohibiting the free exercise thereof; or abridging the freedom of speech, or of the press; or the right of the people peaceably to assemble, and to petition the Government for a redress of grievances.

Amendment II. (1791)

A well regulated Militia, being necessary to the security of a free State, the right of the people to keep and bear Arms, shall not be infringed.

Amendment III. (1791)

No Soldier shall, in time of peace be quartered in any house, without the consent of the Owner, nor in time of war, but in a manner to be prescribed by law.

Amendment IV. (1791)

The right of the people to be secure in their persons, houses, papers, and effects, against unreasonable searches and seizures, shall not be violated, and no Warrants shall issue, but upon probable cause, supported by Oath or affirmation, and particularly describing the place to be searched, the person or things to be seized.

Amendment V. (1791)

No person shall be held to answer for a capital, or otherwise infamous crime, unless on a presentment or indictment of a Grand Jury, except in cases arising in the land or naval forces, or in the Militia, when in actual service in time of War or public danger; nor shall any person be subject for the same offence to be twice put in jeopardy of life or limb; no shall be compelled in any criminal case to be a witness against himself, nor be deprived of life, liberty, or property, without due process of law; nor shall private property be taken for public use, without just compensation.

Amendment VI. (1791)

In all criminal prosecutions, the accused shall enjoy the right to a speedy and public trial, by an impartial jury of the State and district wherein the crime shall have been committed, which district shall have been previously ascertained by law, and to be informed of the nature and cause of the accusation; to be confronted with the witnesses against him; to have compulsory process for obtaining witnesses in his favor, and to have the Assistance of Counsel for his defence.

Amendment VII. (1791)

In Suits at common law, where the value in controversy shall exceed twenty dollars, the right of trial by jury shall be preserved, and no fact tried by a jury, shall be otherwise re-examined in any Court of the United States, than according to the rules of common law.

Amendment VIII. (1791)

Excessive bail shall not be required, nor excessive fines imposed, nor cruel and unusual punishment be inflicted.

Amendment IX. (1791)

The enumeration I the Constitution, of certain rights, shall not be construed to deny or disparage others retained by the people.

Amendment X. (1791)

The powers not delegated to the United States by the Constitution, nor prohibited by it to the States, are reserved to the States respectively, or to the people.

Amendment XIII. (1865)

Section 1. Neither slavery nor involuntary servitude, except as punishment for crime whereof the party shall have been duly convicted, shall exist within the United States, or any place subject to their jurisdiction.
Section 2. Congress shall have the power to enforce this article by appropriate legislation.

Amendment XIV. (1868)

Section 1. All persons born or naturalized in the United States and subject to the jurisdiction thereof, are citizens of the United States and of the State wherein they reside. No State shall make or enforce any law which shall abridge the privileges or immunities of citizens of the United States; nor shall any State deprive ay person of life, liberty, or property without due process of law; nor deny to any person within its jurisdiction the equal protection of the laws.

Amendment XV. (1870)

Section 1. The right of citizens of the United States to vote shall no be denied or abridged by the United States or by any State on account of race, color, or previous condition of servitude.

Amendment XVIII. (1919)

Section 1. After one year from the ratification of this article the manufacture, sale, or transportation of intoxicating liquors within, the importation thereof into, or the exportation thereof from the United Sates and all territory subject to the jurisdiction thereof for beverage purposes is hereby prohibited.
Section 2. The Congress and the several States shall have concurrent power to enforce this article by appropriate legislation.

Amendment XIX (1920)

Section 1. The right of citizens of the United States to vote shall not be denied or abridged by the United States or by any State on account of sex.
Section 2. Congress shall have power to enforce this article by appropriate legislation.

Amendment XXVI. (1971)

Section 1. The right of citizens of the United States, who are eighteen years of age or older, to vote shall not be denied or abridged by the United States or by any State on account of age.

Glossary

A

abate. Put an end to; reduce or lessen.

abet. Ask, assist, command, counsel or encourage another to commit a crime.

absolute immunity. Immunity for judges, prosecutors, witnesses and jurors who cannot be sued for acts undertaken as part of the judicial function.

abstention. A federal court's exercise of its discretion to decline to exercise its jurisdiction in a legal action and to allow a state court to resolve the matter.

abuse of process. Improper use of criminal or civil process.

abuse of writ. Prohibition on filing successive writs of habeas corpus raising the same issues.

accessory. Person who helps a criminal either before or after a crime is committed, but who is not present during the crime.

accessory after the fact. Person who, with knowledge that a crime has been committed, conceals or protects the offender.

accessory before the fact. Person who aids or assists another prior to the commission of an offense.

accomplice. Person who voluntarily and knowingly aids or assists another in committing an offense and thus becomes liable for the offense.

accountable/accountability. Responsible or liable; state of being responsible and punishable for a criminal act. This responsibility is reduced or abolished in some cases because of age, mental defect, or other reasons.

accusation. Accusations of guilt may be made by complaints or affidavits, and sworn to by injured persons or by police officers, especially in minor offenses. Accusations of felonies are made either by indictments (found by grand juries) or by informations (filed by prosecuting attorneys generally following preliminary hearings in magistrates' courts.)

accusatorial system. System of administering criminal justice law, like systems of the United States or Canada, that is based on the assumption that justice and truth can best be attained through a process that resembles a contest between opposing parties—the accused (defendant) and the accuser (state or plaintiff).

accusatory stage. Stage of the criminal justice system which begins when the police identify a suspect and forward information about the crime to the prosecutor's office.

accuse. To bring formal charges against a person before a court or magistrate.

accused. The defendant in a criminal case.

acquiesce. Agree or comply with (assent, consent).

acquit. Absolve a person legally from an accusation of criminal guilt. A finding of not-guilty by the fact-finder (either the jury or the judge) in a criminal trial.

acquittal. A release or discharge (from an accusation) especially by a final determination by the judge or jury that the defendant is not guilty of the offense charged.

action. A lawsuit; a proceeding in a court of law. A plaintiff files a civil action to protect the rights of a private individual, business, or government entity. The state files a criminal action against a defendant in order to determine guilt and appropriate punishment of a guilty offender.

act of omission. The failure to perform an act required by law.

actual authority. Authority intentionally conferred by a principal upon an agent or the authority that a principle allows an agent to believe she possesses. Actual authority includes both express authority and implied authority. Contrast **apparent authority**.

actual imprisonment standard. The standard governing the applicability of the federal constitutional right of an indigent person to have counsel appointed in a misdemeanor case. For the right to be violated, the indigent defendant must actually be sentenced to jail or prison after having been tried without appointed counsel. This standard requires the judge to determine in advance of trial, and without hearing any evidence, whether he or she will impose incarceration. Most states reject this approach and assign indigent defense counsel when there is any possibility that the defendant could ultimately be incarcerated on the charge(s). See, *Scott v. Illinois*, 440 U.S. 367 (1979).

actual innocence. Claim on a petition for writ of habeas corpus that the defendant did not commit the crime (as opposed to the assertion that the state merely failed to prove the defendant committed the crime).

actual possession. Possession of something with the possessor's having immediate control. Actual possession can either be "knowing possession" (with an awareness of the physical possession) or "mere possession" (physical possession without an awareness of the physical possession).

actus reus. Criminal act; "wrongful act," or omission to act when there is a legal duty to act, or possession of unlawful substance that when combined with other necessary elements of a crime, constitutes criminal liability.

ad hominem. Latin. "To the man." Argument against an opponent personally instead of against the substance of the argument.

adjournment. Termination of a session or hearing; continuance to some other time or place.

adjudge. To rule upon judicially; to grant through a judicial process.

adjudicate. To determine or decide judicially.

adjudication. Judicial decision terminating a criminal proceeding by judgment of conviction or acquittal or dismissal of a case.

adjudicatory hearing. Fact--finding process in the juvenile justice system.

administrative courts. Courts created by the legislature and not established by Article III of the U.S. Constitution.

administrative law. Agency created law, for example the Oregon Administrative Rules (OAR's), Contrast, law made through the legislative process.

administrative regulations (rules). Agencies own rules.

administrative review board. Military officers who review decisions of combat status review tribunals.

administrative searches. Searches of premises by administrative agency official to determine compliance with regulations.

administrative-type acts. Ministerial acts performed by executive officers in carrying out duties assigned by law.

admiralty courts. Courts dealing with maritime law.

admissible. Evidence that the trial judge allows to be introduced into the proceeding.

admission. Voluntary statement or acknowledgement, made by a party, that is admissible in court as evidence against that party. Generally, this statement is against the interest of the person making the statement; entry of an offender into the legal jurisdiction of a corrections agency and/or physical custody of a correctional facility.

admonition. Courts' advice and instructions to a jury regarding the jurors' duties or conduct, the admissibility of evidence, or limitations on the purposes for which a jury may consider evidence; judge's statement to the defendant before accepting a guilty plea that informs the defendant of the consequences of entering a plea.

adoptive admission. Statement that a person adopts or agrees to by their silence (or an equivocal response) when made in a person's presence. (Also known as a tacit admission).

advance sheets. Recently decided opinions of the federal or state appellate courts in a particular response. Cases appearing in advance sheets are eventually published in hardbound volumes.

adversary system. The Anglo-American system for resolving civil and criminal disputes. This system is premised on the belief that truth emerges when competing parties challenge the evidence presented by the other side. In the adversary system, attorneys plan an active role, and the judge acts as a relatively passive neutral party who decides the admissibility of proffered evidence.

adverse party. The party on the opposite side of a legal action.

adverse witness. A witness who exhibits hostility or prejudice toward the party who calls the witness to testify on direct examination. The general rule is that a witness cannot be asked leading questions by the party who calls him, but if the witness is deemed an "adverse" or "hostile" witness, then leading questions can be asked of him or her on direct examination.

advice/advisory. An opinion; suggestion; counsel. An advisory opinion does not require obedience, but does let the parties know what the court is thinking.

advisement. (As in, to "take it under advisement" or "the case is under advisement.") A court takes a case under advisement to consider its decision after it has heard the arguments of opposing counsel but before it renders a decision.

advisory opinion. A formal opinion a court prepares on a question of law submitted by a legislative body, a governmental official, or other interested party but not actually presented in a concrete legal action. Advisory opinions are not precedent. Many courts refuse to issue advisory opinions for policy reasons. Federal courts do not issue advisory opinions because their jurisdiction is limited to cases and "controversies."

advice and consent. Constitutional requirement that certain executive branch appointments of individuals (for example, to the U.S. Supreme Court) require the approval, aka "advice and consent," of the U.S. Senate.

affiant. Person who swears to an affidavit supporting a request for a warrant.

affidavit. Sworn statement setting forth the acts that constitute probable cause in a request for a warrant.

affirm. To uphold, ratify, or approve.

affirmation. Solemn declaration made under the penalties of perjury by a person who declines to take an oath. See **oath.**

affirmative defense. Defense to a criminal charge where the defendant bears the burden of proof. Self-defense, necessity, and alibi are examples of criminal affirmative defenses. In civil litigation, an affirmative defense is one in which the defendant asserts in response to plaintiff's claims to limit or negate the defendant's liability. Contributory negligence, expiration of the statute of limitations, fraud, and waiver are examples of civil affirmative defenses.

aforesaid. Previously said or mentioned.

aforethought. Premeditated; deliberate; thought of beforehand for any length of time. See **malice aforethought.**

a fortiori. Latin. All the more. For a stronger reason. The term is used before a statement that is more certain or more necessary than a statement preceding it.

aftercare. Supervision or treatment of a juvenile offender after release from a juvenile correctional facility. Also called juvenile parole.

agent. Person who acts on behalf of another (the principal) in dealing with third parties.

age of consent. Youngest age at which a person may consent to sexual intercourse with another without the other being subject to criminal charges.

aggravating factor. Circumstance accompanying the commission of the crime that increases its seriousness. The judge can consider aggravating factors as a basis for a more severe sanction when imposing sentence. Juries in death penalty cases must find there were aggravating factors before imposing the death penalty.

aiding and abetting. Assisting in or otherwise facilitating the commission of a crime.

a.k.a. or AKA. Abbreviation for "also known as."

Alford plea. Type of guilty plea that allows the defendant to take a negotiated plea bargain while at the same time maintain his or her innocence of the charges. See *North Carolina v. Alford*, 400 U.S. 25 (1970).

alias. Any name used for an official purpose that is different from a person's correct legal name. In criminal history records, an alias may be designated by "AKA."

alibi. Meaning "elsewhere." Defense to a criminal charge that claims the defendant was someplace else when the crime occurred.

ALI standard. Test proposed by the American Law Institute to determine if a defendant is legally insane (the substantial capacity test of the Model Penal Code)

allegation. Assertion or claim made by a party to a legal action.

allege. To aver, assert, claim. A prosecutor will allege certain facts in developing a case against a criminal defendant.

Allen charge. A judge's instruction to jurors who are deadlocked (having a difficult time reaching a verdict) to consider the arguments and reasons of the other jurors and not take an inflexible position. Also called a "dynamite charge." See *Allen v. United States*, 164 U.S. 492 (1896).

allocution (right of allocution). A defendant's right to speak on his or her own behalf during sentencing.

alternate dispute resolution. Procedure in which a criminal case for a minor offense is redefined as a civil one, and an impartial arbiter decides the case. Both parties must agree to the amicable settlement—reserved for minor offenses.

ambiguous. Susceptible to more than one meaning; uncertain or doubtful. Statutes are sometimes said to be ambiguous, or a suspect's invocation of rights may be considered ambiguous. See **equivocal.**

amendment. A modification or addition (for example, amendments to the U.S. Constitution).

American Law Institute (ALI). Private, independent organization currently comprised of 4000 academics, judges, and lawyers formed in 1923 with the objective of clarifying, modernizing and improving the law, and providing a model on criminal law and criminal procedures that the states could follow. The ALI created the Model Penal Code (MPC) and the Model Code of Pre-Arraignment Procedures (1975). The Institute "drafts, discusses, revises, and publishes Restatements of the Law, model statutes, and principles of law that are enormously influential in the courts and legislatures, as well as in legal scholarship and education. ALI has long been influential internationally and, in recent years, more of its work has become international in scope."

Amicus Curiae **brief.** A brief filed by a "friend of the court." This brief is filed by interested persons or organizations who are not parties to the suit in order to educate or persuade the court.

Anders brief. Appointed defense counsel submits an "Anders brief" to the appellate court explaining   that the defendant's appeal has no merit and requests release from further representation of the defendant. See *Anders v. California,* 386 U.S. 738 (1967).

announce. (As in, "the court announced its decision."). To proclaim officially or make known publicly—either orally or in writing.

anonymous tip. Information from an unidentified informant. See **unnamed informant, confidential informant.**

answer brief. Appellee's written response to the appellant's law brief filed in an appellate court.

antecedent. Preceding; prior.

anticipatory search warrant. Search warrant issued based on an affidavit alleging that at a future time evidence of a crime will be at a specific place.

Antiterrorism and Effective Death Penalty Act of 1996. A federal statute enacted to reform the administration of the death penalty by curtailing successive petitions for writ of habeas corpus. See Pub. L. No. 104-132, 110 Stat. 1214 (known as AEDPA .

apparent authority. Appearance of having access, use, or control over some thing or some place. Used in conjunction with a third party consenting to a search. Some jurisdictions require that the third person have actual authority (access, use, control) over the place, and other jurisdictions require only apparent authority.

appeal. Bringing a case from a lower court to a higher court for the higher court's review of the legality of the lower court proceedings. The higher court may reject a petition for review on a discretionary appeal (called petitions for certiorari) from the lower court, but must review "appeals of right" or "mandatory appeals" from the lower court.

appellate courts. Courts that hear appeals.

appellate jurisdiction. Authority of a court to review a decision of a lower court; power to hear cases appealed from the lower court.

appeal of right. Defendant's first appeal after a conviction. Although the right to appeal a decision is not found in the constitution, every state and the federal government allow the defendant to appeal his or her conviction and require the appellate courts to review (called mandatory review) the trial court proceedings. See **discretionary appeal.**

appearance. An act by which a party submits to the jurisdiction of the court, either personally or through an attorney. The conduct of an attorney indicating to a court that the attorney will represent a particular client in a particular action. See also, initial appearance.

appellant—the party who appeals from a lower court to a higher court.

appellate courts. Judicial tribunals that review decisions from lower tribunals.

appellee. A party against whom an appeal is taken.

apply. To be pertinent or relevant to a certain set of facts (for example, "Case X does not apply to this situation"); to make a formal request, usually in writing (for example, "to apply for a pardon.").

a priori. Latin. Valid independently of factual study or observation. Describes a type of reasoning that puts forth a general principle or acceptable truth as a cause and proceeds to derive from it the effects that must necessarily follow.

arbitrary. Not governed by fixed rules or principles; without regard for the facts and circumstances presented. See also **capricious.**

arraign. To bring the defendant before the court in order that the charge may be read and that the defendant may plead to the charge.

arraignment. Appearance before a court of law for the purpose of pleading to a criminal charge.

arrest. To take a person into custody for the purpose of charging him or her with a crime. Case law helps define whether a person is "in custody."

arrest of judgment. When the court refuses to enter judgment in a case after the verdict because an error appears on the face of the record. Entry of judgment is refused because the error would make the judgment reversible on appeal. See **motion in arrest of judgment.**

arrest warrant. Court order authorizing a police officer to arrest a particular person after the judge or magistrate finds there is probable cause to believe the person committed a crime.

articulable facts. Events that can be explained and thus can establish probable cause. Contrast articulable facts with hunches and guesses.

Article III Courts. Federal courts that are established by the judicial branch under Article III of the U.S. Constitution. Article III courts include the U.S. Supreme Court, the U.S. Courts of Appeal, and the U.S. District Courts but do not include magistrate courts (which were established by the Congress under its enumerated power in Article I, §8, Clause 9: "Congress shall have Power. . . To constitute Tribunals inferior to the supreme Court.")

asset forfeiture. Governmental seizure of personal or real property that was obtained from or used in a criminal enterprise. Also called civil forfeiture.

asportation. Carrying away of something. In kidnapping, the carrying away of the victim; in larceny, the carrying away of the victim's property

assign. Point out or specify (for example, to assign errors); to set apart for a particular purpose; to appoint; to designate; to transfer property (technically, to assign rights to property.)

assigned counsel. Defense attorney, not regularly employed by a government agency (like a public defender's office), assigned by the court on a case-by-case basis to represent indigent defendants.

assignment of error. Written presentation to an appellate court identifying the points that the appellant claims constitute errors made by the lower tribunal.

associate. To join with another attorney or law firm on a case; join with others having equal or nearly equal status (for example, appellate judges other than the chief judge are called associate judges or associate justices).

ATF. The Federal Bureau of Alcohol, Tobacco and Firearms. An arm of the Department of Treasury, established by Treasury Department Order No. 211, effective July 1, 1972. (It had previously been part of the Internal Revenue Service).

at large. Unrestrained; free; not limited to any particular place, person or matter. For example, an at large member is one that does not represent any particular group.

attempt. Intent to commit a crime coupled with an overt act, beyond mere preparation, moving toward the completion of a crime. States have adopted various approaches indicating at what point attempt begins.

attenuated. Describes a weak link between an unreasonable search and the resulting seizure of evidence. The exclusionary rule does not apply when evidence is attenuated.

attest. Bear witness to; to affirm to be true or genuine; to certify.

attorney. Anyone who has received a law degree from a recognized law school. Some restrict the use of this title to those who are authorized to practice law in a given jurisdiction. Also called counsel, lawyer, or advocate.

Attorney General. Chief legal officer of a state or the federal government.

attorney-client privilege. Right of a person not to testify about matters discussed in confidence with an attorney in the course of the attorney's representation. The client is the "holder" of the privilege and may waive it. The attorney must assert the privilege on behalf of the client, refusing to discuss what was said in confidence.

authenticate. Establish as genuine.

authority. Power to act for or represent another; person or book that is an accepted source of expert information or advice; statute, text, or judicial decision that sets forth a principle of law that can be used as a precedent or guide in decision-making. Primary authorities are statutes, government rules and regulations, court decisions. Primary authorities must be applied by the court in deciding issues in dispute. Secondary authorities are textbooks, scholarly treatises, law review articles, that do not have the force of law. Secondary authorities may guide the court, but the court may disregard secondary authority. See **actual authority, implied authority, express authority**

automatic reversal rule. Requirement that violation of a fundamental constitutional right during trial results on appeal in the reversal of a conviction.

automatism. Condition where a person performs acts during a state of unconsciousness.

automobile exception. An exception to the Fourth Amendment's warrant requirement that permits police to search a vehicle without a warrant so long as they have probable cause to believe it contains evidence of a crime (based on the exigency of the mobility of the automobile).

a.w.o.p. Affirm without opinion. Appellate courts need not issue written opinions on every case they decide. Instead, they may affirm lower courts' decisions without an opinion.

B

backlog. Court's inability to dispose of the number of cases pending within an appropriate time frame.

bail. Historically the word "bail" referred to the property that the accused had to leave with the court for security to obtain release while awaiting trial. Bail was given to guarantee a defendant's appearance at trial. Now "bail" means pre-trial release typically based on payment of ten percent of a fixed bail amount, but could include any condition that must be met to obtain release during the proceeding

bail bond. Sum of money posted to ensure a defendant's subsequent appearance in court. To "set bail" is a process by which the judge determines the amount of money the accused will have to pay to be released from custody pending the resolution of the criminal case. Those who have posted bail but fail to appear will forfeit the bail amount.

bail bondsmen. Individuals who pay the bail amount to the court in order to secure the release of a defendant. The defendant would pay a percent (generally 10%) of the bail to the bondsmen as a fee. If the defendant failed to appear, the bondsmen would forfeit the money paid to the court. Bondsmen would often hire "bounty hunters" to go and retrieve defendants who had failed to make their court appearances so they would not forfeit the money to the court. Bail bondsmen are also known as "sureties," and bail bond agents.

bailiff. Court officer who maintains order in the court throughout a trial. Bailiffs are also responsible for protection of jurors, seating of witnesses, announcing the judge's entrance into the courtroom. (In some jurisdictions the bailiff is a law enforcement officer; other courts utilize volunteers, and other courts employ workers to act as bailiffs.)

balance of powers. General division of power among the three "equal" branches of government: the legislative branch (established by Article I of the U.S. Constitution), the executive branch (established by Article II of the U.S. Constitution), and the judicial branch

(established by Article III of the U.S. Constitution.)

banishment. Punishing an offender by forcing him or her to leave a geographical area for a specific period of time.

bar. Attorneys admitted to practice law in the jurisdiction (for example, "Attorneys must pay annual fees to the bar association."); railing in a courtroom separating the judge, jury, attorneys, defendant, witnesses from the general public; impediment, obstacle, prohibition (for example, "the judgment of not guilty was a bar to further prosecution."); impede, obstruct or prevent (for example, "His claim was barred by the statute of limitations.").

bench. Judges who make up a court. For example, "bench and bar meetings" are gatherings of attorneys (the "bar") and judges either for social reasons or to discuss issues that may have arisen in dealing with certain types of cases or proceedings.

bench probation/parole. Type of sentence or punishment that allows an offender to remain free in the community under the jurisdiction/supervision of the sentencing judge (instead of a parole/probation officer).

bench trial. Trial in which the judge sits without a jury and acts as the "trier of fact" and decides whether the defendant is guilty or not guilty.

bench warrant. Order from the court directing police to arrest a person. Bench warrants differ from arrest warrants in that they are issued because the defendant failed to appear as directed in court rather than because there is probable cause to indicate he or she committed a crime.

benefit of clergy. Early form of clemency in England that allowed clergy members to escape the death penalty for commission of capital crimes. It allowed cases against clergy to be transferred from the King's courts to the clerical courts (jurisdiction of the church). Eventually, many non-clergy members would claim "benefit of clergy" by proving they were "clergy" because

of their ability to read (or memorize a passage) in Latin (something traditionally reserved for clerics).

"best evidence" rule. Evidentiary rule that requires that the original written document be produced as evidence of a communication or transaction.

beyond a reasonable doubt. Standard of proof required for a court to find a defendant guilty of a crime.

bias. Predisposition or inclination of the mind that prevents a person from impartially relating or evaluating facts presented for determination. See **express bias, implied bias.**

bifurcated trial. Trial in which the guilt or innocence phase is separated from the sentencing-penalty phase.

bill of attainder. Specific legislative act pronouncing an individual guilty and directing that punishment be imposed on the person (or readily identifiable group of individuals) without giving an opportunity to contest guilt through a judicial process. The Article I, Section 9 of the U.S. Constitution prohibits Congress from passing bills of attainder.

bill of indictment. Formal charging document presented by prosecuting attorney to the grand jury accusing a specific person of having committed a certain crime. If the grand jury finds sufficient evidence that the person has committed the crime, it writes across the document "true bill." If the grand jury does not find sufficient evidence it writes, "not a true bill."

bill of particulars. Written statement prepared by prosecution giving the accused more specific details of the crime charged in the indictment or on the complaint. The purpose of a bill of particulars is to help the accused prepare a defense, avoid prejudicial surprise at trial, and intelligently raise the defenses of double jeopardy and statute of limitations.

Bill of Rights. The first ten amendments to the U.S. Constitution.

binding authority. A decision in a appellate case that establishes a precedent that other courts in that jurisdiction must follow. See the **doctrine of stare decisis.**

bind over. Term of art used when a judge finds sufficient evidence at a preliminary hearing to send the case to the next stage in the proceeding in the court of general jurisdiction. The judge "binds the defendant over."

Bivens action. Legal suit against federal agents or officers for violating an individual's constitutional rights or rights under federal law. See *Bivens v. Six Unknown Named Agents,* 430 U.S. 388 (1971).

Blackstone's Commentaries. Treatise on the English common law published in 1769 by Oxford University Professor, Sir William Blackstone. Very influential treatise in the formation of American law.

Blockburger test. Examination of whether criminal offenses have the same elements in order to determine whether subsequent prosecutions violate the constitutional protection against double jeopardy. See *Blockburger v. United States,* 284 U.S. 299 (1932).

bodily injury. Under the Model Penal Code, bodily injury is defined as "physical pain, illness or any impairment of physical condition. Also known as bodily harm.

bookie. Short for "bookmaker." Person who engages in illegal practice of betting on, accepting bets relating to horse and dog races, athletic events, or any other contest or event whose outcome is in doubt. See **bookmaking.**

booking. The process by which an arrest is officially documented and the arrestee is placed into custody. During booking, the arrestee's personal items will be inventoried, and he or she will be fingerprinted and photographed.

bootlegging. Illegally manufacturing alcohol or alcoholic beverages and/or transporting such

contraband for sale; in modern usage, the unauthorized copying of music or movies.

bona fide. In good faith; without fraud or deceit; honest; authentic; genuine.

bond. Any written obligation, especially one that requires payment of a specified amount of money on or before a specified date; written document assuring the presence of defendants at a criminal proceeding; if not, the bail bond (monetary surety) will be forfeited. See **bail.**

bondsman. Person acting as a surety.

border search. A search of persons crossing into the United States. Includes not only geographical borders but also the entry point into the United States by sea, or air.

bounty/bounty hunter. Monetary rewards for capture of persons who escape prosecution by fleeing the jurisdiction. Often such persons have posted a bail bond with a bonding company and the bonding company hires a bounty hunter to track them down and bring them to court.

Brady Bill. Legislation passed by Congress in 1993 that requires a five-day waiting period before the purchase of a handgun so that the buyer's background check may be conducted.

Brady rule. Requirement that the prosecution turn over to the defendant all exculpatory evidence prior to trial. See *Brady v. Maryland,* 373 U.S. 83 (1963). See **exculpatory evidence.**

breach of peace. Violation or disturbance of the public tranquility or order.

breaking and entering. Forceful, unlawful entry into a building or conveyance (such as a boat or motor home). In some jurisdictions, burglaries are described as "breaking and entering" or a "B and E." Breaking and entering is, however, only two elements of many in the crime of burglary.

brief. Written legal argument pointing out trial errors (or claims of error) in an appeal submitted to the appellate court (appellate brief); also means to summarize a court opinion (case brief).

briefing a case. Reading a court opinion and outlining the basic facts, issues and rulings of the decision so that the case can be easily understood and used for legal research.

bright-line rule/decision. A decision in which the court hands down a specific rule, one subject to very little interpretation.

bug. Electronic device enabling a listener to intercept conversations of other persons.

buggery. Sodomy.

burden of production (of evidence). Burden imposed on one party to produce evidence on a particular issue in the case.

burden of proof. Requirement that a party introduce enough evidence on a particular issue to persuade the trier of fact to a certain level of certainty (legal standard) (for example, beyond a reasonable doubt). Includes the burden of production and the burden of persuasion.

burden of persuasion. The burden on a party to convince the trier of fact to a specific legal standard (for example, clear and convincing evidence or proof beyond a reasonable doubt).

"but for" causation. A person is said to be the cause in fact of harm when he or she sets into motion a chain of events that results it the harm. Contrast, legal or proximate cause that focuses on whether the harm was foreseeable. Also called "cause in fact: or "factual causation."

Bureau of Justice Assistance. Federal bureau created to provide financial and technical assistance to state and local units of government to control drug abuse and violent crime and to improve the criminal justice system. The Anti-Drug Abuse Act of 1988 (42 U.S.C. §3750) authorizes the bureau to make grants for the purpose of enforcing state and local laws that establish offenses similar to the federal Controlled Substance Act.

Bureau of Justice Statistics. Bureau created in 1979 to distribute statistical information concerning crime, criminals, and crime trends.

Burger Court. The United States Supreme Court under the leadership of Chief Justice Warren Burger, 15th chief justice of the court, from 1969 through 1986.

C

canons of construction. Rules governing the judicial interpretation of constitutions, statutes, and other written instruments (for example, contracts).

capital crimes. Crimes punishable by the death penalty.

carnal knowledge. Sexual intercourse.

case. Generally refers to a legal suit, cause of action, or controversy contested before a court; matter under investigation for possible legal action.

case-by-case adjudication. Because some cases cannot result in bright-line rules, courts often look to the "totality of the circumstances" when taking a case-by-case approach.

case law. Body of law made up of judicial rulings that are potentially binding on the current controversy.

castle doctrine. Comes from "a man's home is his castle." This doctrine, used in states requiring individuals to retreat before using force in self defense if they can safely do so, allows individuals to use force to defend themselves in their homes without having to retreat.

causation. An act that produces an event or an effect.

caveat emptor. Warning meaning "let the buyer beware."

CCH. Abbreviation for computerized criminal history.

celerity. Speed with which police apprehend a suspect and punishment is applied for the offending.

censure. The non-criminal practice of punishing individuals for particular acts they have committed. For example, if a judge has acted improperly, a higher court may censure such conduct by issuing the judge an informal/formal reprimand. Censures differ from formal punishment for a criminal offense.

certification. See **waiver**.

certiorari. Writ issued by the higher court agreeing to review a case.

cert. petition/petition for cert. Abbreviation for *certiorari* petition. A petition asking a higher court to review a lower court decision.

chain of custody. Chronological documentation (paper trail) showing how police have preserved, transferred, analyzed, and disposed of seized evidence. A record of the individuals who have had physical possession of the evidence at any point during the criminal process.

challenge. See **challenge for cause, peremptory challenge.**

challenge for cause. Means of excluding prospective jurors who cannot be impartial. Prosecutors and defense attorneys have an unlimited number of challenges for cause in criminal cases, and any potential juror with bias may challenged for cause. If the judge finds bias, then he or she will "excuse the juror for cause." See **bias**.

chancery court. Equity court rooted in early English common law where civil disputes were resolved. Most modern courts have merged "courts of equity" and "courts of law."

charge. Formal allegation filed against a defendant in which prosecutors allege one or more crimes. Charging documents include indictments and informations.

chattel. Property of a landowner, generally livestock, but can include tangible personal property or assets.

chicanery. Trickery.

chilling effect. Laws that cause people to hesitate to express themselves because they fear criminal prosecution are said to have a "chilling effect" and may violate the First Amendment.

CHINS. Abbreviation for "children in need of supervision." Typically, unruly or incorrigible children who cannot be supervised by their parents.

churning. Making purchases and sales of securities in a client's account to generate commissions for a broker.

circumstantial evidence. Indirect evidence from which the existence of certain facts may be inferred.

citation. Summons to appear in court, often used in traffic violations; reference to a statute or court decision, often designating the publication where the law or decision appears.

cite and release statutes. Laws permitting police officers to issue citations instead of making arrest for traffic violations or minor misdemeanors.

civil action or litigation. Private lawsuit brought to enforce private rights and to remedy violations of private rights.

civil commitment. Legal confinement to a hospital or other treatment facility for a period of time to undergo evaluation or therapy.

civil contempt. Being held in contempt of court pending the performance of some court-ordered act.

civil death. Practice of terminating the civil rights of convicted felons. No longer used in any state.

civil disabilities. Rights forfeited as a result of criminal conviction. For example, some states limit a convict's right to vote.

civil disobedience. Any illegal public action involving political demonstrations or picketing in order to protest a government action.

civil forfeiture. Taking of property used in or obtained through unlawful activities through a civil lawsuit. The state files suit against the property it wishes to seize. For example, "California versus $15,789.00."

civilian input. Method of citizen input into the complaint review process in which a civilian panel receives and investigates a complaint, leaving adjudication and discipline with the department.

civilian monitor. Weakest method of citizen input that leaves investigation, adjudication, and discipline inside the department. A civilian is allowed to review the adequacy and impartiality of the process.

civilian review. Strongest method of citizen input in which a civilian panel investigates, adjudicates, and recommends punishment to the police chief.

civil law. Law that governs relationships between private parties; includes family law, property law, trusts and estates, contract law, intellectual property laws, etc.

civil liberties. Rights guaranteed by the U.S. Constitution and the Bill of Rights.

civil rights. Rights protected by the federal and state constitutions and statutes. The term is often use to denote the right to be free from unlawful discrimination.

civil service. Employment by local, state, or federal government; public employees are civil service employees.

class action. Any lawsuit on behalf of a large group of individuals with similar claims against a specific party. The class of persons may persist over time and change, but the action is for all current and future members of the class.

clear and convincing evidence standard. evidentiary standard, higher than the standard "preponderance of the evidence" used in a civil lawsuit but lower than the standard "beyond a reasonable doubt" used in criminal prosecutions. Recently adopted as the standard for the affirmative defense of insanity in the federal system. (The defendant must present evidence that convinces the jury that he or she was insane by "clear and convincing evidence.")

clear and present danger. Constitutional doctrine that the First Amendment does not protect those forms of expression that pose a clear and present danger of bringing about some harm that the government has a right to prevent.

clemency. Grant of mercy by the chief executive official (i.e., president or governor) commuting a sentence or pardoning a criminal.

closing arguments or closing statements. Arguments presented at trial by counsel at the conclusion of the presentation of evidence.

closely regulated business. Type of enterprise that is subject to extensive government scrutiny, such that warrantless search is permissible. Examples include liquor stores and firearm dealerships.

code states. States that have abolished the common law by enacting a set of laws through the legislative process.

coerced confession. Confession or other incriminating statements police obtain from a suspect through force, violence, threats, intimidation or undue psychological pressure.

collateral attack. Attempt to change the outcome of a judicial proceeding by challenging it in a different proceeding or court.

color of law. One of two requirements for a successful suit against a public official. An official act under color of law when he or she acts in an official capacity.

Commerce Clause. Article I, § 8, Clause 3 of the U.S. constitution enumerates powers of Congress and gives it the authority to make laws (pass Congressional acts) on matters that relate to interstate commerce. "The Congress shall have Power . . . To regulate Commerce with foreign Nations, and among the several States, and with the Indian Tribes."

commercial speech. Speech in which the speaker is engaged in commerce or the audience is potential consumers, or where the message is commercial in nature. The Supreme Court has held that commercial speech is not entitled to the same level of First Amendment protection as non-commercial speech. In order for the content of commercial speech to withstand constitutional scrutiny, it is subject to intermediate scrutiny. False or misleading commercial speech is not entitled to any protection.

common authority. Mutual use of the property by persons generally having joint access or control for most purposes. See, e.g., *United States v. Matlock*, 415 U.S. 164 (1974)).

common law. Original English legal system adopted by most English-speaking countries. Based on general custom and usage, common law is law found and announced by appellate courts and is not based on a set of written codes.

common law crimes. Crimes originating in the English common law. The definition and interpretations of crimes "at common law" developed over time from the Norman Conquest in 1066 through modern times and often the legal rules depended on the nuance of a particular situation. Judges were able to compare the cases' facts with those of earlier case interpretation of the common law crime. For example, the common law crime of burglary involved breaking and entering of a dwelling place. As common law developed, what constituted breaking or entering or a dwelling place changed as society developed and changed.

common law legal tradition or family of law. Legal tradition is based on the common law of England that emerged after the Norman Conquest in 1066.

compelling state interest. Governmental interest sufficiently strong that it overrides the fundamental rights of persons adversely affected by the government action or policy.

compensatory damages. Amount of money intended to restore what the plaintiff (the injured party) has lost as a result of the defendant's wrongful conduct. See **economic damages**.

competency. Legal capacity to testify and offer evidence under oath or affirmation in court.

complicity. Being liable for a crime because of the actions of someone else.

compounding a crime. Acceptance of money or something else of value in exchange for an agreement not to prosecute a person for committing a crime.

compulsory process. Sixth Amendment requirement that criminal defendants have the right to compel the production of witnesses and evidence—usually accomplished through a *subpoena.*

computer trespass. Offense consisting of the unauthorized copying, alteration, or removal of computer data, programs or software.

concurrence. Requirement that the actus reus (criminal act) joins with the mens rea (criminal intent) to produce criminal conduct.

concurrent sentence. Sentence on multiple charges in which the defendant serves time on each charge at the same time as the other charges.

concurring opinion. Opinion of a judge that supports the judgment of the court but for a different reason.

conditional discharge. Negotiated dismissal or discharge of a case after a deal between the prosecutor and the defendant. The defendant pleads guilty to some specific charge, fulfills certain requirements (such as a treatment plan) and then on successful completion of the requirements, the case is dismissed or discharged.

conditional release. Release from pre-trial custody in which the court imposes conditions which defendant must follow during release. A violation of the conditional release agreement generally results in the offender being taken back into custody pending the resolution of the case; the release of a prisoner who has not yet served his or her full sentence by an executive officer (or agency such as the parole board) from a federal or state correctional facility based upon an agreement to satisfy specific rules of behavior.

conduct. Under the Model Penal Code, conduct is defined as "an action or omission and its accompanying state of mind, or, where relevant, a series of acts and omissions."

confession. When a person implicates him or herself in criminal activity following police questioning or interrogation.

confidential informant. Informant known to the police but whose identity police hold in confidence.

confrontation. The defendant's Sixth Amendment right to be present at his or her trial, hear live testimony of witnesses, and challenge such witness's statements (generally through cross examination) in open court. See **the right to confrontation).**

consanguinity. Kinship; the state of being related by blood.

consecutive sentence. Sentence on multiple charges in which the defendant serves back-to-back time on each charge.

consent. Voluntarily yield to the will or desire of another person. A person may either expressly consent or consent by acquiescence.

consideration. Something of value that is exchanged as part of a contract.

consolidated trial. Trial in which two or more defendants are tried together or when two or more separate charging documents against one defendant tried at the same time.

conspiracy. Crime in which two or more persons agree or plan to commit a crime. The crime of conspiracy is distinct from the crime contemplated by the conspirators.

constitutional law. Body of law dealing with the establishment of, or the interpretation of the U.S. Constitution or of the constitutions of the states. Generally, cases involving constitutional law test whether governmental actions or enactments conform to the provisions in the constitution.

constitutional supremacy. The doctrine that the U.S. Constitution is the supreme law of the land and that all executive, legislative, and judicial actions must be consistent with it.

constructive possession. Legal possession of an object based on the ability to control, manage, and direct it. See **actual possession.**

contemnor. Person found in contempt of court.

contempt power. Court's authority to hold a person in contempt of court; grand jury's authority to hold people in contempt of court for failing to appear before it. Courts may impose either civil and criminal sanctions for contempt.

contest. Challenge or oppose; dispute; defend.

continuance. Adjourning a scheduled case/trial/hearing until a future date.

contraband. Any substance illegally possessed.

contract. Agreement between two or more parties to assume a legal obligation not otherwise imposed by law based upon a "meeting of the minds" and the giving of consideration. See **consideration, covenant.**

contract system attorneys. One system of appointed counsel for indigent defense. Under this system, attorneys are under contract to the county represent indigent defendants.

Controlled Substance Act. Federal law listing

controlled substances according to their potential for abuse. Title II of the Comprehensive Drug Abuse Prevention and Control Act, 84 Stat. 1242. (1970).

conversion. Using someone else's property without his or her permission or treating the property as your own and for your own purposes.

corporal punishment. Physical punishment such as caning.

Corpus Juris Civilis/**Justinian Code.** Form of Roman law that was codified by Emperor Justinian I.

corpus delicti. Latin. "The body of the crime." Essential elements of the criminal act; the substantial fact that a crime has been committed. The material thing upon which a crime has been committed—whether it be the body of a murder victim, or the burned building in an arson.

count. The parts of an indictment or information alleging a distinct offense. Synonymous with "charge."

court. Public judicial body/tribunal that applies the laws to controversies and oversees the administration of justice.

court administrator. Individual who controls the operations of the court in a particular jurisdiction. Generally, the court administrator oversees scheduling, juries, judicial assignments, and court employees.

court calendar. See **docket**.

court of equity. See **chancery court.**

court of last resort. Court that has final jurisdiction over all appeals within a state or the United States.

court of record. Trial court that records proceedings. Contrast **court not of record**.

court not of record. A court, usually a magistrate court, in which judicial acts and proceedings are not recorded and therefore cannot be reviewed on the record by an appellate court. When decisions of this court are appealed, a new trial (trial *de novo*) generally results.

Courts martial. Military tribunals convened to try a person subject to the Uniform Code of Military Justice.

Courts of Appeals for the Armed Forces. Formerly known as Court of Military Appeals, this court consists of five civilian judges who review sentences affecting a general or flag officer or imposing the death penalty. It also reviews cases certified for review by the judge advocate general. This court may review convictions and sentences based on petitions by service members.

courts of general jurisdiction. Main trial courts in the state court system. They usually have jurisdiction over felonies and misdemeanors, and civil controversies over a certain dollar amount.

courts of limited jurisdiction. Courts that have jurisdiction over relatively minor offenses and infractions. Examples include justice of the peace courts, district courts, municipal courts, and traffic courts.

corroboration. Evidence that reinforces the evidence already presented.

covenant. Formal, binding agreement between two or more parties to do something or to refrain from doing something. See **contract.**

credibility. Witness's worthiness of belief. After a court has found a witness to be competent (able to give testimony), it is the jury's duty to consider the witness's credibility and decide whether to believe the testimony.

crime. Act (or failure to act) that violates norms of a community that is prescribed by some penal law (statute, code, common law) and is punishable by some term of confinement; offense against the law of the state.

crime-control perspective. Point of view that emphasizes the importance of controlling crime, perhaps to the detriment of civil liberties.

criminal codes. Set of criminal laws enacted by legislatures. These codes may have abolished common law—or at the very least, streamlined and/or supplemented it.

criminal procedure. Set of rules and guidelines that govern how the police and courts process suspected and accused criminals from arrest through post-trial procedures.

criminal punishment. Punishment prescribed by legislatures.

criminal trial. Trial in a court to determine whether a defendant charged with a crime is either guilty or not guilty of that crime.

critical stage. Any step in the criminal justice process that is so important to a just outcome that the Supreme Court has attached to it specific due process rights.

cross-examination. Examination of a witness at a trial or hearing by the opposing party. Generally, attorneys conduct cross-examination by asking a series of leading questions. Cross-examination is the key feature of the right to confrontation and the accusatorial/adversarial system.

cruel and unusual punishment. Punishment that shocks the moral conscience of the community. The Eighth Amendment to the U.S. Constitution has been interpreted to prohibit punishment that is either barbaric or disproportionate. Some U.S. Supreme court justices do not believe that Eighth Amendment prohibits punishment that is disproportionate due to its length of incarceration.

culpable. Blameworthy; subject to criminal liability.

cumulative evidence. Evidence that is of the same kind and on the same point as evidence that was already presented and accepted. The general rule is that cumulative evidence should not be admitted if the opposing party makes an objection to it.

curative instruction. Statement by the judge to the jury instructing it how to consider a piece of evidence that was admitted in error or for some limited purpose. For example, if evidence of a witness's prior criminal conviction is erroneously introduced to the jury, the judge may instruct it to only consider the conviction as impeachment of the witness.

curtilage. Under English common law, the enclosed space surrounding a dwelling house. Under modern codes, curtilage could include other types of buildings.

custody. Typically, an arrest; detention of a suspect. Courts determine whether a person is "in custody" by looking at the totality of the circumstances.

custom. Habitual practice or course of conduct that has become so established that it has the force of unwritten law.

D

Daubert test/Daubert factors. Test of admissibility of scientific evidence from the case *Daubert v. Merrell Dow Pharmaceuticals.* In *Daubert,* the Court stated that evidence based on innovative or unusual scientific knowledge may be admitted only after it has been established that the evidence is reliable and scientifically valid. A technique's reliability depends on a number of factors, including whether the technique can be or has been tested, whether it has been subjected to peer review, whether the test procedures have been published, whether the test has a margin of error and, if so, at what rate, and whether the technique, as applied, conformed to existing standards for the test. These four tests for reliability are known as the *Daubert* factors or the *Daubert* test. See *Daubert v. Merrell Dow Pharmaceuticals,* 509 U.S. 579 (1993). See also the *Frye* **test**, *Kumhoe Tire* **test**.

damages. Monetary awards in civil cases. See, **general damages, special damages, economic damages, or punitive damages**.

deadly force. Amount of force that is likely to cause death or serious physical injury/bodily harm.

death-qualified jury. Term applied to a jury that has been selected on the basis of the jurors' willingness to consider imposing the death penalty in a capital case if the situation warrants such a result. Individuals who indicate they could never, under any circumstance, impose the death penalty are excused from jury service and cannot serve on a death-qualified jury.

decision. Court decree or determination of an issue in a case.

decree. Judgment of the court; Declaration of the court announcing the legal consequences of the facts the court found.

defendant. Party sued in a civil action or suit. In criminal law, the defendant is the party charged with a crime.

defer. Decide to do something later on; yield to the decision or opinion of another.

definite sentence. Sentence that provides for a specific term of incarceration. Also referred to as a flat-time, fixed-time, or determinate sentence.

deliberate. Weigh the evidence and the law for purpose of determining whether the defendant is guilty.

deliberate elicitation. In the Sixth Amendment right to counsel context, deliberate elicitation occurs when police officers create a situation likely to induce a suspect into making an incriminating statement. See *Rhode Island v. Innis*, 446 U.S. 291 (1980), **express questioning or its functional equivalent.**

delict. Tort; wrong; injury.

demeanor. How a witness appears and behaves or conducts himself or herself. Demeanor includes tone of voice, attitude, gestures, facial expressions, and appearance. A witness's demeanor is important to a juror trying to gauge the person's credibility.

demonstrative evidence. Physical evidence that helps the jury comprehend the testimony of a witness, such as a map or a drawing.

demur/demurrer. Defendant's challenge to the charging document (either an information or an indictment) alleging constitutional infirmities with the charges. For example, the defendant may challenge a charge of stalking, alleging that it violates the Constitutional protection against freedom of speech to be charged for communicating (repeatedly) his undying love for the victim.

de novo. Latin. "Anew, afresh." A trial *de novo* is a complete retrial of a case, usually before a higher court, which negates the initial tribunal's decision.

deponent. Person who testifies at a deposition.

deposition. Out of court testimony of a witness, taken under oath prior to trial and reduced to writing. Generally, (in Oregon and nationwide) depositions are not allowed in criminal cases, but are used widely in civil suits.

derivative evidence rule. See **fruit of the poisonous tree doctrine.**

desecrate. Abuse the sacredness of or to violate the sanctity of. MPC §250.9 defines desecrate as "defacing, damaging, polluting or otherwise physically mistreating in a way that the actor knows will outrage the sensibilities of persons likely to observe or discover his action."

detain. Restrain from proceeding, to hold in custody briefly, or to delay. Detain has different meanings in different contexts. See also **arrest, detention, seizure, stop.**

detainer. Notification filed with a correctional institution in which a person is being held, advising that the person is facing pending charges in another jurisdiction.

detention. Legally authorized confinement of a person subject to criminal or juvenile court proceedings, until the point of commitment to a correctional facility or until release; custodial status of persons held in confinement under arrest or while awaiting the completion of judicial proceedings.

determinate sentence. A sentence to a specific amount of time of incarceration fixed by a statute. Determinate sentencing encompasses, mandatory minimum sentencing, sentencing guideline sentencing, and "three-strikes-you're-out" sentencing.

dichotomy. Division into two parts or lines.

dictum. Comment by a judge on a legal point that is not necessary to the resolution of the case.

diminished capacity/responsibility. Mental condition that is not of such severity as to support a successful insanity defense based upon mental disease or defect, but that is relevant in determining whether the defendant had the required mental state for the offense charged. Some jurisdictions allow a diminished capacity defense to be raised as a mitigating circumstance that may lower the degree of the offense or reduce the offense to a lesser-included offense. Also referred as extreme emotional disturbance.

direct evidence. Proof that tends to show the existence of a fact in question without the intervention of the proof of any other fact. For example, a witness who testifies that he saw something take place is offering direct evidence. Direct evidence is contrasted with circumstantial evidence (also called indirect evidence).

direct examination. First questioning of a witness at trial or hearing, done by the party who called the witness to testify.

directed verdict. See **motion for directed verdict.**

disallow. Refuse to allow; reject. For example, "The court disallowed defendant's motion to postpone the hearing."

disavow. Disclaim responsibility for, or knowledge of, something; repudiate.

disbar. Permanently take away an attorney's license to practice law.

disclose/disclosure. Reveal or make known some important fact.

discovery. Court supervised procedure done in advance of trial in which the parties exchange evidence to be introduced by the other side at trial documents, written accounts of statements made by witnesses to be called, criminal histories and backgrounds, etc.).

discrete. Separate; distinct.

discretionary appeal. Appeals can either be "of right" or discretionary. Discretionary appeals are ones that the higher court may, but does not have to, consider. See **appeal of right.**

disinterested. Impartial; fair-minded; unbiased. A disinterested witness is a competent witness who has no personal interest in the outcome of the case or the matter at issue.

dismissal in the interest of justice. Court's termination of a case (dismissing a case) on the grounds that the ends of justice are not served by continuing prosecution. The prosecution frequently cites this ground on its motions for dismissal when it decides for some generic reason not to prosecute.

dismissal with prejudice. Court's termination of a state's prosecution that bars subsequent prosecution for the same matter.

dismissal without prejudice. Court's termination of a state's prosecution that leaves open the possibility of the state re-filing the same charges.

dispense with. Abolish or do away with; suspend.

dispose. Arrange; to put in proper order.

dispose of. Get rid of; settle finally and definitively.

dispositive motion. Pretrial motion (generally a motion to suppress) the outcome of which will determine whether the case will go to trial. For example, if the defendant moves to exclude evidence from a search claiming the search violated the Fourth Amendment, and the only evidence the state has of the defendant's crime is from that search, the motion is said to be "dispositive." (If the state has additional evidence upon which a jury could find beyond a reasonable doubt that defendant committed the crime, then the motion would be non-dispositive).

dissent/dissenting opinion. Disagree or differ in opinion; opinion written by a judge who disagrees with the majority opinion.

dissipate. Dissolve; diffuse; to cause to spread out.

dissipation of the taint. See **fruit of the poisonous tree doctrine**.

distinguish. Point out the differences in the facts of one case from another case in order to show that the court is perhaps not bound by precedent.

district courts. The primary trial courts in the federal court system. There are 94 district courts in the United States, including 89 district courts in the 50 states and one each in Puerto Rico, the Virgin Islands, the District of Columbia, Guam and the Northern Mariana Islands.

diversion. Generally, a contract between the prosecutor and the defendant in which the defendant agrees to perform certain conditions, the successful completion of which results in a dismissal of the case or charges.

divulge. Disclose; reveal.

dock. Place in the courtroom where the defendant stands or sits in a criminal trial.

doctrine. Legal principle, rule or theory.

doctrine of over breadth. Legal doctrine that prohibits laws which criminalize behavior that is otherwise protected. For example, if a statute limits behavior that is constitutionally protected, the law will be considered to be over broad and will be struck down (or narrowed). Also referred to as "void for overbreadth."

doctrine of vagueness. Legal doctrine that holds that laws that are too vague and do not clearly announce what behavior is criminal should be struck down as unconstitutional. The void-for-vagueness doctrine derives its authority from the Due Process Clause. Laws that fail to give notice are not fair.

domicile. Legal residence; place where a person has his or her permanent legal home.

double-blind lineup. Lineup procedure in which neither the witness nor the investigator staging the lineup knows who the suspect is.

double jeopardy. Fifth Amendment prohibition against retrying a person who has been acquitted or convicted. It also bars the imposition of subsequent punishment for the same offense. There are limitations on the prohibition of double jeopardy, and under certain circumstances a person may be re-tried (for example in another jurisdiction, or when a conviction has been reversed on appeal).

draconian law. Exceptionally harsh or severe law.

dram shop law. Liquor law that allows a person who has served alcohol to a minor or to an intoxicated person to be held liable for subsequent injury or damage caused by the intoxicated person.

drug paraphernalia. Items associated with the use of illegal drugs, such as a "bong."

dual court system. The court system in the United States has both a federal court system and state court systems (which is really at least 50 different court systems).

dual sovereignty doctrine. Although the Fifth Amendment protects against double jeopardy, each sovereignty (state government, federal government, tribal government) may prosecute an accused for crimes over which they have jurisdiction even if another sovereign as already tried the person.

duces tecum. Latin. "Bring with you." A *subpoena duces tecum* requires a party to appear in court and to bring certain documents, pieces of evidence, or other matters to be inspected by the court.

due process of law. Fundamental rights necessary to provide a fair legal proceeding; the safeguards and protections of law given accused of a crime (procedural due process). In substantive criminal law, the right to have crimes and punishments clearly defined in the law and satisfy society's sense of justice (substantive due process).

due process perspective. Point of view that is more concerned with people's rights and liberties than crime control.

due process voluntariness approach. Fourteenth Amendment's due process clause has been interpreted to require every confession to be voluntary under the totality of the circumstances.

duress. The use of illegal confinement or threats of harm to coerce someone to do something he or she would not do otherwise. As a legal defense, duress is an excuse similar, but not the same as, the justification of necessity. See **coercion.**

DUII. Driving under the influence of intoxicants.

duty. Obligation to do something.

DWI. Driving while intoxicated.

Dyer Act. (18 U.S.C.A. §2311 et seq) National Motor Vehicle Theft Act that makes it a crime to transport a stolen motor vehicle across state borders in interstate or foreign commerce.

dying declaration. Statement made by a fatally wounded person. To be admissible under the rules of evidence, the declaration must be a statement of fact from the person who expected to die, about how he or she was injured.

E

economic damages. Monetary compensation awarded by a court in a civil action to an individual who has been injured by the wrongful conduct of another party. Financial estimate of the harm that the plaintiff has suffered.

en banc. French. "On the bench." Designation referring to a session of a court in which all the judges of the court participate (as opposed to a session presided over by a single judge or a small judicial panel).

enjoin. Require a person by an injunction to perform or desist from performing from some act; to order.

enter. Formally place before the court (for example, to enter a guilty plea); to make a notation on a transcript, proceeding, action or record.

enumerated powers. Powers of Congress specifically named or designated in the Constitution.

Equal Protection Clause. The Fourteenth Amendment to the U.S. Constitution provides that "no state shall . . . deny to any person within its jurisdiction the equal protection of the laws." This guarantee prohibits states from denying any person or class of persons the same protection of the law enjoyed by other persons or other classes of persons in similar circumstances.

equivocal. Ambiguous; unable to decide what to do.

ergo. Latin. Therefore; thus; consequently.

Establishment Clause. One of the two First Amendment provisions that address religion.

The Constitution states, "Congress shall make no law respecting an establishment of religion." This clause is seen as bar to a nationalized religion, but it may also have ramifications concerning federal funding of religious-based schools or programs.

estop/estoppel. Stop; prevent; bar. Stopping a person from denying the truth of a fact that has already been settled by a judicial proceeding.

ethics. Rules that govern more formal social settings or groups (including public or professional organizations) which are enforced by members within the group.

et seq. Latin. "And the following." Abbreviation for *et sequentes.*

evanescent. Vanishing; transitory; fleeting.

evidence. Witness testimony, exhibits, physical objects, and documents presented by the parties during a trial to convince the jury about the truth of a fact in issue to resolve a case.

evidentiary. Furnishing evidence; having the nature of evidence.

exculpatory evidence. Evidence that exonerates or helps to exonerate a person from fault or guilt.

exigent circumstances. Unforeseen situations that demand unusual or immediate action.

ex parte. one-sided; by or for one party; done for, on behalf or, or on the application of one party only. For example, "The defense attorney objected to the prosecutor's ex parte contact with the judge concerning the motion to continue."

ex post facto **laws.** Laws that make an act criminal after it is committed. Article I Sec. 9 of the U.S. Constitution prohibits Congress from enacting criminal laws that apply retroactively.

express bias. Inability of a witness or juror to relate or evaluate facts impartially. For example, a juror who indicates during questioning that he or she could not be fair to a person accused of driving intoxicated because a family member had been killed by an intoxicated driver.

expunge. Erase or cancel; delete one's arrest record from official sources.

extenuating circumstances. Facts surrounding the crime that lessen or diminish its seriousness or the perpetrator's culpability. See **mitigating circumstances**.

extradite/extradition. Surrender of a person by one jurisdiction (the asylum state) to another (the demanding state) for the purpose of criminal prosecution.

extraneous. Coming from the outside or external; not essential; irrelevant; not an integral part.

extrinsic. From the outside; external; apart from; not essential; extraneous.

extrinsic evidence. External evidence; facts other than those contained in the body of an agreement, document, or other object; evidence not properly before the court.

F

factual basis. When a defendant enters a plea of guilty to a charge, the judge will require the defendant to recite the facts that make him or her guilty in order to establish that proof is available that defendant committed each element of the crime.

fair hearing. Hearing in which both parties have a reasonable opportunity to be heard, present their case, and make arguments. A fair hearing is a fundamental element of due process.

fair notice. Due process requirement that the government provide adequate notice to a person before it deprives him or her of life, liberty, or property.

false arrest. Either the tort or crime of unlawfully restraining a person.

federalism. Constitutional division of governmental power and responsibility between the national (federal) government and the states.

federal question. Case that contains an issue involving the United States Constitution or statutes presents a federal question.

Federal Speedy Trial Act of 1974— Congressional act setting time standards for each stage in the federal court process. Although the time periods set forth are fairly straightforward, there is a list of exceptions and grounds for stopping the clock (tolling), some of which the court automatically approves, and some of which the court must make certain findings. See, e.g., *U.S. v. Tinklenburg*, 563 U.S. ___ (2011).

felony. Serious crime that is generally punishable by one year or more in prison or by capital punishment (death penalty)

fighting words. Utterances that, because of their content, are likely to provoke a violent response from the hearer.

flag desecration statutes. State laws that prohibit damaging or destroying a United States or state flag.

Franks hearing. Pretrial proceeding in which the defendant challenges the veracity of the affiant's statements in a search warrant application. See *Franks v. Delaware*, 438 U.S. 154 (1978).

Free Exercise Clause. One of two First Amendment provisions dealing with religion. It states, "Congress shall make no law respecting an establishment of religion, or prohibiting the free exercise thereof."

freedom of association/assembly. Person's right to meet with others protected, subject to limitations, by the First Amendment.

freedom of expression/speech. Person's right to express thoughts and feelings through speech, writing, and expressive conduct that is protected by the First Amendment.

freedom of religion. See **Free Exercise Clause and Establishment Clause.**

frisk. Outer clothing pat-down (a limited search) of a suspect by the police after a "stop" based on reasonable suspicion that a crime has just been or is about to be committed by this suspect AND that the suspect is currently armed and dangerous.

frivolous appeal. Appeal lacking in legal merit.

fruit of the poisonous tree doctrine. A doctrine based on the judicial interpretation of the Fourth Amendment holding that evidence derived from other, illegally seized evidence, cannot be used by the prosecution. The Supreme Court held in *Wong Sun v. United States*, 371 U.S. 471 (1963) that when the taint from the initial illegality dissipates through time or circumstances, then the derivative evidence may be admissible. Also known as the derivative evidence rule.

fruits of a crime. Material objects part of or obtained by criminal acts. For example, in a child pornography case, the pornographic pictures would be considered fruits of a crime, and in a bank robbery, the money taken would be the fruit of the crime.

Frye test. Supreme Court holding that, to be admissible, expert testimony must be based on scientific methods that are generally acceptable within the relevant scientific community. *Frye v. United States*, 293 F. 1013 (D.C. Cir. 1923). See also, **Daubert test, Kumhoe Tire test.**

fundamental error. Type of reversible error that adversely affects substantial rights of the accused.

fundamental fairness. Fourteenth Amendment Due Process Clause requires states to have criminal procedures that are fundamentally fair.

G

general damages. Damages are money paid to an injured party by the defendant to compensate for loss or injury. At common law, damages were either compensatory damages or punitive damages. Compensatory damages were either special damages (economic damages to compensate for loss of earning, property damage, and medical expenses) or general damages (noneconomic damages for pain, suffering, and emotional distress). See **noneconomic damages.** Contrast **economic damages.**

general deterrence. Theory of punishment in which the threat of punishing the actor is intended to deter criminal behavior in the general population.

general part of criminal law. Statutory provisions in a criminal code that apply to all crimes. For example, the definitions of the mental states used by the criminal statutes are found in the general part of criminal law.

good-faith exception. Exception to the rule that evidence seized without a warrant must be excluded. Evidence from warrantless search may be admissible if the officer acted in good faith that his or her conduct complied with the Fourth Amendment.

grand jury. A jury comprised of 7 to 23 individuals who meet to determine whether there is sufficient evidence against the defendant to allow the case to go forward to the court of general jurisdiction. If the grand jury determines enough evidence exists, the foreperson will sign a true bill on an indictment (the written accusation listing the charges).

gravamen. Grievance; essential part of a charge or accusation; substantial part of the charge or complaint.

gross. Flagrant; glaring; shameful.

ground. Foundation; basis; reason.

guilty plea. Plea in which the defendant admits that he or she committed the crime(s).

guilty verdict. Decision by the jury in a jury trial, or judge in a bench trial, that sufficient evidence about defendant's guilt exists to prove beyond a reasonable doubt that the defendant committed the crime(s) charged

H

habeas corpus/writ of habeas corpus/petition for writ of habeas corpus. Latin. "You have the body." Remedy sought by a person requesting release from an allegedly illegal or unconstitutional confinement.

habit. Constant tendency to act in a certain way in response to specific conditions.

hand down. Announce or release a judicial opinion, decision, or verdict.

harmful error. See **reversible error.**

harmless error. Error made during the trial that did not affect the outcome of the case and thus does not require reversal of the conviction on appeal.

hearing. Proceeding in which evidence is presented and arguments are heard for the purpose of making a determination on some factual or legal issue.

hearsay evidence. Defined in the evidence code as a statement that is made out of court and then offered in a court hearing for its truth.

heretofore. Before this time; previously; formerly.

hold. Decide; state the ruling of the court on a point of law. For example, "The court held that the arrest was illegal." Bind; restrain; maintain custody or control over. For example, officer Jones held him until the patrol car arrived. Preside over; conduct. For example, "Status hearings are held on Thursdays." Occupy; to have. For example, "He holds the office of chief justice."

holding. Legal principle derived from a decision of a court resolving an issue in a case.

hostile witness. See **adverse witness.**

hung jury. Jury that cannot agree to convict or acquit the defendant. If the jury "hangs," the judge will often declare a mistrial, and the state may reprosecute.

I

ibid (ibidem). Latin. In the same place; in the same book, chapter, article or page.

id. (idem). Latin. "The same;" the same as previously mentioned. *Id* is used primarily in footnotes to indicate a reference previously mentioned.

imminent. Likely to occur at any moment; impending; near at hand.

imminent danger. Impending danger that must be dealt with immediately and cannot be prevented by calling for help.

immunity (see also "use immunity" and "transactional immunity"). Exemption from prosecution granted to a witness in exchange for testimony; exemption from liability, duty, service, jurisdiction that is required or imposed on others; special privilege.

impartial. Not favoring one party over another; unprejudiced; disinterested; equitable. "Impartiality is not a technical conception. It is a state of mind." *U.S. v. Wood*, 299 U.S. 123 (1936)).

impeach. Attack the credibility of a witness, usually through cross-examination.

implied authority. Authority not expressly conferred by a principal upon an agent, but arising out of the language or course of conduct of the principal toward the agent. Implied authority is a type of actual authority.

implied bias. When the law assumes that a juror could not be fair or impartial in the evaluating of facts presented for a determination because of some degree of kinship or relationship between a party or witness in the trial.

implied consent. Consent not expressly given but inferred from words, actions, or circumstances or created by law. For example, state law indicates that drivers give implied consent to a chemical test to determine blood alcohol content (i.e., blow into an intoxilyzer) and have the evidence obtained admitted in court when arrested for a DUII.

impracticable. Cannot be performed or accomplished.

impute. To charge, ascribe, or attribute something disadvantageous to another. 2) To impose, ascribe, or attribute something to a person (e.g., knowledge, notice, or negligence) to a person not because of that person's acts or omissions, but because of the acts or omissions of another for whom the person is responsible.

inadvertent. Inattentive, heedless, or careless; unintentional; unanticipated, unplanned or unforeseen.

inalienable. Unable to be given up, taken away, or transferred to another. Also referred to as unalienable.

in camera. Latin. "In chambers." In a judge's private room or office; in a courtroom with all spectators excluded. Contrast **open court**.

incapacity. Legal disqualification; legal inability to act. For example, children cannot enter into contracts because of incapacity.

incapacitation. Theory of, or type of, punishment that makes the offender incapable of committing further crimes (at least in the community); includes incarceration, capital punishment, castration.

incarceration. Confinement. Generic term for imprisonment in a prison, jail, or other correctional facility.

inchoate. In an early stage; begun but not completed; unfinished; partial; imperfect.

incontrovertible. Unquestionable; indisputable.

incorporate by reference. Make one document part of another separate document by specifically referring to the former in the latter and saying that the former shall be considered as part of the latter.

incriminate. Tend to show guilt of a crime.

inculpatory. Tending to show guilt or blame; incriminating.

incumbent. Person who presently holds an office.

independent source exception (to the exclusionary rule). Exception to exclusionary rule that allows evidence to be presented in court if the state can show that it was obtained from an independent source not connected to the illegal search or seizure.

indict. Action by the grand jury when it finds sufficient evidence that the defendant has committed a felony.

indictment. Charging document or written accusation filed against the defendant after being signed by a grand jury. (The grand jury will return a "true bill" on the indictment).

indigency. Being too poor to be able to afford to hire an attorney.

indigent defendants. Criminal defendants who cannot afford to hire an attorney.

indirect attack. See **collateral attack.**

indirect evidence. See **circumstantial evidence.**

inferior courts. A term sometimes used for magistrate courts or other courts of limited jurisdiction.

in forma pauperis. Latin. "In the form of a pauper;" as a poor person; indigent. This phrase indicates the permission given by the court to bring a legal action without paying costs or other court fees because of a lack of financial resources.

information. Formal, written charging document submitted to a court by a prosecutor without the approval or intervention of a grand jury. An information is similar to an indictment and serves as the indictment in jurisdictions that do not use grand juries.

infra. Latin. Below, under, beneath, or inferior to; within; after or later. When infra is used in a book or other document, it means that the matter referred to appears later in the work. Contrast **supra.**

infraction. Minor criminal offense, which is generally punishable by only a monetary sanction; often considered a ticketable offense.

inherent. Intrinsic; existing as a permanent and essential element or characteristic of something.

initial appearance. First appearance by an accused in the first court having jurisdiction over his or her case. A variety of procedural steps may be taken during the initial appearance. In many misdemeanor cases, the initial appearance may be the defendant's only appearance before the court. In some cases, the accused may be arraigned, enter a plea of not guilty, and have bail set, all during the initial appearance. If any major steps are taken for which the defendant is entitled to counsel (legal representation), then the defendant may need to reappear after the initial appearance with counsel (for example, for arraignment, release or bail hearings, at entry of plea). See **arraignment.**

initial plea. The first plea to a given charge entered in the court record by or for the defendant. The acceptance of an initial plea of not guilty indicates that the arraignment process has been completed and that additional pretrial procedures can be scheduled.

injunction. Judicial process or order directing a person to do something, or requiring a person to refrain from doing some thing. A person who violates an injunction may be found to be in contempt of court.

in lieu of. In place of; instead of.

innocent. Not guilty of a specific crime charged or alleged. The term innocent should be reserved for individuals who are factually innocent of the crime (i.e., they did not do the criminal act) rather than used to describe a not guilty finding by the jury or judge, or a plea of not guilty by the defendant.

in person. In one's own bodily or physical presence. For example, the defendant appeared in person rather than "through counsel."

inquest. Proceeding, often conducted by a coroner, to determine whether a death could have been caused by criminal homicide.

in re. In the matter of; in the case of; concerning. In re is used in the title of some cases that do not involve parties who are necessarily adversarial-- juvenile delinquency petitions, for example.

INS. Abbreviation for the Immigration and Naturalization Service, a former federal agency under the Department of Justice. The agency ceased to exist in 2003 when the Department of Homeland Security was established in response to the September 11, 2001 attack. Now three agencies exist under the Department of Homeland Security: the U.S. Citizenship and Immigration Services (USCIS), the U.S. Immigrations and Customs Enforcement (ICE), and U.S. Customs and Border Protection (CBP

insanity. Legal term describing a defendant's mental disease or defect that makes him or her incapable of committing a crime. Insanity concerns the defendant's mental state at the time he or she is to have committed the crime. There are at least four tests of insanity used by the states and federal government when the defense of insanity is raised.

instance. Legal proceeding or process. For example, the trial court is referred to as the court of first instance.

instruction. Direction or explanation given by a trial judge to a jury informing it of the law applicable to the case before it. Attorneys for both sides normally furnish the judge with suggested instructions.

intelligible principle. Judicial doctrine that allows Congress to delegate legislative authority to executive agencies and officials so long as it provides intelligent and defined instructions. This doctrine allows presidents to execute laws through the adoption of rules and regulations by administrative agencies.

inter alia. Latin. Among other things.

interlocutory appeal. Appeal on some preliminary or subordinate issue asking the appellate court to decide something before the trial court reaches a decision. This appeal will not finally settle the rights of the parties. For example, if the defendant files a motion to suppress, and the judge grants the motion after the hearing, the state/prosecutor may file an interlocutory appeal to the appellate courts. Note that the state may not appeal a final verdict.

intestate. Refers to anyone who died without a will.

irrelevant evidence. Evidence that has no tendency to either prove or disprove an issue in the case.

issue (verb). Send out or put forth officially or authority; promulgate; publish.

issue (noun). Disputed point or question of fact or law. For example, "The main issue in the case was whether the police 'stopped' the defendant."

J

joinder. Combining of multiple defendants or charges in any legal step or proceeding.

judge-made law. Common law as developed n form and content by judges and judicial decisions having precedent for future cases. Sometimes used derogatorily to mean a judicial decision based on a tortured construction of the constitution, or a judicial decision that discovers the law applying to a given case.

judgment. Official decision of the court about the rights and claims of the parties to the action or suit.

judgment of acquittal. In a nonjury trial, a judge's order exonerating a defendant based on a finding that the state did not prove the defendant's guilt. In a jury trial in which the jury found the defendant guilty, a judge's order exonerating a defendant on the ground that the evidence was not legally sufficient to support the jury's finding of guilt. Also referred to as a "judgment of acquittal notwithstanding the verdict" or "JNOV."

judicial notice. Act of a court recognizing the existence of certain facts that are commonly known, without formal proof or evidence being introduced.

judicial review. Review of a legislative, judicial, or executive branch action or law by the courts to see if it complies with the constitution. Judicial review is one of the key features in American jurisprudence and began with the landmark case of *Marburry v. Madison*, 5 U.S. 137 (1803)

jurisdiction. Authority of a court to hear and decide a particular case.

jury. Group of citizens convened for the purpose of deciding factual questions relevant to a civil or criminal case. In a felony case, there may be a **grand jury** used to determine if there is sufficient evidence against the defendant to go forward to a trial. The **petit jury** is the group that renders the verdict and it is comprised of different people than those in the grand jury.

jury deliberations. Process by which a jury discusses the evidence after the conclusion of the trial and determines the verdict.

jury instructions. Judge's explanations to the jury of the law they must apply to the evidence/facts that they have heard in a case.

jury nullification. When the jury members disregard the judge's instructions on the law they are to apply and instead decides the verdict on the basis of their conscience.

jury pardon. Action taken by a jury, despite the quality of the evidence, acquitting a defendant or convicting the defendant on lesser charges.

jury selection. See **voir dire.**

jury unanimity. Most states require that all jurors reach the same conclusion (i.e., guilty or not guilty) on each charge. Two states, Oregon and Louisiana, do not have the requirement of jury unanimity for 12-person juries. The Supreme Court has upheld a 9-3 verdict. (Note some speculate that the Court may be willing to reconsider its holding not requiring unanimity).

K

knock and announce rule. Requirement under federal law and in most states that law enforcement officers first knock and announce their presence and purpose before entering a person's home to serve a search or arrest warrant.

Kumhoe Tire test. The Supreme Court held in *Kumhoe Tire Co. v. Carmichael* that the Daubert test concerning the admissibility of scientific evidence applied to "technical" evidence that is not necessarily "scientific" (in this case an expert's testimony about the tires). The U.S. Supreme Court charged district courts to perform a gatekeeping function on technical evidence to ensure its reliability much in the same fashion that it had in Daubert v. Merrill Dow Pharmaceuticals. See **Daubert test, Frye test.**

L

law. Formal means of social control that involves the use of rules interpreted and enforced by the courts.

lay witness. Witness who is able to testify at court about matters personally known or observed. Contrast **expert witness.**

leading question. Question that suggests an answer. Leading questions are permitted on cross-examination of a witness or direct examination of a hostile witness.

legal. Conforming to the law; according to a law; required or permitted by a law.

legal fiction. Condition assumed to be true in law, regardless of its actual truth or falsity. For example, the Court's holding that corporations are persons is a legal fiction.

legal impossibility. Defense allowed in some jurisdictions when, although the defendant intended to commit a crime, it was impossible to do so because the completed act is not a crime.

legal relevancy. Evidence that survives a challenge under Federal Rule of Evidence, 403, is logically relevant, and is not excluded for one of several reasons (for example, because it is cumulative redundant, confusing, or a waste of time). See FRE 403 for the test of legal relevancy.

legislation. Rules of general application, enacted by a law-making body. In its generic sense, legislation includes statutes, ordinances, administrative regulations, and court rules. Most often the term is used to refer to a statute.

legislative intent. Purpose the legislature sought to achieve in enacting a particular provision of law.

legislature. Elected law-making body such as the Congress of the United States or a state assembly.

lenity (rule of). Rule of statutory construction that, when a statute's terms are ambiguous, the court should interpret the terms in a light favorable to the defendant.

lesser included offense. When it is impossible to commit a particular crime without also committing, by the same conduct, another offense of a lesser grade, the latter is referred to as a "lesser included offense." For example, a person who commits armed robbery also commits the crime of robbery, so robbery is a lesser included offense of armed robbery.

lewd and lascivious conduct. Indecent exposure of a person's private parts in public; indecent touching or fondling of a child.

liability. In civil law, the legal term for responsibility. In criminal law, the term for culpability or guilt.

litigation. Contest in a court for the purpose of enforcing a right; any controversy that must be decided on evidence.

logical relevancy. Evidence that has any tendency to either prove or disprove a fact that is at issue is logically relevant evidence under FRE 401.

M

magistrate. Judicial officer of a court of limited jurisdiction. In addition to trying cases or accepting guilty pleas in minor cases, magistrates generally can issue arrest warrants, search warrants and summons; set bail and order release on bail; and conduct arraignments and preliminary hearings on persons charged with major crimes.

majority opinion. Opinion written by one of the members of a court with which the majority of the court agree.

mala in se. (malum in se = singular) Latin. "Evil in itself." Crime that is inherently evil or bad.

mala prohibita. (malum prohibitum = singular). Latin. "Evil because prohibited." A crime that is not inherently evil, but is a crime because it is prohibited.

malice. Intent to commit a wrong or hurtful act with no reason or legal justification. **Express malice** is actual, overt or specific malice. **Implied malice** is suggested by the actions of the subject. Generally, the term **malice** means wickedness or a tendency toward wrongdoing.

malice aforethought. Mental predetermination to commit an illegal act; pre-meditation.

malign. Slander.

malum. Latin. "Wrong; evil; bad."

mandamus. Latin. "We command." Court-issued writ in which a higher court commands a lower court, administrative body, or executive body to perform a specified legally required act. Commonly used to restore rights and privileges lost to a defendant through illegal means.

mandatory appeal (appeal of right). Generally, the federal government and states allow a defendant at least one statutory appeal of right. If the defendant appeals his or her conviction, an appellate court must review the trial record. The appellate court need not, however, issue a written opinion. The U.S. Supreme Court has decided that indigent defendants are entitled to assigned counsel for these mandatory appeals. Contrast **certiorari, discretionary review.**

manifest. Evident; obvious; clearly revealed; unmistakable; undisputable.

manifest criminality. Requirement that intentions have to turn into criminal deeds in order to be punishable.

martial law. Control of civilian populations by military commanders. Martial law displaces civilian laws, authorities, and the courts. It is an exercise of military power that may be arbitrary and unfettered and is reviewable only by the executive branch and not by the judicial branch.

material witness. Person who possesses information of value in a criminal trial. Judges can force such witnesses to post bond or can even detain them to ensure their appearance in court.

mayhem. One of the common law felonies that involved injuring a person in such a way that he or she was less able to defend himself or herself in battle.

McNabb-Mallory Rule. Rule applicable in federal courts that any admission or confession obtained during an unreasonable delay between the arrest of a person and his or her initial appearance before a magistrate will be

inadmissible in court. See *McNabb v. United States*, 318 U.S. 332 (1943) and *Mallory v. United States*, 354 U.S. 449 (1957).

memorandum of law. Written argument in support of a legal position.

mens rea. Latin. Guilty mind; criminal intent.

merger. When a single criminal act constitutes two distinct offenses, the less serious offense is absorbed by the more serious offense. In order to merge into the more serious offense, the less serous offense must necessarily be established by proof of the more serious offense. For example, the crime of attempted murder merges into murder at sentencing. Conspiracy to commit murder, however, does not merge into murder. Merger presents some tricky legal issues and much room for.

merits. Substance of a legal matter, not the procedural, technical, or extraneous aspects of the matter. For example, the statement, "the court decided the case on its merits" means that the court decided the case based on its facts (i.e., evidence that the defendant committed the crime or not) rather than whether the case was barred by the statute of limitations, double jeopardy, or some other procedural constraint.

military tribunal. Court set up to deal with violations of military law (rules and regulations governing military forces). Military justice is administered by court-martial with no concern for the judicial power or civil law of the United States. Courts-martial are convened for the duration of a particular case; the regulations governing military justice are set forth in the Uniform Code of Military Justice.

misdemeanor. Minor crimes for which the penalty is usually less than one year in jail or a fine.

mistake of fact. Erroneous conclusion or misunderstanding of a factual nature not due to negligence in finding out the truth. A potential defense to criminal liability when an individual commits a prohibited act in good faith and with a reasonable, though false, belief that certain facts are correct. In order to be a successful defense, the mistake must be honest, reasonable and not the result of negligence or poor deliberation. For example, it may be a defense to the crime of theft if the defendant took someone else's umbrella reasonably believing it was hers.

mistake of law. Erroneous conclusion or misunderstanding of the legal consequences of a situation with full knowledge of the facts surrounding the situation. Generally, not a defense to a criminal charge ("Ignorance of the law is no defense.") However, the Supreme Court ruled that ignorance of the law may be a defense, if the law has not been made reasonably well known. (This is, in essence, a due process issue—it is unfair to hold people accountable for behavior that they couldn't reasonably know was criminal). For example, it generally won't be a defense to theft when the defendant takes someone else's umbrella believing that theft is not a crime.

mistrial. Trial the court terminates and declares invalid because of some circumstance that creates a substantial and uncorrectable prejudice to the conduct of a fair trial.

mitigating circumstances/factors. Circumstances or factors that tend to lessen culpability.

Model Penal Code. Published by the American Law Institute in 1962, the MPC consists of general provisions concerning criminal liability, sentences, defenses, and definitions of specific crimes. The MPC is not law; instead, it is designed to serve as a model code of criminal law for all states. Most states have completely revised their penal codes since 1962, and the content and arrangement of these recently revised codes often reflect the MPC approach.

moot. Theoretical; not actual; hypothetical; purely academic; having no legal significance.

moral certainty. High degree of probability. Some states, including Oregon, have jury instructions in that define beyond a reasonable doubt in terms of being convinced to a moral certainty.

morality-based offenses. Category of criminal conduct intended to protect the family and social institutions, including the crimes of lewdness, indecency, prostitution, obscenity, and sex-related offenses.

morals. Principles, practices or values held by individuals or small groups that are self-enforced or regulated through social rejection or approval.

moral turpitude. Base or vile act that reflects depravity and runs contrary to the accepted and customary rule of right and duty between individuals. In some jurisdictions, persons convicted of crimes of moral turpitude may lose the right to hold office or to vote.

motion. Written or oral request a party makes to a court at any time before, during, or after court proceedings, asking the court to make a specific finding or decision, or issue a specific order. Motions in criminal cases can be made by the defense, the prosecution, or the court.

motion for change of venue. Defense motion for the trial to be moved to another area based on adverse pre-trial publicity that would prejudice the defendant.

motion for directed verdict. Defense motion asking the court to direct a verdict of not guilty based upon insufficient evidence being presented by the prosecution during its case-in-chief. In order to grant a motion for directed verdict (and take the case away from the jury), the judge must find that no reasonable jury could find that there was evidence beyond a reasonable doubt that the defendant committed the crime.

motion for judgment of acquittal notwithstanding the verdict. Defense motion asking the judge to acquit the defendant even though the jury has found him or her to be guilty. In order to grant this motion, the judge must determine that no reasonable jury could find there was evidence beyond a reasonable doubt proving the defendant's guilt.

motion for new trial. Formal request of the trial court to hold a new trial in a case that has already been adjudicated (decided).

motion for rehearing. Formal request of the court to convene another hearing in a case in which the court has already ruled.

motion for severance. Motion to separate defendants and/or charges into two or more trials.

motion in limine. Motion asking for a preliminary ruling on the admissibility of evidence. Unlike a motion to suppress, this motion is not limited to constitutional issues and therefore need not be filed prior to trial; however, it is a good idea for both judicial efficiency and trial strategy.

motion to dismiss. Formal request to a trial judge to dismiss criminal charges against a defendant.

motion to set aside judgment. Motion to have a judgment set aside because of errors appearing on the face of the record. A motion to set aside judgment can be made at any time within the statute of limitations.

motion to strike. Motion made during trial requesting the judge to instruct the jury not to consider a witness's statements. Motions to strike should generally be made immediately after the purportedly inadmissible statement is offered.

motion to suppress. Motion to exclude evidence based on some constitutional violation, such as a violation of the Fourth Amendment. Motions to suppress need to be made in advance of trial, and are either **dispositive** or **non-dispositive.**

motive. Reasons for acting.

municipal court. Court of limited jurisdiction whose territorial jurisdiction is limited to a city or town.

N

Necessary and Proper Clause. Clause in the U.S. Constitution that grants Congress power to make laws that are necessary and proper to carry out its enumerated powers Article 1 § 8.

natural law. Theory of law maintaining that law is not crated by human beings, but rather originates from the natural order of things.

negate. Deny; nullify; make ineffective.

negotiable. Capable of being legally transferred from one person to another by delivery, with or without endorsement. (A check is a negotiable instrument.)

no bill. A decision by a grand jury when it declines to return an indictment. Also referred to as "not a true bill."

no contest plea. See **nolo contendere.**

nolle prosequi (nol pros). Latin. "We shall not prosecute." Prosecutor's declaration to the judge that the state has decided to drop charges against the accused. The statement is an admission that the case against the defendant has fatal flaws, that there is insufficient evidence against the accused, or that the prosecutor now believes in the defendant's innocence.

nolo contendere **(no contest) plea.** Defendant's plea to a criminal charge that, although it is not an admission of guilty, generally has the same effect as a plea of guilty. A no contest plea in a criminal case is usually not admissible in evidence in a subsequent civil case.

nominal damages. Monetary damages that a plaintiff may recover when he or she can prove injury caused by the defendant but cannot prove the exact dollar amount. The amount of damages is generally a small, symbolic sum of money. See **economic damages**; contrast **compensatory damages and punitive damages.**

nondeadly force. Force that does not, or cannot, result in death.

noneconomic damages. Nonmonetary losses recoverable in a civil suit including pain, mental suffering, emotional distress, humiliation, injury to reputation, loss of care, loss of comfort, loss of companionship and society, loss of consortium, inconvenience.

nonjury trial. A trial in which the judge determines the facts as well as the law. See, **bench trial.**

non sequitur. Latin. "It does not follow." Something that does not follow logically form or is unrelated to things preceding it.

not guilty plea. A defendant's plea to criminal charges contained in a complaint, information, or indictment, claiming that he or she did not commit the offense(s). In this plea the defendant denies the charge and puts in issue all the material facts alleged in the charging document (complaint, indictment, or information). If the defendant refuses to enter a plea, the court must enter a plea of not guilty. The entry of a not guilty plea, is generally the procedural step that "starts the ball rolling" with regard to setting hearings, trials, etc. The defendant can later change his or her not guilty plea to "guilty" or "no contest."

nullen crimine, nullem poena, sine lege. Latin. "There is no crime, there is no punishment without the law." Doctrine that one cannot be found guilty of a crime unless there is a violation of an existing provision of the law defining the applicable criminal conduct.

nugatory. Of no force or effect; inoperative; voidable.

null (null and void). Void; invalid; of no legal effect.

nunc pro tunc. Latin. "Now for then." Phrase used to describe acts allowed to be done after they should have been done and given retroactive effect as if done timely.

O

oath. Solemn appeal to God or some other sacred object, in witness of the truth of a statement or the binding nature of a promise or undertaking.

object. Oppose an action by the opposing party or by the court because it is illegal or improper. When an attorney objects to the introduction of certain evidence, he or she is said to have made an objection.

obscenity. Explicit sexual material that is patently offensive, appeals to a prurient or unnatural interest in sex, and lacks serious scientific, artistic, or literary content.

of counsel. Phrase used to describe an attorney employed to assist in the preparation or management of the case, but who is not the principal attorney of record; an attorney who is associated with a law firm but is neither a partner nor an associate.

offense. Act committed or omitted in violation of law forbidding or commanding it. The term offense is sometimes used restrictively as a synonym for crime. In broad usage, however, offenses may include crimes, delinquent acts, status offenses, infractions, civil violations, and private wrongs and injuries.

officer of the court. General term for any type of court employee, including judges, clerks of court, bailiffs, sheriffs, marshals. Attorneys are also considered officers of the court and therefore must obey rules of court.

of record. Entered or existing on the official record of a court in connection with a particular case, judgment, or proceeding.

omission. Failure to act or do something the law requires. Some omissions are criminal acts--for example, failure to pay taxes.

open court/in open court. Public court session with spectators present.

opening statements. Part of a trial before the presentation of evidence, in which the attorney for each party outlines what he or she thinks the testimony/evidence will be.

opinion. Official written decision of a court together with the reasons for that decision.

oral argument. Verbal presentations an attorney or party makes to an appellate court to persuade it to affirm, reverse, or modify a lower court decision.

order. (verb) issue a command or instruction. (noun) Mandate, command, or direction issued by a judicial officer in the exercise of judicial authority, entered in the court record. Sometimes viewed as a judgment, a court order is instead the mechanism by which the court directs the course of a proceeding, settles intervening matters, or ensures that actions implementing the judgment occur. Writs and injunctions are orders.

ordinance. Rule and regulation, similar to a statute, passed by local legislative bodies, such as city councils.

ordinary negligence. Failure to exercise ordinary care. Contrast **gross negligence**.

organic law. Essential or fundamental law or constitution of a nation, state, or other governmental unit that establishes the manner in which its government will be organized.

original jurisdiction. Jurisdiction of a court or administrative agency to hear or act upon a case from its beginning and to pass judgment on the law and the facts (trial court jurisdiction rather than appellate court jurisdiction).

outbuilding. Building usually separated from the main house such as a barn, a detached garage, or a stable.

overbreadth. See **void for overbreadth.**

overrule. Overturn the holding in a prior case by deciding a point of law exactly opposite to the decision in the prior case. A court's decision can be overruled by that court or by a higher court with the same subject matter jurisdiction; deny a motion, objection, or other request made to the court during the course of a trial.

overt. Open to view or knowledge; manifest; not concealed or hidden.

overt act. Outward act done toward the accomplishment of a crime from which an intent to commit the crime may be inferred; a visible act done by an individual.

oyez. French. "Hear ye." Word bailiff calls out in some courtrooms to get attention when an announcement is about to be made. Opening call at the commencement of a Supreme Court session.

Oyez Project. "The Oyez Project at Chicago-Kent is a multimedia archive devoted to the Supreme Court of the United States and its work. It aims to be a complete and authoritative source for all audio tapes recorded in the Court since the installation of a recording system in October 1955." See www.oyez.org.

P

pander. (verb) pimp. (noun) One who supplies another with the means to gratify sexual desires.

par. Latin. "Equal."

pardon. An action by the president or a state governor that mitigates or sets aside punishment for a crime.

party. Person who takes part in a criminal offense; person or entity directly interested in the subject matter of a case and who may assert a claim, make a defense, examine witnesses, or appeal the judgment.

pass. Pronounce; render; utter. For example, "the court passed judgment on the defendant. "

penal. Relating to punishment or penalty.

penal law/code. Law that creates an offense and establishes a penalty for it.

pendency/pending. State of a court action after it has begun and before it is completed; awaiting decision.

pen register. Device that enables law enforcement to obtain the numbers that have been dialed by use of a specific telephone.

per. by; by means of; through; by/for each.

per curiam opinion. Unsigned opinion issued by a court as distinct from an opinion attributed to one or more judges.

per diem. By the day; daily.

peremptory challenge. Challenge to the selection of a potential juror for which the attorney making the challenge is not required to state the reason for the objection.

perfect (verb). Satisfy all the legal requirements for; complete; finish.

per se. Latin. "By, of, or in itself." Inherently; intrinsically; without connection or reference to anything else.

personal knowledge. Knowledge obtained by a person firsthand through perception or experience. Personal knowledge is distinguished from secondhand knowledge (commonly referred to as "hearsay"). See **hearsay**.

persuasive authority. Any source of law, such as related cases, law review articles, legal encyclopedias, that a court may but is not required to consult/refer to when deciding a case.

petit jury. The trial jury—usually six or twelve members—whose duty it is to determine the facts in a case and announce a verdict.

petty offenses/petty crimes. Minor crimes for which fines or short jail terms are the possible punishment.

Pinkerton Rule. Rule enunciated by the Supreme Court that a member of a conspiracy is liable for co-conspirator's acts done in furtherance of the conspiracy. *Pinkerton v. United States*, 328 U.S. 640 (1946).

plain error/plain error rule. Error that is evident on the face of the record; judicial doctrine that an appellate court may take notice of error in the proceedings even if no party objected to the error when it was made. The rule applies to errors that are obvious, that affect substantial rights of the accused, and that, if uncorrected, will seriously affect the fairness, integrity, or public reputation of judicial proceedings.

plain meaning rule. Judicial doctrine that if the meaning of a statute or rule is plain and understandable, the court may not interpret it but must simply apply it as written.

plaintiff. Party who can sue for wrongs in civil cases.

plea bargain. Agreement between a defendant and a prosecutor in which the defendant agrees to plead guilty in exchange for some concession. In charge-bargaining, the concession is that the state gives up certain charges; in sentence-bargaining, the concession is that the state recommends a shorter sentence.

plead. Enter a plea on an allegation; assert or urge (as a defense). For example, "He will plead the Fifth."

plenary. Full; complete; entire.

plurality opinion. Court opinion in which a majority of the court agree as to the ultimate result, but in which less than a majority of the court agree as to reasoning. A plurality opinion carries less weight as precedent than a majority opinion under the rule of *stare decisis*.

police power. Power of a government to legislate to protect public health, safety, welfare and morality.

positive law. Theory of law asserting that the source of law is people, not nature, and is found in written word.

positive proof. Proof that establishes a fact or matter in question by direct evidence.

post-conviction relief (PCR). Statutory procedures by which a person convicted of a crime can challenge in court the validity or legality of a judgment of conviction or the penalty or the action of a correctional agency. PCR relief is considered a collateral attack, and deals with matters that could not be addressed in a direct appeal. The rules governing PCR and the remedies are similar to those for habeas corpus. See 28 U.S.C. §2255 for the federal PCR statute.

power of attorney. A written instrument authorizing another person to act as one's agent or attorney.

practicable. Capable of being done or used; feasible.

prayer. Request, in a petition or pleading, for the aid or relief desired from the court.

preamble. Statement at the beginning of a constitution, statute, or other formal document explaining the reasons and purposes of what follow.

precedent. Prior court decision that guides (binds) judges in deciding future cases.

preclude. make impossible; prevent; bar.

preemption. Judicially created doctrine, based on the Supremacy Clause of the Constitution, providing that certain matters are of such a national character, that federal laws relating to these matters take precedence over state or local laws. See e.g., *Arizona v. United States*, 567 U.S. ___ (2012)

prejudicial error. Substantial error in a proceeding that is likely to affect the outcome of the case to the detriment of the defendant. Contrast **harmless error**.

preliminary hearing. Adversary proceeding (meaning the defendant is present and can challenge state's evidence) before a judge to determine if there is sufficient evidence supporting a charge to proceed onto the next stage (generally, with a felony to the court of general jurisdiction.) If the judge finds that there

is, then he or she will "bind the defendant over" and ask the prosecutor to file an information (charging document) on those charges. In some jurisdictions, a grand jury will meet to make this same determination, and an indictment will be filed instead. It is possible for a defendant to waive a preliminary hearing and/or grand jury and just allow the prosecutor to file felony charges without this review (called a waiver of presentment). In some jurisdictions, a defendant may have a right to a preliminary hearing on misdemeanor charges. Often confused with **probable cause hearing** (see below).

present danger. Constant or always present danger. For example, an individual living in constant threat of being attacked or brutalized in his or her own home is said to be in present danger.

presentment. Initial appearance by the accused before the magistrate after arrest; written statement by a grand jury to the court indicating they have probable cause to believe that a person has committed an offense, from their own knowledge or observation. A presentment is made on the grand jury's own initiative without any bill of indictment from the prosecutor and arises from its own broad power to investigate crimes.

presumption of innocence. Fundamental principle in criminal law that a person charged with a crime is innocent of the crime until his or her guilt is proved by the prosecution beyond a reasonable doubt. The prosecutor carries both the burden of production (producing sufficient evidence) and the burden of persuasion (convincing jurors to a high standard of reasonable doubt).

presumptions of law. Legal conclusion required to be drawn from particular facts in the absence of evidence to the contrary. Under most rules of evidence, there are no presumptions of law in criminal cases; at best, jurors are instructed that they may make inferences from certain facts.

presumptive sentencing. Sentencing structure under which a particular sentence is presumed to be typical for a particular offense. The sentencing judge is allowed to depart from that typical sentence, within limited ranges, upon finding certain mitigating or aggravating factors exist.

pretext/pretext stop. Something put forward to conceal the real purpose or object of an action; false justification for an action; situation in which police stop a suspicious person/vehicle on the pretext of a motor vehicle infraction.

pretrial discovery. Process by which the defense and prosecution exchange information and gain access to evidence possessed by the opposing party prior to trial.

pretrial release. Release of an accused person from custody for all or part of the time before or during prosecution upon a promise to reappear or security (bail) being set.

prevention. Theory of punishment based on preventing crimes in the future.

preventive detention. Pretrial detention of an accused based upon the need to prevent future crime and harm to society, rather than on factors indicating the defendant would not show up for hearings and trials.

prima facia. Latin. "At first sight or appearance." Sufficient or adequate on its face without further investigation or inquiry.

prima facia **case.** A case established by *prima facia* evidence which prevails contradicted and overcome by other sufficient evidence.

prima facia **evidence.** Evidence sufficient to establish a given fact, or the group of facts constituting the party's claim, and which, if not rebutted or contradicted, will remain sufficient.

principal. a person who authorizes an agent to represent or act on behalf of him or her; actor or perpetrator of a crime. For example, a principal in the first degree is the person whose acts directly caused the criminal result. A principal in the second degree is a person who aids and abets the principal in the first degree and is present, either actually or constructively at the commission of the crime

principle. An accepted rule of action or procedure; fundamental truth or doctrine which provides a basis for other truths or for action.

principle of legality. Principle in law there can be no crime or punishment if there are no specific laws forewarning citizens that certain behaviors will result in particular punishments.

principle of orality. Principle in law that only evidence developed and presented during the course of a trial may be considered by the jurors during deliberation.

principle of utility. Permitting only the least amount of pain necessary to prevent/deter a future crime.

privacy (constitutional right of privacy). Implied constitutional right allowing individuals to be free of government interference in individual decisions about intimate activities. For example, the Supreme Court has found a constitutional right to privacy in the decision to have an abortion, get married, or use contraceptives.

privacy (reasonable expectation of privacy). Doctrine that the Fourth Amendment protects persons from government intrusion so long as they believe they have an expectation of privacy and their expectation is a reasonable one.

privilege. Special right, benefit, or immunity granted to a certain person or class.

privilege against self-incrimination. Right derived from the Fifth Amendment that a person may not be compelled to be a witness against him or herself. "No person shall. ... be compelled in any criminal case to be a witness against himself. ... "

probable cause. Reasonable belief; reasonable cause; apparent state of facts which would induce a reasonably intelligent and prudent person to believe, in a criminal case that a suspected person committed a crime.

probable cause statement. Statement from police officer who has arrested an individual without an arrest warrant explaining what facts lead him or her believe that the defendant had committed a crime.

probable cause hearing/determination. Judicial determination made within 48 hours of a warrantless arrest of whether sufficient probable cause exists to detain defendant on a crime. See *County of Riverside v. McLaughlin,* 500 U.S. 44 (1991).

procedural due process. Fair and reasonable procedures that guarantee certain minimal standards of notice, hearing, and opportunity to respond adequately before a government agency may deprive an individual of life, liberty or property.

proceeding. Legal action or process; any step or measure taken in a legal action by either party or by the court; instituting or carrying on of a legal action.

proffer. Put before; offer; tender, present for acceptance.

proof beyond a reasonable doubt. Standard of proof in a criminal trial or a juvenile delinquency hearing.

pro se. Latin. "For himself or herself; on his or her own behalf." Acting as one's own defense attorney in a criminal proceeding; representing oneself without retaining an attorney.

prosecute/prosecution. initiate criminal action against a person; state's initiation of criminal action against a person alleged to have committed an offense in order to obtain a conviction.

proviso. Clause in a legal document making some condition, stipulation, or exception.

proximate cause. Cause sufficiently related to, or connected with, a result that justifies imposing liability on the person who produced the cause. One test of proximate cause is whether the result of the person's actions was foreseeable, and whether it would be fair to hold him or her responsible. Also known as **legal cause.**

prurient interest. An excessive or unnatural interest in sex.

public defenders. Attorneys responsible for defending indigent persons charged with a crime.

public forum. Public space generally acknowledged as appropriate for public assemblies or expression of views.

public law. Area of law concerned with the organization of the government, the relation between the government and its citizens, the powers, capabilities, rights and duties of government officials, and the relations between political entities.

public order offenses. Criminal offenses that cause harm to society as a whole (sometimes called crimes against public order); these include, fighting, breach of peace, disorderly conduct, vagrancy, loitering, unlawful assembly, and public intoxication.

punitive damages. Fines imposed in a civil action to punish the responsible party beyond that necessary to compensate the injured party. See **economic damages;** contrast, **compensatory damages and nominal damages.**

pursuant. In accordance with; proceeding in conformity to.

putative. Commonly thought or regarded; supposed; reputed. For example, a putative father is the person alleged to be the father of an illegitimate child.

Q

quasi-criminal action. Civil suit that has criminal remedies (such as the potential for confinement). Some contempt of court charges are quasi-criminal.

quasi-public forum. Forum that, although it is privately owned, has many of the characteristics of a public forum. A private (not public owned) area in which the public will typically be found, and persons may assemble. For example, a shopping mall is a quasi-public forum.

question of fact. Disputed factual issue that is traditionally decided by the jury or the judge in a bench trial. For example, whether the defendant was driving in a reckless manner is a question of fact.

question of law. Disputed legal issue that is traditionally decided by the judge because it involves the application or interpretation of law. For example, whether a careless driving charge is a lesser-included charge of a reckless driving is a question of law.

quid pro quo. Latin. "Something for something." One thing in exchange for another.

R

racial profiling. Practice of singling out members of minority groups by law enforcement officers.

racket. An organized illegal commercial scheme or activity.

ratification. An agreement by a judge to adhere to a negotiated plea agreement.

ratify. Make valid or legal by formal official approval.

rational basis test. The judicial requirement that legislation must be at least rationally related to a legitimate government objective in order to survive judicial scrutiny during a constitutional challenge.

real evidence. Tangible items or objects that can be viewed or inspected, offered as proof in trial, that are identified and associated with the crime. Contrast, testimony.

rebut. To refute or disprove by offering opposing evidence or arguments.

recant. To formally withdraw or disavow something that has been openly stated.

record. An official written account of an act or transaction designed to be preserved as evidence of the act or transaction.

recusal. Refusal; rejection; objection; exception; the process by which a judge is disqualified from hearing a case because of alleged interest, prejudice, or other incompetency.

redaction. Editing out portions of a transcript in order to maintain secrecy of someone's identity or other information.

rehabilitation. Preventing future crime by treating the offender.

release on own recognizance (aka, "O.R Release"). A pretrial release in which an accused person enters into an obligation before a proper judicial officer or law enforcement officer and secures his or her own release by agreeing to appear in court when required.

relevant evidence. Evidence that tends to prove or disprove the truth of a fact or matter in issue that is more probative than prejudicial. Relevant evidence has a tendency to make the existence of any fact that is of consequence to the determination of the action more probable than it would be without that evidence. For example, the "price of tea in china" may be relevant in a lawsuit claiming international price fixing of tea leaves. It might tend to show a rate of price inflation that would make it more likely that a company fixed the rates. The price of tea in china would, however, not be relevant if the trial involved reckless driving.

remand. To send a case back to a lower court from which it was appealed with instructions as to what further action should be taken. When the appellate court reverses a judgment of a lower court, it will often remand the case to the lower court for further proceedings not inconsistent with the appellate court's opinion. 2) to send a prisoner back into custody to await further proceedings after a preliminary hearing.

rendition. Procedure, less cumbersome than extradition, for returning a person accused of a crime and released from custody prior to final judgment by a court of one state (demanding state) and whose presence in another state (asylum state) constitutes a violation of the terms of release.

reparation. Generally, compensation for an injury; redress for a wrong done. In the criminal law context, reparation means reimbursement to victims of crime for the actual loss flowing from the charged offense or from related misconduct.

reply brief. A brief submitted by an appellant in response to an appellee's answer brief.

repudiate. To reject; to refuse; to disown.

res. Latin. "A thing; an object." **res judicata.** "the matter has been decided." The doctrine that a final judgment by a competent court on a particular matter or issue is conclusive upon the parties in any subsequent litigation involving the same matter or issue.

rescind. To void, cancel, or annul something previously granted or agreed to.

respondent. The party who is the defendant on an appeal; the party who contends against the appeal.

retain. To hire a lawyer.

retained counsel. A defense attorney selected and compensated by the defendant or offender, or by other private persons. Contrast **appointed attorney, public defender, indigent defense.**

retainer. The contract between an attorney and the client specifying the nature and cost of the services to be rendered; the fee paid to engage the services of an attorney.

retribution. Theory of punishment based on just deserts.

retroactive. Influencing or applying to matters that have occurred in the past.

reverse. Overthrow, set aside or revoke by a contrary decision, usually because of errors of law; set aside a decision on appeal.

revocation. The taking away of a benefit. For example, a probation revocation hearing is one in which the state must prove that the defendant violated conditions of probation, and if successfully proven, the state requests the court revoke the defendant's release on probation.

revoke. Take away a benefit. For example, "The judge revoked the defendant's release on bail."

right of allocution. Right of a criminal defendant to make a statement on his or her own behalf before the sentence is pronounced.

right to confrontation. The right to face one's accusers in a criminal case.

right to compulsory process. The defendant's right to compel witnesses to testify in his or her behalf.

right to privacy. Constitutional right to engage in intimate personal conduct or make fundamental life decisions without governmental interference. General right of a person to be let alone by other people and the government. Although not enumerated in the constitution, this right has been held to be a fundamental right.

Rule of Four. U.S. Supreme Court rule in which the Court grants certiorari only in those cases where at least four justices agree to hear the case.

rule of law. Principle that the law, and not one person or group of persons, is the highest authority. "We are a government of rules not of men."

rule of lenity. Principle that when judges apply a criminal statute they must follow the clear letter of the statute and resolve all ambiguities in favor of the defendant (and against the application of the statute).

rules of court. Rules or regulations usually established by the highest court in the court system, governing practice and procedure in a court or court system.

rules of evidence. Legal rules governing the admissibility of evidence at trial.

rules of procedure. Rules promulgated by courts of law under constitutional or statutory authority governing procedures for trials and other judicial proceedings.

rules of statutory construction. Rules developed by courts to determine the meaning of legislative acts.

S

scientific evidence. Evidence obtained through scientific and technological innovations.

scienter. Latin. "Knowingly." Guilty knowledge; such knowledge as to make a person legally responsible for the consequences of his or her acts.

scintilla. Latin. "Spark." A barely perceptible amount; the slightest trace. Courts, for example, require that a confession be supported by at least a scintilla of evidence that a crime actually occurred in order to establish "corpus delicti."

SCOTUS. Abbreviation: Supreme Court of the United States. Note, referring to the Supreme Court at SCOTUS is a fairly recent trend.

separation of powers. The United States Constitution has established three co-equal branches of government that are to keep each other in check. Each branch has its own duties, functions, authority, and powers. An agent of one branch should not be acting as an agent of a different branch. For example, the prosecutor (an executive branch agent) should not be issuing search warrants (a function and duty of the judicial branch).

sequestration. Keeping jurors from communicating with the outside world during deliberations or, under extreme circumstances, during the pendency of the trial.

show cause hearing/order. A court order, made upon an applicant party's motion, requiring the adverse party appear in court and explain why a certain thing should not be done or permitted. If the responding party fails to meet the prima facia case made out by the applicant's affidavit, the court will grant the relief.

sic. Latin. "Thus; so; in such manner." The term sic is often used parenthetically to indicate that something has been copied exactly from the original.

silver platter doctrine. Doctrine that evidence of a federal crime obtained in a search by state law enforcement officers which would have been illegal had the search been done by the federal officers, is admissible in a federal prosecution. (The states would hand the evidence over on a silver platter.) No longer possible since the Supreme Court held in Wolf v. Colorado that the Fourth Amendment applies to the states to the same degree as it applies to the federal government.

sine. Latin. "Without."

sine qua non. Latin. "Without which not." An essential or indispensable element or condition.

sit. To hold a session of a court, legislature, or other deliberative body.

situs. The place where something is for purposes of exercising power or jurisdiction over it; location; position.

slander (noun). action of making a false spoken statement about someone that is defamatory.

slander (verb). Make a false and damaging statement about someone; speak evil and ruin the reputation of someone; tell lies about someone.

slip opinion. A copy of the opinion of a court that is published and distributed very soon after the opinion is handed down (before it can be published in the official recorder).

solicitor. Attorney. The chief law officer of a city, town, municipality, or government. In England, a solicitor is the attorney who communicates with the client, and a barrister is the attorney who is hired by the solicitor to present arguments during the trial.

Solicitor General. The Solicitor General in the Department of Justice represents the U.S. Government in cases before the Supreme Court.

special appearance. An appearance made only for the purpose of attacking the jurisdiction of the court over the defendant's person.

special damages. monetary damages that compensate the plaintiff for quantifiable monetary losses such as medical bills, lost wages, or the cost to repair damaged property.

special/specific deterrence. Theory of punishment in which the offender is punished to deter him or her from future criminal conduct.

special interrogatories. Written questions submitted to a jury on one or more material issues of fact to test the correctness of the general verdict.

specific intent crimes. Crimes that require the state to prove not only that the defendant intended to commit the act but also intended to cause the harm or do something beyond the intent to commit the actus reus. For example, the crime of burglary requires not only that the defendant intended to break and enter a home at night, but also that he or she intend to commit a felony while there.

split sentence. A sentence of both a fine and incarceration. 2) A sentence of probation which specifically requires the person serve a period of incarceration as a condition of probation.

spurious. Not genuine; not authentic; counterfeit; false.

standby counsel. An attorney appointed to assist an indigent defendant who elects to represent himself or herself at trial.

standing. The requirement that a person must demonstrate a personal right has been violated in order to be permitted to argue for suppression of illegally obtained evidence.

stare decisis. Precedent. The doctrine of deciding cases based on precedent, i.e., the principle of following previously announced decisions. *Stare decisis* is a hallmark of the common law legal tradition.

state action. Any action taken by an agent of a state (political unit) under authority or color of state law.

state court. A court authorized under the constitution or laws of a state that is concerned primarily with judicial administration of state and local laws; any court other than a federal court.

State's attorney. Prosecutor.

State's evidence. Evidence given by an accomplice or joint participant in a crime who becomes a witness for the prosecution against other defendants in the crime, sometimes in return for a grant of immunity.

status. Who we are, as opposed to what we do. A condition that is not an action cannot be the actus reus of a crime. For example, being an alcoholic is a status, drinking to get drunk is an action.

status offense. An act or conduct that is declared by a statute to be an offense, but only when committed by a juvenile such as violations of curfew, truancy, incorrigibility.

status quo. The existing state or condition of affairs at a particular time.

statute of limitations. A statute that sets out the time period within which a certain type of action must be brought or the right to bring the action will be lost.

statutory law. Law based upon statutes or codes passed by legislatures (or through initiative and referendum process and then incorporated into statutes).

stipulate. To formally agree.

strict liability. Criminal liability based only on the commission of a prohibited act. The state does not have to prove the defendant had any particular mens rea.

strict scrutiny. Judicial review of a government action or policy in which the ordinary presumption that the act is constitutional is reversed. This standard is applied in review of laws involving suspect classifications for example race and voting rights and those rights protected by the First Amendment (e.g., speech, press, religion, etc.).

sua sponte. Latin. "Of itself or oneself." Through its own volition or motion; voluntarily. When a court takes action on its own motion rather than at the request of one of the parties it acts *sua sponte.*

subject matter jurisdiction. The power of a court to hear and determine cases of the general category to which the case under consideration belongs. For example, a juvenile court does not have subject matter jurisdiction over tax appeals.

substantive due process. Substantive due process is the authority of the judicial branch to invalidate legislation and statutory enactments on the grounds of fairness. According to Professor Erwin Chermansky, "Substantive due process asks the question of whether the government's deprivation of a person's life, liberty or property is justified by a sufficient purpose. Procedural due process, by contrast, asks whether the government has followed the proper procedure when it takes away life, liberty or property." An example he gives is one where the state seeks to remove a child from the custody of its parents. Procedural due process would examine whether the state provided notice and a hearing before it terminated parental rights; substantive due process would require that the government must show a compelling reason that would demonstrate an adequate justification for terminating parental rights."

substantive criminal law. The branch of criminal law that defines criminal offenses and defenses and specifies criminal punishment.

substantive evidence. Evidence offered to establish the truth of a fact or a proposition. Contrast, impeachment evidence or bias evidence used to discredit the witness.

subpoena. A judicial order to appear at a certain place and time to give testimony.

subpoena ducus tecum. A judicial order commanding a person (generally the custodian of records) to appear with certain documents or records at a certain place and time (generally grand jury or trial).

sue. To start a legal action (particularly a civil action) against another.

sui generis. Latin. "Of its own kind." Unique; peculiar; in a class by itself. For example, the Court has held that dog searches/sniffs are *sui generis.*

suit. A civil action or proceeding to enforce a right or to obtain compensation for injury.

summary judgment, (motion for, grant of or denial of) . An action in a civil suit in which the judge rules in favor of one of the parties based upon written pleadings before the case goes to trial. A ruling in favor of summary judgment is a way to short circuit clearly frivolous lawsuits that have no legal merit in advance of trial. The court must determine that there is no possible way, after considering the evidence in the most favorable light of the non-moving party, that any reasonable jury could find for the nonmoving party.

summons. A legal order of the court directing a person to appear in court to answer certain charges. (Aka, a citation).

supra. Latin. "Above." The term supra refers a reader to a previous part of a written work.

Supremacy Clause. Article VI, §2 of the U.S. Constitution that indicates the federal government's ultimate power over the states. The clause has been interpreted to mean that states may not interfere in any manner with the functioning of the federal government, federal statutes, treaties, etc. and that the federal actions prevail over inconsistent state laws. Also, the idea that the federal constitution is the supreme law of the land. See, preemption.

surety bond. A sum of money posted or guaranteed by a party to ensure future court appearances by another person.

swear. To give evidence or testimony on oath or affirmation; administer a legal oath or affirmation.

sworn. Made or done under oath or affirmation; bound by oath or affirmation.

syllabus. A short statement appearing at the beginning of a reported court decision that summarizes the facts and legal principles established in the decision; brief statement or outline of the main points of a treatise, lecture, course of study.

symbolic speech. Expression by symbols, gestures, etc. For example, burning a flag is considered symbolic speech.

T

tainted evidence. Evidence indirectly obtained by exploitation of some prior illegal police activity.

take effect. To become operative.

take issue. To adopt or assume an opposing viewpoint or position.

tangible property. Property that has physical form, substance, and value in itself. An iPod would be tangible property; a trademark would not be tangible property.

term. A fixed period of time. Example, the judge sentenced the defendant to a one-year prison term. 2) The legally prescribed time during which a court, legislature, or official body is in

session (used interchangeably with session). 3) The time period during which an appointed or elected official may hold office. 4) (Aka, term of art), A word or group of words with a particular meaning in a particular profession, science, or discipline. For example, probable cause is a term of art in the legal profession.

test. A process, method, or set of criteria for determining the presence, quality or truth of something. For example, the test of insanity in Oregon is the "Substantial Capacity Test."

test case. A legal action whose outcome is likely to set precedent, establish an important legal principle, or determine the constitutionality of a law.

testimonial privilege. A right of a person to refuse to give testimony himself or to prevent another from giving testimony of a certain type, such as a spousal privilege, or the attorney-client privilege.

testimony. Evidence given by a competent witness, under oath or affirmation, as distinguished from evidence derived from writings, or physical/real evidence. Although testimony is just one type of evidence, sometimes the words are used interchangeably.

time, manner, and place restrictions. The Supreme Court has held that the constitution allows reasonable time, manner and place restrictions be placed on the First Amendment's right to assembly and expressive activities.

third-party consent. Consent, usually to a search, given by a person on behalf of another.

three strikes and you're out. (three strikes laws) Popular term for a statute that provides for mandatory life imprisonment for a convicted felon who has been previously convicted of two or more serious felonies.

toll. Cease. For example, hiding out of state tolls the statute of limitations on the prosecution of a crime.

tort. Private wrong, not arising out of contract, for which the wrong doer can be sued and the injured party can recover monetary damages. Many torts have comparable crimes; for example, the crime of murder is the tort of wrongful death.

totality of the circumstances. Circumstances considered in the aggregate rather than individually.

to wit. Namely, that is to say. Outdated legal phrase used in legal documents to call attention to a more particular statement of what has preceded.

trademark. A distinct word, phrase, graphic symbol used to distinguish a commercial product which is a protected property interest of its owner. For example, the Nike swoosh, or the University of Oregon's distinctive O.

transactional immunity. A type of witness immunity that, although requiring a witness to testify, protects him or her from prosecution for any offenses that a witness's testimony relates to.

transcribe. To reproduce in writing or print.

transcript. A written, typewritten, or printed reproduction of an original; a printed copy of the entire record of the pleadings and proceedings of a trial or hearing.

trial. The examination in court of issues of fact and law in a case for the purpose of reaching a judgment.

trial courts. Judicial tribunals usually presided over by one judge who conducts proceedings and trials in civil or criminal cases with or without a jury. Trial courts are courts of original jurisdiction and are the courts in which evidence is developed and presented. Contrast **appellate courts.**

trial de novo. A new trial or retrial in which the whole case is gone into again as if not trial whatever had been held before. In a trial de novo, matters of fact as well as matters of law may be considered, witnesses heard, and new evidence presented, regardless of what happened at the first trial.

trial judge. The judicial officer who is authorized to conduct jury and nonjury trials and who may (or may not) be authorized to hear appeals. (2) The judicial officer who conducts a particular trial and whose rulings are reviewed on appeal.

trial jury. A jury of a statutorily defined number of person selected according to law and sworn to determine, in accordance with the law as instructed by the court, certain matters of fact based on the evidence presented at trial and to determine a verdict. A trial jury's power and duties is to determine matters of fact only. (The trial judge/presiding judge's duty is to interpret the aw of the case.) The size of the jury is set by statute, generally 12 but can be as few as 6.

trial on the merits. A trial on the substantive issues of a case as distinguished from pretrial motions or other technical matters. (Trial on merits determines the ultimate issue—guilt/non guilt).

tribunal. A court or forum of justice; a person or body with authority to adjudicate matters.

true bill. An indictment handed down by a grand jury.

try. To examine and determine by a judicial process. To put an accused person on trial.

U

ultimate issue. Issue that must finally be determined. For example, the guilt or innocence of the accused is the ultimate issue in a criminal case; whether the defendant was insane at the time of the offense is the ultimate issue when insanity is raised.

unanimous. In complete accord; of one mind; having the agreement or consent of all concerned.

unconstitutional as applied. Declaration by a court of law that a statute is invalid insofar as it is enforced in some particular context, e.g., as to a particular person based on a specific set of facts.

unconstitutional *per se.* Statute that is unconstitutional under any given circumstances.

undue. Improper; unwarranted; unjustifiable; unreasonably excessive.

unequivocal. Clear; plain; not ambiguous.

unilateral. Affecting or involving only one side or party; performed by or undertaken by only one side or party.

Uniform Code of Military Justice. Code of law enacted by Congress that governs military service personnel and defines the procedural and evidentiary requirements in military law and the substantive criminal offenses and punishments.

Uniform Jury Instructions. Model set of jury instructions for either criminal or civil trials. Jury instructions are statements of law the judge reads to the jury at the end of the trial instructing it what the law is and how it should consider evidence. For example, if the defendant raises the insanity defense, the judge will tell the jury the test of insanity used in that jurisdiction. Usually the attorneys draw up jury instructions and submit them to the judge who decides which ones to read to the jury. The state bar associations usually draft a set of uniform jury instructions for the jurisdiction, and attorneys may pattern their instructions on those.

unnamed informant. See confidential informant.

U.S. Attorneys. Attorneys appointed by the president with consent of the U.S. Senate to prosecute federal crimes in a specific geographical area of the United States.

U.S. Code. The comprehensive and systematic collection of federal laws currently in effect.

U.S. Code Annotated. A multivolume work published by West Publishing Company that contains the complete text of federal laws enacted by Congress that are included in the U.S. Code, together with annotations of state and federal decisions that interpret and apply specific sections of federal statutes, plus the text of presidential proclamations and executive orders.

U.S. Court of Appeals for the Armed Forces. A court composed of civilian judges for review of court-martial convictions from the various branches of the military forces.

U.S. Courts of Appeals. Twelve intermediate appellate courts of appeals in the federal system that sit in specified geographic areas of the United States and in which panels of judges hear appeals in civil and criminal cases, primarily from the U.S. District Courts.

U.S. District Court. The principal trial courts in the federal system located in ninety-four districts.

U.S. Magistrate Court. Court that fulfills the pretrial judicial obligations of the federal courts. These are non-Article III Courts (i.e., not established by Art. III of the U.S. Constitution, but rather established through Congressional Act). Formerly, the office of the United States Commissioners.

U.S. Marshals. Law enforcement officers of the U.S. Department of Justice who are responsible for enforcing federal laws, enforcing federal court decisions, and effecting the transfer of federal prisoners.

U.S. Sentencing Commission. Federal body that proposes sentence guidelines for defendants convicted of federal crimes.

U.S. Supreme Court. The highest court in the United States, consisting of nine justices, which has jurisdiction to review, by appeal or writ of certiorari, the decisions of the lower federal courts and many decisions of the highest courts in each state.

use immunity. One type of immunity given to a witness who is required to testify. Use immunity protects the witness from being prosecuted for the crimes based on the compelled testimony or any evidence derived from it. A grant of use immunity does not stop a prosecution for offenses based on compelled testimony if there is evidence derived from an independent source. See **transactional immunity.**

utter. Put something into circulation or to offer or pass it to another in trade, representing it to be good or genuine, such as uttering a forged document; express audibly; to speak.

V

vacate. To annul, set aside or rescind.

vagueness doctrine. Doctrine of constitutional law holding as a violation of due process (and therefore unconstitutional) any legislation that fails to clearly inform the person what is required or proscribed.

venire. French. The group of citizens from whom a jury is chosen n a given case.

venue. Location of a trial or hearing.

verdict. Formal decision rendered by a jury in a civil or criminal trial

vicarious liability. Doctrine under which liability is imposed upon an employer for the acts employees commit in the course and scope of their employment.

victim. Person who is the object of a crime or a tort.

victim impact evidence. Evidence relating to the physical, economic, and psychological impact that a crime has on the victim or victim's family.

victim impact statement. Statement read into the record during the sentencing phase of a criminal trial to inform the court about the impact of the crime on the victim or victim's family.

voir dire. French. "To watch what they say." Process by which prospective jurors are questioned by counsel and/or the court before being selected to serve on a jury.

voluntary intoxication. State of becoming drunk or intoxicated of one's own free will

voluntary manslaughter. Intentional killing of a human without malice or premeditation, usually occurring during a sudden quarrel or in the heat of passion.

W

waiver. Transfer of jurisdiction over a juvenile to a criminal court including judicial, prosecutorial, and legislative waivers. Also known as a "certification" or "transfer."

waiver motion or waiver hearing. Motion by prosecutor to transfer juvenile charged with various offenses to the criminal/adult court for prosecution.

waiver of presentment (to the grand jury). Defendant's voluntary, written relinquishment of the right to have the facts of the case presented to the grand jury when being charged with a felony. When the defendant "waives presentment," the prosecution files charges on an information in the court of general jurisdiction.

warrant. Judicial writ or order directed to a law enforcement officer authorizing the doing of a specific act, such as an arrest or a search.

warrantless arrest. Arrest made by police who do not possess a valid arrest warrant.

warrantless search. Search conducted by police who do not possess a valid search warrant.

Warren court. The U.S. Supreme Court under the leadership of Chief Justice Earl Warren from 1953 through 1969.

Wharton's Rule. Named after Francis Wharton, a well-known commentator on criminal law, this rule holds that two people cannot conspire to commit a crime such as adultery, incest, or bigamy inasmuch as these offenses require two participants.

writ. Order issued by a court of law requiring the performance of some specific act.

writ of certiorari. See certiorari.

writ of error. Writ issued by an appellate court for the purpose of correcting an error revealed in the record of a lower court proceeding.

writ of habeas corpus. See **habeas corpus.**

writ of mandamus. See **mandamus.**

Y

year-and-a-day rule. Rule at common law that a person could not be guilty of murder if the victim lived for a year and a day after the injury was inflicted.

Made in the USA
Columbia, SC
11 March 2024

32415919R00233